Transpersonal
Psychotherapy

SUNY Series in the Philosophy of Psychology
Michael Washburn, editor

Transpersonal Psychotherapy

Second Edition

edited by

Seymour Boorstein, M.D.

STATE UNIVERSITY OF NEW YORK PRESS

Published by
State University of New York Press, Albany

For information, address State University of New York Press,
State University Plaza, Albany, NY, 12246

Production by Marilyn P. Semerad
Marketing by Theresa Abad Swierzowski

Library of Congress Cataloging-in-Publication Data

Transpersonal psychotherapy / edited by Seymour Boorstein. — 2nd ed.
       p.   cm. — (SUNY series in the philosophy of psychology)
    Includes bibliographical references and index.
    ISBN 0-7914-2835-4 (HC). — ISBN 0-7914-2836-2 (pb)
    1. Transpersonal psychotherapy. I. Boorstein, Seymour.
  II. Series.
  RC489.T75T75   1996
  616.89'14—dc20   95-44527
                                                                CIP

10   9   8   7   6   5   4   3   2   1

This book is lovingly dedicated to my wife, Sylvia.

Contents

V. Transpersonal Implications of the Birth and Death Experiences

PREFACE TO THE SECOND EDITION

THE IMPETUS TO PUBLISH A REVISED EDITION of this book came from two sources. Historically, the thoughts which led up to the first edition took form in 1978, with the book itself coming out in 1980. At that time, transpersonal psychotherapy and the ideas relating to it had not been widely disseminated, resulting in very few therapists being familiar or comfortable with the approach. Also, at that time, there were very few schools of psychology teaching these ideas. Most of us were groping in the dark to establish theories of how any of this worked. Compared to the detailed and clinically relevant writings of so many traditional therapists, the transpersonal field looked rather primitive at the end of the 1970s. We simply did not have the language, theory, concepts, etc., to do justice to what we were seeing and experiencing with our patients.

In the seventeen years since the first edition was conceived, the field has grown in many ways. As a country, we have become much more interested in spiritual matters. A look at the *New York Times* best-selling book list provides an instant "cultural measure" of what people are reading. Books dealing with spiritual issues and some of the esoteric thoughts associated with them now appear in great number on that list. Since 1978, we have seen, and welcomed, the proliferation of training centers where students are attempting to integrate traditional psychotherapy with spiritual matters.

When the first edition was published, it sold very slowly at first. As interest by the public sector and training institutions increased, sales rose and in ten years the first edition had to be reprinted. Sales and interest continued to grow, and the second printing sold out. A decision had to be made: to go ahead with a third printing of the first edition or to create a newly revised edition.

This leads me to the second initiator of a revised edition. Since the first publication, many new and talented therapists have matured and their thoughts and perceptions have grown. Ken Wilber has written prodigiously and importantly for our field. His pre/trans fallacy concepts should be a cornerstone for all transpersonal therapists. In addition, many of the old-timers in the field have sharpened the focus of their thinking, so that the more traditional clinicians can no longer accuse us of sloppy thinking (as they used to). However, we still have a lot of catching up to do, and it is to that end that we have prepared this revised edition.

There are two events that further spurred me on to edit a revised edition: In 1994, the DSM-IV (official American Psychiatric Association diagnostic category code book) included, for the first time, a category for spiritual problems or relationships to spirituality. The implications of this addition are far-reaching. Since the DSM-IV is used by insurance companies and other payers of therapists, it means that spiritual problems have now been *officially* recognized and legitimized. With all of the new health-care issues emerging, this will probably translate into funding for psychotherapy in the area of spiritual issues.

Secondly, there is an almost explosive interest in Eastern and Western Europe, Russia and its old colonies, and Japan and Korea in the area of the transpersonal. In 1988 the first edition of this book was translated and published in German; a Hungarian edition will be published in 1996; and a Korean edition is in the planning stage.

In preparing this new edition, it was clear that many of the original chapters would have to be omitted to make room for new ideas, concepts, and approaches born since 1978. Approximately two-thirds of the original chapters have been retained—mainly for two reasons. Firstly, they provide a historical view of some of the origins of the field of transpersonal psychotherapy. (The original introductory paragraphs have been purposely left intact to give the reader an idea of how we viewed these matters in 1978.)

Secondly, one can see in many of these chapters seminal ideas, many of which are as relevant today as they were then. For example, I could never have imagined when I wrote *Anger and the Fear of Death* in 1980 how important those ideas would be for the chapter I have just written on relationships for the revised edition.

How was I to select nine or ten new chapters for the revision? It was clear that for every paper chosen there were at least two or three others that simply could not be included because of space limitations. I here offer my apologies to all the clinicians whose work I could not include in this volume. I hope this new edition of *Transpersonal Psychotherapy* will inspire others to carry on the project of presenting the new theories and methodologies emerging in our field.

Not by accident, the new chapters emerge from Hindu, Buddhist, Christian, Jewish, and shamanic traditions. Since the first edition was conceived, the field of past-life regression therapy has mushroomed with training centers, certification, and conferences offered internationally, as well as in the United States. Dr. Roger Woolger is one of the many leading practitioners and writers in the field, and his chapter provides an entry to begin explorations in this rich and very complex area. Drs. Walsh and Vaughan have rewritten their earlier chapter to bring us their current thinking. Also new for this volume are two chapters by Dr. Stanislav Grof reflecting the cutting edge of his thinking on the theory and practice of the transpersonal field. Dr. Charles Tart, another pioneer of the transpersonal field, writes about helping the dying and the possible survival of death.

One of the most distressing and sad occurrences in our present culture is the very high failure rate of marriages and relationships. We see, also, much evidence of relationship failures on the emotional level, even where the relationship appears intact superficially. This sad phenomenon has spawned many fine books to help people in relationships.

About 40 to 50 percent of my practice is working with couples. Where I can introduce a spiritual factor, the healing usually progresses more rapidly. Because I have observed this in my practice, I have included some transpersonal ideas I have in this area which integrate current brain studies and couples' psychotherapy.

Most of the new chapters reflect the degree to which transpersonal therapists are prepared to reveal themselves about their thinking and work. As therapists, we know this takes courage in general and is especially challenging when we reveal our views on spiritual issues. It is my hope that therapists will begin to be more open about their work, so that we can all learn what our colleagues really do and think.

It is crucial that you, the therapist-reader, approach each chapter as a *beginning* guide in the area discussed and that you explore the bibliography for more details. In addition, you might consider further investigation of an area by finding individuals or groups who are already using the approach described.

If any one of these chapters serves as a launching pad for the reader to do further research and/or become involved in utilizing transpersonal concepts in conjunction with traditional psychotherapy, we will have fulfilled the promise we made to ourselves and to you in 1978.

ACKNOWLEDGMENTS

I WANT PARTICULARLY TO THANK MARTHA LEY for her valuable editorial assistance on this edition. I also want to thank Charles Simpkinson who urged me at the spring 1994 Kripalu conference to revise the original edition of *Transpersonal Psychotherapy* and reissue it. I took his suggestion to heart, and this book is the result.

Introduction

Seymour Boorstein

Perhaps the time is now ripe when the mystic can break the glass through which he sees all things darkly, and the rationalist can break the glass through which he sees all things clearly, and both together can enter the kingdom of psychological reality.
—N. Brown, *Life Against Death*

MY OWN INTEREST IN THE TRANSPERSONAL began about nine years ago, around the time of my father's death. It was not long before this personal interest extended itself into my professional work as a classical Freudian analyst. Today, my practice embraces both the traditional and the transpersonal in a way most clearly reflected in the two chapters I have contributed to this collection.

At a meeting of transpersonal psychotherapists in San Francisco in 1976, I met Kathleen Speeth. Dr. Speeth had spent some of her childhood in Gurdjieff's home, and that exposure to transpersonal and mystic concepts provided a rich heritage for her professional life. As she moved from the transpersonal to the classical approach to psychology, I was moving in the other direction. The conversational bridge we built to connect these converging paths eventually led to this book.

We believed that many therapists in this country were practicing transpersonal therapy but that most of them were hidden from public and professional awareness—as was the field of transpersonal psychology itself. There was no easily available forum for the opening up of discussion in this area, so we examined ways of establishing one.

This collection, I hope, begins this process. Together, we collected the names of many authors and practitioners whom we knew to be working in this field, and asked other therapists to suggest potential contributors. Correspondence with one author sometimes led us to another, and thus the collection began to take form.

The ground rules suggested to potential authors were simple: first, we provided each contributor with our broad working definition of the transpersonal; second, we asked that the papers have a clinical orientation and contain illustrations of how the author actually applied transpersonal approaches to his or her clients' treatment. Apart from our explicit intent to represent as many major Eastern and Western approaches as possible, we gave no other guidelines to the contributors, believing that maximum flexibility would facilitate maximum creativity.

Before the final manuscript was ready, Dr. Speeth regretfully had to withdraw from the project; unavoidable delays in publication had created a conflict with her other commitments. So it is that the book bears my name, and I must bear the responsibility for its final form.

This book, then, is a beginning attempt to build a literature to breach the current wall between the sacred and the psychotherapeutic. Recognition of the healing potential hidden in the sacred technologies of the great religious traditions, and particularly of Eastern practices, has been growing in recent years. In 1976, the Group for the Advancement of Psychiatry wrote a report of over one hundred pages entitled *Mysticism: Spiritual Quest or Psychic Disorder?* because it saw that "mysticism has become a significant force in our time" (GAP [Group for the Advancement of Psychiatry] 1976). That same year, *Newsweek* declared that at present there are four major forces in psychology: behavioral, psychoanalytic, humanistic, and transpersonal.

Attributing such importance to the transpersonal may be surprising to many psychiatrists and psychologists; it is an aspect of psychology that has relatively little formal literature and certainly no widely accepted definition.

Early transpersonal thinkers include William James, who systematically explored states of healthy and higher consciousness (James, 1961); Carl G. Jung, whose concept of individuation transcended the personal (Jung, 1933); Roberto Assagioli, who translated certain spiritual practices into workable psychotherapeutic tools (Assagioli, 1965); and Abraham Maslow, whose interest in self-actualizing people, their experiences, and values has exerted a powerful influence on postindustrial America (Maslow, 1968, 1971). Charles Tart, the parapsychologist, was a pioneer in collecting interpretations of human psychology by various spiritual traditions in his massive *Transpersonal Psychologies* (Tart, 1975 [new edition 1992]).

It is uncertain who first used the term *transpersonal psychology*. A. J. Sutich (1976) gave an interesting account of the development of the term, limited by what was known at the time he wrote. He quotes a letter from Abraham Maslow to Stanislav Grof:

> The main reason I am writing is that in the course of our conversations we thought of using the word "transpersonal" instead of the clumsier word "transhumanistic" or "transhuman." The more I think of it, the more this word says what we are all trying to say, that is, beyond individuality, beyond the development of the individual person into something which is more inclusive than the individual person, or which is bigger than he is. What do you think? (p. 16)

Earlier references have come to light since, however. Ira Progoff used the term in his contribution to the 1955 Festschrift on Jung's eightieth birthday, later published (1956); Eric Neumann (1954) had used it the year before; and Dane Rudhyar had applied the word *transpersonal* to astrology back in the twenties. Perhaps yet earlier mentions will still be uncovered.

The *Journal of Transpersonal Psychology* began publication in 1969. Each issue contains this definition of the field: "Meta-needs, transpersonal process, values and states, unitive consciousness, peak experiences, ecstasy, mystical experience, being, essence, bliss, awe, wonder, transcendence of self, spirit, sacralization of everyday life, oneness, cosmic awareness, cosmic play, individual and species-wide synergy, the theories and practices of meditation, spiritual paths, compassion, transpersonal cooperation, transpersonal realization and actualization; and related concepts, experiences and activities." Despite its partial circularity, this definition indicates well the class of interests, experiences, and events gathered under the appellation of "transpersonal."

Those who practice psychotherapy within this general context can be considered transpersonal psychotherapists. One description of the field of transpersonal psychotherapy is provided by James Fadiman and Kathleen Speeth:

> Transpersonal psychotherapy includes the full range of behavioral, emotional and intellectual disorders as in traditional psychotherapies, as well as uncovering and supporting strivings for full self-actualization. The end state of psychotherapy is not seen as successful adjustment to the prevailing culture but rather the daily experience of that state called liberation, enlightenment, individuation, certainty or gnosis according to various traditions. (in press)

From this perspective, transpersonal psychotherapy differs from the traditional approaches not so much in method or technique as in orientation and scope. There may be technical innovations such as meditation, visualization, and awareness training, borrowed from the spiritual traditions of the world, but the essential difference lies in the attitudes of the therapist, attitudes that shape the course of therapy. He neither avoids the issues of value and meaning in a human life nor places them outside the bounds of therapeutic work; rather he explores them, either as they arise in the working through of personal suffering or when their resolution frees the patient's energies for deeper confrontation with the dilemmas we all face.

Without the transpersonal perspective, traditional psychotherapy gives an implicit message of pessimism, which might be stated without too much exaggeration as, "Know thyself and adjust to the absurd!" The transpersonal ingredient alters this implication to "Know thyself, transcend defenses, transferences, projections, and even beliefs, and attain the station of one who has outgrown the need for such childish things, as the great human beings of all times and places have done!" It might be added that this station involves the full realization of human possibilities; it is in no way connected with schizoid withdrawal, megalomaniacal delusions of grandeur, or flashy demonstrations of parapsychological prowess.

As more people in the West turn to meditation and other spiritual practices, and relationship with a spiritual teacher becomes less uncommon, the transpersonal psychotherapist must become adept in discriminating between the uses and abuses of extraordinary or at least extracultural experiences. Just because a technique may have a noble origin does not keep it safe from possible misuse by neurotic or psychotic trends in the personality. To see all spiritual practices as necessarily free of individual pathology is as blind a view as the rigidly orthodox position that all spiritual aspirations and practices are merely symptomatic.

An objective and experienced therapist needs to discriminate, to be willing to put down preconceptions in favor of looking at, listening to, and realizing what is actually happening in each particular circumstance. For example, meditation can put one in touch with a fine and essential part of oneself; it can also be used to rationalize compulsive withdrawal in a family power struggle, or symbolically to blot out a hated world. The relationship to guru or guide can be a lifesaving reorientation; it can also be distorted with transference gratifications. Altered states of consciousness—easily produced with concentration and breathing practices—may help free a person from constricting linguistic schema; or they may feed paranoid ideation, accentuate schizoid trends, and act generally in the service of resistance. And the initial glow and romanticism of inexperienced meditators may be just what is needed to allow for the modification of destructive habits; or it may be used to avoid the here and now of life's problems, including therapeutic transference reaction.

In working on such areas as anxiety, depression, sense of identity, and reality testing, traditional psychotherapy attempts to strengthen the ego so that it can endure the eventual weaning from unreality that human maturity requires. Although meditation or other specifically transpersonal practices used alone might eventually unravel a modern anxiety neurosis or depression, therapeutic techniques are more specifically designed for the usual people and settings with which therapists work. The therapist can greatly hasten transpersonal processes by first using ordinary methods to bring into the patient's consciousness what has been repressed. For example, beneath a depression, a patient may be unconsciously clinging to the idea that his childhood mother should "make up" to him all his previous deprivations. By working with transferences in the traditional fashion, the therapist can help the patient bring to the surface this area and all the feelings it involves. It might then be appropriate for the experienced therapist to offer certain meditative techniques to facilitate the letting go of the ideas and feelings.

But how is the therapist to gain experience? In the two decades since Norman Brown suggested that the mystics and rationalists among us (and within us) might come to an understanding, many psychotherapists of widely differing theoretical persuasions have been tentatively exploring the common ground where this uncommon realization might take place. A rather large body of unshared experience has developed, the communication of which is likely to cross-pollinate and enrich us all. It is to provide a measure of vicarious experience and to support the formation of a community of like-minded individuals within the helping professions that I have undertaken this collection of papers.

The contributions are remarkably diverse. They reflect a spectrum of perspectives—from the tough-minded, precise extrapolations from behavioristic methodology of Les Fehmi and Fern Selzer, through the creative clinical pharmacology and theory development of Stanislav Grof, to the tender empathy of Norman Don. Not all of the papers represent my own orientation. Each, however, is a potentially valuable stimulus to other therapists.

There are possible dangers in working with the spiritual and psychological domains simultaneously. Can therapists be adequately competent in both areas, sufficiently certain to avoid the pitfalls of their own counter-transference traps and spiritual biases? Can therapists work in areas beyond those to which they have personally progressed? Many classical therapists who are atheists or agnostics implicitly endorse their own belief systems by the kind of attention they give to the religious aspirations of their clients. Will transpersonally oriented therapists be guilty of the same kind of suggestion, albeit in the opposite direction? What are the implications of prescribing meditation practices or other techniques derived from spiritual traditions as adjuncts to treatment?

Clearly, the practice of transpersonal psychotherapy requires the very best of which the therapist is capable: experiential knowledge rather than opinion; attention instead of preconception; certainty in place of theory. The papers presented here are like the experiences of the elephant in the dark in the old Sufi fable: one man feels the tail and declares that the elephant is like a rope; the next feels the ear and exclaims that the elephant is like a palm leaf; the third grabs the trunk and yells that the elephant is like a snake; and the fourth runs his hand over the hide and protests that the elephant is like the bark of the tree (Shah, 1971b). The synthesis of many opinions into a fuller picture is the perennial task of each human mind and one of the marks of psychological awakening.

The ultimate goal of the spiritual quest is the experience of oneness with the universe. As Ken Wilber points out in *The Spectrum of Consciousness*, humanity's task is to remember or become aware of those aspects of itself which it has forgotten or repressed (1977). Thus, different parts of the spectrum are remembered or made available by different approaches. For example, the psychoanalytic approach will permit one to remember and accept as part of oneself that which has been repressed in the unconscious; certain body approaches such as Reichian therapy, bioenergetics, and Rolfing permit one to become aware of certain aspects of the body that may have been repressed or made unconscious. Other aspects of the unconscious are elicited in Jungian work where certain archetypes and aspects of the shadow can be owned or remembered. Various kinds of work can be done on the subtle energy fields, and these, too, can become part of our awareness. Finally, through various meditational or contemplative approaches, direct awareness of unity with the rest of the universe can also be achieved.

As you read the following papers, it might be well to keep in mind what the Buddha said in the Kalamas Sutra:

> Do not believe in what you have heard; do not believe in traditions because they have been handed down for many generations; do not believe anything because it is rumored and spoken of by many; do not believe merely because the written statement of some old sage is produced; do not believe in conjectures; do not believe merely in the authority of your teachers and elders. After observation and analysis, when it agrees with reason and it is conducive to the good and benefit of one and all, then accept it and live up to it.

I

The Dimensions of Transpersonal Psychotherapy

To refer to the dimensions of transpersonal psychotherapy in the title of this section is tantamount to presenting myself with a paradox. For the true dimensions of the transpersonal are unseen and boundless. Yet, while the transpersonal field may have no finite limits, it does have—at least in the beginning, novice stages—direction.

To fix direction, it is humanly necessary to take a starting point. While the historical starting point of this field is older than oral or recorded history, the present-day articulation of that direction is most concretely attributed to Anthony Sutich, founder of the *Journal of Transpersonal Psychology* and the parallel association. Without his work, this collection of papers would not be possible in its present form.

To take direction in a theoretical mode, it is humanly necessary to build a foundation. Roger Walsh and Frances Vaughan attempt to provide this foundation by building a comparative model of the person and psychotherapy. It is a model that provides for the concept and potential of consciousness. For this edition, the authors have updated their chapter on the comparative model.

To take direction in a personal mode is as difficult and exciting as formulating a theory—and equally challenging. The journey into consciousness is full of unexpected twists, leaps, and backtracking to take a higher road. Gerald May shares his personal journey with us, a journey that takes him away from "fixing" within a medical perspective to "healing" within a transpersonal perspective. It is a journey as potentially full of light and shadow as the therapeutic journeys I share with my patients.

Stanislov Grof's chapter explores his views on non-ordinary states of consciousness and experiences which transcend the limitations of three-dimensional space and linear time. He explains that, as a rule, the traditional Western culture does not consider the transcendent experiences to be real, in part because they do not fall into the framework of mechanistic science.

Consciousness, once accepted as both a starting point and an infinite end point, then pervades all aspects of human thought and feeling—from the creation of new schools of exploration to the construction of theory, to intimate, personal change in life values and orientation. It provides unique direction for each individual; it only remains for the individual to accept the presence of consciousness in himself or herself.

1

Transpersonal Psychotherapy
History and Definition

Anthony J. Sutich

No one can open this collection so appropriately as the late Anthony J. Sutich. His chapter, perhaps better than any other in the collection, outlines the origins, early definitions, and questions raised by this emerging field of transpersonal psychology and therapy.

Sutich and his chapter are really their own introduction. The content itself demonstrates how the author explored consciousness first within the field of humanistic psychology. One might think that, after having helped to found both the association and the journal for that field, he would have been content to rest. On the contrary, his determination to explore all areas of consciousness that presented themselves to him led to his founding of the journal and association for transpersonal psychology as well.

It is relatively difficult to formulate assumptions for any new field. It is even more difficult to perform the often ignored task of relating those assumptions to what preceded them in the field. Sutich does just this in many of his papers and was instrumental in building a bridge between humanistic psychology and the transpersonal area to which this collection is devoted.

This article is based on a presentation made at a panel discussion (with Stanislav Grof and Thomas N. Weide) at the annual meeting of the Association for Humanistic Psychology, September 1972. The author expressed his "deep indebtedness" to Sonja Margulies and Weide for their assistance in preparing this article. It has been further adapted for use in this collection with kind permission and approval of Miles Vich, editor of the *Journal of Transpersonal Psychology.*

Sutich's classic chapter concludes by raising a number of pertinent questions about the transpersonal field and its relation to therapeutic practice. In concluding his piece with these questions, he has pointed directions for the other chapters in this collection, which consciously or unconsciously address themselves to many of his questions.

IN 1968, I PUBLISHED a brief paper announcing the growth of a new force in psychology which appeared to be a direct outgrowth of humanistic psychology; the paper was titled "Transpersonal Psychology: An Emerging Force." After the publication of this paper, it gradually became apparent to us that this new transpersonal force was more than "an outgrowth"; the assumptions which lay behind the transpersonal position differed significantly from those basic to the "growth-oriented" humanistic position. A new paradigm had emerged.

Probably the most relevant assumptions of the humanistic psychology position appeared in an early paper of mine, "The Growth Experience and the Growth Centered Attitude" (1949, 1967). These assumptions were basic to the launching of the *Journal of Humanistic Psychology* in spring 1961, and to the founding of the Association for Humanistic Psychology in August 1963. By 1966, it was commonly understood that the basic goal in humanistic psychology was "self-actualization" or some equivalent of that.

The major assumptions underlying the transpersonal position continued to evolve (Sutich, 1968, 1969) and were first clearly formulated when we were founding the Association for Transpersonal Psychology, a division of the Transpersonal Institute (Sutich, 1972). These may be summarized as follows:

- Impulses toward an ultimate state are continuous in every person although full awareness of these is not necessarily present at any given time.
- The realization of an ultimate state is essentially dependent on direct practice related to a "path" (course of action or conduct entered into for the purpose of realizing an ultimate state) and on conditions suitable for the individual concerned.
- Every individual has the right to freely choose his or her own path and to change from one personal path to another if or when he or she so desires.

Transpersonally Oriented Therapy

With these assumptions in mind, transpersonally oriented therapy may therefore be described as therapy directly or indirectly concerned with the recognition, acceptance, and realization of ultimate states. As such, it is not new;

rather, it is perhaps the oldest of all the therapeutic approaches. Through history it has played a vital part in most if not all systems concerned with the realization of ultimate states.

Transpersonal therapy is also concerned with the psychological processes related to the realization, or making real, of states such as "illumination," "mystical union," "transcendence," and "cosmic unity." It is also concerned with the psychological conditions or psychodynamic processes which directly or indirectly form barriers to these transpersonal realizations. In both the past and the present, individuals have necessarily had different relationships to their impulses toward ultimate states and emotional growth; they have also varied in their levels of development in these at different times in their life cycles.

Different levels of development, experience, and concern have not always been dealt with in ways of maximal value to either client/patient or therapist. Psychoanalysis, for example, was not originally, and is not now, designed to deal with impulses toward ultimate states. Neither have behaviorism's fundamental assumptions been directly related to the client's transpersonal experiences and concerns. Nevertheless, within limits, both psychoanalysis and behaviorism have often been helpful in dealing with human problems which fall within the primary focus of particular psychological systems.

My own work in and support of humanistic psychology demonstrates the regard I have for the importance and value of its primary concern and effort. However, Baba Ram Dass, former professor of psychology at Harvard, has highlighted in a lecture the discontinuity between the level of work done in relation to self-actualization, the maximal goal of the humanistic orientation, and the work done toward the realization of ultimate states. I have been informed, too, that Roberto Assagioli, founder of psychosynthesis, now uses the term *transpersonal* instead of *spiritual* in his work, because the latter term has so often been misused. It is this area of work—the intrapersonal rather than the interpersonal—that is the primary focus of transpersonal psychology. A high level of spiritual or transpersonal concern is presumed conducive to or facilitative of interpersonal development and vice versa.

Transpersonal Therapy in Relation to Humanistic and Other Interpersonal Therapies

Probably all human beings have some "unfinished business" in the interpersonal psychodynamic realm, whether they know it or not. Those engaged in a transpersonal therapeutic approach, therefore, necessarily deal with such material in themselves and in others. In my own practice, I work with all kinds of "neurotic" conditions in clients—compulsions, phobias, anxiety—whether or not these clients are personally committed to a spiritual path.

Others, such as psychosynthesis therapists, also work with both interpersonal and transpersonal problems. Because the full range of pathologies and positive human possibilities is the appropriate concern of the transpersonal therapist, he or she is interested in and supportive of psychological work being done across the entire spectrum.

If the primary focus of transpersonal therapy can be accepted as valid, it seems appropriate to ask, What are the requirements for functioning as a transpersonal therapist? With the understanding that I consider the crucial issue in transpersonal therapeutic or counseling work to be the perspective, attitude, or orientation of the therapist himself, I suggest the following as a preliminary or tentative statement of requirements.

The therapist or counselor:
- is on his (her) own spiritual or transpersonal path.
- accepts the right of any person with whom he (she) is working to pursue his (her) own path and to change to another if that seems desirable.
- has a commitment to the principle that all human beings have continuous impulses toward emotional growth and ultimate states, and accepts that the chief responsibility of a transpersonal therapist is to function in the best way he (she) knows how, to help in the realization of emotional growth as well as ultimate states.
- has reasonable knowledge, among other psychological principles, of the role of self-deceptive mechanisms throughout the life cycle, including their function in himself (herself).*
- accepts all individuals as having impulses toward ultimate states whether or not they are on a personal path. More specifically, this means working with individuals as much as possible through techniques and forms of relating that are directly relevant to their current state.

Some Pertinent Questions

During the years I have been engaged in transpersonal therapy work, numerous questions have arisen with which I have had to grapple. I conclude this chapter by presenting a sampling of those that seem to merit serious consideration:
- What are the various areas in which transpersonal psychology might be applied?
- What is the role of meditation in transpersonal psychology? Is meditation sufficient therapy for neurotic and other psychopathological states?

---

*I am deeply indebted to Lama Chögyam Trungpa Rinpoche, for corroboration of this long-standing personal and professional observation.

- In what ways can a transpersonal therapist or counselor work with individuals who are not on a spiritual path?
- These days one frequently encounters terms and phrases from the great spiritual traditions, such as the Buddhist terms "expedient teachings," "right attitude," "right understanding," and "right actions." What do these terms mean? In what ways do they relate to transpersonal psychology?
- What is appropriate and inappropriate in accepting payment for transpersonal therapy?
- Is transpersonal psychology a system?
- When using a transpersonal orientation, how does one select appropriate therapeutic techniques for those who are not, as well as those who are, on a spiritual path?
- What is the importance of self-deception, and of awareness of self-deception, in transpersonal functioning?
- What is required in the training and/or development of transpersonal therapists?
- How can transpersonal therapists most harmoniously and helpfully interact with teachers and counselors of various religious practices and spiritual disciplines, Eastern and Western?

2

Comparative Models of the Person and Psychotherapy

Roger Walsh and Frances E. Vaughan

Both theoreticians, practitioners, and authors in the transpersonal field, Roger Walsh and Frances Vaughan combine forces in this chapter to provide a strong yet open foundation for exploring the transpersonal. Moving into areas of inquiry largely ignored by the schools of psychoanalysis, behaviorism, and humanistic psychology, the authors see transpersonal psychology as "the fourth force of Western psychology," a force that draws from both Eastern and Western world views.

The authors view the term transpersonal psychology as still developing. However, they summarize its connotations as having close relationships with health, well-being, and consciousness. Transpersonal psychotherapy, therefore, places greater emphasis and importance on these three elements than traditional psychotherapy while still including traditional therapeutic areas.

In a courageous attempt to develop some testable hypotheses for this rapidly changing field, Walsh and Vaughan first construct a transpersonal model of the person, its four major dimensions being consciousness, conditioning, personality, and identification. As may be expected, the first of these dimensions, consciousness, has high importance in the model. The concept of consciousness is, in the authors' view, greatly limited in traditional schools which allow for no higher states. Correspondingly, whereas consciousness is much more than most of us have hitherto imagined, conditioning is much more tyrannical and pervasive. Personality, on the other hand, is accorded less importance as a psychological concept; in this transpersonal model it is seen as "only one aspect of being, one with which the individual may, but does not have to, identify." While the fourth dimension of this model—identification—bears a superficial resemblance to other models of the person, the concept here is associated with internal as well as external phenomena and processes. The implications of this are important because, as Walsh and Vaughan explain, "identification with mental content renders the individual unconscious of the broader context of consciousness which holds this content. . . . Thus identification sets in train a self-fulfilling prophetic process."

What are the implications of this model of the person for therapy? The most frightening implication is that some of the material presented in therapy and interpreted as psychopathological is, in fact, not psychopathological at all; it is transpersonal. The authors refer, for example, to a recent report that classified mystical experiences as borderline psychotic processes. This is not to say that transpersonal psychotherapy ignores traditional goals of therapy; rather, it adds to them such goals as actually disidentifying from and transcending the traditional psychodynamic processes the clients are already working through. Because the approach to therapy draws on karma yoga principles, the therapist-client relationship ceases to be hierarchical, and the modeling that takes place is more closely aligned with a learning-to-cope model than a competency one. Both therapist and client use their encounters as opportunities for growth. In using any technique, be it yoga or meditation, or another, more traditional one, both therapist and client have a commitment to openness and self-examination.

In comparing the transpersonal approach with classical psychoanalysis, analytical psychology, behaviorism, humanistic psychology, and existentialism, these authors provide incisive insights into the similarities and differences. These insights and their examination of the current limitations of the transpersonal field will likely prove surprising and illuminating to practitioners and cynics alike.

IN RECENT YEARS TRANSPERSONAL PSYCHOLOGY HAS EMERGED as the fourth force of Western psychology. Its distinguishing characteristic is an expansion of the field of psychological inquiry to embrace areas of human experience and behavior associated with health and development beyond conventional levels, areas largely ignored by the first three schools—psychoanalysis, behaviorism, and humanistic psychology. These areas include, in addition to exceptional psychological health and well-being, subjects such as altered states of consciousness, peak experiences, self-realization, meditation, and other techniques which transcend the more traditional limiting models of human potential (Tart, 1975). In so doing, transpersonal psychology draws on the contributions of both Eastern wisdom and Western science.

The purpose of this chapter is to suggest possible theoretical founda-tions for transpersonal psychology and therapy by, first, delineating a model of the psyche; second, explaining and examining transpersonal psychotherapy from this model; and third, comparing transpersonal with other forms of therapy.

Defining Transpersonal Psychology and Psychotherapy

Defining transpersonal psychology and psychotherapy can be difficult. This may be partly because transpersonal experiences raise all the problems of state dependency and cross-state communication discussed by Tart (1972, 1975). Because definitions may be constricting, especially for developing fields, it is useful to consider those for transpersonal psychology as being in process rather than definitive, in order to allow for continuing growth and evolution (Sutich, 1975).

With these caveats in mind, let us consider the following definitions:

Transpersonal experiences may be defined as experiences in which the sense of identity or self extends beyond (*trans-*) the individual or personal to encompass wider aspects of humankind, life, psyche, and cosmos.

Transpersonal psychology is the area of psychology that focuses on the study of transpersonal experiences and related phenomena. These phenom-ena include the causes, effects, and correlates of transpersonal experiences and development, as well as the disciplines and practices inspired by them.

Transpersonal psychotherapy is therapy informed by a transpersonal per-spective which recognizes the value and validity of transpersonal experiences and development.

With the introduction of a variety of consciousness-altering techniques, an increasing number of people, including mental health professionals, are beginning to have a range of transpersonal experiences. Such experiences can be extremely powerful and have far-reaching implications for the individual's identity, lifestyle, and philosophy (White, 1973).

A Transpersonal Model of the Psyche

Four major dimensions of this transpersonal model are consciousness, con-ditioning, personality, and identification. Using these headings, we will sum-marize basic tenets of a transpersonal model and compare them with traditional Western assumptions.

Consciousness

The transpersonal model clearly holds consciousness as a central dimension. Traditional Western schools of psychology have held differing positions with regard to consciousness. These range from behaviorism, which ignores it, to psychodynamic and humanistic approaches, which pay more attention to its contents than to consciousness itself.

A transpersonal model views "normal" consciousness as a defensively contracted state of reduced awareness. This normal state is filled to a remarkable and unrecognized extent with a continuous, mainly uncontrollable flow of fantasies which exert a powerful though largely unrecognized influence on perception, cognition, and behavior. Prolonged self-observation inevitably reveals that normal experience is perceptually distorted by the continuous, automatic, and unconscious blending of inputs from reality and fantasy in accordance with our needs and defenses (Tart, 1975; Thera, 1972; Walsh, 1977; Wilber, 1977).

Optimum consciousness is viewed as being considerably greater than normal consciousness and potentially available at any time, if the defensive contraction is relaxed. Growth, therefore, involves letting go of this defensive contraction and removing obstacles to the recognition of the ever-present expanded potential. This is achieved by quieting the mind and removing the perceptual distortion and constriction imposed by the fantasies (Assagioli, 1965; De Ropp, 1968; Ouspensky, 1949; Ram Dass, 1976, 1977; Speeth, 1975; Walsh, 1977).

> The fundamental task which gives the key to many realizations is the silence of the mind. . . . All kinds of discoveries are made, in truth, when the mental machinery stops, and the first is that if the power to think is a remarkable gift, the power not to think is even more so. (Satprem, 1968)

Traditional Western approaches differ from the transpersonal in implicitly assuming that normal consciousness is close to maximum developmental levels.

The transpersonal perspective holds that a large spectrum of altered states of consciousness exists. Some states are seen as potentially useful, possibly having specific functions. Others are true "higher" states—higher being used here in Tart's sense, namely, possessing the properties and potentials of lower states together with some additional ones (Tart, 1972). A wide range of literature from a variety of cultures and growth disciplines attests to the attainability of these higher states (Buddhagosa, 1923; Byrom, 1976; Goldstein, 1976; Goleman, 1976, 1977; Kapleau, 1967; White, 1973). The traditional view again differs in holding that only a limited range of states exists, such as waking, sleeping, dreaming, and intoxication. Furthermore, the traditional view sees nearly all altered states as detrimental; "normality" is considered optimal.

Conditioning

A transpersonal perspective holds that the "normal person" is much more ensnared and trapped in conditioning than we appreciate, but that significant freedom from this conditioning is possible, at least experientially (Goleman, 1977). The aim of transpersonal psychotherapy includes efforts to begin the extraction of awareness from this conditioned tyranny of the mind (Ram Dass, 1987).

One form of conditioning is attachment. This has been examined in detail by Eastern disciplines. Attachment is closely associated with desire; when attachment is present, it signifies that nonfulfillment of desire will result in pain. Therefore, attachment plays a central role in the causation of suffering (e.g., addictions), while letting go of attachment is central to its cessation. These principles are clearly stated in the Buddha's Noble Truths (Buddhagosa, 1923; Guenther, 1976). Or in Carl Jung's words: "Whenever we are still attached, we are still possessed; and when one is possessed, it means the existence of something stronger than oneself" (Jung, 1962, p. 114).

Personality

Personality has been accorded a central place in previous schools of psychology. Indeed most psychological theories have held that a person *is* the personality. Many books on psychological health and well-being have addressed "the healthy personality" (e.g., Chiang & Maslow, 1969). Health has usually been viewed as primarily involving a modification of personality (Heath, 1977, 1978). Transpersonal psychology accords less centrality to personality. It is seen as only one aspect of being, one with which the individual may, but does not have to, identify. Healthy adult development may involve a disidentification from personality rather than solely a modification of it (Wilber, 1977, 1978).

Identification

Traditional psychologies usually recognize identification with external objects only; they have defined identification as an unconscious process in which the individual becomes like or feels the same as something or someone else (Brenner, 1974). Transpersonal and a variety of Eastern psychologies, while recognizing external identification, hold that identification with internal (intrapsychic) phenomena and processes is even more important. Identification is seen as a crucial concept and is thus conceptually extended beyond traditional Western limits. Furthermore, this type of identification goes unrecognized by the majority of individuals, including therapists and behavioral scientists, because we are all so involved in it; we become so identified that it never even occurs to us to question that which it seems so clear that we are (Wilber, 1977, 1978). Consensually validated identifications go unrecognized because they are not called into question; indeed, any attempt to question them may meet with considerable resistance from others.

> Attempts to awake before our time are often punished, especially by those who love us most. Because they, bless them, are asleep. They think anyone who wakes up, or . . . realizes that what is taken to be real, is a dream, is going crazy. (Laing, 1971, p. 82)

This process of identification has far-reaching implications. Identification with mental content renders the individual unconscious of the broader context of consciousness which holds this content, a process that may be central to trance states. When the individual identifies with mental conflict, this content is transformed into the context within which he or she interprets other content, determines a reality, adopts a logic, and is motivated. For example, if a thought such as "I'm scared" arises, is observed, and is seen to be what it is—just another thought—then it exerts little influence. However, if the thought is identified with, then the individual is scared, and a whole series of fearful thoughts is likely to arise. Nondescript feelings are then interpreted as fear. Thus, identification sets in train a self-fulfilling prophetic process.

> We are dominated by everything with which our self becomes identified. We can dominate and control everything from which we disidentify. (Assagioli, 1965, p. 22)

> As long as we are identified with an object, that is bondage. (Wei Wu Wei, 1970, p. 6)

It may be that thoughts and beliefs constitute the operators which construct, mediate, guide, and maintain this identificatory constriction of consciousness and act as limiting models of what we think we are. Some may be adopted as strategic, defensive decisions about who and what we must be in order to survive and function optimally. Yet, they must be opened to disconfirmation and disidentification in order to allow growth.

It is significant to note the similar conclusions about the powerful effects of thoughts reached by explorers of the mind, even though they may be separated by millenia:

> Within the province of the mind what I believe to be true is true or becomes true, within the limits to be found experientially and experimentally. These limits are further beliefs to be transcended. In the province of the mind there are no limits. (Lilly, 1972, p. 5)

We are what we think.
All that we are arises with our thoughts.
With our thoughts we create the world.
(The Buddha, quoted in Byrom, 1976, p. 3).

Understanding the nature of thoughts and the process of disidentification may therefore help explain transpersonal states of consciousness in which the sense of identity expands beyond the individual ego or personality, even to the extreme of nondual states in which people experience themselves as connected with, or one with, the whole universe. Such states are explored by a variety of transpersonal disciplines (Goleman, 1988; Wilber, 1977).

Principles of Transpersonal Therapy

Before we discuss the principles of transpersonal therapy, it is relevant to consider the importance of a transpersonal perspective for therapeutic work.

Because the transpersonal acknowledges a wider spectrum of psychological well-being than traditional approaches, it affords individuals who are ready the opportunity of working at these levels. Perhaps most important is the fact that the transpersonal recognizes the importance and eupsychian nature of transpersonal or transcendental experiences; these can then be appropriately treated as valuable opportunities for growth. This is very different from some other approaches which fall into what Ken Wilber calls "the pre/trans fallacy" of confusing transpersonal experiences with prepersonal manifestations of psychopathology. Failure to recognize this distinction can easily lead to pathologizing interpretations, with consequent damage to, and suppression of, healthy processes that can lead into the transpersonal realm.

A general principle here is that it is difficult to see beyond our own level, and those individuals and systems that have not recognized the possibility of, or experienced, transpersonal awareness may interpret such experiences from an inappropriate and pathologizing perspective. This is sadly and starkly demonstrated by a report on mysticism by the Group for the Advancement of Psychiatry (GAP, 1977). This document generally interpreted mystical experiences as manifestations of borderline psychotic processes. Its authors thus exhibited a marked lack of understanding of altered states, an understanding readily apparent to anyone with experiential as well as intellectual knowledge of these areas (Deikman, 1977).

The goals of transpersonal therapy include both traditional ones, such as symptom relief and behavior change, and, for appropriate clients, the introduction of a variety of methods aimed at the transpersonal level. The latter include the provision of an adequate conceptual framework for handling transpersonal experiences; information on psychological potential; realization of the importance of assuming responsibility, not only for one's behavior but for one's experience; discovery of the possibility of using all life experience as a part of learning; experiencing the existence and potentials of altered states; and understanding the usefulness, limits, and dangers of attachment to fixed models and expectations. In addition to working through psychodynamic processes, the therapist may also assist the client in beginning to disidentify from them.

The tools used include both Eastern and Western methods. Various forms of meditation and yoga may be added to more traditional techniques. One of the major distinguishing features of such tools may be that their primary aim is not so much to change experiences directly as to change the individual's relationship to them by heightened, mindful awareness.

Approaches such as meditation and karma yoga are largely independent of therapist-client interaction. The client can practice them in daily life and thus make more efficient use of the therapeutic contact as well as begin to use all life experiences for learning. The following cases exemplify some of these processes.

> A forty-five-year-old woman who had been making good progress in therapy for a year and had become increasingly sensitive to her inner experience, developed marked resistance to further exploration and became unable to maintain her former sensitivity. My response as her therapist was initially one of support and encouragement, but when this was unsuccessful, I became less patient and began subtly pressuring her.
>
> Gradually it became apparent to me that I was attached to her maintaining her former gains. The resultant coercion set up a dialectic which only reinforced her defensiveness and my attachment. When I recognized what was happening, I discussed it with her. I pointed out that my attachment had fueled her defenses and vice versa, that this was an example of my attachment to success, and that I would endeavor to let it go and to use this opportunity to work on the attachment as much as possible. For her part she should note her responses to the experience of coercion and communicate whenever she felt pressured, since this would be helpful to both of us.
>
> Although this proved of considerable benefit, she did not overcome her defensiveness more fully until some two months later, when she went on a two-week meditation retreat. She emerged from it with a new level of sensitivity and openness to experience, and progressed in therapy at a significantly faster rate. (Walsh)

One young woman, deeply committed to her spiritual practice of meditation, came into therapy when she was having marital problems.

She was making considerable progress in resolving these problems and reconciling herself to her husband's critical attitudes, when I went on vacation for a month. During my absence my client wanted to continue her work and sought out another therapist. This therapist was unsympathetic to her practice of meditation. She felt misunderstood and discounted, and labeled herself "weird" because the therapist did not share her spiritual values. When I returned, it was evident to both of us that the attitude of the interim therapist, although he had said very little, had had a decidedly detrimental effect on her self-image. (Vaughan)

Two features of the transpersonal psychotherapeutic relationship deserve special mention: modeling and karma yoga. The importance of modeling has now been clearly recognized in the behavior modification and social learning literature, and information on its potency suggests that other therapies may have underestimated its power (Bandura, 1969, 1977b). Since modeling may be a universal, although sometimes unwitting, therapeutic process, the distinguishing factor is that which the therapist models rather than the process itself. For a transpersonal orientation, this type of modeling is closely linked to the concept of karma yoga, the yoga of service.

Traditional psychoanalytic models encourage therapists to minimize their affective involvement, offer themselves as blank projection screens, and put aside their own feelings, reactions, and personal growth for the growth of the client. The humanistic-existential model, however, has emphasized the importance of participation by therapists in all their humanity in the therapeutic relationship, opening themselves fully to the client's and their own reactions (Bugental, 1965, 1976).

To this human participation, the transpersonal orientation adds another perspective: the therapist may serve the client best by viewing the therapeutic relationship as a karma yoga to foster his or her own transpersonal growth through consciously serving the client. The forms this service may take are many and may even be externally indistinguishable from other therapeutic endeavors. But they are undertaken within the context of optimizing growth through service. The situation is seen as one in which therapist and client work together in the ways most appropriate to their particular roles. The therapist's openness and willingness to view therapy as a process of learning and service can provide useful modeling for the client.

The type of modeling appropriate to a transpersonal perspective differs from traditional approaches. In the latter, the therapist is usually portrayed as an expert who can provide information and is thus a model of competency. In a transpersonal approach, the therapist both shares competence and also provides a learning-to-cope model, where appropriate, in a relatively transparent manner. Learning-to-cope models are ones who acknowledge and share their own efforts to learn and cope with issues. Since transpersonal therapists may combine both varieties of modeling, it is of interest that studies of modeling have demonstrated that the learning-to-cope model is frequently more effective than the competency one (Bandura, 1969, 1977b).

Such modeling provides a high degree of mutuality between therapist and client, because both share the same growth-oriented intention for the therapy, are less hierarchically distanced, and each can learn from the other. Indeed, the therapist may enhance this process by interacting with appropriate openness and authenticity with clients working at this level, and by offering the client the opportunity to engage in a mutually facilitating, two-way feedback.

In transpersonal therapy the value and attitudes of the therapist are thus of crucial importance, and the effects of modeling can be recognized not only in overt behavior but in subtle attitudes as well.

A Comparison of Transpersonal with Other Forms of Therapy

Transpersonal psychotherapy can be distinguished from traditional approaches on a variety of dimensions. We shall first discuss the distinguishing general principles and then make comparisons with specific therapeutic schools.

The major aims of traditional approaches might be summarized as primarily oriented toward changing mental contents and sometimes to exploring questions such as, Who am I? or What type of person am I? A transpersonal approach, while it includes these aims, expands them to incorporate further goals derived from the transpersonal model discussed earlier.

Important among these is enhancing awareness. To do this, perception may be trained as in meditation where the individual may learn to observe mental content rather than primarily attempting to change it. As Fritz Perls observed, "Awareness per se—by and of itself—can be curative" (1969a, p. 16). In addition to watching mental content, the individual may also aim to disidentify from it (Vaughan, 1977, 1979), a process which explores not only the question of Who am I? but also, What am I?

For example, a client presenting to a traditional therapist feelings of inadequacy would be viewed as having low self-esteem, poor ego strength, or negative self-attributions, according to the therapist's particular discipline. If a psychodynamic approach were employed, then the therapist might attempt to determine the genesis of these thoughts and to have the client examine their origins. Behavioral and cognitive approaches might attempt to modify them directly by environmental change, differential reinforcement, or thought substitution (Rimm & Masters, 1975; Thoresen & Mahoney, 1974). Whatever the approach, the effective aim would be to modify the client's belief and experience about what type of person he or she is.

A transpersonalist might use these approaches, too, but would also recognize that the problem represented an example of identification with negative thoughts and emotions.

> A young woman who came to therapy suffering from severe anxiety, loneliness, and fear of men, perceived all men as threatening and potentially dangerous. In therapy, as she learned to relax and allow her own violent fantasies to become more conscious, she was able to see how her fears distorted her perceptions of reality to such an extent that she felt continually threatened. Through relaxation training and meditation she was able to acknowledge her negative thoughts and disidentify from them. As self-awareness expanded, she became increasingly willing to take responsibility for her own state of consciousness. Anxiety was greatly reduced, and she was eventually able to establish satisfying relationships with both men and women. (Vaughan)

Such a problem would be viewed as only one example of many types of identification with which the client was unwittingly involved. The distinguishing feature of this particular identification would be that it caused discomfort of clinical proportions. Thus, if the transpersonal therapist chose to employ a meditative approach that involved training awareness with the aim of reducing automatic identification with thoughts, it could result in the client's having not only a different belief about what type of person she was but an alteration in the more fundamental perception of what she was.

The relative extent to which traditional and nontraditional techniques are employed varies with the individual client, and they may well be mutually facilitative. It would seem, however, that the goals of meditation and other transpersonal approaches extend beyond those of traditional Western psychotherapy. Eastern traditions suggest that our usual state of consciousness is colored by illusions and is dreamlike. When this illusion is mistaken for reality, the Western therapist may help prevent the dream from becoming a nightmare, but Eastern approaches to consciousness also aim at awakening (Jung, 1973; Walsh, 1977; Wilber, 1977, 1978).

The expanded version of psychology which the transpersonal perspective offers is not only a general synthesis of East and West but also an integration of various Western approaches. In *The Spectrum of Consciousness*, Wilber (1977) distinguishes three primary levels of consciousness: the ego, the existential, and the level of Mind. The ego level concerns the roles, self-image, and analytical aspects of our mind with which we identify. The existential concerns our basic sence of existence, the meaning of life, confrontation with death, aloneness, and the central experience of being-in-the-world. Together, these two levels constitute our identity as separate, self-existent individuals. It is with these levels that most Western therapies are concerned, assuming that humans are condemned to live out their lives as isolated, alienated individuals, inherently and permanently separated from the rest of the universe. Such approaches aim at strengthening the ego.

Each therapeutic approach may contribute to health and well-being in its own way at its own level and is not necessarily better or worse than another. Rather, each is simply addressed to different levels. Ideally, the transpersonal recognizes the potential of each level and makes optimum use of the contributions of both East and West to intervene at the appropriate level.

The following is an attempt to compare the transpersonal with some other major Western traditions: psychoanalysis, Jungian analytical psychology, behaviorism, humanistic, and existential psychologies.

Classical Psychoanalysis

In psychoanalysis the human being is presumed to be inherently locked in mental conflict which can be reduced but never fully resolved (Brenner, 1974). The individual must therefore constantly guard against and control this conflict. A strong ego, the mediating factor between an irrational id and a controlling super ego, is considered the hallmark of health. Health is often defined, by default, as the absence of pathology.

From a transpersonal perspective, this is insufficient. There is no quarrel with the premise that a strong, healthy ego is an asset in meeting the demands of life, but the transpersonal concept of health goes beyond belief in ego development as the summit of mental health. While the conflicts of the ego may indeed be unresolvable, they can be transcended.

Analytical Psychology

Of all the schools which have developed and departed from Freud's original work, the depth psychology of Carl Jung—also called analytical psychology—has been the one most concerned with transpersonal levels of experience. The in-depth exploration of the psyche in Jungian work extends beyond both the ego and existential levels when it deals with archetypes and the collective unconscious. Jung himself was the first Western psychotherapist to affirm the importance of transpersonal experience for mental health. He wrote that the main thrust of his work was not the treatment of neurosis but the approach to the numinous, or transpersonal dimensions of experience. He claimed that "the approach to the numinous is the real therapy, and inasmuch as you attain to the numinous experiences you are released from the curse of pathology" (Jung, 1973, p. 377).

Analytical psychology recognizes that the psyche has within it the capacity for self-healing and self-realization. A good deal of attention is devoted to the mythological dimension of experience, and the images of dreams and active imagination are valued as powerful therapeutic agents. However, Jungian work remains predominantly concerned with the contents of consciousness rather than with consciousness itself as the context of all experience. It therefore stops short of valuing the direct, imageless awareness attained in the practice of some meditative disciplines.

Behaviorism

The defining characteristic of behaviorism is its insistence on the measurability and verification of behavior and behavior change (Bandura, 1969, 1977b). By careful, methodical, empirically based growth, it has developed a technology which is often highly effective in the treatment of delimited behavioral problems.

However, its strength also dictates its limits. The rigid demand for measurement of observable behavior has tended to remove subjective experience from consideration. Such dimensions as consciousness and, until recently, even thoughts and feelings have been ignored. Classical behaviorism is therefore unable to encompass some of the most central aspects of the human condition and has little to say about positive health and well-being. Rather, it has been limited mainly to the treatment of pathologies that have clearly defined, overt, and relatively simple behavioral characteristics.

At the present time, however, cognition and cognitive mediation of behavioral manifestations are being increasingly investigated in cognitive behavior modification and cognitive therapy (Mahoney, 1974). Self-control is being increasingly emphasized (Thoreson & Mahoney, 1974), and self-efficacy has been advanced as a major mediator of therapeutic change (Bandura, 1977a).

Some transpersonal techniques can readily be viewed from a behavior modification framework. For example, a variety of meditations aim to enhance feelings of love and then to use these feelings to inhibit negative emotions such as anger; clearly these practices are based on a form of reciprocal inhibition, which behaviorists use to replace anxiety with relaxation. The Buddha's explicit instructions for such techniques (Buddhagosa, 1923) suggest that some of the principles of this discipline were recognized over two thousand years ago.

In a similar way, transpersonalists have recognized the importance of modeling, on which behaviorists have amassed a significant body of research data. There is, however, a major difference between the schools, a difference which relates to the subtlety of the behavior and phenomena which are modeled. In general, behaviorists have concerned themselves primarily with relatively gross, easily measured behaviors, whereas the transpersonalists have been interested in more subtle experiences and behaviors.

If the field of transpersonal psychotherapy is to be advanced, it needs empirical testing and validation of many current assumptions and practices. Here, the behaviorists have much to teach us. Similarly, as behaviorists appreciate the need for a broader, less restricted and dehumanizing perspective, they may turn to the experiential psychologies for guidance. Although it may still be far off, some type of rapprochement is clearly desirable.

Humanistic Psychology

At first glance, the distinctions between humanistic and transpersonal psychotherapy are less apparent. Both are growth-oriented models concerned as much with health as pathology, and both are holistic, attempting to deal with the whole person.

However, their central concepts of health are different. From the usual humanistic standpoint, the healthy individual is self-actualizing and aims for a balanced integration of physical, emotional, and mental dimensions. The spiritual dimension, however, may be ignored or even invalidated by the humanistic approach, whereas for the transpersonal it is central.

Humanistic psychology addresses itself predominantly to the ego and existential levels. The development of personality and the achievement of ego goals are central. From a transpersonal perspective, these are accorded less centrality. Here, the human capacity for self-transcendence beyond self-actualization is recognized as a further developmental possibility.

Many humanistic psychologists are not particularly interested in exploring transpersonal experiences. Transpersonal psychologists, however, are expected to have some firsthand experience of such states in order to work effectively with those who seek guidance in dealing with them. A therapist who does not have firsthand knowledge may unwittingly invalidate clients' transpersonal experiences, often to their detriment.

Existentialism

The existential approach comes close to the transpersonal in its concern with the search for meaning and purpose, the confrontation of death and aloneness, the necessity for choice and responsibility, and the demands of authenticity (Bugental, 1965, 1976). The same is true for the view that we shape our reality by our beliefs. For example, freedom seems real when we believe in it; we have to know that we can have it before we can exercise it. The same is true of many other values which we can choose to cultivate.

Facing these questions and challenges at the existential level may lay the groundwork for transpersonal work. This, in turn, can penetrate the mask of our separate and alienated individuality to reveal the transpersonal self, which experiences the underlying interconnectedness of all life. The experience of freedom, with all its paradoxes, and the raw experience of being-in-the-world that the existentialists portray can open the way for the personal transformation which leads to transcendence. Existentialists, however, usually regard the separate, ego-defined identity as inescapable and do not make the leap beyond dualistic knowledge into transpersonal experiences.

Existentialists might be said to have rediscovered the first Noble Truth of Buddhism—namely that life is imbued with suffering—but not to have discovered a way out. The primary recommendation is therefore a heroic attitude of, for example, resoluteness and engagement in the face of apparent existential inevitabilities. However, the Buddha went further, and in the remaining three Noble Truths he pointed a way to freedom from the existential dilemma, leading to the transpersonal realm beyond the ego and existential levels.

Limitations of Transpersonal Psychotherapy

The preceding sections describe some of the characteristics of transpersonal psychology and psychotherapy. What, then, are the factors that currently limit this field?

First, the transpersonal clearly lacks an adequate experimental foundation. Of course, the same can be said of most other psychotherapy schools, but that is hardly an adequate response. Many of the concerns of the transpersonal therapist lie outside the range of interest, competence, and investigative arenas of most researchers. Therefore, many assumptions, though experientially satisfying, remain experimentally untested. There has been an understandable but regrettable and unsustainable tendency to think that if experimenters are not interested in this area, that is their problem. Yet if the transpersonal is truly to be what it claims to strive for—namely an effective synthesis of Eastern wisdom and Western science—its practitioners need to do all they can to ensure that their work is subjected to careful scientific scrutiny. The history of psychotherapy is filled with partisan assumptions and claims of superiority, which have remained intact only as long as they remained unexamined (Karasu, 1977; Luborsky, Singer, & Luborsky, 1975). While there is a growing body of research on meditation, which is supportive on the whole, few other transpersonal areas have been examined.

This raises the interesting question of the applicability of traditional scientific paradigms to the investigation of transpersonal phenomena. The necessity for novel approaches—approaches less interfering, more sensitive to subjective states, and involving the experimenter as a trained participant-observer—has been frequently recognized, but such approaches are still little used (Maslow, 1966; Shapiro & Walsh, 1984; Tart, 1992; Walsh, 1977). With rare exceptions, the transpersonal has to-date been little integrated with other

Western psychologies and therapies. Hopefully, increased knowledge will correct this schism.

To anyone who has explored the transpersonal realms in any depth, it is apparent that intellectual comprehension demands an experiential foundation (Deikman, 1977; Walsh, 1977, 1978). Experiential knowledge is clearly a limiting factor for conceptual understanding. Indeed, the individual needs to recognize this through experience before he or she can appreciate its power and implications. Failure to appreciate it has led to countless misunderstandings, discountings, and superficial and pathologizing interpretations of the transpersonal. Even the most intellectually sophisticated mental health practitioners, if they are experientially naive, may make such errors—errors like those made by the Group for Advancement of Psychiatry's (GAP, 1977) report on mysticism and psychiatry. Both therapists and investigators need to be aware of this and to undertake their own personal experiential work. Since both the transpersonal realm and the potential for growth exceed the explorations of most of us, it is probably safe to say that the limits of our psychological growth represent one of the major limiting factors for this field.

Transpersonal psychotherapy places a number of stringent demands on its practitioners. These are not unique to the transpersonal; rather, they represent subtler, deeper demands than other therapies because the phenomena with which we are working are themselves subtler and deeper. This may perhaps represent an example of a general *principle of increasing subtlety:* as we move toward greater health, the psychological phenomena with which we must work become increasingly subtle, and the tools most suitable for dealing with them become correspondingly less active and interfering, and more simply observing, accepting, and allowing (Walsh, 1976, 1977).

Because we are both the instruments and the models for what we have to offer, we must seek to live and be that which we would offer to our clients. With few empirical guidelines, we must rely heavily on ourselves for guidance and strive for integrity and sensitivity. Nowhere in the field of psychotherapy is the therapist's growth more important for both client and therapist.

Postscript

In the two decades since the original preparation of this chapter for the first edition, the transpersonal field and our thinking have progressed significantly. For updated, expanded discussions of issues raised in this chapter see Frances Vaughan, *The Inward Arc: Healing in Psychotherapy and Spirituality,* Nevada City, Calif.: Blue Dolphin Press, 1995; and R. Walsh and F. Vaughan (eds.), *Paths Beyond Ego: The Transpersonal Vision,* Los Angeles: J. P. Tarcher, 1993.

3

A Pilgrimage of Healing
Personal Thoughts of a Transpersonal Psychotherapist

Gerald G. May

"The world needs places to heal," wrote two women recently at the conclusion of internships at battered women's shelters (Miyazaki & Youngdahl, 1979, p. 2). They were speaking of this need not only for the women with whom they worked but also for themselves. The pilgrimage towards healing or wholeness is as ancient as human existence; the writings about the journey are as ancient as writing itself. Whether it be Odysseus, interns, experienced practitioners, the victims of violence, or anyone else, each traveler knows something about the uniqueness of his or her own journey and has glimpses of its universality.

Gerald May, in this warm, personal chapter, shares both the unique and the universal aspects of his own journey in a way that each of us can understand, no matter how far we have traveled. Who of us has not experienced what May describes—taking the giant step from familiar territory to a region of untested ideas and experiences; feeling the effort, anguish, and excitement of making an important personal discovery and afterward coming home with the knowledge that, though the world about us seems unchanged, inside we shall never be quite the same again?

The familiar territory from which May started his personal and professional journey was that of medicine and psychiatry. With disarming honesty he describes how his training and intense desire to alleviate suffering led to objective distancing, loss of empathy, and a search for personal gratification. In his desire to become a good therapist and to effect change in people, his clients became "things one wishes to fix."

Frustrated and angry at the apparent ineffectiveness of accepted techniques, May moved into unfamiliar territory—meditation, biofeedback, rediscovery of religious roots, mysticism—where he regains some of his sensitivity to and empathy with human suffering. Speaking now from the vantage point of the homeward journey, he shares with us a number of lessons he has learned, deceptively simple lessons that can be simply expressed only because they are profoundly understood. "One thing I've learned," he says, "is that there is a difference between healing and fixing."

To learn thoroughly the lessons that May has learned and continues to learn requires considerable courage, because it requires "the sacrifice, at least temporarily, of both one's self-importance and one's preconceptions and prejudices." In their place, for that time, there is "only space." One of the techniques May uses himself and encourages his clients to use is meditation, which he describes unpretentiously as "just sitting there for a while, letting things come and go." He sees it as a "kind of open awareness" which allows the meditator to begin to see life as-it-is.

May believes that this ability to tell the difference between what is invented and what is not is one of the fundamental issues of transpersonal therapy. It is also, for him, fundamental to growth and healing. In this chapter, then, he challenges us to pursue our own journeys, to live a question posed by those two interns: "Are we willing to give up who we are in order to be who we are not yet?" (Miyazaki & Youngdahl, 1979, p. 2). Odysseus, intern, practitioner, client, person—whoever we are, we would do well to be as honest in our responses as May is in this chapter.

I HAVE NEVER BEEN ABSOLUTELY CERTAIN what transpersonal psychology is. But it has something to do with a recognition of life being more than we perceive it to be. It seems to acknowledge that most of our perceptions are colored and clouded by the images we make of reality, the prejudices, preconceptions, and expectations that we bring to experience. It holds out the hope that, if we could but clear our vision of the world and see things just-as-they-are, the suffering of human minds would greatly be eased. For me, the learning of these lessons has been a pilgrimage of healing.

The meaning of pilgrimage is that one starts from a certain familiar territory where the world makes sense and there are few surprises. Then one begins a journey into lands that are not so familiar and where things don't make the same kind of sense. During the journey, many things seem special, dramatic, promising, and fearful. And one knows that one is learning something very important. Then, when the journey is finished, one goes home again—back to the same old place, with the same old things going on. Nothing has happened to change the world, and on the outside one may not appear to be much different for having taken the trip. But inside, there is a difference. Something has indeed happened, but it is so subtle that its quality escapes definition.

This going-home phase of pilgrimage is often overlooked, but it is the most important part. One cannot have made a pilgrimage unless one goes home afterward. It's like the old Zen saying, "At first the trees were just trees and the mountains were just mountains. Then, when I began to practice Zen, the trees were no longer trees and the mountains no longer mountains. Now, after I have practiced a long time, the trees are just trees again, and the mountains just mountains."

The starting place of my professional pilgrimage was very familiar territory indeed. I saw around me minds that were suffering, and I did not understand why. I wanted to help ease this suffering, so I learned many things—the anatomy and physiology of the human body, the neurochemistry of brains and the psychodynamics of minds, the categorization of people's problems from adjustment reactions to schizophrenia, and all the theories of therapy.

Somehow in this process, people became things. When a student begins to study the behavioral sciences, he or she naturally learns to look at people's problems objectively. And just as naturally the student soon begins to look at people objectively, too: There's me (the subject) studying people (the objects). Perhaps it is necessary to go through this, but it is deeply frightening. It is frightening because you begin with a feeling of empathic sensitivity to the suffering of others, and then, while you're trying to learn how to ease that suffering, you find out that you are distancing yourself from the humanity of those very people. And usually this distancing and objectification grow into a desire for personal gratification—I want to be a good therapist . . . I want to be able to effect change in these people. At this point, the people become things you wish to fix.

When I was in high school, I had a friend with whom I used to spend a lot of time, driving around town, getting root beers at the A&W, looking for girls we could pretend we were going to pick up. One evening while we were driving, he began to cry. I didn't know what to do, so I pulled the car over and asked him what was wrong. He told me he'd been having nightmares, that he'd felt afraid nearly every day during the past several weeks, and that he thought he was going crazy. He ended his story with "Oh, I wish I were dead."

"Ah, come on," I said. "It can't be that serious."

"Yeah? Well, I just talked with Reverend Wilson today, and he said— he said—" He was crying so hard he could barely get the words out. "He said I was a latent homosexual."

I hardly knew what that meant at the time, so I just responded with "Hogwash!" I don't remember what we said after that, but it wasn't long until we were back at the A&W, making comments about the girls.

About a decade later, in the middle of my psychiatric residency, I had been called to see a young woman who had scratched her wrists. "Would you like to tell me about it?" I asked. She proceeded, through her tears, to tell me about a series of broken love affairs, job failures, and drug abuse. "I just can't get it together. I wish I'd never been born."

"Well, I think you'd better come in the hospital for a while, and we can get these problems ironed out."

Somewhat reluctantly she let herself be admitted to the hospital, was given antidepressant medication, and listened to. I saw her regularly to ascertain her progress, and we'd talk about her troubles. I would try to help her explore her background, hoping she could get some understanding of why she had the problems she had. Then, while she was on a weekend pass from the hospital, she met a young man with whom she hit it off very well. Her depression lifted and she was discharged. I never saw her again.

Several years later I was working in a drug abuse clinic and was seeing a young man who had been in therapy with me for eight months. For the past four of those months he had been drug free, but this day he came in high. "You shot up again, didn't you?"

"Yeah. Man, I can't take it anymore. I know you tried to help me and I let you down, but it's just too much."

"Well, let's talk about it some more," I said. I tried to sound professionally optimistic, but I know he heard the anger and disappointment in my voice. We talked for an hour or so, then he left, and that was the last I ever heard of him. That kind of thing had been happening a lot. All these suffering, drug-abusing people, and I'd use all my therapeutic techniques on them, and nothing would work.

Every time I'd try to evaluate this state of affairs, I'd find myself walking a very thin line. On one side of the line I would say, "I'm an incompetent therapist. Somewhere in my training I didn't read that important paragraph which said how to really help people." And on the other side of the line I'd say, "There's nothing that can be done for people like this. They're not motivated. They ought to be in jail instead of in a clinic."

All of this was part of a pilgrimage, but I didn't know it at the time. I had begun with empathy and some kind of open awareness of suffering, and had responded with whatever seemed best at the time. Then, with training, I responded with objectivity and used supposedly tried-and-true techniques to fix people's problems. Later on, when I saw the inadequacy of the techniques in certain situations, I felt frustrated and angry—not out of empathy for the suffering of others anymore, but because I wasn't being an effective therapist.

About that time, I began to speak with people who had overcome their addictive problems. Looking for "the answer," I asked them how they had done it. Their responses all seemed to indicate that they had had some kind of experience, a sort of eye-opening, clarifying, different vision of the world and of themselves. It had had virtually nothing to do with therapy, but somehow it had changed their lives.

Thinking there might be a new technique in this, I tried to clarify what that experience was, how it happened, how to make it happen. And that is what opened the door for me to what is now known as "transpersonal."

For the experience they described was a transpersonal one. It was one in which, at least for a while, all their preconceived images of themselves and of the world dropped away, and they saw life just-as-it-is, without naming, judging, manipulating, or thinking about it in any way.

Many years have passed since then. Years of chasing after that experience, at first thinking it was something special, some altered state of consciousness to be achieved through meditation, biofeedback, psychedelics, or religious conversion. Years of talking and reading and learning the language of mysticism. Years during which I rediscovered my own religious roots with totally new eyes. And, gratefully, years during which some of the objectification of people lessened and some of that naive sensitivity to human suffering returned. I was struck by that not too long ago when a person told me of his distress and I felt it with him saying, "Ah, come on, it can't be that serious." And he said something else, to which I responded, "Hogwash!"

The pilgrimage is far from over, but I can see home coming up on the horizon. And the trees and mountains look a lot more like trees and mountains than they used to. And inside, I think I've learned something.

For one thing, I've learned that there is a difference between healing and fixing. If I try to fix the person that I see before me, I am embarking on a path that will lead both of us into ever-increasing separation and alienation. But if I can blink my eyes and see what's there, and *quit thinking about it*, then there may be some space for healing to occur. For healing is not something I do to someone else, nor is it something one does to oneself; rather it is a process within us, happening—*just happening*—if we can get out of its way.

Getting out of the way is very difficult. Most people suffer because they get in their own way. Then they go to therapists who also get in the way. Though this kind of approach can cause considerable change in a person, that change is likely to encourage greater suffering later on.

For example, a middle-aged woman says: "For years I've been a nobody. I've lived my life for my husband and my children. Now the children are grown, and my husband's running around, and I'm sick of it. I'm tired of being held down. I want to make something of myself. I want to be my own person." She wants to get in control of things, build a new identity, and create a self-image she can be proud of. It sounds admirable, and it's certainly normal, but it's also asking for trouble. For what happens if she succeeds? She will have struggled to build an image of personal and interpersonal competence, an image she'll have to maintain. Having struggled to establish an independent identity, she will need to struggle to preserve that identity, perhaps to increase it. It will feel good to be autonomous, powerful, in charge of herself, but it will require great energy, and sooner or later she will tire. Having come from the one extreme of feeling held down by the world, she will be tempted to go to the other extreme of trying to feel on top of the world. In so doing she will have got in her own way. If you are *either* held down by the world *or* on top of it, you can't possibly feel at one with the world. The sky, which might have been a sister, now becomes a thing to look at. And other people, whom you might have experienced as a shared unity of consciousness, now become objects to be dealt with, things either to be feared or ruled.

So I might want to say, "Of course you need not be held down. And maybe you need some time of self-determination to balance things out a little. But watch out. Because, whether you are derogating yourself or determining yourself, you are indeed making a big deal of yourself. And whenever you do this, you will find you are separating yourself more and more from the world around you, and getting in your own way more and more." And I might go on to say, "Blink your eyes now, and then look around. Take a breath, and listen to the sounds around you. This is the way things are, before any thought about it, before any fear or desire, before you or I do anything to it. This is just the way it is, and here there is no holding down or striving forth, no struggle and no contempt. Anything else is something we add to this, something that comes from our images and desires, something that will make it all very complicated and worrisome, something that will pull us apart and make us forget who we really are."

These are things I might say—things I think I'd like to say in such a situation. But I don't really know whether I'd say them or not. I know that she has her image of the world and I have mine, and one thing I don't want to do is to complicate her images. I hope that I can be blinking my eyes and breathing and practicing what I preach. Then whatever is said is whatever is said—there's no way to predict.

There is a risk in all of this. To see life as-it-is requires the sacrifice, at least temporarily, of both one's self-importance and one's preconceptions and prejudices. And for however long it lasts, there is nothing to replace what has been sacrificed. Only space. For most of us, the thought of this kind of sacrifice is very threatening, and we cannot rationalize ourselves into comfort about it. The more we think about this non–self-defining, nondesiring, noncontrolling realm of being, the more anxious we are apt to become. So there is a need for either faith or trust, or some combination of both, to substitute for thinking.

If faith is present, you are fortunate. You can say something that means "Thy will be done" and go on simply living the best way you can with your eyes as open as possible. But faith, it seems, either is there or is not there. As with healing, you can't make it happen. You can try to get yourself out of its way, but you can't fabricate it. Trust, however, is different. Trust is something built on personal experience, and it is for this reason that I now encourage myself and my clients to practice some form of meditation.

In meditation, you have the opportunity of easing your grip on all your preconceptions, images, and self-importance, the opportunity of allowing them to fade away for a while and finding out that you are still there. The repeated experience of this builds a trust that you do not have to figure life out or cling to a self-image, that you do not have to commandeer your own spirit or jump to fix every problem you detect in yourself. There are times in meditation when life can be seen just-as-it-is. Then you realize that all the neurotic and interpersonal hassles a person struggles with are merely figments of an overzealous mind. This is, of course, very reassuring, and you often find yourself giggling at your emotional turmoil. When this happens, healing is very close at hand.

So meditation, as I see it, is not really a tool of or an adjunct to therapy. It is not something I tell someone to do in order to fix him or her. Rather, it is just a way of seeing. It is not even, in my opinion, an alteration of consciousness. It seems to me that one's consciousness is *already* altered most of the time by thoughts, images, and desires *about* life. Meditation is just a way of opening one's eyes to see what's really there.

There's nothing very dramatic about this kind of meditation. It's just sitting there for a while, letting things come and go. It is simply maintaining some attentiveness while all the thoughts and sounds and feelings rise and fall. Or being watchful while you are eating, talking, working, reading, or whatever—just to *notice* what's going on with a minimum of judgment or manipulation.

There are many ways of facilitating this kind of open awareness. Muscular relaxing, breathing exercises, and different ways of centering attention can all help your mind quiet down a little and allow the clouds to pass away from consciousness. But these are just gimmicks to nurture seeing, and it is probably wise not to become infatuated with any of them. It is best, I think, just to blink your eyes, take a breath, and see. And to stay with that seeing until you begin to add something to it. Then to blink your eyes, take a breath, and see again.

In daily professional practice, I make an attempt to encourage this kind of seeing. When feelings are discussed, for example, I ask people to watch how those feelings seem to rise and fall in consciousness as well as to explore their possible psychodynamic roots. And I ask people to compare their state of mind when their attention is riveted to their problems with their state of mind when they have "momentarily forgotten" their problems. What is the difference, and who is this one who is there seeing both situations? What this nurtures is a growing sense that there are not only many ways of perceiving life, many realms of mental activity, but also a constant consciousness that is not affected by *any* kind of experience.

One comes to learn that neuroses occur totally within the realm of mental images. To work on neurosis within that realm means to invest more energy in that realm, hoping to achieve *another* mental image that is fulfilled, complete, mature, and integrated. There is nothing wrong with this. The only question is how much time and energy one wishes to invest in working with and reacting to these mental images as compared with how much time and energy one has left to live one's life simply and directly as it is.

> Jim and Lisa have been married for twelve years. They have not been getting along well at all. They argue a lot and have many periods of cold silence. They seek counseling and spend most of their therapy time defending themselves. At various times, both Jim and Lisa find themselves doubting whether the marriage can work. This feeling creates even more disturbance, because the prospect of going it alone is frightening to both of them.
>
> One day there is a windstorm, and the tree in front of their house is blown down. No one is hurt, but the front porch is damaged and a window is broken. Immediately Jim and Lisa are working together, clearing the broken branches, repairing the window and the porch. Afterwards, it dawns on them that, in spite of all their troubles, they worked very well with each other. Jim even recalls watching Lisa working on the porch and feeling something tender for her. When they talk about this, they realize that in many areas of their life they *do* work well together—in responding to a hurt child, in preparing meals, in driving to the store—as well as in more dramatic situations.
>
> With a little perspective at this point, it might be possible for Jim and Lisa to see that their problems are, in large part, a result of where their attention is placed at any given time. When their attention is on the day-to-day task of living, with their mundane, automatic solutions, there is no great difficulty. But when they start *thinking about* themselves and each other, when they start reacting to their mental images of themselves, when they become caught up in their concepts of what each is doing to the other, that's when the problems happen.

In reality, there are only two important things in a relationship. One is affection, and the other is living one's life. All the rest is invented.

Distinguishing between what is invented and what is not is, I think, one of the core issues of transpersonal psychotherapy. This way of seeing does not come easily. As it does come, however, it not only addresses the specific psychological problems for which one has sought help but also opens the doors to constantly fresh perceptions throughout the remainder of one's life.

Some months ago, after a particularly strong experience of what seemed real and what seemed invented, I wrote the following. I doubt that I would be able to describe it any better than this:

> With completely open arms I would embrace all this. Just-as-it-is. Nothing added or subtracted. The beauty is indescribable.
>
> By night my mind makes images of life, preparing for the morning. As a dream it does this, and its work is long and hard.
>
> When dawn comes and I wake up, the images are ready—already laid over my consciousness like so many veils.
>
> There is an image of me—of who I am and was and will be. Clinging to this or that characteristic of myself, sensing some kind of identity.
>
> There are images of those around me, of my loved ones, colleagues, neighbors. These are images filled with longing, scorn, prejudice and possessiveness, and, occasionally, fear.
>
> There are images of my environment, of time and space and form, telling me the names and purposes of things. Without these I might try to drink the sunlight or wear a chair upon my feet. Would that be so bad?
>
> And there are images of my own thoughts and feelings. Some energy arises in my chest, and it attracts my attention. Then without a moment's pause my mind selects the appropriate image. "Longing," I say. "Wanting, needing, not having—hunger." A name for this energy in my chest, but it all happens so quickly I don't even know it's my label. It seems I actually *feel* wanting, longing, hunger.
>
> And then the dance of the images begins. Over the raw and pure essence of things as they are, I have placed the many-colored veils and filters of things as I want them to be, and the world becomes dulled, and cumbersome, and very complicated.
>
> My image of me reacts with my image of you and your image of you and your image of me, in an arena of our images of the way things are around us, in a time frame which is only

image; and it is all driven by energy disguised as emotions, striving for concocted goals, running from imagined fears, playing in an invented space between us.

There is a certain quality of feeling about this image-dance. A subtle thing, but recognizable. It feels as if there is some tenseness about my eyes and forehead, and my shoulders scrunch up a little bit. There is something closed-in, tight, confining about my consciousness, almost as if all the images have packed themselves together tightly, encompassing the entire sphere of my vision. There is no space. The air is stuffy.

Recognizing this, seeing this image-of-my-images, my eyes blink hard and I shake my head a little. Take a deep breath and blow it all away.

And then, oh, just for a fraction of a second, just an instant, it all becomes clear. The world sparkles with diamond sharpness of detail and—just then—things are as-they-are. The images have fallen away, simply not there, and beyond them, through them, the indescribable beauty!

Here now in this precious moment there is no difference between me and you, no pulling of this against that, no struggling of feeling—just this, all of it, as-it-is. Wonderful, exquisite, awesome and immense, the universe opens its heart, and love is the very air.

This mind, so busy through the night in its image factory, is resting now. The clouds in its water settle, its surface calms, and in that instant it is pure water, still water, reflecting like a perfect mirror all the things of this life.

But somewhere in the murk, the deep, still cloudy underwater caverns of my brain, a turbulence of death and fear takes place. "Too long," it rumbles, "too long I have been without knowing who I am. Too long in this awesome bliss, too long." It churns the deep and ruffles the surface, and the mirror becomes erratic, distorting again, pretending all over again, and I am caught.

This is the cycle of my days, the changing weather of my mind, evolving, growing, dying, resurrecting, to what end? I think I know, but these are images reflected from a restless mind. I think I was given this gift of consciousness in order that I might appreciate and know the wonder of life. But I have used it to play God. I have changed wonder into wanting, and awareness into mastery and self-preservation. I think this is true, but of course I do not know. All I know is that another time will come, soon, maybe in this very next instant, when it will all be clear again. And then the reasons won't matter anymore.

With completely open arms I would embrace all this. Just-as-it-is. Nothing added or subtracted. The beauty is indescribable.

Whatever transpersonal psychology really is, I hope it will never be defined as objectively as analytical and behavioral psychology have been. If and when that should happen, transpersonal psychology will cease to be the catalyst for pilgrimages in growth and healing that it now is. It will become simply another in the long line of mental conceptualizations which we human beings use to complicate our lives.

4

Theoretical and Empirical Foundations of Transpersonal Psychology

Stanislav Grof

Stanislav Grof emphasizes that transpersonal psychology recognizes spirituality and non-ordinary states of consciousness (NOSC) as important dimensions of the human psyche. In this chapter, he shows that a transpersonal orientation is not only scientifically justified, but that it also leads us to new approaches to many practical problems in the therapeutic area (psychological and medical). Further than that, Grof proposes, it even has particular relevance to solving global problems facing our planet.

The author focuses on the perinatal area of our lives, not only for its own importance, but also because "it represents an important gateway to the transpersonal domain of the psyche." He makes the important differentiation between spirituality, which is "universal, all embracing, and based on direct experience" and religion, which is based on dogma or religious scripture.

Spiritual experiences manifest as the experience of the immanent divine and the transcendental divine, where the latter involve transcendence of the usual boundaries of space and time. Cartesian-Newtonian science finds it very difficult to accept the idea that "everything we can

Revised paper presented at the Twelfth International Transpersonal Conference entitled "Science, Spirituality, and the Global Crisis: Toward a World with a Future," June 20–25, 1992, in Prague, Czechoslovakia.

experience in the everyday state of consciousness as an object has in the non-ordinary states of consciousness a corresponding subjective representation." In addition to the transcendence of space and time, spiritual experiences may involve the extension of consciousness into realms and dimensions that the traditional Western culture does not consider to be real. An important example of this, as described in many of the great spiritual traditions, would be the identification with the mysterious and primordial emptiness and nothingness that is the ultimate cradle of all existence.

In this chapter, Grof reviews the areas of: shamanistic and spiritual practice, the mystical traditions, modern clinical and laboratory consciousness research, experiential encounters with death, spiritual emergencies, parapsychologic research and psychic phenomena, UFO phenomena, multiple personality disorders, and human survival. The common denominator of all these phenomena, Grof writes, is that they "have been dismissed by mainstream psychology and psychiatry as irrelevant manifestations of brain pathology."

The author relates the trauma of birth to global problems such as violence with the suggestion that the study and experience of the transpersonal can contribute to the alleviation of our global crisis. "Transpersonal psychology offers a way of understanding the psyche that is universal—culturally sensitive, respectful to spiritual traditions, and applicable to any culture and historical period.

"There exist," he writes, "important mechanisms of healing and personality transformation that operate on transpersonal levels . . . and clients have to receive encouragement and support to confront unconscious material on all the levels involved."

Grof humbly admits that despite his own personal NOSC and the observation of NOSC of others, it took him "years to fully absorb the impact of this cognitive shock" of the implications and conclusions of his findings. We need to approach this area with the same humility and be open to examining this area for a long time before drawing any final conclusions.

TRANSPERSONAL PSYCHOLOGY IS a branch of psychology that recognizes and accepts spirituality as an important dimension of the human psyche and of the universal scheme of things. It also studies and honors the entire spectrum of human experience, including various levels and realms of the psyche that become manifest in non-ordinary states of consciousness (NOSC). Here belong, for example, experiences and observations from meditation and other forms of systematic spiritual practice, spontaneous mystical raptures, psychospiritual crises ("spiritual emergencies"), psychedelic therapy, hypnosis, experiential psychotherapy, and near-death situations (NDE). More specifically, these are such phenomena as sequences of psychological death and rebirth; experiences of divine light; cosmic consciousness; mystical union with other people, nature, and the entire universe; encounters with archetypal beings; visits to mythological realms; karmic experiences; various forms of extrasensory perception (ESP); and many others.

Transpersonal psychology has been in existence for more than a quarter of a century and has been enjoying steadily increasing influence and popularity. In the last fifteen years, the transpersonal orientation has expanded into other scientific disciplines, including quantum-relativistic physics, biology, medicine, anthropology, art, ecology, politics, and many others. The Association for Transpersonal Psychology (ATP) holds annual meetings in Asilomar, California, and the International Transpersonal Association (ITA) convenes regularly in different parts of the world. There exist universities and other educational institutions that offer advanced degrees in transpersonal psychology, and many national and regional conferences in psychiatry, psychology, and anthropology have featured special symposia dedicated exclusively to the transpersonal perspective. Many journals, such as the *Journal of Transpersonal Psychology* and the *Re-Vision Journal*, specialize in publishing articles on transpersonal subjects, and the number of books in this field has reached many hundreds in the United States alone.

In spite of all this, many professionals refuse to accept that the transpersonal orientation represents a legitimate scientific endeavor. They dismiss it as an irrational and undisciplined product of a group of eccentric, mystically oriented professionals and paraprofessionals who are not familiar with the most basic principles of traditional science. The main reason for this criticism is the fact that the findings and conclusions of the transpersonal disciplines are incompatible with the most basic metaphysical assumptions of the Newtonian-Cartesian paradigm and with the materialistic philosophy that has dominated Western science for the last three hundred years.

However, this attitude completely ignores the fact that many of the pioneers and chief representatives of the transpersonal movement are people with solid academic backgrounds and often impressive professional credentials. They have departed from the traditional conceptual frameworks, not because of their ignorance of the most basic principles of Western science, but because the mainstream conceptual frameworks failed to account for and explain too many of their important observations and experiences.

The purpose of this chapter is to review the existing evidence and show that the transpersonal orientation can be fully scientifically justified, both as a theoretical system of thinking and as an approach to important practical problems. I will first describe in very general terms the essence of the issues involved and then discuss more specifically the findings in various areas of the transpersonal field and the challenges they represent for traditional science.

I will also touch upon the new perspectives that open up when we accept the transpersonal orientation and point out the hopes this brings on a personal, as well as collective, level.

The critical issue and pivotal focus of the controversy about transpersonal psychology is the nature (or the ontological status) of a wide spectrum of experiences that occur in various forms of NOSC, such as death-rebirth experiences, archetypal visions, karmic phenomena, out-of-body experiences, episodes of ESP, and many others. Their existence has been known to psychiatrists and psychologists for many decades. However, they were in the past dismissed as pathological products of the brain, as manifestations of mental disease. The main reason for this was the fact that they could not be explained in the context of traditional conceptual frameworks of mainstream psychiatry. They thus were not seen as having any heuristic or therapeutic value. The main concern of psychiatrists has been to find effective means of suppressing them when they occur.

Serious study of NOSC has proven this position to be untenable. It reveals that these experiences are not random products of brain pathology, but represent phenomena that are natural and genuine manifestations of the deeper dynamics of the psyche. Their existence clearly indicates that we have to radically revise our ideas about the nature and dimensions of human consciousness and that our current cartography of the psyche has to be vastly extended. The traditional model of the psyche used in academic psychiatry is limited to postnatal biography and to the individual unconscious as described by Sigmund Freud. In my own attempt to map the new territories of the unconscious, I found it necessary to add two large transbiographical domains; I refer to them as the perinatal and the transpersonal realms.

The perinatal domain derives its name from the fact that most people associate the experiences on this level with reliving of their biological birth (the Greek prefix *peri-* means "around" or "near" and the Latin root *natalis* translates as "pertaining to childbirth"). Birth is a potentially or actually life-threatening event, which accounts for the fact that perinatal experiences represent a strange combination of a profound encounter with death and a determined struggle to be born and to become free. The emotions and physical sensations involved are extremely powerful, often reaching far beyond what the individual could previously even imagine.

The fact that perinatal experiences transcend all the individual limits makes them a natural bridge between the personal realm and the transpersonal domain that we will discuss later. On the one hand, they contain many memories related to various aspects of the process of birth, such as pressures, physical pains, suffocation, strangulation by the umbilical cord, or smell of anesthesia; on the other, they open up into the historical or archetypal domains of the collective unconscious as described by C. G. Jung. This often adds to the perinatal process such elements as racial, collective, karmic, and phylogenetic experiences, as well as rich archetypal imagery of a mythological nature.

To understand the importance of the perinatal dynamics, it is necessary to realize that at the moment of biological birth, the fetus is born anatomically, but not emotionally. While the newborn is liberated from the mechanical confines of the birth canal, he or she still carries a cellular record of the agonizing experience and an enormous amount of pent-up emotions and physical energies. These were generated during the many hours of delivery and could not be adequately processed because there was no access to peripheral discharge in any form.

Unless the person has the opportunity to participate in powerful ritual practice, undergoes systematic experiential therapy, or has a spontaneous episode of NOSC, this situation does not get resolved and persists for the rest of his or her life. The perinatal reservoir of difficult emotions and physical sensations is an important potential source of future psychopathology and of a generally unfulfilling and inauthentic strategy of existence. It is conducive to a relentless linear pursuit of goals ("treadmill" or "rat-race" existence) that can easily be recognized as surrogates for the incomplete gestalt of birth. This unconscious repository of heavily emotionally charged material also seems to separate the individual from his or her inner spiritual core.

Activation of this level of the unconscious in NOSC results in sequences of psychospiritual death and rebirth. It involves not only full conscious experience, assimilation, and integration of the trauma of birth, but also connection with the rich spiritual resources of the transpersonal domain. The specific symbolism of these experiences comes from the Jungian collective unconscious, not from the individual memory banks, and can, therefore, be drawn from any spiritual tradition of the world, quite independent of the subject's racial, cultural, or religious background. For somebody who connected with this experiential domain, spirituality is not a matter of belief or interpretation of the world, but deep knowing.

People who have experiences of this kind open up to spirituality found in the mystical branches of the great religions or in their monastic orders, not necessarily in their mainstream forms. If they take a Christian form, the subject would feel close to St. Teresa of Avila, St. John of the Cross, Meister Eckhart, or St. Hildegard von Bingen, rather than develop appreciation for the Vatican hierarchy, the edicts of the popes, the crusades or the acts of the Inquisition. An Islamic experience of this kind would bring the subject close to the teachings of the various Sufi orders, not to Khomeini, Saddam Hussein, or to the concept of jihad, or the Holy War against the Infidels. A Judaic variety of this experience would connect one to the Hasidic or the Cabalistic tradition and not to fundamentalist Judaism or Zionism, etc. It is spirituality that is universal, all-embracing, and based on direct experience rather than dogma or religious scripture.

The observations from the study of NOSC confirm the ideas of C. G. Jung concerning spirituality. According to him, the experiences from deeper levels of the psyche (in my own terminology, perinatal and transpersonal) have a certain quality that Jung calls (after Rudolph Otto) numinosity. The subjects having such experiences feel that they are encountering a dimension which is sacred, holy, radically different from everyday life, belonging to another order of reality. This term is relatively neutral and thus preferable to others, such as "religious," "mystical," "magical," "holy," "sacred," "occult," and others, which have often been used incorrectly and are easily misleading.

Direct spiritual experiences appear in two different forms. The first of these, *the experience of the immanent divine,* involves subtly, but profoundly transformed perception of the everyday reality. A person having this form of spiritual experience sees the people, animals, and inanimate objects in the environment as radiant manifestations of the same unified field of cosmic creative energy and the boundaries between them as illusory and unreal. This is the experience of nature as god, *deus sive natura,* that Baruch Spinoza talked about. Using an analogy with television, it could be likened to a situation where a black and white picture would suddenly acquire colors. Much of the old perception remains in place, but is radically redefined by the addition of a new dimension.

The second form, *the experience of the transcendental divine,* involves appearance of archetypal beings and realms of reality that are ordinarily transphenomenal, i.e., unavailable to perception in the everyday state of consciousness. They seem to unfold or explicate—borrowing a term from David Bohm—from another level or order of reality. These two types of transpersonal experiences represent the source of inspiration for the founders of religions, saints, prophets, and spiritual practitioners. This form of spirituality is often first encountered in the context of the death-rebirth process, but then finds full expression in connection with the transpersonal level of the psyche, where such experiences appear independently of the perinatal elements.

The term *transpersonal* means literally "lying beyond or going beyond the personal." The experiences that originate on this level involve transcendence of the usual boundaries of the individual (his or her body and ego) and of the limitations of three-dimensional space and linear time that restrict our perception of the world in the ordinary state of consciousness. The transpersonal experiences are best defined by describing first the everyday experience of ourselves and the world—how we have to experience ourselves and the environment to pass for "normal" according to the standards of our culture and of Newtonian-Cartesian psychiatry.

In the ordinary or "normal" state of consciousness, we experience ourselves as Newtonian objects existing within the boundaries of our skin. The American writer and philosopher Alan Watts referred to this experience of oneself as identifying with the "skin-encapsulated ego." Our perception of the environment is restricted by the physiological limitations of our sensory organs and by physical characteristics of the environment. We cannot see objects on the other side of a solid wall, ships that are beyond the horizon, or the other side of the moon. If we are in Prague, we cannot hear what our friends are talking about in San Francisco. We cannot feel the softness of the lambskin unless the surface of our body is in direct contact with it. In addition, we can experience vividly and with all our senses only the events that are happening in the present moment. We can recall the past and anticipate future events or fantasize about them; however, these are very different experiences from an immediate and direct experience of the present moment. In transpersonal states of consciousness, however, none of these limitations are absolute; any of them can be transcended.

Transpersonal experiences can be divided into three large categories. The first of these involves primarily transcendence of the usual spatial barriers, or the limitations of the "skin-encapsulated ego." Here belong experiences of merging with another person into a state that can be called "dual unity," assuming the identity of another person, identifying with the consciousness of an entire group of people (e.g., all mothers of the world, the entire population of India, or all the inmates of concentration camps), or even experiencing an extension of consciousness that seems to encompass all of humanity. Experiences of this kind have been repeatedly described in the spiritual literature of the world.

In a similar way, one can transcend the limits of the specifically human experience and identify with the consciousness of various animals, plants, or even a form of consciousness that seems to be associated with inorganic objects and processes. In the extremes, it is possible to experience consciousness of the entire biosphere, of our planet, or the entire material universe. Incredible and absurd as it might seem to a westerner committed to Cartesian-Newtonian science, these experiences suggest that everything we can experience in the everyday state of consciousness as an object has in the non-ordinary states of consciousness a corresponding subjective representation. It is as if everything in the universe has its objective and subjective aspect, the way it is described in the great spiritual philosophies of the East (e.g., in Hinduism all that exists is seen as a manifestation of Brahma, or in Taoism as a transformation of the Tao).

The second category of transpersonal experiences is characterized primarily by overcoming of temporal rather than spatial boundaries, by transcendence of linear time. We have already talked about the possibility of vivid reliving of important memories from infancy and of the trauma of birth. This historical regression can continue farther and involve authentic fetal and embryonal memories from different periods of intrauterine life. It is not even unusual to experience, on the level of cellular consciousness, full identification with the sperm and the ovum at the time of conception. But the historical regression does not stop here, and it is possible to have experiences from the lives of one's human or animal ancestors, or even those that seem to be coming from the racial and collective unconscious as described by C. G. Jung. Quite frequently, the experiences that seem to be happening in other cultures and historical periods are associated with a sense of personal remembering; people then talk about reliving of memories from past lives, from previous incarnations.

In the transpersonal experiences described so far, the content reflects various phenomena existing in space-time. They involve elements of the everyday familiar reality—other people, animals, plants, materials, and events from the past. What is surprising here is not the content of these experiences, but the fact that we can witness or fully identify with something that is not ordinarily accessible to our experience. We know that there are pregnant whales in the world, but we should not be able to have an authentic experience of being one. The fact that there once was the French Revolution is readily acceptable, but we should not be able to have a vivid experience of being there and lying wounded on the barricades of Paris. We know that there are many things happening in the world in places where we are not present, but it is usually considered impossible to experience something that is happening in remote locations (without the mediation of the television and a satellite). We may also be surprised to find consciousness associated with lower animals, plants, and with inorganic nature.

However, the third category of transpersonal experiences is even stranger; here consciousness seems to extend into realms and dimensions that the Western industrial culture does not consider to be "real." Here belong numerous visions of archetypal beings and mythological landscapes, encounters or even identification with deities and demons of various cultures, and communication with discarnate beings, spirit guides, suprahuman entities, extraterrestrials, and inhabitants of parallel universes. Additional examples in this category are visions and intuitive understanding of universal symbols, such as the cross, the Nile cross or ankh, the swastika, the pentacle, the six-pointed star, or the yin-yang sign.

In its further reaches, individual consciousness can identify with cosmic consciousness or the Universal Mind known under many different names— Brahman, Buddha, the Cosmic Christ, Keter, Allah, the Tao, the Great Spirit, and many others. The ultimate of all experiences appears to be identification with the Supracosmic and Metacosmic Void, the mysterious and primordial emptiness and nothingness that is conscious of itself and is the ultimate cradle of all existence. It has no concrete content, yet it contains all there is in a germinal and potential form.

Transpersonal experiences have many strange characteristics that shatter the most fundamental metaphysical assumptions of the Newtonian-Cartesian paradigm and of the materialistic world view. Researchers who have studied and/or personally experienced these fascinating phenomena realize that the attempts of mainstream science to dismiss them as irrelevant products of human fantasy and imagination or as hallucinations—erratic products of pathological processes in the brain—are naive and inadequate. Any unbiased study of the transpersonal domain of the psyche has to come to the conclusion that the observations represent a critical challenge not only for psychiatry and psychology, but for the entire philosophy of Western science.

Although transpersonal experiences occur in the process of deep individual self-exploration, it is not possible to interpret them simply as intrapsychic phenomena in the conventional sense. On the one hand, they appear on the same experiential continuum as the biographical and perinatal experiences and are thus coming from within the individual psyche. On the other hand, they seem to be tapping directly, without the mediation of the senses, into sources of information that are clearly far beyond the conventional reach of the individual. Somewhere on the perinatal level of the psyche, a strange flip seems to occur, and what was up to that point deep intrapsychic probing becomes experiencing of the universe at large through extrasensory means. Some people have compared this to an "experiential Moebius strip," since it is impossible any more to say what is inside and what is outside.

These observations indicate that we can obtain information about the universe in two radically different ways: beside the conventional possibility of learning through sensory perception and analysis and synthesis of the data, we can also find out about various aspects of the world by direct identification with them in a non-ordinary state of consciousness. Each of us thus appears to be a microcosm containing in a holographic way the information about the macrocosm. In the mystical traditions, this was expressed by such phrases as: "as above so below" or "as without, so within."

The reports of subjects who have experienced episodes of embryonal existence, the moment of conception, and elements of cellular, tissue, and organ consciousness abound in medically accurate insights into the anatomical, physiological, and biochemical aspects of the processes involved. Similarly, ancestral, racial, and collective memories and past-incarnation experiences provide quite frequently very specific details about architecture, costumes, weapons, art forms, social structure, and religious and ritual practices of the culture and historical period involved, or even concrete historical events.

People who had phylogenetic experiences or identification with existing life forms not only found them unusually authentic and convincing, but often acquired in the process extraordinary insights concerning animal psychology, ethology, specific habits, or unusual reproductive cycles. In some instances, this was accompanied by archaic muscular innervations not characteristic for humans, or even such complex behaviors as enactment of a courtship dance.

The philosophical challenge associated with the already described observations, as formidable as it is all by itself, is further augmented by the fact that the transpersonal experiences correctly reflecting the material world often appear on the same continuum as and intimately interwoven with others that contain elements which the Western industrial world does not consider to be real. Here belong, for example, experiences involving deities and demons from various cultures, mythological realms such as heavens and paradises, and legendary or fairy-tale sequences.

For example, one can have an experience of Shiva's heaven, of the paradise of the Aztec rain-god Tlaloc, of the Sumerian underworld, or of one of the Buddhist hot hells. It is also possible to communicate with Jesus, have a shattering encounter with the Hindu goddess Kali, or identify with the dancing Shiva. Even these episodes can impart accurate new information about religious symbolism and mythical motifs that were previously unknown to the person involved. Observations of this kind confirm C. G. Jung's idea that beside the Freudian individual unconscious we can also gain access to the collective unconscious that contains the cultural heritage of all humanity.

It is not an easy task to convey in a few sentences conclusions from daily observations in the course of more than thirty-five years of research of non-ordinary states of consciousness and make this statement believable. It is not realistic to expect that a few sentences would be able to override the deeply culturally ingrained world view of those readers who are not familiar with the transpersonal dimension and who cannot relate what I say to their personal experience. Although I myself had many experiences of NOSC and the opportunity to observe closely a number of other people, it took me years to fully absorb the impact of this cognitive shock.

Because of space considerations, I cannot present detailed case histories that could help illustrate the nature of transpersonal experiences and the insights which they make available. I have to refer those readers who would like to explore this area further to my book *The Adventure of Self-Discovery* (Grof, 1988), where I discuss in detail the various types of transpersonal experiences and give many illustrative examples of situations where they provided unusual new information about different aspects of the universe. The same book also describes the method of Holotropic Breathwork which opens the access to the perinatal and transpersonal realms for anybody who is interested in personal verification of the above observations. Comparable information about psychedelic sessions can be found in my book *LSD Psychotherapy* that has recently been published in a new edition (Grof, 1994).

The existence and nature of transpersonal experiences violates some of the most basic assumptions of mechanistic science. They imply such seemingly absurd notions as relativity and arbitrary nature of all physical boundaries, non-local connections in the universe, communication through unknown means and channels, memory without a material substrate, non-linearity of time, or consciousness associated with all living organisms, and even inorganic matter. Many transpersonal experiences involve events from the microcosm and the macrocosm, realms that cannot normally be reached by unaided human senses, or from historical periods that precede the origin of the solar system, formation of planet Earth, appearance of living organisms, development of the nervous system, and emergence of *Homo sapiens.*

The research of non-ordinary states thus reveals an amazing paradox concerning the nature of human beings. It clearly shows that, in a mysterious and yet unexplained way, each of us contains the information about the entire universe and all of existence, has potential experiential access to all of its parts, and in a sense is the whole cosmic network, as much as he or she is just an infinitesimal part of it, a separate and insignificant biological entity. The new cartography reflects this fact and portrays the individual human psyche as being essentially commensurate with the entire cosmos and the totality of existence. As absurd and implausible as this idea might seem to a traditionally trained scientist and to our common sense, it can be relatively easily reconciled with new revolutionary developments in various scientific disciplines usually referred to as the new or emerging paradigm.

After this general introduction, I would like to review briefly more specifically some of the most important areas studied by transpersonal psychology. The common denominator in all of these is that the phenomena involved have been dismissed by mainstream psychology and psychiatry as irrelevant manifestations of brain pathology. They have been interpreted in a very superficial and highly unsatisfactory way, or even completely ignored, because their very existence is in a radical conflict with the leading paradigm.

Ritual Life, Spiritual Practice, and the Mystical Traditions

Transpersonal psychologists and anthropologists study very systematically and seriously various spiritual systems and religious practices in ancient and pre-industrial cultures. Among these, great attention has been given to shamanism, the most ancient religion and healing art of humanity. Historically, shamanism spans an extremely long period since the Paleolithic era to the present time. It also shows a universal geographical distribution; it can be found in North and South America, Asia, Polynesia, Australia, Africa, and Europe. Shamanism is a true gold mine of fascinating information on consciousness and on the human psyche. Since it transcends history and race or culture, it seems to be addressing what the anthropologists call the primal mind. An essential characteristic of shamanism is the work with NOSC and perinatal, as well as transpersonal, experiences.

The anthropologists have also described rites of passage, elaborate rituals conducted by various aboriginal cultures at the time of important biological and social transitions, such as birth, circumcision, puberty, marriage, dying, migration, and others. They typically employ powerful mind-altering technologies, and the experiences induced by them revolve around the triad birth-sex-death; like shamanic experiences, they also represent different combinations of perinatal and transpersonal phenomena. Clinical work with psychedelics and various non-drug experiential approaches (such as the Holotropic Breathwork) has helped us understand these events and appreciate their importance for individuals and human groups.

Closely related to the rites of passage were the ancient mysteries of death and rebirth, complex sacred and secret procedures that were also using powerful mind-altering techniques. They were particularly prevalent in the Mediterranean area, such as the Babylonian ceremonies of Inanna and Tammuz, the Egyptian mysteries of Isis and Osiris, the Orphic Cult, the Bacchanalia, the Eleusinian mysteries, the Corybantic rites, and the mysteries of Attis and Adonis. According to a modern study by Wasson, Hofmann, and Ruck (1978) the Eleusinian mysteries represented a psychedelic cult using a potion (*kykeon*) which contained ergot preparations related closely to LSD. The procedure the neophytes were undergoing had to be extremely powerful and compelling, since these mysteries were conducted without interruption for a period of almost two thousand years and disclosure of their secret to the uninitiated was punished by death.

However, of particular interest to transpersonally oriented researchers is the sacred literature of the various mystical traditions and the great spiritual philosophies of the East. Here belong the various systems of yoga, the theory and practice of Buddhism, Taoism, the Tibetan Vajrayana, Sufism, Christian mysticism, the Cabala, and many others. Traditional psychology and psychiatry is dominated by materialistic philosophy and has no recognition for spirituality in any form. It makes no distinction between a mystical experience and a psychotic experience. In its rejection of religion, it does not differentiate between primitive folk beliefs or fundamentalist dwelling on literal interpretation of scriptures, on the one hand, and sophisticated mystical traditions and spiritual philosophies based on centuries of systematic introspective exploration of the psyche, on the other.

Mainstream psychiatric literature contains articles and books that discuss what would be the best clinical diagnosis for founders of various religions and their saints and prophets. St. John of the Cross has been called a "hereditary degenerate," St. Teresa of Avila dismissed as a severe hysteric, and Mohammed's mystical experiences have been attributed to his seizures suggestive of epilepsy. Other religious and spiritual personages, such as the Buddha, Jesus, Ramakrishna, and Sri Ramana Maharishi have, because of their visionary experiences, been relegated into the realm of schizophrenic psychosis. Similarly, some traditionally trained anthropologists have argued whether the correct clinical diagnosis for shamans is ambulant schizophrenia, epilepsy, or hysteria. The famous psychoanalyst Franz Alexander, known as one of the founders of psychosomatic medicine, wrote a paper in which even Buddhist meditation is described as "artificial catatonia."

Traditional Western science relegates religious beliefs of any kind into the realm of primitive superstition, magical thinking, or unresolved parental issues from infancy and childhood, and sees direct spiritual experiences as manifestations of gross psychopathology. It also pathologizes the ritual and spiritual life of all pre-industrial societies and thus much of human history. By seriously studying and honoring the entire range of human experience, including perinatal and transpersonal experiences, transpersonal psychology offers a way of understanding the psyche that is universal—culturally sensitive, respectful to spiritual traditions, and applicable to any culture and historical period. It also acknowledges the deep human need for transcendental experiences and sees, therefore, spiritual pursuit as an understandable and legitimate activity.

Modern Clinical and Laboratory Consciousness Research

Another important source of supportive evidence for transpersonal psychology is modern clinical and laboratory work with non-ordinary states of consciousness. It includes systematic study of the effects of psychedelic substances, experimentation with powerful forms of experiential psychotherapy that profoundly change consciousness (such as primal therapy, rebirthing, hypnosis, or the Holotropic Breathwork), and investigation of laboratory mind-altering techniques—various forms of biofeedback, sensory isolation, sleep and dream deprivation, acoustic entrainment studies, and others.

The experiences and observations from all these areas require a large cartography of the psyche that includes the perinatal and transpersonal domain. Clinical work with psychedelic substances and Holotropic Breathwork has generated many remarkable insights that are of great theoretical and practical relevance. It has shown that psychogenic emotional and psychosomatic disorders have a complex multilevel dynamic structure which includes, besides the usual biographical determinants, also significant perinatal and transpersonal elements. For example, a serious phobia, psychogenic asthma, or addiction can have psychological roots in traumatic experiences from childhood and also significant additional roots in the difficult emotions and physical sensations associated with the trauma of birth. The deepest source of such disorders can then be found on the transpersonal level in the form of dramatic karmic or archetypal matrices.

Since the sources of many clinical problems lie in transpersonal realms of the psyche, there exist also important mechanisms of healing and personality transformation that operate on transpersonal levels. To reach a resolution of such problems, clients have to receive encouragement and support to confront unconscious material on all the levels involved—not only relive and integrate traumatic events from infancy and childhood, but also confront perinatal and prenatal material, as well as karmic issues, archetypal dynamics, and other transpersonal contents of the psyche. For this reason, the transpersonal perspective has very important practical implications for daily clinical work.

Laboratory techniques for inducing NOSC, such as sensory isolation, sleep and dream deprivation, lucid dreaming, and biofeedback, can also evoke a broad spectrum of experiences which includes transpersonal states of mind. Such work therefore naturally leads to and requires a transpersonal perspective.

Experiential Encounter with Death

Some of the most convincing evidence for transpersonal understanding of consciousness and of the human psyche comes from thanatology, a relatively recent scientific discipline studying death and dying. Spiritual literature of various cultures of the world and historical periods contains descriptions of the "posthumous journey of the soul"—complex adventures in consciousness that accompany and follow the experience of biological demise. Special texts have been dedicated to this subject; the most famous among these are the *Egyptian Book of the Dead (Pert Em Hru)*, the *Tibetan Book of the Dead (Bardo Thödol)*, and the *European Art of Dying (Ars Moriendi)*. The Aztec *(Nahuatl) Borgia Codex* describing the journey of Quetzalcoatl through the Underworld and the Mayan *Ceramic Codex* portraying the adventures of the Hero Twins and their death and rebirth belong to this category.

Many aspects of these descriptions, initially considered wishful fantasies and fictional stories of eschatological mythology, have been confirmed by modern thanatological studies by such researchers as Raymond Moody, Elisabeth Kübler-Ross, Kenneth Ring, and Michael Sabom. At the time of Moody's study, published as the best-selling *Life After Life,* only one of the 150 people studied indicated that the attending medical personnel—people dealing professionally with death and dying on a daily basis—knew anything about near-death experiences (NDEs). Since that time, the phenomenology of the NDE—the panoramic life review, passage through a dark tunnel, meeting of ancestors, visions of divine light, and judgment by a Being of Light—have become well-known to professionals, as well as general audiences, and even served as inspiration for popular movies, such as *Resurrection, Ghost,* or *Flatliners.*

The existence of NDEs of a transpersonal nature has been confirmed beyond any reasonable doubt, and it has become increasingly impossible to discard them as being simply hallucinations resulting from biological damage to the body and the brain. It has been repeatedly confirmed that people facing clinical death often experience their consciousness detaching from the body and observe the scene of the accident or the resuscitation procedures from above. When they return to normal consciousness, they are able to give detailed retrospective accounts of all the events that occurred. They know, for example, who was present at the scene, who came and left through which door, what gadgets were wheeled in and out of the operating room, and sometimes even what the little pointers were showing on the gauges of the equipment used for resuscitation.

Occasionally, these people are able to witness accurately what is happening in other parts of the same building or even in remote locations. And there exist case histories of congenitally blind persons who, at the time of their clinical death, were able to observe the environment optically and in colors, only to lose their sight after they regained ordinary consciousness. It is difficult to imagine a more serious blow to the traditional scientific paradigm and a more convincing support for the transpersonal perspective than observations of this kind.

Psychospiritual Crises (Spiritual Emergencies)

Another area where the transpersonal approach offers important theoretical understanding and practical guidance is the problem of psychospiritual crises. These are episodes of non-ordinary states of consciousness that can occur in the course of powerful spiritual practice, as a reaction to various physical and psychological situations, or "spontaneously"—for reasons that we can not identify. They can take many different forms, such as that of awakening of Kundalini energy, a shamanic crisis, John Perry's renewal process by activation of the central archetype, Abraham Maslow's peak experience, emergence of a disturbing past-life experience, precipitous opening of psychic abilities, possession states, and many others. Episodes of this kind have been repeatedly described in spiritual literature of various traditions.

The intensity of emotions and psychosomatic manifestations accompanying these states, as well as the rich spectrum and exotic nature of the experiences involved, make them incomprehensible in the context of traditional psychiatry and psychology. Since they combine in various ways perinatal and transpersonal experiences, a system of thinking that does not recognize these levels of the psyche and which is limited to postnatal biography and the Freudian individual unconscious has to attribute them to brain pathology of unknown etiology.

People experiencing these episodes are therefore labeled as psychotic and routinely treated by suppressive medication. A transpersonal approach using a large encompassing cartography of the psyche makes it possible to understand that these states are potentially healing, transformative, and evolutionary. It also offers sensitive support and guidance through these states as an important therapeutic alternative to the routine suppressive psychopharmacological approach. In the transpersonal context, these episodes appear to be crises of transformation ("spiritual emergencies").

The idea that a pathological process afflicting the brain could in itself produce the rich and complex experiences of this kind, such as a past-life experience in ancient Egypt or in the French Revolution, glorious identification with the dancing Shiva, or abduction by extraterrestrials in a flying saucer, is so bizarre and implausible that it is difficult to believe that it has been seriously considered by respectable researchers. It would be comparable to believing that damage to a computer could transform its program into a completely different one, but equally complex and comprehensible. Damage to the brain can explain disturbances of thinking, intellect, and memory. Transpersonal experiences are clearly genuine manifestations of the psyche as such, but they reveal that the dimensions of human consciousness reach much farther than academic psychiatry and psychology ever suspected.

Parapsychological Research and Psychic Phenomena

The list of areas that are relevant for transpersonal psychology should also include parapsychology. Prominent researchers, such as J. B. Rhine, Jules Eisenbud, Hans Bender, L. L. Vasiliev, Charles Tart, Stanley Krippner, Russell Targ, Harold Puthoff, Keith Harary, and many others have conducted meticulous laboratory and field studies and amassed vast supportive evidence for the existence of telepathy, clairvoyance, precognition, remote viewing, psychometry, telekinesis, out-of-body experiences, and poltergeist phenomena. The results of their meticulously conceived and conducted research have been ignored because of their basic incompatibility with the leading scientific paradigm.

The relationship between parapsychology and transpersonal psychology is very interesting. The results of parapsychological research are in full congruence with the transpersonal perspective. However, in the new context, there is no reason to limit parapsychological studies to their traditional topics, such as telepathy, clairvoyance, psychometry, or telekinesis. As I mentioned earlier, just about every form of transpersonal experience can become a source of information received through extrasensory channels. If in the future transpersonal psychology becomes a recognized discipline, parapsychology might have to expand the range of its activities to other types of transpersonal phenomena, or even lose its separate identity and be completely absorbed and integrated into the new field.

UFO Phenomena and Alien Abduction Experiences

The transpersonal perspective is also very useful in the study of a group of unusually puzzling and confusing phenomena that baffle traditional researchers—the experiences of encounters with extraterrestrial visitors. The reports involving unidentified flying objects (UFOs) are certainly among the most controversial materials of the modern era. Since 1947 when the American civilian pilot Kenneth Arnold first saw them in the mountains near Mt. Rainier and gave them the name "flying saucers," countless people all over the world have reported related experiences. Many of them have described daytime sightings of unusual objects and nighttime visions of strange lights. Others claimed they observed landings of alien spacecrafts and saw their crews or interacted with them. Occasionally, such reports referred to abductions, visits to the interiors of the spaceships, medical examinations and interventions, or even space flights to more or less remote extraterrestrial destinations.

The controversy surrounding these phenomena is of unprecedented proportions and deserves more detailed discussion. On the one hand, the descriptions of alien creatures and their mysterious machines defying the laws of nature as we know them seem to be too fantastic to be taken seriously. In addition, an extensive study conducted by the U.S. Air Force and headed by a special committee at the University of Columbia declared most UFO reports to be results of natural causes or of mental disorders of the observers. On the other hand, serious researchers such as Allen Hynek and Jacques Vallée disagreed with these conclusions. Analyzing the same material, they found the data sufficiently interesting and convincing to dedicate their lives to their study.

A fascinating aspect of the UFO experiences is that they often seem to be associated with events occurring in the material world and it is not rare that they leave some physical evidence. This includes impressions and burnt soil at the site of alleged landings, materials that can not be identified by chemical analysis, photographs and amateur movies, stigmata-like marks on the bodies of abductees, mysterious cattle mutilations, and others. The nature of the evidence is often ambiguous, almost of a trickster quality, and leaves open various ways of interpreting it. In many instances, emotionally stable and intelligent witnesses gave detailed independent descriptions of the same UFO events that were practically identical. The phenomena continue to attract much attention, and the media alternate in seriously reporting sensational events and debunking them. Special conferences and meetings of the UFO abductees are held regularly and have large numbers of participants.

These phenomena are clearly too complex to be ignored or to be dismissed as artifacts of pathological processes in the brain. The discussions in this area are usually limited to the question whether or not the Earth has been visited by material spacecrafts from other regions of the universe. The Newtonian-Cartesian paradigm of materialistic science with its sharp and absolute dichotomies—subjective or objective, material reality and hallucination—has no other alternative. However, it seems that the problems involved are much more complicated and that transpersonal psychology can bring some new light into this confusing situation.

C. G. Jung, who was very interested in UFOs, wrote a fascinating book entitled *Flying Saucers: A Modern Myth of Things Seen in the Skies*. It was based on careful historical analysis of legends about flying discs and actual apparitions throughout the ages that had occasionally caused mass hysteria. Jung came to the conclusion that the UFO phenomena might be archetypal visions originating in the collective unconscious rather than alien hardware or intrapsychic hallucinations. This would explain the frequent synchronicities associated with them and the fact that they have what Jung called a "psychoid" quality—they seem to operate in the twilight zone between intrapsychic processes and consensus reality.

Many studies conducted in the years following the publication of Jung's book have come to conclusions similar to his interpretation. John Mack, a Harvard professor of psychiatry, recently published a study entitled *Abduction: Human Encounters with Aliens*. On the basis of his analysis of more than fifty people who had retrieved memories of UFO abduction, he concluded that the material represents a serious challenge to the entire philosophy of Western science. As could be expected, he encountered the severe criticism of his colleagues and much ridicule from the media. However, there is no doubt that the UFO phenomenon cannot be easily dismissed and deserves systematic study. It seems to offer fascinating new insights into the nature of human consciousness and the nature of reality. This makes them a subject of great interest for transpersonal psychologists.

Multiple Personality Disorder (MPD)

Another fascinating frontier of transpersonal psychology is the study of multiple personality disorders. This phenomenon, once very rare and unusual, has in recent years mushroomed and reached almost epidemic proportions. The traditional approach to multiple personality is to see it as a result of disassociation and splitting off of various aspects of the same personality. The entire problem would thus be contained inside the skull and the brain of the person involved.

Modern research has brought extraordinary new data which challenge the traditional understanding and make the research of MPDs another exciting frontier of transpersonal psychology. The new evidence has profound implications for the understanding of human consciousness and of the relationship between the mind and the body. It indicates that consciousness is not a mere product of the brain and that its relationship to the body is much more complex than originally assumed. This only supports similar conclusions made by foremost brain researchers, such as Wilder Penfield, Karl Pribram, and John Eccles.

There have been instances where one of the personalities showed the symptoms of a serious disease, such as diabetes, and others did not. Similarly, allergies to certain foods can be limited only to some personalities. Each personality has a distinct handwriting which is quite consistently associated with its appearance. In some instances the client has serious vision problems and needs strong glasses to correct them, while some of the alternate personalities show no such difficulties and can see well without glasses. Even colorblindness can afflict only some personalities and not others, as indicated by the results of objective tests used for diagnosing this disorder. All this suggests the possibility that under certain circumstances several separate units of consciousness can compete for the control of the same body. Some researchers have concluded from these observations that even an ordinary personality is composed of a larger number of units of consciousness.

In addition, patients with multiple personalities often have a history of ritual cult abuse. The traditional understanding of this strange phenomenon, whose incidence has also grown enormously in recent years, is very superficial and unconvincing, because it misses entirely the critical role of the perinatal and transpersonal dimensions involved. Transpersonal psychology is thus finding exciting supportive evidence in another area where traditional thinking has failed to provide adequate answers.

Consciousness Evolution and Human Survival

The most important problem area where transpersonal psychology could offer important theoretical and practical contribution is the current global crisis that threatens to destroy the life on this planet. The exploration of the psychological, philosophical, and spiritual roots of this crisis is of great interest to transpersonally oriented researchers. We all have the dubious privilege of living in an era when the world drama is reaching its culmination. The violence, greed, and acquisitiveness that shaped human history in the past centuries has reached such proportions that it could easily lead not only to complete annihilation of the human species, but to extermination of all life on this planet. The various measures of a diplomatic, political, military, economic, and ecological nature that are intended to alleviate the situation seem to make it worse rather than improve it.

In view of the power of the weapons of mass destruction and the continuing deterioration of the natural environment, it is more than obvious that humanity will not survive, unless it can find effective ways to overcome its deeply rooted intolerance, violence, and greed. However, mainstream science has very little to offer to understand these destructive tendencies within human nature and even less in terms of finding promising solutions and remedies. The "naked ape" hypothesis that sees an explanation of human violence in biological killer instincts is not very convincing since there are no parallels in the animal kingdom for the bestiality occasionally manifested by humans (Erich Fromm's "malignant aggression"). Traumatic experiences in infancy and childhood do not adequately explain the extremes of individual violence, let alone the horrors of Nazi Germany, Stalin's Russia, Yugoslavia, Rwanda, and of the South African apartheid, or the atrocities committed by the Chinese in Tibet.

The work with non-ordinary states of consciousness has confirmed that traumatic experiences in infancy and childhood are important sources of aggression. However, it revealed even more elemental roots of violence in the domains of the psyche which lie beyond postnatal biography. The experiences of people reliving the trauma of birth are characterized by murderous aggression and abound in imagery portraying wars, revolutions, concentration camps, and genocide. It seems only logical to see the potentially life-threatening situation of the human birth that can last many hours or even days as an important source of extremely difficult emotions, particularly anxiety and aggression.

The relationship between the trauma of birth and the psychology of wars has been confirmed by the research of psychohistorian Lloyd de Mause who found that the demagogic talks of military leaders around the time of wars and revolutions abound in figures of speech and metaphors related specifically to biological birth. Similarly posters and political caricatures revolve around perinatal images. Sam Keen has shown in his excellent book *Faces of the Enemy* that nations and groups who are involved in war portray each other with the use of symbolic stereotypes. Analysis of these images shows that they are identical with the art of clients depicting their perinatal experiences.

However, significant additional roots of violence and psychological patterns breeding aggressive feelings and behavior can be found on the transpersonal level of the psyche. They are associated with archetypes of wrathful deities, karmic material, consciousness of various animal forms, and other transpersonal matrices. C. G. Jung believed that the archetypes of the collective unconscious not only have a powerful influence on the behavior of individuals, but also govern large historical movements. From this point of view, entire nations and cultural groups might be enacting in their behavior important mythological themes. For example, in the decade preceding the outbreak of World War II, Jung found in the dreams of his German patients many elements from the Nordic myth about Ragnarok, or the twilight of the gods (Götterdämmerung). He concluded from this that this archetype was emerging in the collective psyche of the German nation and predicted that it would lead to a major catastrophy which would ultimately turn out to be self-destructive.

In many instances, leaders of nations specifically use archetypal images to achieve their political goals. Thus, Hitler exploited the mythological motifs of the supremacy of the Nordic race and of the millenial empire, as well as the symbol of the solar eagle and the ancient Aryan swastika. The initial appeal of Communism was partially due to the fact that its presumably atheistic program for the world revolution was using archetypal symbolism of the spiritual death-rebirth process—a bloody upheaval that frees us from oppression and brings about a paradisean future of universal brotherhood and fulfillment of our inner potential. The intolerance of any departure from the Marxist-Leninist and Stalinist dogmas, rigid iconography of the socialist realism, and serious public declaration of Stalin's infallibility further illustrate the similarity between Communism and a rigid religious system. Similarly, Ayatollah Khomeini and Saddam Hussein succeeded to ignite the imagination of their Moslen followers by references to "jihad," the holy war against the infidels. Many similar examples can be found in recent and more remote history.

The best protection against such efforts of dictators and demagogues to exploit people's transcendental needs for political purposes is intimate intellectual and experiential knowledge of the transpersonal realms. In addition, deep experiential self-exploration can result in full conscious experience and transformation of the destructive and self-destructive forces in the human psyche. Transpersonal experiences of psychological death and rebirth and of oneness with other people, with nature, with the entire universe, and with cosmic consciousness can drastically reduce the level of aggression, increase compassion and tolerance, and automatically lead to high ecological awareness.

I have seen over the years profound transformations in many people who were involved in serious and systematic inner quest. Some of these people were meditators and had a regular spiritual practice, others had spontaneous episodes of psychospiritual crises, and many participated in clinical programs of psychedelic therapy and various forms of experiential psychotherapy and self-exploration. Their level of aggression decreased, and they became more peaceful, more comfortable with themselves, and more tolerant of others. Their ability to enjoy life, particularly simple aspects of everyday existence, increased considerably. Deep reverence for life and ecological awareness have been among the most frequent consequences of the psychospiritual transformation that accompanies responsible work with non-ordinary states of consciousness. The same was true for the emergence of universal spirituality of a mystical nature based on deep personal experience.

Experiences and observations of this kind suggest that the theory and practice of transpersonal psychology could be a significant contribution to the alleviation of the global crisis if applied systematically in the life of each of us. It would mean that we would all complement whatever we are doing in our everyday life to ease the situation in the world with systematic deep self-exploration and work on ourselves. In this way, we would be able to tap the deep wisdom of the collective unconscious and use it as a guiding principle in our private affairs, as well as professional, political, and social activities. This is a strategy of existence recommended by C. G. Jung; it involves a constant dynamic interaction and ongoing dialogue between the conscious ego and the Higher Self.

Such an approach to life can mediate a process of inner transformation and individuation, as well as provide guidance for our everyday activities from a source of wisdom that by far transcends any ordinary human resources. From the perspective of transpersonal psychology, this appears to be the optimal strategy to leading a fulfilling individual life and to making the best possible contribution to our collective well-being. Moreover, if it turns out that humanity is on an irreversible self-destructive course in spite of all our efforts to steer in a more positive direction, the same strategy of focusing on inner transformation will prepare us to face whatever has to come with more equanimity.

II

Transpersonal Currents in Some Major Western Therapies

ALMOST WITHOUT EXCEPTION, each transpersonal therapist has arrived at the point of accepting transpersonal implications into his or her personal and theoretical construct by starting at a well-established point—classical psychoanalysis, Jungian analysis, or psychosynthesis. For each, the experience and the embracing and applying of transpersonal concepts is unique; the transpersonal serves to throw the light of consciousness onto an area that already has distinct and undeniable value for that person.

In this section, we have the opportunity to observe how practicing therapists in widely differing fields are blending the transpersonal into current professional practices founded on a more Western base. Quite possibly, some professionals who read these chapters will be surprised to find that many of the techniques considered to be transpersonal are already familiar to them within more traditional therapeutic frameworks. However, this is not so surprising when one considers that any framework is constructed and communicated to others through language or a linguistic perspective.

There is a common theme running through the widely differing chapters of Crittenden Brookes, Joseph Fabry, John Firman and James Vargiu, Harold Bloomfield, Edward Hoffman—and my own chapters. Whether we choose to approach our personal and professional worlds from a construct of id, ego and superego, from the perspective of archetypes or of Buddhist or Jewish mystic findings, we are essentially making the same assumption: meaning exists, no matter how we choose to define or experience it, meaning that is conveyed to others through metaphor, theoretical and experiential.

The risk involved in any of these approaches is not to be ignored. The therapist and the patient are both seekers and, as such, have a responsibility to themselves and others to remember that the construct, the metaphor, the manifestation of an awareness is not the reality, is not the awareness itself. The self must transcend the chosen mode of self-expression or remain confined to finite limits of the expression.

5

Psychodynamic Therapy and the Transpersonal Quest

Seymour Boorstein

Many transpersonal therapists see Freudian psychoanalytic theory as a polar opposite to transpersonal therapy. I suspect that they have come to this conclusion because classical theory has, in the past and in the present, denigrated the transpersonal by classifying its manifestations as mere evidence of regressive, infantile desires to merge with the all-good and all-giving mother or to re-experience oceanic feelings of early childhood bliss.

Though I was trained as a Freudian analyst, my work today leads me more along the lines that Ken Wilber establishes in *The Spectrum of Consciousness* (1977). Wilber speaks of many levels of consciousness, each of which must be dealt with, integrated, and ultimately unified with the others if man is to achieve enlightenment. Some of these levels, he asserts, are best approached from the psychoanalytic stance; others through meditative practices. No one level of approach should preempt or exclude another, since each is necessary. It is a matter of using different tools for different parts of a task; no one tool is better than another—just different.

In his book, *The Atman Project* (1980), Wilber explains the error he believes has been made in psychoanalytic views of the transpersonal: just because superconsciousness experiences involve nondualism, spacelessness, and timelessness is not reason enough to classify them as infantile. To equate infantile experiences with what occurs after the individual struggles through the whole cycle of consciousness to achieve higher states is not only simplistic but incompatible with the experience of persons who have reached those higher states.

It would be inappropriate to comment on classical psychoanalytic theories of the unconscious without first having gone through the rigorous emotional and intellectual vicissitudes involved in its explorations. It is equally inappropriate to criticize the transpersonal area without having had the same kind of intense study and emotional and intellectual involvement. This chapter, drawing on many years' involvement with both approaches, shows how the classical and the transpersonal can successfully interpenetrate.

FREUD'S WORK EVOLVED in an era when classical physics indicated that space, time, and matter were static and stable. Likewise, conflict was seen as occurring among the relatively stable and static superego, ego, and id in their conscious and unconscious derivatives. Much of psychodynamic theory rests on the idea of causality in which time is progressing steadily forward. In the context of this particular scientific stance, certain transpersonal theories have been seen as irrational; the spiritual quest has often been relegated to the position of an infantile, regressive pull to be taken care of, to merge with an all-giving mother.

The work of Fritjof Capra (1975), Jack Sarfatti (1975), and Henry Stapp (1976) seems to indicate that the universe can be seen as particles of energy where everything is related to, and influences, everything else at a speed even faster than the speed of light. Physics even indicates that the direction of time may be indefinite and there may in reality be no cause and effect, just interconnections. In the same way that the original Newtonian and Einsteinian physics are being expanded in the light of newer findings, so perhaps we can expand some aspects of classical psychoanalytic theory in order to understand and include in the transpersonal quest that aspect of man's strivings which goes beyond interpersonal and intrapersonal struggles.

Psychodynamic psychotherapy and the "transpersonal quest" can be seen as on a continuum. They have similar methods, directions, and goals, and similar theoretical backgrounds. I believe that psychodynamic psychotherapy and a spiritual quest can occur simultaneously or sequentially—in any order—and have a positive effect on each other's evolution. Whether the state of consciousness is called the "watcher," "witness," "awakened one," or "observing ego," both psychodynamic psychotherapy and the transpersonal quest seek to cultivate that state where an individual can comfortably tolerate and even learn from the ebb and flow of feelings, thoughts, and fantasies arising in the mind.

A major goal of psychodynamic psychotherapy is to allow the unconscious to become conscious as much as possible so that it may be constructively integrated within the total personality. This goal is remarkably similar to the goals of certain Eastern traditions, Buddhism in particular. A person who thus becomes totally aware of his or her unconscious would be considered in some spiritual traditions to be enlightened. In Buddhist meditation it is accepted as a possibility that one can so refine one's awareness that one can even become aware of atomic processes within the body.

In psychoanalysis, the paradigm of psychodynamic psychotherapy, the patient attempts to follow the basic instruction to stay aware of what is going on at any moment (thoughts, feelings, sensations) and to report it to the therapist. As the patient develops more expanded awareness, he perceives more and more of the processes of his mental functioning. Further, the patient is advised not to be judgmental. Certain Buddhist meditational practices such as Vipassana are almost identical to psychoanalysis in their approach to exploring the mind and gaining insight into ultimate realities. The meditator spends set periods of time becoming increasingly aware of thoughts, feelings, and sensations, and reports progress periodically to his or her teacher.

The psychodynamically oriented psychotherapist and the guru or spiritual teacher have similar tasks. The traditional psychotherapist helps a patient or client become free of infantile modes of coping by first exposing them in the transference relationship. Awareness of these maladaptive modes and their negative effects on the adult aspect of the personality leads to their cessation. In a similar way, the guru or spiritual teacher helps free disciples or students from greed, anger, vanity, and selfishness. In addition, the therapist and the spiritual guide both give the patient or seeker the courage to face unknown fears, whether they take the form of infantile neurotic anxieties or the existential "dark night of the soul," which occur at stages in the spiritual quest.

All of the great religious and spiritual traditions have at their core, I believe, the desire to transcend duality and estrangement and to experience the world nondualistically. The mystics and great spiritual leaders of all ages describe the moment of experiencing nonduality—"at-one-ment"—as the epitome of joy, bliss, and ecstasy. These teachings, their methods, and their disciplines reflect our inherent desire to understand ourselves, our condition, our struggles in life. They also provide insights into life's meaning and techniques for achieving the most gratifying state of consciousness, a state that in the prescientific world was called "enlightenment."

Similarly, the process of psychodynamic psychotherapy can be seen as removing obstacles blocking the way to living at the highest level of functioning, which in this framework is called "genitality." Genitality can be understood as living nondualistically, fully, and creatively, at one with the world. Erik Erikson defines this as "intellectual clarity, sexual mutuality, and considerate love, which anchors man in the actuality of his responsibilities" (Erikson, 1964, p. 128). Perhaps we can relate the desire for genitality to the quest for enlightenment. In genitality, sexual expression serves as the paradigm of that state of consciousness in which loving, caring, gratifying relationships prevail;

in enlightenment, there is an expanded awareness that leads to compassionate, loving behavior.

Freud's formulations regarding the dual instincts, Eros and Thanatos, have within them the seeds of transpersonal orientation. Freud postulates that the instinct for love—Eros—is a desire for union with objects in the world. In its highest form the instinct to love manifests itself in the desire to merge with the love object and to become one with it. This merging can be seen in the momentary loss of individuality and boundaries during the moment of sexual orgasm. In other words, Eros is the desire to transcend separateness and, even for a moment, experience the ecstasy, joy, and bliss of nonduality.

While examining the higher level manifestations of Eros, we should not forget the important earlier developmental stages (oral, anal, phallic, and oedipal) that must later be integrated if the individual is to achieve genitality. In their own ways these earlier stages can be understood as antecedents to the desire for merging and union. Even the anal stage, in which this desire seems less evident, may be understood as providing those locomotor skills which make it possible to move towards a loved one as well as to produce a gift for the loved one.

CASE 1

A twenty-four-year-old computer programmer sought psychoanalytic treatment because the thoughts and feelings about his past continually intruded into his spiritual practices. In spite of an antipsychiatric attitude, he finally came for help because all attempts to work through these feelings in his meditational practice had been unsuccessful. Although obviously very bright, he had "arranged" never to go to college in order not to compete with his father, a prominent physician. His father was a harsh and punitive person, and the oedipal rivalry fears dated back to the age of five or six. It also became clear that success in the young man's spiritual practice had come to symbolize an oedipal victory with the following need to undo it. Traditional analysis of the oedipal transferences afforded him relief from his repeated need to fail in all of his endeavors including his spiritual work.

The blockage of earlier stages leads, according to Freud, to neurosis. Psychotherapy is aimed at eliminating these blockages. Perhaps Wilhelm Reich intuited in Freud's formulations the importance of Eros's striving for nonduality and thus was led in his own work to emphasize the function of the orgasm. We can understand Reich more clearly if we place his emphasis within the context of man's innate drive to seek nonduality.

In the dual-instinct theory, Eros represents the impulse towards expression and preservation of life in the physical body. Traditional psychology and psychotherapy often assume that a wish for death is a negative reaction derived from frustration. However, within a psychological framework that includes other dimensions of existence or awareness and/or continuation of consciousness after physical death, Thanatos might be seen as a desire to come alive into another state of consciousness. Such a state of consciousness might be a mystical experience, an out-of-body experience, or even rebirth or reincarnation into a new life.

Raymond Moody, in *Life After Life* (1976), recounts the experiences of people who are revived and continue to live after having been pronounced clinically dead. They are able to report events that took place around them during the time they showed no vital signs. They also report an awareness of survival of consciousness accompanied by sensations of release and pleasure. In a study of survivors of attempted Golden Gate Bridge suicides, David Rosen (1975) reports a uniform experience of transcendence of the body accompanied by pleasurable physical feelings and expanded awareness. Some survivors report a sense of spiritual rebirth. Grof comments that several of his patients who had attempted suicide realized after LSD therapy that "their previous suicidal urge was actually an unrecognized craving for ego transcendence" (1973, p. 44).

In many mystical, esoteric, or religious traditions, death represents an awakening or rebirth into another state of consciousness. What we call "being awake" is referred to in these other traditions as "being asleep." From the point of view of the body/ego, Eros seeks to preserve and enhance it while Thanatos seeks to end it. If we see Eros as the impulse towards realization of the highest state of loving and awareness through the body, we might see Thanatos as the urge to experience new states of consciousness through the death of the normal waking state of consciousness. In many transpersonal practices, specific meditative and contemplative techniques are used as means of entering into altered states of consciousness. Even death can be understood as a paradigm of an altered state of consciousness. The Eros dimension of man, his living joyfully and fully in this world, operates at the same time as the Thanatos dimension, the desire for transcendence, for altered and expanded states of consciousness, for spiritual experiences.

Traditional psychiatry suggests that man must adjust to his inevitable end. Erikson believes that the most we can hope for is that the despairing vision of a life that will end will be balanced by a wider vision of human problems and responsibility to the next generation (Erikson, 1964). What Erikson offers us—the best that can be had from our classical rational schema—is a pessimistic view, representing for most people a bleak picture. In contrast, psychiatrists and psychologists researching the area of altered states, survival of consciousness (Jacobson, 1973; Moody, 1976), out-of-body experiences (Tart, 1968a), and reincarnation (Stevenson, 1974, 1977) are now presenting possibilities of alternative realities. We should not summarily dismiss matters of "spirit" as regressive phenomena but rather explore these areas further.

CASE 2

A twenty-nine-year-old psychologist reported that as a child he had had an intense fascination with the poem "Richard Cory" (by E. A. Robinson), in which a presumably happy person who "has everything" kills himself. The poem had never made sense to him, although he had pondered its meaning and its effect on him throughout his life. He began treatment with a great deal of bodily anxiety as a result of certain oedipal constellations and preoedipal traumas, anxieties that subsided as treatment progressed. When his treatment was ending, he was motivated—despite his symptoms having largely disappeared—to begin his own spiritual quest. With a classical "aha," he saw the parallel between Richard Cory's situation and that of the Buddha, who as a prince had all of the worldly pleasures possible and yet felt impelled to begin his own spiritual quest to find greater meaning. Both reflected his own life situation where, although he had gratifying family relationships and was symptom free, he felt a need to search for greater meaning. He noted that his former anxiety about death had disappeared, and indeed he sometimes looked forward to his eventual, natural death— not as a manifestation of depression but as a result of his experiences in meditational practice and his desire for transcendence.

A transpersonal approach can help undermine the character armor or personality style that many people have evolved defensively to deal with their conflicts. For example, obsessional persons who have become attached to and rigidified certain behavior sometimes respond, paradoxically, to the Buddhist view of impermanence and constant change, in which there is nothing to hold on to. Another important area in which the transpersonal can help traditional psychoanalytic psychotherapy is in the optimistic atmosphere of the transpersonal approach as opposed to the more pessimistic psychoanalytic view.

Freud quite possibly suspected that psychoanalytic theory was imbalanced. He wrote to Hereward Carrington: "If I had my life to live over again, I should devote myself to psychical research rather than to psychoanalysis" (Jones, 1957, p. 392). Freud was too rational a man to accept what in his culture would have been considered the irrationality of matters relating to the spirit. In our time, however, considering the vast amount of new scientific knowledge available, we need to be open to redefining basic concepts in psychotherapy as well.

Therapists, gurus, and teachers should not deprecate the efforts of the others; rather, each should investigate to see ways in which he or she can benefit from and expand on the other's work. Only through the balanced evolution of both sides of our nature—our inter- and intra-personal development and our spiritual development—will we be able to reach our fullest potential.

6

A Jungian View

Of Transpersonal Events in Psychotherapy

Crittenden E. Brookes

In Crittenden Brookes's words, "Carl Jung was one of the earliest Western psychologists to recognize the relevance of transpersonal psychic events to the development of a complete human psychology." In this chapter, Brookes presents a distillation of many years' experience in many complex areas of Jungian analytic work.

For the author, as a Jungian-oriented psychotherapist, and for Jung himself, the "reality of the psyche" is of central importance to any therapeutic work, and "a transpersonal event may be said to have occurred when there has been a confrontation between personal and impersonal elements of the psyche, involving consciousness of that event. The bringing to awareness of the transpersonal—either spontaneously or through analytic dialogue—can have either regressive or progressive effects. Central to this drama of the psyche is the principle of synchronicity, a meaningful confluence of events for a particular individual. For Brookes the *Book of Changes*, or *I Ching*, and Jung's contribution to its Western understanding is one of the clearest demonstrations of the operation of synchronicity. At the same time he emphasizes the importance of treating such a system as simply one manifestation of meaning rather than a specific technique for reaching the meaning.

From a Jungian perspective the largest danger in the transformation of consciousness is the possibility of ego-inflation, which frequently happens when a patient overidentifies with transpersonal events. If this risk is recognized and dealt with, then the possibilities are great for the patient to attain not only a sound path to individuation but also continuing psychic growth and development. For the Jungian-oriented psychotherapist, increase of consciousness through awareness of transpersonal events and use of Eastern philosophy are not simply useful adjuncts to some therapeutic technique; they are the foundation of analytical psychology.

CARL JUNG WAS ONE OF THE EARLIEST Western psychologists to recognize the relevance of transpersonal psychic events to the development of a complete human psychology. Furthermore, he was perhaps the first Western psychotherapist to identify such phenomena in his psychotherapeutic work and to develop a theoretical mythology to bring meaning to them, both as a part of a general psychology and in the context of psychotherapy itself.

Jung was a pioneer in investigating the connections between psychopathology and the transpersonal element of the psyche; since he was, above all, a psychiatrist and psychotherapist, his theorizing stemmed from direct confrontation with human suffering. His work adds new dimension to more traditional psychodynamics, and psychotherapists familiar with his ideas can bring a broad spectrum of "alternative meanings" to bear on the experiences of their clients, meanings that amplify and deepen the more reductive, instinctual, and interactional explanations. This is a particularly significant contribution; few systems of therapy or theory are equipped to deal meaningfully with states of consciousness exhibiting the unique emotional quality of the transpersonal, a quality Jung called "numinosity" (Jung, 1961). The development of meaning is central to a Jungian view of psychotherapy. Transpersonal events during therapy are examined for the real as well as potential meaning they may have for the client. The development of meaning is seen as closely parallel to the major function of therapy: to increase consciousness.

In a strict sense, there is no single "Jungian view" of psychotherapy as a whole or of specific areas of psychotherapy. Jung's work amplifies ideas and raises questions rather than reducing concepts to final answers. However, it is appropriate to say that there is a view that relies on Jung's orientation. This view takes into consideration the reality and independent meaning of the psyche and psychic events, and makes use of these events without necessarily replacing them with organic or sociologic analogues. Thus from this "Jungian viewpoint," psychic events are seen as meaningful in their own right. Such meaning can be amplified by a "state-specific science" (Tart, 1992, p. 428) whose language is specific to the state of the psyche itself. Since the psyche's language is phenomenological, it follows that the state-specific science evolved from the Jungian viewpoint is a phenomenological one.

The Jungian-oriented psychotherapist deals with clients in a consciously phenomenological, symbolic, and open-ended way.

> A graduate student in his late twenties came to psychotherapy with a complaint of moderate depression and lack of creativity. Early in therapy he reported a dream in which he is standing in front of a church, looking awe-struck at the beautiful spire that soars high above him. After he reported the dream, he commented, "Of course, that was only a penis symbol." This statement is made in a flat, rather depressed way. The therapist responded, "It sounds as though you have been trained to explain your experiences before you have given yourself a chance to experience them." The therapist asked the client to report the quality of *feeling* associated with seeing the church spire in the dream, and then asked what the vision of the church and the accompanying feeling reminded him of.

It is consistent with the Jungian viewpoint for the psychotherapist to bring his own amplification to bear on the client's ideas and feelings, and likewise to bring personal amplification to the theoretical concepts of Jungian psychology, or of any other theoretical system. Working with this open-ended theoretical system, it is a major mistake for the therapist to codify "the words of the master" as if he had made final, definitive statements.

This chapter, therefore, can be most appropriately read as my personal amplification of a loosely defined set of attitudes and concepts attributable to Jung. In addition, the clinical examples provided should not be taken too literally, nor should they be construed as examples of therapeutic "technique." Jung saw psychotherapy as a unique and unreproducible dialectic between two psyches, in which the actions or interventions of the therapist at any moment arise out of the unique history of the two parties to that moment (Brookes, 1977b). Technique, then, arises out of and is secondary to relationship in psychotherapy; the therapist should not impose upon the client actions of his or her own that are inconsistent with the quality of their relationship, because such actions are artificial and detrimental to the process of therapy. For this reason, it would be a mistake to understand the therapist's intervention in the clinical example above as a technical move that any other therapist could arbitrarily repeat at any time. The choice of the particular intervention at a particular moment depended on a melange of factors both impinging upon and making up the therapist's psychic state at the moment the intervention took place. Such factors include the therapist's intuitive assessment of the quality of rapport with the client at the time, the kind and quality of the client's affect, the therapist's own mood and internal state, the therapist's sense of whether the client's ego-functioning at that moment allowed

for a quality of "active listening" to the therapist, and so on. Such considerations should be assumed to apply to all clinical examples given in this
chapter.

From the Jungian viewpoint, then, although science may be brought
into play in a consideration of the phenomena of psychotherapy, the act and
experience of therapy itself is inevitably an art, and any moment in therapy
is a unique and unrepeatable phenomenon.

Psychotherapy is seen as a uniquely *dyadic* event, the interaction of two
psyches, therapist's and client's, as a result of which both psyches undergo
transformation and change. Interpretations or other interventions can be effective *only* if the client has given the therapist *permission* to make them. This
"permission" is a function of the *relatedness* between therapist and client, and
is also a function of the balance between defensive-regressive and assimila-
tive-progressive aspects of the client's ego-functioning during therapy.

From a Jungian viewpoint, it is appropriate to say that an "analysis" is
a psychotherapy in which there is access to a great deal of unconscious
material and an opportunity to work with it thoroughly in order to bring it
into consciousness. Analysis, then, differs from a psychotherapy devoted
primarily to supportive measures, reality-testing, and counseling about life
situations and relationship problems. In this usage, *psychotherapy* is a generic
term under which we might classify analysis and non-analytic psychotherapy.
There is, of course, no absolute distinction between analysis and non-analytic
psychotherapy; in practice they tend to overlap.

Jung termed his theoretical system and therapeutic approach *analytical
psychology,* to distinguish it from Freud's psychoanalysis. However, since the
term *psychoanalysis* has come into generic use as an intensive psychotherapy
dealing extensively with unconscious material, I shall here use the terms *analysis* and *psychoanalysis* synonymously. In this usage, Jung's system of analytical
psychology is one form, or school, of analysis, just as Freudian psychoanalysis,
existential analysis, neo-Freudian psychoanalysis, and Adlerian analysis are.

From a Jungian viewpoint, a particular format or technique is not needed
to identify a psychotherapy as an analysis, reflecting at least in part Jung's
view of therapy as a dialectic or a dialogue between two psychic systems, in
the course of which *both* systems undergo change. For example, many Jungian
analysts sit face to face with their clients, rather than using the couch and the
free-association technique. Also, it is typical for a Jungian analyst to meet
with a client at the most two or three times a week, and often to decrease the
frequency of sessions to once a week or even less. Neither frequency nor
format is a central criterion for analysis. Nor does the Jungian rely heavily on
the concept of *transference neurosis* in order to define an analysis. The primary
criterion for analysis from a Jungian viewpoint is the elucidation of unconscious material.

Because therapy is a dialectical process for Jungians, it is often important that the therapist make him- or herself known to the client as a *real person*. Contrary to the idea that such a position will "dilute" or cloud elucidation of the transference phenomenon, Jungian therapists maintain that the projection of both personal and impersonal elements of the unconscious occurs spontaneously in any human transaction, whether inside or outside of the consulting room. In fact, for Jungians, one characterization of the process of psychotherapy might be the idea that therapy is a process of making continual distinctions between projective (transference) events of both personal and impersonal nature and "literal" (situation-appropriate) elements, at any moment during therapy. As the client (as well as the therapist) learns to identify his or her own projections, he or she is faced with the challenge of "withdrawing" them, of taking personal responsibility for them. Thus, as therapy progresses, the client is, one hopes, increasingly able to relate to the therapist as a person having both strengths and weaknesses.

The specific nature of the transference phenomenon that does develop will vary according to the characteristics of the particular therapist-client dyad. That is to say, specific "real" characteristics of the therapist will trigger specific aspects of the total transference potential of each client. Therefore, Jungians often hold the opinion that clients should work with more than one therapist before completing psychotherapy.

Whatever the format, Jungian analytic work is work with unconscious material, personal and collective. In actuality, much psychotherapy (with the possible exceptions of strict behavior modification and other therapies that deliberately avoid dealing with, or deny the existence of, unconscious material) is of the type currently referred to as "psychoanalytically oriented psychotherapy," in the sense that the degree to which unconscious material is addressed during therapy fluctuates from moment to moment.

However, from the Jungian point of view, what is most important is this: whenever collective or impersonal unconscious elements are addressed during psychotherapy, a transpersonal event takes place. Such a viewpoint goes a long way toward neutralizing the mystique that has arisen around the concept of transpersonal events. Although these events are often powerfully perceived and therefore register themselves in consciousness as uncanny and mysterious, many of these events are quite mundane and should be so treated. If not, there is danger of ego-inflation, a concept and phenomenon that will be elaborated on shortly.

Reality of the Psyche in Jung's Thought

Jung's view of psychic reality is of central importance to an understanding of his thought. It is stressed again here because this simple yet subtle concept is fundamental to his approach and to those of Jungian orientation in identifying and dealing with transpersonal events in psychotherapy.

Jung believed that a dangerous situation had developed during the past few centuries with the increasing emphasis on rationality and cognition as the primary functions or aspects of consciousness. Although great strides have been made in manipulating the physical or material world, rational man has simultaneously lost contact with the "irrational" experiences that impinge on consciousness; he tends to ignore his dreams and fantasies, his inarticulable experiences—in short, all those aspects of experience that cannot be precisely identified by cognition and rationally explained as manifestations of the physical universe. For Jung, this was tantamount to "throwing the baby out with the bath water," because it is precisely that irrational side of experience that carries powerful energy, and brings fundamental meaning to existence (Jung, 1961).

From a Jungian viewpoint, then, transpersonal events, themselves usually inarticulable and irrational in manifestation, are primary to understanding human psychic functioning and psychopathology. Such events are truly "of the psyche"; they often appear to be unresponsive to so-called physical law and are often experienced as unrelated to space, time, or causality.

In the face of such events, alternate conclusions may be drawn. The first is that, since such events do not appear to follow physical law, they must be distortions of perception. Organically oriented psychotherapists and psychodynamic theories often assume that such experiences are functional distortions, manifesting as disguises or "screens" for instinctual experiences or impulses. The Jungian attitude toward this first conclusion is illustrated by an example:

> A Jungian-oriented therapist receives a call from a young woman who tells him that she has been in therapy for some time with another therapist but has recently discontinued it. She says, "God is very important to me, but every time I mentioned God to my therapist, he would just sit and stare at me without changing expression and would ask questions about my sex life." She is seeking another therapist, and although the therapist whom she called has no time in his schedule, he assures her that he will refer her to someone of his acquaintance "with whom you can talk about God."

The second and alternate conclusion is that, although the individual may use transpersonal events defensively, they are part of that person's psychic reality and therefore deserve attention and trust. In our example, the therapist whom the young woman called illustrates this attitude. He makes no value judgment about whether she is using her interest in God to avoid looking at regressive aspects of her sexual nature. He accepts the possibility that her focus on God may be, among other things, a protection against confronting specifically sexual problems. However, he also accepts that in the *psychic reality* of the individual, God may be intrinsically meaningful and vitally important. In telling the client that he will refer her to someone who will talk about God with her, he operates from the assumption that her phenomenal world, her psychic reality, is a primary reality for her, regardless of whether she has difficulty integrating her organic or physical side. He knows that he must move first into *her* reality, in order to be of any help to her. If there is, indeed, a connection between her interest in God and difficulties with her instinctual life, he assumes that his colleague will discover with her whatever connections there are between the two—without denigrating her original fascination with the God-image. Jung would accept wholeheartedly this slightly paraphrased adage: It's not what happens (in the world of physical reality) but how you *perceive* and *feel* about what happens (in the world of psychic reality) that really matters.

Another way of differentiating psychic reality from other reality is to say that physical reality is concerned with *events* and psychic reality with *meanings*. In this sense, transpersonal events are manifestations in imagery of psychological meanings: the phenomena of psychic reality.

The reality of the psyche is primary, Jung believes, for an understanding of human beings. He further states that it is possible to develop a (state-specific) science to deal with phenomenological occurrences, which are the raw material of that reality. The largest body of Jung's work is an attempt to develop such a science.

The Nature of Transpersonal Events

Reference to transpersonal elements of the psyche and to transpersonal events is an intrinsic part of the attitude and armamentarium of the Jungian psychotherapist. In order to focus more precisely on the transpersonal event as it appears in psychotherapy, let us define it from a Jungian viewpoint.

A *transpersonal event* may be said to have occurred when there has been a confrontation between personal and impersonal elements of the psyche, involving consciousness of that event. *Personal* elements of the psyche are further defined as those aspects of individual experience which are a part of the personal history of the individual and which have been recorded by him as such, even if "forgotten" or repressed. They also include the present attitude of consciousness. In the language of analytical psychology, the personal aspect of the psyche includes both *consciousness* and the *personal unconscious*. The impersonal elements of the psyche include those precursors of individual experience which are *not* a part of the individual's personal history but which derive from the psychic reality of the human condition, of which they are the psychological parameters. Their manifest forms or images are not "inherited" per se, but the predispositions or parameters from which specific forms are derived tend to manifest themselves in individuals across historical and geographical boundaries. To these hypothesized "fundamental parameters" of the human psyche, Jung gave the name *archetypes*.

Archetypes are experienced only through the specific forms or images that manifest them; these forms or images are therefore called *archetypal images*. Archetypes are identified through analysis of the themes running through dreams and fantasies. They are also found in creative art and in the legends and mythologies of peoples. Such themes include "mother," "father," "the child," "the wise old man," "the self" or integrating principle of the psyche, and so on.

These impersonal elements or archetypes tend to use one form of imagery or another to intrude on the existing attitude of consciousness; they are particularly intrusive if they represent elements diametrically opposed to that attitude of consciousness. The church spire appearing in our first clinical example is just such an archetypal image; it is in opposition to the attitude of consciousness (ego-alien) and functions as a corrective to the conscious attitude. The image of God in the second example is also archetypal; it is ego-syntonic, or accepted by consciousness, but requires further "constellation" or filling-out in therapy itself.

Utilization and Significance of Transpersonal Events

Jung saw ego-consciousness in a dialectical relation to unconsciousness; elements from the unconscious are in compensatory or balanced relationships with conscious elements. If consciousness rejects or denies the confrontation with the impersonal element, no change in the attitude of consciousness results, although by definition a transpersonal event has occurred. This rejection or denial is demonstrated in the following example.

> A woman in her early twenties entered therapy partially as a result of a series of dreams that had left her puzzled and uneasy. She gave a history of a very conventional life marked by a denial of her own worth as a woman and as an individual. About two years previously she had married a young man from her home town and tried to settle into the conventional role of housewife and be subordinate to her husband, who was quite controlling in a superficially masculine way. He was completing an advanced academic degree that would enable him to begin a career as a university researcher and professor. One of the dreams presented by this woman was recurring: she walks alone through

a kind of enchanted wood to an open clearing on top of a hill. As she walks into the clearing, a figure, at once human and not human, unusually tall and wearing a hooded white robe, advances towards her from the other side of the clearing. There is a vaguely feminine "feel" to the figure. The dreamer is terrified but unable to prevent herself from advancing to meet the figure. In the midst of her terror she is fascinated that in the figure's hands is a white flower, so perfectly beautiful and radiant as to inspire feelings of the deepest awe and wonder, even in the midst of her terror. In each of the recurring dreams, the figure holds the flower out to her as if inviting her to take it for herself. And in each dream the dreamer, filled with terror, forces herself to awaken.

This young woman remained in therapy for over a year. Although it became quite clear that her lifestyle was restricting her far beyond her capabilities, interventions by the therapist along this line had little result, as the client persisted doggedly in an attitude of consciousness entirely consistent with her personal history. She had been raised in a family that stereotyped and sharply limited the feminine role and enforced the limitation by an implied violence to be visited upon any female who "broke the rules." The relationship of female to male in this family was marked by masochistic subservience; indeed, during therapy the client regularly visited her family and resumed the masochistic role that she had been taught to play toward her father and older brother. Toward them and toward her husband she was passively hostile but could not bring herself to assert her own needs and desires. Toward the therapist, who was a male, she remained basically fearful, hostile, and distant, but also masochistically dependent. She finally left therapy when her husband found placement in a university in a distant city. At no time during therapy was she able to develop an attitude other than one of vague fear, fascination, and discomfort toward her initial dreams.

This particular transpersonal event—a dream event—occurred spontaneously and repeatedly, but because of the fixedness of the conscious attitude, it remained unassimilated and therefore unconducive to psychic change, at least during the period noted. Such occurrences are common in psychotherapy; they illustrate well the functioning of the impersonal aspect of the psyche. This aspect virtually proceeds with its own process, sometimes in apparent disregard for the attitude of consciousness and often in a "polar resonance" with that attitude.

The clinical situation described above is, from a Jungian viewpoint, not necessarily seen as a resistance in the traditional sense of an ego-defense mechanism. There are questions of timing in the assimilation of unconscious material; it is important for the therapist to trust a client's psyche, including his or her avoidances. Jung points out that confronting the client prematurely or too forcibly with material to which the client is showing consistent signs of avoidance could be dangerous; in some circumstances it could precipitate a psychotic episode. Furthermore, each individual's course of development is unique; material that is avoided at one time might be made available by consciousness for assimilation at another time. The psyche itself often makes a direct statement of avoidance, as is shown in the following case.

A middle-aged professional man began therapy around concerns involving the termination of his marriage and entering into a new relationship. During several exploratory sessions, it became apparent that the client was functioning from a rather restricted attitude of consciousness, and there were signs of potential danger in several areas of his life. However, the client was nominally successful in his profession and had no conscious complaints other than those relating to his transition from one primary relationship to another. The therapist pointed out a few of the apparent danger signals, whereupon the client had the following dream, which he brought into the session:

> I am hiking up a beautiful canyon, along a flowing river. There is full sunshine, the light sparkles on the water, the air is like spring, birds are singing, and there are beautiful plants growing along the bank of the river. As I hike up this canyon in good spirits, the canyon makes a bend. Up ahead I now see a huge dam, filling the entire canyon. I am fascinated by it and curious to see what is behind it, but at the same time I feel a kind of foreboding. Above and behind the dam I see clouds gathering; a storm might be brewing up there. I see that with some difficulty I might pick my way up one side of the canyon to get level with the top of the dam and see beyond it. I begin the climb, filled with curiosity. But as I climb higher, the sense of foreboding increases; the clouds above the dam now look dark and ominous. I begin to feel most uncomfortable and frightened, and an urgency to leave the area comes over me. I turn and climb back down to the base of the dam and hurry back down the canyon, around the bend, where once again sunshine and a sense of peace and beauty engulf me. Once again my feeling of fear subsides and once again I am contented, as if the disquieting dam were very far away.

The client and therapist discuss this dream quite openly; the obvious metaphor of retreat in the face of a looming and possibly dangerous fear is quite obvious to both. The client offers another obvious association that the dam could break, but adds: "Even so, it's holding for the present, and I really don't feel I want to get into discussing those topics you raised, right now. Perhaps some other time, when things have settled down." The therapist agrees that this seems quite appropriate, and the client discontinues therapy shortly thereafter, after a short-term course devoted primarily to support and reality-testing of his personal relationships.

Now when there is interpenetration or mutual assimilation of personal and impersonal elements, the impersonal event takes on *meaning* for consciousness; the transpersonal event may be said to have produced a change in the conscious attitude itself. Jung called such a change a demonstration of the "transcendent function" of the psyche (Jung, 1921, 1971). When the transcendent function is operative, *transformation* of consciousness occurs. An unusual clinical example elucidates such transformation and illustrates the Jungian approach to transpersonal events in psychotherapy.

A thirty-year-old woman in the latter stages of an extensive analysis had become increasingly dissatisfied with what she felt to be slow but steady progress and too much attention to "details" in her life. She felt that she had worked through some difficult problems and that she was now ready to make some rather drastic changes, including change of career and return to school. This feeling had come up increasingly during her analytic sessions.

The analyst felt that there was indication for caution in regard to this attitude, but admitted to his analysand that he himself was not entirely clear on the issue. He suggested, and they mutually agreed, that she should consult the *I Ching* (the *Book of Changes*)—or "throw an I Ching"—as a way of obtaining both an "impersonal reading" and some perspective on the question. The analysand threw the coins during an analytic session and obtained hexagram 62, "The Preponderance of the Small." This hexagram cautions against "attempting large things," indicating that "one should not strive after lofty things but hold to lowly things . . . since the requisite strength is lacking." The instruction seemed to speak quite directly to the question, but the analysand was dissatisfied with it, feeling that perhaps she had not followed the correct procedure in obtaining the hexagram.

Upon her return home from the analytic session, she consulted the *I Ching* again on the same question, and again obtained hexagram 62 (one chance in sixty-four). She found the repetition of the hexagram very convincing and decided to continue to work slowly on herself, making no large changes in her life for the present.

About a year later she was referred to another analyst, a woman, for the completion of her analysis. Again she had been feeling quite restive with her life and considered the possibility of making some extensive changes. Again she consulted the *I Ching* and for the third time obtained hexagram 62.

Finally, about two months later, again restive with what she considered to be the slowness of changes in her life, she consulted the *Book of Changes* for the fourth time on the same question, and for the fourth time obtained hexagram 62. This final event precipitated an extensive examination with her analyst of her tendency to throw herself impulsively into ill-considered actions, a tendency that included magical thinking and other aspects of a hysterical personality-formation, which had hitherto gone unanalyzed.

Jung became interested in *I Ching*, or the *Book of Changes*, through his studies of Eastern psychologies and through his connection with Richard Wilhelm, the first major European translator. Many readers will be familiar with this book; those who are not are referred to its most complete available edition for further, needed elaboration (Wilhelm, 1967). This ancient book, some three thousand years in the making, is an absolutely central codification of the spirit and thought of Chinese civilization; and, in a sense, it may be thought of as the bible of that civilization. Legend tells us that it was originally written by four holy men, including Confucius, and was a major source for the Taoist thought of Lao Tse and others. It has received attention from and elaboration by eminent scholars down to the present day. Its present form is a collection of sixty-four symbols, or "hexagrams," each with its own central theme and amplification; these flow into and out of each other and together make up a panorama of the situations and qualities of human life and consciousness. Each hexagram describes a typical human situation and gives a "larger perspective," which provides amplification for the questions of concern to the person consulting the book.

The book was and still is consulted as an oracle by persons desiring a "commentary from the gods" concerning their individual human problems. But its major use down through Chinese history has been as a book of wisdom rather than an oracle.

Jung thought he observed an interdependence or "meaningful coincidence" between physical events and the subjective or psychic states of the observer. He termed this "acausal connecting principle" *synchronicity.* He saw it as diametrically opposed to the principle of causality in Western science, which he viewed as a statistical truth but not absolute, belonging only to what Gordon Allport and others would call a "nomothetic" science (Allport, 1960).

The principle of synchronicity applies idiographically; for the individual psyche at a single moment, the universe of conscious experience and potential (unconscious) experience is arranged with all of its parts manifesting a potentially meaningful interconnection. In other words, each part or aspect is in a "synchronous" relation with each and every other part, as if each were an aspect of one unitary reality.

Jung used the principle of synchronicity to bring meaning to psi and other phenomena that are inexplicable within a traditional causal or Newtonian framework. For him, synchronistic phenomena are manifestations of the self-archetype, in turn bringing with them the possibility of a state of consciousness of a "larger order" than that circumscribed by the usual definitions of ego-consciousness. One aspect of individual psychic development, or individuation, is the transcendence of the ego itself—a giving up of the "I" in favor of a larger conscious perspective. Therefore, the assimilation into consciousness of synchronistic phenomena is an important aspect of individuation.

The acknowledgment and utilization of synchronistic phenomena are parts of the formal and informal tradition of human thought, but this connection has been overlooked in recent history due to what Jung believed was overemphasis on the rational aspect of consciousness and on a narrow definition of "science" in terms of materiality and causality. For Jung, dreams, fantasy, and indeed most aspects of phenomenal (psychic) experience are better understood from a synchronistic point of view than a causal point of view.

The *Book of Changes* provides a major example of the formal acknowledgment of the synchronistic viewpoint in human consciousness. (Jung's foreword to the Wilhelm translation [1967] is a major elaboration of his theory of synchronicity, a central concept in his psychology.) Systems of astrology in both Western and Eastern thought are another example.

However, from a Jungian viewpoint, a belief that the planets affect our individual lives or that "the gods speak through the *Book of Changes*" is a gross misinterpretation; it reifies and overliteralizes what are simply formal, systematized acknowledgments of the synchronistic nature of the psyche. It is much more accurate to say that consulting the *I Ching*, sorting the Tarot cards, or casting an astrological chart is simply an attempt to bring a larger perspective of *meaning* to a situation, to put a particular problem into the context of the larger, essentially unitary course of events. In other terms, it is an appeal to the *transpersonal* aspect of the situation in which a particular ego-consciousness finds itself in a given moment. In our clinical example, the therapist suggested consulting the *I Ching* out of his and his client's mutual recognition that such an action would be relevant and bring meaning to her situation and concern.

Jungian-oriented psychotherapists do *not* routinely advise use of the *Book of Changes*—or any other system of synchronicity—as a technique in work with clients. Such an interpretation of this clinical example severely distorts its meaning. Use of the book in this or any other instance arises out of the context of the relationship between therapist and client as it had developed to that moment. At the moment the suggestion was made, this context included some mutual acknowledgment of the personal meaning to the client of synchronistic phenomena, a sense of frustration with the seeming insolubility of the particular issue by the usual rational or analytic methods, and a mutual trust and rapport between client and therapist. Furthermore, a great degree of more traditional analytic work had already been done and use of the *I Ching* was already known to and somewhat accepted by the subcultures to which both therapist and client belonged.

Therapy is not a technical procedure for the Jungian therapist; in fact, all Jung's thinking about psychotherapy may be viewed as a corrective to what he believed to be overtechnical use of method and technique in Western psychotherapy. For example, while it would be inaccurate to conclude that the therapist in the example regularly used such procedures in his practice, it would be accurate to conclude that the *possibility* of using such procedures was part of the therapist's resources in working with clients—just like using medications, interpretations about instinctual matters, free association, or any other of the procedures of psychotherapy.

What about the outcome of the clinical example itself? One outcome of the therapist's suggestion that the client consider the synchronistic aspect of the question was that a series of synchronistic events then did occur. There was clinical importance in the client's having obtained the same hexagram and consequently the same instruction four consecutive times over the next fourteen months; each repetition of the hexagram drew her attention to the same possible correction for her attitude of consciousness. This correction was transpersonal; it was, for example, contrary to the position of the ego, both currently and in its personal history.

The truth or falsity of the principle of synchronicity is not what the Jungian psychotherapist is primarily concerned with. He is more interested in it as a potential source of meaning to the client. The model might be stated as follows: ego-consciousness maintains an essentially conservative function; it tends to remain fixed. In this example, the ego-consciousness of the client remained fixed on her desire to make some major changes in her life. Although at first glance this appears to be an option for change, it is actually a fixed position. The *desire* for change in her physical circumstances actually becomes a defense against any awareness of her tendency to substitute action for self-reflection.

The transpersonal events of the repetition of the hexagram—this synchronicity—finally forced the client to examine factors she had avoided by her fixed determination to effect physical changes in her situation. It is as though "some power larger than herself" (more inclusive than her attitude of ego-consciousness) repeatedly inserted itself into awareness, demanding that she look at herself from another perspective. Thus this series of events takes on the quality if not the intensity of a religious conversion or other "peak experience." While other factors might also have played a part, such as her shift from a male to a female analyst, undoubtedly the accumulation of such events was a factor in her eventual decision to examine herself from an angle previously resisted. This accumulation of events apparently contributed to the interpenetration of personal and impersonal elements, producing a meaning that marked a change in the conscious attitude. Thus, the transcendent function of the psyche manifested itself through an interaction of the impersonal synchronistic events and the previous conscious attitude.

The synchronistic phenomenon implies a bimodal or paradoxical definition of *psyche:* psyche is deeply personal and individual and at the same time a "transcendent" concept that includes the universe of physical and psychological phenomena. It is beyond the scope of this chapter to elaborate on this "psychoid" aspect of Jung's theoretical system, in connection with which the reader is referred to writings by both Jung (1954b) and Aniela Jaffé (1971).

In Jung's theoretical system, the continued tension in consciousness between two opposed psychic elements produces an apparent paradox and eventually activates the transcendent function, that inherent potential for psychic growth and change. One function of therapy, then, is to help maintain such tension *in the field of consciousness*. The ensuing change involves an expansion of consciousness, the inclusion of ever-larger wholes within awareness. The situation for such change bears an obvious similarity to the paradoxical situation deliberately set up for the student by Zen teachers, or by don Juan for his pupil, Carlos (Castaneda, 1971, 1972, 1974). Always, the integration of a personal and impersonal psychic element involves a transpersonal event, in which consciousness sheds some of its overly rigid attachment to the ego or "I." Consciousness is transformed by finding a larger base than the previous self-definition of the ego. And at some point in this process—a point not covered by the clinical example—the ego or "I" becomes only a part or one aspect of identity.

The Danger of Ego-Inflation

In certain cases, the course of the transformation of consciousness to a broader or more ego-less base does not occur; instead, the ego identifies directly with impersonal psychic material and dangerous *ego-inflation* occurs. At times this can prelude a fixed or acute psychosis.

Cases of subtle paranoia are fortunately fairly rare, but they illustrate well the danger of activating and focusing on impersonal psychic material;

here, the client's dynamics include a primitive ego-structure, which copes with its fear of annihilation by identifying directly with archetypal material in a grandiose way. In some instances grandiose overidentification of ego with archetype produces a rather fixed position of ego-inflation; such appears to be the case in this example.

A woman in her early forties had returned to school to complete training toward a doctoral degree in a major helping profession. She had also entered analysis, for the stated purpose of providing herself with additional training.

The woman was brilliant, highly regarded by her colleagues, and in analysis was unusually innovative in her work with her own unconscious material. However, she was always somewhat aloof and impersonal. Her dreaming and fantasy life produced highly archetypal material, and her analyst, a female, found the work with her fascinating and compelling.

The analyst, recognizing a consistent lack of feeling in her client's productions and in the way she related to herself and others, attempted for a time to activate the client's feeling-side by expressing her own feelings more openly. She sensed a certain danger when her client appeared to regard the analyst's feeling as a weakness. However, the woman's introverted brilliance was for a time reassuring.

The analyst, who was indirectly involved with her client's university as a visiting faculty member, began to obtain chance information from the comments of others that caused concern. This information centered around the client's tendency to refer to her own creative genius, apparently seeing herself as a major innovator in her field and interpreter of the ideas of its best-known theoretical figures. The analyst was additionally concerned when she heard that her client had been accusing fellow students and faculty members of deliberately throwing impediments in the way of her career, such as plagiarizing her ideas, passing her over for grants, and so on.

The analyst began to raise questions during sessions about her client's feelings about her graduate work and career plans. The client was immediately resistant to discussing such topics; she wanted to deal only with the dream and fantasy material she chose to bring into the analytic hour. When the analyst continued to push for reality-testing of her client's life situation and ideas about herself versus others, the apparently good rapport broke down quite rapidly. The client became coldly angry with the analyst, accused her of deserting her, and made indirect reference to the analyst's supposed collusion with other faculty members.

An attempt to refer the client to another analyst failed; she coolly informed the analyst that the analysis had been completed for some time and that she had continued sessions only out of pity for the analyst.

In other cases grandiosity is only a prelude to a gross breakdown of the personality in acute psychosis. More frequently, however, individuals exhibit at least brief manifestations of ego-inflation that give cause for concern but are not obviously pathological. Such persons often are professionals and paraprofessionals in fields involved with medicine, psychiatry, and psychology as well as in transpersonal areas of interest such as astrology, psychic healing, body work, and mystical disciplines. People involved in the helping professions are especially vulnerable to ego-inflation and problems involving the use of power for personal enhancement.

The dividing line between demonstrable ego-inflation and optimal functioning as a teacher or healer is often vague in my opinion. From a Jungian viewpoint—perhaps from any viewpoint—transpersonal events in psychotherapy are a two-edged sword: they provide great potential for further growth and evolution of consciousness, but they strongly tempt susceptible persons to succumb to ego-enhancement, manipulation of others through power, and even paranoid and other psychotic states. For these reasons, a careful assessment of the client's ego-functions during every stage of therapy is essential.

Either denial of the existence and significance of transpersonal events or overidentification with them is to be viewed with considerable caution. It is consistent with a Jungian view and mandatory for every psychotherapist to regard human psychological functioning as simultaneously and paradoxically both progressive and regressive. The art of psychotherapy is to distinguish between the two and to make a choice in each moment as to which deserves the focus of therapeutic intervention.

The Nature of Psychopathology

Analytical psychology may be said to be primarily a psychology of the growth of the psyche. It traces the vicissitudes of the individual psyche and particularly of ego-consciousness in its progressive encounter with elements "outside" itself. Other psychodynamic viewpoints focus on the interaction of the ego with the organic and social elements of personal experience; the Jungian viewpoint adds the dimension of interaction with impersonal elements of an archetypal nature—those collective, universal elements presumed to provide an *anlage*, or groundwork, for the actualization or constellation of a particular human psyche at a particular moment of history. Thus, through archetypal theory, the Jungian viewpoint sets up an objective psychological model by means of which transpersonal events may be ordered, investigated, and found meaningful.

Jungian psychology holds that psychopathology derives from blocked, impeded, or distorted psychic development. The mutual assimilation of ego-consciousness and elements outside of consciousness, and/or the movement of consciousness along the axis from ego to self have somehow been interfered with. This interference is usually a function of one of the following mechanisms. First, there may be some inadequacy of the ego in handling input from the unconscious through weakness of ego structure as in borderline or psychotic conditions. Second, it may be a function of conflict, anxiety, and/or depression occasioned by the ego's conservative and defensive stance when confronted by strange, unfamiliar elements often diametrically opposed to its view of itself and the world. Third, the interference may be a function of a defensive fixation of the ego itself, leading to ego-inflation and a denial of the legitimately transpersonal qualities inherent in the psyche as a whole, rather than specifically to the ego.

In the second instance, a neurosis of some kind presents itself, either acutely as gross anxiety and other symptomatology, or more slowly, as in the increasing dissatisfaction of a fixed character neurosis, or so-called character-disorder. The third mechanism is exemplified by the clinical case of ego-inflation outlined earlier. The ego reacted to a perceived external threat to its existence and legitimacy by partially reifying itself, partially "making itself God." This case was accompanied by typical paranoid manifestations of ideas of reference; that is, all elements external to the client's ego—whether inside or outside of herself—were perceived as directed against or inimical to the ego. Ego-inflation—the inappropriate assimilation of impersonal psychic elements to personal identity—may be seen, then, as a primitive attempt to deal defensively with such a threat. In the case described, that attempt was at least partially and temporarily successful—at the expense of adaptation to literal reality and the capacity to engage appropriately in human relationships.

By far the most common antecedent to the activation of transpersonal events is some form of fixed conflict. This illustrates what Jung called the compensatory function of the collective aspect of the psyche, commonly manifested in dreams:

> A thirty-five-year-old woman came into therapy shortly after the death of her father, to whom she had been very attached.
>
>   She exhibited symptoms of rather deep and unmitigated mourning and, in many ways during therapy, resisted her therapist's attempts to "reduce her father to normal size." There remained an overdetermined attachment to him and a stubborn melancholia. In many ways she saw

herself as nothing without her father and used her mourning for him to avoid investigating her own resources and potentials. At times she exhibited a definite suicidal potential, manifested as an almost palpable wish to join the beloved father in death.

She dreamed voluminously, and during the very slow and agonized breaking of the attachment to her father during therapy, a number of vivid dreams lent themselves to developing a broader perspective on her situation. Two of these dreams are related here.

In the first, she is upstairs in her childhood home and hears a knock on the front door. She looks out of the front window and sees her father standing there, looking as real as he ever did, with a suitcase in his hand. She is overjoyed, thinking that at last he has returned to her. She runs downstairs and throws open the door. Her father stands looking at her with an expression of deepest poignancy on his face. She wants to fling herself into his arms, but he restrains her with a gesture, and says: "I've come to say goodbye; I've got to go over the mountains, and you *must* let me go." He turns and motions back over his shoulder. In the far distance she sees a range of mountains, very high and blue.

In the second dream, she finds herself in a beautiful garden. Two gorgeous butterflies are floating in the air near her. The first butterfly flies close to her ear and whispers, "Reality has many forms." The second butterfly then floats near and says, "And death is not what it appears to be."

In this example, the dream events are strikingly transpersonal. The therapist's response was to help the client accept them very literally; they directly spoke to her overfixation on her father, appealing for a broader perspective. The fixation itself was a kind of negative ego-inflation, an overidentification with the impersonal, or archetypal, masculine element in the woman's own psyche, an element represented by the image of her father. In this example, the transpersonal events themselves functioned through phenomenal "personalities" of their own, acting as a corrective to the previous transpersonal fixation. The transpersonal element itself "invited" ego-consciousness to break its own fixation and inflation, to take a broader perspective, to recognize her father and his death as something far beyond her own personal needs in its scope and implication.

From this perspective, psychopathology not only derives from personal historical antecedents but may also arise spontaneously at any moment in life when one finds oneself unable to assimilate unpredicted events from inside or outside. For example, a person in middle life who has previously functioned adequately in meeting the demands of success and material satisfaction may come to the psychotherapist with an unexplained depression or anxiety. Dream content in this instance may reveal highly archetypal themes of death and rebirth, the giving way of old ways of functioning in the material world. New themes may emerge that are more spiritual, more introverted, and so unfamiliar in content as to be mysterious, even frightening.

In summary, psychopathology from a Jungian perspective has to do with a dysfunction of the ego-attitude as it attempts to deal with the emergence of unconscious elements to which the context of the life situation, both inner and outer, has given form. It is generally held by Jungian psychotherapists that specific phases of the individual life cycle lend themselves to confrontation with specific impersonal, archetypal themes.

During childhood and early adult life, aspects of the parental archetypes that have not been given form—or to use Jung's term, *constellated* by personal experience—manifest themselves in an intrusive or problematic way to ego-consciousness. They demand to be given form by further experience. This occurs simultaneously with a regressive manifestation of distorted parental themes deriving from inhibiting or constricting personal experience and the personal unconscious.

During the second half of life, archetypal themes demanding integration of spiritual values often make their appearance. Active work with such themes during therapy involves not only techniques designed to focus the attention of ego-consciousness on archetypal material but also the manifestation and working-through of such material in the transference and countertransference.

There is, of course, considerable overlap between the first and second halves of life. Generally speaking, however, earlier life is usually concerned primarily with questions of autonomy, the developing and strengthening of ego functioning, and mastery of the material world; later life demands a disidentification with the ego and a focus on spiritual and transpersonal concerns. Therefore, a Jungian therapist is cautious when confronted with a young client who is heavily involved with transpersonal elements before personal autonomy and ego-integrity have been fully established.

Nature and Function of Jungian-Oriented Psychotherapy

When obviously regressive elements appear during therapy—as they typically do early in therapy or in severe disorders—Jungians use reductive approaches to the problem much as any other psychodynamically oriented psychotherapist would, provided of course that the rapport and the ego strength of the client allow such threatening intervention.

However, rather constant attention to the progressive aspect is necessary for several reasons: to counteract the constrictive and depressive effect of the reductive approach; to identify obviously meaningful transpersonal events when they do occur; to encourage the inherent growth tendency of the psyche; and to provide the ego-consciousness of the client with a larger arena of self-functioning as a corrective for ego-inflation or constricted identity. One term for this last provision in analytical psychology is progression along the *ego-self axis* in which self is seen as an archetypal entity more inclusive than ego or "I" (Edinger, 1972).

In dealing with progressive and transpersonal elements of the psyche, Jungian-oriented therapists employ a method of *mutual amplification*, which (in contradistinction to free association) involves a conscious collaboration between therapist and client. Contribution of conscious imagery around a particular problem in a collaborative effort by both parties is felt to activate unconscious material in the form of symbols, which are now available to consciousness for further work. It should be noted that Jungians feel that active participation and contribution by the therapist do not *necessarily* have a suggestive effect on the patient; nor does such collaboration necessarily add to the possibility of a "transference cure." However, if regressive elements are dominant in a particular phase of therapy and especially if predominantly hysterical or borderline elements are present, the therapist may choose to minimize his or her own contribution to amplification, in view of the probability of suggestive or ego-disintegrative effects.

The Jungian psychotherapist is alert to the probability that both personal and transpersonal events will manifest themselves during the course of the work with a client. Such a therapist will certainly deal heavily with the usual phenomena of psychotherapy—personal transference, resistance, catharsis, development and utilization of ego strength, interpretation of characterological traits, instinctual and conflictual material, habitual difficulties in interacting with emotionally significant "others," and so on. This therapist is just as alert, however, to working with both the emergence of unconstellated archetypal material (potential for experience that has not yet been given form by actual experience) and the ego's ambivalent attitude toward this material.

When impersonal, archetypal material does appear, the problem for the therapist is not simply one of dealing with regressed ego functioning. Ego states become regressed in the face of external or internal events that induce an earlier, more childlike, stereotyped, and limited level of consciousness. However, the client may be able simultaneously to assimilate a new way of behaving, and that involves integration of these previously unconstellated archetypal phenomena. Therefore, a potentially progressive aspect of the psychic situation is always present. This progressive aspect both complements and brings meaning to the regression. The therapist must often choose whether to intervene with a client from the regressive or progressive point of view. It is the making of such choices which defines psychotherapy as an "art" as well as a science.

A twenty-five-year-old man entered therapy with complaints of pervasive anxiety and inability to "get going" on a career of artistic performance involving what appeared to be considerable talent. He was likable, intense, and talkative, and used most of the first twelve hours of therapy reporting voluminous dreams of vivid content, and stories of altered states of consciousness. These included out-of-body experiences, hypnogogic experiences, and spiritual revelations.

The therapist received this material with interest, and his interventions were supportive and included amplification of the material to help his client bring psychological meaning to these experiences. During the thirteenth hour, the client was, as usual, reporting a series of such experiences when the therapist took advantage of a brief silence to refer to a comment the client had made during the previous hour: "Have you made any arrangements to find a new place to live?" He was referring to the client's casual mention that his landlord had given him a month's notice to vacate his present apartment. The client looked rather blank and stumbled over his words, saying, "No, I haven't gotten around to that yet." The therapist then reminded the client that he had made a number of such casual comments from time to time during previous sessions, each of which added to the illustration that the client's daily affairs, both personal and artistic, were in considerable chaos. Then the therapist said, "You know, you've been reporting to me a number of experiences from your inner life which obviously carry a lot of energy for you, and you need to bring some meaning to them. But I begin to wonder if maybe those far-out experiences don't serve to kind of function for the part of you that resists 'getting it together' in the regular world? It's as if you're so busy with them, and they fascinate you so much, that you just can't bother to get organized."

The young man was startled, looked at the floor for a while, and finally said: "You know, you're right. I've got all my life to find out what leaving my body is all about. But pretty quick I have to find out why I can't just plan things and carry them out."

This rather simple and ideal example illustrates the complexity of factors that contribute to even a brief transaction during the process of therapy, especially the "polyvalent" use of transpersonal factors. Initially, in any psychotherapy, the therapist's task is to gain client rapport and quality of relationship; this will later allow the client to be open to interventions that might involve considerable threat to the relatively fixed attitude of ego-consciousness.

In this example, the therapist reacts supportively to the client's reports of his transpersonal experiences. He says, essentially, "Your experiences are valid and important to you in your unique psychic reality. In order to help you, I must initially go with you to where you are. If you can experience my validation of this level of your awareness, you may later trust me enough to examine the possibility that, in other areas and in other ways, you might be working against yourself." This "working against yourself" included the client's negative use of a positive thing; he had used his very talent for the transpersonal experience as a defense against consciousness of his unwillingness to assume responsibility for his daily life. Uncovering the *source* of this unwillingness was not achieved in the example given; that task remained for future sessions. But in this session, the *fact* of the unwillingness and its possible negative connection with his penchant for transpersonal states of consciousness began to be established. Such a connection and such unwillingness are typical, in Jungian formulation, in clients whose lives are heavily conditioned by the archetype of the *puer-puella,* "the eternal child."

A central concept in Jungian psychotherapy is balance—in this case, between the inner and outer worlds. If alteration of consciousness does not find outward manifestation in a changed way of dealing with the literal world and vice versa, no event of significance for the individual psyche has occurred.

Using a fascination with and talent for transpersonal experiences as a defensive maneuver by the ego does not invalidate these experiences themselves; but the "regressive" or defensive use of the transpersonal event for this client at this time in his therapy obviously took precedence over its potential significance for him. Furthermore, overemphasis on these experiences at the expense of literal reality makes useful integration of transpersonal events unlikely. As another example, a person who has considerable musical talent but lacks capacity or motivation to gain skills necessary for its expression gains nothing from its possession.

There are many situations, of course, where the obvious function of the transpersonal event is progressive; if the conscious attitude is prepared, it represents a potential breakthrough to a more pervasive consciousness. This preparation probably will involve at least a degree of suffering, the development of a kind of desperation; the old ways of adapting and looking at things are no longer satisfactory. One such example is that of the young woman who experienced the recurrent dream of the white flower. In her case, apparently, the experience was premature; the conscious attitude was not yet prepared to be receptive to it.* Although the unconscious process seems to operate in a rather

---

*It could also be said in retrospect that in this particular case, work with a female therapist might have been helpful to the client—especially considering the negative quality of the transference towards the male therapist, the history, and the feminine quality of the dream content.

constant compensatory fashion to the attitude of consciousness, as it did in this case, to the degree that such an attitude remains "fixed," the unconscious material is perceived as intrusive and will be avoided in some way.

Assimilation of transpersonal material is more likely to occur if a buildup of circumstances has made the conscious position increasingly untenable. This is often accompanied by some degree of psychological symptomatology, such as anxiety and/or depression in one or more of their many forms. In addition, ego-strength must be such that some tolerance of the symptoms themselves is possible, rather than such symptoms appearing primarily as unreflective acting-out. This is evident in the following example.

A thirty-four-old man came into therapy after a deliberately planned psychedelic drug session left him deeply moved but also quite symptomatic, with anxiety attacks bordering on panic, difficulty in sleeping, and extremely vivid and sometimes frightening dreams. He attended therapy regularly for about fifteen months, during which it centered heavily on an anamnesis of an extremely difficult childhood and young-adult life. The original drug experience had involved a deeply spiritual "revelation," which could not be well-articulated and which was contaminated by the simultaneous confrontation with negative and frightening archetypal images.

Slowly during the therapy, he worked to separate out these negative elements from the spiritual insight he had undergone, relating them to literal experiences from his own past that had obviously given them their negative coloration. During this period, the therapist not only worked with him on the anamnesis and discharge of feeling connected with the negative personal experiences but also encouraged him continually to make a conscious distinction between such negative experiences and the more deeply meaningful and spiritual images with which they were intertwined.

Gradually the symptoms decreased and essentially disappeared. Quite early in therapy it was evident that the client approached his work on himself with considerable tenacity, showing a stubbornness that allowed him to deal with such material even while experiencing symptoms. This tenacity continued to manifest itself during the entire course of therapy. The client discontinued therapy when he was experiencing no further symptomatology; he wanted to "try it on his own" rather than perpetuating his dependence on therapy.

About eight years later, the client again sought out the therapist. He was not experiencing symptoms of any degree of severity but wanted some help with ongoing dream material that seemed to be pointing him toward additional changes in his life and consciousness. This "therapy" continued intermittently and attained a quality of "consultation be-tween peers" rather than the dependent therapist-client quality that had marked the earlier therapy.

In the interim between the two therapies, the client had contin-ued his own education, both formally and personally, and had obvi-ously deepened and broadened himself as a human being. He was now ready to look at a number of possibilities for himself, including a radi-cal change in vocation and career, as well as entering into significant personal relationships, which had hitherto eluded him.

Ego-strength, in this case manifested by the quality of stubborn tenac-ity, is essential to integration of transpersonal material. Other clients exposed to heavily transpersonal experiences, yet lacking ego-strength, have experi-enced deep regression, sometimes to the point of open psychosis requiring hospitalization.

Jung continually pointed out that activation of the unconscious always carries with it the possibility of the ego being overwhelmed by transpersonal material (Jung, 1935, 1954). All psychotherapy is necessarily concerned with working with the ego. In some instances it helps the ego become more flexible in correcting an over-rigid and defensive attitude toward the images and affects of the unconscious; in other cases, it patiently works with ego-functioning to give it more energy and an objective detachment in order to prevent it from being overwhelmed by the inevitably alien possibilities thrown up by the unconscious.

The vicissitudes of such work with the ego are the guts as well as the nuts and bolts of psychotherapy. The qualifications of the psychotherapist rest to a great extent upon skill in working to induce changes in ego-function. The psychotherapist must not only be familiar with the typical manifestations of the unconscious psyche, both personal and collective, but must be more than familiar with the subtle and sometimes dangerous interface between the unconscious and consciousness itself.

The psyche is *process;* "cure" is not necessarily a valid concept for work with the psyche. The nature of psychic life is such that new problems and new questions continually arise.

The return to therapy of the client just discussed several years after his initial experience illustrates this point. Although many psychotherapy clients come as "patients," that is, with symptoms of one kind or another, symptom removal is not necessarily the end point of psychotherapy. Symptoms are signals that something needs to change and that change is being resisted in some way.

A more appropriate goal of psychotherapy, therefore, might be to help the client to the point in his own consciousness where he can, in a sense, be his own therapist. Even then, there are times when the individual once again needs, for a time, to find in someone else the personification of the archetype of "the physician." For the psychotherapist is truly "doctor of the soul," whether he or she asks to be or not. This is true when and because the psyche demands it to be so.

Essentially, from Jung's viewpoint, transpersonal events in psychotherapy do exist and possess a vital reality of their own, and they may involve great power and energy. Therefore, they have the potentiality to produce psychological effects of great good or great harm. They involve the possibility of ever-continuing psychic growth and development; however, they can overwhelm consciousness and bring personal psychological life to the edge of stagnation and death. The Jungian psychotherapist knows that much of his work has to do with using himself as an instrument to encourage and enhance the former, and to reduce the possibility of the latter to the minimum allowed by the destinies of both parties to the psychotherapeutic transaction.

7

Use of the Transpersonal in Logotherapy

Joseph Fabry

One of the most important practitioners and writers in the field of logotherapy, Joseph Fabry presents an eloquent distillation not only of his own professional experience and knowledge but of the restoration of his personal life order after losing overnight "family, job, country, language, security, and roots." The theories he presents have been subjected to rigorous trial.

For those unfamiliar with logotherapy, Fabry describes its tenets as developed by Viktor Frankl. Logotherapy postulates three inseparable dimensions in the human person: the physical, the psychological, and the spiritual. All three must be given credence for the maintenance or restoration of health, but it is the area of the human spirit to which logotherapy has made its greatest contribution, by leading the client toward new or rediscovered meanings—"the meaning of life" and "the meaning of the moment."

Logotherapy sees meaning as the awareness of order, which may or may not be seen as religious. Treatment directed toward finding meaning for the client consists of four steps: helping the client gain distance from symptoms, modifying attitudes toward symptoms, prophylaxis and attainment of optimal meaning at this stage, and last, letting the client take charge of his or her life, thus making the therapist superfluous.

While there is no single method for achieving these four steps, some particular techniques have proved useful. The principal technique is the Socratic dialogue, in which the logotherapist is an active partner, probing, supporting, disagreeing. Two other techniques developed by

Frankl are "paradoxical intention," which is based on the capacity for self-detachment and humor, and "dereflection," which is based on the capacity for self-transcendence.

How can transpersonal experiences be used in logotherapy? Fabry sees the logotherapist as continually facing the difficulty of motivating his or her clients to accept the hypothesis of an ultimate meaning and to sharpen their inner ears to make them response-able to "the meaning offerings of the moment." He believes the transpersonal experiences of both therapist and client are among the most effective ways of providing this motivation. In the transpersonal experience the awareness of order becomes "immediately apparent," even though it may last for only a moment and then be forgotten or repressed. People can be helped to recall or discover such experiences through group participation, diary writing, free or guided fantasies, drawing, and simply listening to others share their transpersonal experiences.

Fabry observes in conclusion that although any conceivable circumstance can illuminate meaning, it is most likely to appear in five areas, each of which may be the content of transpersonal experience: self-discovery, choice, uniqueness, responsibility, and transcendence. He provides moving, pertinent vignettes from his own work as illustrations for each of these. For Fabry himself and for his clients, these five areas are truly transpersonal because "they lead—if only for a moment—to the awareness of order."

LOGOTHERAPY WAS CONCEIVED by Dr. Viktor Frankl, a student of Alfred Adler in Vienna during the late twenties. It was developed in youth counseling centers during the depression years of the thirties, and was put to a rigorous test in the forties when Frankl spent two and a half years in German death camps.

Frankl had stipulated three tenets for logotherapy: life has meaning under all circumstances; everyone has a will to meaning, which is the prime motivation for living; and each of us has the freedom to find meaning.

Did life have meaning in a concentration camp? Did a will to meaning help inmates survive? Did they have freedom to find meaning?

As readers of Frankl's *Man's Search for Meaning* know, his answer to all three questions was an unqualified yes. Although the suffering in the concentration camps was meaningless, each moment offered meanings within the limitations of camp existence—helping a fellow inmate, applying logotherapy to the despairing, keeping on working in order to avoid the gas oven. The will to meaning—all other things being equal—made the difference between life and death; those who despaired were more likely to die than those who saw a purpose in survival, a purpose like completing a work, being reunited with a child or a wife. And a freedom was available that no barbed wire could destroy—freedom that could not change the situation but allowed room for the individual to take a stand within an unchangeable situation. The inmate could ask himself, Why did this happen to me? What did I do to deserve this fate? and then despair because there were no answers to these questions. Or he could take a different attitude and ask himself, What can I do even under these dreadful circumstances? From here, a path to meaning became visible.

This attention to the present and future, and to the potential meaning in attitudes, was the cornerstone of logotherapy and is applicable to everyone. Sooner or later we all have to go through "concentration camp" experiences, in the sense that we find ourselves trapped, without hope of escape, and through no fault of ours. The philosophy and methods of logotherapy are needed in these situations to help us survive. Sometimes this means purely physical survival but mainly it means survival in order to live a life worthy of a human being, a life in which we see meaning.

In order to understand how logotherapy works and how it can use transpersonal experiences, it is necessary to know something about logotherapy's views of human beings and the world in which they live.

The Human Spirit

Logotherapy sees the human being as a totality consisting of three inseparable dimensions: the physical, the psychological, and the spiritual. All three must be considered for clearer self-understanding and health. The inclusion of the human spirit is new in medicine—or at least it was new in the prewar years when Frankl developed his therapy. The human spirit has been the domain of religion, but religion often discounted the areas of the physical and psychological. Medicine, including psychotherapy, has tended to disregard the human spirit as a source of health. Logotherapy warns against reducing the human being to nothing but a body and a psyche. Such a view would see in Dostoevski nothing but an epileptic and in Joan of Arc nothing but a schizophrenic. Only by including their spiritual dimension can we understand them in their fullness. Only by including their spiritual dimension can we understand patients in general. Logotherapy rehumanizes psychotherapy.

To maintain or restore health, we must consider all three dimensions. The spirit, like the body and psyche, is part of every person, not just the religiously inclined. The spiritual dimension, which Frankl calls the *noös*, contains such uniquely human attributes as our will to meaning, our goal orientation, our creativity, our imagination, our intuition, our faith, our vision of what we can become, our capacity to love beyond the physiopsychological, our capacity to listen to our conscience beyond the dictates of the superego, our sense of humor. It also contains our self-detachment or ability to step outside and look at ourselves, and our self-transcendence or ability to reach out to people we love and causes in which we believe. In the area of the spirit we are not driven; we are the drivers, the decision-makers.

This reservoir of health is available to everyone regardless of religious or secular beliefs. Most of this reservoir is contained in our unconscious, and it is the task of the logotherapist to make us aware of this spiritual medicine chest.

This emphasis on the human spirit, the noös, is logotherapy's contribution to human health. Ironically, it also contains its limitations. Logotherapy can be helpful in five areas, only two of which are strictly medical.

Applications

The first area applies to the increasing number of people whose will to meaning is repressed, frustrated, or ignored. They have, too, developed a feeling of inner emptiness, which Frankl calls the "existential vacuum." These people are not sick but feel frustrated, empty, bored, in limbo, in despair, and in doubt, or have the vague notion that they are not living up to their potential.

The second area where logotherapy is helpful concerns people who believe that life is too short to bother about meanings (hedonists), that meanings cannot be found (fatalists), that people can find a meaning only by following others (conformists), or that they alone know the path to meaning (fanatics).

The third area Frankl calls "medical ministry." It applies to people in "concentration camp" situations of unavoidable suffering. Some suffer from incurable sickness, old age, loss of a beloved person; others must live within limitations like blindness, crippling, or heart attack effects.

The fourth area in which logotherapy is helpful relates to psychogenic neuroses caused, for instance, by a complex or a trauma. These neuroses, having originated in the area of the psyche, can be treated by psychotherapy. But whatever the method used, logotherapy will be helpful as supplementary therapy; it at least helps the clients gain self-confidence or break unwanted behavior problems they acquired during their sickness and directs them towards new or rediscovered meanings.

The fifth area concerns *noögenic* neuroses, those originating in the *noös* or spirit. Because these neuroses are not caused by past events, they will not respond to orthodox psychotherapy. Noögenic neuroses are caused by conflicts of conscience or collisions of values in the present and may show the same symptoms as psychogenic neuroses—physical illness or psychological disturbances like depressions or fears. Worldwide research has found that about 20 percent of all neuroses are noögenic. For those people suffering from this type of neurosis, logotherapy is specifically indicated (Crumbaugh, 1968; Lukas, 1972).

Because logotherapy stipulates the interrelationship of body, psyche, and spirit, an overall diagnosis needs to be made by a psychiatrist who considers all three areas. He might prescribe pharmacotherapy, psychotherapy, logotherapy, or a combination of these. Logotherapy is useful by itself in cases of noögenic neuroses; it is also useful together with or after the application of pharmacotherapy or psychotherapy in treatment of other disorders. The cured phobic, the person with a "successfully" amputated leg, the "cleaned up" drug addict will have to be guided toward a meaningful life. Other people who are not sick but feel the frustrating emptiness of their existential vacuum will also have to be led toward meaning.

Meaning

Logotherapists see meaning on two levels. The first is ultimate meaning, *the* meaning of life. We become conscious of ultimate meaning by our awareness that, in spite of all apparent chaos, injustice, and suffering, there is an order in the universe in which I, the individual, have a part, however minute that might be; it does make a difference what I do—whether I ignore the order, fight it, or cooperate with it. The religious mind calls that order God; the nonreligious may call it life, nature, science, evolution, history, the ecosystem, or any other name that indicates belief in suprahuman laws that can be disregarded only at personal peril. Ultimate meaning cannot be proved or disproved; it must be lived *as if* it existed. Nor can it ever be reached and captured. It is like the horizon. It lures us on, but the closer we get the farther it recedes. Here the pursuit of meaning is important, not its attainment.

But there is a second level of meaning that can and must be attained, if life is to be meaningful. It is "the meaning of the moment." In Frankl's concept, we are all unique individuals living through a string of unique moments, each of them offering us a meaning to fulfill. To realize the meanings of the moment and to respond to them—to be "response-able"—is to lead a meaningful life. The meaning of most moments is prosaic, perhaps even trivial—getting up in the morning, driving safely on the freeway, saying a word of love and concern. But occasionally the moment requires vital decisions—taking on a new responsibility, deciding on a career, proposing marriage, planning a family. In most standard situations in life we are guided by what others have found useful in similar types of experiences. We follow the traditional "values" of our society as they are expressed in the laws, customs, and religious commandments of our cultural heritage. But values can contradict one another and cause conflicts, and then we have no other course but to follow the voice of our conscience, feeble as it may be.

Treatment

The logotherapist achieves his goals in four steps. First, the clients are helped to gain distance between themselves and their symptoms. They must become aware that failures, depressions, fears, obsessions, and physical shortcomings are not anything the clients *are*, but something they *have*. They must become aware that they are endowed with what Frankl calls the "defiant power of the human spirit" to overcome these unwanted conditions—even though they may also require pharmaceutical and psychotherapeutic help at times.

Second, the logotherapist helps clients to modify their attitudes toward themselves and their conditions. They learn to move from blaming parents, society, and themselves and feeling helpless (relying on help from outside sources) to assuming responsibility for their own recovery. At the same time, they also learn not to blame themselves for conditions over which they have no control. An overweight man, for example, can assume responsibility for reducing, unless his excess weight is caused by, let us say, an incurable glandular malfunctioning. Then he is not responsible for his obesity, but he is responsible for the way he lives his life as a person whose physical condition has condemned him to carry a lot of extra pounds.

When the modification of attitudes has been accomplished, the third phase begins. The body reacts to the influence of the spirit and the symptoms disappear or at least become manageable. Now the final step, the prophylaxis, can start. The clients are led toward the optimal meaning possible at the present stage. Again the responsibility remains with the clients: meanings are not handed out. They have to be discovered within the clients' own value system. All possible meaning potentials are discussed, enriched, and expanded. The aim of this phase is to enlarge the clients' meaning reservoirs so that they can draw meaning possibilities from various sources. This will protect them from existential frustration in the future if one source of meaning is lost—the person whose life changes drastically at retirement, the spouse whose partner dies, the couple whose children have moved out.

If the third step, the reduction of symptoms, has been successful, clients experience such a positive feedback from their new attitudes that they are likely to open themselves to a wider orientation toward meaning. The therapist becomes more and more superfluous, and the clients take charge of reorganizing their lives toward a wider range of meanings and values.

Methods

There is no one highway by which the logotherapist can achieve success. Client and therapist go on a common search for some indications from the client's spiritual unconscious, indications which might point the direction of his or her hopes, visions, and goals. Client and therapist together probe into what is important and desirable to the client. The essence of the logotherapeutic method is improvisation. Any technique may be applied, provided it is not reductionistic in treating the client like a machine that can be manipulated or an animal that can be trained. Some techniques have proved especially useful.

The principal technique is the Socratic dialogue or self-discovery discourse. The basic assumption of logotherapy is that in the deepest resources of our human spirit we know who we are, what our potential is, and by what paths we can go from where we are to where we would like to be. The therapist asks questions in such a manner that the clients take on the challenge of finding their own particular way or answers. The therapist acts as a midwife to help the birth process of ideas and attitudes that lie dormant in the client and are not consciously recognized. This is Socrates' idea of education, and it is also Frankl's idea of education to responsibility.

The logotherapist remains an active partner, who keeps probing and challenging and watches out for some indication in the client's meaning orientation. Once the client indicates this by a recollection, by a fantasy, perhaps by a hope or a value expressed, can indicate a direction, a hook to which the therapist can attach his or her support, it heralds the emergence of a new path for the client to pursue, step by self-chosen step.

But the logotherapist also must be able to say no to a client's attitude—not because he or she disagrees but because that attitude is not mentally healthy for the client. He or she will tell an obsessive compulsive, "No, you will not do what you fear you will do. You can be sure it won't happen." Or he or she will say to a depressive patient, "No, it is not true that your life has lost all value and meaning. You are wrong there, and I'll prove it to you."

Two logotherapeutic techniques Frankl developed in the thirties are paradoxical intention and dereflection. Logotherapy literature contains numerous examples and case histories of these. Both methods enable clients to break—even if only for one brief moment—the vicious cycle of fear and anticipatory anxiety in which they believe themselves hopelessly trapped.

Paradoxical intention is useful in cases of phobias and compulsive obsessions, and wherever else undesirable behavior patterns need to be broken. Clients are encouraged not to run away from the feared situation but to face it with humorous exaggeration. By learning to laugh at their symptoms, the clients can disassociate themselves from them. Paradoxical intention is based on the human capacities for self-detachment and humor.

Dereflection is useful in cases of excessive self-reflection and self-observation, such as sleeplessness or sexual dysfunction. Impotence, for example, is cured by dereflecting the man's thoughts away from his performance and from his anxious self-observation, something which is especially strong after previous failure. This is accomplished by taking the pressure off him to "have" to perform and requires the active cooperation of his partner. Dereflection is based on the human capacity for self-transcendence. Instead of laughing at their symptoms, as in paradoxical intention, clients learn to bypass them in their thoughts and, again, find distance between themselves and their symptoms.

The logotherapist faces the difficulty of motivating clients to accept the hypothesis of an ultimate meaning and to sharpen their inner ears to make them response-able to the meaning offerings of the moment.

I have found three ways in which clients can be so motivated. The first is to show them that someone cares about them and their situation, be it friend, counselor, or group. The second is example. If a client is brought together with a person who went through the same difficulty and has overcome it, the client will be encouraged to try, too. No one can so effectively motivate a person getting blind to find new meanings as another blind person. Example as motivation has long been used in such organizations as Alcoholics Anonymous. If in a sharing group a woman is in deep despair because her husband has left her, she can be motivated to change her attitude from one of hopelessness to one of challenge if another woman can tell her: "I know how you feel. I was in the same situation five years ago. I thought the world had come to an end. But now I see that many good things have come from my divorce. I have become independent, have developed talents I never dreamed I had, and have made new friends." The third motivation to do something about a situation is what Frankl calls an *abyss experience*. The client has come to a point so unbearable that he decides his life cannot go on like this. With the support of the therapist, he can discover that he has the defiant power of the human spirit to change his attitude from "I'm the helpless victim of my circumstance" to "I'll do something about it."

Transpersonal Experiences

Transpersonal experiences are a promising tool in logotherapy because they combine all three of these motivations. These experiences can be understood as immediate existential proof that Someone or Something cares, no matter whether the carer is conceived as a religious or nonreligious force, as God, Life, or Nature. Transpersonal experiences also serve as examples—all the more effective because the examples are set by the clients themselves: they know from their own experience that life made sense during one peak moment in the past and that such a moment of recognition may recur. Finally, transpersonal experiences often come during periods of stress and despair; the peak rises directly from the abyss.

Transpersonal experiences are difficult to use in therapy because they are often so unspectacular that the client does not perceive them as extraordinary. They may be forgotten, repressed, disregarded; they may be a source of embarrassment because they are taken as a sign of instability, irrationality, even mental illness. For the logotherapists, *transpersonal* is used to describe any experience that has an effect on the person not explainable on the human level, especially not on a rational level. Meaning and order become immediately apparent. In most cases the message is hidden in commonplace experiences; it may come up when we are watching a sunset, ocean waves, or a fire; when we are listening to music, watching a play, or reading a poem; or when we are in the process of an intense human relationship with a lover, a child, a guru. Suddenly and inexplicably, life, if only for a moment, makes sense.

Transpersonal experiences are also difficult to use in therapy because they cannot be made to happen at will. Although they can be invited by a setting of peacefulness and beauty, or by a mental conditioning through meditation, it is the essence of such experiences that they come unexpectedly. But the therapist can help clients to remember transpersonal experiences, to admit them to consciousness, and to see their message: life is good; there is order; you are part of this order; you are part of a totality; you are secure.

The logotherapist would do well in searching his or her own past for transpersonal experiences; this would enable him or her to help clients ferret out theirs. I have discovered several experiences in my life I consider transpersonal. One of them I regard as pivotal, yet it took me fifteen years to realize it was a peak, and fifteen more until I talked about it because it was so personal that I doubted anyone else would understand its impact on me. Only through my work with logotherapy did I come to realize its potential as a tool for healing myself as well as others through sharing the example.

Meaning had not been a conscious problem during my first twenty-eight years. In March 1938 Hitler's storm troopers marched into my native Vienna and shattered the order of my life. Overnight I lost family, job, country, language, security, and roots. After a chase of five months I escaped to Belgium. One day, in September 1938, I sat under a pine tree in a forest, in deeper despair than I had known to exist. My mind was filled with a chattering of fear and confusion. My family was being shipped to German death camps. I had no place to go, no future. I cannot say today that I was consciously searching for meaning in a situation that obviously had none, but my anguish was an indication that I was desperately trying to make sense of my life.

Then it happened. My eyes fell on a small pine twig on the ground. It was an ordinary twig, shaped regularly, three shoots on each side, each pine needle in place. Most needles were dry and brown, but on each tip there was fresh, light-green growth. An Indian-summer sun broke through the clouds and a shaft of light fell on my little twig. That was all.

I did not understand. I was not even conscious of the branch. Only years later its memory was dredged up from the depths. All I felt at that moment in 1938 was a sense of calm. The chattering ceased, the weight lifted, and I felt refreshed and hopeful. The rejuvenation did not last; I was to go through many moments of despair. But I know now that the memory of the pine twig helped me regain my balance in subsequent situations of chaos and grief. The experience had directly shown me that order existed, even in the smallest twig, that new, green growth springs from dead and fallen stems, that the sun is there even if it is temporarily hidden behind clouds.

The healing effect of such experiences has been discovered by many people without the help of a therapist. A friend, also a refugee from Hitlerism, had been trapped in Shanghai and finally, just before Pearl Harbor, received his saving visa to the United States. As his boat left Shanghai, the setting sun silhouetted the Chinese junks and fishing boats against the flaming sky. The sense of peace was so strong that my friend is able to revive that image in situations of stress. He calls it self-hypnosis. The recall always gives him assurance, and he often uses it to fall asleep when his mind is troubled.

While most people have had transpersonal experiences, it is not easy for them to see them for what they are—cogent guideposts to meaning. In the supportive atmosphere of a logotherapy group participants may recall past incidents and see their significance for the present. A minister, for example, found the strength for the first time to unburden himself of a memory about which he had felt guilty for years. He had just buried his wife, a long-suffering cancer victim. He had fought for her life with her, and now it was over. After the funeral, in heavy grief, he boarded a plane. When it broke through the layer of clouds into the clear sky, he felt a tremendous release, a sense of joy, which he, especially as a man of the cloth, "should not have felt." Now, in the caring environment of the group, he understood the message: Life is not over, and it is beautiful.

Frankl's own examples also illuminate commonplace experiences of the past. He describes the inexplicable uplift he received at finding a carrot growing in the mud of the concentration camp (1973b). This episode released a memory in a group member who had spent time in jail. One day, he recalled, during a hunger strike, he saw the sky behind the barred window suddenly glow and felt soothed, he said, as he had not felt since his mother stroked his head when he was a child.

Several techniques can be applied to prompt the recollection of these messages "from beyond." One of them is diary writing and discussing the writings in the group. One participant, a carpenter who had temporarily gone blind, described his unbounded joy at seeing the grain in the wood floor of his room when the bandage was taken off his eyes after a successful operation. In talking about his diary notes he realized that the message was not merely the obvious "You are no longer blind," but "There is a grain in the universe." As a carpenter he knew well that one has to work with the grain, and not against it, if one does not want to get hurt. Now, years later, he faced the agony of divorce. What was the "grain" of his present situation?

Fantasies, free or guided, are another method of helping participants in groups to recall transpersonal experiences. In the relaxed stage in which free associations are encouraged to float, a woman relived the unaccountable comfort she had felt years ago by looking at a diamond ring she had inherited from her mother. The mother's sudden death had brought the woman to the depth of depression. She was contemplating suicide when a ray of sunlight fell on the ring on her finger, releasing the colors of the rainbow. Mysteriously, the load had lifted. Now, in the group, she sat silently, under an electric light, playing with her ring. For some time she had felt trapped in an unbearable work situation. Suddenly she said, "I know I'll find a way out." When asked how she knew, she answered: "There is green, red, orange, and blue in my white diamond."

A third method of bringing out transpersonal experiences is drawing. Participants are given sheets of paper and a set of colored crayons and told to draw how they see their life up to the present and how they visualize their future. The drawings are placed on the floor and each is discussed. In discussing his life's picture, one elderly man described the greatest catastrophe in his life: he had lost both parents in a car accident. He had drawn this event as a lightning bolt in orange. His lifeline took a plunge and only slowly crept upward until it rose sharply when he had met and married his wife and started a family. He suddenly stopped and shouted excitedly, "Look! I drew my wife and children orange, just like the accident of my parents!" In the ensuing discussion he explained how he understood the transpersonal message he had received right then and there: the death of his parents, which had seemed a crushing blow, had actually opened many potentials that had lain dormant, just as his marrying and having children had done later. It helped him mature, take on responsibilities, make a man out of a boy. That realization lifted a great weight from him.

The incident had a chain reaction in the group. A woman recalled the despair she had felt when her husband had left her. She could not sleep at night, she said, and one morning she got up early and took a walk through some nearby woods. "A new world was opened to me. I had never heard stillness so consciously, never seen trees at predawn, never heard the first bird break the silence with a song. I suddenly realized how much life there was still to explore, and that I now had the chance to explore it." Looking back at her divorce now, she saw that it had helped her to stand on her own feet, to discover new interests, to start her own career. And her recollection had still another effect in the group. A woman who had spoken about her despair of having to go through a divorce said quietly, "I feel better now."

Transpersonal experiences often achieve in one split second what the goal of logotherapy is: the awareness of an ordered totality in the universe of which the individual is a part. Under ordinary circumstances, this realization may be accomplished only in weeks or months, often never. Almost everyone has had fleeting perceptions of oneness and belonging, under a starry sky, on a mountain top, in a concert hall, in a moment of love-making. These may be forgotten, repressed, or ignored, and may have to be reclaimed to consciousness. Sometimes these incidents are more explicit. A woman recalled driving on a country road when a fox walked across it. The fox stopped in the middle of the road, and she also brought the car to a halt. "He stood there calmly," she said, "looking at me with large yellow eyes, and all of a sudden I had this tremendous feeling of being one, not only with the fox but with all of life. After a while he turned and slowly ambled away. I felt uplifted, and still have something of that feeling of unity when I think of that meeting."

Areas of Meaning

In my work I have found that, although meaning can become illuminated under all conceivable conditions, it is most likely to shine forth in five specific areas. Each one of them may be the content of transpersonal experience.

The first area is self-discovery. Whenever we have a glimpse of our authentic self—not as we are pretending to be but as we, in our spiritual unconscious, know we are—meaning will manifest itself. A forty-year-old man wrote, in evaluating a ten-week sharing group, "When Greg told us about his joking, it hit me: all my life I had been the life of the party, but something was wrong. I knew something was wrong. I used the clowning—what for? To hide my insecurity? To gain popularity? To avoid serious discussions? I have to find out, but I know now I am no joker." A woman with a limp said, after seeing *Cyrano de Bergerac,* "Cyrano is a fool. Just because he has a big nose he thinks no woman can love him. And I've been doing the same thing to myself because of my short leg. I've been a fool, too." A young man, after having completed college, went through an unexplainable depression. During a symphony concert, he suddenly realized that he did not want to go out and start working from eight to five. "I realized I was lazy, irresponsible, immature. Yet, I felt wonderful. The depression lifted. I had found out what kind of person I was but also that I didn't have to remain that way."

The second area where meaning becomes revealed is choice. Whenever we see choices, we see meaning. Conversely, life becomes meaningless when we feel trapped, without options. I remember an instant from my own life. After the war I worked as a script writer for CBS in New York. I was married, had two small children, and life in New York seemed unbearable after having lived in California. In New York I had an interesting, well-paid job. In California, I had nothing. I felt trapped. Then, one day, I did what all my friends thought was the most foolish thing to do: I quit the job. Yet, I'll never forget my feeling of exhilaration when I stepped out of my boss's office after having given notice. All my life I had gone the reasonable way. For this first time I had extended my choice to the "unreasonable." The lesson was not to be unreasonable from now on but to extend choices.

Unexpected choice can be an eye opener about meaning. A happily married San Francisco woman found herself alone in Denver while her husband attended a conference. She stepped out of her hotel, with an inexplicable feeling of ecstasy. She realized that this was the first time in her life she could remember having had complete freedom to do what she pleased—the first eighteen years of her life her father had limited her choices; the past nine, her husband.

The third area of meaning is uniqueness. When we feel irreplaceable, life has meaning for us. A professor of zoology collected pebbles and driftwood on a beach and glued together a statue. He experienced a satisfaction he had never experienced with his research. He said, "In zoology, I know that if I don't make a discovery, someone else will. But here I know that if I don't make this driftwood figure, no one else will make it just that way." Uniqueness is often experienced in works of creativity, and also in human relationships. "I love to be with my granddaughter," confessed a retired engineer. "She says, 'Follow me, Grandpa,' and I do whatever she wants me to do. Nobody does this for her, not even her mother—she doesn't have the time." One student will never forget a workshop led by Margaret Mead. In the discussion, Mead asked the student about his opinion on bringing up children. "Imagine that! Margaret Mead asking me for my opinion!" To make it a peak experience, it needn't be Margaret Mead. *Anyone* really listening to us, giving us full attention, can make us feel life is worth living.

The fourth area where meaning materializes is responsibility. In logotherapy terms, whenever we respond to the meaning of the moment, especially when the response emerges from our own conscience, there will be a glow of satisfaction. A young man who had refused to be drafted during the Vietnam War felt a strange elation when he was taken to prison. A married woman related her experience on a vacation trip to Acapulco without her husband. A handsome young man had become interested in her, and she was flattered by his attention. He begged her to let him visit her hotel room, and she finally agreed. She had never been unfaithful to her husband, but now she had been separated for two weeks and felt sexually starved. She waited for her man in great excitement, but when he knocked at her door she felt sudden pangs, a change of heart. While his knocking became more insistent, she thought of her husband and decided not to open the door. "Then," she reported, "I heard his footsteps going away and went to the window. When I saw him leaving, I experienced the most intense orgasm of my life."

The meaning potential of responsibility can also be expressed as a direct message from a dimension beyond human experience. An old man reported a feeling he had had as a young husband when he went to the hospital to have a first look at his newborn baby. "Her eyes were closed, and she had a very red and rumpled face. I didn't feel anything, but suddenly she opened one eye and looked at me. I'll never forget it. I'd had an easy childhood and had slid into marriage without thinking much about it. But when the kid looked at me, it hit me. Here was a human creature whose life depended on me. I was responsible for her. I was a responsible person."

The final area where meaning breaks through to us is transcendence. It is really a synthesis of the other four areas. In transcending ourselves, we get a glimpse of our authentic self, we do make a choice, we feel unique, and most of all, we assert our responsibility. We extend our self-interest to at least one other person, possibly to more, or to a cause. Meaning through transcendence is not always pleasurable, as anyone will know who has stayed awake nights to nurse a child, or who has been ridiculed in a women's liberation march, or who has been beaten up in a sit-in against nuclear weapons. Meaningful transcendence comes from self-chosen commitment, not from a commandeered duty. A former Peace Corps volunteer objected to Frankl's emphasis on obligation. "He brings the old puritan ethic in by the back door," she said. When it was pointed out to her that her life in the Peace Corps had been a meaningful obligation, she recoiled and explained, "But it was one I had chosen myself!" Then she stopped and laughed. Better than through any lecture she had understood transcendence as a path to meaning.

It can be argued whether these experiences leading to a glimpse of meaning through self-discovery, choice, uniqueness, responsibility, and transcendence are truly transpersonal. To my way of thinking they are, because they lead, if only for a moment, to the awareness of order that I have proposed as a definition of meaning. For that one moment we feel exposed to direct knowledge of ultimate meaning. It is a gift that life, or the circumstances, bestows upon us without our having especially sought it. Without asking, we sense our being part of an order. In religious terms, this is revelation, grace. But it would sell short the experiences of peaks if we limit them to the majestic heights of revelations. As Maslow's research has shown, peaks can come as summits, hills, and even molehills so small that we hardly notice them and certainly do not grace them with the term *peaks*.

The height of transpersonal experiences cannot be measured, but it can be "weighed." A load is taken off us. We feel we belong and are comforted. We are granted a fresh insight, and the freshness lingers, even if only in the unconscious from which it may emerge later. We are allowed a glimpse of life as it could be, and are challenged by the demands we face in this and every other moment of our lives. To respond to this challenge can be therapeutic, and logotherapy makes use of this possibility for healing.

Much work still needs to be done to discover the uses of transpersonal experiences in therapy. Logotherapy contends that our past contains not only traumas that can be used to explain present failures but also peaks that give assurance and hope. These peaks may be brief, often hidden in everyday experiences; they come in situations of stress and may not be immediately recognized. They offer us a glimpse of a pattern, a meaning most reassuring during times when we see nothing but chaos and emptiness.

8

Personal and Transpersonal Growth
The Perspective of Psychosynthesis*

John Firman and James G. Vargiu

In John Firman and James Vargiu's chapter, it is possible to see how the traditional field of psychoanalysis laid the foundation for yet another kind of transpersonal therapy, this one in many aspects almost identical to Buddhist approaches to the evolution of the Transpersonal Self. The authors make sure that the dangers of developing only the personal self or only the Transpersonal Self are clearly explicated; both need to be developed simultaneously and in balance. The approach used in psychosynthesis is well recognized for its contribution to this balanced development, and both authors of this chapter not only were trained by Roberto Assagioli himself but are considered leading spokesmen for the approach.

Firman and Vargiu describe the basic tenets of their chapter in this way:

> The conceptual framework of personal and transpersonal unfoldment underlying this paper is that of psychosynthesis. As an inclusive approach to human growth, psychosynthesis dates from 1911 and the early work of the Italian psychiatrist Roberto Assagioli. Although he was one of the pioneers

*Abridged from "Dimensions of Growth" by John Firman and James Vargiu in SYNTHESIS: The Realization of the Self, No. 3/4, copyright 1977, the Psychosynthesis Institute of the Synthesis Graduate School for the Study of Man, San Francisco.

of psychoanalysis in Italy, Assagioli maintained that Freud had given insufficient weight to the higher aspects of the human personality; he recognized the need for a broader concept of the human being.

Psychosynthesis asserts that there is in us not only a primitive or "lower" unconscious—the source of our atavistic and biological drives—but also a higher unconscious—a superconscious, which is the realm from which our more highly evolved impulses originate: altruistic love and will, humanitarian action, artistic and scientific inspiration, philosophic and spiritual insight, and the drive for purpose and meaning.

To respond fully to the emerging needs of the human being psychosynthesis maintains that we must be concerned with both these levels of the unconscious. In fact, the etiology of psychological disturbances can be found not only in a repression of our "lower" drives but also in a "repression of the sublime"—the failure to accept our higher nature.

Psychosynthesis works toward the integration of the personality, the recognition and actualization of the energies of the superconscious, and the realization of the self—first the personal self, the center of identity around which the personality becomes integrated and then the Transpersonal Self, that deepest center of consciousness and will in which individuality and universality blend. (Personal communication to the editor.)

MODERN LIFE HAS FAILED TO MEET the human need for meaning. The experience of meaninglessness, the lack of values and direction, has reached epidemic proportions. And yet our underlying need persists, the urgent questions remain: What is really meaningful in life? What is truly important for me to achieve?

We need to find two different kinds of meaning: first, the meaning of our own individual existence and second, the meaning of the world we live in, which is ultimately the meaning of life itself.

Our first concern as developing individuals is the search for meaning in our personal existence. Whether as a child learning to walk, as a student struggling with a mathematical problem, or as a businessman closing an important deal, we have a similar experience of this personal meaning. When we succeed in achieving a goal, we experience ourselves and our lives as having greater significance and value. Accordingly, we seek to accomplish larger and more important goals, and in so doing we develop our capacities and add to our skills and knowledge. This pursuit of personal meaning and goals leads us to grow as human beings, to form an increasingly well-integrated, creative personality, which is more and more effective in the world. This process takes place along what we may call the *personal dimension* of growth.

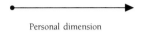

Personal dimension

But as the scope of our active involvement in the world increases, we find that our sense of world meaning also needs to grow. We leave the shelter of home and go to college; we leave school and go to work; we marry and raise a family; we seek to make a worthwhile contribution. At each step, experience calls on us to clarify and deepen our values, to explore, to re-examine the beliefs we live by. If we respond to this call and pursue the quest far enough, we shall eventually be concerned with such self-transcendent questions as: What is the true nature of the world? Can there be a peaceful and loving humanity? What are time, space, consciousness, good and evil? Is the universe evolving in a positive direction? We may approach questions of this sort intellectually, seeking insight into the truth, or we may reach for a direct experience, an expanded awareness that we hope will reveal the meaning and purpose of the larger reality. This search will lead us to the transpersonal or spiritual dimension of growth.

Transpersonal dimension

The Personal versus the Transpersonal

The personal and the transpersonal dimensions are distinct but not separate. Both are natural to human unfoldment. But a person generally tends to be more in touch with one dimension, experiencing it as more real, more important. This tendency to favor one dimension is often reflected in approaches to growth currently offered in our own culture. Many of them have been categorized as following one of two general orientations commonly and loosely described as Eastern and Western.

The Western view values most highly the person who is a strong individual, who can fully invest himself in his activities, function effectively, accomplish tasks, and demonstrate skill and success in handling the practical realities of life. With his strong intentionality, he orients the many aspects of himself toward a unified focus. He wastes little time and effort in internal conflicts, ambivalence, or confusion. Accordingly, he has considerable energy available for the business of achieving a rewarding and productive life. He is likely to regard the transpersonal dimension as secondary and, possibly, as a distraction from what is most important.

However, the Eastern view values most highly the individual who cultivates the inner, spiritual life. Emphasis is placed on achieving clarity of vision, serenity, love and compassion, a sense of joy and harmony, and, ultimately, oneness with all life.

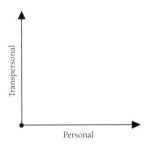

To reach these goals the individual develops the ability to master inner processes and to expand awareness. It is considered necessary to simplify or even largely to transcend daily life and the material world, attachment to which is seen as a distraction from what is most important. Thus the person who leads a contemplative life—the sage, the guru, the ascetic—is most revered and valued.

Despite the age-old tendency of people—and even whole cultures—to emphasize one dimension to the exclusion of the other, the possibility of unifying both has been splendidly realized by certain individuals throughout history. In our times, increasingly many people involved in spiritual life are realizing the need to develop well-integrated, capable personalities in order to make their spiritual values work. And, conversely, increasingly many people who have been successfully expressing themselves in practical ways are reaching for the transpersonal to find deeper meaning, more certain direction, and greater effectiveness.

Unifying the Personal and the Transpersonal

In the last decades a growing number of psychologists have said that both dimensions are essential to full human growth, and they have begun to explore the relation between these dimensions. Andras Angyal (1965), for example, discusses the individual's need not only to achieve autonomy but to experience "homonomy," union with a greater whole.

Similarly, Roberto Assagioli has recognized and developed two interrelated aspects of psychosynthesis: personal psychosynthesis, which aims at the development of a well-integrated, effective personality, and spiritual psychosynthesis, which leads to realizing one's higher nature.

Abraham Maslow, who introduced the term *transpersonal,* arrived at parallel conclusions through his observations. The similarity between Assagioli's and Maslow's conceptions is especially interesting, because while both men were deeply concerned with the spiritual nature of man and based their work on strong empirical foundations, they worked in very different environments and at different periods. In his later work Maslow recognized three groups of people: the first group, self-actualizers, have well-integrated personalities, strong, effective identities, and minimal experiences of transcendence; the second, transcenders, have strong contact with the spiritual dimensions,

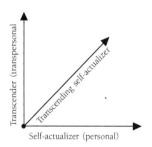

frequent transcendent experiences, but personalities that are often underdeveloped; the third, transcending self-actualizers, not only have strong and effective personalities but are also capable of transcending the limitations of personal identity and thus have a deep sense of eternity and of "the sacred" (1971).

In order to realize more and more of our essential humanness, we need to include both personal and transpersonal dimensions. As personal meaning and world meaning develop and then fuse, as both the the scope of our vision and our ability to express it expand, as our sense of individuality blends with our sense of universality, we find that we move toward a lived unification with our higher human nature, toward realizing our true Self. Therefore *Self-realization,* the realization of our Transpersonal Self (Assagioli, 1965, 1973; Carter-Haar, 1978; Miller, 1978), involves the progressive unification, at higher and higher levels, of the two dimensions of growth. It is important to remember that Self-realization is not something we should *do* or *make happen.* Self-realization is a natural process, and it occurs spontaneously.

However, we can begin to understand the process better and by doing so cooperate with and facilitate it.

Before we can unify the two dimensions in ourselves, we need to develop them. Whether we develop both simultaneously or first one and then the other depends on many different factors such as our individual makeup, our awareness, our environment. In practice, people often tend to proceed a long way primarily on one dimension before even becoming aware of the existence of the other.

If we feel more drawn toward one of the dimensions and this path seems right and fulfilling to us, clearly it is the one for us to follow; at the same time, it is helpful to develop and maintain awareness of the other dimension. Experience has shown repeatedly that if we proceed too far in one direction, sooner or later we shall need to include the other. When that time comes, we can include the other dimension by a conscious, deliberate choice, provided we have the awareness and the understanding needed to recognize what is missing. The alternative to conscious choice is to fall into a crisis of reorientation; this, too, eventually leads to the missing dimension, but often at the cost of much time, effort, and pain.

In short, whatever path we may follow as individuals, it is best to keep in mind the whole picture, the entire "territory" of human growth.

This chapter looks more closely at both the personal and the transpersonal dimensions of growth, at how we experience these dimensions, at the crises of reorientation that may occur if we proceed too far along one dimension exclusively, and at how we can more closely unify the two dimensions in our lives.

The Personal Dimension

From the moment of birth on, we experience urges and needs that motivate us into activity. What motivates us at any moment is the sense that there is something worth achieving, something that has value and meaning. Our first and most basic meaning lies in simple physical survival. However, when this need is satisfied, we do not merely sink into contented satiety; something else arises, some new goal with different or greater meaning.

To fulfill these goals we successively develop various aspects of our personality. As children we see that it is meaningful to master our body, to have physical competence, so that we can act effectively. The child's relentless urge to walk, his persistence through frustration after frustration, and finally the joyful elation that comes with success is a beautiful example of this process.

As we grow older, it becomes increasingly meaningful to establish satisfying and warm relations with others. We learn to experience and share sensitive, deep emotions. During adolescence, relations with our peers—romantic relations in particular—become the most significant focus of our life; consequently the subtlety and richness of our feelings may flower. During later adolescence, in response to the desire to understand ourselves and learn more about the world, our interest often shifts to developing the mind. At first, this motivation is likely to be in the form of simple curiosity. Gradually, however, we may become more and more involved in the pleasures of learning and develop increasing mental discipline. When this happens, the mind takes a central place in our life.

In adulthood, we may find that in order most effectively to achieve the goals we set for ourselves—whether pursuing a career, raising a family, or attaining success of some other kind—we need to coordinate and integrate all our inner resources so that they work in a unified way and in line with our aims (Vargiu, 1977). Our feelings must be developed and harmonized so that we can avail ourselves of their energy and relate to other people in a satisfying way. Our mind must be further trained so that we can think creatively, flexibly, and with the power to do broad planning as well as work with specific details. Finally, body, feelings, and mind must be harmonized and integrated with one another so that they can work synergistically.

The full, harmonious integration of the personality functions is a long process, a goal toward which most of us are still working and moving. This process of integration is represented by the horizontal arrow in our diagram.

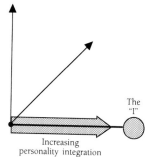

The
"I"

Increasing
personality integration

There are many approaches available to assist one during any of the various aspects of personality integration. The central concern of most forms of psychotherapy is to deal with deficiencies in specific personality functions or with conflicts between functions. The best approaches to self-actualization that have appeared in recent years aim at the positive development of particular aspects of the personality and contribute to their gradual integration into a unified, dynamic whole. There is, as well, the growing recognition that self-actualization consists not only of the harmonization of all the aspects of the personality but also of the gradual emergence and empowering of the "I", the center of personal identity. It is through the action of the "I" that the personality aspects are harmonized; the integrated personality gradually forms around the "I." Psychosynthesis provides many resources for this dual process of self-actualization. Some focus on the harmonization of the personality through the integration of subpersonalities—the many characters on our inner stage (Vargiu, 1977). Others deal with the means by which we can achieve the discovery of, and our identification as, the "I"—the center of personal identity, awareness, and will. (Carter-Haar, 1978).

As we have seen, whether or not we deliberately seek self-actualization through the various approaches, it proceeds naturally through the pursuit of meaningful goals. In recent times, increasing numbers of people have achieved a high level of self-actualization and have reached their goals with increasing success. This has led to an interesting phenomenon: many people have attained their personal or career goals only to find that the satisfaction, the value, the meaning of these goals is less than they had expected. They eventually abandon them. And they often abandon them just when things seem to be going best for them, when they appear to be the most successful. These people often take up a new and perhaps completely different pursuit, one they believe will be more meaningful than the previous one. But each new goal that they achieve also is likely to provide only limited or temporary satisfaction. Paradoxically, the greater the success, the more they experience what was expected to be highly satisfying as uninteresting and empty.

After this happens a number of times, an individual may simply imagine seeking new goals, pursuing new avenues to their conclusion, and then realize before even making a move that there will be no more meaning in these pursuits than in the previous ones. Here the individual enters a difficult period. If contact has not yet been made with the transpersonal dimension, the stage is set for what may be called the existential crisis, the crisis that challenges the meaning of an individual's very existence (Frankl, 1970; Assagioli, 1965).

The person now begins to wonder whether fulfillment is ever to be found. An increasing sense of meaninglessness pervades all normal activities. Pastimes and interests which he or she formerly found rewarding no longer bring the same pleasures. Family, friends, and career simply do not provide the same interests. As this progresses, the person may experience at various times apathy, fear, even despair. What is missing? The person has a strong identity and a well-integrated personality, can function very well in the world, is not neurotic, has more than successfully attained *normal* functioning by modern mental health standards. Logically that individual should be happy.

But although the person can seemingly accomplish almost anything, he or she is at a loss as to what or why to choose: I have been able to create a fine life for my family and for myself, but to what end? What does it mean? As the educator and Gestalt therapist George Brown puts it, "After the individual can stand on his own two feet, what does he do then? Just stand there?" (1977, p. 33)

The Existential Crisis

The nature of this crisis and the pattern that leads to it are illuminated by Leo Tolstoy's striking account of his own struggle:

> Something very strange began to happen to me. I experienced moments of perplexity and arrest of life as though I did not know what to do or how to live, and I felt lost and became dejected. These moments of perplexity began to recur more and more often. . . . They were always expressed by the questions: What is it for? What does it lead to?
>
> At first it seemed to me that these were aimless and irrelevant questions. I thought that if I should ever wish to deal with the solution it would not cost me much effort: just at present, I had no time for it, but when I wanted to I should be able to find the answer. The questions however began to repeat themselves frequently and to demand replies more and more insistently. . . . They seemed such stupid, simple, childish ones; but as soon as I touched them and tried to solve them I at once became convinced, first, that they are not childish and stupid but the most important and profound of life's questions; and secondly that, try as I would, I could not solve them.
>
> Before occupying myself with my Samara estate, the education of my son, or the writing of a book, I had to know *why* I was doing it. As long as I did not know why, I could do nothing and could not live.

All this happened to Tolstoy when he was having enormous personal success and showing great vitality and capability.

> All around me I had what is considered complete good fortune. I was not yet fifty; I had a good wife who loved me and whom I loved, good children, and a large estate which without much effort on my part improved and increased. I was respected by my relations and acquaintances more than at any previous time. I was praised by others and without much self-deception could consider that my name was famous. And far from being insane or mentally diseased, I enjoyed on the contrary a strength of mind and body such as I have seldom met with among men of my kind; physically I could keep up with the peasants at mowing, and mentally I could work for eight and ten hours at a stretch without experiencing any ill results from such exertion.

Yet, in spite of his fruitful life and his remarkable talents and abilities, Tolstoy makes this comment:

> I felt that what I had been standing on had collapsed, and that I had nothing left under my feet. What I had lived on no longer existed, and there was nothing left.
>
> There was no life, for there were no wishes the fulfillment of which I could consider reasonable. If I desired anything, I knew in advance that whether I satisfied my desire or not, nothing would come of it. If in moments of intoxication I felt something which, though not a wish, was a habit left by former wishes, in sober moments I knew this to be a delusion and that there was really nothing to wish for.
>
> (Tolstoy, 1951)

Tolstoy describes the existential crisis with penetrating clarity. It is a crisis in which the very basis of individual existence—an existence which had been unfolding primarily along the personal dimension—comes into question. The map of the two dimensions of growth suggests the strategy for the resolution of the crisis. This resolution is found when the individual is able to expand the meaning of his existence beyond the boundaries of his own personality in order purposefully to participate in the life of the whole. This can begin as he reorients his attention toward the greater life revealed by exploration of the transpersonal dimension.

The period of the existential crisis is a particularly appropriate time to seek or renew contact with the transpersonal. Seen from the vantage point of the Higher Self, the existential crisis is precipitated by an increasing flow of superconscious, or transpersonal, energy directed by the Self toward the

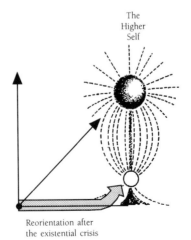

Reorientation after
the existential crisis

personality (Assagioli, 1965). In particular, as the energy of the Self increases, it attracts the personal self or "I" toward it. Before the existential crisis, the "I" was attracted primarily by the pull of the personality life and of the environment. The existential crisis occurs when the increasing pull of the energy of the Self becomes equal in intensity to, and therefore *neutralizes,* the pull of the personality and environment. This is a period of transition. It is like being suspended in space at a "zero gravity" point; the earlier meaning of the personality life has vanished and a new meaning has not yet appeared.

The needed reorientation toward the transpersonal can involve a sudden, life-changing peak experience in which superconscious energies spontaneously become conscious. More often, it is a gradual, purposeful reorientation, a quest that can take many directions—from remembering and reclaiming past peak experiences to exploring realms beyond the normal world view.

Discrimination and motives are critical to the fruitfulness of this quest. Discrimination needs to be practiced in interpreting transpersonal experiences and inner messages, in determining the appropriateness of a teacher or particular spiritual practice, in evaluating all information from outside resources. In addition, as spiritual teachers of all times have stressed, our motivation needs to be founded in an honest search for truth rather than in a selfish desire for spectacular phenomena or special knowledge with which to increase our own self-importance or security.

If such a quest is pursued far enough, it results in a reorientation toward the transpersonal dimension, and the existential crisis can then be overcome. Its resolution is found in an expansion of our perception of who we are and the world we live in. In other words, we begin the process of disidentifying from our personality and of achieving a broader, more inclusive state of awareness and identification (*SYNTHESIS* 2 Workbook, 1978), one that *includes* our personality within a larger context. It is from this larger context that, as individuals, we can begin to participate meaningfully in the greater whole. This expansion of identification is the turning point in the crisis.

Disidentification from the personality in no way implies that we are to destroy our personality, "kill our ego," give up all our activities, resign from life, or take any similar action that would impede or even reverse our natural growth process. Disidentifying from the personality means recognizing experientially that our personality is not what we are but what we have—not the source of our identity but the means by which we express that identity in the world. By disidentifying from it, we do not destroy or abandon it; rather, we transcend its limitations and the self-centered and separative tendencies these limitations can bring.

Deliberately entertaining the hypothetical existence of a realm of higher meaning not yet perceived can be most helpful in disidentification. We can purposefully decide to turn from an insistence on a meaninglessness similar to that of certain existentialists; in an open-minded way we can see whether there is something greater than ourselves. This attitude is no less realistic than the physicists' search for the unseen principles of nature and the universe (*SYNTHESIS* 3–4, 1977).

Countless people have demonstrated that, as we increasingly disidentify from the limitations of our personality and search for what is more than ourselves, we begin to see the world as an interconnected and unified whole, a world in which personality can find its rightful place. Then all that had lost its meaning as an end in itself acquires new and greater meaning because it is now recognized as an intrinsic part of the whole.

For Tolstoy, light broke in on despair as he walked one day alone in a forest. He says he began thinking about his life and that which was greater than his life—as yet undiscovered. It was the lack of this greater element that was the source of his despair. There, in the naturalness of the woods, he sought to trace in himself this sense of something greater. Suddenly he experienced the first awakenings of a renewed sense of meaning and purpose in life. This "something greater" was life itself, and it was all around him. He was filled with an appreciation of the richness and depth of life, and of his own place in it. After this experience, Tolstoy wrote:

> Things cleared up within me and about me better than ever, and the light has never wholly died away. Just how the change took place I cannot tell. As insensibly and gradually as the force of life had been annulled within me, and I had reached my moral deathbed, just as gradually and imperceptibly did the energy of life come back.
>
> (Tolstoy, 1951)

So the existential crisis is, fundamentally, an opportunity to expand our sense of reality. When the crisis is resolved, purpose, meaning, and values become part of our lives in a new way and our personal life takes its meaning from a more universal, inclusive, and lasting source.

At the point of personal development when one would normally reach the existential crisis, it is possible, although rather uncommon, for the personality to be impervious to the influence of the superconscious. This is especially so when a strong, well-integrated personality is fed by an overweening drive for personal power, and such power is seen either as the source of meaning or as the way to gain that which one considers to be meaningful. In such a situation, the existential crisis may not appear or not be felt very strongly, as the personality is likely to be well equipped to resist it. The resistance of the personality is greatly increased if one is working with a therapist or guide who does not recognize the crisis for what it is and thus fails to encourage, or even allow, the emergence of the superconscious energies. One's development may then tend to continue solely along the horizontal dimension. If followed for too long before making a stable connection with the superconscious, this path leads one in an antisocial direction, to seek more and more personal power, and can be harmful both for oneself and others. In extreme cases it can even lead, eventually, to draw on superconscious energies and use them to achieve personal, separative goals, thus perverting their essential nature.

There can also develop a confusion of levels and an illusion, by which one attributes to his personal self, or "I," the qualities of the Transpersonal Self (Assagioli, 1965). One then unwittingly arrogates to himself—and *himself only*—those powers that justly belong to the Transpersonal Self: the transcendent focus in which *all* humanity participates. In other words, such a person sees his personal identity as the ultimate reality and, to use a current phrase, "goes on a power trip." He increasingly perceives other people and his environment as mere objects to be used in support of his personal identity and may even go so far as to see them as extensions of himself. A most extreme example is that of a political dictator who has exaggerated his sense of identity to the extent that he sees it as absorbing even his country—such as Hitler, who stated, "I am Germany."

The Transpersonal Dimension

The reorientation that saved Tolstoy from his "moral deathbed" is a dramatic example of one person's encounter with the transpersonal. It should not be thought, however, that transpersonal experiences are only the results of life crises, of pain and struggle, or that they are reserved for the exceptional few—great artists, scientists, or religious figures. In fact, experience of the transpersonal dimension is neither exotic nor unusual. It is a characteristic of being human.

There have been many studies of transpersonal experiences from the point of view of the psychology of the normal individual. This tradition in psychology, which goes back as far as Richard Bucke (1901), was carried forward by William James (1902/1961), Roberto Assagioli, Carl Jung, Abraham Maslow, and others. A good description of the characteristics of transpersonal experiences by Maslow is to be found in his chapter "Various Meanings of Transcendence" in *The Farther Reaches of Human Nature* (1971).

Recently, social scientists Greeley and McCready conducted a research study on mystical experiences in which they interviewed 1,400 people chosen as a representative sample of the population in the United States (Greeley, 1975). To a key question, "Have you ever felt as though you were close to a powerful spiritual force that seemed to lift you out of yourself?" 35 percent replied "yes." Of these, half also indicated that such experiences had occurred "several times" or "often." Almost as many said that they had experienced "feelings of peace, a certainty that all things would work out for the good, a sense of need to contribute to others, a conviction that love is at the center of everything, and a sense of joy and laughter." Also 29 percent stated that during their experience they had "a sense of the unity of everything and my own part in it."

Their findings, which are consistent with those of a recent Gallup Poll, are of considerable interest because of the quantitative, statistical approach taken in researching these experiences and because the study is based on a large cross-sectional sample of the American population as a whole (Gallup, 1976). It is also significant that the people surveyed described their experiences in ways similar to the autobiographical accounts of many great spiritual figures.

The following report of one woman's peak experience shares many of these characteristics:

> I was sitting quietly in the kitchen after getting the kids off to school. I was alone in the house and in the quiet I began thinking about my life, where I was now, and where I was going. Gradually, I began seeing my life as one flow, a flow which was only one stream in the larger flow of life in the universe. Suddenly I was unexpectedly overwhelmed by an intense feeling of joy; I felt intensely alive and saw my life filled with meaning and direction. Mixed with the joy was a deep love—a love for my life, my family, and a love for humanity as a whole with its struggles to grow and change. I felt that all of us were moving toward this joy and love.

Clearly, during her experience she moved into a state of consciousness beyond her everyday awareness, a state in which she saw deep meaning not only in her own life but in the life of humanity as well. The experience was indeed transpersonal; in it she transcended her normal identifications, saw her connection to a larger system of life, and felt a deep sense of love and joy from this connection.

The orientation toward the transpersonal may begin in different ways and at different times. The various periods of life—childhood, adolescence, and adulthood—all have typical patterns of transpersonal activity that are well known although not often recognized for what they are.

That the child is often a "philosopher" has been observed by such widely disparate figures as Piaget and Wordsworth. Wordsworth's description is classic:

> Thou best philosopher . . . Seer blest!
> On whom those truths do rest
> Which we are toiling all our lives to find . . .

A child's intense curiosity and wonder at first seeing a snowfall or taking apart a flower are often expressions of natural early interest in the transpersonal dimension. Even a very young child may sometimes seem the true philosopher, delving into the meaning of things—the nature of birth, death, space, time.

In adolescence, interest in the transpersonal may be kindled by a peak experience, by facing the challenge of a new situation, or by confronting deep philosophical questions. Often, the adolescent's quest is unsupported or merely tolerated by an environment that is not receptive to the transpersonal. If this is the case, he may keep to himself or even repress this whole area of his life.

Transpersonal awareness in adults may emerge as the result of a positive search for meaning in religion, the sciences, or the arts, or as a result of a major life disruption—a divorce, an accident, an encounter with death—which forces a disidentification from habitual attachments and a deeper look at existence. In general, transpersonal experiences have a reality that seems deeper than normal day-to-day existence. They carry an intrinsic validity, a noetic quality, and convey a broadened sense of meaning and values.

However, the transpersonal dimension is subtle. Our connection to it can be tenuous at first and may have to be nurtured and deliberately strengthened. We can do this by first learning to recognize such an experience when it occurs, then by exploring the experience through meditation, introspection, or other means, and finally by integrating the experience, by expressing in our life and activities what it brought us.

The Path of Transcendence

When people search for meaning along the transpersonal dimension, the results vary greatly. For some, the process is slow and laborious; for others, quick and spontaneous. Whatever the rate of progress, many people sooner or later go through a phase of having increasingly frequent transpersonal experiences with decreasing effort.

Because these experiences of transcendence are fascinating, gratifying, even ecstatic, some people are gradually so drawn to this activity that they turn away from their personality development and participation in the world. By comparison, the world and their personal existence in it may begin to look drab, ugly, even unreal. At this point, people whose personality is not sufficiently integrated may tend increasingly to neglect everyday life and activity. Eventually they may come to ignore their personality and its further integration altogether, further increasing the imbalance between personal and transpersonal development. A person may devote his whole life to penetrating into increasingly exalted superconscious levels, with the mistaken assumption that, if one can experience the transpersonal intensely enough, one will be able to maintain that state indefinitely and live all of life in the higher consciousness thus achieved. It is as if one sees an image, a reflection of the Self, and moves directly toward it, not realizing that it is a reflection, that the real state of unity inherent in the Transpersonal Self, and the joy, the serenity it brings about, must necessarily include the integration of what one is trying to leave behind.

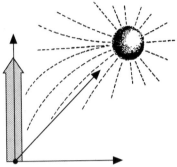

The path of transcendence

Some people who pursue the path of pure transcendence can be temporarily successful. They may be fortunate enough actually to bridge the gap and experience unity with the Transpersonal Self. But when unity is achieved in this way, the experience is only transient and is inevitably followed by a profound and painful sense of loss. Assagioli points out that

> one cannot go to the Goal directly, except momentarily. In a moment of ecstasy, it can be done. But one must distinguish between mountain climbing and airplane flights. You can fly to the top, but you cannot remain always on the airplane, you have to go down. The flight is very useful in order to show you the reality of the mountaintop, inasmuch as there are clouds and mist which prevent one from seeing it from the plain. One also sees the road better, the different steps, and so on. But eventually one has to come down, and go through the laborious process of gradual, organic development, of real conquest. (1966)

If one persists exclusively along the path of pure transcendence, the increasing awareness of what appears to be an unbridgeable gulf between oneself and the transcendent goal will lead to the *crisis of duality*.

The Crisis of Duality

Like every other crisis, once correctly understood, the crisis of duality is an opportunity for growth. The one-sided, single-minded focus along the path of transcendence that leads to it can be a necessary, appropriate, and even important phase of development. But sooner or later, the inevitable pull of nature to re-establish balance will require the shift of one's orientation to include the personal dimension as well.

The first sign that one is entering the crisis of duality is an ever-increasing difficulty in proceeding further along the vertical dimension. The difficulty, and the ensuing realization of the need to include the personal dimension, can be experienced in a number of ways. Some people report that eventually their higher experiences stop happening, and after a period of depression they realize both the necessity and the wisdom of accepting their personality and the world in which they find themselves. After this acceptance, contact with the superconscious gradually returns, as they find that their personalities can be vehicles for transmitting this energy into the world.

Other people find that beyond a certain point the way is barred as long as they tread it alone. Others see the way to be wide open before them, but out of a powerful, deepening love and compassion for humanity and its suffering, they freely make the choice to turn back toward the world and help others in their own journeys. Still other people, by proceeding in this direction, recognize that the transcendent unity toward which they are yearning is the culmination of a process of unification in which *all* mankind participates; without "getting there" all together, getting there has no meaning. They comprehend that attempting to reach and maintain this unity by oneself is not only a practical impossibility but a contradiction in terms.

There is a fascinating paradox here. Because the Higher Self is in fact our true being and transcends normal time and space, there is a sense in which "we are there" already and eternally. From this high point of view there is nothing to seek, nowhere to go. There is, however, the gradual process of becoming aware of who we really are and of learning to act accordingly. The apparent paradox is resolved by distinguishing between what in philosophical terms can be called "life" and "consciousness": what is, and our awareness of it. The process of reaching toward the Self is thus a very real one, one that involves the expanding of our consciousness to become increasingly aware of that which eternally is.

After the Crisis of Duality

Having made the decision to reorient life to include the personal dimension, people typically encounter a number of problems and opportunities. After making significant progress in exploring the transpersonal realm, they have now turned to the task of expressing their vision in the world. Full of that vision of the way things could be, such people may approach the task of transforming the world with great confidence and enthusiasm, assuming first that they can do it alone and second, that they can do it this week. At first, they may believe that all they need to do is tell what they have seen of the right way to do things, and others will speedily and gratefully follow. When the others do not respond, these crusaders may begin to become more zealous, assailing and haranguing them. With the best of motives, they may even get angry, take a militant approach, and proselytize to the point of fanaticism. Clearly, if they are to make progress and be effective, they must accept that the world is slower and more resistant in responding to their vision and ideals than they had expected.

What is needed here is a working sense of proportion: a sense of how grand the transpersonal vision really is, coupled with a realistic assessment of the state of the world. A superconscious experience can be so powerfully vivid and immediate that one may forget that it is still very much *potential* in the dimension of daily life, and that true actualization of this potential will require considerable time, patience, and skill, in addition to a well-developed personality.

Thus individuals who become filled with a love for humanity or convinced that all people need to become more loving may discover that it takes considerable examination of the nature of love and many changes in their own lives for them actually to become more loving themselves. For example, they may discover that they need to overcome a fear of loving and being loved, and to do work on personality patterns developed in childhood. Clearly, experiencing love in a peak experience is very different from making one's personality and life an expression of love.

To take another example, the person who has a vivid insight into what society would be like if it recognized deeper humanness may see the need to improve social structures. In looking carefully, he might see that society would profit from a more positive approach to the development of the human being. He might then decide that if children were raised with their higher potential in mind, many of the ills in society would fall away, because we would be producing healthier human beings. Understanding now the scope and complexity of the task of actualizing his insight, he might start by searching out the best of what is already known in psychology and education, and begin to develop his own understanding and knowledge in order to create a better educational approach.

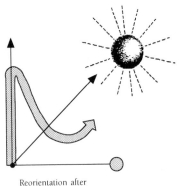

Reorientation after
the crisis of duality

By developing a realistic plan in this way, people who have been oriented toward the transpersonal dimension move closer to making their vision happen. Taking time to balance transpersonal growth with personal development may seem, at first, to be a sacrifice of the glories of transcendent experience. But as these people develop needed personality functions and skills and their vision begins to become a reality, they gain access to reaches of the transpersonal vaster than ever before and experience increased communion with others, together with a sense of participating in the evolution of the larger whole.

Toward Self-realization

As we have seen, no matter which path we have been following, sooner or later we experience a compelling pull to include both the transpersonal and the personal dimensions of meaning—the vertical and the horizontal, transcendence and self-actualization, reception and expression of superconscious energies.

Throughout history humans have used a very wide range of methods to reach for superconscious energies and to facilitate their flow and expression. These methods include myriad forms of prayer and meditation, chanting, dancing and rituals, many types of yoga, fasting and other ascetic practices and disciplines for the body, purification and sublimation of the emotions, mental training, group experiences and activities, different kinds of psychotherapy, and a variety of approaches to action and service to others. In earlier times, such methods were known only to an initiated few who were also limited by the cultural traditions of their particular society. Today, because of rapidly growing knowledge—in psychology, sociology, anthropology, history, comparative religion—combined with the communications explosion, these techniques are becoming increasingly accessible.

This unprecedented circumstance provides great opportunities; it also presents unique problems. Many methods, especially those of recent development, tend to be relatively or sometimes excessively specialized, to address only one part of the overall process of Self-realization. They must be very well suited to one's needs during a particular phase of growth but not during another. Clearly, such techniques can be effective, but only temporarily.

However, if a method is focused on shortcuts or quick results for their own sake, it may have dangerous or even harmful side effects. For example, striving to increase an already adequate inflow of superconscious energy, if one has not yet learned to use what is available, can be irresponsible and dangerous—even despite the possibility that the results may turn out to be positive because of the inherent synthesizing nature of the higher energies. Also, popular methods that focus on the physical body, such as special diets and taking particular postures, can help prepare the personality to handle superconscious energy, but they cannot in themselves get that energy to flow. They can be useful if used at the right time in conjunction with other techniques; by themselves, they are eventually sterile and often lead either to discouragement or to the illusion that making a considerable effort means making progress.

People in growing numbers are using one method of growth after another. Often they derive benefits from each, but in each case they eventually gain all that particular method has to offer them, need to abandon it, and look for something else.

In summary, to use the many available methods most effectively and according to individual need, it is helpful to understand development in respect to the two dimensions of human growth. A study of the great spiritual traditions and the lives of their followers shows that the integrative path of Self-realization has always taken into account all phases of the process along both dimensions. This is true, for example, of the Raja Yoga of India, the

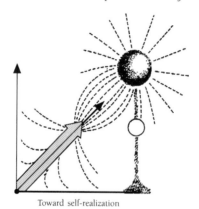

Toward self-realization

Eight-Fold Noble Path of Buddhism, and some parallel approaches in the Judeo-Christian tradition. All these traditions show that as we proceed along the path of Self-realization we need to avail ourselves, simultaneously but in various proportions according to our point of development, of the three complementary aspects of that path:

- reaching upward toward the superconscious, through various methods of meditation, visualization, and prayer;
- understanding the nature of the superconscious, our personality, and our world, so as to be able increasingly to harmonize them with one another; and
- serving or expressing the best we know so as to achieve the greatest good.

Let us examine each of these and some of their main methods.

Reaching Upward

Prayer is a universal method of reaching upward. Seen psychologically—that is, independently of the validity or nonvalidity of specific religious beliefs associated with its particular forms—prayer can be described as that inner action in which our feeling function is directed toward or through our higher nature or to even higher realities or powers. It is a bringing together of the many divided aspects of our emotional nature, first through desire, then through aspiration, affirmation, dedication, and gratitude. Consequently, prayer has a harmonizing and transmuting effect on feelings. Whether or not the prayers hold the conscious desire to obtain something or to have that something "descend" on ourselves or others, the upward projection of feelings has the effect of "lifting" the center of consciousness in some measure into subtler levels of the inner world. It is a process of elevating feelings and desires, and thus transmuting them into aspiration toward higher goals.

Imaginative techniques are another means of reaching upward toward superconscious inspiration and insight (*SYNTHESIS* 2, 1978; *SYNTHESIS* 3–4, 1977). These techniques are based on visualization, the conscious and deliberate use of images. By visualizing the appropriate image or symbol, we establish with the corresponding superconscious pattern a reverberation through which the needed energy can flow. The visualized image then takes a life of its own, and the energy reaches the personality with beneficent results. This purposeful use of imagination is valuable because it makes use of mind as well as feeling, it can tap a wide range of superconscious energies, and it can be used with both flexibility and precision. For example, while symbols formed by the imagination are often polyvalent—carrying many meanings, reverberating to many energies—and therefore full of surprises in their effect, they can also have selective properties and specialized uses which give access to specific qualities of transpersonal energy.

Meditation in one of its most basic forms is described in the following account of Robert Frost, written when the poet was still living:

> When Frost was a freshman in college, his fraternity brothers worried about him because he took long walks alone in the woods. Finally a delegation of seniors waited on him, and after some fumbling preliminaries, one asked, "Frost, what do you do walking by yourself in the woods?"
>
> Freshman Frost looked at them and replied, "Gnaw bark." Thereafter, they left him alone.
>
> Actually, what Frost was doing in the woods was meditating. He still takes long walks and he still meditates. In part, it is his ability to do so which makes him America's greatest living poet.

There is one kind of meditation which is passive, a quiet sinking into the self, a sort of contemplation. But with most of us, what passes for thought is a purposeless stream of consciousness, like an uncut motion picture with our own confused inner dialogue attached.

Robert Frost's kind of meditation is neither passive nor meaningless. It is directed, tenacious and purposeful. He is able to take a word, or an idea, and hold his mind to it while he looks it over from all angles, turns it inside out, dissects it. By doing so, he sees new aspects, new meanings, new beauties even in tired and timeworn phases. (Cole, 1960)

This focused and purposeful type of mental activity is one of the most effective forms of meditation. It has enabled people like Einstein and Teilhard de Chardin to gain direct awareness of what they called the "Universal Mind." Its patient and regular application has proven invaluable in establishing a rich and reliable channel between the personality and the superconscious.

Understanding

The development of a reliable and inclusive understanding, an understanding that grows as we grow, is the second essential aspect of the integrative path of Self-realization. It means understanding the nature of the transpersonal realm, of ourselves as personalities, and of the world in which we live, in light of our best awareness of the purpose of the larger whole. It can be achieved by seeking the deeper meaning, the hidden causes of outer events. If, for example, we understand the world as moving toward transcendent unity, then we shall examine particular events to see how they relate to that unity. Do they, as is true in the case of many historical occurrences, reveal obstacles to evolution with which individuals and society must deal? Or do they indicate positive and growing trends which we shall choose to encourage and support? Events having great impact on society—the Renaissance, the American Revolution, the Great Depression, the Civil Rights movement, the Vietnam War, Watergate—can be examined in this way, as can more personal events and turning points.

Study of the outer world and the inner world are, therefore parallel and complementary. We can then use our understanding more and more to bring our personalities and the world into meaningful correspondence with transpersonal reality. In this way, the generalized visions we have attained in our transpersonal experiences become particularized and can be practically applied to ourselves, to society in general, and to our part in society.

But in order to build this progressive and dynamic understanding, our thinking must be, in the most profound sense, our own. For much of our lives, our primary source of learning has been what we absorb "by osmosis" from the ideas, feelings, and actions of others. Through this contact we gain access to the combined experience and understanding of humanity through thousands of years. This is both inevitable and good, provided that this richness is neither lightly accepted nor automatically dismissed. At each important step, we must strive to be aware of what we are exposed to, what idea or new knowledge is becoming available to us, and we must decide whether or not we want to accept it. We need to develop an awareness of what flows into us and a capacity to regulate that flow. Just as regulating this inward flow is our responsibility to ourselves, so regulating the *outward* flow is our responsibility to others. This is the significance of such traditional spiritual watchwords as "right speech" or "harmlessness." The issue is not only whether a certain idea, principle, or value is good or bad, true or false; rather, we cannot truly make it our own if we absorb it without understanding it.

It is interesting to observe that many spiritual guides of the past, whose followers were oriented primarily along the vertical dimension—the path of transcendence—emphasized devotion, unquestioned belief, acceptance of the teacher's authority, and obedience to the teacher's wishes and precepts. Now, as more people reach the path of Self-realization, spiritual guides are increasingly abandoning such approaches and adopting techniques more appropriate to this path. Rather than asking for unquestioned belief and obedience, they stress the importance of clear thinking, of ascertaining for oneself what is true or false, important or trivial, and of acting on what one sees. They emphasize one's inner resources and responsibility, and guide one to rely more and more on oneself, and eventually on one's Self. While this orientation is rapidly spreading at present, it is far from new. It has always been at the core of the greatest spiritual teachings; it was, for example, a central teaching of the Buddha at least twenty-five centuries ago:

> We are earnestly enjoined to accept nothing whatever on faith; whether it be written in books, handed down from our ancestors, or taught by sages. The Buddha has said that we must not believe in a thing said merely because it is said; nor in traditions because they have been handed down from antiquity; nor rumours, as such; nor writings by sages, merely because sages wrote them; nor fancies that we may suspect to have been inspired in us by a Deva (that is, in presumed spiritual inspiration); nor from inferences drawn from some haphazard assumption that we may have made; nor because of what seems an analogical necessity; nor on the mere authority of our own teachers or masters. We are to believe when the writing, doctrines, or saying is corroborated

by our own reason and consciousness. "For this," says he in concluding, "I taught you not to believe merely because you have heard, but when you believed of your consciousness, then to act accordingly and abundantly." (Olcott, 1971, pp. 62–63)

Service

Acting thus, abundantly and according to one's best vision, is the essence of service. It completes the path through which the superconscious energies can flow in the same way that completing the circuit at an electrical power station energizes and illuminates a city.

Just as breathing is a natural activity of our body, service is a natural activity of our Higher Self; and at a certain point of development, it becomes natural to the personality as well. Its precursor in the personality is the urge to make things better. This is perhaps our most human tendency, that which most clearly distinguishes us from animals. As we make contact with the superconscious and begin to understand the larger whole as it is at present and as it is also evolving, we are spontaneously drawn to use our energies to assist that evolution, to help the gradual work of perfecting humanity and the world. We recognize that service in line with our transpersonal vision is the most effective way to make things better and, therefore, the best and most meaningful thing to do.

We can also be drawn to service before having made a clear contact with the transpersonal, perhaps out of a sense of obligation or guilt, perhaps from following the example of others, or perhaps from feeling for the pain of those in need. Many are motivated in these ways at first, and much that is good and valuable has been accomplished out of such motivations. But in the long run, if the transpersonal energy is missing, difficulties will occur. If we give more and more of our energy, the need to refill ourselves will inevitably emerge. If we act only out of an emotional urge without a clear vision and plan, we may find that the results, although worthwhile, may not be commensurate with the effort. Increasingly, there will develop the sense that our work is more difficult, more unconnected than we instinctively know it should be. We feel that something is missing, something that needs to be found. What is missing, of course, is our connection with the transpersonal vision and source. And as we search for what is lacking, we reorient our personality and make that connection possible. As our vision and knowledge of the whole then become clearer and we become able to express the energies of our superconscious as well as those of our personality, we can serve more freely and energetically. We see the forward moving currents in the larger world and we are nourished, sustained, and strengthened by them—and by the knowledge of their inevitable triumph. Feelings and mind become aligned with each other and with our higher nature, and the work of perfecting the whole then becomes at the same time the most reasonable and desirable thing we can do with our lives.

This leads to a new and more realistic perspective on our own growth. We discover that there is no contradiction between serving the whole and developing our individuality; as we serve the whole, we also develop our unique gifts and overcome our particular limitations. Gradually our individual growth becomes integrated with our commitment to do useful work in the world. But no longer do we strive to improve our personality for its own sake. We see clearly that our personality could be improved, but we also see that there is an almost endless possibility for improvement. Although there are many ways our personality could grow, and many limitations we could elimi-nate, it is most practical to work on some and postpone others according to what specific service seems particularly right for us to do. The shy man who sees that having direct contact with people is an intrinsic part of his next contribution will choose to work on his shyness. Another shy man, however, who sees that writing is his next best vehicle, may ignore his shyness for the moment and work on some other limitation, such as a lack of persistent will.

Interestingly enough, people invariably report that after having made their individual growth dependent on the needs of their service, not only did that growth refuse to slow down but it gained increasing breadth, momen-tum, and ease. The apparent paradox is resolved if we keep in mind that the commitment to serve our larger vision and express our transpersonal values in action calls for the sustained flow of superconscious energy through our personality and out into the world. Thus service becomes the most effective and most direct way to organize the patterns of our personality in harmony with the superconscious in order best to transmit its energy. And that energy will now work with us—and also spontaneously, by itself—to remove blocks and clear the way.

The integrative path of Self-realization has in it, then, an inherent *joy-ousness*. It is the joy of becoming who we really are by living our higher values, the joy of *Self*-expression. It arises from the increasingly immediate sense of our true identity, as we learn to manifest it in daily life. We realize that as the Self, we are one with the larger whole, that our essential nature is what we would have to describe by such words as *transcendent, immortal, divine*. Yet we deal with such joyous realizations realistically, because we also understand our need to cooperate progressively with and find our place in the larger context, as it is continuously revealed to us.

With all this comes maturity—not the drab and mere "getting older" that is often falsely taken to be maturity, but something rich and ripe—an enlightened maturity, full of joy and will, acceptance and discrimination, wisdom and love.

We may well end with Goethe's thought from *Faust* (part 2): "Everything that changes is a symbol." In other words, any action, habit pattern, feeling, thought, or word, all processes—indeed our life as a whole—can be seen as symbolic patterns. As we learn to live the patterns of our life according to our best values and vision, these patterns become more attuned to the higher patterns of our superconscious energies. The Hermetic aphorism "As above, so below" becomes then not only an inclusive description of reality but also a fundamental method of individual unfoldment and, at the same time, an affirmation, an imperative, a way of life. As we increasingly identify with the whole and help to create it, any sense of separateness, of alienation, gradually fades away and is replaced by a certain knowledge of being at home—indeed, of being at one—both with ourselves and with the world.

9

Transcendental Meditation as an Adjunct to Therapy

Harold H. Bloomfield

Transcendental Meditation (TM) was probably the first major Hindu meditation tradition to break onto the Western scene on a large scale. Harold H. Bloomfield, widely recognized as the psychiatric spokesman for the TM movement, here speaks to the value of practicing this form of meditation for both patient and therapist.

Noting that spiritual awakenings are becoming widespread among Western populations today, Bloomfield observes that such awakenings can, at times, be the source of great happiness and joy; at other times, they can produce great anguish and suffering, to which present-day therapists would do well to give credence, understanding, and aid. The spiritual crisis that is always part of awakening is often confused by health professionals of all persuasions with direct physical or emotional problems—an easy mistake to make as many of the symptoms are similar. However, the spiritual crisis cannot be resolved with two aspirin or a tranquilizer. The crisis presents the individual with a great opportunity for growth out of pain and must be approached with respect and openness by both patient and therapist.

In the recognition and use of the individual's need for deeper significance, for spiritual validation of Self, Transcendental Meditation can play an invaluable part as a practice by itself or as an adjunct to

Portions of this chapter were previously published in *Happiness: The TM Program, Psychiatry and Enlightenment* (Simon and Schuster, 1976) and *The Healing Silence* (Simon and Schuster, 1978). I would therefore like to acknowledge my co-author of these two books, Robert Kory.

therapy. Why Transcendental Meditation? In Bloomfield's opinion and the opinion of a number of researchers, TM is highly effective "not because it is some kind of religious opiate or fashionable cultivation of Eastern culture but because it fosters very tangible spiritual development: growth toward enlightenment." This process of becoming enlightened, according to the author, "is one of systematically and naturally unfolding the full potential of the human biomachinery." Not only, then, can TM provide the potential for enlightenment, but it can play an active part in relieving stress and strain.

Enlightenment through TM, asserts Bloomfield, is not achieved by seeing visions in a cave and retreating from work, family, and friends forever; rather, it is achieved by practical exercises that enhance and increase contact with the external environment. The enlightened person is characterized by a deep-rooted happiness, a sense of freedom, ease of activity, and spontaneity. The enlightened patient can terminate therapy knowing that the source of nurturance is within himself or herself, not the therapist. The enlightened therapist can tap deeper resources for personal and therapeutic benefit.

THE PHENOMENON OF SPIRITUAL AWAKENING has received so little attention in the mainstream of psychiatric literature that most practitioners are unprepared to diagnose and treat the personality changes resulting from it. Psychiatrists Carl Jung (1933), Karen Horney (1945), Roberto Assagioli (1965), and Abraham Maslow (1965) have discussed the stages of spiritual realization, but their writings have not yet infiltrated the standard curriculum in psychiatric training. Too many therapists still think "spiritual" is synonymous with mysticism and the occult. Spiritual refers to the experience of wholeness and integration, irrespective of religious belief or affiliation. It is neither a statement of belief per se nor a measure of church attendance; indeed, an atheist can have a profound spiritual life.

Spiritual experiences of an extraordinary as well as a more general nature have been recorded through history and in every culture. There are indications that spiritual awakenings are becoming widespread among Americans today. A Gallup Poll conducted in 1962 asked: "Would you say that you have ever had a 'religious or mystic experience'—that is, a moment of sudden religious insight or awakening?" One in five adults answered "yes" to this question. This percentage represents approximately twenty million people in the whole adult population. At the National Opinion Research Center of the University of Chicago, Andrew M. Greeley and William C. McCready conducted a survey in 1974 among some 1,500 representative American adults (1975). They asked, "Have you ever had the feeling of being very close to a powerful spiritual force that seemed to lift you out of yourself?" Forty percent reported having had at least one such experience and half of these had had it several times, indicating that forty million adults have experienced the symptoms of spiritual awakening, twenty million of them repeatedly. These surveys suggest that the number of people reporting spiritual experiences has more than doubled in a decade.

An overwhelming feeling of happiness, an ecstatic joy that fills the person with a deep sense of peace, security, understanding, and certainty are what usually characterize a harmonious spiritual awakening. People of all ages, races, nationalities, and occupations report a virtually identical experience of ecstasy, rebirth, being lifted out of themselves, knowing the "way things really are." This experience of "absolute" knowledge gives people an unshakable conviction and profound understanding of life's basic goodness and unity and leaves them totally comfortable with their place in the larger scheme of things. Though difficult for many to put into words, this knowingness—what Maslow called "Being cognition" (1968)—leaves all who have had it significantly changed, never to be quite the same again.

Spiritual awakenings are ecstatic and enrapturing when they occur and have profound significance for the people who have them, but they may also be alarming and disruptive. The majority of people who have these experiences never speak of them to anyone, not even a close family member or friend, for fear of being thought "crazy" or because the awakening is so deeply personal that they believe it cannot be adequately communicated, so why bother? Unfortunately, many health workers view reports of these spiritual awakenings as psychopathological and the episode itself as a form of regression, an escape, a mini-psychotic episode, or a symptom of schizophrenia. This is unfortunate because many healthy and stable individuals have such experiences, but need support and understanding from a knowledgeable guide if they become initially unsettled or confused. The Greeley and McCready survey was doubly remarkable because the most frequent "mystics" were not drug-taking hippies or fundamentalists but well-educated, disproportionately Protestant, solid "middle-America" types.

With the rise in spiritual awakenings among contemporary Americans, and the consequent difficult path of adjustment which may at times ensue, psychiatrists will have to address spiritual health, spiritual crises, and their differential diagnosis with increasing sophistication and understanding. "Spiritual health" refers to an overall sense of personal fulfillment and satisfaction with life, a sense of peace with oneself and the world. It may also include a sense of unity with the cosmos or a personal closeness to God, or with nature. Spirit differs from the physical or emotional dimensions of the personality in that it reflect one's total satisfaction or dissatisfaction with living, a deeper sense of purpose and meaning.

The issues of spiritual growth are usually concerned with value and purpose. What do you value in life, what do you want from life, what do you find satisfying and meaningful? These issues differ greatly from physical health issues like fitness, weight, and life habits, and from emotional issues like interpersonal skill, self-esteem, and emotional maturity. However, a spiritual crisis can throw the whole personality into turmoil. Among the physical and emotional consequences potentially precipitated by a severe spiritual crisis are: physical illness, depression, anxiety, and self-destructive behavior like drug abuse and alcoholism.

Recognizing a Spiritual Crisis

One of the most serious problems with a spiritual crisis is recognizing it. The physical and/or emotional symptoms can be so intense that the physician or psychiatrist may be led to focus exclusively on the symptoms of free-floating anxiety, depression, or somatic complaints. Failure to recognize a spiritual crisis frequently prolongs it. Patients may get involved in one treatment program after another in hopes of curing their symptoms. But the symptoms will not abate because tranquilizers, antidepressants, and conventional psychotherapy do not solve the underlying problem. In frustration these victims might try travel, more work, or affairs, again only to find themselves further confused and still in turmoil. Until they finally begin to recognize the spiritual nature of their crisis and take steps to meet their deepest needs, the turmoil will continue.

Although a spiritual crisis can occur anytime after childhood, research has shown that it is especially likely to occur between the ages of thirty-three and forty-five. Few people reach fifty without going through some measure of spiritual turmoil. Those who manage to avoid it may be either the most healthy or the most fortunate (Sheehy, 1976). A spiritual crisis during midlife may be a necessary step toward discovery of inner creative resources that can bring renewal to the second half of life. Through successful resolution of a spiritual crisis, a person seems to be able to give up hidden childhood legacies of fear and dependency that block the full blossoming of self-reliance and self-actualization. In many cases, this process involves a major life adjustment—the break-up of a stifling marriage, resignation from an unsatisfying job, the beginning of a new career. While initially trying and sometimes painful, these steps away from the past lead to a future of increased personal fulfillment and enhanced joy in living.

Spiritual stagnation is all too common and can result in the gradual asphyxiation of personalities, what Thoreau referred to as "lives of quiet desperation." An individual may become dull, lifeless, resigned, and bitter. Such a person may turn forty or fifty and find life holding no deep satisfaction or meaning. A job may become just a way to pay the rent, a spouse just someone to take care of the kids, and the children just a financial burden. The past may rise up as an endless series of regrets, and the future may appear as little more than a road to the grave. Willy Loman in Arthur Miller's *Death of a Salesman* vividly portrays the spiritually asphyxiated person. One of my patients, a "successful" middle manager in a large electronics firm with a suburban house, a wife of twenty-two years, and three teenage children, revealed his spiritual stagnation all too plainly; head in hands he sighed, "My life feels like a prison, a punishment, damn it, and I don't know why."

Like all crises that accompany transitions from one life stage to another, however, a spiritual crisis is not just a dislocation but also an opportunity for tremendous personal growth. At the root of a spiritual crisis, there is a powerful force pushing upward into consciousness, requiring that individuals break free from the unexamined conventions of the past and discover what is truly meaningful and important to *them*. The disruptive elements of this crisis force them to stop postponing the discovery of real needs, and begin what Jung called the work of individuation (1933). One may have to surrender the psychological security of merely programming one's life according to the wishes of parents, employers, or the expectations internalized without question from one's culture. One may also have to stop pushing aside those ultimate issues—the inevitability of one's own death, how long one has left to fulfill creative desires or leave a mark on the world. But, by letting go of programmed security and taking the time for the reflective self-examination that the spirit requires, one stands to make a great discovery—one's deepest needs and the personal power to fulfill them. Fortunately, it is never too late to resume spiritual growth.

A Case of Spiritual Crisis

Tom, a successful married architect with two young children, faced the precipice of his first spiritual crisis at thirty-three.

Tom was a classic young superachiever. Soon after graduating in architecture, he joined a leading firm. Through a combination of outstanding work and aggressive drive, he became the firm's youngest full partner at thirty-one. He bought a new house, started collecting primitive art, and tried to keep up his reading, but soon found little time for it. While he enjoyed travel and sports cars, his increased workload also forced him to spend less and less time with these pursuits. After his promotion, he began using most of his afterwork hours to entertain prospective clients. Fortunately for him, he had married an attractive, intelligent, and capable woman who could provide the support he needed to make his rapid career ascent. When he called late in the day to announce that he was bringing a client home for dinner, or when he couldn't take his children to the beach on Saturday as he had promised, or when he came home late and exhausted, Cynthia understood.

By modern cultural standards, Tom thought he really had "made it." He had a lovely family and home, a well above average income, and a bright future in his chosen profession. Within two years of achieving his dream of becoming a partner in a leading architectural firm, however, his sense of security and well-being began to vanish. In its place arose a powerful gut feeling that he was missing out on life and that he was slowly choking under the weight of his responsibilities.

What followed for Tom was a plaguing sense of panic. Little analysis was necessary for him to see that he had committed himself to a lifestyle that required an enormous expenditure of his time and energy at work. The mortgage, clothes, parties, cars, and eventually his children's education—all had to be paid for, and that was a lot of money. He was already making enough and would make more, but he was finding less and less time to do those things that mattered most.

"I began to face the futility of my life," he said. "I worked hard to provide my family with a high standard of living but never saw them; I owned a sports car but could never work on it, liked to travel but didn't have time for vacations. In college and graduate school, I buckled down to get top grades with the idea that I'd be in control of my life when I got my degree with honors. I got a top job but then had to put my nose to the grindstone again to land a partnership; then I made it but had less control over my own time and destiny than ever. I had to be totally committed to the firm in order to support the lifestyle I had established for my family."

Tom fought his growing despair for a while by trying to make more time to have fun. He took weekend vacations with his wife, went to parties frequently, and even experimented with marijuana. To his surprise, he soon discovered that these efforts yielded only fleeting enjoyments that reinforced his deep-seated feelings of futility and purposelessness. He hadn't yet realized that his efforts to have fun were merely extensions of his adolescent desire for kicks, while his real search was for meaning and lasting satisfactions. He was still looking for fulfillment outside himself in the reflection of something he did rather than within his own sense of personal autonomy. He was still trying to find fulfillment according to someone else's expectations rather than his own. Consequently, all his efforts to "get more out of life" resulted only in more strain and anxiety.

Soon his persistent inner turmoil began producing physical and emotional symptoms. He stopped sleeping well and became restless, fatigued, and depressed. He also noted a slight pain in his chest, which he interpreted as the early sign of coronary artery disease that he thought would eventually kill him. He even feared that his psychological defenses were crumbling and that he might become psychotic. When he went to his family doctor, he learned that the pain in his chest was simply a "pulled muscle" and that his other symptoms were "apparently no more than a case of nerves." His doctor prescribed Valium p.r.n. for anxiety and Dalmane as needed for insomnia. Tom took the pills, but his condition worsened.

He began to show signs of a gradually worsening depression. He started losing interest in personal and professional affairs and felt that he was losing his capacity to enjoy life. He became preoccupied with questions about the purpose of life, the meaning of his own despair, and the likelihood of death cutting his life short before he had a chance to discover what living was all about.

When he tried to share his concerns with Cynthia, she became anxious and communication broke down. She had great difficulty appreciating his existential doubt because she was younger, presently fulfilled as a mother, and not yet ready for her own spiritual crisis. This breakdown of communication unfortunately generated a major strain in their marriage. Tom began to feel that Cynthia did not understand him and could not always be relied upon after all. He felt let down and angry; she felt hurt and worried. When Tom finally blurted out that he felt trapped by the house, the children, and his commitment to Cynthia, a full-scale marital crisis ensued.

By the time Tom sought professional help, he was convinced that he was having a nervous breakdown. He described himself as trapped in a box with his inner self pounding the walls. With relatively little insight into what was happening to him, he entertained ideas ranging from quitting his job to leaving his marriage and even began contemplating suicide. His decision-making and reasoning abilities were clearly impaired. The prospect of failing to fulfill his commitment to his family filled him with guilt and remorse.

Tom's crisis developed over an eighteen-month period, and once he finally recognized it, he spent another year resolving it. Later, when we examine strategies for the management of a spiritual crisis, we shall come back to Tom. For the present, his case illustrates the enormous potential impact of spiritual health on total well-being.

The Dynamics of a Spiritual Crisis

Once a person has gained a measure of success in his struggle for achievement and financial independence, the need for an underlying sense of integrity, satisfaction, and wide horizons of psychic fulfillment becomes more critical to his psychological health. Jung put the matter plainly:

To be normal is a splendid ideal for the unsuccessful, for all those who have not yet found an adaptation. But for people who have more ability than the average, for whom it was never hard . . . to accomplish their share of the world's work—for them, restriction to the normal signifies the bed of Procrustes, unbearable boredom, infernal sterility, and hopelessness. (1976)

For individuals who have not yet experienced adult security and independence, a rich spiritual dimension to the personality can be a great asset, but its need does not usually emerge as critical. During the twenties and early thirties, people's formative struggles to find a mate, a career path, and a degree of financial independence displace spiritual needs. For this reason, most people enter midlife poor in understanding of their spiritual needs and consequently get caught by surprise when these powerful forces finally press into consciousness.

A spiritual crisis usually assumes a focus around one of several major issues. One of the most common—and the principal issue in Tom's crisis—is a lack of authenticity. To achieve his rapid success and cope with his own security needs, Tom chose a wife and a career path early in life. To do this, he had to set aside a whole range of feelings and needs that might interfere with achieving success as rapidly as possible. He denied his insecurity, his fear of failure, and his own fallibility. He rejected his need for some time without the pressures of school, family, or work to discover how to enjoy the simple things of life and not just major achievements. He also suppressed the dark side of his personality—anger at being pressured to excel, envy of those stronger and brighter than he, and promiscuous desires for intimacy with many women. When Tom finally achieved success, the reason and the will to suppress these hidden parts of himself vanished. His fears, passions, and unfulfilled desires began to surface, and a vague sense of discontent crept into his life. He had achieved success, but he lacked inner wholeness that would make his success worthwhile. Panic and crisis ensued.

Another focus for spiritual crisis is a feeling of self-recrimination for having failed to make a meaningful contribution to social betterment. This is especially common among thirty-five-year-old men and women who ten years earlier were highly committed social activists. Few twenty-five-year-olds realize that the unbending idealism of their twenties will almost inevitably give way to realism and compromises in their thirties. When the thirties finally arrive, this gap between ideals and compromises can become fertile ground for spiritual doubt. Today, this focus for spiritual upheaval is just as likely for the business school graduate determined to make a large corporation more receptive to consumer issues as for the peace corps worker who goes into social work.

One of the most common issues in spiritual crisis is an inability to come to terms with aging and death. In our youth-oriented culture, the subjects of aging and death have become taboo. As a result, it has become commonplace to fight the signs of aging with face lifts, hair transplants, breast lifts, and long stays at health spas. Inexorably, however, the grim reaper approaches and generates in many people a panic that they are running out of time. Among the most common ways for both women and men to cope with this anxiety is to bed one new partner after another. This may stave off anxiety for a while, but eventually the spiritual issues surface, and the individual must ask what real fulfillment she or he has experienced.

Whatever the focus of each person's crisis, the dynamic is essentially the same. For some months or even years prior to the major upheaval, doubts and anxieties about the purpose and value of living are present consciously or preconsciously. These remain relatively mild until an event like a business failure, an illness, or a death in the family occurs and shatters youthful feelings of invincibility and immortality. Abruptly, the questions What have I accomplished? What am I getting out of life? and Where am I headed? become major concerns. Doubt and self-recrimination may grow to the point of causing significant emotional and physical distress. Eventually, the person may feel that his or her innermost self is being asphyxiated. At this point, the crisis has reached its climax.

Spiritual Crisis versus Neurosis

Gauged by ordinary standards, a spiritual crisis resembles in many ways a serious psychoneurosis or borderline schizophrenic state. Tom's case is a good example. By the time he sought psychiatric assistance, he had deteriorated mentally and emotionally. His reasoning ability and judgment were impaired; he exhibited high levels of anxiety; and his productivity and efficiency had dropped significantly. His physical symptoms—perhaps heart palpitations, shortness of breath, or numbness and tingling—suggested anxiety neurosis, while his loss of interest in work and home, and overall despondency, indicated depression. He had not been spared his family doctor's superficial diagnosis of a "bad case of nerves," and he was taking tranquilizers and sleeping medication as needed. How could we be sure that Tom was suffering symptoms secondary to a spiritual crisis and not ordinary pathogenic conflicts?

Several important factors may differentiate a spiritual crisis from an ordinary neurosis or preschizophrenic episode (Assagioli, 1965). First, the unconscious stirrings of a spiritual crisis are distinctly progressive; those of ordinary neurosis are clearly regressive. For example, the person in a spiritual crisis seeks a greater participation in life, while the neurotic shows avoidance behaviors and seeks to withdraw. Second, the person in a spiritual crisis does not resort to manipulative, deceitful ways of avoiding responsibility; the neurotic may try to seek refuge in illness or invalidism in hopes of lessening the pressures of work or family life. Third, a person in spiritual turmoil may show anxiety, depression, and wide mood shifts but usually exhibits a reasonably high degree of emotional maturity and is both willing and able to express feelings. In contrast, the neurotic almost always shows clear evidence of emotional immaturity such as inability to express feelings easily or appropriately. Finally, the personal history of the person undergoing a spiritual crisis reveals symptoms emerging from vague discontent; the neurotic's personal history is quite often laden with signs of poor adaptation in childhood and adolescence.

If the person undergoing a spiritual crisis seeks professional help, the therapist must have some special skills and use caution to be effective. The therapist must, quite obviously, be sensitive to the issues and dynamics of spiritual growth as well as those of ordinary emotional illness. The treatments for these two kinds of patients are quite different. The people in spiritual crisis need help in expanding emotional and intellectual horizons to allow those deepest spiritual needs a proper place in the personality. They also need guidance in recognizing their innate power to realize those long-neglected needs. The neurotic, however, must be assisted in eliminating fears, inhibitions, and dependency, and in developing a mature ego that appreciates self and others. Sometimes a spiritual crisis unearths neurotic fears or inhibitions, and then the therapist must encourage spiritual growth while assisting the patient in resolving a specific neurotic symptom.

Commonly, many patients show both neurotic symptoms and those secondary to spiritual growth. Some people may achieve a high degree of spiritual development but remain handicapped by certain infantile fears or interpersonal hang-ups. The therapist must be sensitive to such a person's needs for spiritual validation while fostering the working through or unlearning of neurotic constellations.

Management of a Spiritual Crisis through Transcendental Meditation

Knowing how to treat a person in a spiritual crisis depends first upon understanding its cause. The origin of a spiritual crisis is lack of spiritual experience. A person can feel empty inside in the midst of material comfort when he has never known the profound inner experience of wholeness. Without such a well-spring, the small ego can start to feel asphyxiated by the boundaries of everyday living even though everyday pleasures are many.

The Transcendental Meditation (TM) program is ideally suited to the treatment of spiritual crises because it permits the direct experience of inner wholeness. When a person transcends during practice of the TM technique, the small ego throws off the shackles of bounded perception and gains the status of unbounded pure consciousness. This experience, coupled with knowledge about it, provides a way for a person in a spiritual crisis to emerge at a higher level of personality integration.

Let's take a look now at how Tom's case was handled.

By his second consultation visit with me, it was evident that his problem was spiritual, not just neurotic. I told Tom about the TM program and suggested that he look into it, as an adjunct to psychotherapy.

After attending the introductory lectures, Tom and his wife decided to take the TM course. Within several weeks of completing the course, Tom began noticing a dramatic reduction in symptoms. His insomnia cleared and his anxiety lessened. With the easing of psychic pressures, he no longer felt trapped. He began to recognize his power to give his life whatever direction he chose. Largely due to the reduction in anxiety and depressive feelings, his reasoning ability and productivity quickly returned to normal. He also stopped blaming his wife for his distress and began to rediscover how much he loved her and how much she had helped him.

These initial effects of the "healing silence" seem dramatic because indeed they were. At the root of this improvement is the simple fact that the TM program directly provides the experience that a person undergoing a spiritual crisis is desperately seeking—inner wholeness and satisfaction. Once this experience is gained and cultivated, the clouds of crisis begin to lift. For growth to continue and fulfillment to become lasting, however, meditation is not enough. The real work of individuation must begin. Needs must be reassessed and a life course recharted to fulfill those needs. Transcendental experience generates an inner platform for this task; psychotherapy, a major channel for its support and integration.

Several months after starting the TM program, Tom began, in his psychotherapy visits with me, to reassess his desires and goals. He recognized that one of his principal sources of dissatisfaction was constantly having to buckle under to what he considered the overcommercialized standards and practices of his firm. For the first time in his life, he decided to take a major risk, starting his own architectural firm. Before resigning from his firm, he used accumulated vacation time for an eight-week trip to Europe, where he saw the latest European developments in design. When he returned, he went ahead full steam setting up his own firm. He realized that he would take a substantial cut in income for a few years, but he and Cynthia had decided they were making the right move. He also agreed with Cynthia that he would spend time with the children every day, and that the whole family would spend at least one afternoon together each weekend. Though Tom realized he had not chosen what would be considered the safest career path, he was happy and optimistic about his long-term success.

Tom's case illustrates clearly that spiritual development is not easy; it also shows how much the healing silence can help. He saw me for ten sessions over six months. The TM program very naturally became the major means for fostering his autonomy and growth. Two years later, his firm was well established, he had discovered a new enthusiasm for living, and he literally radiated energy and well-being. The rewards of spiritual growth were self-evident.

Sudden Spiritual Awakening

Spiritual crisis also commonly occurs in the period immediately following a dramatic and sudden spiritual awakening. This is well illustrated by Anne, a twenty-five-year-old woman who unexpectedly one morning had a profound spiritual awakening:

> It was incredible. I opened my eyes to find the room filled with light, a golden glow that left everything fresh and radiant. It was like I saw the world again for the first time. It brought me to tears. Everything was so beautiful, so precious. I felt sanctified and made whole. Life was profoundly good; wars, bickering, and complaints seemed silly. Love, universal love, was the only reality. I understood myself, history, my family, the world situation, everything. But I wasn't thinking, I just knew. There was no fear—just light, love, and a peace that defies all description. It was all-encompassing; time stood still, each moment seemed infinite and blissful.
>
> But as great as the feeling was while it lasted (it lasted for about eight hours and then gradually receded over the next ten) that's how crushed I felt when it left. It was worse than if I had all at once lost my husband, child, parents, and best friends. I felt

like I had been cast out, had the door to the spiritual kingdom slammed in my face. I felt unworthy, more so than I had ever felt before. My existence seemed shallow and futile without that larger loving awareness.

An ecstatic state may last for moments, hours, or even days, but it is bound to cease. When the knowingness and experience of life's oneness, love, and joy begin to fade, a personal crisis may ensue. As Assagioli so poignantly describes it,

> the personal ego re-awakens and asserts itself with renewed force. All the rocks and rubbish, which had been covered and concealed at high tide, emerge again. The man, whose moral conscience has now become more refined and exacting, whose thirst for perfection has become more intense, judges with greater severity and condemns his personality with a new vehemence; he is apt to harbor the false belief of having fallen lower than he was before. (1965)

Anne had never suffered from any emotional disorder or abused drugs. Following the "coming down" from her awakening, however, she became so full of despair that, at the encouragement of a friend, she sought me out. When Anne first came to see me, she was no longer certain whether her experience had been real, a fantasy, or "just plain crazy."

Anne felt very relieved when I validated her experience. I read her passages from Maharishi Mahesh Yogi, Thomas Aquinas, Plato, William Blake, and William Wordsworth to help her appreciate the universality of what she had experienced. When she realized that she had glimpsed life's deeper reality, the transcendental field, her spirit began to pick up. But her pressing questions remained: Why would such a supreme experience come and go, and how can I regain it?

Our discussion of enlightenment helped her with these questions. I again read passages of Maharishi's that distinguished between temporary experience of the transcendent and the permanent experience of it in the state of enlightenment. Anne had heard of enlightenment but had always thought it a mystical state with little practical value and, whether practical or not, attainable only through many years of effort. A brief discussion of psychophysiology helped dispel these misconceptions. I showed her how enlightenment is simply the normal state of the human biomachinery free from the backlog of old stresses; I explained how the TM program can unfold this state naturally. When she saw that the TM program would bring her back to the heights of pure consciousness step by step, she was eager to begin. She recognized that the "fall" she had experienced was natural and that she could now plant herself firmly on the path to total enlightenment.

Anne learned the TM technique the weekend after her visit with me and thoroughly enjoyed it. During her first meditation, she once again glimpsed the transcendent, not with all the fireworks of her first experience but in a stable and rewarding way. After two more visits with me, twice daily TM practice and advanced lectures at the TM center were all she needed. She did beautifully and, at last contact, was on her way to a TM teacher training course.

The Healing Silence and Spiritual Growth

The cultivation of inner silence has long been recognized as a cornerstone of spiritual growth. Meditation, after all, has been passed down for thousands of years not primarily as a means to relieve insomnia or overcome depression but as a way to reach the heights of spiritual development. During TM practice, deep in meditation, a person is likely to achieve what may be called the core spiritual experience. This experience is essentially simple. Daily experience is made up of an unending cascade of thoughts, emotions, sensations, and perceptions. Transcendental Meditation creates an opportunity for the mind to disengage itself from these continuous impressions. The mind settles down to a profound inner silence, a state of expanded awareness in which one recognizes one's innermost self as distinct from the roles, programs, and conditioning of one's external, more bounded existence. This experience is generally very satisfying and produces lasting positive effects. Perhaps because such expanded awareness is difficult to describe and rarely achieved under ordinary circumstances, it has been called "mystical."

Despite this shroud of mystery, this experience has been esteemed in almost every culture. In the West, we are advised to "Seek the Kingdom of Heaven within." In the East, the great spiritual masters explain the immense value of achieving *samadhi* or *satori*. The cornerstone of ancient Greek wisdom was the simple statement, "Know thyself." Humanistic psychologists express this same idea today in their discussions of the importance of self-actualization. Behind all these statements, the message is the same. Directly experience your spiritual essence in order to reap rewards in all aspects of life.

This experience is the goal of all meditation techniques. It appears, however, that some techniques result in this experience more easily and effectively than others (Bloomfield & Kory, 1976). The TM technique appears to be particularly effective. Interest in the TM program has actually been due less to spiritual considerations than to research demonstrating its significant value in stress reduction and in the unfolding of full human potential. The regular practice of this simple technique appears to bring about profound benefits for normal individuals, as well as for those in medical, psychiatric, and rehabilitation settings (ibid; Carrington & Ephron, 1975; Glueck & Stroebel, 1975; Shafii, 1973a; West, 1974).

Advocates of the TM program assert that while TM is a simple, mental technique, it is more than just a relaxation exercise. They emphasize the need for a trained TM teacher and the availability of systematic follow-up. When taught and practiced in the prescribed manner, the TM program accomplishes more than relief of stresses and strains; it can lead naturally to a state of enlightenment.

Growth toward Enlightenment

It is important to emphasize that the TM program is effective not because it is some kind of religious opiate or fashionable cultivation of Eastern culture, but because it fosters very tangible spiritual development: growth toward enlightenment.

The process of becoming enlightened is one of systematically and naturally unfolding the full potential of the human biomachinery. Far from a state of self-delusion or self-denial, enlightenment represents the ultimate development of what we ordinarily consider the most valuable qualities of human life—intelligence, creativity, compassion, freedom, and the capacity for spontaneous, life-supporting responses under any circumstances. Enlightenment results from the continuous and progressive neurophysiological refinement or "purification" of the nervous system until a state of perfect psychophysiological integration is achieved (Bentov, 1977; Wallace, 1975). This physiological state of maximum ease and order supports the state of enlightenment.

This theme is not new; it has become central to much current psychological thinking. Fritz Perls, the founder of Gestalt therapy, frequently pointed out that most people use only a tiny portion of their full potential. At the turn of the century, the father of American psychology, William James, wrote:

> I have no doubt whatever that most people live whether physically, intellectually or morally, in a very restricted circle of their potential being. They make use of a very small portion of their possible consciousness and of their soul's resources in general. Much like the man who, out of his whole organism, should get into the habit of using and moving only his little finger. (1963, pp. 275–276)

In discussing enlightenment in therapy, I find that patients frequently have misconceptions about it. Perhaps the most common is that gaining enlightenment requires withdrawal from the world to sit meditating in a cave for many years. This kind of misunderstanding has led naturally to the belief that enlightenment may be a state of "eternal bliss" but is impractical for a dynamic person and tantamount to renunciation of the material world. Enlightenment requires neither spending years in a cave nor denial of the world.

If enlightenment is a natural capability of the human biomachinery, what prevents most people from living that state right now? What obstructs a person's immediate access to his full creative intelligence? Research on the TM program suggests that what restricts a person from living fully is lack of complete ease and order in the functioning of his nervous system. Deep-rooted stresses appear to play the major role in keeping the human biomachinery in a state of "dis-ease" and "dis-order." As the deep rest and self-desensitization of the TM technique neutralizes these deep-rooted stresses, the nervous system gains a higher mode of functioning; enlightenment progressively dawns.

In my discussions with patients, I like to use an excellent analogy by Maharishi to illustrate how this process of purification transforms the small, bounded self to a Self that is more universal. Maharishi compares the nervous system to a muddy pond reflecting the sun. When the mud is stirred up in the pond, the reflection of the sun may be very poor. On the other hand, when the mud settles and the water becomes pure, the reflection can become so perfect that it shines with nearly all the brilliance of the sun itself. Similarly, the nervous system may be thought of as a reflector of creative intelligence, and deep-rooted stresses may be compared to mud obstructing the nervous system's reflecting capacity. As long as the nervous system remains cluttered with stresses, the individual poorly reflects the highest values of creative intelligence. One experiences oneself primarily within the boundaries of daily living—one's body, job, interests, family, friends, thoughts, feelings, and so on. Maharishi notes that the word *self*, written with a lower case *s*, usually refers to this quality of self-consciousness. On the other hand, when the nervous system becomes a perfect reflector of pure creative intelligence, in the state of enlightenment, one experiences the universal and unchanging values of the self in all activities. Maharishi adds that in describing this state of self-consciousness, the *S* of *Self* deserves to be written in the upper case. The process of becoming enlightened, then, may be described as raising one's level of self-consciousness to an individual state that reflects universal values. The impetus for this growth is purification, dissolving the backlog of deep-rooted stresses.

Albert Einstein described the universal need for expanding individual awareness when he wrote:

> A human being is part of the whole, called by us "universe," a part limited in time and space. He experiences his thoughts and feelings as something separate from the rest—a kind of optical delusion of his consciousness. This delusion is a kind of prison

for us, restricting us to our personal decisions and to affection for a few persons nearest to us. Our task must be to free ourselves from this prison by widening our circle of compassion to embrace all living creatures and the whole nature in its beauty. (1972)

And William Blake succinctly described the whole matter in his verse: "If the doors of perception were cleansed, everything would appear to man as it is— infinite." His poetic vision further portrays how, once enlightened, one is able "to see a world in a grain of sand, and heaven in a wild flower, hold infinity in the palm of [one's] hand, and eternity in an hour."

Another misconception about enlightenment frequently voiced by patients is that achieving a universal Self-consciousness will result in a loss of individuality. But it is not the dissolution of deep-rooted stresses that makes people uniform. On the contrary, stresses tend to foster stereotyped behavior and to inhibit creativity and self-expression. When stresses dissolve, only then can one truly discover one's unique talents and capacity to contribute to the world. In putting people in touch with their maximum energy, intelligence, and creativity, enlightenment does not obscure but enhances individual differences. At the same time, enlightenment assures harmony among differences and unity amidst diversity by structuring a universal awareness in each person's consciousness.

The Enlightened Individual

What are the characteristics of the enlightened individual? Is it possible to pick an enlightened person out of a crowd? Patients sometimes ask these questions with the expectation that I shall give some dazzling description of the enlightened person walking on water or performing other remarkable feats. This expectation stems from the belief that enlightenment is a supernormal state, far removed from the realities of everyday living. In fact, the enlightened person does show some remarkable characteristics but at the same time appears more normal and natural than the so-called normal person. A backlog of deep-rooted stresses causing dis-ease and dis-order may be common to most people today, but this condition hardly deserves to be called normal.

Enlightenment is not some esoteric state requiring great self-manipulation and striving; rather, it is the most natural and comfortable state of human experience. What could be more normal than a person functioning at full potential? Abnormal or subnormal is the failure to use full creative intelligence due to the accumulation of stress. These stresses can be systematically eliminated by the TM program so that normal functioning is assured. Because enlightenment is the most normal, natural state of living, its special characteristics are not extraordinary but, rather, fully developed qualities already present to some degree in the unenlightened state. I believe that enlightenment will provide the criterion for which modern psychology has been looking in order to define the fully healthy individual.

The enlightened person enjoys a virtually unshakable baseline happiness. Underlying all shifts in mood or emotion is an inner contentment that assures maximum enjoyment of whatever is at hand. Enlightened individuals do not walk around thinking how happy they are or how much they are enjoying themselves. On the contrary, a natural innocence, almost childlike, characterizes their interactions with others—just as children enjoy the spontaneous happiness that wells up from the most basic element of their being. Childhood is often regarded as an enviable time because children are not self-conscious about their feelings; they just express them. The strong baseline happiness of the enlightened person permits a re-emergence of that childlike spontaneity against a background of emotional and intellectual maturity. The enlightened individual wastes no energy on worries or anxieties. Perfect balance in the autonomic nervous system allows for a smooth and unruffled flow of energy. Fatigue, dullness, or loss of alertness are foreign. At the same time, enjoyment and excitement are infinitely available. Indeed, the enlightened person discovers ripples of pleasure in everything. In no way should enlightenment be thought of as a state of dry serenity. On the contrary, enlightened individuals enjoy such an inner happiness that they overflow with laughter and expressions of warmth and friendship.

Another important characteristic of enlightenment is freedom. In the process of becoming enlightened through the TM program, people discard their deepest fears and inhibitions. As a result, the barrier that most people feel between their inner and outer lives melts away and harmonious integration occurs spontaneously. No longer do unspoken wishes or pent-up feelings keep individuals cut off from themselves and others. Game playing disappears and intimacy becomes the natural way of relating to others. At the same time, the unshakable quality of inner contentment keeps enlightened individuals from losing their equanimity and from becoming overly caught up in other people's problems or even their own pleasures. Because they are free from deep-rooted stresses, they are also free from unconscious cravings or unfulfilled desires that distort thinking or behavior. They are free to perceive their own feelings, the feelings of others, and the world around them as they are, not as they appear to be through the screen of their own stress, which inevitably clouds perception. Their sense of self is so strong that they experience an independence of their innermost being from all the changing aspects of living.

Another characteristic of enlightenment is ease of activity. Straining to be happy or to achieve is a classic feature of the neurotic, but nature does not work according to the principle of strain. Physicist Lawrence Domash points out that nature is always maximally economical in its expenditure of energy; the law of least action operates everywhere in nature. For example, when a beam of light passes from air to water, it bends because in doing so it travels from one point to another in the least possible amount of time. Nature automatically computes the path that gets the light from the one point to the other with the greatest economy. In getting back in tune with the natural, the enlightened person acts more in accordance with the law of least action. For this reason, meditators typically report that they are doing less but accomplishing more. As a result, work becomes more pleasurable. Strain for achievement can yield some success but it loses all the joy of the process. William Blake made this point well when he wrote:

> He who binds to himself a joy
> Does the winged life destroy;
> But he who kisses the joy as it flies
> Lives in eternity's sunrise.
> (Poems from mss.)

Perfectly attuned to the law of least action, the enlightened person enjoys the process of achievement as well as the goal itself.

Spontaneity is another quality of the enlightened person. Stressed people are not spontaneous, in part because they cannot afford to be; when people are spontaneous, they display their innermost feelings to everyone around them. Anxiety and tension play such a large role in stressed individuals' emotional make-up that spontaneous expression of feelings would not be rewarding. But once a strong baseline happiness begins developing, the inner controls on spontaneity start to wither away because they are no longer necessary. Enlightened people can enjoy maximum spontaneity, for their actions spring from a comprehensive vision and are naturally appropriate.

Toward an Enlightened Psychotherapist

Even though psychiatrists face the same stresses and strains that affect almost everyone today, people expect them to be free from emotional distress. This expectation may not be unreasonable; an auto mechanic whose car never ran properly would hardly deserve confidence as an auto mechanic.

"It is particularly often noted by laymen as well as professional observers," wrote Albert Ellis, founder of Rational Therapy,

> that most psychotherapy practitioners are themselves hardly the
> very best models of healthy behavior. Instead of being minimally
> anxious and hostile, as on theoretical grounds one might expect

them to be if their own theories work well, they are frequently seriously emotionally disturbed, even after they have undergone lengthy psychoanalytic or other treatment. (1962, p. 377)

Psychiatrists are motivated to alleviate suffering in themselves and their patients, and, in quiet moments, most wish they could better reflect the ideals of emotional health and well-being that they try to foster in their patients. However, psychiatrists have few quiet moments. They belong to a very difficult and demanding profession with one of the highest rates of suicide and drug addiction of any group. The general failure of psychiatrists to enjoy a high degree of mental health does not reflect so much on them as people as on the limited efficacy of psychotherapy as an efficient way of producing emotionally healthy people. If psychotherapy alone does not cure the patient, it cannot be expected to cure the doctor. Psychiatrists who learn the TM technique often take to it immediately because they quickly see its potential value for their personal and professional lives (Carrington & Ephron, 1975).

In his discussion of transference, Freud was the first to describe just how intimate psychotherapy becomes when the patient transfers all repressed feelings about parents onto the therapist. No matter how much therapists may wish to remain objective, they also transfer some of their wishes and needs onto the patient. This phenomenon of countertransference may be damaging to the best interest of the patient. For example, therapists may tell themselves that they want to make their patients more self-reliant, while all along they encourage dependency because the therapists transfer their need for people to be dependent on them onto their patients. Because the TM program daily exposes the whole fabric of the nervous system to deep relaxation, it promotes the kind of psychological integration that helps therapists avoid countertransference.

I would add, too, a very human note to how the TM program helps therapists. It enhances their ability to love. Unconditional love is often a patient's most important need; most have been love-starved throughout their lives. Patients need to be accepted fully and without blame in spite of their incompetencies, misdeeds, disturbances, and complaints. If the patient feels the doctor's genuine love and compassion, a helping relationship can blossom. Ironically, psychologists and psychiatrists are often just as guilty as many physicians in remaining aloof and cold behind their professional exteriors. I believe that unloving therapists may often do harm instead of good for many patients despite their best intentions.

In the therapeutic relationship, psychiatrists lend their own ease, orderly thinking, and emotional well-being to each patient; they therefore must sustain an ample supply of these qualities. In his 1957 presidential address to the American Psychiatric Association, Dr. Francis J. Braceland emphasized that "the ideal goal of the psychiatrist is to achieve wisdom—to reflect those human qualities most important to helping another person" (1975, p. 22). All aspects of therapy—verbal exchanges, feelings, suggestions—can reflect only as much wisdom as the therapist has. Where a surgeon may be a lousy person but technically a great surgeon, a psychiatrist who is a lousy person is going to be a lousy psychiatrist. Psychiatry is not just technique; human elements remain of paramount importance.

Most patients are surrounded by other stressed people who reinforce dis-ease, dis-order, and emotional chaos. The effective psychiatrist introduces a new element of ease, order, and happiness into the patient's human relationships. In one sense the psychiatrist assumes the responsibility of a lighthouse in a sea of darkness. He or she radiates ease and order, which guide the patient toward a strong baseline happiness. The TM program can give the psychiatrist access to his or her own unlimited reserves of creative intelligence and thereby contributes substantially to effective therapy. Once the patient begins the TM program, he or she starts drawing on his or her own creative intelligence and gradually needs to "borrow" less and less ease, order, and happiness from the psychiatrist. Soon, the patient no longer needs the therapeutic relationship. When patient and therapist both practice the TM technique, the termination of therapy is joyful and easy because the patient does not feel cut off from his source of nurturance. He knows that he is genuinely able to keep growing on his own.

10

An Introduction to Kabbalistic Psychotherapy

Edward Hoffman

Edward Hoffman introduces us to an area of spirituality that in the past has been very hard to access without going through Orthodox Judaism. Further than that, not just *any* path through Orthodox Judaism would lead one to this spiritual path; one would need to be in the *mystical branch* of Orthodox Judaism, for it is only within that branch that one would have access to the secrets, knowledge, and wisdom of the Jewish mystics passed down, preserved, and honored from ancient time.

Hoffman explores this esoteric branch of Judaism—with particular emphasis on its relevance for transpersonal psychotherapy. He points out frequent and intriguing parallels with other psycho-spiritual systems; for example, the thirteenth-century *Zohar* (Book of Splendor) posits the concept of boundaries of our perceptual world as being illusory. Hoffman demonstrates how Jewish mysticism contains many of the essential features of Hinduism, Catholicism, Buddhism, Taoism, North American shamanism, Kundalini yoga, and Tantrism, as well as of current psychological disciplines, such as Gestalt therapy and Freud's theory of the unconscious.

This Jewish system seeks to balance the physical and the spiritual by achieving, in the *Zohar's* words, "harmony, peace and union, both above and below." Within this system, bodily needs and desires are not seen as innately wrong, but they need to be transformed in order not to be allowed to dominate the mind.

Highlighting the background principles of the Kabbalah, Hoffman clarifies the concept of the Ten *Sefiroth* (rays or emanations) which have often been identified with Jewish mysticism. "All mysteries of faith," says the *Zohar*, "are contained in these Palaces."

Hoffman's descriptions of the Kabbalistic higher realms are strikingly similar to those described in other mystical systems, especially Buddhism. All the practices of the Jewish mystical system are grounded in concern for daily life and "our ethical conduct toward family members, friends and those in our workplace and community." One can see this as an excellent way to discern and uproot aspects of the personality that in psychology we would call narcissistic.

Hoffman's chapter explores the Kabbalah's warnings to practitioners seeking to navigate the rigors of non-ordinary consciousness. The Kabbalah stresses slow and careful progress to mitigate the real potential for self-harm which can arise in such states if one is unprepared.

In the second part of his chapter, the author illustrates various techniques and approaches he uses with his clients. He provides a number of case histories that illustrate the implementation of his ideas in the therapeutic setting. One approach is to help clients see their lives in the context of a higher philosophical perspective. In addition, meditation, reading of sacred texts, and dream work within a *Kabbalistic framework* are proposed as important psychotherapeutic tools.

Hoffman helps us see that the Kabbalah is timeless—a relevant and modern spiritual path from antiquity.

THE KABBALAH (from the Hebrew root-word meaning "to receive") has for many centuries entranced people of diverse faiths and backgrounds. This esoteric branch of Judaism provides a detailed, massive, and coherent worldview of the nature of human existence and our relation to the cosmos. Its powerful, poetic vistas have excited the imagination of Jews and non-Jews alike in nearly every country of the globe. Yet, beginning in the early nineteenth century with the dominance of the mechanistic outlook of science, the Kabbalah fell into increasing obscurity. It has only been since the late 1960s, with the rediscovery in the West of many long-standing spiritual traditions, that the Kabbalistic allure has been felt once more. Throughout the world, Jewish mysticism today is undergoing a true renaissance of interest.

Certainly in the fields of psychology, therapy, and counseling, spiritually oriented practitioners are increasingly recognizing that the Kabbalah provides an immensely valuable system of knowledge. Within its vast realm, we can find considerable wisdom for expanding the relevance of today's helping professions. Rather than merely offering a theoretical framework for transpersonal therapy, the Kabbalah also provides specific guidelines for therapeutic intervention with all those seeking greater direction, wholeness, meaning, and fulfillment in their lives.

In this chapter, I will first highlight six major principles that serve as a vital backdrop for basic therapeutic activity with individuals. Certainly, these ideas bear fascinating parallels to those of other psycho-spiritual systems. I will then present specific recommendations for incorporating Kabbalistic insights into the therapeutic process. As we shall see, such time-honored methods include dreamwork, meditation, sacred reading, and journal-keeping.

1. *The cosmos is a unity, with all aspects in interrelation,* is the first Kabbalistic principle. This notion, it may be said, is the most essential concept in the Kabbalah. It is repeatedly summarized in the thirteenth-century *Zohar* (Book of Splendor) by such aphorisms as, "For as it is above, so it is below," (vol. 3, p. 84) or "So, too, does the lower sphere affect the upper." (vol. 3, p. 127)

Underlying virtually all Kabbalistic teachings and practices is the notion that all parts of the universe intimately affect one another. Nothing in the cosmos exists in true isolation from the whole. Rather, our all-too-common perception of separateness is deemed an illusion, sustained by our particular focus of consciousness. The Kabbalah stresses that from the movement of the stars to the flights of birds, everything is interconnected and interrelated.

In one of its central concepts, the Kabbalah indicates that in order for the universe to exist, the "Divine Essence" (known as the *Ein Sof*) was filtered, or channeled down, in degree, through ten separate but inextricably linked energy-spheres of vibration. Known as the *Sefiroth* (rays or emanations), and sometimes grouped in three sets of trinity with the highest demarcated separately (hence, in part, the interest of Catholic mystics in the Kabbalah), these consist of: *Keter* (enlightenment), *Hokhmah* (wisdom), *Binah* (understanding), *Hesed* (mercy), *Gevurah* (judgment), *Tiferet* (beauty), *Nezah* (eternity or victory), *Hod* (reverberation or glory), *Yesod* (foundation), and *Malkut* (kingdom).

The ten *Sefiroth* are said to be in constant interplay, and together, underlie all aspects of the universe. Alluding to the *Sefiroth*, the *Zohar* informs us that, "All the mysteries of faith are contained in these Palaces." (vol. 1, p. 213)

The Kabbalah further postulates four distinct but interrelated worlds of existence, each composed of these ten divine energy manifestations. For example, any human idea, such as a carpenter's conception of a chair to be built, would pass through several worlds of existence before emerging into physical reality. These four worlds are identified as those of Emanation, Creation, Formation, and finally Action or matter, in descending order to our own world. It is interesting to note that the Hopi Native Americans similarly suggest that our world is the fourth and last of several which were created.

Despite the vastness of the realms around us, the Kabbalah emphasizes that each individual's actions reverberate like an echo throughout the cosmos.

There is a strong ethical imperative in Kabbalistic thought, and human acts are considered to be far from inconsequential. In a universe where all elements are in continual interplay, even the slightest action has an effect upon the functioning of the whole. Thus, the *Zohar* declares that, "Every word that a person speaks, whether it be good or bad, causes a vibration in the higher sphere." (vol. 4, p. 409)

2. *The forces of creation represent an eternal interplay between an active force and a passive one.* It is surprising, indeed striking, to those initiating study of the Kabbalah, how similar is this second key principle to that of the yin/yang formulation in various Far Eastern spiritual systems. Again and again, the Kabbalah affirms that the cosmos as a whole, and all of its components, represent manifestations of these passive and active forces.

"Now observe a deep and holy mystery of faith," declares the *Zohar* in one passage, "the symbolism of the male and female principle of the universe . . . which together form a perfect unity." (vol. 2, p. 89) Or, as it is stated elsewhere in the *Zohar,* "every figure which does not comprise [these] elements is not a true and proper figure." (vol. 1, p. 177) The Kabbalah repeatedly stresses that everything in the universe manifests this principle. Though such qualities as active and passive, strong and weak, light and dark, appear to ordinary consciousness as separate and indeed mutually contradictory, the Jewish visionary tradition insists that all are in fact one.

In one acute commentary on the biblical line from Genesis, "And God divided the light from the darkness," the *Zohar* aptly explains:

> Up to this point, the male principle was represented by light and the female by darkness; subsequently, they were joined together and made one. The difference by means of which light is distinguished from darkness is by degree only; both are one in kind, as there is no light without darkness and no darkness without light. (vol. 1, p. 147)

This concept is, of course, virtually identical with that of Taoism and other Far Eastern philosophies. The terms yin and yang, for example, originally stood for two sides of a mountain, both terms compounded with the Chinese character for "mound of earth." These terms eventually came to be associated with the two pulses of the Tao as it moves in the world—one perceived as active and thrusting (in the Kabbalistic tradition, known as the "King"), and the other as receptive and enclosing (known as the "Queen" or "Shekinah").

According to the Kabbalah, all dimensions of creation, from the origin of the universe itself to the simplest human innovation or action, involve a balance or synthesis between these two seemingly oppositional forces. The wise person is able to discern this harmony in all things; and indeed, perception of this harmony is considered basic to higher states of consciousness. Thus, within each individual, the needs of the intellect must be balanced by the needs of the body or emotions. Similarly, the urge for extroversion must be balanced by the urge for solitude, and vice versa.

The Kabbalah would also suggest that our current technological, analytic approach to knowledge (*Keter*) inevitably leads to a limiting view of the human potential, without a complementary receptive and holistic approach (*Binah*). In this vein, scientific research on human brain hemisphere function suggests that both intuitive and objective orientations are central to effective sensory processing of the world.

The Kabbalistic tradition also asserts that not only do material objects comprise active or passive qualities, but time and its various sub-components do as well. Thus, according to the *Zohar*, even particular seasons or moments are "ruled" to varying degrees by the King or *Shekinah*. Interestingly, research on human bio-rhythms has strongly intimated that men and women, in the course of their day-to-day lives, undergo countless subtle rhythmic shifts in their biological processes. Though the evidence is as yet far from conclusive, it does appear that for optimal mental and physical health, we might profitably monitor our activities to harmonize with those underlying diurnal, monthly, or seasonal cycles.

3. *The human individual is a microcosm of the universe.* The third, and one of the most central beliefs in the Jewish mystical system, is that every person represents a direct manifestation of the "Divine Essence." To fully understand the functioning of the universe, it is necessary that we comprehend the human mind and body, the Kabbalah repeatedly affirms. "For there is not a member in the human body," the *Zohar* explains, "but has its counterpart in the world as a whole." (vol. 2, p. 36) Or, as the *Zohar* declares elsewhere, "It is plain that the substances composing an individual's body belong to two worlds: namely, the world below and the world above." (vol. 3, p. 79)

A basic Kabbalistic goal is for each of us to harmonize or balance these seemingly conflicting forces, within and without. Both are seen to mirror the larger forces intrinsic to the universe itself.

Another related Kabbalistic concept is that the human mind and body are closely linked. Like other spiritual traditions including yoga and those of the Native Americans, the Kabbalah insists that all emotions, such as anger, joy, or sorrow, have an effect upon our overall biophysical functioning. For example, the *Zohar* states that, "Anger, in contradistinction to sins which pollute only the body, pollutes also the soul, and in fact, the whole being." (vol. 4, p. 118) In recent years, a growing number of psychotherapists and other health professionals have become convinced of the importance of the mind-body relationship. Such emotions as chronic anger and resentment are seen to be particularly destructive.

According to the Kabbalah, too, our mind-body composition is modeled directly after the pattern of the cosmic, primordial human being, *Adam Kadmon,* and is therefore viewed as good and praiseworthy in itself. To perceive this pattern accurately is a mark of high spiritual achievement, and thus, a heightened awareness of the sensory world is regarded as a valuable path to inner development.

In the Jewish mystical system, our bodily needs and desires are not to be condemned as innately wrong. Rather, our goal ought to be the transformation of our lower emotions (such as anger, fear, jealousy) so that they are recognized and observed—or "witnessed"—but not allowed to dominate the mind. This viewpoint is strikingly similar to that of other spiritual traditions including Sufism and Kundalini yoga. Also, in current psychotherapies such as Gestalt therapy, there is a growing emphasis on "re-educating" individuals to become more fully aware of both their inner and outer environments. In this regard, the Kabbalah suggests that sustaining a strong respect for our bodily and emotional needs is basic to a systematic effort in self-growth.

In addition, the Jewish visionary tradition teaches that our total personality or Self is composed of three distinct but ultimately interrelated aspects. These consist of: (a) *nefesh,* the most physical and material; (b) *ruach,* a subtle bio-energy that is likewise ultimately physical in nature; and (c) *neshamah,* or over-Self, which is our physically transcendent, spiritual aspect, and which, ultimately links everyone with the universal "Divine Essence."

For optimal mental and physical health, the appropriate goal for each individual is, in the *Zohar's* words, "to achieve harmony, peace and union, both above and below." (vol. 3, p. 414) Or, as the *Zohar* states elsewhere, "These three grades (nefesh, ruach, and neshamah) are harmoniously combined in those persons who had good fortune to render service to their Maker." (vol. 2, p. 280)

4. The fourth Kabbalistic principle states that *in daily life, we are attuned to only one state of consciousness among many.* Jewish mystics suggest repeatedly that we typically move through daily, waking life as though surrounded by veils, which hide other possible dimensions of perception from conscious awareness. "Each person, whilst in this world," observes the *Zohar* in one passage, "considers not and reflects not what he is standing on, and each day as it passes he regards as though it has vanished into nothingness." (vol. 1, p. 323) These other states of consciousness exist, the Kabbalah insists, even though from birth onward, we tend to become oblivious to them.

Of course, this intriguing concept is central to a variety of spiritual approaches from Sufism and yoga to Native American shamanism. That is, what we commonly perceive as "reality" (what philosopher Alan Watts once jokingly referred to as "how the world looks on a bleak Monday morning") is regarded as simply one level of consciousness to which we have become habituated in our mundane society.

Relying upon a variety of poetic similes and metaphors, the Kabbalah stresses that the cosmos manifests a dazzling radiance that we may more fully experience in higher realms of awareness. In the *Zohar* and other lofty writings that span the centuries, Kabbalists describe the "tens of thousands of worlds" and their multitude of wonders, "for there is door within door, grade behind grade, through which the glory. . . is made known." (vol. 1, p. 332)

Jewish visionaries have sometimes described ecstatic states of consciousness as incorporating new perceptions of sound and light. Individuals may hear exalted strains of music or behold unseen colors (which today we might term "unperceived vibrational frequencies"). These colors are said to possess a brilliance and beauty which far surpasses what we ordinarily experience in the natural world. Once more, Kabbalists explain, it is our ordinary consciousness which typically shuts these perceptions out. "There are colors disclosed and undisclosed," the *Zohar* declares, "but people neither know nor reflect on such matters." (vol. 3, p. 77) This sacred text goes on to explain that, "the visible colors represent reflections of higher colors, of which the spiritually advanced, such as the prophets, were not entirely ignorant." (ibid.) In frequent references to mystical adepts like Rabbi Simeon bar Yochai of ancient times, the *Zohar* indicates that they were sometimes transported into such realms of bliss that they forgot to eat or drink for several days.

The Jewish mystical tradition also emphasizes that negative human emotions, such as anxiety or unhappiness, should be recognized as stemming from lower and hindering states of awareness. In one well-known, Zen-like simile, the late eighteenth-century Hasidic master Reb Nachman of Bratslav pointed out that just as our hand can blot out the sun's potent rays from our eyes, so, too can our lower emotions obscure the universal splendor and harmony which we can experience in higher states of consciousness.

Quite frequently, the Kabbalah's central metaphor to describe these altered states is the perception of dazzling, ineffable light. During the highest states of consciousness, individuals feel themselves suffused through their total being in this radiance. As the *Zohar* relates, "The primal point is the innermost light of a translucency, tenuity, and purity passing comprehension." (vol. 1, p. 84)

This fundamental Kabbalistic notion is again strikingly similar to that of other spiritual systems such as yoga and Zen Buddhism. Such traditions likewise emphasize that in ordinary consciousness we are not typically aware of the inherent beauty, wonder, and harmony of the cosmos; except in generally unusual and fleeting circumstances, we remain oblivious to these other realms of awareness. Within American humanistic psychology, bold thinkers like William James and later Abraham Maslow (the latter coining the term "peak experience" to describe such wondrous moments) have suggested that ordinary waking consciousness represents only one highly specialized or "trained" type of consciousness, with others definitely possible to attain.

Similar to Far Eastern spiritual masters, Jewish mystics have taught their initiates how to gradually expand their perceptions in order to attain loftier inner states. Like Hinduism with its notion of the veils of *Maya* with which this world is surrounded, the Kabbalah both cautions and admonishes us not to accept mundane reality as the only valid perception of the universe.

5. *Each person may attain higher states of consciousness, but careful preparation is necessary,* according to the fifth Kabbalistic principle. Throughout its long history, Jewish mysticism has taught that we all have the ability to transcend ordinary, daily consciousness, but wholly according to our degree of intent and diligence. There is nothing inherently impossible or insurmountable about the quest for higher spiritual awareness, only that we must be prepared for the rigors involved. This striving, the *Zohar* declares, "must be approached with proper preparation, not only of the mind but also of the body." (vol. 1, p. 243) In addition, we must be patient about the journey and not expect dramatic or overnight breakthroughs to occur.

As we shall see, the Kabbalistic tradition has incorporated a variety of specific methods for inner development. But, in general, the most important concern is for our daily life and our ethical conduct towards family members, friends, and those in our workplace and community. Even our simplest habits or acts are to be approached from an integrated and holistic mental-physical perspective. Parables abound in the Kabbalah which are designed to illustrate this point.

In one Hasidic legend, a renowned eighteenth-century mystical adept is said to have commented how the greatest piece of knowledge he acquired from his own teacher was "how to sleep properly." In another parable, a disciple is said to have sought one Hasidic master, "in order to see how he ties his shoelaces." Similar to Zen aphorisms with their emphasis on everyday holiness, the *Zohar* states that "all depends on the kind of speech, action, and intention to which a man habituates himself." (vol. 1, p. 324) For it is in daily life that we must be grounded for all inner growth.

The Kabbalah affirms that our most typical daily habits and thoughts are precisely of the utmost importance in the process of inner growth. For example, we cannot expect to benefit much from even intense meditation if we spend the rest of the day involved in selfish or hedonistic pursuits. Contemporary humanistic psychological approaches, such as gestalt therapy, have arrived at the same view, in which our simplest everyday acts, from eating to gait or posture, are considered to reveal the essence of our personality. This vital Kabbalistic concept is also found in spiritual traditions such as Zen Buddhism and Taoism, which similarly stress the importance of our objectively "witnessing" our ordinary daily thoughts and behaviors.

Jewish mysticism also emphasizes that the perception of higher reality ultimately depends upon our own degree of spiritual awareness. Thus, the *Zohar* relates in one parable that the patriarch Abraham saw the dazzling but ethereal form of Adam beckoning to him in the ancient Cave of Mechpalah. Meanwhile, the owner of the cave "saw only darkness within," (vol. 2, p. 14) and therefore could not understand why Abraham was interested in it. Similarly, while dreams are regarded as potential wellsprings of knowledge, the *Zohar* states that, "no person is shown anything in a dream save what falls within his level." (vol. 2, p. 79)

Another related, Kabbalistic concept is that of *kavana*, or intentionality-willpower. Modern psychodynamic theory has contributed much to our understanding of the extent to which we may be ruled by unconscious drives, such as the need for dominance or sexuality. It is therefore obvious that people often act from motives that are seldom wholly pure. Yet, Jewish mysticism indicates that all humans also possess a higher motivating force that can be mobilized for great achievement, and without which certainly little individual growth can be accomplished.

"Kavana is the mystery of a soul directed to a goal," wrote Martin Buber in *Hasidism and Modern Man*, "it is given to [us] to lift up the fallen and to free the imprisoned. . . . [We] can work toward the redemption of the world." (p. 46) Unfortunately, modern psychology has generally slighted our human innate need to make the world a better place. Rather than simply serving as conscious willpower, *kavana* refers to an intentionality that emerges from our entire being: at a certain inner juncture, each of us, with both conscious and unconscious impulses, strives to help redeem the surrounding world.

The Kabbalah cautions that intentionality is not in itself typically sufficient for immediate inner development and external change. But, the Jewish visionary tradition has always contended, this motivating force to help renew and perfect the world is a basic human attribute. Significantly in recent years, a growing number of humanistic psychologists have sought to reassert the primacy of intentionality in self-growth. A pioneer in this regard was the Viennese-born medical psychologist Alfred Adler, who called this quality "courage" and directly influenced with his optimism such key theorists as Rollo May and Abraham Maslow.

The Kabbalah has also emphasized that the path to higher realms of awareness must be trod slowly and with the utmost caution. Although our ordinary, daily consciousness is compared to that of the blinders around a horse's eyes, this everyday consciousness serves an important protective role. That is, none of us without considerable training could possibly sustain the experience of all the "doors of perception" being opened at once. The Jewish mystical tradition is filled with legends of would-be spiritual masters who hurriedly and without proper guidance sought to storm the celestial doors. In instance after instance, such practitioners are said to have perished, or gone mad, with the onrush of knowledge and vision which they were unequipped to receive.

This notion, which is fundamental to other spiritual traditions like yoga and Native American shamanism, has inspired significant empirical research. For instance, several psychological investigators have theorized the existence of a filtering process within our central nervous system. This filtering system is believed to effectively screen out most of the extraneous sensory stimuli from potentially overwhelming us. Other studies in experimental psychopathology suggest that the inability to selectively process incoming stimuli may be an important feature of both autistic and schizophrenic syndromes. In addition, research on the effects of psychedelic drugs such as LSD and mescaline has indicated that such substances can provoke a potentially sudden, explosive, and dangerous rush of visual, auditory, or tactile stimuli through altering the biochemical balance of our ordinary consciousness. Indeed, various groups such as Native American peoples, have deliberately sought to attain altered states of consciousness through such plants as peyote, but under carefully ritualized ceremonies.

Thus, there appears to be growing research evidence for the Kabbalistic notions concerning everyday versus non-ordinary consciousness. Transpersonal therapists are similarly becoming more aware of the importance of adequate guidance and supervision for novices who undertake meditative and other consciousness-altering techniques.

6. According to the sixth Kabbalistic principle, *to achieve such transcendent states of consciousness, various specific practices and techniques must be utilized.* In a variety of ways, these methods strikingly parallel those of extremely diverse traditions ranging from Tibetan Buddhism to Native American shamanistic practices. First of all, Kabbalistic techniques emphasize bodily vitality as an important prerequisite for attaining loftier realms of consciousness. Typically, special diets and fasting have been recommended, with a total avoidance of gluttony in eating or drinking.

Abraham Abulafia, the great thirteenth-century Kabbalist, wrote over two dozen treatises for achieving higher mental states. His techniques incorporated yoga-like bodily postures, special rhythmic exercises, and cloistered seclusion from others for unhindered meditation. Abulafia cautioned initiates on the care needed in these exercises, lest in contemplation, "a fire which proceeds from one's own body" (Jacobs, p. 31) precipitate severe damage to oneself. Similar admonitions are common to many spiritual paths, such as

Kundalini Yoga, which likewise warns of prematurely unleashing one's "serpent energy" to cause potential self-harm.

Typical Kabbalistic practices have also involved the recitation of special rhythmic prayers and chants, resembling partially the *mantras* of the Hindu traditions. The effect appears to be related, in which our mind becomes stilled and our whirlpool of thoughts is put in order. For instance, individuals are encouraged to meditate or quietly chant the Hebrew word *shalom* (meaning "peace" or "wholeness"). It hardly seems a coincidence that it incorporates the yogic sound of *Om* for inducing a calmer, deeper inner state. The early Hasidim utilized wordless melodies (called *niggunim*) combined with exuberant dancing to help release the ego from its daily bonds. In general, music has been accorded a significant role in the Kabbalistic tradition. It declared that in the highest contemplative states, we may inwardly hear the "divine singing" that permeates the entire universe.

Interestingly, celibacy has decidedly not been encouraged by Jewish mystics as a means for inner development. Kabbalistic initiates have been encouraged to marry, and the act of lovemaking on the Sabbath was deemed particularly beneficial for one's spirituality. In fact, not unlike Tantric yogic belief, the Kabbalah has taught that the act of sexual intercourse, in conjunction with intense mental concentration, is an extremely powerful means for experiencing the divine in its earthly indwelling (known as the *Shekinah*). Moreover, the same Hebrew word is used to indicate both sexual intercourse and knowledge, as in Adam "knew" Eve. Sexual intercourse with love is regarded as among the most potent experiences possible for men and women in altering the daily functioning of the conscious mind.

According to the Kabbalah, dreams are another important source of inner wisdom. "A dream is more precise than a vision," the *Zohar* explains, "and may explain what is obscure in a vision." (vol. 2, p. 79) Adepts consider it crucial that we pay close attention to our dreams, for "a dream uninterpreted is like a letter unopened." (vol. 2, p. 200) In his intriguing book on Sigmund Freud and Jewish mysticism, David Bakan (1958) explicitly compared Freudian dream analysis with Kabbalistic techniques, which rely heavily on the use of symbols. It should be added that while the Kabbalah attributes to dreams the power to reveal hidden truths, its mystics also suggest that our dreams generally reflect our degree of spiritual development in waking life.

Finally, Kabbalists have typically recommended various methods of mental concentration to elevate daily consciousness. Among the most widely used techniques have been those involving an inner focus upon the ten *Sefiroth* and also upon the twenty-two Hebrew letters. Through various prescribed permutations and rearrangements of these letters and numbers, the initiate's higher soul *(neshamah)* is awakened to experience higher realms. Such practices reflect the esoteric Jewish notion that each letter is an archetypal form that exerts a particular effect on our consciousness.

Also, as Rabbi Zalman Schacter-Shalomi has observed, three main practices have traditionally been utilized. These have included (a) *Gematriyah,* in which the numerical value of particular words are analyzed to reveal correspondences between words; (b) *Notarikon,* which breaks words into sentences comprised of individual letters; and (c) *Timurah,* in which the sequence of letters within a word are rearranged to change its meaning. It is interesting to note that such traditions as yoga and Tibetan Buddhism similarly utilize methods in training their initiates to develop intense mental concentration through a "narrowing" of external stimuli.

Methods of Intervention

The aforementioned principles are meant to provide a conceptual overview of Jewish mysticism and its psychological relevance. But what specific methods can be actually incorporated by practitioners involved in psychotherapy and counseling? Based on my own years of clinical experience in this domain, four basic guidelines can definitely be recommended. Of course, these are not intended as all-inclusive, but rather as representative of an immensely beneficial system of knowledge.

1) Understand your client's life—his or her challenges and problems—from a higher perspective: that is, encompassing a unique *tikun* (mission, task) on Earth. Based primarily on the inspiring teachings of the sixteenth-century sage Rabbi Isaac Luria and later emphasized by the early Hasidim, Kabbalists have long insisted that each person on Earth is here for a specific purpose. This typically entails vocational, familial, and social aspects of life. The more we are able to comprehend and carry out our unique, divinely mandated mission, the more fulfilled and joyful we feel. Conversely, the more we have strayed from our personal *tikun,* the greater our unhappiness and sense of emptiness. It is important to realize that one's *tikun* does not automatically translate into earning a full-time livelihood. Such an event is certainly possible, and may be even desirable for most of us, but it is not guaranteed. Rather, the key therapeutic issue is to help the client identify his or her *tikun,* and then to actually find ways to express it (not just think about it) in the context of everyday life. This is because Kabbalists teach that in the World of *Assiyah* or Action which we inhabit, our deeds are the most important thing. Your role is to help the client see more clearly, or discover his or her *tikun,* but you must never cajole or force an interpretation, however sensible it seems to you.

CASE 1

Peter was a talented twenty-eight-year-old pianist who earned a living playing at bars in a resort area. He was a sensitive person and intensely disliked the raucous, unsavory atmosphere in which he was obliged to work nightly. Peter had begun turning to street drugs for solace and sought my professional help when he found himself becoming addicted to cocaine. In the first few sessions of therapy, Peter decided that song-writing above all gave him a sense of purpose and direction in life. That was definitely his *tikun*. But he initially felt that the sensitive ballads he wrote were uncommercial and therefore unworthy of his effort. In therapy, Peter came to understand that his *tikun* was independent of his specific livelihood, and that he could write satisfying songs for himself and small, like-minded audiences without having to feel inadequate. Initially, Peter was resistant to putting aside ample time for creative song-writing; he complained of feeling too tired due to his piano-playing hours. But as Peter actually began to compose lyrics and music in a meaningful manner, he found himself becoming purposeful, self-directed, and strong. He eventually gave up all illegal drug usage and felt ready to become involved in a meaningful love relationship.

2) Meditation is almost always a useful adjunct in the therapeutic process. As discussed earlier, Kabbalists teach that the meditative state is a key avenue for inner development. Not only does it increase our sense of emotional calmness and well-being, meditation is regarded as a key means to strengthening our higher sensitivities including intuition, creativity, and spiritual discernment. In American society, most people would benefit from two daily meditative sessions—one lasting a few minutes before leaving for work and the other session taking place in the evening after dinner. Each session can be ten or fifteen minutes in length.

Dozens of Jewish meditative techniques have historically existed. Several cogent books are now available with elementary exercises clearly explained. The important thing is that your client choose one that appears beneficial and then practice it consistently over a period of several months. Kabbalists recommend that, as much as possible, individuals select the same time and place each day to meditate. Sometimes within just a couple of weeks, dramatic benefits arise as a result.

CASE 2

Alicia was a fifty-four-year-old woman who had recently taken early retirement at her job. She had spent the past fifteen years working as a computer technician for a large bank. Overweight and in only fair health, Alicia had been increasingly bored and unhappy doing this work and had eagerly accepted the offer of early retirement. Now, Alicia felt exhilarated, yet simultaneously anxious and worried, about what to do next with her life. Although sensing that care-giving rather than computer technology appealed most to her, Alicia was quite uncertain about all the possibilities that loomed and panic feelings were beginning to assail her. Alicia also lacked a strong sense of conviction about what career to choose in mid-life.

Alicia was advised to meditate at least twenty minutes per day, and chose to focus on the creative energy of the *Ein Sof* and the ten *Sefiroth* of the Kabbalistic Tree of Life. With my guidance, she systematically sought to embody the unique strengths of each *sefirah* into her own being. Within two weeks, Alicia felt herself gaining a stronger sense of confidence, and after three months of daily meditation, she had gained considerable insight and mental clarity. Alicia decided that a career in pediatric nursing would be most fulfilling; she enrolled in a public university, and also began to take better care of herself physically in terms of diet and exercise. For the first time in years, Alicia felt confident and optimistic about the future.

3) Encourage your clients to pay close attention to their dreams. Kabbalists have long taught that all persons can gain tremendous insight and clarity about their lives through attentive dreamwork. Particularly in psychotherapy, it is useful for individuals to heed their dreams for personal guidance. Kabbalists definitely believe that dreams have symbolic import, but point as well to concrete actions we need to take in this World of *Assiyah*. In other words, a significant dream can help induce clients to enact specific deeds that can strengthen their *tikun*.

CASE 3

Paul was a forty-eight-year-old businessman who lived alone and experienced great difficulty in forming friendships and love relationships. He had been involved in psychotherapy for more than fifteen years with several different therapists and had made only slight progress. Paul had learned to intellectualize his problems and found it very hard to look within for guidance. He was encouraged to keep a dream journal and record all his dreams, however fragmentary. More so than meditation, which Paul found hard to sustain, he enjoyed this diary-like activity and quickly began to see consistent themes in his dreams—especially a yearning for parenthood. With my direction, Paul also practiced the "dream incubation" technique recommended by medieval Kabbalists; that is, actively soliciting one's dreams for advice on important matters. This practice gave him impetus to study his own Jewish tradition more seriously. After approximately four months of regular dreamwork, Paul had acquired greater insight into his tendency to distance himself in relationships and had begun to take adult education classes for a social outlet.

Paul was also encouraged to directly contact those living relatives who appeared in his dreams—such as by initiating a phone call or letter—for it was explained to him that Kabbalists always stress that dreams must be understood concretely and not just symbolically. Paul was willing to follow up his dreams in this way, and such efforts helped him to "break the ice" of immobility after years of self-imposed isolation and estrangement from family members.

4) Encourage your clients to read sacred texts as a way of strengthening their higher qualities, such as *kavana* (intentionality), intuition, and creativity. Bibliotherapy may seem to be a new field, but its antecedents in the Kabbalah certainly date back many centuries. Jewish mystics have long taught that by immersing ourselves daily—even for just a few minutes—in sacred, soul-stirring writings, we immeasurably strengthen our *neshamah*. From my experience, it's not necessary to read these in the original Hebrew; many excellent translations exist. Some of the most effective texts include *Pirkey Avoth* (Ethics of the Fathers), *The Way of God* by Rabbi Moses Luzzatto, the *Zohar*, and the Hasidic teachings and tales of Reb Nachman of Bratslav. You can encourage your clients to record their reactions to specific aphorisms, concepts, and stories, and then appropriately discuss these during therapy sessions.

CASE 4

Madeline was a forty-five-year-old woman suffering from multiple sclerosis. She was depressed about her condition and continually demanded to know why she had been made to suffer in this way. For years before the onset of her illness, Madeline had experienced tense and conflicted relations with her elderly parents, her husband, and business partner in the preschool they owned. Madeline was half-hearted about practicing meditation and regular dreamwork, but was willing to read various sacred works that I recommended to her. Almost immediately, she began to feel spiritually inspired and intellectually challenged as well. During therapy sessions, Madeline engaged in much less self-pity and began looking at her own condition more hopefully. With my assistance, Madeline put together a special reading list and applied herself to it with a zeal that initially surprised me. For the first time in many years and antedating her illness as well, Madeline felt excited about her life and interested in using her abilities to the fullest.

Conclusions

In summary, the Kabbalah offers a tremendous wealth of theory and technique for those involved with psychotherapy. Jewish mystical teachings have much to offer therapeutic practitioners interested in incorporating the insights of an ancient, time-honored, and still-relevant spiritual system into their transpersonal work. In a time when a new vision of the human potential is now sought by many, the Kabbalah speaks to us with a relevance perhaps unprecedented since its inception.

11

Clinical Applications of Transpersonal Psychotherapy

Seymour Boorstein

In this chapter, I describe aspects of my personal spiritual evolution from a traditionally trained Freudian psychoanalyst to a therapist who amalgamates the best of what I know in psychoanalysis with spiritual knowledge and practices. I have seen that the addition of the spiritual can help heal and consolidate the ego at more fragile levels of psychological development.

This chapter takes an approach that is more conservative than some of the others in the book: I use classical diagnostic categories together with some of my theoretical views which have been greatly influenced by Self Psychology to explain the clinical pictures presented.

The six vignettes offered cover the diagnostic categories from psychosis to borderline to character pathology (narcissistic) to neurotic to existential problems. I explain the histories using psychodynamic concepts, and I chose them because, in each case, the patient worked with a specific spiritual practice as an adjunct to traditional psychotherapy. The effectiveness of our work lay in the conjoining of the two; a balance was found by the patients that I suggest would not have been found so easily nor so quickly through psychotherapy alone.

In some instances, the patients were involved in the practice of a faith tradition, such as Christianity or Buddhism, and in others, select practices were "borrowed" from a religious tradition and practiced in a secular context.

Traditional transpersonal wisdom indicates that only at more advanced psychosexual levels are certain spiritual practices appropriate. A surprising finding is that patients at all levels of ego development have a certain inner wisdom which enables them to use spiritual traditions selectively, taking from them those elements needed for personal growth—thus, my conclusion that transpersonal and psychodynamic approaches complement and augment each other.

OVER THE PAST FIFTEEN YEARS of my more than thirty-five years of psychiatric practice, I have consciously urged my patients to include and value the spiritual dimension of their lives as part of their healing process. This has been in contrast to my earlier stance which saw religion as, at best, a benign social custom, and, at worst, a pathologic reflection of infantile ego development. With patients whose lives have included a religious path that they have valued, I have supported even stronger investigation and practice of that path. With patients alienated from, or ignorant of, religious paths, I have shared my own. With rare exceptions, the addition of a spiritual dimension has facilitated positive results. My therapeutic style continues to be psychodynamically traditional, working in the transference to uncover defenses, resolve ego conflict, and heal pathologic self-systems. This chapter is an overview of my theoretical understanding of why (or how) spiritual practice facilitates healing by presenting examples of my work with specific patients.

My evolution from a totally traditional and conventional therapist was, as it obviously needed to be, a reflection of my own experience. I don't believe that it would be possible for anyone to make this change out of academic or professional curiosity alone, as one might in a decision to use a new drug protocol.

The recommendation of meditation, contemplation, prayer, spiritual or philosophical study needs to come, I believe, both from the experience that these work as techniques and the conviction that the wisdom that gave rise to these techniques matters. Personally, my father's death when I was forty years old significantly awakened my concerns about the existential dilemmas of life and death, meaning, and purpose. Furthermore, although I had completed a long course of psychoanalysis with a respected analyst, I still recognized in myself habitual patterns of fear and melancholia that, although manageable, I knew inhibited my ability to live fully and joyfully. My own spiritual search included the daily study of *A Course in Miracles* for several years, attending Buddhist (Vipassana) retreats, and reading widely in both Western and Eastern philosophical traditions. I was convinced that this exploration, which changed my world view, also lessened my fears, clarified my previous self-analytic work, reduced my anger, and thus increased my ability to be loving.

I think it would be fair (and honest) to admit that my openness about the spiritual dimension of my life with my patients was spontaneous rather than premeditated. Later on, when I began to share with colleagues the positive results my patients were reporting, I started to reflect more carefully about the theoretical explanations for how (and why) transpersonal psychotherapy works. Also, since transpersonal psychotherapy, by its nature, requires a certain self-disclosure on the part of the therapist, I felt that it was important to consider the effects of such disclosure on the transference in order to validate its appropriateness. These theoretical considerations came out of my respect for psychodynamic theory and practice, since these were the professional tools that I was primarily using, and I wanted to be able to explain the facilitative effect of spiritual practice in terms that were scientific so it could be taught in a systematic way.

I have chosen the clinical vignettes that follow to demonstrate the value of spiritual practices across a wide spectrum of emotional difficulties. Typically, transpersonal psychology has presented spiritual systems as the growth tool appropriate for persons at a relatively mature, post-neurotic level of ego development (Wilber, Engler, & Brown, 1986). The shift from a predominantly self-preoccupied (or immediate family–preoccupied) stance to a position of identification with (and concern for) people and life in general is noted in the last stages of ego development described by Erik Erikson in the *Eight Stages of Man* (1950b). It was perhaps best summarized by Engler (Wilber, Engler, & Brown, 1986) when he wrote that you have to become a somebody before you become a nobody.

What I believe I can add from my own clinical practice experience is that while spiritual practice, in theory, promotes ego transcendence, it also serves as a healer and consolidator of the ego at more fragile levels of psychological development. To demonstrate this, the next six vignettes are presented in ascending order of ego development.

John is a seventy-four-year-old man whom I have been seeing on a once-a-month basis for the past thirty-two years. His clinical diagnosis is paranoid schizophrenia. He has been able, with Mellaril (a phenothiazine), to maintain a solitary existence and (until his recent retirement) to handle a non-stressful job; however, on those occasions when he stopped the Mellaril, he became disorganized, confused, and his paranoid ideation became severe enough for him to require hospitalization. Until he began working with *A Course in Miracles* (which I suggested to him when he retired, hoping it might occupy his otherwise empty days), his attitude toward all people was angry and aversive. Working with *A Course in Miracles*, where a great emphasis is placed on the pleasure and peace of mind that comes from the practice of forgiveness, seems to have lessened his fear system. He read the *Course* several hours each day and reported that he was smiling at strangers in the supermarket, a new behavior he recognized as a major breakthrough.

It is important to add that, although he has breakthrough experiences of kind feelings and experiences less paranoia, his underlying psychosis remains intact. When his neighbor's dog soils his garden, rather than rage at his neighbor, he faults himself for not sending his neighbor enough loving thoughts. He seems to have used spiritual truth to substitute a less harmful delusion for a more abusive delusion. The net result, however, is that he feels calmer, less depressed, and more friendly to his family and others. John has spontaneously noted, and mentioned to me, that in periods when he neglects his daily practice, his level of antipathy toward others increases, and more benign feelings return when he resumes daily practice.

Kathleen was a fifty-year-old woman who sought therapy as a relief for bouts of obsessive worrying about issues for which she felt (unreasonably) responsible and guilty. Her parents, fearful and dogmatic in their interpretation of Catholicism, had sent her to boarding school where the nuns had reinforced the idea that she was guilty if she experienced pleasure, especially if others were experiencing pain. At the time she came to see me, her sister, recently widowed, was wanting to live with her. Kathleen's husband was opposed to it, and Kathleen herself didn't want it, but the conflict and guilt she felt over her "dilemma" were unmanageable. Her other "dilemma" was her husband's recent retirement and his wish that she accompany him in his pleasant leisure activities. The more pleasant the activity, the more anxious Kathleen became.

Her mood was generally tense and irritable, with minimal ability or interest in self-reflection. The source of her problem, Kathleen insisted, was external. If only her sister (or husband) would not present her with "dilemmas," she would, she insisted, be fine. Her general lack of empathic depth, her frequent outbursts of anger and rage at her husband, and her sense of outrage about everyone in her life who had "done her wrong" seemed typical borderline pathology. She did not appear at all to be a candidate for exploratory therapy, since her frenzy about her "worries" left her no space to witness her behavior as possibly being related to factors within herself. She probably would have been a good candidate for drug therapy, but she refused to consider it since her aunt had been hospitalized for "mental illness" and, to Kathleen, taking drugs would mean that she, too, was "crazy."

Kathleen wanted relief from her pain, immediately. When I suggested that meditation might attenuate her worrying, she was interested. However, she felt sure that sitting down to meditate in the middle of worrying "will only make me more agitated!" She agreed to try a form of moving meditation—walking briskly and repeating to herself (silently or aloud), "May I be happy! May I be peaceful!" with each step. I told her this was a practice that came from Buddhism, and she agreed to do it in spite of what she called her "bad feelings about religion."

She was an avid walker and lived conveniently close to many hiking trails. If she stayed alert as she walked along, if she noted the early onset of a worrisome thought and immediately began her meditative resolves ("May I be happy! May I be peaceful!"), Kathleen discovered she could avert a full-scale barrage of obsession. Learning that she had some control over her mind states made them less frightening and led to a general lessening of her anxieties. This might have been an appropriate time to do some depth psychotherapy to try to repair some narcissistic damage and/or resolve some of the roots of her guilt, but Kathleen wasn't interested.

The recitation of these phrases (Metta meditation) was used by Kathleen as a tool to concentrate her mind. Experienced meditators report that two capacities of a concentrated mind are calmness and one-pointedness. Kathleen's ability to focus her mind on these phrases kept her mind free of the "trigger" thoughts that resulted in obsessive guilt. Whatever calm she experienced was an antidote to her anxiety, and her mood seemed much improved.

I think it was important that I suggested these particular phrases to Kathleen. She probably could have developed concentration saying, "One, two" or "Pepsi-Cola, Coca-Cola," with every step. However, I think the message of these Metta phrases—that it is permissible (and not selfish) to "pray" for one's own happiness and peacefulness—was specifically valuable for her. Furthermore, I believe the fact that I "prescribed" them made it possible for Kathleen to internalize an image of a more nurturing, caring parent than either of her actual parents had been.

Paul was another person whose diagnosis (borderline psychotic) reflected his high level of anger and inability to control his rage. When he was referred to me he was on psychiatric disability leave from work because of depression and suicidal thoughts. He was unable to take any psychiatric drugs because his work involved operating heavy machinery.

Paul had little capacity for introspective reflection, so in our sessions we talked mostly about his world view and his thoughts about life. As he was more comfortable with ideas than with feelings, I suggested that he read various spiritual books that I was interested in at that time. I think it was beneficial to Paul to feel that I respected him enough to share with him books and ideas that were important to me.

Since Paul particularly enjoyed reading *The Experience of Insight* by Joseph Goldstein, I encouraged him to attend a ten-day Vipassana meditation retreat. The technique taught at these retreats involves noting (internally, silently) what one's experience is in every moment. The goal of this noting is ultimately to observe the ephemeral nature of all experience. In this tradition, the deepening awareness of the inevitability of change through moment-to-moment experience allows the individual to live more calmly with all experiences, pleasant as well as unpleasant.

In the early stages of this form of meditation, precise noting is used as a way of concentrating the mind, of cultivating the ability of the mind not to wander. It is believed that this level of concentration is a prerequisite for clear understanding of the fact of change. Although the practice of "noting" continues at all levels of practice, in the beginning it is used to develop concentration, whereas at later stages it serves to bring the attention to the direct intuition of impermanence.

Paul became a fantastic meditator in the sense of being able, almost obsessively, to note what was happening at every moment. He made no attempt, nor did his teachers encourage him, to use his concentration to reflect more deeply into the nature of his experience. He was very pleased with his meditation as the concentration he developed improved his mood, his rage diminished, and his suicidal thoughts disappeared. He felt proud of himself as a "good meditator" in the company of people whose ideals he admired.

I think there were aspects of Paul's fragile self-system, probably the result of his childhood experiences with unempathic, distant parents, that were healed by his sense of doing a practice that he knew was important to me. I believe this healing happened in the realm of "idealizing" and "mirroring" transferences as described by Heinz Kohut and other Self-Psychologists (Roe & MacIsaac, 1989).

> In our conversations together, Paul talked about his interest in this new (for him) philosophic system and his pleasure about how effective his meditation was in promoting his sense of well-being. He imagined me to be a much more accomplished meditator and to be more spiritually a sage than I actually was. While I certainly didn't pretend any higher level of sophistication or attainment than I had in either category, neither did I strongly protest. I felt that this was a form of idealizing transference in which Paul idealized me by doing "my" practice and espousing "my" ideals of good will and kindness.

In fact, I was pleased that Paul had such good results from his meditative practice, and I was delighted that his life circumstances seemed to be improving. I am sure that Paul sensed this pleasure in me. In terms of Self-Psychology, this "mirroring back" to a person the fact that he/she is well liked is a major component in the developing ego's consolidation of self-esteem and self-confidence. These two aspects of early childhood positive transferences do not call for interpretation. Indeed, interpreting them would be counterproductive.

After leaving the retreat, Paul was able to continue his practice of noting and included a regular period of walking (with noting) in his daily regime. The concentration he maintained by doing this stabilized his improved mood sufficiently for him to be able to return to his job. Although he had previously had difficulties at work, with frequent outbursts of rage at co-workers, he continued his "noting" practice at his job and found he was able to maintain his good feelings there as well. Probably helped along by the positive feedback from his wife and co-workers, Paul has maintained his meditative practice and psychological well-being for fourteen years.

Paul, like Kathleen, used a piece of contemplative practice from the Buddhist tradition for a specific purpose. For people who are able to reflect on their noting experience and intuit the changing nature of phenomena, Vipassana meditation often has the effect of loosening ego defenses and allowing neurotic conflicts to emerge. The next clinical vignette presents an example of this. The experiences of Kathleen and Paul suggest that the psyche will select what it most needs for healing. For both of them, concentration (with its benefits of a sense of calm and well-being) was what was most beneficial.

Frank was a thirty-seven-year-old engineer who sought treatment for anxiety and depression which had been increasing since the death of his father one year previously. Although he loved his two sons, he felt stuck in his marriage, unable to assert himself with his wife who was harsh and critical. Like his mother, she was beautiful and seductive, but narcissistically preoccupied and unable to intuit or respond to the needs of others. Frank, as a child, had felt ashamed of his father's timidity.

I saw no evidence of narcissistic character pathology in Frank. He was respected by his co-workers and had some cordial, although not intimate, friendships. His manner with me was genial and sincere, but guarded. I thought that Frank's anxiety about asserting himself with his wife was a repetition of his relationship with his mother and that his depression probably masked his anger toward his father for not protecting both himself and Frank from his wife's wrath.

Treatment with Frank was traditional in the sense that he was encouraged by me to free associate, to say his thoughts and feelings as they arose. Over the course of two years, he spoke often of his difficulties with his wife, and, indeed, began to be more assertive (with my encouragement) about his feelings and needs in that relationship. In time, he could intellectually speculate about the roots of his anxiety, but I did not feel that major unconscious material emerged.

Frank expressed interest in meditation as a way to calm his anxiety, and I suggested to him that he attend a ten-day Vipassana retreat. Although these retreats are held completely in silence, Frank "fell in love" with the woman sitting next to him in the meditation hall, a woman he didn't know at all. He was amazed and dismayed to find his mind constantly preoccupied with intense sexual fantasies of all varieties with this woman as his partner. When her place was vacant the morning before the retreat was to end, he was heartbroken, and, when he observed her in the parking lot leaving with another man, he was furious. In fact, he was aware of wanting to kill the man.

When Frank returned from the retreat and came for his next appointment, he was eager to tell me the content of his experience since it had been surprising in its forcefulness. However, as he recounted his story, he became increasingly anxious. Suddenly, he was convinced that I would be critical of him, that he had been a "bad meditator," had "missed the opportunity to meditate," or "spent the time entertaining himself with sexual fantasies."

We then spent several months working through, in depth, the meaning of Frank's triangular (Oedipal) experience with the man and woman at the retreat. Many previously unconscious memories arose from his own childhood which expressed his triangular relationship with his parents. At the same time, his reactions to me as an invalidating mother became clear to him. He began to see how he (unconsciously) continued to populate his world with "invalidating mothers" and how his general timidity was a characterological defense against the pain of humiliation. While he had previously only been aware of positive feelings toward his father, he now discovered that he had also been angry at his father for not protecting him from his mother. His guilt about his oedipal strivings had prevented him from expressing this anger. Probably his father's death had reactivated Frank's guilt about his aggressive feelings toward him and accounted for his depression. As these childhood guilts were uncovered and worked through, both his anxiety and depression subsided.

Frank was able to communicate more effectively with his wife as unconscious material was resolved. And, as he began to stand up for himself against her criticism, she was initially startled and defensive.

Frank also reported, however, that she said he was more "manly" now that he was assertive and that she found it attractive. My recommendation to Frank as he terminated therapy with me was that he might later want to do some couples' work with his wife, perhaps attending some "marriage encounter" workshops since they both had Catholic backgrounds and these workshops, in the Catholic tradition, emphasize empathic communication.

The next two vignettes have been included because, in both cases, the recommendation of spiritual practice had positive results and was suggested instead of, rather than in addition to, psychotherapy. In the first situation, there certainly were issues present that might have been helped by therapy, but there was not enough motivation present to make therapy successful. In the second situation, I did not see any major psychological lesions or unconscious conflicts. I felt that the most significant source of emotional pain was the awakening to the existential dilemma of the fragile and changing nature of life, issues more appropriately addressed in the realm of philosophy and religion than in psychotherapy.

Elliot was a thirty-nine-year-old computer programmer who had quit his job a year previously when he had been passed over for a promotion. Since that time he had been living on his savings, brooding about the unfair way he had been treated, and struggling in an acrimonious relationship with a woman with whom he had been living for six years. She apparently loved him and wanted to marry and have a family with him, but he experienced her urging that he get a job as "hassling" and was afraid that marriage would mean he wasn't "free." He had "tried therapy" some years earlier and thought it was "worthless," but he had heard good things about me from a friend, a former patient of mine, and came to see me for what, he announced, was "just one visit."

Elliot's childhood had been difficult. Both of his parents drank excessively, although both managed to maintain their status as university professors. Although Elliot was physically well cared for (there were always students available to babysit), he felt his parents were remote, enjoying their status with students more than they enjoyed spending time with him.

As a boy, Elliot was bright enough to do well in school with no effort at all. He often stole money from his parents, went to movies instead of school, and lied about where he had been. He felt he was "smart enough not to have to do what everyone else did." As an adult, he began to drink excessively, and his two previous relationships with women had ended because they found him "too selfish."

I knew that I had only one session to work with Elliot. I felt that his narcissistic character pathology, his sense of being entitled to do whatever suited him, was his defense against the fear and sadness he must have felt by being "abandoned" by his parents. My experience is that character pathology changes slowly, over years of therapy. Also, Elliot's previous therapeutic experience had not been helpful, and he wasn't motivated to try more.

I made as many empathic remarks as I could about the degree of pain he must be feeling to cause him to continue to drink excessively and about his pain in his relationship. I asked him about the role of religion in his life, and he said that his parents had mocked it, considering it unscientific and childish. The woman he lived with attended church each week, and he sometimes accompanied her since she liked it when he did. He admitted that he often felt soothed by being in church, but he felt "weird" about praying, didn't understand a lot of what he heard there, and felt inhibited about asking.

I suggested that he buy a copy of *A Course in Miracles* and see if it interested him at all to work with it. I told him that I thought he had psychological problems (no news to him) but that this did not seem the right time for him to work on them. I said that I felt that his psychological problems, causing him to be "stuck" in his life, were now bringing up existential problems. His life was passing by, without particular meaning or goals. *A Course in Miracles* offers a framework of meaning in life. Also, for those people who appreciate its style and are motivated to do the exercises, it has a soothing effect.

I had a note from Elliott three months later, thanking me for my suggestion of *A Course in Miracles* and reporting that he was feeling much better. He has kept in touch with me at regular intervals. It is two years since our meeting, and he has returned to work, married, and had a child. He reports that he was so profoundly moved by the message of forgiveness of *A Course of Miracles* that he experienced a "change of heart." His former brooding style, finding fault with others in his life for not attending to his needs, had been, he said, consciously replaced by forgiveness. The immediate positive feedback from this change dramatically increased his energy level, helping him get a job. He had recognized that he needed to stop drinking alcohol entirely and had begun attending AA twelve-step meetings. He began to go to church regularly with his wife and eventually organized a weekly *Course in Miracles* discussion group as part of his church's adult education program.

My theoretical guess about Elliot's dramatic "recovery" is that the *Course* provided him with the sense that he was loved in much the same way that an empathic therapist would have done over years of therapy. According to the *Course*, all beings are interrelated, "at one with God." Sin, rather than relating to "bad" behaviors, is forgetting the oneness we all have with each other and with God. Elliot understood the "bad" behaviors of his youth (which had damaged his self-esteem system) as acts of ignorance rather than malevolence, allowing his guilt to give way to remorse and then to compassion for himself as well as to the people he had hurt. As Elliot's self-hatred diminished, he was able to stop his self-destructive behavior (e.g., poor work performance and selfish relational style). As he began to like himself, he was able to identify with Jesus, or the Holy Spirit, as a compassionate being concerned about the well-being of others and acting out of kindness. This positive identification could replace the unconscious (and painful) sense he had as a child that he was not worthy of his parents' attention.

I believe the *Course* was particularly the correct therapeutic tool for Elliot for two reasons. The first, obviously, is that he wasn't interested in psychotherapy. The second is that the practice of the *Course* is private and controlled by the practitioner. Elliot's narcissistic wounding was so painful and the shame about disclosing how badly he actually had felt when stealing, or cutting school, or drinking, was so deep that it would have taken him a long time to do that in the presence of another person. Even a skilled therapist would require a long time to develop that degree of trust. Also, since the *Course* has a built-in soothing mechanism, in the form of daily phrases to be repeated to oneself, the experience of self-discovery and self-acceptance can be titrated by the practitioner to the speed that he or she can best tolerate.

> Larry came to see me because he had begun to experience catastrophic thoughts and fears about the well-being of his twin sons, freshmen in high school. He knew that his worries had begun suddenly when he had heard about the death of his college rommate's son in a skiing accident. He felt that his worries were "unreasonable," that his sons were as cautious and reliable as he was. He was concerned that his fears, leading him to strictly supervise his sons' activities, would alienate them from him. He said that every time he saw them leave the house he would wonder if he would ever see them again. He reported that he never before recognized how fragile life is, and it was terrifying to him. He worried that he might be "going crazy." He looked at his friends and was amazed that they didn't appear to see things as he did (since they seemed at ease) and that made him feel *more* crazy.
>
> I met with Larry twice, leaving a week between the sessions to see if any significant material (which might indicate a need for psycho-

therapy) arose in response to our first session. My first impression, confirmed when we met again, was that he was psychologically quite healthy. His childhood seemed to have been untraumatic, and he liked his parents. He had been married for sixteen years, had a warm and loving relationship with his wife, was successful in his career, and, until this recent onset of fears, had been congratulating himself on constructing a perfect life for himself and his family.

I agreed with Larry that life is, indeed, fragile and told him that many people protected themselves from recognizing that truth by diverting themselves or by imagining that, if they were always "in control," they would be immune to life's pain. I said that I felt that the shock of his friend's son's death had made it impossible for him to avoid confronting this truth and that his currently excessive anxiety about his sons and his attempts to control and supervise their behavior were his reaction to this discovery.

I told Larry I didn't think he needed psychotherapy, that the issues confronting him seemed primarily spiritual ones. He had no interest in religion, since the reform Judaism of his youth had seemed like a social club, without spiritual meaning. He was interested in my suggestion that meditation might relax his anxiety and took an introductory Mindfulness Meditation course (Vipassana) being given at a local junior college. This interested him enough to try a weekend retreat and, some months later, a ten-day retreat. He telephoned me a year after our initial visit to thank me for referring him to meditation practice and for reassuring him about his mental health. He reported that his anxiety level had subsided and his terror about the possibility of something sad happening to one of his loved ones had mellowed into a heightened appreciation of the love he felt for them and gratitude about their current wellness.

Larry had a hard time with the Vipassana meditation technique, since he found it hard to concentrate. He spent the time at retreats thinking about his family and speculating about philosophy. He found he experienced the most support and solace from listening to the teachers explain Buddhist philosophy. He said, "I never heard so many people talk so much about suffering who seemed so happy!"

I believe it was helpful to Larry to have the support of teachers validating his intuition about the truth of suffering. The fact that they spoke candidly about the fragility of life, and yet seemed able to live relational, committed, enthusiastic lives was very reassuring to him. His perception that his frightened thoughts meant that he was "going crazy" was replaced by the sense that he now saw things clearly and had become more mature. A by-product of his changing awareness was his resolve to lighten his heavy work load and spend more time with his family.

These case studies of patients at different levels of ego development clearly demonstrate how various aspects of spiritual traditions (e.g., meditation, reading, studying, support of a spiritual community) can be used by the ego in healing. Furthermore, patients seem to have an intuitive wisdom as to which practice will be beneficial, and this adds additional conviction to my recommending spiritual practice to my patients. This may, indeed, be the root of a transpersonal approach—*to trust in and appreciate the power of spiritual experiences.*

III

Western Psychotherapy and Eastern Traditions

The earliest explorations and establishment of European trade routes and relations with the East resulted in a perfectly logical, yet unforeseen, side effect: an introduction to, and creation of a need for, the spiritual wares as well as the exotic material wares of the East. However, wisdom and enlightenment are not as easily transported or assimilated into the life of the westerner. Gold is gold no matter how far it has traveled, enlightenment is not.

This section represents the work of practitioners who have attempted the near impossible, namely, the integration of Eastern spiritual ways with Western psychological ways, while at the same time preserving the discreteness and purity of each. The contributors to this section examine major Eastern traditions, including Buddhism, Sufism, yoga.

Once again, these authors all face squarely up to the questions of meaning and of self-transcendent consciousness—two questions without absolute answers. It is their contention that Eastern approaches offer us more potential ability to pursue the answers for ourselves. These traditions do not simply hand us food and tell us how to cook it; they offer us the possibility of growing our own.

Integrating Eastern thought into the Western mind can happen in many ways. Stephen Schoen focuses on transcendence of ego; Olaf Gary Deatherage describes his use of mindfulness meditation as a therapeutic technique; Daniel Goleman focuses on the attainment of mindfulness and insight as a way to inhibit unhealthy states; Arthur Deikman examines the contribution to meaning and changing consciousness made by Sufi stories; and John Enright looks at the way renaming symptoms can contribute to enlightenment and shifts in consciousness.

In this new edition, W. Michael Keane and Stephen Cope explore an innovative integration of yoga and psychotherapy; Sylvia Boorstein contributes her perspective on the interconnection between psychological and spiritual insights, discussing both their potential and their limitations; John Nelson explains his view of the need for an expansion of the traditional Western psychiatric diagnosticians' viewpoint to include the transpersonal, recognizing the significance of the chakras in the spiritual evolution of the individual.

The contributing authors included in this section—like all of the contributors to this collection—give us hope that Eastern wisdom is transportable to the West. While it may not have the same external form, it can be even more powerful in a form that retains its essence but has been adapted for Western understanding.

12

Gestalt Therapy and Buddhist Teachings

Stephen Schoen

Stephen Schoen's observation that "therapists may face here the letting go of a culture form" is an appropriate description of the provocative tone and content of his own chapter. Schoen examines first the similarities and the differences between Gestalt therapy and Buddhist belief, and then some of the implications of this comparison for present therapeutic modes.

The two approaches, according to the author, have these elements in common: first, both have faith in the human capacity to control habit creation; second, both allow one to consider how one creates one's own suffering. There the commonalities end. The first main difference Schoen sees between the two approaches is that Gestalt therapy "does not differentiate between the 'I' separable from experiencing and the 'I' inseparable. . . . This distinction," he says, "is normative in Buddhism." Gestalt therapy strongly validates a belief in "subject-I"—a validation that is greatly needed. However, subject-I can result in a prima donna attitude towards life and can turn itself into an object of fetishism.

From this point on, Buddhism is needed to expand the concept of ego. "It becomes obvious," says Schoen, "that Buddhists have a saltier conception of mental health" than westerners. The Buddhists way challenges not only the concept of "egoitis" but also the concept of "ego." Here, both therapist and patient have some hard work to do, because all too frequently both have a serious investment in the perpetuation of the illusion of ego.

Schoen's perspective, extending as it does the scope of Gestalt therapy as traditionally presented and meshing it with views on the spiritual quest, especially the Buddhist view, offers each of us a challenge to re-examination and transformation.

THROUGH THE CROSSCURRENTS of twentieth-century ideas on mental health and disorder, Gestalt therapy flows as a philosophy of consciousness. The powers ascribed to the Freudian unconscious—its passion, its irrationality, its eruptiveness in the service of the pleasure principle—all belong, says Gestalt therapy, to an unusually wide scope of conscious living. Full life exists in presentness and personalness of awareness, and in responsibility for oneself.

This life is intrinsically exciting. It invites and challenges us to vigilant freedom and flexibility with ourselves. By contrast, the life deficient in, or disturbed by, freedom and flexibility continually pushes freedom away. This dissociation creates a kind of unconscious which the person fears as much as diabolical possession. It is alien and brutal, and strong.

Fundamentally, we are our own chosen oppressors. As T. S. Eliot (1943, line 101) wrote, we are "distracted from distraction by distraction" in the strainings of the conscious; we are distracted by the "chattering of our minds," as Krishnamurti (1969, p. 24) says. This view does not deny the physiological unconscious; we live chiefly by functions we have no awareness of: cells metabolize, the heart beats, eyes see. However this unconscious is a far cry from Freud's "seething cauldron." (1965, Lecture XXXI, p. 65). It is a marvel of efficiency, order, balance. Crucial to the increasing numbers of psychosomatic diseases is how we look to oppressions by consciousness again, how we drive or cramp ourselves. We take the conscious as the source of mental problems, whether these appear in maladaptations of waking life or in dreams; in fact, dreams are themselves the branchings of consciousness in sleep. We also consider that the conscious is able to bring about its own cure.

These views also lead to the realm of religious wisdom; here, too, consciousness sees its own sickness and works its own cure. Lao-tse exhorts: "Surrender yourself humbly. Then you can be trusted to care for all things" (Feng & English, verse 13). The teachings of Buddhism, in particular, detail the problems of surrender, the reluctance of the conscious mind to give up its anguish, at the same time announcing the infinite wholeness of the enlightened state.

Gestalt thought approaches this wisdom and joins with it in two ways. First, both have a faith in the human capacity for rehabituation. We do not stand still in thought and feeling, and it is death to want to do so. The inner injunctions from which we suffer ("I should be better organized," "You should not disappoint me") must be recognized and allowed free play in awareness in order for the *Gestalten* of which they are a part to complete themselves and let go of us. That is the art of therapy. Onward flowing with awareness is the essence of human life. If, for example, my genetic code decreed that I could *not* play wrong notes in a Chopin étude, I would have a sense of fated facility as a pianist that I do not have now. However, I would lack the awareness, the alert supervision, sense of power, and esthetic mettle that comes with developing a skilled habit and attuning it to a musical end. This conscious control of habit creation—evaluating the habit's fitness, keeping it on course, relinquishing it as my needs and purposes determine—is the special prerogative and responsibility of the human being. According to Zen, eating when hungry and sleeping when tired are not mere reflexes either; they are my achievement and my responsibility.

Awareness together with response to what goes on in the present is always awareness of something new, although the parts of any situation may be familiar. I see my car, for instance, and approach it. I reach in my pocket for the key to unlock the door. I quickly survey the parts of the situation: key, car, locale, time of day, mood. However, in the very act of placing the key in the lock, I encounter something new; a new and unforeseen pattern is present. We live always in unique, freshly disclosed patterns—a sudden doubt, a sudden quarrel, a sudden pleasure—and trying to understand them in the light of their separable parts results only in confusion and self-torment.

There is a second major bond between Gestalt therapy and Buddhist psychology. I reach into my pocket for the key—and it isn't there. I go back to my house and search. I can't find it. Now the newness of the situation is dramatic. I feel a tingling of uncertainty, which grows quickly to panic oddly touched with exhilaration. Then I set to worrying in earnest. I have serious plans for the day, meetings, appointments. Everything is interrupted. I sit down to collect myself, to make new plans. I don't want to let others down. I wish, if at all possible, to feel composed. Then, suddenly, I ask myself: *Must* I be upset? At this level of self-awareness I confront, to my surprise, very deep premises indeed: the importance of my keeping to a plan, the expectation that a program of action must work out, the assumption that I must count on stability and dependability in my environment to feel good, the idea that I must harbor a sense of permanence not only about plans but about my own self in order to feel that I am intact. All this, in one stroke, has been thrown open to question. I face, in the onrush of daily routine, what Chögyam Trungpa calls "a gap." I allow myself to consider how I create my own suffering.

The example is trivial, but the issue resembles the most sustained psychological work. In psychotherapy I discover how I have come to consider myself in a particular way—dependent on my mother, cowed by my father. I then see that I do not have to depend or subjugate myself. I also begin to perceive that I am different according to the actual situation—now I am dependent, now I am independent. My "self" lacks a stable meaning altogether. It takes on, in Gregory Bateson's words, "a sort of irrelevance."

The Abyss between Gestalt Therapy
and Buddhism: Subject-"I"

"The true nature of man," Fritz Perls writes in *The Gestalt Approach* (p. 49), "is integrity. Only in an integrated spontaneity and deliberateness does he make a sound existential choice." The aim of therapy is to develop the patient's capacity for self-support. To this end, characteristically, patients are asked to begin a series of sentences with "Now I am aware . . . ." In this way, they focus on the variety and continuous change of their present experience, and take responsibility for it.

But responsibility to what? To what kind of "I"? Am I learning that the actual present shows me to be something more than I had formerly noticed or imagined? Or do I learn that the present is something more than the "I" which seeks to experience it so that the present which I am is all that I am? Gestalt is ambiguous here. Gestalt welcomes the inner immensity which Keats describes as the acceptance of life beyond its good and evil; Gestalt also approves Emerson's large discourse on the "transcendent simplicity and energy of the . . . deep power in which we exist." (1951, para. 3) However, Gestalt philosophy fails to distinguish sharply between *particular* Gestalts. It does not differentiate between the "I" separable from experiencing and the "I" inseparable about which Keats and Emerson are speaking. This distinction is normative in Buddhism. And it clarifies what I believe is always at stake in the Gestalt goal of "organismic unity."

There is a distinction between a stationary "I" and a fluid "I"; between a subject-I, which is a stable entity, and a predicate-I, which varies in each different context; between an "I" that is enduring substance and an "I" that, when taken for substance, is illusory.

Gestalt therapy gives vivid evidence of subject-I. First, the work as a whole regularly slopes in this direction, although for a while the slope is imperceptible. The therapist asking the patient to be alert to each element of an inner process sounds similar concern to the Buddha's directing attention to the precise events of the present, as, for example, in his teaching a village woman to be aware of each moment as she draws water from a well. By means of this present-centeredness, the Gestalt viewpoint seeks to reconcile—to quote Fritz Perls's words about the contents of a dream—"essences of the personality" (1975). In this way, we complete unfinished situations from the past (the colloquial expression for this is "cleaning up my shit"). In this liberated awareness, we now often accept a "true me," a "natural me," and suddenly the liberation is curtailed again. From the open immediacy of the moment, and somehow not noticing the shift, we return over time to a few set attitudes and stability. It is as if we slid smoothly over a polished rounded edge onto a new position for the I, which is more secure and durable than the past's. We hold on again; this time it is to "my real self," "my authentic, centered self," not faithful to our awareness that what at bottom is incompletable is the Me and that to complete is to let go.

What is this "real me" like? People speak at length about "my rights." The phrase is thrown down as a challenge, spoken as one might speak of real estate property lines, sanctioned and sanctified by natural law. The phrase asserts what one feels entitled to from the world: "My right to speak and to be heard. My right to my way. And to get you, if I possibly can, to give me my way. I stand up for myself. I know how to get tough." For these people, anger is a particular allegiance. They are ready for a state of feud. They know how to remain *against* someone or something. Demanding, protesting, quick on the draw, explicitly egocentric, they may feel quite liberated from depriving and intimidating persons in their own past. But in their liberal provocations of the environment, we may uneasily suspect a provocative parent styled up to date.

Assertion itself is not what I am derogating. The issue, rather, is the boundary of assertions, the "contact boundary" with the surroundings that Gestalt therapists look to as vital for the individual's functioning. This boundary has one meaning for the person full of subject-I and occupied with "my rights"; it has quite different meaning for the person without this I, who has no lasting Me to defend, free to be open, or to share. Gestalt thought does not ordinarily dwell on this distinction. It emphasizes the importance of being clear about oneself, and it sets no value on any one inner state over another.

However, in the Buddhist view, clarity itself has consequences. It means attention to the actual flow of experience, to all this flow, including fundamental not-clinging to a sense of personal permanence and stability. So clarity also appraises qualities of contact. The Buddhists value "generous fearlessness," an attitude of warm welcome toward others which is both unsentimental and candid. Certainly, the person without subject-I needs withdrawal as well as contact. He tries. He has his own boundaries—but he does not have to patrol them.

Subject-I is also famous today for defense of "my space." Property lines again! Here the geographical reference is literal. Or is it? Do these people have a physical space in mind, a space they need for growth or replenishment like a plant? Or are they talking of a power they want to possess, invisible to others, tangible to them, a kind of separate being, invoked like a "familiar" from the spirit world to stand by them? "I need more space," they say. "You are invading my space." The emphasis is on "you" and "my." And the tone, abrupt. The attitude is insular; it does not ask for the nurture which requires not only space but time and support from the environment. Instead, the impetus is to push the environment away. "I could be bounded in a nutshell," confided Hamlet, "and count myself a king of infinite space, were it not that I have bad dreams." (Act II, Scene 2, lines 252–254) One could wonder what the bad dreams of Hamlet's modern equivalents contain.

Again I have sketched a type of difficult prima donna whose insistent separateness in living is on guard against the surroundings. While there is such a thing as the natural spaciousness of unself-conscious life, as Chögyam Trungpa describes it, a great deal of the "emotional space" cultivated today seems to be directly linked to limitations put on the inner life by the needs of the subject-I—"my satisfactions," "my activities." This I, intent on self-demonstration, on flexing its muscles and proving its control, tends to be claustrophobic about *Lebensraum*. It pushes against its own barriers as though these were in external space; but the barriers are made of its graspings to secure itself. In this process, creativity has no space, even though the creative life actually requires relatively little physical space. Schubert wrote songs while eating dinner in a café; Jane Austen worked on complex, meticulous novels at a table in the parlor with family members walking round. Seclusion and privacy are important for much work and self-nourishment. A woman, for example, needs to get away from the demands of a job, a baby, housework. But the preoccupation with "my space" adds a further obstacle; it shuts off awareness of the space at *hand* in personal openness.

Rights, space. These two are, in a sense, preliminary to the main concern of subject-I: "my wants." The problem is subtle because desire is indefinitely variable in spontaneous living; isn't awareness of "what I want" a simple good?

However, if I want most of all to feel solid and whole, then out of the flow of impulse I build a multifaceted structure. This structure is not my narrow self prior to therapy, a self that chose approved responses and avoided the others. This is a new version of my old self, more complex, self-tolerant— a faceted self embellished with acceptance of my wishes, my moods, fascinated with my different ways of being and the "interesting spaces I get into," full of "my existential integrity." I may pursue many relationships, take drugs to expand my mind. I may invite varieties of stress—go without sleep for several days, for example, because I am intrigued with the range and diversity of my power to experience.

This savored power, however, remains restless and threatened. It seeks continual shots in the arm. Experiences are hoarded; experiencing becomes a program. Enjoyment—at what price? "Nothing is more hopeless than a scheme of merriment," Dr. Samuel Johnson once observed (Boswell, p. 337). Wanting to be intact and durable, I can only fear the possibility of my exhaustion and cannot perceive that exhaustion may indeed be a great chance for new discovery because predicate-I always finds "myself" simply and exactly in what is happening to me. I am aware of but not separate from my situation. However, when I no longer hold on to my variability, then the variability I find in myself without drugs, the other person I respond to free of fantasy and design—unrestricted experience, as the Buddhists say, in its "original state"—emerges.

Chögyam Trungpa uses the word *ego* for subject-I. At first glance, this is not the ego that Freud defined, the ego that exemplifies the reality principle and works hard to accommodate both psychic demand and the external world. Yet, from another viewpoint, it is the same ego—and the Buddhists have shifted this viewpoint fundamentally. The ego does not bring together different realms, the inner and the outer. It takes one realm apart. And having divided the self from the environment, all its well-intentioned efforts on behalf of the reality principle remain harassed and uneasy. In the ego's wish to establish its own permanence and composure, reality itself is given an ironic twist, because ego's stable, solid existence is actually stable, solid hallucination. The very word *ego,* as used here, connects its familiar English connotation of foolish and unreal self-importance with Buddhist teaching.

The word *ego* deserves an extension. When the ego acts to maintain itself by clinging to and defending its structure with hue and cry, when it is full of management, determination, and cunning, it is inflamed. We have egoitis. As with physical inflammation, the ego at this time is painful, tender, and swollen. It musters itself first against assaults from the environment, then against its own internalization of these assaults. It is just this congested, defensive gathering together of oneself that is usually termed *neurosis.* All the symptoms of neurosis—anxiety, depression, obsessional thought, phobic avoidance, and self-belittling—express the pain and tenderness of egoitis. All the neurotic mechanisms—the defensive manipulations of the surroundings, the inattention to what actually goes on in the environment and in one's own response to it—contribute to keeping egoitis stable and to warding off awareness of the illusions that maintain it.

In schizophrenic psychosis, the individual has been battered more drastically. The ego he has put together is itself under assault; he is, in Gregory Bateson's words, "penalized for the basic function of pattern formation" (1966, p. 32). He finds the I intolerable and pushes it from him. In our time, the psychotic state has often been championed as a state of personal freedom. It is true that the schizophrenic is a radical critic of the people who thwart him and that he excels at avoiding or caricaturing them. But also he avoids subject-I, and remains phobic toward it, flees from it, and deflects it in unidentified metaphor, games, or babble. He maintains himself by virtue of this disorder; and thus predicate-I cannot exist either. To discover his own inner harmonies, he must first of all have an environment at once hospitable yet confronting to invite his awareness of his habit of flight.

This view of mental illness, neurotic and psychotic, centers on ego in the closest Buddhist sense. Among Western psychotherapies, Gestalt therapy in particular shares this picture of neurosis and seeks for the individual a clear discrimination of his spontaneity: "what is himself," as Fritz Perls says, "and what is not himself" (1973, p. 26). However, it becomes obvious that Buddhists have a saltier conception of mental health; not only eogitis but solid ego is the problem. And ego, even when clearly recognized or deeply experienced as illusionary, is not about to go away. It will not be dispatched. It may be an inevitable referential structure for human learning in early life. This is the subject-I—whom Buber (1958b, p. 24) pictures so eloquently in *I and Thou*—grown separate from basic predicate-I "shrunk from substance and fullness" and taking the world as a thing to isolate, objectify, and use.

By its holding on like an unvarying mirage, ego asks us to believe in it. "Desire engenders belief," Proust observed. "If we are not usually aware of this, it is because most belief-creating desires last as long as we do" (1966). We are hard put to see through the desire for permanence to its unreality.

Illusions about Therapy

The consequences for therapists of clear seeing in both thought and practice are radical. For example, there is no "correct way" to do therapy. Correctness is a derivative of stability. Correctness is an illusion. There is no "right doctrine" for therapy. Doctrine implies permanent truth. Doctrine is illusion. There is no "correct approach" to cure. Once again, correctness is an illusion. There is, indeed, no cure. "Cure" refers to correctness in behavior. Cure is an illusion.

These statements may seem to abolish psychotherapy itself. Yet if the concern of therapy is to work toward acceptance of experience, then being clear about the illusory nature of experience is what makes therapy possible. The familiar illusions about therapy need to be abolished; without them, therapy is free of rules and manipulation. Rules and manipulation imply illusory stable standards of what is right. How can we really find words for what the conduct of therapy "should be"? "The Tao that can be told," Lao-tse's book begins, "is not the eternal Tao" (Feng & English, verse 1). In therapy as in life, then, reality is unnamable. Therefore, questions about comparative merits of psychotherapeutic approaches and techniques and even the issue "good clinical results" also misrepresent the real thing. The real thing is experiencing what is. At the same time, maintaining the notion of rightness by redefining it as "self-acceptance" is, too, simply a new and dangerous invitation to illusion; "rightness" returns us to illusory objective standards and their illusory evaluation.

The real aim of therapy has nothing to do with correctness or evaluation. It is to be at one with one's experience. This is illustrated in the two examples below.

CASE 1

An earnest young man in a Gestalt training group says to me, "I believe in doing Gestalt thoroughly. I don't learn enough techniques from you."

I ask, "How do you feel now?"

"Very serious. A little depressed."

"Well, be as thorough, as single-minded as you possibly can with a particular technique. Let's see. Choose someone here as a client consulting with you. Observe his or her tone of voice and body language. Then ask your client to exaggerate what you observe."

"Wait a minute. Do *you* believe in this?"

"I believe in your doing whatever you do fully."

A young woman volunteers to be his client. They begin working. He comments scrupulously on her voice and movements. After a minute she starts on her own to exaggerate what he observes. The exercise of technique takes on the spirit of a game.

He turns to me, grinning. "This is *not* what I had in mind."

"Say more."

"I'm feeling perplexed about my original request. And I'm also lighter."

"You are less sure and more free."

He nods thoughtfully. "That's so."

CASE 2

In my office a woman says to me, "When my husband won't give me the warmth I want, I feel it's up to me to make him. The problem is all mine.

"You sound oppressed."

"I feel awful. I feel so driven! God, I sound exactly like my damned driven mother!"

"Let's not try solving anything now." I wait a moment. "That's your approach, isn't it? To solve the difficulty."

"Of course."

"When you're solving a difficulty, you're separate from what you do. I mean, it's different from what you really can do. Like talking to your husband."

"I can do that." She adds grimly, "For what it's worth."

"What it's worth is that you can do it, naturally do it. That it's easy to do."

There is a long pause.

"My mother is on my mind again," she resumes. "She never believed that anything worth doing should be easy to do."

"Poor woman."

"Yes." She begins to weep. "I'm crying for her. For *her.* I never thought I would." She sobs convulsively a few times; then she looks at me and suddenly smiles. "I really am surprising myself."

I touch her arm. "To me you're more alive."

She continues smiling. "And to me."

Buddhism helps us in these clarifications both by its consistency about the illusoriness of ego, of our solid, fixed view of ourselves, and in its appreciation of the difficulty with being clear. Not only are patients anxious to keep ego intact; so are therapists. The ego types have been learned in good measure from Gestalt teachers. The same ego problems are present in religious tradition. The guru approves the fidelity of the disciple; the disciple copies the guru and cannot find his way because of too much modeling of good advice. However, when the powers of ego attachment are at their height, one can do no better than to acknowledge and respect them. The story is told of how upset the guru Marpa was at the death of his son. "Isn't it illusion?" a disciple asked. Marpa answered, "My son's death is a super-illusion" (Trungpa, p. 49). The pain of Marpa's loss will not be gainsaid, yet admits no other realization than this—poignantly comic, poignantly stern. Buddhist teachings themselves advise drily about the spiritual path: "Better not to begin . . . unless you must." But then, once begun, "Better to finish it" (p. 47).

This interweaving of Buddhist and Gestalt perspectives affects many therapists outside of Gestalt. Since Freud's first studies some eighty years ago, the twentieth century has become the era of voyages over unknown waters of the inner life, and of discovery and annexation of its various domains. Freud, Jung, Adler, Reich, and later in this country Sullivan, Erikson, and Bateson have gone out like the European explorers of the sixteenth century seeking—and finding—a new world. By now many basic territories have been charted, and the last twenty-five years have seen them subdivided and evaluated. At the same time, a new psychological vigor has developed in religious thought, especially through the work of Buber in Judaism, Tillich in Christianity, and the influx from Asia in recent years of traditional Buddhist, Taoist, Hindu, and Sufi understanding. These ideas have nourished psychotherapists wanting increased awareness within their own disciplines.

The provinces of the therapist and the guru will remain distinct to the extent that their followers have different goals. People come to therapists out of distress in their living. They are concerned with the content of their distress, and they leave therapy when they feel well enough. They may remain as unenlightened as they please. Seekers of religious wisdom, on their part, look for an inner liberation which religion offers to teach. For them the relevant content may be a spiritual discipline not touching on therapeutic issues like dependency or confusion.

But there is a significant middle place at which the viewpoint of the guru may change clinical psychotherapy as we have known it. This is where the vision of psychological life and spiritual life as one gives therapy a new set of norms and a new dedication. And in this respect, the psychological purity of Buddhist teaching, its constant attention to the pain that comes with our endeavors to feel stable, its clarity about the illusoriness of ego, its practice of seeing precisely, simply, and warmly—all this is a profound contribution to psychotherapy, both within Gestalt and beyond. Whether indeed this approach to the therapeutic in any way satisfies the traditional roles of "therapist" and "patient" is an open question. To complete is to let go. Therapists may face here the letting go of a culture form, the completing of roles which is their transformation.

13

Mindfulness Meditation as Psychotherapy

Olaf G. Deatherage

Olaf G. Deatherage's chapter, on mindfulness meditation, is one of the few in this book that correlate in detail a traditional spiritual practice with traditional psychotherapeutic practice. His findings are particularly interesting because they are drawn from the combined use of both practices with classical psychiatric problems of patients in and out of the hospital.

The use of mindfulness meditation is founded in Buddhist practices directed towards the goal of enlightenment. It also has strong roots in the work of Bhikku Soma, Mahasi Sayadaw, and Nyanoponika Thera. Deatherage studied mindfulness meditation with Joseph Goldstein, a student of Anagarika Munindra, who in turn was a student of Sayadaw, acknowledged as one of the greatest Buddhist meditation teachers living today.

The first techniques of mindfulness which need to be mastered are breathing observation and naming of interruptions. These are the requirements for "bare attention." Observing one's breathing or, in some cases, some other physical process enables one to identify the constant mental interruptions that usually break concentration without conscious awareness. These interruptions are named according to this form: remembering, worrying, hearing, imagining, fantasizing. Whatever the interrupting factor might be, the individual usually tends to use one more than the rest. As Deatherage says, "becoming aware of one's primary interrupting factors can be diagnostically and therapeutically significant because one can clearly see unhealthy, habitual mental processes."

All of these interruptions may be viewed as successful and neurotic ways to avoid spending energy in the not-too-comfortable present. Mindfulness training is, therefore, indicated for "neurotic, anxious, or depressed clients." It is not indicated for "psychotic, senile, or brain-damaged clients." A third mindfulness technique may be practiced to help the client gain distance from either the interruption or the neuroses brought on by confrontation with present reality: the "watcher self." The watcher self is not intended to be a permanent fixture but a means of objectively observing one's own psychological functioning. This part of one's self may be used to examine either emotions or thoughts that occur with monotonous and frightening regularity.

Deatherage states strongly that mindfulness training is not suited to all clients. While it may be used as a primary, secondary, or supplementary part of any psychotherapeutic program, it requires a certain degree of rationality and motivation on the client's part. If the client does not have both of these, then the therapist should be perceptive enough to withhold or defer mindfulness training. When the client does have these qualities, then the training may be used on either a short-term or long-term basis with positive results, as documented in the cases Deatherage provides.

The author believes that mindfulness training also has benefits for the therapist. First, it is possible for the client to continue his or her "therapy" outside the therapeutic hour and thus make more progress. Second, the therapist may gain a great deal personally by practicing these ancient yet modern techniques himself or herself.

MINDFULNESS MEDITATION, like any other approach, is most powerful when employed as part of an overall program of psychotherapy designed specifically for the individual client. It can be a primary, secondary, or supplementary part of any therapy program, depending upon what is appropriate for the client.

This approach to psychotherapy derives directly from Buddhist teachings. It is therefore relevant to mention the philosophical foundation of the techniques. Buddhist thought and practice have always been directed toward providing the individual with a way to gain insight into life experiences, to perceive more clearly the nature of internal and external realities and the relationships between the two. People continuously and rapidly cycle through a multiplicity of moods and emotional states. This cycling process—sometimes termed *samsara*—is inescapable. But it can be seen and accepted, thus providing people with freedom unavailable to others who are unknowingly entrapped in states of psychological distress.

Buddhism uses both philosophy and direct "therapeutic" intervention to accomplish its goal of enlightenment. Therefore the Buddhist approach establishes logical tenets and then provides a way of personally verifying them. For example, the beginning teachings in Buddhism—the so-called Four Noble Truths—observe that everything is impermanent, including one's own life, and that the impermanence of the material world is a primary and direct cause of unhappiness (things and people deteriorate and pass away). Any rational mind can accept the existence of suffering and unhappiness, can perceive the impermanence of the material world, and can to some degree accept the relationship between them. There are ways out of this dilemma, however. Buddhism offers a pathway of coming to know the mental processes and of working directly with these processes to gain insight into—and thus to some degree freedom from—entrapment in the samsaric cycling process.

The mindfulness meditation described here, when practiced diligently and progressively, can potentially lead the practitioner to experience directly the ultimate realities described in Buddhist scriptures. Soma (1949), Sayadaw (1972), and Thera (1972, 1973) describe the Theravada Buddhist mindfulness as *Satipatthana—sati* ("awareness") + *patthana* ("keeping present"). These forms of meditation are the basis of the mindfulness meditation that is discussed here. It is designed to enhance mental health. First it allows one to see one's own mental processes; second, it allows one to exert increasing degrees of control over mental processes; and finally, it allows one to gain freedom from unknown and uncontrolled mental processes. This seemingly impossible task is accomplished through what Thera calls "bare attention" (1972): the accurate, continuous registering at the conscious level of all events occurring in the six sensory modes—seeing, hearing, touching, tasting, smelling, and thinking—without qualitative judgments, evaluation, mental comment, or behavioral act.

Techniques of Bare Attention

How is such an investigation of the mental processes carried out? First, a set of meditative exercises teaches and refines the techniques of bare attention. If one sits quietly with the body comfortable and relaxed, one can practice bare attention through consciously observing the breathing process as one breathes in, pauses, breathes out, pauses longer, and then breathes in again. This concentration on a physical process quickly produces interesting results. Soon, mental events begin to occur and interrupt breath observation. Events external to the body impinge on consciousness—a dog barks, a door closes, the day grows hot, a fly lands on one's face. Awareness of the breathing process is interrupted momentarily as awareness shifts to the sound or other sensation. Awareness arises that breath observation has been interrupted by something particular; breath observation is resumed. Perhaps a memory rises to consciousness, again disrupting the observation process and shifting awareness to the memory for a time; then, realizing that a memory interruption has occurred, one resumes breath observation. Awareness of the breathing process may soon be lost again as a fantasy arises and is played out—what to do during vacation, how to ask the boss for a raise; again awareness eventually arises that breath observation has been interrupted, and it is resumed.

After only a few minutes of breath observation, one realizes that a continuous chain of mental events is taking place, that awareness is flipping from what one is intentionally attending to, the act of breathing, to innumerable others things—bodily sensations, external factors, memories, fantasies. This constant losing and regaining of conscious awareness of what one is doing takes place thousands of times a day. The initial observation of breathing, or any other ongoing process on which attention can be focused, clearly demonstrates the frequency with which this shifting takes place.

Through such observation and through neutral, nonjudgmental naming of each interrupting factor (remembering, worrying, hearing, imagining), one begins to see and appreciate that mental events jump from one event to the next with a staccato rapidity that is seemingly random and chaotic, even frightening. Naming the interrupting factors begins to provide insight into one's unique mental processes and identifies the area with which one must work. One person is interrupted again and again by memories from the past; another is plagued by fantasies of performing heroic acts; a third is interrupted by bodily discomfort, sleepiness, or boredom. Becoming aware of one's primary interrupting factors can be diagnostically and therapeutically significant because one can sometimes clearly see unhealthy, habitual mental processes.

Using Mindfulness Training with Neurotic Patients

While mindfulness training is not indicated for psychotic, senile, or brain-damaged clients, it can be useful with the large group of so-called neurotic, anxious, or depressed clients. Buddhist psychology, in fact, views almost everyone as neurotic to some degree. The person seeking psychotherapeutic help is only slightly more neurotic than the one who does not seek help. Neurosis may be characterized by ongoing internal dialogues ("I want to find a new job"; "No, you had better not—you might fail"; "You are probably right, but I hate this one so much"). These I's who populate our minds reflect our neuroses, sources of discomfort, hang-ups, and disunity.

Mindfulness training, then, can be used to see and name mental processes in action. What use is this? If we believe that the most powerful way to live is in the present, dealing with each moment and situation effectively, then it follows that excessive mental energy spent remembering the good old days or the bad old days is not available to use in the present, where every-thing is happening. Mental energy expended in fantasies of other circum-stances and other places also takes energy from dealing effectively with the present. These are all varieties of neuroses for which mindfulness training can sometimes be effective. Here is a simple clinical illustration of how mindful-ness techniques can be used with a client.*

CASE 1
A twenty-three-year-old, newly divorced female patient complained that her thoughts about her former husband's bizarre sexual demands were triggering bouts of depression and severe anxiety attacks. She was trained to observe these retrospective thoughts carefully, using Satipatthana techniques, and to label them as "remembering, remembering." Within a few days, she reported that while there was no significant decrease in the frequency of the thoughts, the way they affected her had changed. The labeling process helped her to break the causative relationship between these thoughts and the depression and anxiety attacks, thus allowing the gradual disappearance of those symptoms. What remained at that point were regret about the past and considerable guilt, which were worked on in a traditional group psychotherapy setting during the following weeks.

The Watcher Self

When straightforward breath observation techniques are used with clinical patients, many potentially positive benefits can be gained. One benefit in-volves what we shall call the "watcher self." This is the aspect of one's mental "self" which is discovered through and carries out the task of mindfulness. It is the part capable of consciously watching and naming interruptions or bothersome mental habits and events. While only one aspect of the total personality, the watcher can be useful and important for certain clients be-cause it always behaves with calm strength. The watcher can see the remem-bering of some painful event and label it objectively without becoming involved in its melodrama. The watcher can therefore put psychological distance be-tween the "me" who experienced the painful event and the "me" who is presently remembering it. The watcher is neutral and can be identified with intentionally. The individual who feels weak, inadequate, indecisive, and defeated can, by intentionally identifying for a time with this watcher, de-

---

*The case studies provided are typical of the population of the psychiatric ward, and therefore young, married female clients predominate. All except for Case 7 first appeared in *J. Transpersonal Psych.*, No. 2, 1975.

velop new strengths, motivations, and abilities to participate more fully in and benefit from an overall psychotherapy program. Here is a case in point.

CASE 2

A twenty-seven-year-old divorced woman had been hospitalized for $2\frac{1}{2}$ months for a condition variously diagnosed as manic-depressive psychosis, depressive psychosis, and schizophrenia. She had responded to chemotherapy to the extent that she was able to begin group psychotherapy free of psychotic symptoms. However, she still suffered from recurring episodes of depression, anxiety, loss of interest in life, and loss of self-esteem. Several weeks of intensive group psychotherapy failed to produce symptom relief, and she was readmitted to the hospital suffering from severe depression and thoughts of self-destruction. Her primary concerns, in addition to feelings of depression, were loss of concentration and racing thoughts.

Mindfulness technique was presented to the patient as a "concentration exercise." She was asked to sit quietly, look at the second hand of an electric clock, and try to attend fully to its movement. She was instructed to notice carefully when she lost her concentration on the moving second hand, to identify what constituted the interruption, and to name it. She quickly found her concentration constantly broken by thoughts. On inspection, the nature of the thoughts racing through her mind was always the same—concern with her past, her misfortunes in the relationship with her ex-husband, and her regrets about that situation.

She was instructed simply to label such thoughts, "remembering, remembering." The labeling process seemed to allow her to withdraw some of her involvement in those depressing thoughts about the past and to let her realize that more than just those thoughts was present in her mind; there was also a "she" who could watch and name thoughts. She learned to identify herself as the objective watcher of her disturbing thoughts instead of the depressed thinker, and she began to feel some relief from her psychiatric complaints.

On reflection, the patient reported that, as a result of this psychotherapeutic endeavor, she had come to see more clearly the nature of her former illness. She subjectively perceived that she had become totally immersed in thoughts and regrets about the past, thus becoming less involved in what was happening around her in the present. She consequently lost any involvement in her future as well. Because her thoughts of the past caused her discomfort and depression, even anxiety, she used large amounts of energy to defend herself against them and make them go away. She felt that during her illness all of her energies had been consumed in thinking about the past and simultaneously fighting to stop such thoughts. This left her no energy to run her life. The mindfulness technique of labeling was effective here because it allowed the patient to stop expending energy in fighting the remembering.

After only a few days of using the exercise, the patient reported a significant increase in her concentration span. This increased concentration, accompanied by decreases in frequency and intensity of disturbing thoughts, allowed her to begin reading again, to carry on meaningful personal interchanges without the usual loss of awareness of what was happening, and to devote more time and energy to her personal appearance, which had been untidy during her illness.

With the additional benefits coming from the slightly disguised Satipatthana techniques, she could then investigate the nature of the watcher self which she had come to identify. This allowed her to come in contact with the calm and peaceful aspects of her own mind—her "center" was how she identified it at the time—and to re-establish some enjoyment and pleasure in her life. These dimensions had been missing for many months. This, too, helped with her interpersonal relationships. Within a few weeks of these observations, she was able to decide to terminate therapy, after which she moved to another city, where she intended to begin a new life.

All of the "selves," "I's," and "me's," including the neutral "watcher," are of course the products of continuous brain processes. All of these selves are collectively termed the "ego" in Buddhist psychology (not to be confused with Freud's use of "ego"). When we employ mindfulness meditation with clinical patients, it is not our purpose to establish the watcher as anything permanent or "real." The watcher is used only as a tool for grounding some of the patients' mental energies in the present, providing a temporary, psychologically stable center for them to operate from and providing a perspective from which their own psychological functioning can be objectively observed.

Many clinical patients, especially those we would label depressive, anxious, or neurotic, have problems either contacting or controlling emotions. Continued work with mindfulness techniques often yields results in these areas, because emotions and emotional states can be made the object of contemplation. Emotions, too, can be watched and labeled (anger, joy, fear), and when seen objectively, they can be allowed to return to their proper place within a healthier psychological system.

CASE 3

During a group therapy session, a twenty-two-year-old married woman who suffered from what had been diagnosed as an endogenous depression expressed despair at her inability to "feel anything any-more," relating a total lack of emotion. The only feeling she could identify was one of gloom and depression. She was asked to begin to get in touch with her feelings, becoming more aware of, and carefully and accurately labeling any emotion she experienced as she sat quietly watching her breathing or even during her normal daily activities.

Over the next few weeks she found herself increasingly naming anger as her predominant emotion, and it became possible to identify the source of that anger in her marital relationship. She then gradually became aware that she had been misinterpreting her emotions over many months, mistakenly believing that she had been experiencing depression whereas strong elements of anger, hostility, self-abasement, and disappointment had also been present. This recognition of the feelings she had been inaccurately labeling depression freed her to identify other feelings as well. Soon she was back in touch with the full spectrum of human emotions. Her depression disappeared and was replaced by a greatly improved self-image and understanding of her feelings.

In a similar way, thoughts, intentions, and even the task in which one is involved can be made the objects of contemplation within the psychotherapeutic setting, yielding insights into psychological processes that can be useful in helping the patient to grow in positive directions.

CASE 4

A devout Mormon woman of twenty-nine, who was married to a teacher, spent her days at home with her two children. At the beginning of their marriage, both she and her husband had been university students, but soon she quit to take a job. After her husband received his degree, they moved to a city where he had been offered a job, and she did not finish her studies. The husband went out to work each day, and she became a housewife. After only a few years of marriage, a definitely unhealthy pattern emerged in their relationship, the husband becoming more involved in his job and spending more and more time there. In fact, job and church activities left him little time or energy for his wife and family.

She began to suffer the classic symptoms of "housewife's syn-drome." She became depressed, edgy, anxious, and had no motivation or energy to care for the children or to do housework. She ceased going out because she felt even more anxiety outside her home. She could not even sit completely through a church service because her anxiety level would increase until she had to flee, usually using her youngest child as an excuse. At home, she could make no decisions of her own, did not want to be left alone with the children, and berated her husband when he went out for any reason. During the day she just sat, not even watching television or listening to the radio, unable even to bring herself to do simple tasks like dishwashing.

At the urging of her husband and mother, she finally came under the care of a psychiatrist who placed her in the hospital on the psychiatric unit. As was that psychiatrist's custom, the patient was referred to group therapy immediately upon admission. She also received chemotherapy and individual daily sessions with ward staff and her physician. In the group, she proved to be remarkably intelligent, verbal, and supportive of others, but initially totally lacking in insight into her own life. She was consistently whiny and often weepy when interacting with ward staff and other patients.

After a few group sessions in which she was able to describe her problems as she saw them, and after a session with her and her husband alone in which the family dynamics were well delineated, the therapist decided to use some mindfulness techniques as a supplement to her therapy program. This proved initially difficult. She rebelled against any kind of introspection because it tended to raise her anxiety level. The therapist finally had her imagine she was back home, prior to hospitalization, just sitting during the day as she often had done. Then she was asked to look at the thoughts which had been taking place there and to attempt to relate them to the therapist. Although she accomplished the task with some difficulty, it became quite evident over time that her predominant mental process was imagining. She used all kinds of fantasies to take her away from her anxieties and depression and poured great amounts of energy into that process.

Though we had not established the watcher through the usual set of mindfulness procedures, we had discovered the patient's main interrupting factor. It was then pointed out to her that she was using most of her energies in fantasizing, and she could easily see this. She was then told she would have to work on this if her problems were to be alleviated. Though she expected some mysterious psychological procedure to accomplish such a thing, she was, in fact, instructed to bake a cake mindfully in the treatment center kitchen, trying to attend fully to every detail, to notice when she began to imagine and to return to full concentration on the task. She did this and found that she could use some of her energies in a present-oriented task, observing when she was interrupted by the persistent fantasies.

A substitute for breath observation, the cake-baking routine was used as an example of how she could attempt to attend fully to the present moment, no matter what was happening. She began to work hard at this and slowly improved. She had a mechanism for noticing when fantasies began, and she found that they were decreasing in length and frequency. She could intentionally return to the present, and she learned that, with this intention, she could initiate behaviors, such as cooking, sewing, reading, and piano playing, which she had neglected for some time. She played the piano at the treatment center very well and found music a very good way to stay grounded in the present.

In group therapy, she worked on relationships between her and her husband. This was supplemented by family therapy sessions in which he participated fully. She also worked on her extremely dependent relationship with her mother who constantly told her what to do; she gained independence and confidence, slowly losing her anxieties. She continued group and family therapy for several months after she was released from the hospital. During that time she began again to attend church without anxiety, to care for the house and children, and to get out and involve herself in activities that interested her and helped her grow. Although the mindfulness techniques were not the only psychotherapeutic tools employed, and perhaps were not even the primary ones that aided her, they proved to be the key approach in getting her moving and growing in a positive way again.

Suiting Technique to Client

A psychotherapist-as-guru approach is not being advocated here. Neither is sending the client to meditate advocated as the best therapy. The word *meditation* is seldom mentioned to patients. What is being advocated is the adaptation of certain useful techniques of mindfulness meditation to the treatment program for selected clients. Mindfulness training does not work for everyone. To look directly within requires a great effort, and any psychotherapist realizes that many clients, particularly those just beginning therapy, are not capable of this kind of intense work. As I have pointed out before, mindfulness training is most appropriate for clients with an intact rational component and sufficient motivation to make the effort required. Only with these two factors present will the techniques be successful.

In short-term psychotherapy, breath-observation techniques or some modification of them are usually most appropriate. Discussion between client and therapist about insights gained is the primary indicator of the techniques' effectiveness for a given client. In long-term applications of mindfulness techniques, basic breath observation and interruption naming are first accomplished. Then the client can observe mental processes during everyday activities without needing breath observation as the focal point. Emotions, thoughts, and thought subject matter can be observed in any life situation once the watcher is trained. Awareness is then focused directly on what is happening in the present and on the mental processes of perceiving and reacting to external and internal stimuli which are gaining access to consciousness. Insights into the perceptive process—how external events are translated into internal reality—seem to occur if the "meditation" is directed toward seeing the external situation clearly and objectively from the perspective of the watcher self, which does not react emotionally, verbally, or behaviorally but simply sees. The watcher can suddenly see old and persistent patterns of reacting to certain standard problem situations. This frees the client to respond volitionally in new and different ways. The automatic response of fear or anger to a particular set of stimuli—an authority figure perhaps or a frustrating situation—will suddenly be seen occurring, due to concentration on the incoming stimuli of the present moment. These can be valuable, insightful occurrences for the individual who goes to the trouble of practicing and refining the mindfulness techniques. A simple, nonclinical example illustrates this.

> If I am driving during rush hour, a dangerous near collision with another car can be a good situation to observe mindfully. The near collision may have been due to the failure of a traffic light, rather than either driver. Yet the other driver directs abuse at me. The other driver's statement is an event external to "me." If I am being mindful, "I" will note that "I" perceive the event in a particular way, namely that the other driver is being unfair and unjust. This perception of the event leads to an immediate intention to reply, to assert "my" point of view. There is great freedom available to me when I see that intention clearly, because many possibilities exist for action or inaction. If I do not see the intention and resultant emotions like anger and frustration early, I can only react to the situation instead of experiencing its freedom. Seeing the intentional process arising allows a choice of responses: verbal action ("The same to you, fellow!"), physical action (crashing my car into his to teach him a lesson), early cancellation of either the verbal or physical action, thinking vindictive thoughts about the other driver; it even allows for the continuation of mindfulness—operating in the present, continuing to drive mindfully, and letting the negative thoughts and emotions produced by the event dissipate, instead of preserving them in my consciousness and going over and over them in memory. It does not matter whether I choose thoughts, words, actions, or cancellations as long as these things are done at a level of awareness where I can suddenly come to understand and say, "Oh yes, now I see why I always do that." These are everyday insights that come with increased mindfulness.

Mindfulness training, then, can create a space between life's events and the ego's reaction to those events. The ego itself begins to be seen and known. Mental processes basic to the ego are sometimes seen in operation. Slowly one becomes capable of dealing more effectively and intelligently with each life event as it occurs. At this stage of development, the watcher's role begins to shift and diminish. Occasional, total conscious immersion in present events begins to occur without the watcher consciously watching. In this state of total involvement no mental energy is held back for consciously operating the watcher, and none is used to escape in fantasies or memories; one is functioning at heightened effectiveness. Emotions associated with total involvement are purer. They are uncontaminated by reactions to involuntary memories and fantasies typically projected onto ongoing situations. A state of mental health without the neurotic internal mental dialogue's constant comments and digressions has been temporarily achieved. Total concentration is directed to the task at hand, whether it be washing the dishes, solving a family disagreement, or driving to work. For a time all the "I's" and "me's" are quieted, and the whole person, with all capabilities intact, is allowed to function.

The goal of mindfulness training, then, is to work directly with the ongoing train of experiences, to practice directing "bare attention" to those experiences, to develop patience with and compassion for oneself as well as others, and to deal effectively with neurotic disturbances of mind. This, of course, is asking a great deal. Many clients find it difficult, painful, and even overwhelming to look at their own troublesome and persistent mental processes. A greatly agitated, depressed, or otherwise disturbed individual is not an immediate candidate for such direct therapy, although he or she may later derive great benefit from this approach.

The following case study demonstrates the use of mindfulness techniques with a woman in long-term therapy.

CASE 5

A twenty-seven-year-old woman, married with two young children, was referred by her psychiatrist for group therapy because of increasing depression and inability to cope with family and life responsibilities. She was an intelligent, beautiful woman who was cool and aloof in interpersonal relationships. She attended group therapy for a few sessions and identified some problems with her husband, who traveled extensively and was away from home on business four or five nights each week. She suspected he was being unfaithful, and he admitted he had had an affair a few weeks earlier with a woman in another city.

After about her third week of group therapy, I received a frantic call from her husband one morning saying she had attempted suicide by overdosing with sleeping pills. She was comatose and in the intensive-care unit of the hospital at that time. While we waited for her to regain consciousness, the husband related his understanding of the family problems and stated that the attempted suicide had resulted from his wife's reduced sense of self-worth because of his confessing to the affair. He felt guilty about it, vowed to quit the job, and began to search for another that day.

As she awoke, the woman was upset to learn she had failed in her suicide attempt, and repeatedly said she wanted to die. However, on later learning her behavior had caused serious reconsiderations on her husband's part, she soon agreed to a no-suicide contract and was transferred to the psychiatric ward by her physician. Her temporary but apparently sincere agreement to remain alive left her with little choice but to attempt resolution of the conflicts which had brought her to this point.

Although she was still unable to express herself openly in group therapy and soon even refused to attend the group, she proved a willing and capable client in an individual setting. So all subsequent work with her was on a one-to-one basis. She received the usual chemotherapy for approximately two weeks while in the hospital. She finally admitted in a private session that she had been experiencing strong feelings of friendship, warmth, and perhaps even sexual attraction for an older woman whom she had met a few months earlier. The woman was outgoing, artistic, and in the client's view, everything she was not. She felt guilty and even abnormal about these unwanted feelings. We were able to make some progress in helping her to accept, understand, and work with those feelings during the first few days of her hospitalization.

Before leaving the hospital, she began the basic mindfulness practices of thought and feeling observation. She found no difficulty in thought observation because she was a persistent intellectualizer. However, she claimed to be able to identify no feelings at all. Over some weeks after leaving the hospital, she began to identify two feelings. These were not identified during breath observation but only during situations which arose during the day. She was able to identify strong anger at her husband and children at times and fear in certain interpersonal situations, particularly in meeting male strangers in new social settings. She worked hard on the social fear and soon lost much of her former aloofness by consciously trying to be open, attentive, and receptive in social encounters. At that point, with her depression alleviated and some of her problems part solved, she chose to terminate therapy. She had not yet really looked at her barely repressed homosexual desires toward her friend.

Approximately one year later, she came to my office saying she felt minor recurrences of her old depression and was afraid. In talking with her, I learned that with her husband home each night, her marriage had slightly improved but was still less than perfect. The friendship with the older woman had developed into a sexual relationship, and she was again feeling guilty about it.

She specifically requested that we continue the mindfulness training she had begun months before. This time we worked not on breath observation, but on increasing awareness during ordinary life events, especially in stressful situations. She progressed rapidly, finding that her social fears produced a characteristic response of coldness and near withdrawal, which made her seem conceited to others. She was able to see this mechanism coming into play, and thus to stop withdrawing. She began to derive some of the fulfillment from social situations previously denied her, and to accept more fully the bisexual nature of her sexual relationships. Although this channeled some of her energies away from her marriage, she seemed to have more satisfaction from both relationships.

This woman has come to feel very positive about herself; her occasional minor bouts of depression ended, and she has remained apparently symptom free for a year. Since her hospitalization, she has coped well at home, has grown greatly in personal satisfaction, and has completed two years at the university, something she had previously wanted to do but never felt capable of doing. No further suicide attempts or serious depressions have occurred to date.

This case study is fairly typical of long-term employment of mindfulness training. It takes months, even years, for most of us to grow out of psychological difficulty. It takes persistent application of the techniques to ensure growth, and each person has to grow at his or her own pace. If there is time available, if the therapist can provide the appropriate guidance, and if the client has the motivation and perseverance to work through problems, only then can the mindfulness approach be considered appropriate for a client.

Implications for the Therapist

Mindfulness meditation techniques, when used in psychotherapy, have several things to offer the psychotherapist. First of all, the approach is very client centered; it allows the client the freedom and dignity to work with himself under the therapist's guidance. This, of course, is efficient because it does not confine therapy to the hours when therapist and client meet. Also, It does not condition, direct, or shape the client's behavior into some preordained pattern decided by the therapist. Instead, the course of therapy is more one of the client's seeing, knowing, and accepting his mental processes and then allowing them to re-form and grow in new ways that are healthy for him. However, it is not a cure-all as is shown in this case.

CASE 6

A slightly disguised set of Satipatthana techniques was employed with a twenty-three-year-old male patient who had been hospitalized for extreme periodic agressiveness, fighting, and alcohol abuse, which had occasionally led to brief periods of amnesial or fuguelike states. This young man, who was married and had young children, had been extremely irritable and explosive at home, often losing his temper over minor events and striking out physically or storming out of the house for up to three days. A typical though infrequent pattern was for him to go to a bar with friends for a few drinks during the evening and become intoxicated. In this condition he would often steal a car, get in a fight, or even threaten homicide, but he failed to have any memory of these acts the next day. He was hospitalized twice after such unlawful behavior.

The second time he was admitted to the psychiatric unit, he proved warm and cooperative but experienced high anxiety levels when the staff wanted to discuss why he was in the hospital. He chose to characterize himself as an alcoholic. After a few days of chemotherapy, his psychiatrist referred him for group therapy. For the next few weeks, he received a therapeutic program consisting of brief daily visits by the psychiatrist, chemotherapy, twice-weekly group therapy, a weekly session of conjoint family therapy with the group therapist, and whatever sessions the patient chose to initiate with the psychiatrist nursing staff. This program was continued throughout his four weeks in the hospital and four more of outpatient care.

During the initial group and family therapy sessions, numerous identifiable martial problems became evident; these were the focus of the family therapy. Group and individual therapy revealed personal problems of expressing anger, self-image, hostility toward women, and extreme competitiveness with other men.

Since it did not appear that this man would be receptive to the usual mindfulness approach, a modified version was tried. His tendency to deny anger and then express it explosively seemed to be a good place to begin. It was mentioned casually during a group therapy session, when the topic arose naturally, that one could perhaps come to know quite accurately the causes of one's behavior. The young man took issue with this, saying he did many things he could never hope to understand. It was suggested that he attempt to look at and name the emotions he experienced during the next few days. He tried that suggestion and reported that what he felt most of the time was fear (of people or sometimes of nothing he could identify) and psychological pain. He was instructed to keep watching and naming emotions. Over some weeks, he began to see anger arising in certain interpersonal situations. He was also able to experience his feelings of irritability and to see what events produced them. Most important, he began to be aware that he did not express anger and often was not even cognizant of it until it had overwhelmed him. He was taught to verbalize his anger, to vent it as he experienced it, and to view anger as something all people normally feel. This seemed to free him to progress in psychotherapy. He stopped seeing his problem as alcoholism and spoke of alcohol intoxication as another way of trying to hide from his anger. Soon he stopped mentioning alcohol at all.

Other mindfulness techniques were then used with this man, particularly thought contemplation, which made him aware of his ineffective and inaccurate self-image. This helped him to start correcting misunderstandings about male-female relationships. At the end of eight weeks of this treatment, he took a job. Ten months later, he was still functioning effectively at home and at work, with no recurrences of drinking, fighting, or fugue-states. The mindfulness techniques used here constituted one part of an overall therapy program which proved to be effective.

A few months after this case history was first published, the man again behaved erratically. Even at the behest of his family and friends he refused to seek help and continued to encounter more problems, primarily with his family and his job. He finally fired a rifle through the window of a house, critically injuring a woman he did not know while apparently trying to injure his wife. At this writing, he is confined awaiting trial.

This case is an isolated but striking example of a person who did not continue to grow after terminating therapy, but instead slowly lost the benefits he had gained. The psychotherapeutic gains achieved through the use of this technique, like most other forms of therapy, can erode over time if the client ceases to practice mindfulness and stops growing.

It is usually a mistake to expect predictable, linear progression through therapy for a patient using the mindfulness techniques, as the following case demonstrates.

CASE 7

A twenty-one-year-old female sought help for her increasingly frequent anxiety attacks. Although the attacks could come upon her at any time, she was particularly troubled by crowded places such as classrooms. Her case was complicated by her having been previously treated unsuccessfully by two other psychotherapists. One had apparently attempted desensitization procedures, treating her case as a phobic reaction to crowded places; the other had served only as a counselor discussing her problems with her. Both had failed to alleviate the symptoms, and she had terminated therapy after a few months in each case.

After some preliminary sessions, we decided to try mindfulness techniques. She was shown the basic breath observation techniques of noting interruptions and naming them. After this, most sessions consisted of discussing her experiences with the mindfulness practices. After she had become fairly adept at noting and naming interruptions to breath observation, and after the watcher had been investigated, she began to work on observing emotions. She reported that, as she sat quietly observing interruptions and emotions, fear would arise within her from no detectable source, panic would follow, and she would then have to struggle with that anxiety—effectively ending her observation as she became involved with the anxiety. Slowly she became aware that the watcher could see but did not experience anxiety, and she could sometimes get a little space between the "me" who was so afraid and the watcher.

Suddenly unexpected progress began to occur in our sessions together, progress that seemed to have been impelled by the mindfulness training. The case became almost classically psychoanalytic for a time, with our discussions proceeding backward in time to the point where she discussed a sexual experience with an aggressive older boy when she was twelve. From that almost cathartic session, other sessions followed in which she discussed a long period of sexual promiscuity. At that point in therapy, her crowd-induced anxiety attacks began to subside, allowing her to go into places which had been previously troublesome. Then she related in great detail a long-repressed incident that she had mentioned slightly in one of our first sessions. When she was nine or ten, her father had—at least in her perception of the event—attempted to seduce her. Telling her mother about the incident had caused family difficulties, and she had incurred much guilt about her parents' relationship. All of this poured out as well as her hostility toward males. All her later life had been concerned with rewarding, punishing, and controlling males with her sexuality; at last she began to see this important fact.

By this time her anxiety attacks had grown infrequent and were far less terrifying mainly because she was able to experience them more from the watcher's point of view. The attacks tended to occur only when she was alone, and she felt more capable of dealing with them. Her therapy was finally terminated when she and her husband moved to another city, where she apparently continued with another therapist.

The mindfulness approach to psychotherapy has proven to be compatible with chemotherapies, somatotherapies, and various other psychotherapies. It can provide valuable and timely insights for most clients with whom it is used appropriately, insights that can be deepened and broadened through discussion as therapy progresses.

However, the clinician who plans to use this approach needs first to become personally familiar with the techniques. He or she should verify the insights potentially available by practicing the techniques personally before employing them with clients.

People almost never seem to reach a condition of total psychological stability. Change is constantly required of us as we age and encounter new experiences. Mindfulness training can help the client to continue to adapt successfully long after formal therapy has ended.

14

Meditation and Consciousness
An Asian Approach to Mental Health

Daniel Goleman

Daniel Goleman, one of the pioneer workers, thinkers, and writers in the area of consciousness and meditation, provides here a bird's-eye view of the Buddhist approach to mental health. Like other contributors to this collection, he contends that what is possible within the Eastern system far exceeds almost anything aspired to in the West.

Starting with the premise that Buddhist teachings and other major Eastern religions "embody a psychologic system as well as a cosmology," Goleman then presents the Abhidhamma model of the mind and its method for dealing with mental disorder. From this viewpoint, mental factors are divided into the pure and healthy, and the impure and unhealthy. The key principle for achieving mental health, explains Goleman, "is the reciprocal inhibition of unhealthy mental factors by healthy ones." The principal healthy factors are mindfulness and insight.

How does one achieve the goal of experiencing only healthy states? The method recommended in the Buddhist system is meditation combined

Reprinted from the *American Journal of Psychotherapy*, 1976, *30*, pp. 41–54. This paper was originally presented at the Fifteenth Eilhard Von Demarus Memorial Conference, March 20, 1975, in New York City, and was supported in part by a Research Training Fellowship from the Social Science Research Council. The author is indebted to George Goethals for his helpful comments on an earlier version of the paper.

with "behavioral and affective self-control" and "self-regulation of perceptual and cognitive processes, particularly attention." By the strategies of concentration and insight, the meditator reaches a point where he or she can replace unhealthy mental patterns with healthy ones. "The net effect of [this] mindfulness," explains Goleman, "is deconditioning of habitual response patterns."

One progresses from mindfulness to insight step by step. These steps are closely related in Goleman's view to certain recent studies and theories of human behavior, and the flow model he describes may be interpreted in terms of neurophysiology.

Goleman sees great value in meditation as an adjunct to therapy, just as a number of other contributors do. Its usefulness relates more to the general mental state of the client than to the solution of specific problems. He describes the difference between the classical analytic approach and the classical Buddhist approach: "Freud sought through analysis to help his patients face, understand, and reconcile themselves to this 'tragic' condition of life. Buddha sought through meditation to eradicate the sources of suffering in a radical reorientation of consciousness."

Psychotherapy and meditation are complementary in the opinion of Goleman and many other theorists. He puts it this way: "Consciousness is the medium which carries the messages that compose experience. Psychotherapies are concerned with these messages and their meanings; meditation instead directs itself to the nature of the medium, consciousness."

WHILE IN INDIA AND CEYLON, I had the opportunity to study a system of psychology developed in India fifteen or more centuries ago and which throughout much of non-Communist Asia continues to be applied in various forms as a guide to the workings of the mind. Known as *Abhidhamma,* this system stems directly from the insights of Gautama Buddha in the fifth century B.C., which have subsequently been refined and evolved into the various lineages, teachings, and schools of Buddhism, in a process of evolution akin to that by which Freud's thought has developed into disparate schools of psychotherapy. As a psychologist I was surprised to see that Buddhist teachings embody a psychologic system as well as a cosmology. This psychology is an esoteric teaching which the more popular and widely known cosmological teachings of Buddhism often obscure from the westerner's view.

My contacts and readings in other major Asian religions—Hinduism, Islam, Eastern Orthodoxy, and others—have led me to a similar psychologic system at the core of each major faith (Goleman, 1972), a psychology generally little known to, or followed by, the mass of adherents to that faith, though quite familiar to the appropriate "professionals"—be they yogis, monks, or priests. These psychologies seem to undercut the ostensible differences between faiths in belief system and theology; while beliefs emphasize differences between religions, these esoteric psychologies show remarkable similarity of thought and method.

The most systematic and intricately laid out Asian psychology I have encountered is that of classical Buddhism. Many of its concepts and principles, however, are in the main representative of the psychologic teachings at the common core of these faiths, rather than Buddhism per se. As such it seems emblematic of a prototypic Asian psychology which presents us with a set of assumptions and concepts for understanding mental activity and methods for healing mental disorder which differ markedly from our contemporary psychotherapeutic outlook. Virtually every Eastern meditation system transplanted to the West—transcendental meditation, Zen, and the like—stems from a set of assumptions about human psychology which seems in essence derived from this same source, or from common roots in an even older protopsychology (Eliade, 1969). This Asian psychology has proved remarkably durable, surviving two to three millennia or longer, while our present-day therapeutic theories and techniques are less than a century old. Though our tendency often is to view spiritual belief systems from other cultures through the lenses of our own constructs, it may serve us to look at this Asian psychology on its own terms, to consider what of value we may find applicable to our own needs.

Abhidhamma: An Asian Psychology

Let me briefly outline the Abhidhamma model of the mind and its method for dealing with mental disorder (Narada, 1968). This model of mental activity is an "object relations" theory in the broadest sense: its basic dynamic is the ongoing relationship of mental states to sensory objects. "Sense object" includes percepts in the five main sensory modalities, plus thought or cognitive activity, which in this system is seen as a "sixth" sense. Mental states are in continuous change and flux; in this analysis the rate of change of the smallest unit of mental states—a "mind-moment"—is incredibly fast, described as arising at the rate of millions in the time of a flash of lightning. The level of analysis is much finer than that which contemporary psychology applies; our categories for psychologic states apply to referents with a much longer duration than mind-moments.

Each successive mental state is composed of a set of properties of mental factors which combine to flavor and define it. No mental state exists apart from its constituent factors. There are fifty-two categories of these properties; a subset of these properties is present in every mental state, whereas others arise only occasionally. The basic dichotomy in the Abhidhamma analysis of mental factors is that between pure, wholesome, or healthy, and impure, unwholesome, or unhealthy mental properties. In this system one's mental health is contingent on the quality of the factors which compose one's mental states from moment to moment. While there is a subset of seven perceptual-cognitive properties universally present in mental states, most of the remaining forty-five perceptual, cognitive, and affective factors are categorized as healthy or unhealthy.

Of the fourteen basic unhealthy factors, the major perceptual factor is *delusion*, a perceptual cloudiness or misperception of the object of awareness. Delusion is seen as the fundamental source of unhealthy mental states; it leads directly to a cognitive factor, *false view* or misdiscernment, though its role in other unhealthy factors is less direct. False view entails miscategorization and so is the natural consequence of misperception. Other unhealthy cognitive factors include: *shamelessness* and *remorselessness*—attitudes allowing viewing evil acts without compunction, disregarding both others' opinions and internalized standards; and *egoism,* an attitude of self-interest where objects are viewed solely in terms of fulfilling one's own desires or needs. *Perplexity* is the inability to decide or make a correct judgment.

The bulk of unhealthy mental factors is affective. *Agitation* and *worry*— elements in anxiety—are two primary factors in this category. *Greed, avarice,* and *envy* form a cluster characterized by grasping attachment to an object; *aversion* is the negative pole on the continuum of attachment. *Contraction* and *torpor* contribute a nonadaptive, rigid inflexibility and moribund clinging to unhealthy mental states.

These unhealthy factors are opposed by a set of fourteen factors which are always present in healthy states. The key principle in the Abhidhamma program for achieving mental health is the reciprocal inhibition of unhealthy mental factors by healthy ones. Just as in systematic desensitization, where tension is supplanted by its physiologic opposite relaxation (Wolpe, 1958), healthy mental states are antagonistic to unhealthy ones, inhibiting them. In the dynamic of this system, the presence of a given healthy factor disallows the arising of a specific unhealthy factor. The major healthy factor of *insight* or understanding—"clear perception of the object as it really is"—suppresses the fundamental unhealthy factor of *delusion*. These two factors cannot exist together in a single mental state: where insight is, delusion cannot be. *Mindfulness* in healthy mental states allows continued clear comprehension of an object and is an essential concomitant of *wisdom*. Insight and mindfulness are the fundamental healthy factors; when they are present the other healthy factors tend to arise in the same mental state.

The twin cognitive factors of *modesty* and *discretion* arise only when a healthy mental state has as object an evil act; they function to inhibit committing such acts and so directly oppose shamelessness and remorselessness. These factors are supported by *rectitude,* a more general cognitive factor of correctness in judgment. An associated affective factor is *confidence,* a sureness based on correct perception or knowledge. *Nonattachment, nonaversion,* and *impartiality* together oppose the cluster of unhealthy factors formed by greed, avarice, envy, and aversion, replacing it with an evenmindedness toward whatever object may arise in relation to a mental state. The factor of *composure* reflects the calm and tranquil feeling tone arising from allaying strong positive and negative emotions of attachment. A final affective group of factors acts on both mind and body: *buoyancy, pliancy, efficiency,* and *proficiency,* which together supplant contraction and torpor, lending attributes of flexibility, ease, adaptability, and skillfulness to the configuration of mental health. These core healthy factors, besides supplanting unhealthy ones, further provide the foundation for a set of positive affective states which cannot arise in the presence of unhealthy factors. These include compassion, loving kindness, and "altruistic joy"—a joy which arises when the happiness of another comes into awareness.

These factors tend to arise in groups—either unhealthy or healthy—but any mental state which has a single unhealthy factor present is seen as entirely unhealthy. Indeed, in this system the operational definition of mental disorder would be the presence of any unhealthy factor in the psychic economy of the person: mental health is the absence of unhealthy factors, and presence of healthy factors, in the person's mental states. All of us are most likely "unhealthy" by this criterion. Still, each of us probably experiences wholly "healthy" mental states for greater or lesser periods as mind-moments come and go in our stream of consciousness. Very few if any of us, however, experience *only* healthy mental states. But this is precisely the goal of psychologic development in Abhidhamma.

Meditation: Means to Mental Health

The practicing Buddhist embarks on a multilevel program for attaining a plateau of purely healthy mental states. He must undergo a coordinated effort of behavioral and affective self-control, combined with self-regulation of perceptual and cognitive processes, particularly attention. The basic practice is meditation, which can be more rigorously defined as the self-regulation and retraining of attentional habits.

Meditation is seen as most effective when the meditator voluntarily desists from actions or disinvests interest from thoughts which would lead to strong affects, or which would otherwise distract attention. The meditator does not directly confront unhealthy factors with healthy ones (except occasionally when certain unhealthy factors, such as lust, are particularly distracting). The essence of meditation is the consistent attempt to achieve a specific attentional set. In doing so, the optimal facilitating mental state consists in the group of healthy factors. Attentional stability and mental states are interactive, but the meditator's effort is oriented toward the target attentional stance, not toward the generation of healthy factors per se. These factors come to predominate in the natural course of success in his attentional efforts. This is an organic equivalent of biofeedback procedures: a specific attentional set is accompanied by a sought-after internal state (that is, healthy factors), the induction of which state is achieved by the maintenance of the attentional set. This parallels the situation in, for example, EEG biofeedback procedures of the person who is achieving "alpha" by seeking to maintain a target signal (a tone or light) which accompanies the alpha rhythm.

There are two fundamental attentional strategies for meditation: *concentration* and *insight.* Concentration entails sustained attention directed toward a single object or point of focus. Insight involves the continual maintenance of a specific perceptual-cognitive set toward objects as they spontaneously arise in awareness. In concentration the aim is one-pointed attention to a single percept; in insight the aim is full awareness or mindfulness of any and all contents of awareness.

In the course of developing meditative concentration, the meditator must surpass what we think of as the normal limits for sustaining a single object in awareness. William James (1962), after trying it himself, proclaimed that it was impossible to hold a single thought in awareness for more than three or four seconds. In our culture we have generally left it at that. In Asia, however, it has long been recognized that attentional processes are semi-autonomous, and with practice can be regulated and retrained to a far greater degree than has been thought possible by James and psychologists since.

In the process of acquiring meditative skills, the meditator seems to reprogram basic patterns of perception and cognition. For example, in developing either meditative concentration or mindfulness, it is essential to inhibit the "unhealthy" factors, all of which produce distractability. As inhibition of unhealthy factors is inculcated, healthy ones are elicited: meditation entails a simultaneous unlearning of old perceptual-cognitive habits and acquisition of new ones. To the degree that this new pattern becomes an enduring trait, the meditator undergoes a fundamental transformation of his experience of himself and of the world.

The essential skill in meditation is the ability to hold a specific mental set, or a specific object of awareness, while inhibiting any contrary perceptions, thoughts, or other intrusions. This attentional retraining can produce meditation-specific altered states (called *jhana* in Pali, *samadhi* in Sanskrit), characterized by the total exclusion from awareness of normal sensation, percepts, or cognitive activity, and accompanied by bliss and rapture. These states are totally disjunctive with normal consciousness, and represent the culmination of hyperfocus developed within concentrative techniques. Though there is an afterglow from this state, on emerging from meditation one is still susceptible to the patterns of old mental habits. For this reason, in Abhidhamma this experience is seen as relatively trivial, since it produces no lasting change.

The attentional strategy which is said to produce such change is mindfulness, purposeful dehabituation of stereotyped patterns of perception and cognition. This method involves facing each mind-moment, each experience, each event, as though it were occurring for the first time, rather than allowing perception to become habituated or overridden by cognitive coding. Attention is restricted to bare noticing of mind and its objects. If a subsequent associational train, categorization, or affective reaction arises, that too is in turn taken as an object of bare attention; it is neither rejected nor pursued, but dismissed from awareness after being noted. Each and every object of awareness is given equal valence; nothing is to be isolated as figure, nothing relegated to ground. The net effect of mindfulness is deconditioning of habitual response patterns. As mindfulness progressively matures into insight, there is a gradual transformation of consciousness whereby, in a series of step-functions, subsets of unhealthy factors are said to be eradicated from one's psychologic economy. At the culmination of this process one attains the status of *arahat*, "one worthy of praise," where not a single unhealthy factor arises in the stream of mental states.

The *arahat* embodies characteristics common to the ideal type in most every Asian psychology of consciousness: the *arahat* is the prototypic saint. From the Abhidhamma point of view, the *arahat* represents the essence of mental health. From our perspective, the *arahat* can be seen as having achieved an altered state of consciousness, a stable, transmuted configuration of psychologic structures. A partial enumeration of a traditional list of these changes includes:

1. *Absence* of greed for sense objects; anxiety, resentments, or fears of any sort; dogmatisms such as the belief that this or that is "the Truth"; aversion to conditions such as loss, disgrace, pain, or blame; feelings of lust or anger; experiences of suffering, need for approval, pleasure, or praise; desire for anything for oneself beyond essential and necessary items; past conditioning as a major determinant of present behavior; and

2. *Prevalence* of impartiality toward others and equanimity in all circumstances; ongoing alertness and calm delight in any and all situations; strong feelings of compassion and loving kindness; quick and accurate perception; composure and skill in actions; openness to others and responsivity to their needs; immunity from conditioning.

Meditation and the Quality of Life: Speculations

While empirical studies as yet have not been designed to assess the specific formulations of Abhidhamma regarding the impact of meditation on consciousness, there are enough data to begin building nomological nets which, though going beyond the data given, allow consideration of the possible implications of these changes for daily living and for mental disorders. I would like to outline the converging evidence from Asian psychology and from empirical studies as they connect with some recent theories of human behavior.

The *arahat*, it is said, at all times and in every circumstance experiences an internal state of calm delight, is keenly attentive to all important aspects of the situation, and exhibits "skillful means" in response to the requirements of the moment. A similar state has been described in contemporary psychology by Csikzentmihalyi (1975), who has studied a broad range of intrinsically rewarding activities, all of which are marked by a similar experience, which he calls "flow." The key elements of flow are: (*a*) the merging of action and awareness in sustained, nondistractible concentration on the task at hand, (*b*) the focusing of attention on a limited stimulus field, excluding intruding stimuli from awareness in a pure involvement devoid of concern with outcome, (*c*) self-forgetfullness with heightened awareness of functions and body states related to the involving activity, (*d*) skills adequate to meet the environmental demand, (*e*) clarity regarding situational cues and appropriate response. Flow arises when there is an optimal fit between one's capability and the demands of the moment. The flow range is bordered, on the one hand, by anxiety-inducing situations where demand exceeds capability and, on the other hand, by boredom where capability far exceeds demand.

In a related work Hartmann (1973) proposes a pattern of "inhibitory sharpening" in cortical arousal patterning, which represents optimal specificity of organismic response to environmental demand. Thus a situation of focused attention with exclusion of unwanted stimuli entails clearly demarcated small areas of cortical excitation surrounded by areas of inhibition.

When blurring occurs in the demarcation of excitation and inhibition, there is a "spillover" of arousal to functional areas irrelevant to the task at hand. This, proposes Hartmann, characterizes a less balanced, less delicately adjusted cortical functioning as is found during tiredness. Such an excitation "spillover" may also occur in the global arousal of acute anxiety and may account for the inability to integrate perceptual cues and organize functional coping responses in anxiety states. Finely tuned cortical specificity, on the other hand, characterizes well-rested waking functioning, with optimal reality testing and other adaptive ego mechanisms, allowing flexibility in meeting environmental demands with skilled response. This should be one aspect of the neurophysiologic substrate of flow.

As I interpret the flow model in terms of neurophysiology, Hartmann's formulation points up a significant characteristic of flow: it requires both precision and fluidity in neurologic patterning, so that activation can change tailored to fluctuating situational requirements. This in turn may demand the potential for delinking neurologic systems which normally may covary, but which must fractionate as finer patterns of excitation and inhibition are called for. The flow state is not a given pattern of ongoing arousal: rather than state-boundedness, it demands state-flexibility. The person who is chronically anxious, or habitually locked into *any* given configuration of arousal, is likely to confront more situations where his internal state is inappropriate for optimal fit with environmental demands—that is, nonflow. Changing circumstances require changing internal states.

There are two ways of increasing the likelihood of a flow experience: regulating environmental challenge to fit one's skills, as in games, or self-regulation of internal capacities to meet a greater variation in external demands. The disadvantage of the first approach is that flow remains situation-bound, relying on a given set of environmental cues for its elicitation. I propose that meditation may be a functional equivalent of the latter strategy, producing a change in internal state which could maximize possibilities for the flow experience while lessening one's need to control the environment. Moreover, meditation does not entail increasing flow by the attempt to perfect a specific skill, but rather by altering a broad range of basic processes of consciousness so that situations more frequently can be met with the elicitation of flow.

"Some people," notes Csikzentmihalyi in passing, "enter flow simply by directing their awareness so as to limit the stimulus field in a way that allows the merging of action and awareness"—namely, attentional focus with the exclusion of distracting stimuli. This is identical to the basic skill practiced in meditation: it is the essential core of every meditative discipline (though techniques may vary according to the degree of attentional effort expended). A constellation of findings on the enduring effects of meditation suggests that this central process may generalize in a spectrum of changes, which include: perceptual sharpening and increased ability to attend to a target environmental stimulus while ignoring irrelevant stimuli (Pelletier, 1974; Stein, 1973); increased cortical specificity—that is, arousal of the cortical area appropriate to a given task with relative inhibition of irrelevant cortizal zones, a pattern underlying skilled response (Schwartz, 1975); increased situation-specific cortical arousability with limbic inhibition (Goleman, 1995); autonomic stability and lowering of anxiety level (ibid.; Hjelle, 1974; Orme-Johnson, 1974;

Seeman, Nidich, & Banta, 1972); and equanimity and evenness in responding to emotionally loaded and threatening stimuli (Kasamatsu & Hirai, 1966;
Garfield, 1974).

To the extent that these diverse findings were true for any individual
meditator, these traits should operate so as to lower the threshold for entering
flow by bringing into its domain those instances where flow would otherwise
have been excluded by misperception, distractability, global and non-
differentiated arousal states unsuited to specific requirements, or functioning
impaired by anxiety. As the range of flow and its sense of the intrinsic rewards
of activity expands, there would be a concomitant shrinkage in the domains
both of anxiety-inducing and of boring situations in daily life. Indeed the
fitting of one's internal state to the demands of specific action, as in flow, has
been an ideal of many Asian systems for self-development. In the words of
the Zen master Unmon: "If you walk, just walk. If you sit, just sit. But
whatever you do, don't wobble."

The intentional cultivation of such a state should have salutary behavioral consequences. For one, the intrusive psychologic effects of heightened
limbic activation have been linked to schizophrenic symptoms, specifically
"pre-emption of consciousness by characteristic fear, sense of unreality,
or . . . disturbed sexual and sensory perception" (Stevens, 1973). Similarly,
uncontrolled and ongoing autonomic arousal patterns typify both anxiety
neuroses and certain psychosomatic disorders. The flow state stands in direct
opposition to those conditions, as well as offering an alternative to the negative aspects of stress-induced global arousal, where limbic and cortical activation are combined. The flow state should facilitate essential cortical functions
while minimizing the debilitating limbic excitation which is implicated in a
range of disorders. The phenomenology of flow shares many attributes of the
meditation adept's mental state as described in Abhidhamma: clarity of perception, alertness, equanimity; and pliancy, efficiency, and skill in action. To
the degree that the lasting effects of meditation approach this ideal, the flow
state can be seen as one possible benefit of meditation.

In this sense the goal of meditation training coincides in part with the
qualities of skilled behavior and, more generally, with flow: action unimpeded
by anxiety, clarity of perception, and accuracy of response, pleasure in action
for its own sake. The nature of this experience is aptly capsulized in Merton's
translation of a poem by the Taoist master, Chuang Tzu:

> Ch'ui the draftsman
> Could draw more perfect circles freehand
> Than with a compass.
> His fingers brought forth
> Spontaneous forms from nowhere. His mind

Was meanwhile free and without concern.
(Merton, 1969, p. 112)

Meditation and Psychotherapy: Further Speculations

While the specifics of the lasting changes produced by meditation are by no means certain, some general consideration is possible of the potential utility of this Asian approach to mental health. Present therapies were generated as treatments for particular symptoms and syndromes; meditation was not. The clinical utility of meditation is more likely to be in terms of providing a general psychologic pattern of positive mental states rather than as a response to any particular presenting problem.

For example, Gellhorn (1965) posits a changing ratio of ergotropic-trophotropic balance or "tuning" as causing behavioral changes ranging from deep sleep through wakefulness to emotional excitement. Gellhorn and Kiely (1972) suggest that the physiologic changes observed in meditation are due to a shift in this balance in the trophotropic direction, which reduces sympathetic responsivity and accelerates sympathetic habituation to arousing or stressful stimuli. Gellhorn and Kiely propose the clinical use of meditation in the treatment of psychosomatic tension states, anxiety, and phobic reactions, reasoning that the meditation state effects of trophotropic tuning (lower limbic activation) would counter an imbalance in the ergotropic direction seen in such disorders. Meditation in this view is a global strategy for improving health, a neurophysiologic "retuning" process.

The Abhidhamma ideal type of the healthy mental state and empirical findings of enduring meditation effects are both congruent with a related speculative neurophysiologic interpretation deriving from my own research. In meditators in a stress situation I found a psychophysiologic configuration suggesting increased motoric readiness to respond, heightened global arousal in anticipation of the stressor but more rapid limbic inhibition in recovering from confrontation, accompanied by more positive affect and lower situational anxiety throughout the situation. In response to initial threat cues the meditators showed a significantly greater cortical excitation and a simultaneous limbic inhibition. This combination delinks the cortex and limbic systems, two major neurophysiologic units which more often tend to covary along an activation continuum, most notably at the extremes: emotional arousal or stress reactivity at the hyperarousal pole, and boredom or drowsiness at the hypoarousal pole.

This delinked neurophysiologic pattern is in contrast to Benson's view (1975) of meditation as inculcating a "relaxation response" marked by diffuse low arousal: while a hypometabolic state usually accompanies meditation,

meditation effects during waking activity are by no means a simple, global lowering of arousal. With appropriate situational demands, meditators may be characterized by a differentiated pattern of greater cortical alertness with limbic inhibition (Goleman, 1995) and certain meditative disciplines have been found to increase cortical specificity (Schwartz, 1975). I suspect that what transfers to normal waking activity from meditation practice is not simply a relaxed state, but in addition the capacity for focused attention, which is the basic skill acquired in meditation, and which, as Hartmann proposes, is accompanied by heightened specificity of cortical excitation and inhibition. This combination of situationally appropriate arousal plus specificity of excitation areas is the most likely neurologic substrate of flow, where attention is focused, perceptual and motor systems function optimally, and anxiety is minimal.

The most efficacious clinical application of meditation may not be as an antidote to specific end-organ symptoms; strategies such as biofeedback or behavior therapies may be more suited to self-control and relearning of adaptive responses to stress within a given physiologic target system. Specific therapies may be most appropriate for the treatment of given psychopathologic syndromes. The clinical utility of meditation may be in providing a general pattern of stress-responsivity less likely to trigger specific overlearned maladaptive responses, whether psychologic or somatic. Selye (1956) sees the disease process as contingent upon a complete disease-producing situation, the specific agents of the disease requiring appropriate organismic conditions—for example, stress in combination with lowered systemic defenses—to produce illness. He points to the need for a "stress therapy" which would not function against any one disease producer or ameliorate any specific symptom, but rather would be preventive, working in a manner favorable to the organism as a whole in interactions with the environment. The pattern of stress reactivity I found among meditators is one of differentiated arousal in response to threat clues (cortical excitation with limbic inhibition), and a global arousal in direct anticipation of stressor confrontation which is counterbalanced post-impact by a more rapid limbic inhibition. Thus the meditator is more alert but composed in response to threat cues, may seem more "stressed" in anticipation, and recovers more efficiently. To the degree that the recovery phase of stress confrontation is the key to chronic anxiety symptoms and psychosomatic disorders, meditation may function as a stress therapy, on the psychologic as well as the purely somatic levels, facilitating more rapid recovery from the psychologic and physiologic coping processes mobilized in stress situations. As such, meditation may prove a useful adjunct to any modern psychotherapy.

Some aspects of meditation have already been incorporated into modern therapies—for example, Gestalt therapy and psychosynthesis in the United

States, autogenic training in Europe, and Morita therapy in Japan (Naranjo, 1970; Assagioli, 1971; Luthe, 1969/1970; Chang, 1974). Processes intrinsic to meditation may coincide with aspects of therapy. For example, as the meditator turns his attention inward he becomes keenly aware of thoughts, feelings, and states drawn from the stored pool of his total experience which arise spontaneously. Since the meditator is at the same time deeply relaxed, the whole contents of his mind can be seen as composing a "desensitization hierarchy." Unlike the desensitization paradigm, this hierarchy is not limited to those items which therapist and patients have identified as problematic, though these are certainly included, but extends to all one's life concerns, to whatever is "on one's mind." In this sense, meditation may be natural, global self-desensitization.

This may account for the lessening of tension usually associated with repressed material when meditation has been used as an adjunct to therapy, thus allowing formerly painful material to surface with greater awareness (Carrington & Ephron, 1975). After meditating, the patient's free association has been found particularly rich in content while at the same time the patient is more able to tolerate this material. In this way meditation seems to improve access to the unconscious. (Meditation may not be appropriate for all patients. A schizoid may possibly develop poor reality-testing, becoming overly absorbed in inner realities; those in acute emotional states might be too agitated to begin meditation; obsessive-compulsives might, on the one hand, be too closed to new experience to try meditation or, on the other, overzealous in their efforts.) Meditation may benefit the therapist as well as the patient. Meditation training has been found to increase empathy in a counseling situation (Lesh, 1970; Leung, 1973); a therapist in flow should be able to tune in and respond to the client in an optimal manner.

Many contemporary therapies begin from an understanding of the human condition similar in certain respects to that of Abhidhamma. Freud, for example, saw the "universal neurosis in man," Buddha saw that "all worldings are deranged." While the insight was similar, the response differed. Freud sought through analysis to help his patients face, understand, and reconcile themselves to this "tragic" condition of life. Buddha sought through meditation to eradicate the sources of suffering in a radical reorientation of consciousness.

Psychodynamic therapy since Freud has worked within the constraints of the fundamental processes of consciousness to alter the impact of the contents of one's past as it affects the present. Asian psychologies have largely ignored psychologically loaded contents of awareness, including psychodynamics, while seeking to alter the context in which they—and all other information—are registered in awareness. Conventional psychotherapies assume as givens the mechanisms underlying perceptual, cognitive, and affective processes, while seeking to alter them at the level of socially conditioned patterns. Asian systems disregard these same socially conditioned patterns, while aiming at the control and self-regulation of the underlying mechanisms themselves. Therapies break the hold of past conditioning on present behavior; meditation aims to alter the process of conditioning per se so that it will no longer be a prime determinant of future facts. In the Asian approach behavioral and personality change is secondary, an epiphenomenon of changes, through the voluntary self-regulation of mental states, in the basic processes which define our reality.

Consciousness is the medium which carries the messages that compose experience. Psychotherapies are concerned with these messages and their meanings; meditation instead directs itself to the nature of the medium, consciousness. These two approaches are by no means mutually exclusive, but rather complementary. A therapy of the future may integrate techniques from both approaches, possibly producing a change in the whole person more thoroughgoing and more potent than either in isolation.

Summary

The Abhidhamma, a classical Buddhist phenomenology of mental states, represents an Asian "protopsychology." In this model, fifty-two basic perceptual, cognitive, and affective properties arise in varying combinations to give each successive mental state its distinctive characteristics. An "unhealthy" subset of properties is inhibited by an opposing "healthy" subset. Buddhist meditation aims to eradicate these unhealthy properties from the psychologic economy. The operational definition of mental health is their complete absence, as in the case of the *arahat,* or saint. Characteristics of the *arahat* ideal type coincide with the elements of "flow," an intrinsically rewarding state arising from absorption in a situation of optimal fit between one's capability and environmental demand. Empirical findings on meditation, in light of a neurophysiologic interpretation, suggest that meditation may extend the domain of flow within daily activity. Meditation may serve as a complementary adjunct to psychotherapy.

15

Sufism and Psychiatry

Arthur J. Deikman

In this chapter Arthur J. Deikman, a well-known pioneer in the areas of meditation and change of consciousness, demonstrates how Sufi stories can provide a much needed philosophical backdrop for modern psychiatry and can serve as instruments for alleviating psychological pain. He uses a generous sampling of stories to clarify and advance his argument.

In reviewing the psychiatric approaches to meaning, the author concludes that it is possible that "the greatest problem confronting psychiatry is that it lacks a theoretical framework adequate to provide meaning for its patients." Frequently it also fails to provide meaning for its practitioners.

By contrast, Eastern disciplines do focus on meaning. In Deikman's view, however, they "have employed a strategy in which the use of intellect and reason is neither central nor basic to the process of investigation." While this approach is valid and relevant for the Eastern traditions, Deikman asserts that "modern westerners need technical means specific to their time and culture." And this is where the Sufi approach enters the picture.

Sufism, according to many authorities, is not some "Middle Eastern mystical religion"; it is a "science" in that it presents a particular body of knowledge, possesses certain fixed principles, and has a specific result. Both Idries Shah, whose stories are used in this chapter, and the author himself contrast the "fossilization" of traditional religions and psychiatry and the freshness of the Sufi approach. The knowledge of

Reprinted and revised by permission of the *Journal of Nervous and Mental Disease*, 1977, *165*, 318–329.

how to achieve "conscious evolution," according to the Sufis, existed long before the Islamic religion, from which many believe Sufism to be derived. Sufis see Moses, Christ, and Mohammed all as Teachers, each proclaiming the same message in different forms. The use of one external form as *the* means to the end of "conscious evolution" is a current and ongoing tragedy to Deikman and other Sufi authorities; too many people see meditation, special diets, chanting, or ritualistic religious practices as the end rather than one means among many. "The analogical form [as in the teaching stories of the Sufis] can evade the categorizing of our rational thought and reach other sectors of our mind."

About his own connection with Sufism, Deikman says:

> Since the early 1960s, I have been conducting research on meditation and the mystical experience. In 1972 I began the study of Sufi teaching stories and have been increasingly impressed with their power as instruments for clarifying and modifying one's own behavior, as well as for clarifying the human situation, in general. Furthermore, the psychological sophistication of these materials and their emphasis on motivation fit in well with my education and practice as a psychotherapist.
>
> Western psychotherapists can benefit from the perspective that Sufism provides because its essence is universal. However, it does require considerable study and the application of suitable materials in the correct manner and sequence, just as does the learning of psychotherapy. Idries Shah's writings and translations of teaching stories are designed for that purpose, and I recommend them to those who would like to assess the matter for themselves.

PSYCHIATRY CAN BE DEFINED as the science of reducing mental suffering and enhancing mental health. To date, the field has been primarily concerned with the first part of the definition. For example, in the index to *The Standard Edition of the Complete Psychological Works of Sigmund Freud* the word "neurosis" has over four hundred references while "health" is not even listed (Strachey, 1961). The imbalance is also present in contemporary texts. This is understandable; psychiatry originated to deal with disordered function. The question, What is the function of a healthy person?—which necessitates the further question What is the purpose of human life?—is not usually asked. It is assumed to be answered by simple observation of the everyday activities of the general population (Strachey, 1961).

Freud did consider that question in his later, philosophical writings; and when he did, his answer was more in keeping with mystical literature than with modern psychology: "I may now add that civilization is a process in the service of Eros, whose purpose is to combine single human individuals, and after that families, then races, peoples and nations, into one great unity, the unity of mankind" (Strachey, 1961, p. 121).

Underlying all of our activities are purposes that give meaning and direction to our efforts. One might go to college to become a lawyer or save money to buy a car or vote to elect an official; all these actions are vitalized by purpose. If the purpose is removed, the activities may cease. That being the case, what is the purpose of human life itself? What answer do we have to the question Why am I? A direct answer is not usually attempted in our culture but an indirect answer is there, implicit in scientific publications and in the world view that permeates from scientific authority to the public at large. We are told either that the question lies outside the scope of science or that the question is false because the human race has developed by chance in a random universe. The physicist, Erwin Schrodinger, commented on this problem:

> Most painful is the absolute silence of all our scientific investigations towards our questions concerning the meaning and scope of the whole display. The more attentively we watch it, the more aimless and foolish it appears to be. The show that is going-on obviously acquires a meaning only with regard to the mind that contemplates it. But what science tells us about this relationship is patently absurd: as if the mind had only been produced by that very display that it is now watching and would pass away with it when the sun finally cools down and the earth has been turned into a desert of ice and snow. (Schrodinger, 1969, p. 149)

We pay a price for the non-answer of science. Psychiatry has recognized the existence of "anomie"—an "illness" of meaninglessness, of alienation or estrangement from one's fellows. Anomie stems from the absence of a deeply felt purpose. Our contemporary scientific culture also has had little to say about meaning itself, except to suggest and assume that humans *impose* meaning; they do not discover it. That this assumption may be incorrect and productive of pathology is a possibility that needs to be considered.

It may be that the greatest problem confronting psychiatry is that it lacks a theoretical framework adequate to provide meaning for its patients, many of whom are badly handicapped in their struggle to overcome neurotic problems because the conceptual context within which they view themselves provides neither meaning, direction, nor hope. That context derives from the modern, scientific world view of an orderly, mechanical, indifferent universe in which human beings exist as an interesting biochemical phenomenon—barren of purpose. Survival is a purpose, but not enough. Working for the survival of others and alleviating suffering is a purpose, but it loses its meaning against a picture of the human race with no place to go, endlessly repeating the same patterns, or worse.

The issue of meaning increases in importance as one's own death becomes less theoretical and more probable. Life goals of acquisition become utterly futile, for no achievements of money, fame, sex, power or security are able to stop the relentless slide towards extinction. Our bodies age and our minds grow increasingly restless in seeking a solution to death. As former goals lose their significance, life can easily appear to be a random cycle of trivial events and the search may end in the most profound despair or a dull resignation. The widespread use of sedatives, alcohol, and narcotics is related to the wish to suppress despair and substitute sensation for meaning.

Such "existential" despair is so culturally accepted that it is often defined as healthy. Consider the following extract from *The American Handbook of Psychiatry*:

> To those who have obtained some wisdom in the process of reaching old age, death often assumes meaning as the proper outcome of life. It is nature's way of assuring much life and constant renewal. Time and customs change but the elderly tire of changing; it is time for others to take over, and the elderly person is willing to pass quietly from the scene. (Hunt & Issacharoff, 1975, p. 1166)

And so we should end, according to the voice of reason, not with a bang or a whimper, but in a coma of increasing psychological fatigue.

The problem is illustrated concretely and poignantly by the dilemma of many psychiatrists themselves. A recent article in the *American Journal of Psychiatry* concerned a number of professional therapists, ages thirty-five to forty-five, mostly of a psychoanalytic background, who formed a group which at first provided peer supervision and later attempted to function as a leaderless therapy group. Its members, as it turned out, were in a crisis:

> The original members of the group we have described were remarkably homogeneous in their purposes in joining. The conscious reason was to obtain help in mastering a phase in their own development, the mid-life crisis. We refer to that stage of life in which the individual is aware that half of his time has been used up and the general pattern or trajectory of his work and personal life is clear. At this time, one must give up the normal manic defenses of early life—infinite faith in one's abilities and the belief that anything is possible. The future becomes finite, childhood fantasies have been fulfilled or unrealized, and there is no longer a sense of having enough time for anything. One be-

comes aware that one's energy and physical and mental abilities will be declining. The individual must think of prolonging and conserving rather than expanding. The reality of one's limited life span comes into sharp focus, and the work of mourning the passing of life begins in earnest. (Ibid., p. 1166)

The "healthy" attitude recommended here would seem to be a stoic and courageous facing of a reality defined by certain assumptions prevalent in our culture: limited human capacity and limited meaning to life. From this point of view, it can be maintained that the second half of life should be used to adjust oneself to the final termination of individual consciousness. The grimness of such a goal may have resonated in the authors' minds because they go on to brighten up the picture.

In Erikson's terms, the individual must at this time struggle to achieve intimacy and creativity and avoid isolation and stagnation. If the work of mourning one's lost youth is carried through and the realities of the human situation are fully accepted, the ensuing years can be a period of increased productivity and gratification. (Ibid., p. 1166)

"Increased productivity" and "gratification" are invoked to suggest that something good is still possible after forty, but the possibilities still would seem to call more for resignation than for vitality and continued growth. This ultimately circumscribed view of human life is widely held by psychiatrists. Even in the relatively affirmative writings of Erikson, the "Eight Stages of Man" has some of the flavor of a survival manual (Erikson, 1950).

Eastern Approaches

In contrast to our scientific culture and its psychology, Eastern introspective (mystical) disciplines have focused on meaning and purpose but have employed a strategy in which reasoning is not central to the process of investigation. They have employed procedures such as meditation, fasting, chanting, and other practices unusual in the West as part of an integrated strategy whose exact pattern and content depend on the nature and circumstances of the individual and of the culture in which the teaching was taking place.

Unfortunately, the literature of Eastern psychological disciplines has not been of much practical use for contemporary Western readers. Academic study of such texts does not seem to develop wisdom or improve personality functioning, and exotic practices themselves have proven to be elusive, tricky instruments. For example, procedures such as meditation, which were once part of a unique and individually prescribed pattern of development, are now extracted from their original context and offered for consumption as if they were a kind of vitamin that was good for everyone, ridiculously cheap, and devoid of side effects. Users of these components of a specialized technology may obtain increased calmness, enjoyment, and improvement of efficiency—but without noticeable gain in wisdom. They answer the question Who am I? by reciting dogma, not by realization, and for all the "bliss" that may be displayed, the person's essential knowledge appears unchanged. For those who fare less well with meditation, schizoid withdrawal, grandiosity, vanity, and dependency flourish under the disguise of spiritual practice. Perhaps the worst effect of indiscriminate and unintegrated use of these techniques is that people come to believe that the effects they experience are the measure of Eastern esoteric science. The end result is that these casual experimenters confirm and strengthen their conceptual prison, from which they desperately need to escape.

The crux of the problem is that modern westerners need technical means specific to their time and culture. Although such a statement makes perfect sense to most people when the subject concerns the training of physicians or physicists, training in the "spiritual" is believed to be different. Programs and techniques two thousand years old are assumed to be adequate to the task. Indeed, it seems that the older and more alien they are, the better they are received.

The Sufi Approach

Fortunately, some traditional materials have recently been made available in a form suitable for contemporary needs; they offer practical benefits of interest to psychiatry as well as the general public. These materials address themselves to the question Why am I? but they do so in a unique manner.

Why We Are Here

Walking one evening along a deserted road, Mulla Nasrudin saw a troop of horsemen coming towards him.

His imagination started to work; he saw himself captured and sold as a slave, or impressed into the army.

Nasrudin bolted, climbed a wall into a graveyard, and lay down in an open tomb.

Puzzled at his strange behavior, the men—honest travelers—followed him.

They found him stretched out, tense and quivering.

"What are you doing in that grave? We saw you run away. Can we help you?"

"Just because you can ask a question does not mean there is a straightforward answer to it," said the Mulla, who now realized what had happened. "It all depends upon your viewpoint. If you must know, however: *I* am here because of *you,* and *you* are here because of *me*." (Shah, 1972a, p. 16)*

"Why We Are Here" is a teaching story adapted from the classical literature of Sufism. Teaching stories, in a form appropriate to the modern reader, are now being made available to prepare Western intellects for learning what they need to know. Stories such as "Why We Are Here" are built of patterns, depth upon depth, offering resonance at the reader's level, whatever that may be. Teaching stories have more than one function. They provide the means for people to become aware of their patterns of behavior and thinking in order to refine their perception and develop an attitude conducive to learning. Some stories are also designed to communicate with what is conceived to be the innermost part of the human being. Speaking metaphorically, Sufis say the stories make contact with a nascent "organ" of superior perception and supply a type of "nutrition" that assists its development. This latter function is particularly important; it is the key to the possible role of Sufism in helping to diagnose and cure, eventually, the basic illness that afflicts psychiatrists as well as their patients.

Sufism is usually thought of as a Middle Eastern mystical "religion." According to Idries Shah, that description is misleading. Referring to copious Sufi classics, he states that Sufism is a *method* of developing the higher, perceptual capacity inherent in human beings and vital to their happiness.

Classical Sufi authorities call this method a "science" in the sense that it is a specific body of knowledge, applied according to the principles known by a Teacher, to achieve a specific and predictable result. That result is the capacity to *know* directly (not through the senses or the usual intellectual functions) the meaning of human life and the inner significance of ordinary events. The change in consciousness that results is regarded as the next step in the evolution of the human race, a step that we must take or perish.

Ordinarily, we do not consider that the zone of normal perception may be so limited as to preclude the experience of a significant dimension of reality, the one with which mystical disciplines were concerned. According to the Sufis, meaning is just such a perceptual problem.

An illustration of this issue from the standpoint of biology has been described by C. F. Pantin, former chairman of trustees of the British Museum:

> A danger in this sort of behavior analysis—one which I fell into myself—is that it looks so complete that if you are not careful, you may start to imagine that you can explain the whole behavior

---

All the stories quoted in this article are copyrighted by Idries Shah and are reproduced with his permission. He has written many books on Sufism and his position as spokesman for contemporary Sufism has been accepted by many authorities. (See L. F. Williams, 1974).

of the sea anemone by very simple reflexes—like the effect of a coin in a slot machine. But quite by accident, I discovered that apart from reflexes, there was a whole mass of purposive behavior connected with the spontaneous activity of the anemone about which we simply know nothing. (Actually, this behavior was too slow to be noticed; it was outside our sensory spectrum for the time being.) (Greene, 1969, p. 60)

Similarly, the purpose of human life may be outside the perceptual spectrum of the ordinary person. To widen that spectrum, to provide "sight," is the goal of Sufism.

The Sufis claim that humanity is psychologically "ill" because people do not perceive who they really are and what their situation is. Thus, they are "blind" or "asleep" because their latent, higher capacity is underdeveloped—partly because they are caught up in the exercise of their lesser capacities for purposes of vanity, greed, and fear. The development of the necessary perception is called "awakening"; the perception, itself, is called "knowledge." It is often said that the science of awakening humanity has been present for many thousands of years, but, because of the special nature of the process and of the knowledge it brings, and partly because of the resistance it provokes, dissemination of the science has fluctuated throughout history and has never taken place on a large scale (Shah, 1971b, p. 23).

Radios

I was once in a certain country were the local people had never heard the sounds emitted from a radio receiver. A transistorized set was being brought to me; and while waiting for it to arrive I tried to describe it to them. The general effect was that the description fascinated some and infuriated others. A minority became irrationally hostile about radios.

When I finally demonstrated the set, the people could not tell the difference between the voice from the loudspeaker and someone nearby. Finally, like us, they managed to develop the necessary discrimination of each, such as we have.

And, when I questioned them afterwards, all swore that what they had imagined from descriptions of radios, however painstaking, did not correspond with the reality. (Shah, 1972c, pp. 13–15)

If we substitute "intuition" for radio receiver, the meaning of the analogy might be clearer. Ordinary intuition, however, is considered by the Sufis to be a lower-level imitation of the superior form of intuition with which Sufism is concerned. For the moment, however, consideration of the place of ordinary intuition in the activity of the scientist may help to illustrate the practical reality of the Sufic position.

Although the scientific method is taught as if data plus logic equal discovery, those who have studied how discoveries are actually made come to different conclusions. Wigner, a Nobel Prize–winning physicist, comments:

> The discovery of the laws of nature requires first and foremost intuition, conceiving of pictures and a great many subconscious processes. The use and also the confirmation of these laws is another matter . . . logic comes after intuition. (Greene, 1969, p. 45)

An extensive, detailed study of the process of scientific discovery was made by Polanyi, formerly professor of physical chemistry at the University of Manchester and, later, senior research fellow at Merton College, Oxford (Polanyi, 1958). Polanyi studied scientists' descriptions of how they arrived at their "breakthroughs" to a new view of reality. He found, like Wigner, that logic, data, and reasoning came last—another channel of knowing was in use. Since there was no word for that channel in ordinary vocabulary, he used an analogy to convey its nature:

> And we know that the scientist produces problems, has hunches, and, elated by these anticipations, pursues the quest that should fulfill these anticipations. This quest is guided throughout by feelings of a deepening coherence and these feelings have a fair chance of proving right. We may recognize here the powers of a dynamic intuition. The mechanism of this power can be illuminated by an analogy. Physics speak of potential energy that is released when a weight slides down a slope. Our search for deeper coherence is guided by a potentiality. We feel the slope toward deeper insight as we feel the direction in which a heavy weight is pulled along a steep incline. It is this dynamic intuition which guides the pursuit of discovery. (Discussed in Greene, 1969, p. 60)

Not only do the Sufis contend that people need more than intellect and emotion to guide them, but that those two "servants," in the absence of the "master," have taken over the house and forgotten their proper function:

The Servants and the House

At one time there was a wise and kindly man, who owned a large house. In the course of his life he often had to go away for long periods. When he did this, he left the house in charge of his servants.

One of the characteristics of these people was that they were very forgetful. They forgot, from time to time, why they were in the house; so they carried out their tasks repetitiously. At other times they thought that they should be doing things in a different way from the way in which their duties had been assigned to them. This was because they had lost track of their functions.

Once, when the master was away for a long time, a new generation of servants arose, who thought that they actually owned the house. Since they were limited by their immediate world, however, they thought that they were in a paradoxical situation. For instance, sometimes they wanted to sell the house, and could find no buyers, because they did not know how to go about it. At other times, people came inquiring about buying the house and asking to see the title-deeds, but since they did not know anything about deeds the servants thought that these people were mad and not genuine buyers at all.

Paradox was also evidenced by the fact that supplies for the house kept "mysteriously" appearing, and this provision did not fit in with the assumption that the inmates were responsible for the whole house.

Instructions for running the house had been left, for purposes of refreshing the memory, in the master's apartments. But after the first generation, so sacrosanct had these apartments become that nobody was allowed to enter them, and they became considered to be an impenetrable mystery. Some, indeed, held that there was no such apartment at all, although they could see its doors. These doors, however, they explained as something else: a part of the decoration of the walls.

Such was the condition of the staff of a house, which neither took over the house nor stayed faithful to their original commitment. (Shah, 1970a, pp. 211–212)

The Sufis specify that the development of man's superior capacity has its own rigorous requirements: adequate preparation of suitable students, the correct learning situation, and the activity of a Teacher—one who has reached the goal and by means of that special knowledge is equipped to teach according to the needs of the particular culture, the particular historical period, and the particular person. Because of these requirements, no set dogma or technique is used as standard: the form is only a vehicle and is constantly changing.

All religious presentations are varieties of one truth, more or less distorted. This truth manifests itself in various peoples, who become jealous of it, not realizing that its manifestation accords with their needs. It cannot be passed on in the same form because of the difference in the minds of different communities. It cannot be reinterpreted, because it must grow afresh. (Shah, 1970b, p. 264)

Thus Sufis differentiate their science from traditional religions, whether Christian, Judaic, Buddhist, Moslem, or Hindu, because such religions have solidified around set rituals, forms, exercises, and dogmas that tend to be handed out to everyone regardless of the context and individual differences. According to Idries Shah, even organizations designated as Sufi Orders may undergo this " . . . crystalization into priesthood and traditionalism. In the originally Sufic groupings where this fossilization has indeed taken place, their fixation upon a repetitious usage of Sufi materials provides a warning for the would-be Sufi that such an organization has 'joined the world'" (ibid., p. 259).

We have examples of this problem within the field of psychiatry itself. In Freud's time, for example, the Vienna Circle was open to all who had sufficient interest and capacity to participate, regardless of what formal degrees or titles they possessed. Today, the American Psychoanalytic Institute will not accord full membership to anyone without an M.D. degree, even though the functional relevance of a medical degree for the theory and practice of psychoanalysis can scarcely be discerned. A similar stiffening, sclerosing process seems to invade every human organization. With this in mind, we can understand the Sufic contention that religions were initially based on the development of a higher form of perception but inevitably became ossified, lost their capacity to function in that way, and now persist as archaic structures, hollow shells good only for fulfilling social and emotional needs. Furthermore, most "mystical experiences" are regarded by the Sufis as primarily emotional and having little practical importance—except for the deleterious effect of causing people to believe they are being "spiritual" when they are not. Self-deception is at work in such cases and blocks progress towards the development of higher perceptions.

Strange Agitation

Sahl Abdullah once went into a state of violent agitation, with physical manifestations, during a religious meeting.

Ibn Salim said: "What is this state?"

Sahl said: "This was not, as you imagine, power entering me. It was, on the contrary, due to my own weakness."

Others present remarked: "If that was weakness, what is power?"

"Power," said Sahl, "is when something like this enters, and the mind and body manifest nothing at all." (Ibid., p. 182)

The ordinary man is said to suffer from confusion or "sleep" because of his tendency to use his *customary* thought patterns and perception to try to understand the meaning of his life and reach fulfillment. Consequently, his experience of reality is constricted and dangerously so, because he tends to be unaware of it. Sufis assert that the awakening of man's latent perceptual capacity not only is crucial for his happiness but is the principal goal of his current phase of existence—it is man's evolutionary task. Rumi, the great Sufi poet, stated this explicitly:

This Task

You have a duty to perform. Do anything else, do any number of things, occupy your time fully, and yet, if you do not do this task, all your time will have been wasted. (Ibid., p. 110)

How Far You Have Come!

Originally, you were clay. From being mineral, you became vegetable. From vegetable, you became animal, and from animal, man. During these periods man did not know where he was going, but he was being taken on a long journey nonetheless. And you have to go through a hundred different worlds yet. (Ibid., p. 102)

According to the Sufis, only with the knowledge that perceptual development brings can human beings know the meaning of human life, in both the particular events of a person's life and the destiny of the human race.

City of Storms

Once upon a time there was a city. It was very much like any other city, except it was almost permanently enveloped in storms.

The people who lived in it loved their city. They had, of course, adjusted to its climate. Living amid storms meant that they did not notice thunder, lightning and rain most of the time.

If anyone pointed out the climate, they thought he was being rude or boring. After all, having storms was what life was like, wasn't it? Life went on like this for many centuries.

This would have been all very well, but for one thing: the people had not made a complete adaptation to a storm-climate. The result was that they were afraid, unsettled and frequently agitated.

Since they had never seen any other kind of place in living memory, cities or countries without some storms belonged to folklore or the babbling of lunatics.

There were two tried recipes which caused them to forget, for a time, their tensions: to make changes and to obsess themselves with what they had. At any given moment in their history, some sections of the population would have their attention fixed on change, and others on possessions of some kind. The unhappy ones would only then be those who were doing neither.

Rain poured down, but nobody did anything about it because it was not a recognized problem. Wetness was a problem, but nobody connected it with rain. Lightning started fires, which were a problem, but these were regarded as individual events without a consistent cause.

You may think it remarkable that so many people knew so little for so long.

But then we tend to forget that, compared to present-day information, most people in history have known almost nothing about anything—and even contemporary knowledge is daily being modified—and even proved wrong. (Shah, 1972b, pp. 140–141)

Most psychotherapy focuses on uncovering the fantasies that shape neurotic action and on clarifying and resolving the conflicts of wishes and fears that lead people to the repetitive, self-defeating behaviors for which they usually seek therapy. These functions of psychotherapy are necessary and important. However, while the resolution of neurotic problems may be a necessary first step for an individual, it is the measure of neither health nor human potentiality. Freud's model of man as an organism seeking relief from tension, forced to negotiate a compromise among instinct, reason, and society, leaves even the most successful negotiator in a position of impoverishment as pathological, in its own way, as any illness listed in the diagnostic manual. This is because the usual psychiatric concept of health is both barren and narrow.

Even the most "humanistic" of current psychologies that offer, in principle, equal attention to the playful, the creative, and "the spiritual" in human experience have no clear concept of the nature of the problem and little to suggest for its solution. "Self-realization" is advocated, but just what the self is that is to be realized and what that realization might be is not made explicit.

All these therapies and theories are in the same boat because they share the fundamental limiting assumptions about humans that are basic to our culture. Unwittingly, they help maintain the lack of perception that is the basic dysfunction of the human race and the chief obstacle to development of the higher capacities that are needed. In this sense, psychiatry, whether neurochemical, psychoanalytic, or a combination of both, perpetuates the endemic illness of meaninglessness and arrested human development; it has no remedy for the cultural affliction that cripples normal people. Thus, we arrive at the dilemma of the group of psychiatrists in "mid-life crisis" described earlier. They illustrate the point. Their science is caught within the same closed room in which they find themselves; indeed, it helps to bar the door. Psychoanalytic theory, the masterpiece of a genius, is so powerful and encompassing a schema that all phenomena seem to be contained within its walls; its proponents have come to love their city—storms notwithstanding— and they are almost never forced to re-appraise their world.

However, existentialism has helped some psychiatrists look to the underpinnings of their profession. Rychlak, writing in *The American Handbook of Psychiatry*, summarizes: "Building on the theme of alienation first introduced by Hegel, and then popularized in the writings of Kierkegaard, the existentialists argue that man has been alienated from his true (phenomenal) nature by science's penchant for objective measurement, control, and stilted, non-teleological description" (Rychlak, 1974, p. 162). Through existentialism, purpose and meaning have come to have advocates such as the psychoanalyst, Avery Weisman: "*The existential core of psychoanalysis is whatever nucleus of meaning and being there is that can confront both life and death. Unless he accepts this as his indispensable reality, the psychoanalyst is like a man wandering at night in a strange city*" (Weisman, 1965, p. 242). But how can he find that nucleus of meaning, let alone accept it? Our group of psychiatrists in mid-life crisis are missing that center because it is missing from the very discipline they practice and teach. Psychiatry cannot address the issue of meaning because of its limited concept of humans and its ignorance of the means needed to develop the capacity to perceive meaning.

In contrast, Sufism regards its task as the development of the higher perceptual capacity of man, his "conscious evolution." According to Sufi authorities, the knowledge of how to do this has always existed. It had a flowering in Islam during the Middle Ages, during which the term *Sufis* came into use, but it had other names, centuries before. The Sufis regard Moses, Christ, and Mohammed as Teachers of the same basic process; their external forms and the means they employed were different, but the inner activity was the same. The traditional forms we see around us today are said to be the residue of a science whose origins extend back to the beginnings of man's history. The problem is that we have been conditioned to associate "awakening" with vegetarian diets, chanting, chastity, whirling dances, meditation on "chakras," koans and mantras, beards and robes and solemn faces—because all these features of once vital systems have been preserved and venerated as if they could still lead us to the original goal. We mistake the parts, or a collection of them, for the whole. It is as if a car door, lying on the ground, were labeled "automobile" and hopeful travelers diligently opened and closed its window, waiting expectantly for it to transport them to a distant city.

Meditation, asceticism, special diets, and the like—all these should be regarded as technical devices that sometimes had a specific place in a coherent system prescribed for the individual. When used properly by a Teacher, they formed a time-limited container for a content that is timeless. Now, many old and empty containers labeled "spiritual" litter the landscape. The importation and wide use of these unintegrated forms attest to the immortality of institutions and customs rather than to the present usefulness of the activities.

The Sufis maintain that, nevertheless, amidst all this confusion, the science of "conscious evolution" continues in a contemporary form, invisible to those expecting the traditional. "Speak to everyone in accordance with his degree of understanding" was a saying of Mohammed (Shah, 1968, p. 18). Idries Shah states that he is one of those speaking now to contemporary man, Eastern as well as Western, in a way appropriate to the task of educating people who do not realize how much they have to learn. R. L. Thomson, writing in *The Brook Postgraduate Gazette,* agrees: "The problems of approaching the Sufis' work are such that Idries Shah's basic efforts do seem necessary. Little help is to be found in the academic approach based on linguistics and history" (1973, pp. 7–9).

Most of Idries Shah's writings consist of carefully selected and translated groups of such teaching stories, including the ones I have quoted. His translations are exceptionally clear and digestible to a modern reader. The stories provide templates to which we can match our own behavior. We accept them because they are so deceptively impersonal; the situations are presented as the history of someone else. The story slides past our vigilant defenses and is stored in our minds until the moment comes when our thinking or situation matches the template. Then it suddenly arises in awareness and we "see," as in a mirror, the shape and meaning of what we are actually doing. The analogical form can evade the categorizing of our rational thought and reach other sectors of the mind.

The Design

A Sufi in the Order of the Naqshbandis was asked:

"Your Order's name means, literally, 'The Designers.' What do you design, and what use is it?"

He said:

"We do a great deal of designing, and it is most useful. Here is a parable of one such form.

"Unjustly imprisoned, a tinsmith was allowed to receive a rug woven by his wife. He prostrated himself upon the rug day after day to say his prayers, and after some time he said to his jailers:

" 'I am poor and without hope, and you are wretchedly paid. But I am a tinsmith. Bring my tin and tools and I shall make small artifacts which you can sell in the market, and we will both benefit.'

"The guards agreed to this, and presently the tinsmith and they were both making a profit, from which they bought food and comfort for themselves.

"Then, one day, when the guards went to the cell, the door was open, and he was gone.

"Many years later, when this man's innocence had been established, the man who had imprisoned him asked him how he had escaped, what magic he had used. He said:

" 'It is a matter of design, and design within design. My wife is a weaver. She found the man who had made the locks of the cell door and got the design from him. This she wove into the carpet, at the spot where my head touched in prayer five times a day. I am a metal-worker, and this design looked to me like the inside of a lock. I designed the plan of the artifacts to obtain the materials to make the key—and I escaped.'

"That," said the Naqshbandi Sufi, "is one of the ways man may make his escape from the tyranny of his captivity." (Shah, 1972c, p. 176)

Teaching stories, such as the above, are tools that depend on the motivation of the user and his or her capacity or skill. As understanding increases, the tools can be used for finer and deeper work. The more one experiences and uses them, the more remarkable they seem to be. They lend credence to Idries Shah's claim that Sufism is a science whose boundaries contain modern psychology but go beyond it. He states, " . . . Sufism is itself a far more advanced psychological system than any which is yet developed in the West. Neither is this psychology eastern in essence, but human" (Shah, 1971b, p. 59).

According to Shah, the initial step most human beings need to take is to become aware of automatic pattern-thinking, the conditioned associations and indoctrinated values that limit human perception and receptivity. The teaching story is used for this purpose, illustrating at one step removed the egocentric thinking of which we are usually oblivious.

That's Why They Bunged It Up

Nasrudin was very thirsty and was happy when he saw by the roadside a water-pipe whose outlet was bunged with a piece of wood.

Putting his open mouth near the stopper, he pulled. There was such a rush of water that he was knocked over.

"Oho!" roared the Mulla. "That's why they blocked you up, is it? And you have not yet learned any sense!" (Shah, 1971a, p. 48)

Personal Wisdom

"I don't want to be a man," said a snake.

"If I were a man, who would hoard nuts for me?" asked the squirrel.

"People," said the rat, "have such weak teeth that they can hardly do any gnawing!"

"And as for speed . . ." said a donkey, "they can't run at all, in comparison to me." (Shah, 1972b, p. 157)

Teaching stories such as these have clarified patterns of my own thought, permitting me to notice similar patterns in my patients and to make appropriate interventions. One such story, whose content is explicit, is the following:

Vanity

A Sufi sage once asked his disciples to tell him what their vanities had been before they began to study with him.

The first said, "I imagined that I was the most handsome man in the world."

The second said, "I believed that, since I was religious, I was one of the elect."

The third said, "I believed I could teach."

And the fourth said, "My vanity was greater than all these; for I believed that I could learn."

The sage remarked: "And the fourth disciple's vanity remains the greatest, for his vanity is to show that he once had the greatest vanity." (Ibid., p. 47)

Having read this story, I later observed myself doing the same thing as the fourth disciple. In my case, I was berating myself for a personal failing. The context was different from the specific situation of the story, *but the pattern was the same*. The story came to my mind like a mirror and I understood the role of my vanity in what I was doing. That understanding provoked a wry smile and ended my self-flagellation. Later, hearing a patient present feelings in a similar pattern, I could recognize it and respond by eliciting and pointing out the concealed intent:

A young male patient with whom I was working began castigating himself for having made such a "mess" out of his opportunities, particularly as he was generally recognized as highly intelligent and likable. After listening to him for a while, I offered an alternative view:

"I think you're doing yourself an injustice. You're not a good guy who's making a mess of things—you're a mess who is doing a good job."

He stopped in his tracks—wide-eyed—then threw back his head and roared with laughter. We both laughed until our sides hurt. The next session, he reported that he felt much better. The self-recriminations were noticeably reduced.

My recognition of his concealed vanity and offering of an appropriate interpretation were matched by the patient's recognition and followed by laughter, relaxation, and the disappearance of the behavioral symptom. Would it be equally correct to say, from the point of view of behavior modification, that I had applied an aversive stimulus and therefore extinguished his response—a case of instrumental conditioning? Judging by my own experience, the "stimulus" does not feel aversive at all, it feels like relief, it is *recognition*. Distress is suddenly clarified and disappears, leaving a delightful sense of new freedom.

Let me give another example of what I am talking about: A woman whom I had been seeing in once-a-week psychotherapy entered my office almost frantic with distress, proclaiming anxiously that she was about to "go to pieces." Ordinarily, I would have listened, drawn out some explanation of the precipitating circumstances, and worked to clarify her irrational fears and bring into awareness the emotions or ideas that presumably were being repressed and were now increasing in intensity to produce her current symptoms. That would most likely have been helpful, to a greater or lesser extent. What actually happened was that, despite myself, I began to smile, feeling amused. The woman's distress was genuine by all the criteria customarily used in such situations. She was not prone to having crises and her statements were not hysterically exaggerated. Yet, I found myself smiling. The situation seemed funny to me because I perceived her as being in no actual danger but completely caught up in her imagination. Her observing self was not part of all that commotion but, instead, was reporting it.

The woman suddenly became aware of my facial expression. She stopped and indignantly demanded the reason for my "unfeeling" smile in response to her desperation. Her question stimulated me to smile even more broadly, and I actually began to laugh. She stared at me in disbelief with a look of outrage. However, in the midst of her rising anger, despite herself, she started to smile also. "Damn you!," she exclaimed and began to laugh. We laughed together for a long while. The desperate air of crisis, the emergency, the impending breakdown vanished in that laughter like fog evaporating in the sun. The "going to pieces" never happened. The woman's psychotherapeutic progress took a leap forward in succeeding sessions.

This is not an example of a brilliant new therapy. Explanations can be constructed for the incident, using standard theory. However, as far as I can tell, I responded the way I did because the stories I had been reading communicated a particular way of viewing the human situation.

The point of view and the learning principles presented in the teaching stories are tough-minded and emphasize the responsibility of each person for his or her own conduct and fulfillment. Such an attitude is not unfamiliar to psychiatry. However, developing a correct attitude is only the first step in Sufic science, a step called "learning how to learn." Responsibility, sincerity, humility, patience, generosity—these are not ends in themselves but tools that must be acquired before a person can proceed.

It is what comes after this first step that sharply distinguishes Sufism from all the psychotherapeutic and "growth-oriented" disciplines with which we are familiar. The Sufis regard their system as being far in advance of ours because it extends beyond the conceptual and technical limits of psychology and embodies a method for assisting humans to develop the special perception upon which their welfare, and that of the human race, depends. When asked to prove their assertion, Sufis insist on the necessity for undertaking preparatory training and then *experiencing* the domain in question. Such claims and requirements often provoke a haughty dismissal:

Three Epochs

Conversation in the fifth century:

"It is said that silk is spun by insects, and does not grow on trees."

"And diamonds are hatched from eggs, I suppose? Pay no attention to such an obvious lie."

"But there are surely many wonders in remote islands?"

"It is this very craving for the abnormal which produces fantastic invention."

"Yes, I suppose it is obvious—when you think about it—that such things are all very well for the East, but could never take root in our logical and civilized society."

In the sixth century:

"A man has come from the East, bringing some small live grubs."

"Undoubtedly a charlatan of some kind. I suppose he says that they can cure toothache?"

"No, rather more amusing. He says that they can 'spin silk.' He has brought them with terrible sufferings, from one Court to another, having obtained them at the risk of his very life."

"This fellow has merely decided to exploit a superstition which was old in my great-grandfather's time."

"What shall we do with him, my Lord?"

"Throw his infernal grubs into the fire, and beat him for his pains until he recants. These fellows are wonderously bold. They need showing that we're not all ignorant peasants here, willing to listen to any wanderer from the East."

In the twentieth century:

"You say that there is something in the East which we have not yet discovered here in the West? Everyone has been saying that for thousands of years. But in this century we'll try anything: our minds are not closed. Now give me a demonstration. You have fifteen minutes before my next appointment. If you prefer to write it down, here's a half-sheet of paper." (Ibid., p. 25)

If history has any value as a guide, it indicates that we should pay attention to the information now being provided to us by contemporary Sufism. Robert E. Ornstein, in his textbook *The Psychology of Consciousness*, concludes: "A new synthesis is in process within modern psychology. This synthesis combines the concerns of the esoteric traditions with the research methods and technology of modern science. In complement to this process, and feeding it, a truly contemporary approach to the problems of consciousness is arising from the esoteric traditions themselves" (1972, p. 244).

Psychiatrists need to recognize that their patients' psychological distress stems from three levels: from conflicts of wishes, fears, and fantasies; from an absence of perceived meaning; and from a frustration of the need to progress in an evolutionary sense, as individuals and as a race. The first level is the domain of psychiatry. The second and third levels require a science appropriate to the task. The special knowledge of the Sufis may enable us to put together materials already at hand—our present knowledge of psychodynamics, our system of universal education, our technology, our resources, and our free society—to create the conditions that will permit the development of humanity's full capacities, as yet unrealized.

16

Change versus Enlightenment

John B. Enright

Opening with the observation that the concept of enlightenment is particularly foreign to Western psychotherapy, John B. Enright illustrates with myth and case study his view of enlightenment. "Things are perfect the way they are, and if I don't see that, I have misconstrued the events or inaccurately assigned value to them." He further asserts that enlightenment, contrary to widespread belief, is not an "all or nothing" event; rather, it is something that happens in segments and can be aided in the therapeutic setting by deceptively simple tactics.

Among the tactics Enright has evolved in his work with clients, *renaming the symptom* is foremost. This involves a shift on the client's part, when he or she learns to see the "problem" in a positive light by giving it a new name with no pejorative overtones. Naturally, this process is unique for each client. The purpose behind it is twofold. First, the client "experiences . . . that he is the assigner of both meaning and value to the events . . . [and that] there is nothing intrinsically and forever good or bad" about his behavior. "Laziness," for example, can be renamed "taking an unauthorized but well-deserved break" by one client, and "surrendering to the Tao" by another. Second, because the original name for the problem or symptom apears to be an integral part of the client's life and orientation, a renaming that includes all levels of thought and feeling can result in a shift in consciousness. "New vistas . . . open up when people begin to appreciate the value of the very qualities they have been putting down."

When external resistance becomes internalized, a person has the choice of knowing the impulse fully or suppressing it. The enlightenment model encourages bringing that impulse "fully back into awareness," embracing it, being energized by it, living it out. This process transforms the impulse into something creative and positive. This is achieved to a large degree by the client's becoming aware that there was a very good reason for making the original choice to suppress it. As Enright says with kind wisdom, "Each choice . . . looked like the best idea at the time . . . [and] the way in is the way out." This type of enlightenment is not achieved by simply adopting someone else's re-evaluation of one's life, because that would only add another "layer of outside pressure" on the individual. The client must achieve the enlightenment by experiencing the old pattern of behavior fully and then recontacting the original impulse.

Enright clarifies the differences between the enlightenment therapist's encouragement of the client to experience old behaviors—no matter how delusional or unrealistic they may be—and the application of the principle of paradoxical change; the enlightenment therapist differs in being able truly to delight in a client's decision to stay with the "negative" if that is what the client really wants. In contrasting strategies of change and enlightenment, the author defines change as "a shift in relationship between two elements: *what is* and *what might be*. Change is made when the person moves from *what is* to *what might be*. Enlightenment, on the other hand, sees health or goodness located in *what is*.

The author sees the enlightenment approach as a dynamic force in therapy. He has recently found that people can be just as trapped in their fixed positive evaluations as they are in their negative, and that "these can be just as limiting." He does not present his model (which he developed from Gestalt and existential concepts) as being better than a change model; rather, he thinks there is room in therapy for both. He advises us to refrain from seeking after the transpersonal as something bigger and better; the transpersonal is already there. Like many of the other contributors, Enright suggests that as therapists we each start the healing process with ourselves.

THE CONCEPT OF ENLIGHTENMENT IS foreign to Western civilization in general and Western psychotherapy in particular. Life to us is certainly perfectable (through plenty of planning, effort, and "progress"), but it is certainly not perfect the way it is. Voltaire demolished that notion quite thoroughly in his ridicule of Pangloss in *Candide*. Free association with the word *enlightenment* would probably produce images of foreigners endlessly sitting cross-legged or exchanging riddles with Zen Masters—certainly not anything practical and usable for curing mental illness and alleviating human suffering. The purpose of this chapter is to spell out and demystify the concept of enlightenment and show that in it lie the seeds of a very practical body of theory and technique in psychotherapy.

Part of the phenomenon of enlightenment is the *experience,* not merely the concept, that *what is* is perfect just the way it is. Any thought to the contrary indicates lack of perspective, or less than complete understanding of the situation (though that lack of perspective would itself be perfect at that time). A frequent response to this point of view is to ask What about failure, anxiety, bad behavior, and bad traits?

There are two essential ways to miss experiencing the perfection of *what is.* One is an error in the assignment of value to events. There is a story of an old Chinese man, the only man in his village who owned a horse. Having a horse meant he could plow more land than the other villagers, and he was therefore relatively wealthy. Everyone called him fortunate until the day his horse ran away. Then they called him unfortunate. To both of these evaluations he was noncommital. A couple of days later, his horse returned, bringing another, wild horse with it. Since that horse was now his, everyone commented on his good fortune, until the next day when his son, attempting to tame the new horse, was thrown and broke his leg. This the villagers called unfortunate until the emperor's press gangs, drafting recruits for the army, came by—and of course, left the man's son behind as unfit for duty. The story goes on, but the point is clear; the value of the event can easily be misassigned by someone taking a narrow view. Only from a fuller, more complete view can the perfection of an event, trait, or action be seen, once it has been evaluated as not okay from a narrow point of view.

The other error resulting in failure to experience the perfection of everything is more subtle and fundamental. There is a story of two umpires who are talking about their work. One of them says, "I calls 'em like I sees 'em." The other comments, "They ain't, till I calls 'em." The very *what is* that enlightenment is about is not concepts such as "failure," "anxiety," or "horse ran away" but the fundamental energy events themselves. The moment we talk about these events to ourselves, we limit, categorize, and participate in the creation of the meaning, going well beyond *what is.* It turns out that it would have been more accurate for the Chinese man to have said, when his horse was not in the stable, "Oh, how nice. He's gone out recruiting more horses for me!" The only "is-ness" in that incident was the empty stable; the *rest were thoughts and considerations.* The very description of an event or trait is actually a set of theories, and already is hopelessly interlarded with preconceptions and assumptions. It is not surprising that it is hard to see the perfection of things, since most of what we are seeing is not the things but only our unacknowledged assumptions!

To restate, there are no "bad" habits, traits, or symptoms. There are only recurring events that people persistently construe to "mean" something, and to which they persistently assign negative value. "I have a bad habit" more precisely is "I do something, have the thought that I've done it before, and that it means something that I've done it before; then I have the additional thought that it's bad." "Habit" is a theory about repeated behavior, not a fact; and that it is "bad" clearly exists in the one who calls it bad, not in the event.

This chapter is devoted to applying to psychotherapy this point of view about enlightenment—that things are perfect the way they are, and if I don't see that, I have misconstrued the events or inaccurately assigned value to them. One more small point needs to be made first. Enlightenment is occasionally described or implied to be an "all or nothing" event. In my experience, enlightenment has so far always happened in segments. I can become enlightened about—see the essential perfection of—some one aspect of my life without immediate major shifts in other aspects. Essentially, this chapter is about getting people to experience *segmental enlightenment.*

The Tactics of Enlightenment

Some years ago I was working with a woman on her "problem" with jealousy, which manifested as anger when the man with whom she was living showed interest in other women.* She considered this a terrible symptom; her dislike of her jealousy was so great, and her reaction to the very word so strong, that I found it difficult to look with her for the possible, unacknowledged value of the jealousy. The strategy of finding a new name for jealousy thus occurred to me as a means of being able to talk about it more naturally. As we struggled to rename it, some memories and feelings about having been left by her father when very young came up with new relevance and intensity. After a few minutes, the new name emerged: "Early warning signal against the panic of being left unexpectedly." To my surprise, instead of this discovery making therapeutic work possible, as I had hoped, it seemed to finish it. She burst into tears, saw immediately that the jealousy, far from being an enemy, was a friend and protector, and that she had no intention of being without it. Not only did the "problem" shift from dealing with her jealousy to dealing effectively with the life situation that was threatening her well-being, but she knew immediately what she needed to do, and went home and did it.

Such dramatic results from ten minutes of work obviously made me attend very closely to what had happened, and from this incident emerged the basic tactic of the enlightenment approach to therapy: Renaming the symptom.

---

*The clinical illustrations in this chapter are mainly drawn from my practice of brief intensive therapy, or from one-time consultations—interviewing clients of another therapist, with the other therapist present. The brief illustrations are usually drawn from seminars in which participants were all practicing renaming the symptom as an exercise.

Renaming the Symptom

In this procedure, we press the client to find a new name for the "symptom," or rejected trait, that describes it in actual behavior as accurately as the original name but with as positive an evaluative tone as the original name had negative. Thus, if "stubborn" is the rejected trait, the new name might be "persistent." The two terms refer to the same behavior; only the evaluation is different.

The effect of this procedure is twofold. In the very process of doing it, the client experiences quite clearly that he or she is the assigner of both meaning and value to the events in question. There is nothing intrinsically and forever good or bad about "repetitively engaging in similar behavior in the face of opposition." Whether it is to be called stubborn or persistent depends entirely on how it works out.

The other effect is an almost universal tendency to grin with relief, amusement, or recognition at the moment of successful renaming. It is this moment of lightness and experienced perspective, even if only in one segment of one's life, that justifies calling this "segmental enlightenment."

I would like to give a few examples of renaming and some of the steps involved. There are very few "symptoms" that humans develop to which the technique has not been applied. "Temper outbursts against my children" became "dynamic limit-setting"; "procrastination" became "spontaneous reprioritizing"; "secretive" became "mysterious"; "irresponsible" became "willing to find out by inaction what really needs to be done." I should hasten to say that there is no glossary of renamed symptoms. Experience is individual, and rarely do two people with the same symptom come up with the same new name. (This suggests to me, of course, that the symptoms were never the same in the first place. Two unique experiences had, on the basis of some accidental similarity, been given the same abstraction as a name.) Thus for one person "laziness" was "surrendering to the Tao"; for another, more pragmatically inclined, it was "taking an unauthorized but well-deserved break."

The technique works most clearly with a symptom that is slightly stale, that has been around for a while. Some people find it useful as a first step to describe the actual behavior involved in the symptom, stripped of all evaluation. For example, this step applied to "stubborn" would take the form suggested above: "repetitively engaging in similar behavior in the face of opposition." It helps some people to suggest they create a puppet show to demonstrate this trait or symptom, and ask how they would manipulate the puppet to show the trait. Another useful suggestion is to break down the incident or trait into its components, both actions and thoughts, labeling each carefully. Thus in the previous example, "withholding" became "I was talking with a friend, thought of telling him a secret about myself in response to his sharing, had the additional thought that I should tell him, then decided not to" and the new name became "ability to resist blabbering about myself, even when invited to."

When the client has had some success in specifying the behavior involved, as free as possible from evaluation, it is useful to ask him to recall a time when that behavior was appropriate, and then to ask, "What did you call it at that time?" For example, a young man put out "too easily frightened" as his symptom. On one occasion, his anxiety about some tough guys in a bar turned out to be only too accurate; his name for his tendency then was "prudent."

One way of looking at recurring behavior that does not seem presently adaptive is that it worked so well when it was first learned that the individual is still partially committed to it, still half-convinced it will work, and not willing to give it up. Calling it a bad name ("symptom"), far from helping get rid of it, leaves the behavior present but drives underground the awareness that it may be useful, and leaves the individual in mystery about why he or she is doing it. Renaming the symptom calls back into awareness the old benefits of the behavior and leaves the individual feeling more integrated. Much of the excitement and humor of renaming springs from this recognition of the re-remembered value of the behavior. Bringing the old value back into awareness also leaves the individual in more flexible control of the behavior. The man who renamed "avoidance" as "giving unpleasant tasks plenty of opportunity to disappear" immediately has more control over his "avoidance." Knowing he was giving tasks the chance to disappear, he could apply the technique more precisely to tasks that were more likely to disappear and not apply it to tasks more likely to stay around. Instead of being the victim of a bad habit he was the possessor of a valuable skill, which he occasionally misused. The more I have worked with renaming the symptom, the more clearly I have seen not only that in persistent "symptoms" or "bad habits" there is always some unacknowledged benefit but also that it is *precisely* this unacknowledged benefit that has held the "symptom" in place.

The Ground of Being of Enlightenment Tactics

So far, it sounds as though renaming the symptom is a technique; to some extent, it can be used as such. On a deeper level, it seems that there is a particular stance toward life of which this exercise is one manifestation. It may not be immediately obvious, but somehow this stance assumes the denigrated trait or act—the "symptom"—is in reality deeply and rightfully part of the client; any appearance to the contrary springs from some limited and partial view that the client has taken of the trait. The point is not that he has a symptom that can be made tolerable, but that *it is a symptom only because he calls it that.* (Remember the umpire: "They ain't, till I calls 'em.")

Now it is true that the original negative evaluation of the trait came from the outside—a well-meaning parent, teacher, therapist, friend, or weight chart—but somewhere along the way the client "bought" the negative evaluation and made it his or hers. It is also true that at the moment he or she bought it, doing so was the optimum survival-oriented step for him or her to take; it is also true that he or she is presently getting some subtle secondary gain from clinging to this negative evaluation. The trouble is that these externally derived, negative evaluations—and the negative evaluations of the negative evaluations such as "I shouldn't be so self-critical"—have become a top-heavy pile of contradictory tendencies and countertendencies, blinding them to their own reality.

The enlightenment model says very simply: just peel off these pieces of contradictory stuff, *one at a time, starting at the top.* Suppose I criticize myself a lot and then criticize myself for criticizing myself. Life would at least lighten up a little if I stopped the meta-criticism and saw my "ultrasensitivity to incipient problems so that I can mention them first" as the lifesaving virtue it undoubtedly was once, and still may be at times.

A woman who was occasionally beaten by her alcoholic husband criticized herself harshly for "putting up" with the beating, called herself "too dependent," and thought that something must be wrong with her. Now while it was probably true that a life without beatings might be preferable, that her life would be better were she more independent, and that therefore some change would be in order, all her self-criticism had not led to change. She was spending so much energy in the self-criticism (partly designed to forestall others from saying the same things first) that she had lost sight of the value of what she was doing. It *was* valuable, of course, or she wouldn't have been doing it, but she was quite unable at first to see the value as we worked with renaming the symptom.

When she renamed her "symptom" as "willing even to endure abuse to ensure that my daughters have a home," she suddenly began to appreciate herself and lighten up. When she looked at the positive purpose of the action, it also didn't take her very long to suspect that other, less uncomfortable ways of ensuring a home for her daughters might exist. She left the session clearly thinking along these lines. It is very difficult for someone who has not been at a renaming session to appreciate the shift in consciousness and the new vistas that can open up when people begin to appreciate the value of the very qualities they have been putting down.

Renaming can even work with someone else's "symptom."

A woman in consultation complained that her husband often seemed preoccupied at home. The children complained, "Mommy, what's wrong? How come Daddy won't talk to us any more?" She accepted, even fostered their complaints and felt very bad about her husband's deficiency. She had nagged him considerably about this to no avail; if anything, his preoccupation and withdrawal became more pronounced. When pressed as to what he was doing during these times, she acknowledged that at least part of the time he was thinking through work-related problems which he could not think through at work, where he was under considerable pressure. In fact, she began to see that this preoccupation had some value to him and therefore to the family. With the symptom thus reconceived, she decided that she and the children would begin to "give Daddy the space to finish what he needs to do to support and take care of us." She and the children began enthusiastically to support and validate these periods of homework, and instead of family relations being disrupted, everyone in the family developed a feeling of participating in the task of material support for the family.

Although I was not able to check later, I suspect that the husband's periods of work absorption at home grew shorter.

The Process of Enlightenment

As we develop in life, our impulses are met with resistance from the outside. Occasionally, we partially internalize this outside resistance and identify with it, and this leads to an apparent "contradiction" in our personality. (I put *contradiction* in quotes because from one point of view, given all the assumptions and previous learning of the organism, there is no contradiction, just complexity.) More and more energy becomes caught up in the dynamic tension of these apparent contradictions, leaving less and less energy to live with.

Now, in one way it does not matter how complex and apparently contradictory the tendencies and impulses in a person's life are, so long as that person is fully and equally aware of them. The problem is not the amount of apparent contradiction but that awareness has become distorted and incomplete. If a person has some impulse to beat children and a stronger impulse to be a kind parent, he is likely totally to suppress the weaker impulse in favor of the stronger and live his life busily not beating children, but not being very actively and spontaneously kind either because he is using that energy to suppress the beating impulse. If his choice in life is "to have impulse to beat children versus not to have that impulse," clearly he chooses the latter. However, given that he has such impulses, the choice is to know them fully or to suppress them. Most people, at that point, choose to suppress and problems begin. The enlightenment model would say: bring that impulse fully back into awareness, embrace it, let yourself be excited and energized by it and live it out. Now, in the process of living it out in the full light of awareness and balancing it with all other impulses and forces in life, more and more appropriate and elegant ways of expressing it will emerge. Eventually, as he embraces, expresses, and practices this impulse in the context of his whole life, what looked, in his unenlightened days, like a dreadful wish to beat children will turn out to be exquisite sensitivity to the dangers of spoiling children, and exceptional ability to use discipline well. In the enlightenment model, a weed is a flower in the wrong place, and every "fault" a virtue misapplied. The first step toward proper application of the virtue is at least to stop misperceiving it as a fault and give it the space to flower into the virtue it might be.

If a person has wandered deep into a swamp, there are several ways to get out. The enlightenment model would tell him to "turn around and retrace your steps exactly." He would know the route very well, since that's the way he got into the swamp. Since his impulses and unacknowledged urges are what got him in, he will be very familiar with each choice point. *The way in is the way out*—in reverse of the exact order he came in!

It is crucial to realize that on his way into the swamp, *each choice*, though it may in fact have brought him deeper into the swamp, *looked like the best idea at the time*, given his knowledge and assumptions about the situation. Calling his choices "bad," instead of acknowledging them as the best possible, leaves him farther out of touch with the knowledge and assumptions from which he was working, one step more mystified about himself and life, and more likely to stumble deeper into the swamp. Being enlightened by knowing that his choices were the best possible ones at the time, leaves him more in touch with the knowledge or assumptions he has, and able to see more accurately where he is.

In this model, wisdom external to the client's frame of reference is likely to function as a barrier. Everytime we buy someone else's well-meaning evaluation of our life and call some part of ourselves "bad," we lose touch with the rightness of that part *for us now*. We try to reject it, but organismically, still believing it to be somehow prosurvival, we cling to it even as we resist it. Mother said, meaning only the best for us, "Your assertiveness is bad," and we became compliant. Compliance was a useful survival strategy at the time, though it did drive underground our lingering awareness of the value of assertion; so we became covertly assertive. Now the nice therapist, meaning only the best for us, tells us, "Assertion is good and I'll show you how to get more." This attempt at change may succeed, and if it does, all is well. When it does not succeed, it may become just another layer of outside pressure that functions to complicate the picture a little more. Then, instead of being people who suppress our natural assertion, we become people who suppress our natural assertion *and* paste a layer of artificial assertion on top; this drives us yet further from our integrity, our potentially unified self. The enlightenment therapist would encourage and support the surface meekness and give us the space to experience it fully. After we had experienced it fully and achieved segmental enlightenment about it, it is possible that we would tire of it, see how pointless it was, and spontaneously contact our natural assertiveness again.

> A young widow with three children came to see me at the insistence of friends. They had told her it was ridiculous for her after three years still to be mourning her first husband instead of meeting other people, and perhaps finding another husband and father for her young children. I completely validated this choice to stay at home and mourn her dead husband, commenting that such love was rare these hasty days, when people no longer seemed to care very deeply and forgot old loves quickly. I praised her for her constancy. When she said that she visited her husband's grave at least once a week—expecting me, I think, to challenge this as being too frequent—I questioned her closely to see if this were really enough and wondered out loud whether she was beginning to "slip" in her devotion to him. Within a few minutes she was rather irritably saying that enough was enough, that perhaps it was time for her to begin to live a little more, and that looking for another man would *not* detract from the memory of her husband.

Since the consequence of this therapeutic interaction was to change rather than accept *what is,* the interaction needs a closer look to distinguish what I did from the tactic of paradoxical change. The key difference is that I was completely behind the choice of mourning her husband the rest of her life. I thought it would be a fine way to live, if that's what she wanted, and I remember getting a little carried away and poetic about the beauty and rarity of it. Unlike the paradoxical changer, I would have felt I had participated in a therapeutic triumph if she had gone home with new resolve to mourn the rest of her life and stand up for this choice to her nosy friends. Her "problem" was that she was not fully savoring and appreciating the value of her choice, and therefore could not quite finish it. This vignette also illustrates that people do not always immediately appreciate having behavior-as-it-is so enthusiastically supported. People have a lot invested in rejecting and bad-mouthing what they are doing and will resist the enlightenment approach.

The last vignette in this section also illustrates the resistance to accepting the "symptom" and the need for persistence in supporting it.

A fifteen-year-old girl had run away from, or made herself thoroughly unwelcome at, three foster homes in one year. Surprisingly, she showed no other signs of disturbance or delinquency and was doing quite well in school. Her troubles were strictly in her foster homes. She claimed she wanted to live with her mother; her mother, however, refused to take her. In the view of her social worker, her impossible wish to live with her mother was the stimulus for her misbehaving in the foster homes, though she seemed to understand and accept the impossibility of living with her mother.

After a few introductory minutes, a segment of our conversation went something like this:

T: "Well, what *would* you like to do?"
C: "I'd like to live with my mother."
T: "So, why don't you?"
C: "She doesn't want me."
T: "Oh, come on now; she's your *mother.* [1] Surely you can guilt her into keeping you somehow." [2]
C: "I can't seem to get her to." [3]
T: "Well, just go knock on her door and be there when she opens it." [4]
C: "I did, but she locked the door."
T: "Well, bring a sleeping bag and sleep on the porch!"

(1) At this point, in the enlightenment model, we accept her wish to live with Mother as somehow, in some unknown way, perfect. Rather than argue with or reject it, we get behind her wish and support it. She does not, organismically, fully believe it is impossible—and it may not be! In any case, being told once more from the outside that it is impossible will certainly have no value.

(2) Though the suggestion seems to come from me, it seems probable that she has brooded on this possibility hundreds of times. Though my saying it out front may startle her, the *content* will be no surprise.

(3) This validates my suspicion that this is a familiar idea.

(4) Again, she has no doubt played out this fantasy many times.

After a few minutes, in a mixture of annoyance and sadness, she announced that it was silly to talk about living with her mother. We went on to talk about the problems in her foster home. However, very soon, as we looked at the difficulties there, she commented again on how much better and easier it would be to live with her mother. I immediately told her I would waste no more time talking about these dumb foster homes and that we would leave no stone unturned in her effort to get back with her mother. We discussed suing her mother; suicide threats; poison pen letters to the man with whom her mother was living, and a major barrier to the daughter's living there; becoming his absolutely obedient servant; and a number of other quasi-feasible and bizarre ideas—all of which had occurred to her one time or another. Finally, with intense sadness, mixed with anger at me for taking her dream away, she truly, from inside, gave up hope of living with her mother. Though before she had *seemed* to accept that it was not possible, she had clung to little pockets of unexpressed hope through all the talks with her social worker. The negative effect of the hope, of course, was that it eroded her willingness to try hard in the foster homes. Giving up the hope was deeply painful.

It is interesting that she perceived the situation as my taking her dream away, when all the time I had been enthusiastically supporting the dream and coming up with possible ways of achieving it. Though the hope was the big barrier to her living her life successfully, she had clung to it, and the way she clung was to not look at it too closely. Only my grossly exaggerated and unreasonable support of her dream got her to experience it enough to let go. Again, the difference between this enlightenment approach and paradoxical change is that I had no investment in change. For her to continue to run away from foster homes and dream of living with her mother would be fine with me. Somehow, with an enlightenment therapist helping her to do it better and better, something fascinating would emerge from that particular experiment in how to be a human in this weird world.

Contrasting Strategies of Change and Enlightenment

People come to therapy to *change* or, frequently in the beginning, to get someone else to change. They may be overweight and wish to weigh less, or feel guilty about having an affair and wish to be comfortable, or be lonely and wish to be in a relationship.

"Change" can be diagrammed as a shift in relationship between two elements: *what is* and *what might be* (figure 16.1). *What is* could be tipping the scales at 180 pounds, and *what might be*, tipping them at 150. *What is* could be being and going places alone frequently, and *what might be*, being and going with another, special person.

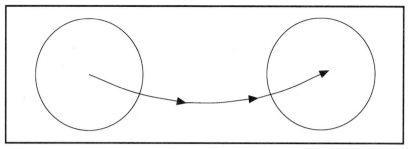

Figure 16.1   A model of change

Other names for *what is* are reality and behavior. Other names for *what might be* are image, dream, goal, standard, or ideal. Change, then, is making the dream real—being with the special person, reaching the goal (weighing 150 pounds), meeting the ideal or standard (stopping the affair). When it happens fully, it includes such feelings as success, completion, and satisfaction.

When change is happening though not yet complete, when there is some movement of *what is* toward *what might be*—losing some weight, beginning to meet possible people—the feelings associated are anticipation, hope, and excitement. When there is no movement in spite of effort, when *what is* and *what might be* remain distant—the scales still read 180 pounds in spite of dieting, activities are endlessly alone—the associated feelings are frustration, stagnation, guilt should, and despair.

These are the feelings that bring people into therapy, seeking to get back on the track of change. From this point of view, "health" and goodness are defined as *what might be,* and illness or badness as *what is,* the symptom.

This is the change model for bringing *what is* and *what might be* together. It is sometimes successful and sometimes not. There is, fortunately, another way to bring the two together: to bring *what might be* over to fit *what is.* This is to realize, rather than just having the concept, that *what is* is okay *just as it is.* That is enlightenment (figure 16.2).

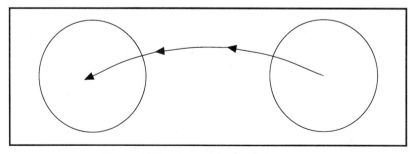

Figure 16.2   A model of enlightenment

The experience of completion and satisfaction in enlightenment is as full as in the change model, though instead of being tinged with "success," the completion feeling in enlightenment is tinged more with peacefulness and a sense of "coming home." In this enlightenment model of completion, health or goodness is located in *what is*; illness or badness is in *what might be*, in the crazy illusion that things should be or could be any different from how they are.

Let us apply this model in some depth to the 180-pounder, a man in his fifties who has been 30 pounds overweight all of his adult life, and supports this judgment by showing us weight charts that give 150 pounds as the optimum weight for a man his height and quoting physicians about the heart and organ damage caused by being overweight. Success in "change" of course, would leave this man at 150 pounds, though his contentment with his success might be marred by constant worry about regaining weight, "watching his diet," and other concerns. In the enlightenment model, trying to lose weight after thirty-five years of failure is seen as insane; he might almost as reasonably look at his weight chart, find out the height at which 180 pounds is perfect, and try to grow to that. He is a 180-pounder with a delusional system, and this delusional system, which leads to chronic guilt, self-loathing, and negative self-image, is his problem.

Before getting into the full implications of the enlightenment point of view in this case, I would like to consider for a moment another man with a weight problem. I met a man in Osaka who is 5' 5" tall and weighs 240 pounds. His weight problem is that he needs to regain about 10 pounds to get up to the optimum weight to hold his championship title in sumo wrestling. Now, weighing 250 pounds makes some sense for him. True, there is damage to some organs and an extra strain on his heart, but his life *as a whole* is better at 250 pounds than at whatever the weight chart says it "should" be. If he ever reached that "right" weight, he would be a broken has-been instead of rich and famous. It is definitely arguable that being "over-weight" is right for him or more precisely (remember the umpire), 250 pounds is not over-weight in terms of his whole life. There are other considerations that make 250 pounds the right weight for him.

My point is this: the same argument applies to the 180-pounder except that the considerations that make 180 pounds right for him, though just as valid, are not as visible and clearly defensible as those for the wrestler. There are some unacknowledged benefits to 180 pounds and/or some unacknowledged drawbacks to 150 pounds. The unacknowledged benefits could be anything; perhaps eating heartily is a deeply satisfying experience for him. The unacknowledged drawbacks could also be anything; perhaps he is un-willing to "give in" to and please his wife by losing weight.

The position of the enlightenment model would be that, given every-thing that is true for him, 180 is his perfect weight, and his persistent self-nagging to lose weight is his pathology. As for the weight charts, they no more apply to him as a unique individual than they do to the wrestler. They apply only to the nonexistent, abstract "average." Further, if he should ever experience his perfection at 180, he would be likely to see all the hitherto unacknowledged benefits of it. With these benefits in awareness, as time goes on, without effort or self-nagging, other ways to achieve these benefits would be likely to emerge in the course of living, and he might lose some weight—or he might not. In any case, the guilt and self-nagging would lift, and he would live a happy and self-accepting life, whatever he weighed.

Five additions and caveats are necessary to complete this presentation.

1. The perfection must be fully and deeply *experienced* in enlightenment, not just theorized. The enlightened person, in the life-segment in which he or she is enlightened, is not "resigned" to something, "thinking positively" about it, passively "accepting reality" or "convinced it's okay." With a sense of finally seeing the truth, he or she joyfully embraces and welcomes the hitherto rejected "symptom" as a true and fully valid part of himself or herself. This quality of joyful embracing, rather than grim acceptance is useful in practice. It is quite easy to tell when a client has not reached this stage but is only accepting the intellectual argument. It is useful to remember that the word *enlighten* includes the word *light*.

2. Everybody changes all the time; this includes enlightened people. The "change" that I have contrasted with enlightenment refers to deliberate, preplanned, goal-directed, usually effortful change. Spontaneous change, though it happens continually, is more likely to happen in someone who has let go of self-nagging and "trying" and is aware of his or her full nature. However, the enlightenment point of view is not another gimmick to induce paradoxical change. The enlightened client is indifferent; he or she is fine with or without change.

3. I have used the phrase "get behind the client's choices" a number of times, and need to clarify it. Reading transcripts of enlightenment-oriented sessions might leave the impression I am giving some wild advice. I have lyrically praised and found the essential goodness in outrageous lifestyle choices. Yet, in context, it is always clear to clients that I am not seriously advocating any life action. I don't think they should do or not do anything; I just throw my weight in whichever way they are leaning so that they can see that way more clearly. If I seem briefly to favor some step, it is only to help bring into fuller awareness some of the murkier fantasies which they have kept around without inspecting closely. I don't care what

people do. I do care that what they do furthers their aliveness. Any notions I may have about *what* would further their aliveness, however, are just my notions, more potentially complicating outside stuff, and I would not dream of seriously asserting them. However much clients may beg me not to, I treat them as queens or kings in their universes, the ultimate authorities on meaning and value in their lives.

4. Though probably also consistent with steady, long-term work, the enlightenment model works especially well in the discontinuous, intermittent therapy I favor. Enlightenment tends to come segmentally, in short, intense bursts followed by periods of action and consolidation, which in my opinion people can do very nicely on their own. They can then come back when they are ready for another segment of therapy.

5. After some months of successful development of the idea of renaming the symptom, I began to sense that something was missing. Not only are people trapped in their negative evaluations; *they are equally or more deeply trapped in their fixed positive evaluations.* If someone has the concept she is "generous" for example, she will cease trusting her real wisdom about when and with whom to be generous. Acting out of that *self-image* of generosity, she may lend money to someone even though she doesn't feel quite right about it. When she is not repaid, there are ripples of negative consequences—suppressed irritation in her own life, as well as guilt, rationalization, and distancing in the person unwisely trusted.

Out of this realization came a parallel exercise, "renaming the virtue," with which I could demonstrate to people that they were as trapped by their apparent positive evaluations as they were by their negative. I say "apparent" because it gradually emerged that the "good" traits that seemed to be the opposite of the "bad" ones were equally narrow, limiting, and ultimately unsatisfying. If "bad" is the opposite of "good," then there is some greater, more profound Good ("is-ness") that is the opposite of "good/bad" (evaluativeness). It now seems to us that it is precisely by the tissue of narrow (good/bad) evaluations, both of self and others, that the individual maintains excessive individuality and dampens or cuts out potential Good, "transpersonal" experiences of oneness and connectedness with others and the universe. If evaluations could be dropped, these so-called transpersonal experiences are right there, waiting to be had. A clever but still profound way of saying this is that paradise follows immediately after the last judgment. There is a trap, of course, in talking of dropping evaluations. If we call an evaluation bad, we have just added not subtracted to the net number of evaluations! Hence the emphasis on renaming, on finding the core of "good" in the apparent "bad"—and "bad" in the "good"—on the way to nonevaluative "is-ness."

Because this chapter has focused on the enlightenment model, it may sound as though I think it is a better approach to therapy than the change model. Not so. There is a time and place for each; a time to work hard for change and a time to focus on the perfection of things-as-they-are. The therapist who is skilled in both points of view and has no commitment to one over the other will have as easy a life as a therapist can have. Every argument a client brings up about how hard change is, becomes an argument for acceptance; the more intolerable the client finds *what is,* the more energy to work for change the therapist can ask of him or her. A rule of thumb for the ambidextrous therapist conversant with both points of view is this: any feeling of effortful straining on the therapist's part is a sign it may be time to switch strategies. When the third "yes, but—" follows the third "why don't you," it may be time to say, "You know, you're right; it looks like it *is* impossible. Let's look at how good it may be just the way it is."

This chapter has presented a point of view about life which, though actually developed from Gestalt and existential practice, seems highly consistent with enlightenment. In this view, whatever is happening in a person's life is somehow right for him, given fully who he is. If he does not experience this rightness, it is because he has taken some narrow and incomplete view of his life, based on some internalized outside evaluation. If clients can only experience the perfection of *what is,* including all of what was previously seen as pathology, their lives will immediately and spontaneously begin to normalize, and life will get as good as it can, as fast as it can, in ways that would have been impossible to see from the pathology point of view.

If there is advice or an action message in this chapter, it is to refrain from seeking after the transpersonal as something different from and bigger than life, from getting special training in psychic phenomena, or from indulging in excesses of meditation in search of powers; instead, heal the personal or transpersonal split in everyday life by letting go of hyperindividuality, effortful ambition, and narrow evaluation. Even *letting go* is too strong a phrase; given the hypertrophy of conscious striving in our culture, we would soon find ourselves "trying" to let go. The transpersonal is *already there,* under the separating layers of effort and evaluation. And the way through the layers is not by rejection and yet more ambition and evaluation, but by finding, accepting, and loving the wisdom and rightness of every action and choice just the way each is.

The best way to do this for our clients is to begin this process in ourselves.

17

When the Therapist is a Yogi
Integrating Yoga and Psychotherapy

W. Michael Keane and Stephen Cope

In this chapter, W. Michael Keane and Stephen Cope show us how the wisdom and techniques of the Yoga Sutras, formulated in the third century B.C. by Pantanjali, can form the basis of an excellent therapy of the mind, body, and spirit.

The authors discuss the linking of spirit or life force (*prana*) with the yogic goals of aligning our personal vibrational energies with those of the universe, and they explain how these can be influenced by the defensive mind-body patterns developed to protect our psyches.

Yoga sees the lodging of all mental and emotional inhibitions in the body where patterns of contraction developed as a defense. By holding a yoga position while breathing and focusing on physical sensations, feelings can begin to be witnessed without contracting.

Through resistances and reactions, the mind can impede our operating through the wisdom of *prana*. The authors describe how concentration and mindfulness meditation practices can be used to work with the impediments, which are called *samskaras*. When removed, these blockages reveal our true nature.

Keane and Cope remind us that emotions are rooted in bodily, not intellectual, experiences. For many patients who find it difficult to verbalize, the yogic approach—starting with bodily feelings—can frequently be an excellent way to access those blocked emotional feelings.

The authors explain that the therapist "moves out of the pathologically based concept of the client's predicament to a model in which the client has only obscured his resources for change and growth." They present an important discussion of the integration of yogic kundalini techniques with psychotherapy.

Along with some clinical examples, Keane and Cope give specific instructions on how to systematically work with this system, both with individuals and with groups.

EACH DAY THE PSYCHOTHERAPIST is witness to the struggling and suffering of human beings. He or she is a listener, a problem solver, a priest, a shaman, a parent, a consultant, a friend, a teacher, a seeker, an explorer, and a container for deep emotions. Sometimes he or she is a yogi and a meditator.

What does it mean for the therapist to be a yogi in terms of personal identity and what techniques come from the yogic tradition that are useful in psychotherapy? This chapter explores how this 2,500-year-old science of inner exploration can be applied to the problems of living in our fast-paced modern civilization.

The Problem Space

People come to psychotherapy because their lives are not working. They come looking for the alleviation of symptoms. They come to resolve conflicts in relationships. They seek to understand the anxiety of an identity crisis which occurs at a developmental milestone. They come to deal with their loneliness or to discover purpose in their lives. The situations are as endless and as varied as the lifestyles that people lead. Yet, consistently, clients want relief from the stressful emotions of anxiety, depression, fear, grief, hopelessness, and despair. They also want more of the positive emotions such as joy, happiness, peace of mind, and love.

Western psychotherapy, with its emphasis on talk and understanding through cognitive structures, has been able to solve some but not all of the many human dilemmas that life presents. The methods, whether psychodynamic, cognitive, behavioral, Gestalt, transpersonal, Jungian, or bioenergetic continue to evolve. Each is just one map to guide clients to explore alternative perceptual realities and behavioral and emotional choices. The emotional waters that flow in psychotherapy constantly shift and change from person to person and from context to context. Many maps are needed for the therapist to fully navigate and explore the alternative routes required to help someone get unstuck.

The philosophy and techniques of yoga which originated over 2,500 years ago contain a very powerful atlas with many directives for exploring and healing the human condition. In the third century B.C., Pantanjali formulated his Yoga Sutras (see Feuerstein, 1979), describing a means for achieving total physical and mental health. Through intense self-observation and experimentation, the yogis developed a holistic system that worked with the mind, the emotions, the body, and the spirit. For the yogi no one aspect of human functioning is more important than the other. To work with the emotions you need mind and body. There is no separation. Change the emotional state then you affect mind and body. Change the physical experience then you affect the mind and the emotions. Change the mental representations then you affect the body and the emotions. At the core of all experience is the spirit, the life force.

The Overall Map of Energy

The concept of energy is the foundation for all body experiences, all emotions, and all mental activity is key to understanding yoga. Here the mystics and the physicists agree. The universe is simply vibrating waves and particles taking form and shape. All the elements of our world—stone, wood, fire, air, and water—are different vibrations of particles. Our words and our thoughts emerge as vibrations of our nervous system. All our emotions are expressions of the energy of our mind/body systems. For the yogi, the goal is not just the adjustment of a symptom but the alignment of personal energy with universal energy.

The Body as Energy

The energy that each thinks of as his "essential self" is contained in his physical body, itself a mass of energy more or less contained in a solid form. Our being is grounded in the body. All experiences go through the body. When there is trauma or neglect of the body early in life, the body literally contracts to protect itself. In these protected contractions the natural flow of energy is blocked. Muscles tighten, shoulders hunch, the stomach churns, the breath is contained. The emotional response may be fear, frustration, or anxiety. Patterns of contraction develop which become part of a defensive structure to all experience. With these energy blocks the person's perception of the world is limited.

Yoga seeks greater consciousness beginning with the body. The yogi perceives that all mental and emotional inhibitions, no matter how or when they originated, are lodged in the body. The body is the grossest layer of our experience, and is a dense reflection of all other aspects of us. As yogi Amrit Desai said to me,

> Through the body, we can begin to address our energy blocks while we bypass the entanglements of our conditioned mental reactions. By focusing on physical sensations as we breathe and

hold a yoga posture, we begin to be witness to the feelings in our bodies. We learn to tolerate the direct experience of life force energy without having to suppress or contract around it.

Unless therapy addresses physical blocks, there is limited success in healing psychic pain. A clinical example will help.

CASE OF ELLIE

Ellie came to therapy on referral from another therapist because she heard that I worked with body memories. She described how she felt completely out of touch with her body and was actually terrified of what she might feel in the body. She had been in several twelve-step recovery programs and was tired of escaping through alcohol, drugs, and now food. She was somewhat overweight and described her eating as being out of control. Despite years of recovery and therapy, she felt depressed most of the time and helpless to change much of her life. Historically, she had been sexually abused by her father who was a Holocaust survivor. The result of this abuse was a fragmentation of the self in order to survive. She had many somatic symptoms from headaches to muscle spasms. She had undergone many operations including a hysterectomy. She had done a lot of work in which her ego could now look at the abuse and describe what had happened. She could have feelings and feel her anger and her despair. Yet, she still felt split off from herself, as an alien in her own body. We began very slowly just teaching her to stand and scan her body, reporting out loud what she experienced. Body scanning is used in many meditative traditions as a way to focus and settle agitations from the body. We have refined it for our use employing a model developed by Phoenix Rising Yoga Therapy (Lee and Reynalds, 1992). Repeatedly Ellie found discomfort and shame. She felt a blockage in her throat as if she were being choked and told not to speak.

In order for her to begin to develop comfort in her body and to begin to make distinctions in what she was feeling, we began each session with a simple yoga warm-up that involved deepening the breath and some elementary yoga stretches. I encouraged her to allow whatever sounds might be present to emerge. We worked with the Lion pose in which you literally open the jaw, stick out the tongue and roar. This gave her some relief and she could laugh about how much she wanted to roar at her father to make him stop molesting her and to howl at her mother to protect her. Repeatedly we worked in a supported Fish pose in which she was supported on a bolster and blankets in such a way that the chest and throat area were opened, while the pelvic area dropped down and was supported on the floor (Lee and Reynalds, 1992). For most people this is a restorative pose that induces relaxation. For Ellie, it was terrifying. Recurrent images of her father coming into her room at night arose, and she would feel the choking in her throat. As she more and more gave voice to the terror, she was able to invoke the image of a wise woman to protect her. In addition, she began to develop a relationship with the split off little girl part of herself that was so terrified and had no voice. She said that despite the discomfort of the sessions, she felt her only hope for a full life was to come more into her body, to actually own what she felt had been taken away by her father.

Initially she was afraid to do yoga in a class for fear she would start crying and not be able to stop. In the meditation at the end of each session, she requested her "higher power" to guide her. The message over and over again was to communicate, to give voice to her experience and eventually her healing. She began to write. At first, all her writing was preoccupied by the abuse. Over and over again in prose and in poetry she wrote of the abuse. Eventually as she became more and more able to stay in her body and be aware of the sensations, she could write from the perspective of the wise woman or the playful imp. She could now witness her experience from different perspectives. As her symptoms shifted, so did her view of life. She could now reach out to others and help them with their suffering. As she said, "through the yoga and body psychotherapy, I finally began to get an inkling that it would be okay to be at home inside myself. I don't feel the shame and disgust that separated me from others." She has now arrived at a stage of self-compassion that gives her space to explore deeper spiritual practices. She has gone on several women's retreats where she has hiked, canoed, and meditated. She said, "I am experiencing my body and my life from a new place."

In this work we see how listening to the body led to intense emotional work. Her mental insights that came from questioning and writing allowed her to integrate the energy of emotional/body experience in a way that her beliefs about her essential self began to change. She also was able to move into the transpersonal connection to a higher universal power.

It is important to note that for the yogi, energy and life force are synonymous. As Desai says,

> At the most basic level our life force or energy expands and contracts our hearts, digests our food, heals our physical wounds and breathes in and out of us in a reliable way. This higher life

force has many higher evolutionary potentials that are meant to work through all human experience—the physical, emotional, mental, and beyond. The higher potentials manifest themselves fully only as we learn to access this power and cooperate with its innate wisdom. Yogis call this life force *prana*, which functions in perfect harmony with universal laws. (1993, p. 4)

The Mental as Energy

From the beginning of language formation, a person applies his intellect to justifying and explaining the world to himself and to directing his behavior. Intellect is basically the cognition of knowing and learning. All thought is energy of the nervous system manifest in thoughts and words. As with the physical body, the intellect develops patterns or habits to protect the organism. We use our intellect to confront and understand the emotions and bodily experiences. The individual utilizes cognitive processes to make sense out of the past, see the effect on the present, and work out the changes for the future (Rosenberg, Rand, & Asay, 1985).

For the yogi, it is the identification with the thoughts, beliefs, expectations, and predictions of the mind that keeps the individual from operating from the pure wisdom of *prana*. The mind, which is itself a tremendous evolutionary gift to man, becomes a liability when it impedes the functioning of *prana* through mental resistance and reactions. The mind can block energy at all levels of our being so that life becomes very constricted (Desai, 1993).

The primary yogic tool for working with the impediments of the mind is meditation. On the yogic path, as in most meditative traditions, there are two basic types of meditation: concentration practices, which create one-pointedness of mind; and insight practices, which create wisdom through learning to reality-test one's experiences of the world.

Through the concentration practices we begin to contain the mind's tendency to wander, grab onto, and categorize experiences. We learn over and over again to come back to the awareness of the breath or an awareness in the body. Through the process we begin to develop full absorption that eventually leads to altered states of consciousness where we connect to the universal. As we access the flow of our own *prana*, we become more willing to surrender our habitual ways of thinking and acting to its infinite wisdom. In the process of letting go of our conditioning to this universal higher power, we become even more conscious. The transformational process is self-reinforcing (Desai, 1993).

Through the insight practices we expand our attention to include many mental and physical events exactly as they occur over time. We attend without judgment to all phenomena—thoughts, feelings, sensations, or fantasies that predominate the field of awareness. As the mind begins to become more and more subtly adept at inspecting its own processes, it sees how thoughts arise and pass away. We learn to get out of our own way and be in the experience of the moment.

The human condition can be compared to a cloudy day. The fact that there are clouds in the sky does not mean the sun is not shining—it means that the sun has been obscured from sight. In each of us, the sun of consciousness is always shining. Our thoughts, our negative predictions, our fantasies, our mind reading are obstructions that cover it up. These obstructions create limited vision, creating darkness and suffering. Yogis call the individual obstructions *samskaras* and the entire covering as *avaran*. The *samskaras* are deeply grooved, patterned, and conditioned complexes of thought, feeling, and behavior which are unconsciously held. They impair our reality testing, influencing perceptions and choices of behavior. The work of meditation is to remove, step by step, the *samskaras* that block the light and energy of our true nature.

How is meditation brought into clinical practice?

CASE OF JAMES

James is a forty-two-year-old married man with two children who came to therapy because he felt that he had lost meaning or purpose in his life. He had many vague somatic complaints, mostly connected to tiredness and a lack of energy. He had been in therapy before and said that he wanted tools with which to work rather than more insight about his past.

Initially I taught him the body scan (Lee and Reynalds, 1992) as a way to focus his attention. He quickly felt more present. Over time we moved into several explorations using the full yogic breath. This is a three-part breath, that takes the breath in three sips—first to the belly, then to the mid-thoracic area and then to the upper chest—pauses briefly and then reverses the flow on the exhale (Taimni, 1961). The result is usually a state of calm and internal focus. James easily learned to reconnect to himself through these techniques. He looked forward to each session as an opportunity to "come inside himself." He began a meditative practice at home, saying, "I feel like I slow down and savor what I have in my life rather than focusing on what I am missing." Eventually one of his young sons, intrigued by his sitting, came and started sitting with him. The result has been a deep energetic bond between father and son.

As James became more adept at taking himself into a meditative state, I guided him to focus on the thoughts and distractions that arose and to verbalize them from his inner state. As he allowed his attention to rove he let go of obsessive ruminations of the past or worry about the future and often found metaphors or images that described his experience. These metaphors served as vehicles for him to integrate some of the trauma of his upbringing in an alcoholic family. For instance, he once had an image of being a raven who kept pecking at him to shape up and get his life together. As he explored the image, the raven became his critical parents who always wanted him to do more. He realized that the image of the raven was inside him and that he constructed a reality of internal self-criticism to keep himself motivated. The result was that he felt driven and constantly dissatisfied. As the raven image returned on occasion, it turned into an all-seeing eagle who could fly over great terrain. As he said, "Now I can see whole situations, and I have this witness consciousness with which to observe my experience with perspective. This is such a different type of insight for me." He began to take better care of himself, altering his diet without effort and beginning to do more yoga. He had much more energy for himself and his family.

For James, the meditations became tools to truly transform his experience of himself. When we develop witness consciousness through consistent practice of self-observation without reaction, misperceptions dissolve and the limited view of reality is greatly expanded.

Emotions as Energy

Emotions are a body experience not an intellectual one. Emotions fire the nervous system which triggers the release of hormones which in turn affect and produce more emotions. Fear and anger shoot the body full of adrenaline so that we are ready for flight or fight. Love relaxes us so that our energy flows more freely and we become expansive. Hate contracts us, stifling our energy, creating tension (Rosenberg, Rand, & Asay, 1985).

The yogis observed that emotions are constantly moving. When we don't hold onto them, they flow through us quickly. Look at the child who moves from pain, to angry tantrum, to smiles within a brief time frame—all in response to some small frustration. As a result of the feedback, both internal and external, we hold on to or block an emotion. The more traumatic the feedback, the greater the holding.

We develop attachments to pleasurable emotions and aversions to painful ones. When we become overwhelmed with the experience of the energy of the emotion in our body, we seek to control it by manipulating both internal and external experience. In vain, we try to hold on to the pleasure and avoid the pain. The patterns of attachment and aversion that get locked into the system become a character structure that is impermeable to corrective feedback. Rather than feeling or experiencing our feelings directly, we tend to have our habitual reactions to them. We then live in reaction rather than in direct experience.

Resisting "what is" creates suffering. Pain is part of life. It exists to show us what works and what doesn't, what is in alignment with universal laws and what isn't. If we experience pain as our teacher, we can experience its lessons and let it go. The pain goes as soon as we have the learning fully and our consciousness has been expanded. If we fight and resist, then not only do we hold the pain in our body-mind, but we also build up layer after layer of tension and distress around the original discomfort. We become afraid of our fear, angry about our shame, and guilty about our anger.

Creating layers of secondary pain is a means to protect us from an original hurt that we are unwilling to face. For instance, it may seem easier to focus on anger and outrage then to fully experience something like shame and humiliation. However, the very process of protecting ourselves from the emotions adds conflict and discomfort to our lives. The actual core trauma is kept from healing. It stays buried in the subconscious and body tensions. Eventually we have to go back through all the layers of tension and protection that we have built up so we can experience the original hurt and release it (Desai, 1993).

Yoga is an incredible tool to cut through the layers and come to original pain. Let's examine a clinical situation.

CASE OF JOHN

John came to see me after attending a program for men in yoga at the Kripalu center. John reported that he had discovered a vitality that he had not known he had within him from his experience. He was a tall, very thin man who seemed very disconnected from the distant limbs of his body. He was very soft-spoken and had little insight into his predicament. He felt that he did not know how to talk about what he was feeling and could not imagine how a talking type of therapy could help him. He had therefore sought me out in order to be able to deepen the experience of himself that he felt in yoga. He reported that he was in a difficult marriage in which his wife controlled everything. He felt shamed and unable to speak up to her. He said that he was aware of passive aggressive ways that he got back at her by not listening when she spoke, doing things at his own time, and ignoring her requests. This only led her to shame him more.

Because John had so little capacity to make body distinctions which would allow him to know his feelings, the body scans revealed very little. He could only notice a tightness in one shoulder or in the hips. We would open each session with a series of warm-ups and postures geared to energize his body. The vigorous nature of the postures allowed him to feel more sensations in his body. From this place we could begin to work on the emotions and the images attached to the emotions. For John, we worked with the warrior postures, which involve a big step forward while simultaneously lifting up the hands over the head. (See Mehta *et al.,* 1990 or Tobias & Sullivan, 1992 for pictures.) The various warrior postures are energetic standing postures that require concentration and a deepening of the breath. For John they came to represent his capacity to step forward into life with new vitality. When he stepped into the warrior, he could feel the sense of power and fullness with him. Over time he began to connect feelings of being small and contracted to his childhood in which he felt shamed and not important. Sometimes he became frightened of the feelings of bigness that he felt from the yoga, fearing on some deep level that he would be overwhelmed and humiliated if he were too visible. At the end of each session he was guided into a meditation of sitting with himself in his fullness. Along with the yoga this became part of his daily practice. He began to speak directly to his wife, ultimately and with much relief separating from her. In this separation he has been more fully able to be with himself and connect with others, particularly his six-year-old son. Together they now have a very powerful father and son bond— one he longed for but did not have in his own childhood. He feels that he can now have compassion for his ex-wife without having to please her and compromise himself. John has learned to listen to cues from his body when he is not being genuine or truthful and to examine the consequences of his behavior. Again we have the development of the witness consciousness. Without the yoga, it is likely that John would have taken a very long time to reach the levels of awareness that he achieved over the six months. As he says, "I probably would not have stayed in therapy because I wouldn't have had anything to say from week to week. I am so amazed at what I can get from listening to my body and knowing my feelings."

Putting Body, Mind, and Emotional Energy Together

The different energies of the body, the mind, and the emotions weave together creating an incredible tapestry of consciousness, awareness, and perception. As seen in the case examples, to work with one thread, whether it be one off the spool of body energies or one off the emotional spool, affects the entire pattern of experience. The pattern of the weaving of the energies ultimately reveals our spirit, our true Self.

Utilizing yogic philosophy and techniques in psychotherapy offers the possibility of going beyond reformation of symptoms and habits to full transformation. Through the methods of yoga and psychotherapy the individual can de-hypnotize himself, clear his body, know his emotions, and then release from his mind illusions and unconscious conditioning so that there is full access to all of the human potential. The yogi believes that ultimately the potentiality of the Self is to connect with the entire cosmos. When we connect with our inner Self with all of its energy we realize that we are truly divine, truly one with the universe, truly God in human form (Mishra, 1987).

How is the therapist to bring the divine into his practice? His clients want relief not religion. The answer is to do nothing, but allow and trust that as he works, the inherent natural, evolutionary urge toward wholeness or unity spontaneously emerges. When the therapist has practiced yoga, he develops faith in the intelligence of the natural internal energy of *prana*. He also develops a heightened tolerance and capacity to tolerate raw sensation, feeling, and thought. His container of Self is large so that he has an abiding self from which he can work with his clients without moving into reaction. Freud himself once wrote that the kind of attention required by the effective therapist is "an evenly suspended or hovering attention"—a concept very much like the witness consciousness found in yoga. The major task for the therapist from this viewpoint is to be in witness consciousness with the client. When he does this, he moves from the bind of thinking that there is something wrong with the client that he has to fix. Instead, he sees that everything that he needs for healing already exists inside. The therapist moves out of a pathologically based concept of the client's predicament to a model in which the client has only obscured his resources for change and growth. His task as therapist is one of facilitator rather than of manipulator. He moves away from the role of therapist as giver and client as recipient. The more that the therapist is connected to his source, the more room exists for the client to connect to his full potentiality. In developing his own consciousness, he is able to shift his vision of the healed self from one of independence and individualism to one that possesses a full acknowledgment of interdependence and unity consciousness. When he can hold the posture that there is nothing wrong with the present moment and there is nowhere else to go, there is a huge space for healing.

How and where does the therapist learn to connect with his own source? The answer in one sense is that he has to turn to his Self and open to the awakening of his full energy of his body, mind, and emotions.

Kripalu Center for Yoga and Health in Lenox, Massachusetts, has been a pioneer in aiding therapists to explore the connections between yoga and psychotherapy (Cushman, 1994). Kripalu yoga itself is the yoga of consciousness. It blends the classical eight-limbed raja (royal) yoga prescribed by Pantanjali in his Yoga Sutras (Feuerstein, 1979) with ecstatic kundalini techniques. Raja yoga teaches the discipline to control the powers of the energies within us while kundalini yoga invites a surrender to the flow of internal energy. According to the principles of kundalini yoga, there is a very powerful spiritual energy known as *kundalini-shakti* which resides in all of us. It is an evolutionary life force that can take us to higher levels of consciousness. It is literally experienced as energy streaming through the body and can be awakened by intense spiritual practice.

Within the Kripalu yoga framework, the awakening to the fullness of inner energy occurs in three stages. The first stage involves a "willful practice" in which, as in other forms of hatha yoga, the body is deliberately guided through classical yoga postures and breathing techniques which strengthen and purify it. In the second stage, postures are held for long periods of time so that long held tensions and energy blockages can be released. This stage can often trigger powerful catharsis with weeping, shaking, and shouting. Often old memories, long held in the body, are released. This can be seen as the beginning of the release of the kundalini energy and unless understood can be threatening to the individual.

In the third stage, the energy that has been released is allowed to temporarily take over the body. All rules of alignment and form are set aside and postures emerge spontaneously from the movement of the *prana*. As the liberated energy courses through the system, it sweeps the *samskaras*—the patterns of holding from the past that are still imprinted on the body and mind—like floodwaters clearing clogged debris from a riverbed. If fully surrendered to, this spiritual energy, the kundalini, will shape not only the practitioner's yoga postures but all other areas of his or her life as well (Cushman, 1994). Consciousness is dropped as the body moves spontaneously from one posture to another, moved from within. One surrenders to the impulses of the body and follows them. It is like a divine dance, a dance with oneself. Surrender practice at this point is a letting go of the ego and of self-concept. It involves surrendering more and more of the self-image that has been strengthened in the willful practice and letting the "fortress of the self be shaken." When the *prana* or the inner energy is allowed to move in this stage of practice, one can experience bliss or one can experience painful images and thoughts. Oscillating experiences often run one after another. It takes a tremendous amount of abiding self or witness consciousness to allow the process to emerge.

Psychologists might describe the experiences at this point of surrender practice as a letting go of the self. There is a dismantling of the self concept and an opening into the true self, the *Atman*, which is connected to the universal flow of energy.

It is important to note that this process of will and surrender is not linear, but circles back upon itself over and over. The process inevitably pulls to the surface parts of the self that are not fully integrated. More yoga can just aggravate the tremendous conflicts that arise. Without guidance, some people abandon yoga at this point as too stressful or too overwhelming. This is where psychotherapy is very powerful to provide methods to integrate emerging experiences or parts of the self which may have been split off at early levels of development.

Yoga Therapy Groups

We have integrated the three stages into our yoga therapy groups. We begin each group with a meditation invoking the wisdom of the body. This is followed by some yoga warm-ups and *pranayama* or breath techniques to guide people into the sensations within the body. As we slow the breath we move more into feeling and sensation. Participants then work in pairs, with the leader directing them into specific postures.

We have discovered in these groups that certain postures tend to bring up specific feelings. For example, those that open the groin area often bring up anger while others that open the chest bring up sadness, grief, or joy. Standing postures can bring up power and strength. (Examples of the postures can be found in Lee and Reynalds, *Phoenix Rising Yoga Therapy Training Manual,* 1992.)

Once the person is in the posture, the leader encourages the breath to deepen and directs attention to listening to the sensations and letting the body speak. Each assistant takes note of his partner's dialogue. Having dropped the normal mode of relating, the body often speaks through metaphor. For example, when one man was asked to have his body speak while in a posture, he replied, "There is a being called 'Klutch' in my hip, and every time I move forward in life he is there to jerk me back and keep me in my place. I need to listen to him before my back goes out of alignment. He is there to remind me to slow down."

Sometimes images of the past come up. One man reported that he could remember his mother sitting on him to control him. "I have the feeling in my body that all she needed to do was come near me and my pelvis would freeze up to protect myself." Over several sessions, he began to move more freely and began to talk with his wife about some of his frustrations with situations in which he felt controlled.

Sometimes the experience is peaceful and meditative. Sometimes it is filled with shaking and a need to shout or yell. At other times there is shaking that runs through the body.

At the end of each group we share the experience. At least once a month, we draw *mandalas* of the experience to open to the creativity and the symbology that emerges. There is a spirit of safety, excitement, and exploration in these groups. As one woman said, "It is like we move into the sacred territory of the psyche, where the doors of the unconscious open from the body outward."

Conclusion

Clearly for the clinician there is very sophisticated technology within yoga that can be utilized directly with individual clients and groups. These techniques aid in the exploration of the experiential self. The *asanas*, the postures, open up parts of the body where we hold our emotional tension. The *pranayama*, the breath control techniques, help to create altered states within the individual, making him more open to change. Meditation in its various forms provides a means to develop inner space for the individual to come into a deeper relationship with himself.

On a larger level, as the therapist himself does his own work, exploring the will and surrender within his own self system, he creates the possibility for ongoing evolvement with his client. The therapist is able to create a large container for the healing of the experiential self, while at the same time coming into consciousness of the transpersonal or divine Self.

As noted in the clinical examples, individual clients found that the practice of yoga stabilized the changes which they had made. Furthermore, they continued to seek experiences in yoga and meditation that allowed them to come into touch with the spiritual.

People in the group are often in awe both from what emerges from them and from what they are able to facilitate with each other. One group member said, "Yoga [has] become a way to deepen every aspect of my being. The power of having group support to explore so deeply goes beyond anything I ever expected to find in yoga or psychotherapy."

The integration of modern psychotherapy with the wisdom of the ancient yogis provides a fertile space for personal evolvement. The threads off the spools of bodily, emotional, and mental energies can be woven into an integrated tapestry for healing. We are in the process of creating this tapestry which will provide healing for the body, mind, and emotions, and ultimately free the spirit.

18

Potential and Limitations of Psychological and Spiritual Insight

Sylvia Boorstein

Sylvia Boorstein is both a psychotherapist and a Buddhist meditation teacher. She makes the point that spiritual insights, like psychological insights, have the potential of promoting growth and health. She also states that integration of insights, both psychological and spiritual, is dependent on healthy underlying ego structure. Just as in the psychological arena we know not to "add insight to injury" (i.e., where there is an injured structure), so we need to know that spiritual insights likewise can be an agent of disintegration. As meditation becomes more and more acceptable and accessible to westerners, therapists who encourage their patients in spiritual practice need to be assured that the spiritual practice is appropriate.

Although the author focuses on the Buddhist spiritual truths in this chapter, they are, in fact, basically the same for all spiritual traditions. Boorstein describes the realization of *dukkha* (the experience of pain in life), of impermanence (that everything is constantly changing), and of how clinging and attachment traps us, leading to further suffering. Her examples of some ego-impaired individuals attaining these realizations are very instructive.

In the illustrations given it becomes clear that intense meditation practice can lower psychological defenses with resultant flooding of repressed memories. In addition, intense meditation can uncover hidden psychotic or manic conditions. Also, the acceptance and integration of certain paranormal powers that sometimes arise as a result of intense meditation practice is difficult for ego-impaired individuals.

Loss of one's sense of separateness or ego boundary, a desired spiritual goal, can be terrifying and threatening to someone who does not have a strong sense of his/her ego boundaries. Boorstein cautions us very wisely to be alert to the dangers of using the spiritual insights for selfish (narcissistic) ends. For example, the insight of " 'we are all one' does not mean 'I can use you for my personal gain.' " Nor do the insights: " 'Everything is empty' and 'Everything is temporal' mean that we do not need to be actively responsible for each other and our world." Unfortunately, all too often we see leaders of various spiritual communities making these errors, leading to all kinds of abuse of their followers.

WHEN I WAS LEARNING to be a psychotherapist, thirty years ago, insight into the unconscious derivatives of conflict was held as the key cure of emotional problems. When I began practicing Vipassana meditation, twenty years ago, I learned that insight into the essential nature of all experience was the key to spiritual freedom. In both instances, the idea that "The truth will set you free" was very exciting to me. In both realms I have been both a consumer and a provider. My own psychoanalysis, with a kind and skilled analyst, gave me considerable symptom relief and much more ease in my life. My ragged edges, my startle mechanisms, my habituated tendencies, remained. I see that to be true with my clients as well. They get better, but not new. Likewise, insights in meditation practice have been thrilling, and things I previously thought might be true I now *know* are true. *And,* I live in a dualistic world with a large family net of attachments and am easily caught in appearances. I see that as true with my meditation students as well. We know a lot of truth, and we often feel and act as if we don't.

The degree to which both categories of insight may be transformative depends, I believe, on two other parameters. One is the degree to which the ego in the individual for whom the insight, psychological or spiritual, arises is able to tolerate it. The second is the degree to which the individual is prepared to make conscious effort to integrate that insight into her/his personality style. This chapter is a summary of how I see that insights, in degree dependent upon the integrity of the ego structure in which they arise, have the capacity for making us free-er. In terms of psychotherapy, we might call this "the use of ego strength to effect further psychological growth." In Buddhist terms, it would be called "using Right Understanding and Right Aspiration" in the development of wisdom.

I field-tested the question How much does insight set us free? with a group of Vipassana Buddhist teachers with whom I meet regularly. All of us have done years of meditation practice, presumably accompanied by insights, and many of us are psychotherapists. Probably all of us have been in psychotherapy at some time. When I asked, "Did insight set you free?" most people laughed. But, we all agreed that we are free-er, and managing our suffering more gracefully.

When I asked my teacher friends, "What was it that changed you? Was it insight? Was it teachers or therapists who were supportive and inspiring? Was it teachings or understandings that led to a broader vision? Was it the altered states that are part of the experience of meditation and of psychotherapy? Are altered states themselves healing? Is it the support that we get in both venues—the support in our life that comes from our therapist and our family and friends, and in our spiritual practice from our teachers and our spiritual community? Is it support that generally helps us to face what is difficult for us so that we are able to grow and change?" The answer from most people was "All of the above."

Years ago, when I first became interested in psychotherapy, "insight" was the main word that we used to talk about change. When someone was asked, "How are you doing in your therapy?" a normal response was, "I'm doing very well. I'm getting a lot of insights!" That was taken to mean, "I'm getting better!" These days I think we generally acknowledge that insights, no matter how dramatic, do not suddenly erase decades of maladaptive responses. What was formerly a "defense mechanism" often endures as a "character style."

In the 1950s, when psychoanalysis and psychodynamic psychotherapy were the prevailing models, TV scripts would portray a seriously inhibited person who would go to a therapist and, in the course of one session, would discover the unconscious derivative of his/her problem, respond fully and emotionally to the discovery, and leave entirely freed of inhibitions. I don't know anyone who has had that experience. I do, however, know many instances of people who were able to use psychological insights constructively.

Here is an example from my practice. What I think this demonstrates is the possibility, given a relatively strong ego, of using an intellectual understanding about one's own dynamics to make constructive life changes. I do not believe this person has been "cured" (if cures actually exist) from her original trauma, but I think that the constructive changes she is now making in her life might enable her to progressively heal.

Sara began therapy at age thirty-three because she had continuing somatic symptoms, primarily headaches, that were not signs of any particular disease. She had been married for one year when she began therapy, and the headaches had increased since her marriage. Sara was the only child of two mild-mannered, shy people. Her parents were forty years old when she was born and had treated her with great affection. Her marriage seemed relatively gratifying, although her husband, while seemingly mild-mannered like Sara's father, was also quite stubborn and unconciliatory, unlike what she had expected.

Sara was a first-grade teacher, very popular with parents and children because of her gentle disposition. She was referred to me by her physician who suspected that her ailments might be a sign of internal stress, but she was unaware of being upset about anything in her life. She was thrilled to be married and felt that she loved her husband. She said that although she sometimes felt dismayed with his stubbornness, she never got angry. My mildest suggestions that perhaps she might feel anger were met with resolute conviction that she felt sorry for him for "being so stuck in his ways" and perhaps a bit annoyed that she needed to accommodate him, but she wasn't really angry.

One day, soon after we began therapy, Sara came in to report that on the previous day, when she had been having a headache, her husband had himself suggested that perhaps she was mad at him. She had protested that she was not, but he apparently had stubbornly continued to insist that she was. Indeed, he had persisted so long in provoking her that Sara had lost her temper and shouted at him, using uncharacteristically vituperative language. She reported to me that at the end of her outburst, although she was shaken by what she had said, her headache had vanished. We both laughed.

Sara's insight did not cure her headaches forever. It was important for her to begin to acknowledge that she did, indeed, feel angry from time to time, which she had not been aware of before. There had not been opportunity, in her family, to discover that anger was a manageable emotion. Her parents, devout Mormons, combined temperamental mildness with cultural determination to maintain a peaceful home. Sara's gentle nature pleased her parents and earned her a lot of community respect. Therapy was a place for her to talk safely, with someone whom she respected and trusted, about her angry feelings. Sara's temperament did not change much after therapy. Indeed, she often found that she would begin to have a headache *before* she knew she was angry. What she learned to do was to speak about her anger to whomever it was she was angry at, in a way that was not frightening to her or out of character. Since she was relieved to have her headaches, and her other ailments, so easily cured, she worked hard at finding ways to speak of her displeasure as soon as her symptoms started so that they stopped being a problem.

Sara's insight was probably not an ultimate insight. Perhaps with depth therapy she might have discovered that she had been angry at her parents for the strictness of their religious household, their supervision of her social life so that it had been hard for her to meet someone to marry, their insistence that she study to be a grade-school teacher because it was a secure job instead of trying to make her music a career, which she would have preferred. Perhaps at some point she will need to discover more about herself, if problems come up that depend on this knowledge for resolution. In the meantime, she is relatively symptom-free and more content and sure of herself in her work and in her marriage. The crucial change factor for Sara was her determination, once she was clear that it was a pattern in her own character style that was causing her discomfort, to be vigilant to it arising and try hard to find alternative, more healthy means of expressing her needs.

It has long been understood that insight is not helpful to people with severe characterological problems. When I was studying psychotherapy, I was taught "do not add insight to injury." We understood this to mean that people who had been seriously traumatized by abuse or neglect by their parenting figures would not have the ego strength to tolerate re-experiencing the pain and/or fear they had felt as children and would either resist doing so or disintegrate further from the experience. We did not have good language to discuss the supportive, ego-building therapy that we instinctively offered people until Self Psychology became widely accepted through the writing of Heinz Kohut. Since then, we are able to talk about empathic attunement, the kind of "insight" that says, "When that experience happened to you, you must have felt very frightened (or lonely, or sad, or unseen)." This kind of supportive insight, I believe, builds ego structure, which then allows people to feel more self-confident, perhaps make more constructive choices, perhaps begin to be more self-reflective. Ultimately, it should lead to better ability to perceive one's patterns of behavior and then make more gratifying life choices.

Spiritual insights, like psychological insights, need a relatively secure structure to support them so they can be tools for freedom rather than agents of disintegration. The hoped-for insights of Buddhist practice, the realization of the impermanence of all experience, realization of the truth of *dukkha* (the cause and end of suffering), or the emptiness of phenomena, are not that rare. We have many flashes of insight in the course of regular living, and, certainly for people doing intensive meditation practice, they can occur quite regularly. Often these insights are followed by the thought, I'll never get caught in confusion again! When I first heard about Buddhist meditation and the freedom that came from insight, I thought, If I just get that, I'll be totally free. All clinging will drop away. Theoretically, it should. But, it hasn't for me, or even for anyone else I know. But it *starts* dropping away, and I am convinced that changes in the direction of freedom are what inspire continued devotion to both spiritual practice and psychological growth. Spiritual insights can be disorienting since they involve paradigm shifts and allow us to see and evaluate our experience in a new way. When the psychological structure that is present is marginally able to maintain itself in the "old" paradigm, it may be unable to accommodate the new one.

I think it is difficult to tolerate the awareness of impermanence when there is no sense of integrity about one's life. Erik Erikson, in *Childhood and Society,* wrote eloquently about the ego consolidation which begins in young adulthood, as the sense of being a person able to manifest competently in work and in relationship which then continues to develop throughout the rest of one's life. I believe that, for people who feel that they have not yet begun to manifest fully in their lives, the discovery that life passes so quickly is insupportable.

> Andrew was a middle-aged businessman, unfamiliar with meditation or Buddhism, who had come to a meditation retreat because he thought it would help him deal with what he characterized as a stressful life situation and generalized anxiety. As the week progressed, he appeared more anxious, rather than less. He expressed his anxiety quite suddenly one afternoon, in the middle of a meditation session while I was giving instructions.
>
> I normally give instructions for awareness meditation couched in terms that I hope will facilitate the arising of insight. For example, instead of asking students to simply rest the attention in the phenomenon of breathing, I will say, "Notice how the breath is arising and passing away." Similarly, I will say, "Notice as you walk, how each step arises and passes away," or "Notice as you eat your meal that the appetite that was present at the beginning of the meal has disappeared by the end of the meal." In other words, rather than ask people to focus on *what* is happening, I ask that they focus on what is *true* about what is happening. Insights about truth, rather than simply calming down and focusing are understood to be the goal of practice.
>
> On the occasion of Andrew's outburst, I apparently had said something like, "Notice how every moment of experience is temporal. It arises and passes away." Andrew spoke out, in a dismayed and almost pleading tone, "Why do you keep *saying* that?" "I say it," I responded in what I hope was a kind way, "because it's true." "I know that," he said, "but I can't *stand* it." I didn't know Andrew well enough to understand what it was about impermanence that was anxiety-provoking to him, but clearly it was not a calming nor freeing insight.

Norma, a woman who I believe had more emotional maturity, came to that same retreat dealing with grief over the death of her husband six months previously. She felt calmed by the quiet, by the use of the breath as a focusing tool, and, indeed, by the awareness of impermanence. Although she would have periods of deep sadness arise, she was able to notice that her mood changed during the mealtimes when she was interested in eating and looking at the people around her. Her awareness of the impermanence of her feelings of sadness made her more relaxed about them, less dismayed when they arose. She said to me, in one interview, that based on her experience she could even consider the idea that at some time in the future her experience of grieving would feel complete, that it, too, would pass. Norma made a healthier adjustment to the insight of impermanence.

Impermanence is also a difficult vision to hold for people who have sustained some life trauma that they have, thus far, been unable to assimilate. When intimations of impermanence arise in a mind dismayed and confused with unresolved heavy emotion, the sense of injustice about one's trauma can seem even greater. Sometimes people report a deepening sense of loss when they discover, along with the awareness of impermanence, how much of their life has been held hostage to impermanent, empty events long past.

The story of Alexa, which I will present here, is particularly important because although Alexa's experience is uniquely her own, the experience of uncovering severe, previously unconscious childhood abuse as a result of meditation practice is not unusual. People for whom this is their experience are often later able to corroborate their memories with reports of other family members, showing them to be valid memories rather than artifacts of meditation.

Alexa had been doing Vipassana meditation for some years with deepening concentration ability and considerable pleasure from hearing Buddhist teachings and being part of the community of meditation students. She undertook a month-long period of intensive practice, and part of her experience was a pervasive sense of the pain of life experience. This "spiritual" insight seemed to be the precondition for the arising of images of sexual and physical abuse which she began to recognize as memories from her own past. At first, she was incredulous, and then she became emotionally shaken. As she attempted to continue to meditate, using her ability to concentrate to calm herself, she found that she was flooded with memories. It was as if the initial breaking down of the defense against those memories then allowed the entirety of her abusive history to present itself.

Although Alexa had seemed, prior to this experience, fairly well integrated psychologically, her behavior became regressed. She retreated to her room, spent days sobbing and shaking, refused to eat and was frightened to be touched by anyone. The teachers at the retreat were not particularly trained psychologically, but provided support in terms of empathy, reassurance, and general caregiving, bringing her meals, etc. After some days, Alexa was able to maintain a conversation and begin to talk about the need to seek out professional psychological help. The follow-up of Alexa's experience is that she did enter into therapy, remained in touch with her meditation teachers, and was able to let them know of her continuing positive results with treatment and, eventually, after some years, of her successful termination of therapy.

In Alexa's case, her discovery of her abuse and subsequent ability to integrate it psychologically are examples of the way in which psychological and spiritual insights augment and reinforce each other.

A particularly potent aspect of the insight of dukkha, suffering, is the awareness that the cause of suffering is craving or clinging, and that the tendency of the mind to cling is so conditioned that the very attempt to avoid it is itself another form of clinging. We are, in a certain sense, trapped in clinging. Becoming fully aware of the tendency of our own minds to cling and feeling the suffering that is the impact of that clinging, we become able to appreciate the monumental amount of suffering that is part of the human experience. If one's own personal story is relatively gratifying, I believe it is not only possible to open to the truth of suffering, but that it provides the necessary key to the development of true compassion. I think it is not accidental that many of the people I know who have dealt with the insight of suffering in their meditation practice choose a healing profession as their work in the world.

The mind sometimes struggles with the arising of the dukkha insight, especially if it is fatigued with pain, but it usually recuperates if its essential structure is secure. There are situations in which people with healthy ego structure, under extreme duress (which might be situational, or the arising of dukkha insight, or a combination of the two) experience psychotic-like ideation. This might be accompanied with the awareness that absurd or bizarre ideation is currently happening, with observing ego able to understand the experience as a temporal altered state. Sometimes, however, the observing ego seems to disappear, and periods of altered and unpredictable behavior can follow.

Olivia was referred for psychotherapy by the discharge physician at an acute psychiatric facility where she had been treated for an overnight stay. Describing the course of events that had led to her hospitalization, Olivia told me that she had been married for twenty-five years when her husband took ill with cancer. Slightly less than two years elapsed between his diagnosis and his death, during which time Olivia and her husband had spent intense time together in conscious preparation for his death. They were both committed to making his death and their separation as conscious as possible as part of their spiritual practice. Olivia did all of the bedside care and was with him at the time of his death.

After the death, Olivia felt that she was aware of her husband's presence remaining with her. She also reported that she had been sure that she had developed an enhanced ability to feel other people's moods and know their thoughts. She had felt exhilarated by what she had felt was an expanded awareness capacity. Days had passed without her eating or sleeping, and her sense of heightened perception had increased. She had felt a certain sense of "calling" to help other people on the verge of death and had entered, uninvited, into the hospital room of a casual acquaintance who was dying. The family reacted negatively, demanding that she leave, and she became distraught. She was confused about people's reactions to her and became agitated. Later that day, some close friends, responding to her agitation, brought her to the local acute psychiatric facility where she was treated with Haldol. When she awoke the following morning, she was entirely clear-minded and remembered her weeks of sometimes frenetic behavior with chagrin. At our first meeting she expressed concern that she might be mentally ill and concern that her grasp of reality, which seemed to have been temporarily absent, was fundamentally tenuous.

Olivia was completely clear and appropriate in affect in our first meeting, and there was nothing in her psychological history prior to her husband's death that seemed significant. I assured her that I thought that her altered perceptions and strange behavior had been the result of her practicing intense concentration for almost two years, coupled with her extreme sadness and sense of loss about her husband's death. I explained that it is not unusual for people to develop extrasensory perceptions as a result of meditation practice, and that when these are accompanied by calm, they may even prove helpful. I also told her that not sleeping and not eating contributed to altered perceptions, and I suggested that she maintain a normal lifestyle, exercising and eating and sleeping as regularly as possible. I saw Olivia weekly four times, to reassure her (and myself) that her situation was stabilized and to allow her to talk further about her sadness about her husband's death. She continued to meditate, eventually attending week-long meditation retreats, and her symptoms have never recurred.

The third insight which Buddhist meditators hope to achieve is that of emptiness, *anatta,* non-separate self. This insight arises in various ways. One might suddenly have the direct awareness that one's mind/body organism, marvelous and complicated as it is, is essentially a process of change happening with nothing at all solid or permanent about it. This is often a freeing awareness, unless there is a psychological sense of shakiness about who one is in the world. If a person is psychologically secure, with this awareness she/he is often able to shift from a personal focus to a universal focus. This is what I believe is meant in spiritual practice when people talk about "losing one's ego." I believe that if people have a level of personal maturity and ego integration they can make the shift from "Life is happening to me" to "Life is happening." It is a happy shift, a shift from an inside out, "me-focused" view to a cosmic or universal overview. Instead of saying, "This drama is happening to me. I am the victim of it!" one is able to say, "What a far-out drama! This is all happening. Birth and death, pain and joy, all the extraordinary story of form!"

Even one's own death can be faced with a degree of tranquillity, and many instances of this demonstration of composure are available. There are many notable accounts of serenity in the face of death in the spiritual literature, and readers are particularly referred to the books of Stephen Levine for detailed accounts.

Being able to see that our stories are *just* stories depends on a relatively high level of ego integrity. Otherwise, for people with fragile egos, the awareness of non-separateness, or interconnectedness, is too threatening.

Maxine's experience provides an example of a person whose personal drama, already apparently complicated by some inability to evaluate situations realistically, became more intense as a result of meditation practice.

> Maxine arrived at a ten-day meditation retreat to discover that a former therapist of hers was one of the seventy other retreatants present. The therapy had ended some years previously, not smoothly, with Maxine leaving therapy because her therapist refused to have a personal relationship with her. In the opening days of the retreat, Maxine reported to all of her teachers that her entire focus of attention was on the presence of this other person and what she felt were the messages this person was sending her. Retreats are in silence and the other person was unaware of Maxine's dilemma. No attempt by any teacher to help Maxine see her preoccupation as a disturbing obsession, and not the reality of the situation, had any effect.
>
> Although "egoless," in the sense of not identifying with current drama, is held as a spiritual insight that is ultimately freeing, it is not useful unless the person experiencing the non-identification has aware-

ness of its presence and can maintain reasonable judgment. Maxine's judgment was impaired. She began writing notes to the former therapist, accosting him in hallways and insisting that they talk, generally upsetting the established boundary codes of meditation retreats. She sobbed loudly in the hall. Ultimately, she was asked to leave by one of the teachers, citing her disturbing behavior, which she denied having done. Another teacher, someone who had not been involved previously in the situation, was able to approach her as an ally, citing the pain she seemed to be having and firmly insisting that leaving would be in her own best interest. This particular teacher, himself a therapist, suggested strongly that she seek some psychiatric help to deal with the upset that attending the retreat had precipitated.

Clearly, this was an example of someone with fragile ego structure not being able to maintain reasonable perceptions when confronted with the stress of a conflictual situation as well as the stress of a retreat situation in which usual avenues for staying psychologically grounded are not present.

Emily, a fifty-five-year-old woman with no significant psychiatric history was one of ninety meditators at a meditation retreat where the practice was the development of high concentration through the repetition of mantra. Normally, intense concentration produces states of increased rapture in the mind and body and intensified feelings of good will and compassion. As is customary, except for interviews with teachers, the retreat was held in silence. On the fourth day of the retreat, Emily reported to her teacher that she felt elated by her practice and felt in love with all the people around her. She seemed a bit euphoric, but not inconsistent with the experience of other meditators with good concentration. Two days later, she reported that she felt ecstatic, flooded with feelings of love, "at one with everyone." The teacher interviewing her did notice her excited mood, but again, accepted it as a particularly strong example of the generation of a sense of universal good will. Three days later, Emily was clearly disoriented, talking in disconnected and irrational sentences. Staff members and teachers spent time with her, attempting to reorient her and trying to help her integrate her experience. All attempts failed, and Emily needed to be hospitalized and treated with phenothiazine. One week later, follow-up indicated that she had been discharged to her daughter's care, was less agitated, but still confused and irrational, and had been referred for ongoing psychiatric care.

Emily's situation is fairly unique. She had no previous psychiatric history. My speculation is that, although she had not previously exhibited any defects in ego structure, they had been present. The "stress" of discovering non-separateness, the same experience of "at-one-ness" that is liberating to meditators with more secure ego functioning was, for Emily, more than she could integrate.

Here is one final connection between psychological and spiritual insights. Not only does the degree to which insights are useful in either realm depend on the level of ego integrity, the level of development in both realms either supports or retards development in the other. A high level of genuine spiritual understanding can be very helpful to a person dealing with difficult psychological issues. I am encouraged when my psychotherapy clients are devoted to a spiritual practice, as I find it usually is supportive to them in their therapy. Also, it is important to recognize that spiritual insights cannot manifest at a higher level than the highest level of psychosexual development. I believe that it is possible to have clear insights and genuine flashes of understanding which, when coupled with lacunae of ego development, may be misinterpreted and expressed incorrectly. "We are all one" does not mean "I can use you for my personal gain." "Everything is empty" and "Everything is temporal" do not mean that we do not need to be actively responsible for each other and our world. These misinterpretations, when they are expressed in behavior, represent, I believe, a limitation of insight.

Psychological insights become part of healing when they are met with conscious resolve to explore them fully and integrate new understandings as they arise in our lives. Spiritual insights also require internal character integrity in order to be expressed in wholesome ways.

19

Madness or Transcendence?
Looking to the Ancient East for a Modern Transpersonal Diagnostic System

John E. Nelson

In this chapter and in his book, *Healing the Split,* John E. Nelson makes the important point that a rapprochement is needed between the orthodox psychiatric diagnosticians, who are not open to the mystical and transcendent states of consciousness, and the transpersonal psychotherapists, who feel that a diagnosis dehumanizes the patient. Furthermore, Nelson argues that we not only need the traditional diagnoses, with their wisdom and practical value (insurance, therapy payments, etc.), but we need to expand the orthodox diagnoses to include issues which impede spiritual growth.

The author suggests that adding the three-thousand-year-old Tantric yoga seven-chakra system to the traditional diagnostic system is one way the necessary rapprochement can be accomplished. In Eastern philosophy and medicine, the chakras are said to be real physical centers that tap into subtle forms of energy. Whereas our Western minds tend to see consciousness arising from the brain, the Eastern systems hold that the mind and body arise from consciousness (spirit) from "its first quickening within a living embryo, through its painful separation from its universal Source as it forms a worldly ego, to its struggle to transcend that ego and return to a state of unity with the spiritual ground of its being."

It is in the first (having to do with survival and relating to the world through the mouth), second (having to do with desire, including early sexuality), and third chakra (having to do with power and control) that we see patients who fall into the more traditional psychiatric diagnostic categories. The fourth through the seventh chakras represent the spiritual levels.

"In an ideal lifetime," writes Nelson, "the chakras open in sequence, each standing firmly on the lesson and growth experience of the last. But in reality, life seldom follows this ideal script."

Occasionally, a therapist may meet a patient, who, while working on advanced spiritual levels, will temporarily have an ego regression to the levels of chakras one, two, or three. With an understanding of higher spiritual levels, a knowledgeable therapist will be able to help such a patient resume his/her primarily higher chakra-level functioning. On the flip side, a therapist may encounter patients, who, while struggling with the more traditional issues in ego development, have premature or inappropriate openings to higher spiritual level experiences which temporarily overwhelm the ego. These experiences can become disorganizing for the patients and may appear, to a traditional therapist, to fit into one of the more conventional diagnostic categories.

By viewing all of the chakras as being important in the spiritual evolution of the individual, Nelson affirms the important concept that traditional psychotherapy or use of medication, if viewed appropriately, can be seen as a part of spiritual psychotherapy.

Nelson discusses the cases of Stuart and Lydia, and, in doing so, clarifies Ken Wilber's important *pre/trans fallacy* concept which cogently argues for the importance of traditional therapists to understand spiritual issues. Likewise, the two case histories presented also argue for transpersonal therapists to have a greater appreciation and respect for the more traditional psychiatric conditions and not try to spiritualize the psychological issues—sometimes known as taking a spiritual bypass to life's problems.

TRANSPERSONAL PSYCHOLOGY has long been wary of traditional psychiatry and psychology's insistence on making diagnoses. Many feel that the process somehow programs a therapist to follow predetermined lines of thought that may not reflect the essential reality of those who come to them for care. Diagnoses, they argue, are impediments to authentic I-Thou relatedness.

Others follow the reasoning of R. D. Laing and his radical antipsychiatry movement of earlier decades. Laing argued that a diagnosis dehumanizes a person experiencing spontaneous alterations of consciousness, insidiously creating an iatrogenic disease by pressuring vulnerable psychiatric patients to conform to expectations that they assume a deviant role.

A third and more synoptic line of reasoning is that orthodox diagnostic categories are simply not broad enough to encompass the astonishing range of experiences inherent within the full human potential, which includes mystical and transcendent states of consciousness. This latter argument moves away from the first two, which would simply eliminate the practice of classifying clusters of symptoms, but which also cut off the therapist from the hard-earned experience of others who have treated similar maladies. More practically, therapists who refuse to diagnose their patients/clients remain hopelessly isolated from parties who pay the bills of all but the wealthy.

If transpersonal psychology is to remain relevant to the real world in which therapists earn their living by treating people who suffer from a wide range of afflictions—from the primitive to the exalted—it follows that we cannot abandon the venerated diagnostic process. A holistic transpersonal view instead recognizes that we need *more* diagnoses rather than fewer, that we must expand our categories to include impediments to spiritual growth from the rudimentary consciousness of early childhood, through ego-based stages, to phases in which an individual struggles to free himself from personal and social obstacles to spiritual advance.

Two important transpersonal philosophers, Ken Wilber and Michael Washburn, have written cogently about discrete stages or levels of personal and spiritual growth. Although they disagree about several important details, both hold that an individual must develop a healthy and strong ego before he can successfully transcend that ego, and that failure to do so results in a pathological state, often accompanied by great subjective distress. Both also agree that a well-prepared individual can progress to *trans-egoic* states that foreshadow ultimate reunion with the Absolute (Wilber, 1983; Washburn, 1995).

Wilber's and Washburn's ideas form a strong foundation for a transpersonal diagnostic system based not only on pathology, but on transcendence, one that can distinguish psychoses based on metabolic disorders of the brain from superficially similar spiritual emergencies in which a person may temporarily regress before continuing his spiritual progress.

I have found that the system of the seven chakras from ancient Tantric yoga provides a near-ideal way to determine an individual's level of personal and spiritual growth. Using this system, modern transpersonal therapists can respond to their patient's spiritual stumbling blocks with techniques that are specific to that level, techniques that neither demand more of a patient than he can accomplish, nor devalue the higher strivings of spiritually advanced individuals.

The Chakra System

The system of the seven chakras—a three-thousand-year-old way of integrating body, mind, and spirit—is an ancient idea that has passed the test of time. Originally intuited by contemplative sages involved in the disciplined practice of Tantric yoga, it remains an integral part of modern esoteric Hinduism and Buddhism and forms the theoretical bedrock for acupuncture, a proven technique of healing used throughout much of the world.

Caught up in a narrow materialistic world view, the Western psychology tends to systematically exclude humanity's spiritual aspects from its models of the psyche. This omission causes it to ignore what is arguably the most important dimension of our full human potential: the study of consciousness—Spirit—itself. Fortunately, Eastern psychological systems have avoided this error, so they offer us a more complete view of our authentic nature as participants in a universal mind with purpose and meaning. Because of its demonstrable usefulness, the time is right for us to integrate the chakra system into Western models of biological science and psychology.

In Oriental medicine, the chakras are considered to be real physical centers that tap into a subtle form of energy that vitalizes the human body. These lotuslike "wheels," each with a specific location in the human body, are said to be vortexes for accumulating life force—*prana*—from a universal source. But for the purpose of this discussion, we will consider the chakras as *metaphors* for psychological stages of development, both for individual humans and for humanity as a whole.

In this psychological sense, the chakras are archetypes, comprehensive themes around which human life revolves, discrete stages of consciousness that guide physical, mental, and spiritual growth throughout life. Specific psychological symptoms accompany difficulties in passage through each of these life stages. Because each chakra level has a unique mode of cognition, relationships, ethics, values, religious attitudes, drug preferences, and psychotherapies, this system can be used as a sophisticated diagnostic system that can guide us in developing level-specific therapies to aid ourselves and others in our lifelong quest for spiritual growth.

The Eastern philosophy from which the chakra system arose offers the Western mind an opportunity to reconsider the mysterious connections between body and mind. Western materialism holds that matter is superior to mind, and that consciousness (Spirit) somehow arises from the molecular activity of the brain, akin to the way the kidneys secrete urine. In contrast, the Eastern view assigns consciousness a primary place in the universe, with matter partaking of the eternal play of Spirit at the lowest and grossest level of a great chain of being. The brain is a unique and complex organ that *attracts* rather than generates consciousness, imparting to amorphous Spirit the unique shapes and forms that allow a human being to survive and reproduce on the surface of this third planet from the sun.

By reflecting a more comprehensive view of human nature, the chakra system elegantly maps the progress of personal consciousness from its first quickening within a living embryo, through its painful separation from its universal Source as it forms a worldly ego, to its struggle to transcend that ego and return to a state of unity with the spiritual ground of its being.

1. Muladhara—The "Root" Chakra

As a human sperm penetrates an ovum, merging its millions of genes with an equal number awaiting it, a soft whisper gently permeates the background hum of consciousness that fills the universe. A new being is forming within its essence.

As the cells of this tiny new being divide and multiply, they act as a vortex of Spirit, condensing it and imparting the unique attributes that comprise a human personality. At this point, the rudimentary awareness of first chakra consciousness begins to guide the destiny of a unique individual.

First-chakra consciousness forms the cornerstone of human life. During the crucial three-year span that follows conception, the foundations of selfhood fructify within what was initially an unbounded field of consciousness. As elementary psychic boundaries gradually separate self from its universal Source, they form a supporting framework that later bears the weight of human emotions, reason, and relationships. When these self-boundaries are poorly formed because of genetic flaws or unsound parenting, the outcome is often a tenuous grounding in the shared realities of a culture, or even psychosis.

Traditional Tantric charts place the physical location of the first chakra in the perineum, between the anus and genitals. It is said to govern the legs and intestines, grounding the individual on earth and governing what Freud called the oral stage of life. The primary mode of first-chakra consciousness is *survival*, and the principal way of relating to the world is through the mouth. A primitive ethical system imbues the infant with the simple rule that whatever fosters survival is good, whatever imperils it is bad.

Western psychologists such as Jean Piaget and Margaret Mahler have described this stage in meticulous detail. Their contributions stand as pillars of scientific psychology. Mahler called it the "symbolic" stage to emphasize the child's psychic merger with its mother, and Piaget called it the "sensorimotor" stage to describe an infant's primary mode of relating to the world through instinct and reflex. However, both fall short of giving us a complete picture of infant development because they fail to take into account that an infant is already nine months old when he is born. We don't know exactly what kind of learning takes place in the womb, but it seems certain that Western psychologists habitually underestimate it. Many sensitive women feel aware of a subtle telepathic rapport with their unborn child, a kind of *sub rosa* conversation in which they feel the fetus' presence deep within their own being. Obviously, this subtle communion can be for better or worse.

In his landmark book *Beyond the Brain*, Stanislav Grof described how an infant's passage through the birth canal leaves permanent impressions on its vulnerable psyche, and how various kinds of impediments to a smooth birth can distort one's personality for a lifetime (Grof, 1985). Immediately after birth, a crucial stage of bonding takes place, a symbiosis in which infant and mother temporarily share their self-boundaries. The essential first-chakra task is for the infant to emerge from its primal, undifferentiated unity with Spirit into early stages of selfhood. The child discovers that when he bites his thumb there is pain, but when he bites his blanket there is no pain. When he feels movement in his arm, his hand waves before his eyes, but his teddy bear's hand remains still. This early "I/Not-I" split creates a rudimentary psychic "membrane" that parts his fledgling self from the universal consciousness of its Source. He connects these first sensations of selfhood with his physical body, an identification that persists until an ego forms much later in life.

The next step is for the infant to separate from his mother, or other primary caretaker, to rupture his symbiotic merger and form a self that is not only apart from its Source, but also apart from his parents. Innumerable repetitions of what Mahler called "separation-individuation" experiences cleave the mother-child dyad from the fourth month of life through the transition to second-chakra consciousness early in the third year. As he approaches the final stages of this period, the ever more emboldened child repeatedly wanders away from his mother, then hurriedly returns seeking the solace of her consistent presence. If she handles her child's initial thrusts toward individuation sensitively, he will gradually and contentedly form his own self-boundaries separate from hers. There will always be a shared area of the psyche, however, where the feelings of one resonate with the feelings of the other. Self-psychologist Heinz Kohut called these permanently overlapping boundaries "self-object" to indicate that our selfhood is never quite powerful enough to stand completely unsupported by others.

Although so-called "borderline" personalities, who are exquisitely vulnerable to self-fragmentation and transient psychoses, may solidify during one's passage through the root chakra, it is unlikely that psychoses so profound as schizophrenia can be attributed solely to poor early parenting without a hefty contribution from one's genes. Yet sometimes severe psychotic regressions can cause a fragile psyche to revert to this primitive stage of life. An adult whose consciousness descends to the first chakra is painful to behold. He will be preoccupied with food, coffee, or endless cigarettes consumed obsessively without savor. His relationships with others are dependent and clinging. Such oral and anal fixations are appropriate for an infant struggling to survive the first years of life, but when an adult carries back dislodged patterns of higher-chakra consciousness, they are inevitably cast in a grotesque light.

A psychotropic drug that typically operates on first-chakra consciousness is Thorazine, or related antipsychotic medicines. By restoring certain chemical balances in primitive parts of the brain, these agents may partly restore one's grounding in a reality shared by most adult humans. As I wrote in some detail in my book *Healing the Split,* such powerful medicines have serious side effects and must be used with requisite artfulness, even in the most severely psychotic individual (Nelson, 1994).

Appropriate therapies at the first-chakra level include simple behavior modification techniques or other methods that improve one's social skills, ability to delay gratifications, and firm self-boundaries. Higher level therapies will generally be counterproductive or confusing for both patient/client or healer.

2. Svadasthana—The Sexual Chakra

Transpersonal philosopher Ken Wilber has called the consciousness of the second chakra "typhonic," after the Typhon, a mythological being who is half-serpent, half-human. This is an apt symbol for a time of life when a child rises from the murky realms of undifferentiated selfhood to form that uniquely human, but ultimately self-limiting psychic organ, the *ego.* Although many spiritual disciplines teach that we must eventually vanquish the ego if we are to regain our connection with Spirit, it is certain that we must first fully develop this essential faculty if we are to survive as members of civilized society.

Traditional Hindu texts place the second chakra just below the naval where it is said to govern the sexual organs. It is not surprising, then, that the classic Freudian Oedipal conflict takes place during this stage of life when a toddler first identifies himself as a person with an individual identity and gender. In common with adult sexuality, the consciousness of this phase of life is characterized by a magical world of wish-fulfilling fantasy that is only partially affected by socially defined reality. The primary mode of second-chakra consciousness is *desire,* as the child gradually turns away from unlimited communion with Spirit and toward objects and people of the material world.

Although emotions rule the consciousness of the second chakra, a kind of thinking and logic first becomes possible as a child grows toward adolescence, although it is not as disciplined and precise as that of the higher chakras. A child tends to make logical connections by linking similarities as if they were identities. For instance, he may conclude that a stuffed doll has the same thoughts and feelings as a live baby. There is a concreteness to thought at this stage that might cause a child to interpret the meaning of a proverb such as, "People in glass houses shouldn't throw stones," as, "Of course not, they'd break the glass." Adults who regress to this level often make similar errors in reasoning that lead to outright paranoia: "The FBI follows guilty people. I feel guilty. Therefore the FBI is following me."

Relationships during this phase of life are idealized and tinged with fantasy. Imaginary playmates are common. The child views others as larger than life and superhuman in their capacities for good or evil. Like the notorious "borderline personality" that has become fixated at this level, the child tends to cast powerful people in his life as either all good or all bad, with very little gray area, although people can change from friend to foe with little provocation. Ethics are based on fulfilling desires as expeditiously as possible, the chief ethical maxim being: *don't get caught*. Religious feelings take form as fantasies of an all-powerful protector and ethical enforcer, an imperious male God vaguely located in the sky.

People who have advanced beyond the second chakra, and then for some reason regress to this level, may experience otherworldly hallucinations, as if they have opened an inner door to a netherworld populated by beings of relentlessly malign intent. As one's ability to share the realities of our adult, third-chakra world slips away, bizarre delusions, usually with a paranoid cast, can form around such hallucinations. When abused, drugs such as alcohol, barbiturates, or opiates reactivate second-chakra consciousness by blurring the line between fantasy and consensual reality and releasing unbridled primitive emotions.

Representative second-chakra figures include novelists Stephen King and J. R. Tolkien, cartoon character Calvin of Calvin and Hobbes, Alice from *Alice in Wonderland*, the early Beatles, and the Ayatollah Khomeini. Appropriate therapies for individuals whose self is based in the second chakra includes behavior modification or other socializing and ego-strengthening techniques that foster one's ability to get others to conform to his worldly aspirations. For all their drawbacks, antipsychotic medicines can act as agents of mercy for people who have regressed to the second chakra.

3. Manipura—The Power Chakra

The consciousness of the third chakra infuses a young adult throughout his quest for a career and a suitable mate as he establishes himself as an effective and competent force in the world. The primary mode of this phase of life is *power and control*. The ego inflates to its utmost strength, with maximum alienation from Spirit as it turns away from its inner roots to focus on manipulating people and physical objects to its own ends. As Michael Washburn put it, the ego's task is to keep the psyche myopically close to the five senses and blind to Spirit.

At this historical epoch, a majority of human beings on earth have evolved to the third chakra and are deeply involved in the countless variations of giving and getting that make up the acquisitive world of commerce. An individual in this stage of life tends to take life as it comes without wondering much about its meaning, worth, or purpose. He seeks enjoyment through the senses, or by cultivating emotional pleasures, material security, or achievement of personal ambition. Because of the limited view afforded by ego-based consciousness, he believes that the only reality is that of the physical world, and therefore he is strongly attached to earthly goods (Assagioli, 1986).

Thinking and logic take a quantum leap forward as a young adolescent first rises above wishful fantasy and engages a world of science, technology, and fierce competitiveness for wealth and desirable sexual partners. This is the stage that Piaget called *formal operations,* indicating one's expanding ability to manipulate ideas as well as objects. Thinking becomes linear, bound to syllogisms that have governed clear reasoning since the time of Aristotle: *A* is always *A,* never *B; A* must either be *A,* or not be *A,* with no intermediate state allowable; *A* cannot be *A* and not-*A* at the same time and place. Therefore five strawberries do not make an apple, frogs do not become princes, and modern mental patients are not Napoleon, no matter how intense their wish to be powerful and famous. Children are suffered to bend these rules, but when adults tamper with them, they are considered flaky at best, psychotic at worst.

As we gain capacity to reason accurately and reflect upon various outcomes before committing ourselves to action, another new capability comes to the fore: free will. This is a power that has only recently emerged in human evolution, one that is not held in equal measure by all men and women. Our legal system is embarrassingly confused about the limits of will, but it is clear that a modicum of reflective reason is necessary for free choice. People whose mental capacities have regressed below the third chakra should not be considered fully culpable for all of their actions.

Third-chakra religious beliefs are outward and conventional, with a preference for authoritarian and dogmatic religions. The ego perceives God as separate from the self, wholly other, watching and making judgments from "on high." Once a person feels that he has conformed to the injunctions of his church and shared in its rites, he concludes that he has accomplished all that may be expected of him spiritually, and that no further growth is possible. He usually notices a vague discomfort when in the presence of people who speak of higher realms of spirituality, and he usually does not cultivate their friendship. The inflated ego assumes a throne located vaguely behind the eyes, where it struggles to override the body's incessant strivings by means of a sexually repressive morality. The ethics of third-chakra consciousness is simply: don't lose!

A classic power-chakra drug is cocaine, which fuels the aggressiveness and exuberant acquisitiveness that characterizes a materialistic orientation to life. Traditionally, the aggressive third chakra is considered a yang, or masculine phase of life. Representative third-chakra figures include Donald Trump, John Wayne, Sadaam Hussein, and Lyndon Johnson.

Appropriate power-chakra therapies include psychoanalysis, which traditionally focuses on removing lower-chakra impediments to successful work and mating, and other "rational" therapies that employ cognitive strategies and intellectual insight to aid an individual to become more "mature" and effective within social hierarchies.

4. Anahata—The Heart Chakra

An exquisite galloping antelope adorns the mandala of the Anahata chakra as depicted in ancient Tantric texts. It is said that this shy, fleet, and graceful animal symbolizes spiritual experiences that move quickly from the ego's eye, vanishing before it can grasp them.

Traditionally depicted in mid-chest, the Anahata chakra opens the heart to universal love that transcends the impetus to possess or manipulate that characterizes relationships in the second and third chakras. The ancient Greeks honored this dichotomy through their god Eros who appears in two manifestations, the worldly and the heavenly. Agape—their word for universal love—was distinguished from the romantic raptures of the second and third chakras, which are characterized by seduction and jealousy, dominance and dependence, and attachment to an idealized object. The aim of lower-chakra love is to quell a feeling of emptiness. But at the heart chakra, love is no longer tainted by need or craving; instead, one feels an inner abundance that saturates the self with a desire to share freely for the good of all.

The heart chakra is the center of healing, which in turn depends on two qualities, *empathy* and *compassion*. By itself, an empathic ability to imagine oneself in the place of another is not exclusively a heart-chakra attribute, and it can even be used to manipulate others. But coupled with compassion, empathy becomes the most potent force of healing known. Compassion is a readiness to respond to the pain of another without aversion or resentment. It includes a compelling impulse to relieve the suffering. Unlike pity, which is really a defense against pain, compassion acknowledges all human suffering as a reflection of one's own anguish. Compassion embraces the other's sorrow and shares his wound as a reflection of shared humanity. Yet this is not a passive or impotent act, but one that mobilizes healing love from one's deepest spiritual connection.

At this point in life, an urge spontaneously arises for commitment to something beyond the ego, perhaps a social cause, a spiritual path, or another person. Relationships at the heart move beyond competitiveness and self-aggrandizement to become selfless and magnanimous. The self starts to transcend its exclusive identification with the ego and begins to identify with humanity as a whole. Once empathy and compassion enter one's life, there can be an overpowering sense of guilt for past acts of selfishness toward others. With this comes a strong temptation to step back, to reaffirm materialistic values, to muffle the beckoning call from above, often with alcohol, cocaine, or other heart-numbing drugs.

Opening the heart chakra heralds yet another advance in thinking, which changes from predominantly linear to lateral. The "first A, then, B, then C . . ." rationality of the third chakra yields to a loosely connected, zigzag flow of ideas, something like the way a knight moves on a chessboard. Formal operations thinking—thought by some to be the highest human capability—thrives on distinctions and polarities. But fourth-chakra reasoning transcends this undeniably useful way of thinking by reaching beyond polarities toward reconciliation and synthesis, toward a higher logic that condenses opposites into mutually sustaining unities. For instance, instead of seeing mountains and valleys as opposites, the higher thinking conceives a "mountainvalley" as a unitive whole, neither of its parts existing independently of the other. Other polarities—good/bad, liberal/conservative—also yield to this unifying logic of reconciliation.

At this stage, *awe* replaces fear as the primary religious emotion. God no longer seems so distant from self, and a "higher power" is felt to reside within. Ethics are now based on the "golden rule" that guides us toward an empathic appreciation of the responsibility we all share toward each other. Every religion provides a symbol for heart-chakra compassion. In Christianity it is the Virgin Mary, and in Buddhism the Bodhisattva, an evolved soul who reaches the threshold of nirvana, but then chooses to remain in the world to teach and heal as long as there is ignorance and suffering. Saintly figures like Mother Teresa, Mahatma Gandhi, Albert Schweitzer, and the Dalai Lama epitomize the consciousness of the heart chakra.

Because the fourth chakra is the first spiritual level, representing the initial tentative step back to communion with our Source, meditation now becomes possible, or even mandatory as a therapeutic technique if a seeker wishes to progress on a spiritual path. This powerful tool for overcoming the constraints of the ego would also be helpful for third-chakra individuals, but most are unable to muster the motivation or discipline for contemplative practice, finding it boring or a waste of time. Meditation is often harmful and generally contraindicated for people whose selves have been arrested at, or regressed to, pre-egoic levels. These people need to consolidate their ego rather than impoverish it. We can't transcend what we never gained.

A representative fourth-chakra drug is MDMA, sometimes called Adam, or XTC. This "empathogen," which until recently was summarily banned even from legitimate research in the United States, has potential to open new realms of compassion if used therapeutically by skilled practitioners who have been trained in its benefits and pitfalls. Like all higher-chakra medicines it has potential for harm if used casually or chaotically.

Appropriate therapy at the heart level is designed to increase awareness of subtle inner feelings, body states, and connectedness to our fellow humans on a deep compassionate level. Meditation, Bhakti yoga, and other devotional practices can aid a spiritually opening individual toward the first steps of overcoming the worldly constraints of the ego while deepening his connection with spirit.

5. Vishudda—The Inspiration Chakra

In ancient Tantric texts, the fifth chakra is located over the throat, where it governs the organs of self-expression. This chakra of visionary artists and philosophers is associated with higher creativity, grasping the "big picture," opening to inspiration that seems to flow from an otherworldly source. Its primary mode is a kind of *grace* that commits one to a path that identifies the self not just with humanity, but with all living beings.

Many artists and profound thinkers describe a distinct feeling that their creations do not arise from within their ego-based selves, but come *through* them from a higher source, as if their awareness has been fine-honed into an antenna attuned to archetypal knowledge beyond reach of the senses. This is especially true for improvisational artists, such as jazz musicians or Indian classical musicians who often spin their intricate webs of sound while in a kind of a trance with eyes closed.

Thinking and logic undergo another significant expansion at the throat chakra, one that incorporates *synergy*, a word that describes complex systems in which the whole is greater than the sum of its parts. Once synergistic thinking is in gear, relationships among events are neither proportional nor additive, but are intimately interconnected in a way that suggests an emerging global order. Meaning no longer emerges from definition, but from interaction, from *process*, in what Buddhists call *pattica samuppada*, a merger of self and object at the heart of reality (Macy, 1991). And the very act of playing the game has an unsettling way of changing the rules.

Like the view from an orbiting spacecraft, fifth-chakra thinking enables a person to mentally soar above any system of which he is a part so that he may contemplate the whole from a vantage inaccessible from within that system. Once informed about the nature of the whole, he can devise ways to manipulate that system once he is back inside. Because he no longer interprets events in terms of his personal feelings about them, but where they fit into the grand scheme, he gains a *long view* of human affairs—an historical perspective so often lacking in our political leaders. A prime example of fifth-chakra thinking is the Gaia hypothesis of James Lovelock that envisions the earth and its ecosystem as a single, interdependent living organism.

To illustrate further, when an altruistic person centered in the fourth chakra is confronted with the spectre of people starving in Ethiopia, his immediate reaction is to take steps to bring food to that unfortunate region in order to directly relieve the suffering of the refugees. In contrast, a fifth-chakra perspective *includes* a compassionate desire to directly reduce suffering, but one's reaction would also require an in-depth analysis of the cause of famine in that region. Do the people there need training in modern agricultural techniques or population control measures? Has the climate permanently changed so that we would achieve a higher good by directing our resources to relocating the refugees to another part of the world? These kinds of questions naturally arise from assuming a whole-systems view.

At least since the time of Plato, the fascinating connection between madness and creative genius has intrigued thinkers who observe the troubled lives of many philosophers and artists, some of whom would be certifiably psychotic by today's standards. Recent refinements in definitions of mental disorders clarify this enigma somewhat. People who work in the "trenches" with the mentally ill will quickly recognize that patients who conform to modern definitions of schizophrenia have regressed to the pre-egoic second or first chakras and are seldom creative except in a bizarre and generally incomprehensible way.

But other research reveals a strong connection between the manic phase of manic-depressive disorder and extraordinary creativity. Such luminaries as Hemingway, Van Gogh, Churchill, and Schumann were probably manic-depressive. However, biochemical changes in the brain that accompany these troublesome states often open the self to infusions of higher-chakra consciousness before an immature, ego-based-self is ready. The natural timing of a first manic shift is in the early twenties, a time when most individuals are appropriately absorbed in third-chakra tasks. This accounts for the well-known psychological turbulence that can accompany breakthroughs in the arts and sciences, predisposing many avant-garde iconoclasts to tumultuous lifestyles (Redfield-Jamison, 1993).

Ethics at the fifth chakra expand toward an active commitment to uplifting the consciousness of humanity. Nothing is undertaken that does not foster spiritual growth, either at an individual or collective level. During this phase of life, religious feelings are based on a direct connection with a guiding force in life and a willingness to surrender to that power as one's personal destiny. God is brought down from the sky and perceived as *residing within the self*, but there is not yet a radical identification of self with deity.

Premature opening of higher-chakra consciousness can be extremely disruptive to one's pattern of spiritual growth and can foster a severe life crisis. Yet when the chakras open sequentially with an adequate foundation in place for each new stage, an individual does not lose the capabilities of the lower chakras when he reaches a higher plane. Like a nest of Chinese boxes, each stage incorporates the lower stages, surrounding them with a larger and more comprehensive field of awareness and possible choices. A person may still fall back on a lower-chakra response when a particular situation calls for action on that level. For instance, a fifth-chakra philosopher might still give direct aid to the downtrodden (fourth chakra), or aggressively promote his books for profit (third chakra), or enjoy passionate sexual relations with his beloved (second chakra), or eat joyfully when hungry (first chakra). It is just that these lower-level responses are no longer his primary mode of relating to people and things.

Examples of those rather rare individuals who have fully integrated fifth-chakra consciousness in their lifetimes include Einstein, Kant, Beethoven, Freud, and Gorbachev, geniuses who broke through the restraints of conventional mentality to radically alter the course of human thought and history. Examples of fifth-chakra drugs include low doses of psychedelics, such as peyote or psylocybin, and marijuana, although the latter agent can also inhibit creativity because of its unfortunate propensity to diminish memory, concentration, and will. Amphetamines and similar psychostimulants can temporarily enhance creativity by inducing a manic-like state, but few people who have evolved to this level would take these drugs because of their well-known toxic effects.

Appropriate fifth-chakra therapies aim at disrupting the last remnants of narrow, ego-based thinking, opening the individual to direct perception of archetypal forms, and enhancing awareness of long-term cause-and-effect relationships. While a fifth-chakra sage certainly does not close his heart, he disciplines himself to look beyond his immediate urge to relieve suffering toward revising the static, habitual attitudes and norms that created it. Zen koan study, contingency "brainstorming," insight meditation (Vipassana), practicing deep ecology, and rigorous analysis of history and philosophy foster the forms of higher consciousness that mark one's passage through the throat chakra.

Western psychology accepts and includes these first five stages of consciousness, and in many ways characterizes them more precisely than Eastern psychology. Yet Western models usually hold that fifth-chakra consciousness represents the highest human potential, so they tend to pathologize the higher two chakras and exclude them from study. To correct this persistent error, we must turn to ancient Eastern models of the psyche to explore the higher reaches of our human potential.

6. Ajna—The Shamanic Chakra

A striking aspect of the ancient Egyptian death masks that signified royalty and priesthood was the head of a cobra projecting from mid-brow at the location of the Ajna chakra. This symbolized opening the "third eye," awakening spirit within the domain of secret knowledge. A person so evolved was said to have gained power to alter consciousness—and therefore reality—at will.

Traditional Western religions tend to abhor manifestations of the higher two chakras, either attributing their appearance to works of Satan or simply holding that such lofty powers are too godlike for human aspirations. Orthodox psychological schools generally ignore them, usually denying their reality without further investigation. In contrast, adepts of ancient Eastern traditions held quite a different view. Although they rarely wrote of their arcane practices, they passed them on from generation to generation through oral teachings and direct transmission. Certain shamans and medicine-men of ancient preliterate cultures also gained access to this powerful level of awareness, which they transmitted to their tribe through ritual, healing, and prophesy.

The primary mode of sixth-chakra consciousness is *intuition,* which essentially replaces observation and logic as a reliable means of apprehending reality. The seer who operates at this level makes *direct* contact with universal archetypes that underlie reality, bypassing the ordinary senses. By manipulating these archetypes, he changes reality in ways that seem miraculous— outside the laws of physics—to less evolved beings. Although traces of ego-based consciousness persist through the fourth and fifth chakras, at the Ajna chakra the ego is transcended, just as are the dependent connections between consciousness and brain, which Western materialist scientists insist are necessary for even rudimentary awareness.

As Arthur Koestler pointed out, *not* to believe in the existence of paranormal phenomena like telepathy and precognition implies a conspiracy to deceive the public among hundreds of reputable scientists using time-honored tools of empirical science in dozens of universities around the world (Koestler, 1972). What confuses many Western thinkers is that most people experience these capabilities erratically and inconsistently, like many other higher-chakra breakthroughs that surprise people who operate within lower levels. The difference is that a sixth-chakra adept gains full and conscious control over these faculties and calls upon them *at will.*

When people who lack grounding in the first five chakras experience spontaneous breakthroughs of powerful intuition, telepathy, or premonitions, they can become stunned and confused, recoiling from them in fear. Sometimes an acute manic episode can expose an unprepared young adult to startling insights about fundamental workings of reality, but this nearly always deranges an ego-based psyche and can be followed by rapid psychotic regression to second-chakra consciousness until metabolic balance within the brain is restored. Careless or de-ritualized use of certain shamanic plant medicines can have a similar atavistic effect.

The higher compassion of the Ajna chakra surpasses that of lower levels as it embraces not just humanity or all living beings, but the entire breadth of creation, for it recognizes that even material objects are manifestations of a single universal Spirit. Religious expressions at this level are personal, deeply contemplative, and usually solitary. A sixth-chakra seer may withdraw from the social world, the better to quietly uplift the consciousness of humanity *from within.*

Plant medicines that open sixth-chakra consciousness include peyote, various psylocybin mushrooms, ibogaine, and *auyasca,* used by tribal shamans of the Amazon. Examples of sixth-chakra adepts include the Indian siddhi-master Swami Muktananda; the medieval physician Paracelsus; Plato, who first described archetypal realms of the mind; Socrates, who conversed with a prescient inner voice; and countless forgotten shamans and tribal healers who broke through the constraints of ordinary reality to become technicians of the sacred for their tribes.

Sixth-chakra therapies are generally unknown in the West, which neither honors the power of the adept nor finds much use for shamans. Preparing for the next and final stage of spiritual growth requires more than simply transcending the ego, but transcending the very foundations of individual selfhood. Esoteric *Siddha* yoga techniques, intensive breath-control methods, various advanced asanas, and other contemplative tactics designed to break down the last vestiges of separateness help prepare the adept for the final reunion with Spirit that awaits the next advance.

7. Sahasrara—The Unity Chakra

The seventh chakra represents the crowning evolutionary goal of humanity, the culmination of our long and painful exile from and triumphant return to our Source. At any given time in history, only a handful of human beings exist who have reached this exalted level of development.

Whereas the lower chakras are bursting with uncountable bits of information about the physical world and its endless chains of cause and effect, the sagely consciousness of the seventh chakra is nothing if not simple. No longer is there an ego to maintain the illusion of separate selfhood that parts one from All. No longer does time split the present from eternity, nor does space part here from everywhere. At this level there is perfect Unity, known through an absolute "withinness" that paradoxically encompasses the entire sweep of creation. When the self confronts this, all it can do is surrender to the irresistible power of the Absolute.

The hallmark of the Sahasrara chakra is the mystical experience, described with remarkable similarity by saints, sages, monks, yogis, and contemplatives throughout the ages. It even occasionally happens to ordinary people centered in lower chakras, inevitably transforming their lives.

Because its primary mode is unity, an authentic mystical experience transports us far beyond the distinctions necessary for language, logic, and ordinary communication. With ego suspended, perceptions, thoughts, and actions happen of themselves, with no doer, no see-er, no hearer, only doing!, seeing!, hearing! Personal selfhood gives way to the power of a much larger identification—the entire universe. Logic yields to a state of pure knowing beyond need for rational demonstration. The state of virginal consciousness, empty of form or content, directly reveals the Ground of Being, transcending even the naked archetypes of the sixth chakra.

Of course, suddenly forfeiting one's individual identity would make it difficult to write an article or drive on the freeway. But a seventh-chakra sage does not live in a state of perpetual transcendent rapture, unable to get along in the world because he is busy merging with the cosmos. Far from it. Because the higher chakras surround and include all the capabilities of lower ones, he commands the full range of human potentials, which confers a distinct advantage over people able to call upon only a fraction of those potentials. What is unique about him is that he has integrated the mystical experience and identifies with Spirit itself, not merely with a split-off part, like the ego or even an individuated self. From this vantage, he can operate from the whole, if that is appropriate to the situation, or from any part, depending on the circumstances.

The mystic now readily relinquishes any need that he once may have had to renounce the world; it is enough that he severs his ego's attachments to it. With this freedom, the sage lives *in* society with unblemished integrity, but is no longer *of* the social world and its customs and rules that can be obstacles to enlightenment. From his passage through the sixth chakra, he clearly perceives repetitive archetypal patterns underlying these social conventions; from the fifth he has learned how to creatively symbolize those archetypes for the benefit of all; from the fourth he draws upon his heartfelt commitment to his fellow men and women; from the third, he grasps the rules, customs, and expectations of society, which he chooses to follow when there is no reason not to; from the second he is playfully receptive to his unconscious mind, but never ruled by it; from the first he maintains a firm grounding in the world of objects and people.

Although many people throughout history have had mystical experiences, very few integrate these to the point that they can operate from the seventh chakra by choice. To the best of my knowledge, there are no drugs that can reliably confer seventh-chakra consciousness, although some people gain intimations of this highest level following intensive periods of fasting and meditation. These experiences can lead to significant personal growth. Because the sage has reached the ultimate epiphany of human experience— radical reunion with the Absolute—therapy is no longer necessary.

Spiritual Growth and Regression

Spiritual growth does not necessarily mean meditating for long hours, entering altered states of consciousness, or cultivating mystical experiences. *Spiritual growth means actively engaging tasks appropriate to one's chakra level which foster movement to the next higher chakra.* For a small child, this may mean learning to brush his teeth and play peacefully with peers. For a teen it may mean ego-building tasks related to social skills and gaining material security. It is only in the late stages of the third chakra that ego-transcending strategies first become appropriate. Prior to that time such techniques can be harmful.

In an ideal lifetime, the chakras open in sequence, each standing firmly on the lessons and growth experiences of the last. But in reality, life seldom follows this ideal script. When chakras open prematurely out of sequence, or when an unfortunate person undergoes *regression*—a backward motion to an earlier, more primitive state of development—the results can be extremely disruptive. Stanislav and Christina Grof coined the term *spiritual emergency* to describe such untimely derailments. These can take various forms from full-blown psychoses to "mini-regressions" that briefly slow spiritual advance in order to marshal strength for the next step upward (Grof & Grof, 1989).

People whose selves have expanded only to include the three lower chakras usually lack adequate grounding to integrate spontaneous intrusions of higher-chakra consciousness. When these suddenly flood one's consciousness, such as during a manic episode, an individual may desperately struggle to make sense of his uncanny insights by casting them in the symbolism of a lower level. The result is usually bizarre and often frightening to others.

For instance, following a feeling of union with the Divine (seventh chakra), such an individual may conclude that he is Jesus (but other people aren't). He may interpret telepathic inputs (sixth chakra) as witchcraft or government thought control. The universal symbolism of popular songs (fifth chakra) may communicate "personal" messages that suggest a grand conspiracy. Overwhelming feelings of compassion (fourth chakra) might lead a college student to give away his meager possessions to the homeless. Although most observers would find such assumptions merely weird, they also impart to many psychotic states a paradoxical appearance of having both regressive and mystical characteristics.

The Pre/Trans Fallacy

There are other ways in which *pre*-egoic lower-chakra states can be confused with *trans*-egoic higher-chakra ones. For instance, the first and seventh chakras may seem alike because both a selfless infant and self-transcended mystic bask in blissful unity with their Source. But an infant has no choice but to surrender to the immense power of Spirit, while an evolved sage willfully regulates its flow so that he can function in the world in an uncommonly effective way. During his passage through the lower chakras, a mystic suffers the exquisite pain of separateness and alienation, both of which he finally transcends.

The second and sixth chakras bear a similar relationship. Both are stages in which self-boundaries are semipermeable, relatively open to free communion with pure Spirit. Both the accomplished seer and the preadolescent child rely on feeling and intuition rather than logic to guide them. But the similarities end there. The child has little control over his emotions, instincts, or visions, and he uses logic based on wishful thinking as his primary means of processing information. The self-realized adept, in contrast, is a master of logic, which he willfully transcends in favor of a kind of awareness in which reason no longer separates him from an intuitive grasp of reality. He alters his consciousness at will, engages paranormal powers with precision, and asserts his will over emotions and instincts, which he nonetheless values as important sources of information.

The third and fifth chakras also bear superficial similarities. When a creative thinker reaches the fifth level, he has begun to transcend the ego, but is far from completing that task, as a short conversation with some of our most creative artists and scientists quickly demonstrates. Both the power chakra (third) and the inspiration chakra (fifth) confer skill for manipulating concepts and objects, but in the former case the focus is on obtaining material security, while in the latter case creativity is a means of higher self-expression to benefit humanity.

The fourth chakra stands alone at the capstone of the pyramid (Campbell, 1974). It is paradoxically a stage of maximum ego differentiation and a momentous turning point when the self tentatively reopens to Spirit, allowing its essence—universal love—to flow inward and alter the course of life. This *agape* love, directed first toward humanity, then toward one's own higher Self, then finally toward all of creation, quickens the journey back to our Source.

The important point is that *one must possess a strong and whole ego before one can begin to transcend it.* Transpersonal philosopher Ken Wilber has aptly named the failure to distinguish between *pre-* and *trans*-personal levels the pre/trans fallacy (Wilber, 1983). This common error has long bedeviled the antipsychiatry movement and its apologists such as R. D. Laing and Thomas Szasz, who blurred the distinctions between madness and transcendence.

The following two case histories illustrate how ignoring pre/trans distinctions can lead to therapeutic errors:

CASE 1
Stuart is a nineteen-year-old grocery clerk whose mother brought him to see a marriage, family, and child counselor who advertised herself as

a "holistic therapist." Stuart was raised alone by his mother after his father committed suicide during one of several psychiatric hospitalizations. His mother said that Stuart recently shaved his head and superficially cut his wrists in response to "orders from the mob," which he later revealed to be hallucinated voices. His mother said that Stuart was an introverted child and a fair student until his last year of high school when he began spending long hours alone in his room. His grades declined, and he quit school six months before graduation. He had no close friends. Because his mother often heard him laughing to himself when he was alone, she was sure that he was using drugs, but none were ever found, and Stuart denied drug use except for occasional experimentation with marijuana.

Stuart's therapist found him to be a pale, thin, and rather unkempt young man dressed in oddly mismatched clothes. Because she suspected poor nutritional habits, she requested that his family obtain a battery of blood tests and hair analysis to determine any metabolic deficiencies. She then recommended that he take large doses of several vitamin and mineral supplements. The therapist also noted that Stuart spoke in an expressionless voice and lacked spontaneity, although he was always polite. He had great difficulty in making minor decisions and seemed to be too distracted to discuss his life issues with her. When asked about career plans, he said he wanted to be a psychiatrist, but had no idea how to achieve that goal. He often smiled during serious moments of their conversation, but when she asked what was funny, his reply rambled off the point.

Stuart's therapist concluded that he was "tense and emotionally constricted" and needed to "loosen up and get in touch with his repressed feelings." She felt that his symptoms represented "blocked emotional energy" from early in life, or possibly from a past lifetime, and that these blockages needed to be released if Stuart was to be free from his symptoms. After teaching Stuart a relaxation technique, she then engaged him in a series of "rebirthing" experiences that included deep and rapid breathing and suggestions for visual imagery that simulated his passing through the birth canal. She also prompted Stuart to strike a mat with a soft bat while shouting how angry he was at his father for abandoning the family when Stuart was five years old. Stuart was instructed to practice the relaxation technique and concentrate on his breathing at least once a day.

Stuart cooperated with the therapy, but seemed dazed following the first of these sessions. When he returned for his next appointment, he was initially distant, but then coolly told his therapist that he planned to kill her because she was "in cahoots with the mob to steal my brain."

When she picked up the phone to call for help, he bolted from her office. Later that day he was apprehended by police when he threatened to jump from a freeway overpass into oncoming traffic.

CASE 2

Lydia is a thirty-six-year-old successful trial lawyer who sought help from a psychiatrist when she began having panic-like feelings that ordinary events in her life were unreal, as if her surroundings had somehow changed or she were dreaming when she was awake. At other times, she felt that her way of perceiving her own thoughts and feelings was different from usual. As she put it, "It's like I'm losing my identity." On two recent occasions, she felt herself to be outside her body, during which she could see her physical body resting immobile at a nearby location. She also described several recent dreams that later came true, including one especially vivid and detailed dream in which a close friend was seriously injured in a skiing accident. This information was unwanted and frightening to her, and she feared that she was going insane.

Lydia was in the midst of an acrimonious divorce from a marriage that she entered "to please my parents." She was also uncertain about the future of her career and was starting to renew a lifelong ambition to write children's books. Having been raised a strict Catholic, she had undergone a spiritual crisis several months earlier when she began a program of yoga and meditation that led her to question her lifelong beliefs in orthodox religion. However, she recently stopped attending her meditation classes and simultaneously increased her daily meditation time from forty minutes to two or three hours. Shortly after this change, she noticed that she was unusually sensitive to bright lights and loud noises. Lydia's psychiatrist made no comment about her meditation practices, but advised her to begin psychoanalytic psychotherapy with him. He prescribed a small dose of Valium to take when she felt an anxiety spell coming on. Initially, Lydia began to feel less anxious, but during her fourth session with the doctor, she suddenly informed him that she had died and gone to hell. She meant this literally, adding that the world was collapsing upon her from all directions, and that she had been abandoned by God. She spoke of vague surges of "energy" flowing upward from her pelvis, through her body, and into her head where they would leave colorful "trails of light." She also felt that there were demonic "presences" in her home who were trying to possess her, although she was able to say that she knew these were not "real." When she threatened suicide to cease her turmoil, the psychiatrist felt he had little choice but to commit her to an acute psychiatric hospital.

In the hospital, Lydia was given Haldol, an antipsychotic medicine. Within a few days, she no longer spoke of being threatened by demons, the bursts of inner light had subsided, and the frightening feelings of unreality had ceased. But she also complained of feeling dull-witted and constricted in feeling, "like a part of me is dead." She also complained that she could no longer recall her dreams and that she could not concentrate on her meditation practice, which she then ceased altogether. Although her psychiatrist gradually tapered the dose of Haldol, the most disturbing of her symptoms did not return. Yet for months afterward, Lydia complained of periodic anxiety attacks, "as if something evil is threatening me from within," and unaccustomed episodes of depression, "as if I've lost something very important."

After six months of psychotherapy that focused on her childhood relations with her parents, Lydia felt that she was not getting to the root of her problem and quit therapy. Her anxiety and depression progressively worsened, and she was admitted to the hospital on two more occasions after attempting suicide.

Both Stuart and Lydia showed clear manifestations of psychosis. Both found their way to healers whose assessment and treatment fit the accepted paradigms of their particular disciplines, but whose responses were unsuited to the symptoms with which they were confronted. In Stuart's case, a lack of previous social adjustment, insidious onset, belief in bizarre delusions, paranoid defenses, critical auditory hallucinations, and an inability to engage in psychological exploration indicates a regression to the second chakra strongly suggestive of malignant schizophrenia.

In Lydia's case, the presence of incipient paranormal abilities, a history of previous high social accomplishment, onset precipitated by a life crisis and intensive spiritual practice, maintenance of reality-testing, inner visions, and lack of paranoia indicate a premature opening of higher-chakra consciousness without adequate foundation in life experience to support it. Although it could be argued that each patient would have been better served if he or she had consulted the other's therapist, a healer who could combine both ways of thinking and apply them precisely would have come closer to the ideal.

Powerful ego-bending techniques such as intense meditation or unguided use of powerful psychedelic drugs can be harmful to individuals who either have not fully integrated third-chakra tasks or who have tentatively done so, but later regressed below this level, such as schizophrenics or borderlines. Authentic growth to higher planes of consciousness is possible only through the persistent exercise of universal love that flows through the heart chakra at the peak of one's estrangement from the Source. This stage simply may not be bypassed.

A Rebirth of Feminine Ideals

Ancient yoga texts assign a *yin* or *yang*, feminine or masculine, characteristic to each chakra. The first chakra, in which the fetus penetrates into the world and struggles for survival, is a *yang*, or masculine level. The second chakra, a stage of passively receptive fantasies, playful openness to worlds beyond that of consensual reality, is *yin*, or feminine. The third, characterized by competitiveness and the warrior Spirit is masculine, ruled by patriarchies and competitive values, as are most cultures in the world today. The fourth, the opening of the compassionate heart that is receptive to the suffering of the world, is feminine. The seminal creativity of the fifth, or throat chakra, reaffirms masculine values, and the intuitive receptivity of the sixth is feminine. The seventh, of course, resolves the *yin/yang* dichotomy in nondual unity that is beyond such polarities, beautifully symbolized in Hindu mythology as the cosmic merger of Shiva and Shakti.

Just as earlier epochs offered women few role models for third-chakra empowerment within the competitive world of masculine values, men now find few role models to guide them in opening the feminine heart chakra. Opening one's inner self to compassion often means confronting leftover guilt for manipulative and exploitative behavior that once seemed proper during a stage of lower consciousness. Men are faced with a great temptation to retreat and numb the heart through addictions to alcohol and cocaine, both of which release mindless aggression and acquisitiveness. Many naturally creative men simply skip the fourth chakra, catapulting ego-bound in the fifth. Lacking empathy and compassion, they direct their higher reasoning capacities toward selfish ends, or in other cases become egomaniacal artists who lack the inner balance of the *anima*.

Women face similar pitfalls, sometimes skipping the male-oriented tasks of the third, or power chakra, making a quantum leap from the second to the fourth chakras. Lacking empowerment and a warrior ethos, they become impotent "bleeding hearts," or co-dependent "women who love too much," identifying with the downtrodden, but lacking sufficient personal resources to heal suffering in the world.

In the waning stages of the second millennium, the most evolved democratic societies on Earth have now progressed to the upper reaches of the third chakra. Yet there are still many theocratic cultures that operate predominantly from second-chakra consciousness, just as did the Western world during the Dark Ages. A few subsistence-oriented first-chakra cultures still exist in isolated areas of the world. Modern societies generally regard the behavior of these cultures as "crazy," just as we define individuals from our own culture as insane when they regress to the first or second chakra. Of course there are many people within any culture who are well above or below the mean of their culture's general stage of evolution.

Biologists know that personal development within an individual parallels the evolutionary development of the human species as a whole. The historic first chakra that spanned tens of thousands of years of precivilized human existence ended when primitive humans relinquished their arboreal isolation to forge social communities. This momentous advance forced the naive consciousness of our animal Spirit into new and complex patterns. Humanity's second-chakra phase ended about the time that the ancient Greeks and related cultures wrested the Goddess from the earth, changed Her sex to male, and put Him in the sky. We now stand at the closing stages of a masculine historical epoch led by patriarchal warrior sky-gods who tamed nature while simultaneously generating the means to sterilize the surface of the mother planet through gradual toxic pollution or cataclysmic nuclear holocaust.

If we are to participate meaningfully in the next evolutionary step for humanity—opening the heart chakra and renewing our earth-mother Gaia—a clear challenge awaits us: *We must reaffirm feminine values.* This means moving from competitiveness to cooperation, from conquest to affiliation, from custodians of earth to participants in its natural evolution, from fighting each other to nurturing each other. Once we accept this task, we will joyfully realign ourselves with the supreme evolutionary mission of humanity: fostering growth of personal and collective consciousness toward reunion with our Source.

IV

Innovative Techniques in Transpersonal Psychotherapy

The diversity of chapters in this section is almost overwhelming. Yet the contributors share a common attitude toward their work: the capacity and courage to innovate. Whether they are working with innovative approaches that have their roots in Eastern traditions or whether they are experimenting with new therapeutic technologies, each is attempting to enhance the potential for transpersonal experience in therapist and patient alike.

These innovations are not simply theoretical. Each experimenter is applying and evaluating theory in his or her daily practice. Richard Yensen evaluates his use of audio-visual material in Perceptual Affective Therapy and its contribution to the development of new identity out of an old ego, and Norman Don combines a wide range of therapeutic modes in unique healing approaches for one patient whose prognosis was highly pessimistic.

Lester Fehmi and Fern Selzer describe "open focus training" and biofeedback in the treatment of stress and point out the contribution these techniques can make to the experience of the transpersonal at the highest level. My chapter in this section explains that in my work with couples I am frequently able to interject a spiritual component which then becomes a powerful tool for healing in the relationship; Roger Woolger theorizes in his chapter that past-life patterning on the mental, emotional, and physical levels can be altered. Donald Evans provides in detail his approach of working with the bodily-emotional and spiritual aspects of clients, with a shamanistic awareness of the spirit, and, finally, Stanislav Grof details some of his extraordinary work with non-ordinary states of consciousness (NOSC).

Once again, by reviewing such a diversity of approaches we see that there is no royal road to the transpersonal. Each therapist and each patient must find the road that is right for him or her. These chapters, then, do not represent opposing views but simply offer different paths suited to different explorers.

20

Perceptual Affective Therapy

Richard Yensen

Many of the chapters in this book describe therapeutic techniques which have evolved from Eastern traditions like meditation and are used and practiced to gain access to and to develop certain realms of the mind. In this chapter, however, Richard Yensen describes a new, essentially Western and modern approach which provides access both to traditional psychodynamic aspects of conflict and to transpersonal realms beyond psychodynamics.

In developing this new therapeutic modality, Yensen draws on the work of four theorists—Freud, Rank, Jung, and Grof—and applies their insights to the therapeutic environment in a fresh way. Just as Grof found psychedelic drugs to be successful adjuncts to therapy and effective ways of achieving altered states of consciousness, so does Yensen find audio-visual technology helpful—without the use of drugs.

Perceptual Affective Therapy is oriented toward "producing a regression in the service of the ego." To do this, it uses an audio-visual environment in a number of fundamental ways: eliciting and reinforcing, facilitating and supporting, defining, and, finally, producing therapeutic regression. After regression is achieved, continued use of audio-visual aids can facilitate going beyond regression to integration. Once integration is accomplished, the patient is then able to take the originally regressive experience to its final stage of resolution: transcendence.

Audio-visual aids in Perceptual Affective Therapy are so effective in Yensen's experience that they can produce—together with carefully interwoven traditional verbal theory—extreme states of altered consciousness. These deep states often contain the theme of death and rebirth, of transition. "The severing of the ego from an old identity and the creation of the experience of being reborn into a new identity are both at the core of Perceptual Affective Therapy."

To be fully effective, this modality requires two elements: ego strength in the patient so that he or she can deal with the profundity of the changes taking place, and sensitivity in the therapist in choosing appropriate music and images as the patient progresses from one stage to the next. What is particularly interesting is that both Yensen and Norman Don describe using their techniques successfully in quite ill patients such as borderline psychotics, patients about whom traditional psychiatry has been pessimistic in the past. Grof, too, indicated that approaches evolving from altered states, whether or not drug-induced, could be used with psychotic individuals with good results.

Perhaps one of the main contributions Perceptual Affective Therapy can make will be in creating an experience of being reborn with a new identity. This is one of the most difficult problems facing the clinician: to change basic identification patterns which may reflect not only psychopathology but also an entire personality style which leads the patient into painful mind states.

PSYCHOTHERAPY HAS BEEN TRADITIONALLY conducted in dry and constant surroundings. Psychoanalysis and subsequent approaches which evolved from Freud's original experience aim at treating a more strictly neurotic population than today's clinician is likely to see; contemporary psychotherapists encounter more severe ego disorders than classical neuroses. Whereas verbal therapy facilitating insight is adequate for the treatment of neurosis, today's pre-Oedipal ego-development defects require a broader, more flexible therapeutic approach. In searching for such a flexible adjunct to psychotherapy, I became interested in ways in which the environment could be arranged to increase the depth of the psychotherapeutic process. Audio-visual technology has opened up a vast array of possibilities for creating a flexible therapeutic milieu which amplifies and exteriorizes the unconscious. Through experiments with the combination of audio-visual technology and altered states of consciousness, I have synthesized a new therapeutic modality, Perceptual Affective Therapy.

The Nature of Perceptual Affective Therapy

Perceptual Affective Therapy enhances the recall of repressed memories, thereby increasing the intensity of the associated emotions and facilitating the emergence of integrative transpersonal material from deeper realms of the psyche. The theoretical framework guiding the way the therapist utilizes the environment is a synthesis of three approaches: Freud's psychoanalysis, Rank's birth trauma, and Jung's analytical psychology. This theoretical framework was suggested by Stanislav Grof (1975). Grof developed this theory as a result of studying thousands of sessions where psychedelic drugs were used as adjuncts to psychotherapy. Perceptual Affective Therapy alters the environment so that perceptual and emotional experiences resembling those encountered when using psychedelic drugs in psychotherapy are facilitated without the use of drugs (Yensen, 1975).

I have explored the use of an audio-visual environment as a device for enhancing the therapeutic relationship in seven basic and complementary ways: (1) as a way of inducing an altered state of consciousness and modulating its intensity; (2) as a diagnostic projective device employing a multitude of ambiguous stimuli; (3) as a way of exploring a patient's coping mechanisms; (4) as an instrument to elicit or amplify a particular experience or emotion; (5) as a way of providing a facilitative and supportive environment in which an already released experience may unfold and develop more profoundly than otherwise; (6) as a way to define a specialized setting in which intense affective release is favored; and (7) as a way of facilitating the emergence of preconscious and unconscious material even in resistant individuals. These techniques are the primary ingredients of Perceptual Affective Therapy.

The physical setting is very important when dealing with a person in an altered state of consciousness. A warm, homey atmosphere is essential to Perceptual Affective Therapy. The first therapy meetings draw on the warmth of the setting and are devoted to establishment of rapport and trust between patient and therapist. The therapeutic alliance fostered during these interviews must be substantial before using the audio-visual environment. Since the therapist manages the sensory input from the environment, the patient immediately regresses. He or she is no longer at the experiential wheel and cannot seek or avoid experiences so easily. This state of affairs clearly parallels the situation of the young child or infant, and often this parallel alone is enough for a patient to recover a memory or experience a strong emotional response.

A combination of audio and/or visual stimuli is used to create the mind-altering environment. A four-channel sound system provides an encompassing sound field; an extensive collection of records and tapes allows the choice of sound from classical music to sound effects, from ethnic and folk music to contemporary music and jazz.

The visual environment is created by projecting slides and motion pictures, at times using several screens simultaneously. Images are chosen from a large collection of 35mm slides depicting every imaginable human situation including birth, death, sex, beauty, ugliness, happiness, sadness, joy, terror, peace, and war.

There is ample technical capacity to create a completely disorienting, sensory overload experience. More often, however, the environment is carefully modulated to elicit and work through unconscious material in a less overwhelming way. In early interviews I usually request pictures of the patient's childhood and then make 35mm slides from these to help the recall of childhood events. I try to use these slides unexpectedly so that the surprise element aids the release of repressed memories and emotions. The therapeutic impact of this procedure depends upon the patient's ability to perceive therapeutic intent in the surprise. Therefore a strong therapeutic alliance is necessary.

In a Perceptual Affective Therapy session, the therapist is guided in the ongoing selection of new stimuli by the patient's emotional, physical, and ideational responses to the present environment. The therapist selects new stimuli, which will be consonant with the implied or expressed content of the patient's experience and which will guide the exploration of deeper levels. This technique, which allows the patient's unconscious or preconscious organismic responses to lead the uncovering process, produces profound regressions. When the environment is managed in this way, the potential for insight and integration is maximized.

Transcendence and Integration

Perceptual Affective Therapy is oriented toward producing a regression in service of the ego. Integration is the result of the patient's re-experiencing previous psychological traumas in a supportive setting. The insight may be clear cut, as in the case of most childhood memories, or it may be more global, as in perinatal, transpersonal, and mystical experiences.

Transcendence, "going beyond," is the goal of Perceptual Affective Therapy. It aims to facilitate "going beyond" the limits of the present personality structure to a superior level of integration. This is achieved by fully experiencing the unconscious determinants of existing personality traits. Transcendence, "going beyond" by "going through," occurs repeatedly on different levels, and it is a basic ingredient of this therapy. Each time the individual transcends, there is a deeper understanding of self and more profound insight into the human condition. Transcendence also implies experiences of God or divine spirit. While this experience does occur in Perceptual Affective Therapy, it is usually preceded by intense relivings and actual resolution of painful infantile conflicts. Thorough exploration of more traditional psychodynamic issues allows the patient to integrate mystical experiences without narcissistic inflation or deflation. Therefore the individual is able to accept the direct experience of collective unconscious material without feeling separated from others or abidingly insignificant in relation to the overwhelming qualities of the experience.

Perceptual Affective Therapy emphasizes the integration of insights occurring during an altered state of consciousness. As I mentioned before, some experiences are intense enough per se to produce a reorganization of the personality. However, I still use a good deal of conventional face-to-face therapy between altered state sessions. This ensures a complete understanding before proceeding to the next experientially oriented session. In these conventional sessions I use contemporary ego psychological views on personality dynamics and extend my theoretical stance to the transpersonal when necessary. The following case vignettes will serve to illustrate this form of psychotherapy.

CASE 1

Kathy came into therapy as a referral from a behavioristically oriented psychologist. She had been in treatment with several therapists for the last seven years and had been a serious management problem. Kathy was an attractive thirty-one-year-old college student. She had been married and divorced once and was remarried at the time of the therapy. She had adopted a child with her first husband and then felt uncontrollable urges to destroy either the child or herself. A subsequent suicide attempt resulted in a short hospitalization.

The previous therapist found her too intensely emotional and quite inaccessible to rational discussion of her problems. On her first visit to my office I quickly found out what he was talking about. Kathy was alternately crying, screaming and angry, or dissolute from the moment she entered the door for her first interview. She called immediately after one of our early conventional interviews to complain that she was so overcome by emotion that she had driven home at eighty miles per hour and felt strong impulses to run into pedestrians. I dealt with her firmly over the phone, indicating that if she were unable to contain her feelings enough to function outside of the therapy then hospitalization would be in order. I told her, however, that I felt she could deal with her feelings more effectively than she claimed and that I was sure she could manage to pull herself together. After several moments of seemingly uncontrollable crying, she said she felt much better and would see me for her appointment the following week.

My assessment of Kathy after several interviews was that, although she displayed superficially hysterical features, she had a more profound developmental disorder. I wanted to proceed with caution in the use of media because obviously there was no need to provoke further emotionality; if anything, the problem was that she seemed to have no sense of relief after these emotional displays.

I therefore decided to use only music and eyeshades with Kathy. For several months she would arrive for her weekly appointment seeming quite distraught. As soon as I put on the eyeshades, she would launch into a display of yelling and screaming. The emotional release was accompanied by considerable verbal material. Kathy never seemed to communicate directly with me during these early sessions. Instead she became so internally absorbed that she seemed to be talking to herself. She described how miserably she had been treated by her parents. Kathy described her father as an extremely weak man who ignored her mother's numerous affairs and was very cold. Her mother was extremely inconsistent, alternating public displays of blatant seductiveness with private conversations condemning sexuality. Religious indoctrination combined with this family milieu to create a confusing picture of sex, which Kathy perceived as an act of aggression.

In an altered-state session after three months of therapy, she described a vision of her parents in a casket. After all of her condemnation of them, I suggested that she close the lid and bury them. She began to cry and admit that she really wanted them to be different but that she loved them even as they were. She went on to speak with each of the important people in her life and related how much it hurt to love and depend on such depriving figures. There was a profound discharge of feeling in this session. In our next session Kathy reported that she was able to have satisfying sexual experiences with her husband for the first time.

It is possible to explain Kathy's experience through currently accepted psychodynamic formulations. As a transpersonal practitioner, I welcome the psychodynamic and explore it thoroughly while aiming for the transpersonal. I therefore saw Kathy's session as beginning a process that, if deepened, would eventually lead to ego death and rebirth. She was abandoning her previous cognitive model of her parents, a model which could only see them as depriving and herself as miserable enough to deserve the deprivation. From observing her body in the session, I could see that this view of her parents was deeply rooted in her image of the world and of herself. In order to restructure such aspects of personality, patients working with this kind of conflict on a deeper level frequently have images and feelings of dying, letting go, and subsequent rebirth.

CASE 2

Miriam was a fifty-year-old widow who had been in therapy for six months. During a prior therapy session, Miriam had experienced a sequence of slides graphically portraying birth, death, and rebirth. The purpose of the stimulation was to activate feelings related to these issues and to suggest that resolution of seemingly irresolvable conflicts was possible. Miriam had learned over the course of therapy how to enter an altered state through environmental effects and short verbal inductions. Eyeshades and music were used in this session. After being given a simple early learning set hypnotic induction (Erikson, Rossi, & Rossi, 1976), Miriam was instructed to free associate to the music while maintaining a bioenergetic tension position (Lowen, 1967). A specific suggestion was given: "Listen to the music in a new and deeper way than usual. Breathe in the music and allow the music to play you."

Miriam began to speak of her sister and their rivalrous relationship in childhood. I encouraged her to speak directly to the sister as though she were right in the room with us. After yelling at the sister in a childlike voice, she began to recall beating up one of the sister's friends in grade school. Miriam described how she couldn't beat up the sister but could beat up the friend as a substitute. She recalled that the sister was quite gifted and that she felt she couldn't gain attention by being good; instead, she decided to be the bad girl and get some recognition that way.

All during this time, angry-sounding musical selections were played to encourage Miriam's discharge of these emotions and recall of these memories; the music indicated that it was acceptable to feel that way and to express it. Miriam began telling about an incident during an Easter parade when she was deprived of her position in the procession, and her bouquet of flowers was given to another child to carry. She experienced feelings of humiliation and rage at the actions of the teacher who ordered her back to the end of the line. As the intensity and aggressive tone of the music were raised, she spoke of feeling crushed and trampled by lack of parental love. Her feeling of being unwanted and unloved was incredibly painful, and she expressed it with deep sobbing, racking of the body, and screams of anguish. The feeling of being crushed became extremely intense, and she said she felt crushed by life itself. I managed the environment by listening carefully to the emotional tone of Miriam's voice and the nature of the content she revealed; I matched the tone of the music to the experience. Work with psychedelics has shown me that when an experience becomes sufficiently intense, eventually it will be transcended; therefore no attempt was made to guide the patient out of difficulties. Rather, explicit encouragement was given to surrender, confront, and experience all feelings in the safety of the treatment environment.

Miriam then reported feeling that life was being crushed out of her, that life was full of pain and suffering and not worth living. She described herself as being ground into the earth under the feet of life. She remained with these difficult feelings for about twenty-five minutes, then there was silence and a relaxation of her body. Miriam spoke of experiencing a beautiful flower. The emotional tone of the voyage shifted toward wonder, and the musical ambience was correspondingly shifted toward more inspirational and uplifting music. Miriam said she felt as though she had died and was surprised to be experiencing a deeper sense of herself. She described herself as a very beautiful flower rising out of the guilt and shame of her childhood. The flower was peaceful. I shifted the music to some Balinese Gamelan selections with a superficially discordant sound in order to test the stability of this apparently positive state. Miriam at first responded to this change by asking why the music had been changed to this dissonant piece. She began to accuse me, the therapist, of trying to destroy the beauty of her experience but quickly changed in tone and demonstrated the depth of her integrating experience. She went on to state that the music was like her life, apparently dissonant and unmelodic on the surface but, when experienced fully, revealing hidden beauty and meaning. The discordant and grating painful experiences in her life fit together with the rest of it to form a consonant and melodious whole which was magnificent beyond beauty. She went on to describe a sense of transcendent energy and love interpenetrating all life.

In this case an integration of previously separate good and bad representations of the self and the world was observed.

The Death-Rebirth Cycle

Our social matrix deprives individuals facing major transitions in their lives— transitions from child to adult, adult to parent, life to death—of socially sanctioned and meaningful rituals of transition. The severing of the self from an old identity and the creation of the experience of being reborn into a new identity are both at the core of Perceptual Affective Therapy. The therapeutic environment enhanced through audio-visual stimuli is a socially sanctioned space where meaningful transitions may occur. In order for this space to be effective, it must have both physical and psychological ingredients. The psychological space is one that the patient learns to create and experience in the physical milieu of the treatment suite. The environment of stimuli is managed by the therapist in order to foster the development of a specialized altered state of consciousness. This altered state offers a temporary relaxation of boundaries in the therapy session and a restoration of necessary boundaries afterwards. Death-rebirth cycles and the profound feelings associated with them are separated from the ordinary consciousness by occurring in an altered state. The state which Perceptual Affective Therapy can induce, like the altered state which psychedelic drugs can induce, is extremely useful for releasing a powerful influx of profound and usually unconscious material. However, the material must be partitioned from ordinary consciousness because it arrives in a form initially incompatible with the linear, logical, sequence-oriented, secondary-process thinking necessary for daily living.

Perceptual Affective Therapy is conducted with stimuli which are musical and visual-spatial in nature. This permits the therapist to interact directly with the unconscious through its language of personal and transpersonal symbols and of emotional links between events in the person's history. In using this approach I believe it is important, where possible, to allow fantasies to be fully experienced and released through complete affective discharge before giving any interpretation. Interpretation is in many cases unnecessary; after the complete discharge of affect, patients become aware of the source and meaning of their experiences. The therapist should, therefore, be reticent about interpreting experiences prematurely. The patient will discover the meaning of his or her experiences and will eventually, through this process, be able to attribute deep meaning and significance to life itself.

The experience of the death-rebirth cycle which can be activated through Perceptual Affective Therapy is extremely vivid. Complaints of difficulty in breathing and the activation of deep reflexes such as vomiting are possible and are accepted by the therapist as a meaningful part of the experience. My attitude toward patients and their difficult experiences is a quiet and firm belief in their ability to face the experience unleashed in the session no matter what its nature. I also have complete confidence in the unconscious as the synthesizer of the experiences ultimately necessary for the curative transformation of the patient's mental life. I therefore attune myself to the process of the patient's unconscious and communicate directly with that process through stimuli selection.

Suitability for Treatment

To be amenable to treatment with such a profoundly mind-altering approach, the patient must have adequate ego strength. Perhaps the two most important factors contributing to the practicability of Perceptual Affective Therapy as an approach are: first, the patient's ability to form a strong therapeutic alliance; and second, the patient's ability to maintain insight and simultaneous awareness of various levels of reality. The patient must be able to gain the awareness that much of the session material constitutes reliving of feelings connected with past events. Patients unsuited to this type of therapy usually indicate some forebodings of insurmountable distress and display a loss or weakening of the therapeutic alliance in the initial altered state session.

CASE 3

Gina was a thirty-five-year-old divorcee. After one month of preparation and traditional therapy, an altered state session was scheduled. In this early session Gina regressed to the age of seven or eight and re-experienced being cruelly beaten with a belt. The beatings were given by a sadistic schoolmaster in a boarding school. Although the material appeared to be well integrated after the session, Gina called several times over the following weekend relating to the therapist as if he were the schoolmaster and was unable to recognize the transferential nature of these feelings. The continuation of regressively oriented sessions with such a reaction would court disaster. During several strictly verbal therapy sessions, the negative transference was ameliorated, but the therapeutic alliance was tenuous and the patient terminated therapy.

In cases where there has been any question of loss of insight, the patients themselves have expressed the desire to discontinue this type of therapy. The therapist need only agree that perhaps this is the best course at the present time. It is usually possible to continue therapy with a more traditional approach and, depending upon the clinical picture, perhaps return to altered state sessions later in therapy. Perceptual Affective Therapy sessions can be used as screening and diagnostic devices. If well managed, these sessions will produce no lasting ill effects, yet they clearly reveal severe borderline individuals who would be unable to undergo this type of procedure without inpatient facilities. Less severe borderline individuals have been treated as outpatients with favorable results.

CASE 4

June had been in therapy for ten months. She had experienced intense rejection in childhood and developed hysterical traits as a result of a seductively attentive father. A visual presentation of childhood pictures intermingled with pictures of starvation and violence was followed by instructions to wear eyeshades and listen to music while free associating. The patient's associations were:

> I'm thinking of all the times I've tried to give love. It hurts so much when you're rejected. I see my mother in the kitchen, she turns her back on me. How that hurts. How many times will it happen? How many times will people tell me that I have misunderstood and that I'm really not wanted. I have to be worth something or else life's not worth living. I have to do something special to get their attention.

> Never enough, whatever I do it's never enough, they're never satisfied. What do you want me to do, kill myself trying? I hate you for making me do that. You're making me choke. I hate you for doing that. I don't want to have to always prove that I'm the best. I want to get that out of me. Nobody wants just plain me. I don't even know what that is, I've lost that somewhere.

At this point June began to vomit violently and I encouraged her to get rid of that sense of worthlessness by feeling it intensely and vomiting it out. She then continued:

> I still have the fantasy that someone will come along and tell me that I'm the one they have been searching for, the perfect person. Then I'll know that I'm okay and be able to say to the world, "See! He loves me!"
>
> I wonder what it feels like when a seed is growing inside. Saying I'm nothing is an insult to that seed. I'm afraid for that seed to grow from myself. I'm afraid to give up hiding behind a shell of rejection. I'd have to be plain and raw and people might not like me. If that happened, they would reject the real me all over again. I'll never have any guarantee. I'm crazy, so crazy.
>
> It's like I'm being born all over again. I'm so dependent on the right climate to grow. It takes guts . . . I'm so alone. It makes me want to go back to doing everything right. I wish I could see your face then maybe I could tell if you approved of this. Whether I'm special or nobody. To get that message from you rather than explore myself, rather than feel this pain.
>
> I wonder if I could stand just being myself. What I'm worth to me all alone: comfort, aloneness, fullness, exploding? I've become so small, such a tiny me inside. Yet I feel quality. A quality dot.
>
> How can I take it? A tiny real worth back from a long time ago. From before the time of my parents. Before my father. Not right, not pretty, not without mistakes, not with talent, not with neatness. I didn't know what to be for him. What should I be, Daddy? What am I supposed to be? Agreeable? Never rebellious? Never fight, say no or talk back? Just be quiet and good, but for God's sake be clever. Don't be like the other kids. Oh Daddy, I can't do that [deep sobbing].

Mom, I want to be special. Look at me. If you only looked you would see. I have something, look and see. Will you please find out something good about me? [deep sobbing continues].

God damn you, go away, go away and leave me alone. You don't want me. No, no, no, no, you don't love me! Where is the real me? There is so much emptiness. I'm so small without any stuffed up importance. Do others feel this way? Other diamonds inside waiting to be seen not for achievements or outside appearances. Does anybody ever really see you? I hope so!

Daddy, I can't say it. Was there something in you I didn't see, something tiny and good, hidden and covered? Was there some playfulness, some joy, some caring? I don't let myself see that in you now. I know why. I'm afraid, it hurts too much.

Wow, I feel like some kind of jellyfish or emerging tadpole or something. I feel unformed. Floating! Floating in the universe. Tender and soft, pliable and amorphous, impressionable and weak. I don't have much power. Except I do seem to be floating free. Not attached to anything else, sort of supported by this warmth. Woman! Not exactly only woman, but female, like receptive, kind of waiting to be united with something. Not to complete me because I am complete, but to expand beyond and create more. It's exciting. It's that tadpole feeling. It's not the end, it's the beginning. You can see if you look closely. It's irregular and it will grow. It feels real and honest, not phony, but true.

There is like a core going up and down inside of me. I realize it's a very sexual symbol. I do. I do feel open. It's funny and sad.

June's experience makes clear the complex interweaving of personal and transpersonal elements in a Perceptual Affective Therapy session. One may also observe that the session has some overall coherence and structure in keeping with the aim of producing a modern healing ritual.

Perceptual Affective Therapy blends theories and techniques from diverse origins. It creates a unique environment for gaining therapeutic access to personal and transpersonal material; the transpersonal nature of music and visual images amplifies the patient's ongoing experience. This is a new way of conducting psychological healing, and Perceptual Affective Therapy will certainly undergo a continuing change and refinement. At present, it offers promise as an amplifier of the healing process and as an innovative transpersonal approach to psychotherapy.

21

The Story of Wendy
A Case Study in Multi-Modality Therapy

Norman S. Don

Norman Don, in his description of his treatment of Wendy, draws the outlines of hope on what would otherwise be viewed by traditional psychiatry as a pessimistic canvas. Almost every aspect of Wendy's case in the treatment she receives and the theoretical foundation for that treatment could become a chapter of a book.

In a vivid descriptive narrative interleaved with theory, Don presents the most challenging therapeutic problem of his professional life—how to help Wendy, whose withdrawal has insulated her from fifteen years of varying kinds of psychotherapeutic assistance. The author's approach embodies a number of different therapeutic modalities, beginning with an exploration of Wendy's dreams and the establishment of physical contact and trust. After tentative establishment of this trust, Don puts to use his own extensive studies of the nature of, and relationship between, consciousness, mind, and energy, applying particularly the Japanese Reiki methods of unblocking energy. Concurrently he also works in activating the dynamic, positive aspects of what Jung calls the positive Mother archetype and then in moving through the alchemical process for transforming conscious experience. He makes extensive use, too, of Reichian and Eastern yogic approaches and techniques at various points in the treatment. From a traditional psychiatric viewpoint, the results he reports are as atypical as the treatment.

Not only does Don's chapter communicate in moving ways the intensity and uniqueness of the therapist-patient relationship, but it also opens up the interesting possibility that some patients classified as "borderline" or "psychotic" may actually have disorders other than those existing on the plane of psychodynamic, intrapsychic problems. Such a contribution can provide a springboard for discussions of possible approaches to these problems and, it is hoped, stimulate a spirit of investigation in these new areas. One of the important questions raised here is whether interpretive, verbal therapy can be used before the body itself can begin a process of integration out of the psychopathology.

IT WAS A SUB-ZERO EVENING WHEN Wendy first came into my office and my professional life. She had been seeing a counselor for one and a half years, and had been referred to me by a psychiatric colleague for treatment of her chronic insomnia. Wendy was expecting the psychiatrist to be present during our first meeting, and she became increasingly withdrawn when she realized that he would not be there.

My first questions were answered in a soft, barely audible voice. Within the first ten minutes she became mute, covering her face with her hands and hair. Finally she took off her mackinaw and put it on backwards, with the hood covering her face. There she sat for about five minutes. At that point I went across the hall to my colleague's office to make sure that this was indeed my insomnia patient. It was, but there was also much, much more— as I was to find out over the next eighteen months.

When I returned to my office, Wendy got up and left, glaring hostilely at me as she departed into the night. She returned within fifteen minutes, during which time my associate assured me that she was easily frightened but not in crisis. Since it was by then time for me to leave and she lived in my neighborhood, I offered her a ride, which she accepted with a nod of her head. She would not speak to me during the ride home and every so often would turn her head and glare at me. When I stopped near her home, she stepped out of the car, took a bottle out of the paper bag she was carrying, threw it on the ground and went on her way into the night, kicking the bottle in front of her.

During the next few weeks, Wendy and I had several appointments during which I attempted to treat her insomnia with biofeedback and relaxation training, but it became apparent that this could not succeed given her mental state. She was eventually given medication for the insomnia.

Wendy and I gradually were able to communicate somewhat better, and she finally asked if I would be willing to become her psychotherapist. I considered her request very carefully over the next week before I agreed to what I knew would be an extraordinarily difficult and possibly fruitless undertaking. I decided that she was robust enough to withstand a very aggressive and intensive therapy without psychotic decompensation. I was not willing to be merely another supportive therapist for her—she had had at least four such relationships by that time with psychiatrists and psychologists. I made it clear to her that this was going to be a frontal assault on her condition, not a palliative. Thus began the most extraordinary therapeutic project of my career.

Getting information from Wendy was almost impossible because our verbal contact would dissolve during the first few minutes of each session, at which point she would withdraw into a fetal position on the floor. After a few minutes her chest would heave as if she were crying, but there would be no sound and no tears. This pattern was to be repeated countless times, and it was to take well over a year for me to get something resembling a complete history on her background and previous treatment.

At the time we started treatment, Wendy was a slender, single woman in her early thirties. She had been raised in a rural setting in an eastern state, the second oldest of three siblings, the other two being male. During her first few years, she lived on a farm with her parents, brothers, and paternal grandmother. Her family moved a few years later into the local town, where her father worked.

Wendy was completely rejected as a human being by her mother from her earliest memory. Various reasons were given for this rejection. She was a tomboy, unsociable; she read too much; and she was irreligious—these last two being inexcusable sins in the eyes of the family's fundamentalist church. Wendy's father and his brothers were passive men, bound to and dependent on their mother and sisters. Wendy's mother was very much an outsider and came increasingly to resent Wendy's closeness to her grandmother and aunt.

After Wendy's older sibling was born, her mother gave birth to two other children, who died soon after delivery. Wendy felt that her conception was completely unwanted and that her mother was living in a very difficult situation. In Wendy's own written words about her mother—*the* mother, as she always referred to her:

> The mother didn't treat me badly. She took care of me all right and all that. But there was clearly a sense of something smoldering, which i thought was a justified disapproval of and impatience with me because i was an impossible child. She took care of me all right but she didn't relate to me much. She didn't really relate, but still i'd be all tense inside and ashamed and scared if we were in the same room—but i don't want to get into those feelings now—i could feel them again from just thinking about it. The thing is, there were a few unexpected outbursts of anger here and there, not because of anything i did particularly, so i never understood. I just chalked it up to the same old thing. But i'd feel humiliated

(because i was bad and now this was being underlined) and bewildered (because nothing specific would set this off usually) and angry. Also very lonely and depressed, i'd get, and then i'd get spaced out, even when i was little. (Wendy's capitalization)

From age seven on, Wendy would never allow her mother to touch her. Her father was a passive, weak individual and had very little to do with the children. Wendy increasingly found her solace by herself in the outdoors. The earth became her mother; the wind, her father; and the sun, her friend and God. This was not merely a childhood fantasy; she came completely to accept the transpersonal parentage of these archetypes.

As Wendy mentioned, she experienced being "spaced out," even when she was little. These dissociative states were very prevalent during the early part of therapy. While in these states, she became tongue-tied, her breath became very shallow and restricted to her upper chest, and she would curl up in a fetal position. She also would experience unusual internal body sensations out of the ordinary range of feeling, conventionally called coenesthetic hallucinations. She described these sensations as being like "electricity" and "pressure." More will be said about these sensations later. Wendy would enter these states during very stressful periods in our sessions and would leave them usually within thirty minutes. They also occurred spontaneously while she was going about her daily activities, when they sometimes lasted several days.

Despite her unusual personality, Wendy was brilliant. She was offered scholarships for college study, but her parents opposed it because she was a woman. Since officials of the state university considered her to be an unusually promising student, they visited the home. They prevailed upon the parents to let Wendy attend the university, and she turned in a very distinguished performance.

During her college years her emotional problems intensified, and she was hospitalized several times. On at least one occasion she became anorexic and was unable to eat for several weeks, which led to hospitalization. Food and eating became a continuing problem for her. She would wake up in the morning and sometimes find that during the night she had eaten a large quantity of food in her sleep. This could be a whole loaf of bread, a large bag of cookies, and sometimes a whole meal, which she had cooked and eaten entirely in a somnambulistic state.

In order to relieve the sensations of electricity and pressure in her head, Wendy would often wait for nightfall, when she could go to a park and bang her head on a bronze plaque for hours. At other times, to relieve the sensations of splitting apart at the level of the navel due to a buildup of pressure there, she would go into a fetal position to contain the pressure.

As her condition came to the attention of the university psychiatrists, she received treatment as an outpatient and an inpatient. She was befriended eventually by a professor of psychiatry and his family who helped her greatly during her college years. For this was the pathology of a sensitive, highly intelligent, kind, and generous person.

After college, Wendy entered graduate school at another university. She was academically successful there, too, but her emotional problems persisted. She was hospitalized at the university psychiatric unit and seen as an outpatient by a university psychiatrist for eighteen months.

The phenothiazines did little to relieve her symptoms; she continued to live in a chronic borderline state. Eventually she terminated treatment with the psychiatrist and somewhat later began treatment with a psychological counselor. He also treated her for eighteen months until we began our therapy.

Therapy to Wendy had come to mean a supportive crutch, not a cure; that possibility seemed to be long dead to her. Thus, when I told her that I was unwilling to do supportive therapy with her but would attempt a cure, she was skeptical and incensed at my use of the word *cure*. I employed this word intentionally to let her know that we were going to go to war together.

Typed on the inside cover of Wendy's dream notebook was:[1]

On a Picture of a Black Centaur by Edmund Dulac
Your hooves have stamped at the black margin of the wood,
Even where horrible green parrots call and swing.
My works are all stamped down into the sultry mud.
I knew that horse-play, knew it for a murderous thing.
What wholesome sun has ripened is wholesome food to eat,
And that alone; yet I, being driven half insane
Because of some green wing, gathered old mummy wheat
In the mad abstract dark and ground it grain by grain
And after baked it slowly in an oven; but now
I bring full-flavoured wine out of a barrel found
Where seven Ephesian topers slept and never knew
When Alexander's empire passed, they slept so sound.
Stretch out your limbs and sleep a long Saturnian sleep:
I have loved you better than my soul for all my words,
And there is none so fit to keep a watch and keep
Unwearied eyes upon those horrible green birds.

(W. B. Yeats)

My first therapeutic goal was to intrude on the withdrawal.

In order to open a channel of communication between Wendy and me, I suggested that she write down her dreams and bring them to our sessions.

She was able to do this since she had good recall of her dreams. She would come in, hand me her dream notebook, and—since she was afraid of falling from chairs (although she could do it when it was unavoidable)—we would sit together on the floor, side by side. Her dreams were highly symbolized and not very comprehensible at the beginning of therapy. Dreams and writing became the major means of following her inner life because verbal contact was so difficult. As therapy progressed, her dreams became considerably less chaotic, though still symbolized—often at an archetypal level. Only rarely would something overtly personal come through, such as the dream in which Wendy was riding in the back seat of the family car and her mother was in the front. Without warning her mother swung around holding a gun and shot Wendy dead. Because of the problem with verbal contact during the sessions, our therapy shifted to body contact forms of therapy though we continued to look at her dreams. The usual verbal and imaginative methods of the transpersonal therapist were impossible to use in this instance.

I was well aware of the terror of annihilation which led her to curl up in a fetal position session after session. It took over a year of therapy before Wendy could articulate this terror to me. So, when Wendy would curl in a fetal position I would wrap my arms around her back and legs and exert pressure, thereby exaggerating the fetal withdrawal. The heaving of her chest and the soundless, tearless sobs would increase and finally become audible.

The first few months of this frontal assault on the withdrawal were very stormy. Sessions averaged two hours, and I saw her twice a week with extra sessions added when she was in crisis. While I held onto her, she would eventually start to express her rage by striking out at me. I would hold on tightly, keeping just out of the reach of her fists—most of the time. These sessions were nothing less than wrestling and punching matches. Once I lost my temper and struck her back after she kicked me in the groin. Any attempt on my part to interpret her early childhood situation to her would send her into a rage, and she would strike at me.

The drain on my time and energy was great, and I knew that if I were to have another patient like Wendy in treatment with me at the same time, I simply could do no other therapeutic work.

Often I reached the point of despair, but Wendy would write me or call me and let me know that what was happening in our sessions was hell, but she wanted to go on. Also, she told me that she appreciated that I was the only therapist she ever had who was not willing to sit back and let her withdraw by herself.

Over several months Wendy became somewhat less defensive, and I was able to change my method from an invasive form of contact to a nurturing one. I would hold her gently and she would sob softly. The interpretation of, or active working with, her dreams was still not possible, since she would regress so quickly during the sessions. Sprinkled among these body contact sessions were a *few* sessions when verbal therapy was possible.

During the twelfth month of therapy Wendy experienced *kairos,* a flash of unusual psychological movement; what Gendlin (1969) would call a major "felt shift." In the fading light of a winter's afternoon Wendy slowly teased apart her existential situation of separation. She suddenly experienced a profound shift (a *moment juste*), the deep psychological and physiological opening of her being. Wendy experienced that *she* could reach out to people and hold them. It was a profound moment, a moment of high drama, of explorers reaching the shore of a new world. I told Wendy to hold me. "Are you *sure* it's okay?" she asked me over and over. "Are you sure you won't let me hold you but hate it?" She finally held me, while I embraced her. She sobbed openly and joyfully, as did I.

During the next two sessions we sat beside each other on the floor, my arm over her shoulder and her arm tentatively on my back, while we laughed and giggled. It was shortly after this time that my ten-year-old son, who had seen Wendy on several occasions, said, "That lady looks like a *real* person now!"

Various people who knew Wendy began to report about these significant improvements. Wendy remarked herself how much less withdrawn she was. Soon after, she found the full-time employment she needed financially and then worked successfully until she was awarded a scholarship and resigned to finish her studies.

We had finally turned a corner in our work, but much remained to be done. The core issue for Wendy was *existence:* her right to be on the face of this Earth. The etiology of Wendy's difficulty has been described by Arieti (1955) and many other writers: from infancy onward the child experiences the mother's hostility and the utter hopelessness of obtaining parental love and approval. The victim of such circumstances comes to experience himself as the "bad one":

> When, on the other hand, the patient realizes that the world is bad for him only, he also feels that the world is bad for him because *he* is bad or worthless. He feels that if he has always done wrong, it is because there is something wrong *with him.* He feels that if he has not been loved, it is not because love does not exist in this world, but because *he* is not lovable. The malevolent authorities which populate the world are malevolent only toward him and with good reason. He must hate himself more than anybody else hates him. His self-esteem undergoes the most injurious attacks.

The defense mechanisms become more and more incapable of coping with these situations. Anxiety is not covered any longer; on the contrary it is felt more and more and finally it is experienced with the same violence with which it was experienced in early childhood. Through generalization it spreads like fire to all situations which are similar to the original unpleasant situation. The behavior becomes more and more symbolic; it continues to be distorted by the power of the repressed experiences. Finally the anxiety is experienced as actual panic, unless other defenses—this time psychotic—are mobilized. (Arieti, 1955)

The treatment of such individuals is very difficult for many reasons. Among them are the lack of contact with feelings and the person's fear of his feelings when he finally becomes aware of them:

He fears lest they be used against him to demonstrate how bad he is, just as he originally feared his parents would do. He is still afraid that feelings will bring about rebuff, anxiety, and attacks on his self-esteem. (Arieti, 1955, p. 65)

All these difficulties surfaced during the course of the therapy. Her severe regressive behavior during therapy is characteristic of the borderline personality and has been described by Kernberg from a psychoanalytic viewpoint (1965, 1966, 1967). Chessick has commented upon the "enormous undifferentiated primitive rage that goes way back to the patient's earliest days" (1977, p. 112), this due here to the mother's hostility and intrusiveness.

Another expression of her deep-seated problems occurred one day when I received a letter from her with a check and a note stating that she could not tolerate the "killing" any longer. I was very puzzled by this, but did not take it as a suicide note. Then she dropped out of sight for several days and I had the police enter her apartment. She was not there but phoned later from New York where she had flown to escape from me. A mutual acquaintance there helped her and enabled her to return after a few days. She explained later that she had suddenly become terrified (after a session during which her mother figured significantly) and had left for the airport and taken the first available plane. Wendy could not figure out the source of the terror, who could so endanger her life. The only person with that power now was, of course, me.

As Wendy and I continued our work, she would hold on to me, but several times during every session a shudder would rack her body and she would pull herself away. I would encourage her to return, and she always did, and we would renew our physical contact. The fear, of course, was of her possible annihilation through such close contact and also my annihilation by her. Thus, month after month, we went right up to and over the edge of terror together. I would gently suggest to her where all these feelings and fears arose. Gradually she stopped striking out at me and began to listen. One day during the fifteenth month of therapy she came in with her history, which she had written without my request. In a rage she threw the papers on the floor and lunged for my throat. We had had many tests of our physical capabilities by this time; and so, knowing that I could easily extricate myself, I resisted only slightly and let her act out the rage. She never exerted full pressure and after a few minutes let go, enabling me to help her experience that her rage need not be homicidal or annihilating for either of us.

Thus, although Wendy was beginning to deepen the quality of her human contact, her primitive rage and terror were surfacing, generally within our sessions. A symptom that surfaced continually although briefly during sessions, and for longer periods between some sessions, was her dissociative behavior. She would "space out" and would be unable to function fully. For example, once when I was away, she spent two days on her apartment floor wrapped in towels to keep her body from falling apart. Medication was not effective in controlling these symptoms.

I turn now to these feelings of dissociation—the pivotal sensations of "electricity" and "pressure" in her body, and her archetypal parentage—because these help to clarify the dissociative process and its treatment in a new way.

Thus far, our therapeutic picture has been quite conventional, except for the experiential nature of the therapeutic relationship. Wendy's difficulties and their origin could easily fit into either psychodynamic or existential-phenomenological models of the mind. It is, however, Wendy's "electricity" and other symptoms that lead us to quite another dimension. The issue is whether these symptoms are pathological or whether they derive from another level of reality experienced in an altered state of consciousness.

Contemporary science views consciousness as stemming from the biochemical and neurophysiological substrate of the brain. Consciousness and mind are something that the brain "does." Although this is the prevailing scientific position, it is by no means unanimous. Several of the most distinguished neuroscientists of recent times have disagreed with it (Eccles, 1965; Penfield, 1975; Sherrington, 1951). The most common alternative scientific position is based upon a kind of interactive dualism between brain and mind (Campbell, 1970). Thus, brain damage or psychotropic drugs will alter conscious experience, but only so long as the brain functions as the transducer of sensory experience. Learning to perceive sensorially without the brain usually requires training. It may be stumbled upon while in a high-energy state such as psychosis, when the normal coupling between mind and brain is weakened. Psychosis, then, may stem from a malfunction of the biological substrate or from purely psychological sources in the mind or from both together.

Scientific evidence for some kind of "field phenomenon" embracing the human and other organisms has been reported in the literature. A full review of this literature is not relevant here, but the work of several investigators is important. That of Yale professor Harold S. Burr (1952–53, 1972) and L. J. Ravitz (1963) on electrically detectable field effects which vary with condition of the organism has been reported in numerous scientific publications. There is the published work of L. E. Eeman (1947) and J. C. Maby (1966) in England on subtle forms of energetic effects whose action transcends the limits of the physical body. Electrophysiological research on the acupuncture meridians by Motoyama (1974) and others strongly suggests that channels exist for the flow of the *Chi* or *Ki* and that these energies are linked with the surrounding environment. Stanford University professor William Tiller has reported on a host of experiments with various psychotronic devices which couple the subtle aspects of energy and consciousness to instruments (1974).

The dualism of mind and body is articulated in scholarly studies of yogic texts (Eliade, 1969). Part of the yogic practice involves detaching consciousness from the normal senses—the practice of *pratyahara*. This practice can result in the complete splitting of perception from the physical organism. Intense interest has recently focused on reports of people who were briefly clinically dead, or nearly so, their vital signs having severely weakened or failed (Kubler-Ross, 1975; Moody, 1976). Many of these people perceived the frenzied efforts of nurses and doctors to revive them, and they had excellent recall despite their apparent physiological debility. Controlled studies of this phenomenon have been carried out by Tart (1974) and Green (1968).

Viewed psychiatrically, the splitting of consciousness and body, often involving the perception of one's own body from a distance, is called the autoscopic hallucination and is conceived as a purely intrapsychic aberration. I submit that the scientific and clinical evidence suggests the contrary: that the mind and body are separate entities and that the limits of ordinary states of consciousness are altered in these states of dissociation.

Indian Vedanta elaborates a series of "bodies" and states of consciousness experienced through their particular "organs" of perception (Meher Baba, 1967; Isherwood, 1969). The basic schema involved a series of levels or bodies. The physical body is the bottom rung in the hierarchy. The next rungs are other embodiments or "energy." Beyond these are various embodiments of "mind." *All* these are lower levels, relegated ultimately to the status of illusion. The only "reality" is an undifferentiated unity within which this play of illusion occurs.

Here we may see three levels of reality: the material level of contemporary science, a higher-order series of subtle levels embracing energy and mind, and a level of complete, undifferentiated unity out of which all phenomena at all levels come forth. The classical statements about this level of undifferentiated unity include the writings of Shankara (Prabhavananda and Isherwood, 1947) and the Buddhist Sutra, Prajna Paramita (Kapleau, 1971). A contemporary statement by David Bohm, a theoretical physicist, posits the interrelationships of these levels:

> Intelligence and material process have thus a single origin, which is ultimately the unknown totality of the universal flux. In a certain sense, this implies that what have been commonly called mind and matter are really abstractions from the universal flux, and that both should be regarded as different and relatively autonomous orders within the one whole movement. (1975, pp. 13–18)

Thus what is ultimately real is this totality. The lower-level material forms and processes of consciousness are relegated to the status of a collective hallucination. This is not to say that one person's hallucination is as good as any other one. Each level of the hierarchy has its own laws.

Psychotherapy has branded, however, certain altered states as intrapsychic aberrations, and has been quite oblivious to the energetic basis of the symptomatology. As in Wendy's case, a person may be thrust unexpectedly into these states because of energy buildup from intense psychological conflict. In such a case the experiences have quite a different quality from what they have when entered into voluntarily (as part of a consciousness-altering practice, for example). Here, use of normative data or naturalistic observation can be risky, because to project the possible from the probable may be completely unjustified.

Although Freud originally formulated his theories in terms of an *energy variable*, the psychoanalytic movement gradually relegated this description to the status of an unnecessary metaphor.

The work of Wilhelm Reich (1972, 1974) has formed the basis of the energy-oriented body therapies in the Western world. Reich and his followers—most notably Lowen (1971, 1976), Pierrakos (1975), Brown (M. Brown, 1971), Kelley (1971), Keleman (1975), and Baker (1974)—have continued to treat patients and develop systems of therapy based upon the release of energy and muscular stases in the body, coupled with psychological interpretations.

The Reichian movement has been very controversial for a host of reasons. Reich's concept of energy or "orgone," as he termed it, has been impossible for most therapists to grasp because most people cannot perceive it. Therefore, most body-oriented therapists take their cues from such factors as flesh tones, the development of various muscle groups, and the symmetry and attitude of the body. There is a fairly widespread use of certain Reichian and bioenergetic techniques today to facilitate the discharge of affect; however, the full system involves a knowledge and awareness of the body energies and of methods for integrating the emotions and the body through the medium of this energy flow. Of primary difficulty is the lack of physical evidence for orgone. Physics fails us here because these energies are not physical but psychobiophysical; they are not directly transducible by the ordinary measuring devices of science.

Pierrakos has carried bioenergetic work in a direction which links Reichian and bioenergetic therapy with yoga, through the *chakras* or energy centers of the body. These energy centers are elaborated in yogic texts (Avalon, 1974) and are mentioned in more recent works (Eliade, 1969; Yogananda, 1975). Conscious experience is ultimately linked with them. The system of yoga conscious experience, including its aberrations, is involved with energy flows in these chakras and associated structures. While there are rough correspondences between the chakras and various nerve plexuses and endocrine glands, the classic texts make it clear that the chakras themselves are independent structures whose seat is in the transphysiological self. The serious practice of a yogic discipline such as *pranayama* (yogic breathing), or the deeper stages of meditation, usually leads to the perception of these structures. Associated structures comprise the most important portion of this system. Most notable is the *sushumna,* a central channel piercing the chakras from the *muladhara* chakra at the base of the spine up to the *sahasrara* chakra just above the crown of the head. There are, however, thousands of energy channels, seven major chakras, and many more minor ones.

Pierrakos (1975) has illustrated the energy flows through these various chakras as a function of the conventional diagnostic categories. In addition, his illustration of schizoid dissociation depicts the actual displacement of the transphysiological self from the physical body. This schema is based upon Pierrakos's own direct clinical perception of these energy effects; it is not a theoretical model.

In a work entitled *Kundalini: Psychosis or Transcendence?* (1977), psychiatrist Lee Sannella has reviewed a number of cases which conventionally would be interpreted as psychosis, but which were actually due to the release of the potent energy of *kundalini* from the base of the spine during meditation. The symptoms caused by this release included sensations of energy rushes in the body, particularly up the spine, heat, jerking movements, and drastic alterations in mood and perceptions of the body. Before the *kundalini* release took place, the people experiencing these effects were normal, asymptomatic individuals. Over a period of time, sometimes with an alteration in their meditation practice, these effects subsided. Sannella's cases illustrate the similarities between certain symptoms conventionally considered to be pathognomonic of psychosis and phenomena due to releases of normally dormant sources of energy in the body. Details from the last six months of Wendy's therapy reveal that these same forces were responsible for her dissociations, and that they were not merely intrapsychic aberrations.

Reich made it clear that the recall of traumatic memories was of much less therapeutic consequence than an attack upon the *"present-day biophysical anchoring* of the historical experiences" (Reich, 1972, p. 446). In Wendy's case such an attack was the only feasible therapeutic path because of the severity of her dissociations and the ease with which they occurred. The surfacing of any highly charged emotional material would trigger a large energy release from the base of her spine. This would flow up to the level of the navel, building up sufficient strain on the biophysical structure that a rupture in the integrity of the organism would result there. Figures 21.1 and 21.2 (pages 367 and 368), drawn by Wendy, illustrate this process clearly.

Bioenergetic and Reichian therapy have, then, evolved methods for working on the body and its energetic patterns. However, these methods could not be used with Wendy because of the ease with which she dissociated. Instead, the Reiki method was employed.

Reiki is a Japanese method of interacting the energy field of two or more people to alter defective patterns. A Reiki master, through training and initiation, is empowered to alter a Reiki therapist's energetic flow so that it can act as a catalyst in this process. The effect of Reiki therapy is to rebalance the energy flow in the recipient's body. During a Reiki session, specific areas of the body are systematically contacted and treated.

During the thirteenth month of therapy, I began to use Reiki on Wendy in order to unblock her system. This procedure was followed for some twenty sessions, which also included the type of therapeutic interventions already discussed. At a later date, the treatments were limited to a few specific areas, namely around the eyes, the throat, the navel, and the area between the navel and the pubic bone. These sites are not specified in a Reiki pharmacopaeia but were clinically indicated to me during the initial treatments as being the source of the major energetic blocks. It so happens that these loci correspond to four of the major chakras, and they were independently identified by Reich as the areas of major energetic stasis in Wendy's type of condition. This treatment had very dramatic effects on her.

One might wonder what Wendy's attitude was about the energy work. She did not understand what it was or what was supposed to happen. She agreed to the treatment because I recommended it. We had made significant gains in our work together, and she had confidence in me, a confidence which gave her the courage to weather some unexpected experiences.

The intensive energetic treatment of the four body centers began quickly to dissolve the energetic stases at those places and to make an unimpeded flow possible, which would enable Wendy to maintain her psychobiophysical integrity. One night she was lying on the floor of her apartment listening to poetry records when she first experienced what Reich called the orgasm reflex, a hallmark of full—not merely normal—health and functioning: ". . . I noticed that I was experiencing a feeling that made it seem that a sea-tide was washing back and forth, surging gently up and down in my body."

Still lying on the floor, Wendy began to think about Steve, her male friend, how open and trusting his face was, how direct his eye contact was with the world. As Wendy described it:

> The openness, the vulnerability he exhibits when he lies there—
> a vulnerability I felt now first in my cheekbones, and which has
> to do with the broadness of Steve's head—how I sometimes no-
> tice precisely that, and am struck by how trustingly he lies there,
> with his face, as it were, open to the air. So I FELT all this now
> (not just thought it only)—first in my cheekbones. Then I real-
> ized it's Steve's eyes also which give me the feeling that he's trust-
> ing himself, to an extent I find nearly jarring when I see it, to the
> world around him. He lets himself just BE there, and then he
> looks at you.

The function of the "ocular block" is to reduce contact with an environment of life-threatening hostility. The ocular block is a major pathognomonic indicator. It may originate in a hostile intrauterine environment as Reich suggested—but it is present at least by early infancy. This block does not necessarily cause a deformity in vision, but it impedes energetic contact with the environment.

While Wendy was thinking about Steve, the phonograph was playing a poetry reading of T. S. Eliot's *The Waste Land.*

> I kept tuned in to the sound of the record, even to the words and
> their meaning. That seemed important, and ESPECIALLY so when
> another shift occurred, and a surprising thing happened: I began
> to tremble throughout my body. Exceedingly surprised—but not
> really frightened, because I felt safe. It didn't feel like my old
> "electricity" at all, although I began sort of convulsing, bodily, as
> I used to with electricity. (But then, it was much more violent,
> plus painful, which this wasn't.) What reassured me most, how-
> ever, was simply the fact that this WAS so different from electric-
> ity. The trembling increased in intensity; also, I was surprised at
> how long it lasted—I expected it to cease at any moment, but it

kept on for some time . . . The concentration of energy in my eyes continued, and although they were closed, they became damp with tears. By "sort of convulsing" . . . I noticed, my knees would pull up, then relax again—but mainly the jerkiness was something I felt happening at the stomach/abdomen/solar plexus area of my body. . . It kept on quite a while . . . And I knew there's more which I am already forgetting . . . Later, at one point, I felt a gentle sea-tide surge again, but it subsided.

Such experiences are common in bioenergetic work. They indicate the opening of the organism to its deeper levels of feeling and energy. Here Wendy's empathy and deep feelings for Steve and the themes of *The Waste Land* enabled her to surrender, despite the emotional charge, to her own inner sources of life and strength, to those sources which are ultimately transpersonal. I also have experienced the orgasm reflex during Hatha yoga, orgasm, meditation, bioenergetic work—and even during Monday afternoon staff conferences.

The opening of the ocular block proceeded to a level where Wendy's intuitive functions and her capacity for deep, inner contact were increased greatly. This kind of opening includes a sensation of flow to and from the surroundings through the activated chakra, in this case the Ajna or "third eye":

It seemed as though I were Steve—or as though I were my mind but inside Steve's body—or as though (to say the LEAST, and really it seemed more than this) I were feeling how Steve must feel when he assumes that particular posture. . . . Here again, the relevant correspondence between my present body sense of myself and my memories of Steve; the feeling of my own head, physically present there and opening to the surrounding air; the dampness in my eyes; the thoughts about what the relevant correspondences were—all these were mixed up together in me.

Such experiences are not instant cures, but they are solid indications that a process of deep change is occurring within the person. There were many expressions of deep change as the therapy progressed. I mentioned that from an early age Wendy chose to disidentify herself from her biological parents and instead embraced the parentage of archetypes, specifically earth mother and wind father. This came about, of course, as a compensation for the horror of her existential situation and was one expression of her need to split from a life-threatening reality and from her subsequent memories and feelings of that reality. Thus the process of dissociation initially served her well by reducing her anxiety and feelings of powerlessness in a life-threatening situation. Even at the time therapy began, she would become very anxious by looking into a mirror because no one was supposed to be there; she did not have permission to exist.

Psychoanalytic writers like Arieti (1955) treat Wendy's kind of alter-parentage as a clear example of delusional thinking due to regression because of the life stresses to more archaic modes of thought. Jung took quite a different view.

For Jung, Mother Earth, Father Wind, and the Sun God are not merely delusions; they are expressions of the underlying structure of conscious experience, the archetypes. It is commonly thought that such images *are* the archetypes, but Jung made it quite clear that a specific image is merely one of many possible *contents* of an archetype. As Jung puts it, archetypes are "ideas in the Platonic sense, that preform and influence continually our thoughts and feelings and actions" (1968, p. 79). These historically predate all personal experience and constitute a mold, as it were, for the expressions of consciousness. According to the Platonic notion, these forms are stored as eternal, transcendent forms. The contents of the archetypes are experienced, not the forms themselves. Images are one articulation of archetypes; energy is another. An analogy drawn from high-energy physics is the creation and annihilation of particles which are represented in *potential* form as mathematical functions. Certain mathematical or experimental operations serve either to bring the particle into "existence" or to destroy it. Another concept very similar to that of archetypes is found in the Sanskrit term *sanskara* (Meher Baba, 1967; Stcherbatsky, 1956). *Sanskaras,* according to Hindu usage, are forms stored in the upper reaches of the mind, forms which condition the content of conscious experience. Thus this repository contains all the forms or *sanskaras,* which have evolved since the very creation of the universe. In certain altered states of consciousness it is possible to re-experience the consciousness of more primitive forms of life, such as the life of reptiles or even stones. My clinical work and Grof's work with LSD tend to support this model. It is possible to experience psychologically the various stages of evolution of the cosmos, and this evolution is supposed to represent the material aspect of the supervening evolution of consciousness. Thus, cosmogeny recapitulates psychogeny.

An archetype is not a univalent entity; it may find expression in several, conflicting modes; the Indian Goddess Kali is, at once, "the loving and terrible mother." In Sankhya philosophy, the mother archetype has the qualities of goodness, passion, and darkness. At her roots she is all these things simultaneously. According to Jung, the initial pathogenic experiences with the mother trigger the development of infantile fantasy, and if this process goes far enough, it eventually constellates the archetypes and brings them into the foreground of the personality, which they then dominate.

It is, of course, likely that Wendy's mother was seldom overtly hostile and that her hostility was quite unacceptable to her at a conscious level. Such mothers "love" their children and often have a way of communicating that "you exist; therefore *I love you.*" The other side of this, experienced by the defenseless child, is that "Mother hates me, therefore I must not exist." The mother's ambivalence creates tremendous anxiety in her and she works grimly at being the "good" mother and controlling her hostile impulses toward the child. One major confusion that grows from this situation is this: should the mother ever express what she really is feeling, a homicide would result. Thus, having a particular feeling is no less than acting out that feeling, both for mother and later, for child. Here, strong feelings must be controlled at any cost; ultimately it is dissociation. The mother experiences tremendous guilt because of her rejection of the child, and the guilt worsens the situation. Because feelings equal behavior to the child as well as to the mother, the child's gaze may become lethal: her simple, angry glance could kill. And the voice may also be poisonous and must be hushed. Thus mother and child have acquired power which makes them larger than life. Jung argues that the depth of this experience does not ultimately derive from the existential situation, despite its negativity. Rather, it served to call forth the negative aspects of the mother archetype which are cosmically destructive and to project them onto the biological mother, thereby imbuing her with a numinous, annihilating quality.

If the positive aspects of the mother archetype are contracted—which is, of course, the ultimate solution—quite a different experience ensues. The dynamic aspect of contact with the archetype is experienced as energy.

Wendy was, by now, slowly becoming more able to surrender to this aspect of "the Mother." Poetry could open her up to it:

I wanted to go to sleep. I lay down, and put on a poetry record. First Yeats reading Yeats, then Auden reading Auden, specifically "In Memory of W. B. Yeats":[2]

> Earth, receive an honored guest:
> William Yeats is laid to rest.
> Let the Irish vessel lie
> Emptied of its poetry.
>
> In the nightmare of the dark
> All the dogs of Europe bark,
> And the living nations wait,
> Each sequestered in its hate;
>
> Intellectual disgrace
> Stares from every human face,
> And the seas of pity lie
> Locked and frozen in each eye.
> (W. H. Auden)

I was lying on my face, listening. When it got to the third, rhymed verse section, that begins "Earth, receive an honored guest . . ." i was startled for a moment, and nearly looked up and behind me to the right, because something seemed present there. Then i started to feel it, so i kept still and concentrated on the poem. But i still felt it. It was very different from what i call Neo Electricity, but had this in common—there was a sort of surging, wave-like, that i felt. The other time, a wave seemed to be washing inside, and through me. But this time it felt as though i were lying on a beach facing away from the sea, and as if the tide were washing up around me. It seemed to surge up toward, and over my shoulders, filling every space around me. It was almost heavy. I also thought it felt like maybe a blanket being laid on top of me. Yet it seemed more like water, gently surging up, around, over— partly because my legs began to feel buoyant, as though buoyed up by water, and my knees naturally moved somehow so my legs rose up, sort of. Anyway, it seemed like water was surging forward, in the space under the calves of my legs which were buoyed up, and then over my shoulders, which felt pressed down by it. All the space around me was filled, in any case, by something either like water or like a blanket. I kept listening to the record until after one more poem ("Still Falls the Rain"). Then i turned off the record. Now i write. One more thing i remember: when this happened, i thought immediately of the recent dream, about being inside the earth before birth and going back in the earth with the dead.

The differentiation of the child from its mother and the mother archetype is a necessary step in the maturation, a step Wendy was beginning to take. The emergence of these symbols into consciousness and the subsequent release of the orgasm reflex clearly indicated this. There was an increasing surrender to the primordial grounding of existence, which made possible further growth. "Grounding" is also an important goal in bioenergetic therapy, wherein it is an open state of energy flow in the organism. Here we realize the initial confluence in the work of Reich and Jung, and, as we will see, with yoga.

The emergence of the archetype of the wind was particularly important in the therapy. This archetype has the double significance of wind and spirit, which is a procreative effect. Discussing a particular delusion of a chronic paranoid schizophrenic involving the sun and the wind, Jung (1968, pp. 51, 52) states that an association between the wind—as the procreative *pneuma* of the Greeks—and the sun occurs frequently in ancient symbolism. The sun is a common archetype of the self.

Jung emphasized that the road to health lies in enlisting the cooperation of the "motive forces" of the archetypes. This is frequently done in Jungian therapy or psychosynthesis (Assagioli, 1971) by active imagination or guided fantasy methods. In Wendy's case, it was not possible to do this; instead, the anchoring of these "motive forces" and energies through the body had to be undertaken.

Tantric Yoga (Avalon, 1914) regards the body as a "microcosm of the macrocosm" as Evans-Wentz (1960) describes it. "The Buddha himself is hidden in the body" (Eliade, 1969, p. 228). In this path of realization the structure and function of the transphysiological body is centrally important. The various chakras, nadis, and energies are used to enter an expanded domain of conscious experience. Also, yoga treatises such as the Hatha Yoga Pradpika (Rieker, 1975) detail the role and techniques for working with these structures and energies. The breath, or prana, is of special interest to us, for it was the archetype of the wind that Wendy perceived to be her father.

In yoga the respiration is not merely a physiological function but is an expression of a more inclusive principle which contains it. The Indian Vedas homologize the breath with the cosmic wind: "The wind is called breath" (Eliade, 1969, p. 385). Five breaths, generically termed pranas, are identified. But this is inner breath. The control and awareness of these five pranas or energies through the methods of pranayama is a central practice in yoga. The cosmic wind "weaves" the universe just as the "breath" weaves man. Further, the transphysiological counterpart of the spinal column, the sushumna, becomes the "cosmic axis" because through this one may be tied to unity with the cosmos. This description of several important aspects of yoga will clarify the following unusual features of our therapy from the sixteenth to eighteenth month.

Starting with the fifteenth month, I intensified the energy contact in the region of the lower abdomen and navel using Reiki principles. We had by then clearly identified these areas as the sites of the panic which led to her dissociations. Two intensive sessions focusing on those centers served to mobilize her panic so that she called to request an extra session. She came then to the office appearing somewhat anxious and withdrawn. She sat on the floor, her knees drawn up to her chin, head down, and said, "The sun is black, the sun is black." After I treated the lower abdominal region for twenty minutes, she suddenly twisted around and looked over her head and said, "Something cold just shot over my head!" Her voice, which had never in fifteen months been more than barely audible, was strong, clear, and resonant. She said, "I'm coming alive, I'm coming alive!"

I do not consider these perceptions hallucinatory. Rather, they indicate that a very significant shift in energy occurred. She perceived this shift as a release. Such releases are in fact quite common during the course of deeper practices of the energy therapies, and Reich was familiar with such occurrences. Furthermore, this release led to her "coming alive," because her energy flow was not diverted before it could complete its natural circuit. Thus the release led to an unimpeded rising of energy in her body and made her a "real person," transforming the quality of her internal states.

Her initial, unbidden statement, "The sun is black, the sun is black," has a very significant archetypal and energetic meaning. It deserves far more than the following cursory treatment.

Jung writes of alchemy as a process for transforming conscious experience. He divides it into four stages, the first of which is the *melanosis* or *nigredo*, meaning "blackening." The *nigredo* is clearly seen as a psychological state: the "darkness of our mind" (Jung, 1953a, p. 259). As Jung further elaborates:

> The first state is the hidden state, but by the art and grace of God it can be transmuted into the second, manifest state. That is why the *prima materia* sometimes coincides with the idea of the initial stage of the process, the *nigredo*. It is then the black earth in which the gold or the lapis is sown like the grain of wheat. . . . It is the black, magically fecund earth that Adam took with him from Paradise, also called antimony and described as "black blacker than black" (*nigrum nigrius nigro*). (p. 313)

This process occurs in an alchemical vessel, a perfected skull or *rotundum*. The *rotundum* is also the sun, and thus in alchemy is found the symbolism of the *sol niger* or "black sun." Jung reproduces a medieval painting in which the *nigredo*, depicted as a skeleton, is standing on the *sol niger* or black sun (1953a, p. 85). What the person undergoing the alchemic process of transformation perceives at this point of darkness is data from his own unconscious projected onto matter.

It would be an error, however, to consider the *nigredo* as the first part of a linearly unfolding process of transformation, which will eventually abolish this quality. Rather, the "darkness of the void" is always inherent as a potentiality. The unity of the complete process of transformation is illustrated by the *uroboros*, the serpent devouring its own tail, with its front half black and rear half white (Jung, 1953a, p. 281). The whole contains all qualities and at the same time transcends them. However, in terms of transformation as an unfolding process, Wendy was clearly into the first stage of it, and there were other indications of this in her dreams.

One can, of course, treat Wendy's statement and the other events of the session from a totally different point of view. But the present perspective becomes increasingly more convincing as we follow the course of the therapy.

During the next four weeks, I continued to treat Wendy's lower centers with energy and I continued to hold her. Sometimes extreme fear was mobilized. Exactly one month after the preceding session, she had another crisis and had to be seen on Saturday evening. We sat on the floor, as usual, with the lengthening shadows of sunset filtering into the room. I worked on her head center for forty-five minutes. She then asked if she could relax in my arms, "like a baby, but it must be safe and not dangerous." I reassured her, and she snuggled close to me like an infant with complete trust—for the very first time.

I worked on her upper centers for about thirty minutes while she continued to coo and snuggle. I next started work on the solar plexus. After a few minutes she started to gasp for air, finally bending over almost double. It appeared that something was being released; whatever it was, a raging struggle ensued. She gasped for breath and I was very concerned that she might lose consciousness. Yet I had a strong feeling that there was to be no turning back here, and I knew I could resuscitate her should she lose consciousness.

After ten minutes she straightened up. The struggle was over. She asked if I had seen "that." What I saw was the release of a subtle emanation which drifted away from Wendy, similar to what I have observed with several other clients. I consider them to be an energetic release phenomenon and attach no other significance to them. She described the sensation as a wind which left her solar plexus and went up to and out of the top of her head.

We were silent for a few minutes. She said, "Is it okay for me to breathe?" I assured her and told her to take three deep breaths. My hand was still on her solar plexus and I could feel the deep, abdominal breaths, fully and easily filling her whole chest. The downward and upward movement of the diaphragm pushed the viscera in and out deeply and rhythmically. She finally said: "I can breathe, I can breathe . . ." We both wept. ". . . and the breath hooks your body all together so you don't come apart." We wept a lot more. Breath "weaves" man, proclaims the *Atharvaveda* (M. Bloomfield, 1964).

Wendy's next session was three days later. She could fully breathe. She had had difficulty sleeping the previous night and so had lain on the floor and breathed deeply, promptly falling asleep. She later talked about babies and how they breathe with bellies that "pop out and then fill them so they can cry loud." Wendy now realized that full breathing mobilizes feelings.

Wendy came again in two days. I worked on her energy centers and then held her. She sobbed gently but more deeply than previously. Gradually she stopped, climbed onto my lap with her head upright, which had previously been too frightening for her. She said that prior to the session when the release occurred she had always been afraid of being killed; now she was not. Her fear now was of being abandoned. She had an image of having just been born and feeling that she was going to be abandoned.

According to the bioenergetic developmental sequence, Wendy had largely cleared the first life crisis—that of existence, which is the schizoid core issue—and was now into the second or oral stage, where the issue is abandonment.

Five days later Wendy came in strong. Her voice was three times as loud as ever before. Her head was erect and her eyes were clear, with no sign of the ocular block. We talked for about twenty minutes, and then she climbed into my lap and held me firmly while she gave in to her sobs. Later, she said that her cycle is to cry, and after the crying stops she can breathe. She asked me repeatedly at the end of these sessions if I minded holding her, and she said that her mother wanted nothing to do with babies. She asked me if I loved my sons; when I told her that I did and that they loved me, she said that this was hard for her to understand.

During the next session she remarked that when I held her she slipped into feeling exactly like a baby. Also, she *clearly remembered* being a baby and how Mother hated her and did not want her. She finally said, "It's sure strange to be held and not feel that it's dangerous."

It was a long way to have come. Finally things were out in the open. But much work remained, and some very intense experiences lay just ahead for us.

In the next session Wendy sobbed quietly. When she could speak, she said—and I elicited this from her very delicately—"The small ones died today." I asked if small ones were babies. "Yes," she said, "they were." Gradually a story emerged that the small ones were born, but then they found that they weren't supposed to be there, so they became quiet, turned themselves inside out and swallowed themselves; now they were dead. While relating this to me syllable by syllable, Wendy was holding her hands to her uterus and said that the dead babies were "in there." She didn't want me to touch there, as if it were tender and precious.

I talked to her about letting the dead babies come out and letting them come alive. She asked how and also said that it was no good to let them out when they were not wanted. I said that I would show her how to let them out, that we would take care of the babies and love them and help them to grow up feeling good about themselves. Wendy started gasping and struggling for breath and holding her uterus. I asked her if she were ready to let them out. Finally she said, "Yes." I lay her on her back on the floor, spreading her legs with the lower leg folded against the upper leg in delivery position. She began breathing much more fully now. In ten minutes she delivered.

I held her, stroking her back, welcoming her, for she seemed soft and open and infantlike. She relaxed next to me and kneaded my breast. I told her that since there was no milk she could suck her thumb, which she did, moving her fingers in an infant-like grasping while she sucked. Slowly she became calmer and calmer. Finally, sucking ceased and I held and soothed her like a newborn. The session lasted two and a half hours. Wendy looked strong, grounded, and clear as she strode out. Just as she went through the doorway she rolled her eyes up in mock disbelief, as if to say, "Did *you* see *that* too?"

Clearly, a complete discussion of the events of this session is not possible here. The rebirth could be viewed from existential, psychodynamic, or transpersonal perspectives. One might argue that Wendy had been aware, probably at an unconscious level, that Mother's rejection of her was closely related to the death of two children born before her. Thus Wendy was going to reenact it, setting things right. The issue of turning oneself inside-out and swallowing oneself is undoubtedly related to her eating problems with their underlying issues of aggression and nurturing.

From a transpersonal perspective, rebirth or being "twice born" is not at all bizarre or unusual. Grof has observed this occurrence many times in his work with serial LSD sessions. And Jung has this to say:

> The idea of a second birth is found at all times and in all places. In the earliest beginnings of medicine it was a magical means of healing; in many religions it is the central mystical experience; it is the key idea in medieval, occult philosophy, and, last but not least, it is an infantile fantasy occurring in numberless children, large and small, who believe that their parents are not their real parents but merely fosterparents to whom they have been handed over. (1968, p. 45)

The regressive therapies in which rebirths are not uncommon have found that many such rebirths are necessary in the case of severe, deep-seated problems. Furthermore, turning oneself inside-out and swallowing oneself is an expression of the *uroboros*, or snake that swallows its own tail. This is one of the formal elements of mandala symbolism (cf. Jung, 1953a, pp. 91–213) and is an expression of the reunion of opposites. There are many other expressions of this principle of reunification. One that Wendy started drawing during the course of therapy was the Klein bottle, a mathematical equivalent of the *uroboros*. The Klein bottle is an exquisite modern expression of the *uroboros*, for it shows how the inner and outer worlds connect. Wendy was fond of drawing people with a Klein bottle on their head, or sometimes lying inside a Klein bottle with the sun either in their solar plexus or in the outside space of the bottle. The expression of this reunification in yoga will shortly bring us back to the psychobioenergetic explanation of the dissociation process.

I next saw Wendy after a three-week break because of my summer vacation. She related a dream to me. In the dream, she and her friend Steve were walking and unexpectedly came across my Saint Bernard, with whom

Wendy had a very affectionate relationship. Upon seeing the dog and feeling its love and acceptance for her—an acceptance "no real person would ever give me"—Wendy felt that in "one, simple step" energy could rush up her spine. This would actually lift her physically as well as energetically, thereby making her "a real person."

Here I reiterate that Wendy had no knowledge of yoga, meditation, Jungian or metaphysical writings, and such symbolism was a complete mystery to her.

I worked on her with energy for forty-five minutes and then held her while she sobbed. She held on to me firmly and with assurance. After thirty minutes of this she began to calm down, and she said, "Norman, Norman"—she had started using my name during the past three sessions. Over and over she asked me, "Is it really okay if I hold on to you?" She finally articulated to me that she was not a real person, the reason being "energy or some spiritual thing like that." It was clear to her that it was not the dissociation of her consciousness from her body, which had occurred, that made her "not a real person." Rather, the answer lay in what happens in the region of her navel and below it. What happened there made the crucial difference between being a real person or not.

Wendy realized now that energy does in fact come up her spine, just as she dreamed. When the energy gets to the region of the navel it may continue its course all the way up her spine, thereby making her "a real person." However, the energy can also "go haywire and then it feels like it's ripping me apart."

Wendy thus identified the region at her navel and just below as the "center of myself." It was clear to us both from the dream and her own growing awareness that, with love and acceptance, this energy could rise all the way from the "center," thereby making her a real person.

The region Wendy identified is considered in Zen and the Oriental martial arts to be the center of the self. It is called the *hara* or *tanden*. It also coincides with the second and third chakras, the *svadhisthana*, and *manipura*. The root of the second chakra is farther down the spine, but its vortex is generally perceived in the region between the navel and the pubic bone.

Wendy brought in two drawings which illustrate how dissociation occurs (figures 21.1 and 21.2).

Figure 21.1 illustrates how the full-blown acute attack begins. Once under way the other centers in figure 21.2 may also be affected. Note that in figure 21.2 the body can be split in five planes: the top of the head, right above the eyebrows, just below the navel, at the bottom of the spine, and at the knees. All these are chakra loci, the knees being a minor chakra. Note too the diaphanous *parts* of the body that then dissociate out along these trajec-

Figure 21.1   Wendy's drawing of the energy movement during an acute attack.

tories. There are also outside forces which can impinge at the throat chakra and at the center just below the navel.

The plane at the navel has been identified by bioenergetic therapists as the main split in the organization of the schizoid. A severe schizoid has a clearly observable crease across the trunk of the body at that point. Thus Wendy had decided that because of these energies ("electricity"), and energy centers, and their sometimes severe effects, she was definitely not "a real person." She was of a different, afflicted species. Reich agrees in essence with this evaluation, but he believes that "real people" are too far removed from their "roots" to experience high energy states. Briefly, Wendy's need was to merge with the energy process and to allow it to complete its circuit at the top of the head. It must be emphasized that, during severe attacks, Wendy experienced being torn apart. She could not speak and her motor control became impaired.

At this time Wendy had a dream. She was on a ship crossing a storm-tossed ocean. The captain of the ship—an old "caretaker" who walked around carrying a staff—warned her not to go too close to the railing, lest she fall in. Just after this she did fall overboard and as she was falling she realized

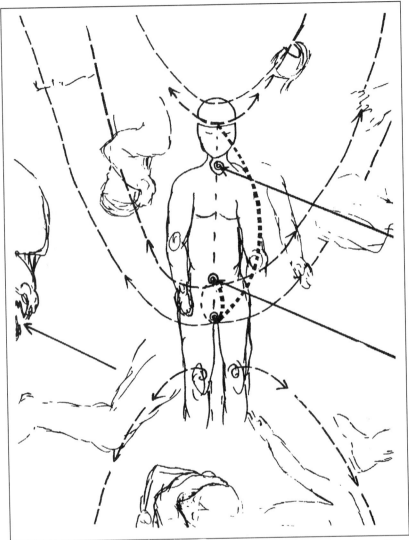

Figure 21.2   Wendy's drawing of the energies, energy centers, and planes where dissociation can occur. Broken lines indicate a dissociative flow, while broader, dotted lines indicate an integrative flow.

that rescue was impossible under these violent conditions. She did not actually fall into the water, but next found herself back on the ship. The caretaker came to her, lent her his staff, and told her that this would keep her from falling into the water again.

The "caretaker" is of course a representation of the archetype of the Wise Old Man, while the ocean is the unconscious. The staff is particularly important to us here, for it is the *caduceus*, representing the healing process through unification and the rising of energy. The energy is the *kundalini* and the staff is the central channel for its ascent, the *sushumna*. Another yogic aspect of the transformational process Wendy experienced is the existence of the *brahmarandhra*, or the central channel rising up through the crown chakra, the *Sahasrara*. It is through this subtle channel that the final liberation and unification occurs. As Eliade puts it:

> Viewed in projection, the *chakras* constitute a *mandala* whose center is marked by the *brahmarandhra*. It is in this "center" that the rupture of plane occurs, that the paradoxical act of transcendence—passing beyond *samsara*, "emerging from time"—is accomplished. (1969, p. 244)

This level of reality has been experienced cross-culturally. The *caduceus* symbolism is found in Egypt, India, the Yucatan, and other places. "Holed" monuments and statues of people and serpents with a hole in the top of the skull are similarly distributed. One such monument was discovered in the Solomon Islands. Others were found in Russia.

Hubert Benoit, a French psychologist writing on Zen, recognized the existence of the subtle energies: a "natural" current ascending from below, and a "normal" current descending from above (1959, p. 113). The ascending current is always present to some degree, but the descending current is a potentiality. If it *does* occur, both currents join at a point and the person "dies" and is "reborn." Thus, Don Ramón, in D. H. Lawrence's *The Plumed Serpent,* says, "I am lord of two ways. I am master of up and down."

The "caretaker's" staff thus represents this process and the therapeutic goal at this point was to open up Wendy's heart and throat centers, in order to let this flow complete its natural, upward flow, thereby making her "come alive" and be a "real person." In order to accomplish this opening, I continued the holding and nurturing, and also concentrated the energy treatment on the heart and throat centers. By this time Wendy seldom dissociated. Her medication had been reduced and she was well on her way to finishing her graduate studies. We could discuss her feelings and her past without any of the old withdrawal occurring. Her posture was erect and her voice of normal volume.

At her last session, Wendy arrived humiliated and depressed because she had become anxious and somewhat out of touch in a social function which she had been ambivalent about attending. She was disappointed with herself and fearful that I would reject her for not doing better. Despite the intensity of her feelings, she did not dissociate, an observation which I mentioned to her.

I worked on her heart and navel chakras with energy and we talked about her embarrassment and fear of rejection. After sixty minutes she began sobbing deeply and held me strongly. I then began to direct energy up from the base of her spine with my right hand and to receive it through the left, placed at the top of her head. After fifteen minutes, she started to gasp. It was clear that the energy had come up to her throat where it had hit a block. I directed energy to the throat and within two minutes the gasping stopped; she sat up very erect and her face was a picture of bliss. Later she told me that there was "an explosion of light in and around my head, like I was inside the sun." She was breathing fully and deeply and there was no trace of the ocular block.

The process of transformation had completed its course for the first time.

The (alchemic) stages succeeding the *nigredo* are the *albedo* or daybreak, the *rubedo* or sunrise, and finally a culmination stemming from the union of these last two states: the great white light. According to the Tibetan Book of the Dead, this issues "from the heart of Vajra-Sattva, the Father-Mother, with such dazzling brilliancy and transparency that thou wilt scarcely be able to look at it" (Evans-Wentz, 1960, p. 109). The *albedo*, the second stage, is often mistaken for the actual goal, since it is a primary emergence into light from the darkness of the *nigredo*. The experience of inner light is well known in all mystical traditions and is the experience of full contact with the *atman* or "higher self." Ancient texts such as the Upanishads posit this experience to be of supreme importance, since it constitutes a major step in the realignment of the personality with the center of consciousness and will. In psychosynthesis in particular, this realignment is a major goal of therapy (Assagioli, 1971). Contact with the "higher self" is of extreme importance since it is the kernel of the process of transformation in *all* therapies since all inner energy derives from it. One such experience is not an instant cure, but once the pathways have been opened to the energies, they will eventually take the person the rest of the way.

This brings us up through the eighteenth month of treatment, where this account ends. Therapy is continuing and I expect that the further nurturing and energy work will soon reveal deeper layers of feelings and lead to the further opening of her energy blocks. I foresee that the rising of her energy will strengthen, at which point she should be completely asymptomatic. Whether we continue the process of transformation from there depends upon Wendy's desires.

The energies and psychic structures involved in this process thus constitute a hierarchy within the undifferentiated unity of all consciousness. It has become commonplace to consider energy as a neutral entity which can be turned to any purpose, just as one may use ordinary electrical power. But the ancient texts, research of our age, and Wendy's experience warn us otherwise. Each chakra has its own pantheon of archetypes, each with its own energies. When the first through third chakras become highly energized, demonic-like experiences may come into consciousness—*unless* the higher chakras have been activated and can balance the lower center processes. It is for this reason that many transpersonal approaches focus exclusively on the upper centers and their transpersonal qualities, without *any* explicit recognition of the subtle structures we have elaborated (Meher Baba, 1967, 1977). Only when the higher qualities are fully developed are the lower centers activated.

This differentiation between upper and lower has been related to the difference between "transpersonal" and "extrapersonal" (Green & Green, 1977). Briefly, this distinction between self-transcending, universal states of conscious experience on the one hand and extradimensional personal experiences on the other. These latter include the planes of power of the sorcerer, but these are not transpersonal.

From the living presence of the archetypes and the subtle yogic energies she experienced, it should be clear that Wendy's dissociation experiences were not merely intrapsychic events. The development of her condition and its psychological aspects followed well-understood psychotherapeutic principles. What was not understood by the many therapists who treated her for more than fifteen years was the archetypal and energetic substratum of her symptoms. Once the personality comes under the direct control of the archetypes the energies operating are more powerful than the energy of words. But the therapist who has learned to work in this domain of heightened energy can be effective—which is not to say that the process of change will be brief, or simple to carry to a successful therapeutic conclusion.

Twenty-four months later the long-term dissociations had stopped, the sleep disorder was significantly better, and her ability to relate to people was greatly improved. Her ocular block was mostly dissolved as were the other blocks; however, a tendency to weaken at the solar plexus remained. Wendy now was much more vital looking, with a full, resonant voice and a contactful, energetic gaze.

The therapy became less dramatic as the "primary process" material diminished, and issues such as individuation and separation moved into the foreground and were being worked through. Writers such as Masterson (1976) have dealt with this from a psychoanalytic point of view. Thus we may view the first phase of Wendy's therapy as a pretherapy, addressed to a "primary process" level of functioning and the most fundamental issues of existence. Foremost this includes the crystallization or individuation of the self out of the cosmic matrix. If this most basic of all development stages is not successfully completed, the basis upon which further growth occurs is severely impaired. This impairment includes not only the self-image but the personal energetic matrix of the character and its physical body. It is for this reason that the psychic history of a person can be read from his body structure.

At this point therapy concentrated on further strengthening of her ability to contain higher and higher levels of emotional charge. Verbalization of early memories and feelings was now becoming possible without dissociation; however, not always. Sometimes, after we had dealt with emotionally charged issues, the rising wave of excitation would break through the weakness at the waist and course upward. A sure sign of the process was the coughing and sometimes gagging, as the neck area was charged. Next what remained of the eye block would be activated and might require my exerting some pressure at the base of the skull and at the side of the nose where it joins the orbit of the eyes.

The final exit of these overcharges is most interesting. These releases are always from points on the right and left sides of the top of the head, usually the left. These points are acupuncture points, but the energies discharged are not those of the acupuncture system. Rather, these points are used since they are a low impedance path out of the body. As we went through this cycle countless times, Wendy became stronger and more capable of containing higher levels of emotional intensity, without this process being activated. What we were doing was the same thing as a yogi who practices various cleansing *kriyas* in order to open up the passageways through the subtle parts of the self.

With Wendy and several other patients I have been party to this same process. The exiting of the energy from the right and left sides of the top of the head is suggestive of the shamanic costume, which may employ animal horns worn at these same places. Also, the shaman often uses the symbolism of the bird in his regalia. One of the frequent inner experiences upon the final release of the upward moving wave of excitation, is of birds—either singing or of their white images. The archetype so activated is well-known cross-culturally, both in its valence of release from bondage—the white birds—and as entrapment by the black birds of prey.

In Qabalistic philosophy the Tree of Life has three pillars. The mystic, wholly concentrating on union with God, will pursue either consciously or more often unconsciously, the middle pillar, or the "path of the arrow." The working of the side pillars, which are considered to be the paths of power, is quite different and can be fraught with dangers. In yoga there is a striking parallel, there the paths being the *ida, pingala,* and *sushumna nadis.* One of the benefits of being associated with an accomplished teacher is his ability to keep the student properly channeled, and to help him out of deep water, should that become necessary for his survival.

It is most natural to consider development as a biopsychological, maturational process. Accordingly, genotype plus environment yields phenotype; constitution plus psychosocial factors yields personality. Thus man ascends from the primitive to the complex. I think, however, that if we are willing to look more deeply, we can see man in terms of his descent from the cosmic. In the process of this descent, it is the unfolding of his lower order systems which occurs (Don, 1977/78). The higher levels of the self, which are completely ignored in the mainstream of Western psychotherapy, are intact at birth and before.

The help of the higher-level systems of both therapist and client can be enlisted during the therapy. Thus the therapist can covertly meditate on appropriate themes such as love and cooperation during the session. It's even more potent to engage the desired qualities by meditating on specific archetypes. In Wendy's case meditating on the compassionate, loving mother aspect of the Goddess Kali was helpful, and its effects were very obvious. This level of therapy is therefore a cooperative undertaking of the higher-order systems of both therapist and client, working in harmony so as to reorganize the lower-order ego levels. Thus we see that transpersonal processes are being engaged which go far beyond the domain covered by such terms as empathy, transference, and countertransference.

The most humbling experience I have been repeatedly confronted with, as clients·become capable of entering superconscious states, is their ability to read me like a book. My defenses and pretensions have by this time suffered dreadfully. My next most humbling experience when working with clients is that, despite my skills as a therapist, the depth and pacing of therapy will vary greatly with different clients. What worked so well for Wendy would be much more difficult with a client with much holding or armoring. Wendy's lack of containment, which is characteristic of her condition, made more available healing and transpersonal communication, as well as the experiences of the nether world.

It should be clear that, when working with people like Wendy, the therapist's state of consciousness, intentionality, and energy level are being perceived by some level of the client's consciousness. There really is no way to disguise who you are at that moment. If you really are not interested in "going to war together," don't expect much to happen.

It is a serious error to attempt therapy exclusively on a transpersonal basis. Even in the early stages of the therapy, on a few occasions, Wendy quite suddenly burst into giggles. I have been party to the same phenomenon with several of my hospitalized and office clients. This kind of laughter is very special and has a quality which clearly distinguishes it from "inappropriate affect." It is a manifestation of *Kensho* or *Satori*. The laughter comes from the sudden, deep intuition of the ridiculousness of one's ego games. From the perspective of the higher levels of the self, to have identified with great seriousness with the suffering lower-order ego levels, is nothing short of hilarious. Unfortunately, such flights into true sanity tend to be short-lived, because major conflicts at the ego levels severely bind consciousness, and so the trap closes down once again. In order fully to lay claim to our freedom and capacity for ontological openness, the conflicts must be released. The energies, feelings, images and thoughts so activated must be brought down and grounded in the life of the person. This grounding is considered to be essential both in bioenergetic work and in Qabalistic philosophy (Fortune, 1979). If this grounding does not occur, then one has a spiritual person whose life still does not work.

Grounding must ultimately be in the body and its vitality. This leads, ideally, to contactfulness in all areas of life.

At this point it was deemed that Wendy's abilities to contain a high level of emotional excitation were sufficient to permit further work on her grounding. Whereas grounding is most often the first step in therapy, here we had to work toward it slowly. This work is the bioenergetic expression of the separation, individuation process.

The grounding involved getting Wendy onto her feet more and more, and away from the regression-promoting work on the mat. The energetic fracturing at the joints had to be dealt with in order to facilitate the union of the earth energies and personal energies of the self. This process can be triggered starting with the pelvis, by activating a descending wave of excitation which, upon contacting the ground, enlists the ground energy to rise and combine with the personal charge.

With most people this process is very helpful therapeutically in that increasing the charge promotes expression of affect. With severely undercontained structures the affect may never be reached since the heightened charge may surge upward "like an enormous dragon," as another client put it, who was almost knocked unconscious in the process.

Thus my advice to therapists interested in this work is "Easy does it." I give the same advice to people involved with yoga and meditation. Handled properly these methods have an enormous potential for healing; however a Pandora's box may also be opened. To guide another person on this path you must have gone there first yourself, which is true of any form of psychotherapy. Thus the therapist's own powers of containment can moderate and channel what otherwise could become catastrophic.

What I have described is obviously a blending of Eastern and Western approaches to healing. It is clearly not the only way to work, but I submit that when healing occurs, these processes are somehow being invoked, but perhaps secondarily. What I have described is characteristic of a "middle ground" of reality, an area where most yogis operate, to some extent. There are indeed higher levels and within the range of a fully enlightened teacher the entire domain I have dwelt upon is merely a reality fantasy. I would say that ultimately there is no substitute for the power and contactfulness of love (Meher Baba, 1967). If one can open up to this, especially its transpersonal expression, the "middle ground" is affected positively and naturally.

As Wendy progressed in her therapy, she gave me a mandala. On a spiral form its periphery inward was written the following:

> As a blind man, lifting a curtain, knows it is morning,
> I know this change:
> On one side of silence there is no smile;
> But when I breathe with the birds,
> The spirit of wrath becomes the spirit of blessing,
> And the dead begin from their dark to sing in my sleep.[3]
>
> (T. Roethke)

Notes

1. Copyright 1928 by Macmillan Publishing Co., Inc.; renewed 1956 by Georgie Yeats. Reprinted from *Collected Poems of William Butler Yeats* with permission of Macmillan Publishing Co., Inc.

2. "In Memory of W. B. Yeats," by W. H. Auden. Copyright 1940 and renewed 1968 by W. H. Auden. Reprinted from *Collected Poems* by W. H. Auden by permission of Random House, Inc.

3. "Journey To The Interior." Copyright © 1961 by Beatrice Roethke, administratrix of the estate of Theodore Roethke. Reprinted from *The Collected Poems of Theodore Roethke* by permission of Doubleday & Company, Inc.

22

Biofeedback and Attention Training

Lester G. Fehmi and Fern Selzer

Lester Fehmi and Fern Selzer provide here an important link between traditional approaches to emotional illness through biofeedback and Open Focus attention techniques, and the transpersonal experiences which derive from these practical clinical methods.

From the time we are born, observe the authors, we are constantly pressed into focusing our attention on something particular. We are rewarded extrinsically and intrinsically for doing so; we survive in many areas only because we learn how to do so—and we also suffer for doing so. In order to focus so narrowly and exclude all distractions, our bodies attune themselves for the task, and in the attuning, they accumulate mental and physical tension which, if not released, becomes psychophysiologically chronic.

Open Focus training has been developed in order not only to alleviate these conditions but also to enhance well-being. The process is deceptively simple. In the words of the authors, "The form of the exercise is to ask a question which relates to the client's imagining something other than a concrete object or experience, an 'objectless image.'" Among numerous benefits derived quite quickly from the practice of Open Focus are a significant reduction in tension and improved use of attentional abilities.

The editorial assistance of Dale Patterson, Paul Diederich, Paul Diederich, Sr., George Fritz, and Terry Meade is gratefully acknowledged.

Open Focus training is most often used in conjunction with bio-feedback techniques; these latter help in learning to control physiological processes not normally under voluntary control. By providing the subject with a feedback mechanism which reports information on a range of physiological conditions, the therapist can aid the subject in treating "a variety of functional, psychosomatic, and stress-related disorders."

The authors comment on the differences between Open Focus training and biofeedback training: "The practice of Open Focus training and the development of physiological self-control with the use of bio-feedback training techniques are different approaches; their goals are the identical. Using attention training and biofeedback techniques together increases the clients' opportunities for a new perspective on the disposition of attentional processes."

FROM THE TIME WE ARE INITIATED into social activities, we are encouraged to "pay attention," "try to focus" on what we are doing, "watch out," and "be careful." These and other similar phrases communicate to us that we should make an effort to focus our attention narrowly on certain stimuli to the *exclusion* of other available stimuli. We are trained to try to repress or resist the distraction or attraction of certain stimulation in favor of focusing upon those aspects of our environmental stimulation that have survival value or that our society or family considers more important.

The use of narrowly focused attention is also reinforced independently of social factors. Most personal gratifications, both in experience and performance, result from our learning to narrow and direct our attention. Many complex and subtle tasks, most goal-oriented behavior, would be impossible to learn or perform if we had not developed this ability to focus our attention narrowly. In addition, most individuals in a competitive society do not frequently seek out or practice activities which, by their nature, would promote a broad and multisensory field of attention; most gradually develop a habitually narrow focus of attention as well as rigidly programmed directional sequencing of their narrowed focus to aspects and objects of their environment.

Narrow focus represents the *inhibition* or *repression* of most modalities of sensation in favor of attention to and enhanced awareness of a limited number of elements or objects in one or a few modalities. In order to limit perceptions and body and eye positions to only those relevant to a particular narrow focus, certain muscles in the body must be tensed in a particular way. The particular configuration of body tonus necessary for a specific focus depends upon the nature of the focus as well as the nature of irrelevant stimulation present in the internal or external environment. When the necessity for narrowness of focus is terminated, equal muscle tonus may be re-established throughout the body. However, if we continually function in a narrowly focused mode of attention, without at least intermittent broadening of our focus, then that portion of the existing neuromuscular tension which supports the narrow scope of attention tends to become chronic in nature. Thus, habitually functioning in the mode of narrow focus results in the accumulation of tension, the physiological representation of inhibition or repression of awareness. In this case, when narrowness of focus of a different scope is required for a subsequent purpose, more effort and tension are necessary to override the existing attentional set and associated configuration of chronic neuromuscular tension; continuous functioning in narrow focus leads to a reduction in the flexibility of the attentional and neuromuscular system.

Our physical and social environment offers an ever-present direction toward, need for, and reinforcement of narrow focus; most individuals, therefore, in modern society accumulate mental and physical tension. Concomitant with the development of chronic tension, we gradually lose our facility to allow our attention to broaden to include a wider scope of our sensory and perceptual environment. Thus, many so-called "symptoms of stress"—tightness, narrow-mindedness, and many diagnostic categories of mental disorder including psychosomatic disorders—may be maintained by this dis-ease of attention, the habitual rigidity of scope or field of attention.

While many of the specific internal and external factors leading to stress are different in each case, individuals suffering from psychophysiological stress disorders commonly share an inability to deal efficiently with their own attentional processes. When individuals function habitually with narrowly focused attention, their chronic tension contributes a stress which predisposes them to overreact to stimuli which would not otherwise be particularly distressing. Therefore, clients suffering from psychophysiological (psychosomatic) disorders are caught in a habitual cycle of stress and rigid focus. Even completely removing "stressful" stimulation from the environment may not be sufficient to reduce stress, because the clients' attentional rigidity causes them to react with stress even when confronted with rather innocuous stimulation.

As the clients develop their ability to broaden their attention when narrowness of focus is not required, tension accumulated in the past begins to dissipate. As a result, narrow focus is utilized when appropriate and is achieved with less effort and tension. When stress reactions do occur, they tend not to be overwhelming, because trained individuals can become aware of their attentional responses to the situation as they occur. That is, using learned attentional skills, they are able to move toward Open Focus to dissipate inappropriate fixation responses before they become entrenched; as a result, lingering stress-related symptoms do not develop.

In practice, the general didactic and therapeutic purview presented in this chapter is not exclusive of other treatments. Many variables in the client's life are examined and explored, including diet, relevant history, and environmental, social, and personal factors. However, for clients with a transpersonal orientation and a desire for personal growth or functional enhancement, and for persons with stress-related symptoms, the treatment and teaching program emphasizes the development of less effortful and more diverse modes of attention. Thus, the major theme of this chapter is describing how biofeedback and attention training are used as tools to teach the transcendence and release of one's habitually narrow focus of attention, as well as the development of one's ability to re-establish narrow focus when it is appropriate. Transpersonal experience and psychophysiological well-being are viewed as valuable side benefits of developing attentional flexibility by the methods described here.

Open Focus Training

Over the last ten years, our major research and clinical emphasis has been in the development and use of biofeedback training with special emphasis on multichannel and phase sensitive electroencephalographic (EEG) biofeedback techniques (Fehmi, 1976).[1] Benefits of an individual's development of control over physiological processes include remission of specific symptoms under treatment and a general increase in feelings of well-being.

During our early research and clinical experience, it was observed that extremely goal-oriented individuals who habitually function with a narrow scope of attention find it very difficult to adopt the gentle approach necessary to control the feedback. They tend to fluctuate between trying too hard and feeling frustrated; they do not reach the point of letting go and maintaining a less focused orientation toward the training task. Once trainees establish active, effortful volition in the feedback session, many training sessions are often necessary to dampen their effortful ardor.

A verbal description of the permissive conditions for successful physiological control is not sufficient to teach inexperienced trainees how to produce the state of mind associated with the production of desired physiological activity. In fact, if trainees attempt to duplicate a state of mind with which they have had no direct experience, the goal orientation and effort involved may actually interfere with the letting-go process which supports the reintegration of experience and the associated feelings of well-being.

Since most clients begin biofeedback training after having unsuccessfully attempted other methods of treatment, biofeedback trainees often lack the faith and persistence necessary to continue treatment in the event that they feel unsuccessful in their early attempts to control the feedback. For these reasons, a technique was developed to facilitate the training process by moderating the client's initially tense and narrowly focused goal-orientation toward the biofeedback task and thus to facilitate an errorless learning paradigm. The technique developed consists of a series of attention exercises called Open Focus training.

The objective of Open Focus training is to create permissive conditions for letting one's narrow focus of attention expand to encompass all modalities of experience simultaneously, an attentional expansion observed to be associated with the normalization of physiological functioning. The specific orientation of the exercises developed as a result of the observation of the EEG activity of hundreds of trainees who successfully practiced EEG biofeedback training. Informal observations were made of EEG responses to many types of traditional and nontraditional relaxation procedures, such as progressive relaxation, autogenic training, and many types of meditation. In addition, many successful trainees described strategies they developed in order to deal with an effortful, highly focused orientation to the feedback task. Of specific benefit in the development of Open Focus training was the observation that several items from a guided imagery inventory were conducive to the production of high amplitude alpha activity. From these initial findings, the orientation of the Open Focus technique was developed. As experience with the actual practice of Open Focus training accrued, the Open Focus exercises evolved to the present format.

A series of six cassette tapes was developed for use with clients practicing Open Focus training away from the training laboratory. The cassette series includes: (1) instructions; (2) Open Focus with emphasis on the head and hands; (3) a longer version of Open Focus; (4) a short version of Open Focus; (5) an Open Focus procedure for dissipating or dissolving physical or emotional pain or any focal experience; and (6) encouragement to practice Open Focus independently, that is, without verbal guidance.

The form of the exercise is to ask a question which relates to the client's imagining something other than a concrete object or experience, an "objectless image." For example, space, distance, or volume tends to convey an objectless image; when asked to experience the space, distance, or volume between one's eyes, one does not focus on something which exists as an object. While the eyes may be experienced as objects, the space, distance, or volume between them is *not* experienced as a concrete object. When one orients awareness to space, distance, or volume, one is left with the task of broadening focus and moving toward dissolving or letting go of objective perceptions and experience, moving toward "no-thing-ness." Specifically, imagining the space, distance, or volume *between* points in the body or within specified body regions leads one to broaden and distribute focus equally over the region demarcated by the objective boundaries to which the question refers. The permissive act of allowing one's attention to distribute simultaneously and equally over regions and modalities of experience—as opposed to focusing it narrowly upon a point, object, or experience—gives rise to the states of consciousness and existence associated with diffusion of emerging release phenomena and other ongoing experience, such as anxiety, competitiveness, tension, inhibition, repression, and active goal-seeking behavior.

The logical extreme of narrow focus is one-pointedness of attention; the logical extreme of Open Focus is a state in which diffusion of the attentional field proceeds to the point at which one experiences loss of self-consciousness, loss of a preoccupation with time and space. This extreme and expanded state of mental processing, readily achievable during the practice of Open Focus, is called "No-Time."

The goal of Open Focus and EEG biofeedback training is to develop the trainee's ability to vacillate flexibly and appropriately among the attentional states of No-Time, less extreme states of Open Focus and narrow focus, and one-pointedness of attention. Most trainees have a narrowly focused mode of attention; therefore, training initially emphasizes the development and practice of Open Focus and No-Time. Time spent in these states has been observed to correlate with an increasing sense of clarity and well-being, and a corresponding reduction of anxiety, tension, and associated behaviors. There seems to be clear correspondence between high amplitude brain wave synchrony and the appearance of subtle, simultaneous awareness and unselfconsciousness. The following instructions for the practice of Open Focus are presented to and discussed with the client:

> The Open Focus exercise consists of a series of questions about your ability to imagine certain experiences. Can you imagine letting your mind and body naturally respond to the questions, without giving any particular effort to achieving any one of these images or experiences? For example, when I ask, "Can you imagine the space between your eyes?" you might naturally experience your eyes and then let your imagination flow to the region between your eyes and imagine the distance between them. Your objective is not to come up with some number or other abstraction, such as "There are two inches between my eyes." The objective is very gently to imagine or experience that distance or region between your eyes. You initially may imagine or experience the distance as a very small region or vague feeling and the distance may then expand or change as you continue to maintain your orientation in that region. The experience often changes with continued practice. Your opening awareness of all your emerging experience is a continuing process.
>
> There will be approximately fifteen seconds between questions, and for that period I would like you to maintain your attention

on the subject of the last question. If you have any difficulty experiencing any particular image or experience, don't let that trouble you, just permit your imagination to remain oriented toward the object of the questions and let your experience evolve naturally. If nothing particular seems to happen or your mind wanders, don't be disturbed. In the event that you happen to notice that your attention has wandered and is focused upon some thought, image, or feeling, neither resist nor encourage this process, merely allow your attentional focus to expand to include also the image of the current Open Focus question, in addition to the perception to which your mind has wandered.

While most people find it helpful to close their eyes while practicing, after some facility is gained the practice may be done with eyes open or half open. Practicing with eyes fully or partially open enhances the transfer of the Open Focus to daily life situations. Again, in order to facilitate transfer of Open Focus effects to daily life situations, a relatively erect body posture is recommended, sitting or standing. Reclining positions often are not effective after some period of practice, since they encourage the onset of sleep. Although drifting in and out of sleep may be a necessary developmental stage in the course of practice, deep sleep and associated loss of muscle tone are to be avoided.

(Open Focus cassette tape)

Open Focus Exercise

The reader may wish to participate experientially in the exercise. If so, in order to experience beneficial effects, it is important to allow at least fifteen seconds for each image. For instance, can you imagine the space between your eyes . . . (fifteen seconds), ears . . . (fifteen seconds), throat . . . (fifteen seconds)?

Is it possible for you to imagine—

—the space between your eyes . . . ears . . . throat . . . shoulders . . . hips . . . thumb and first finger on each hand . . . first, and middle finger on each hand . . . middle and fourth finger on each hand . . . fourth and little finger on each hand . . .

— the space between all your fingers simultaneously . . .

— that your thumbs are filled with space . . .

— that your first fingers . . . middle fingers . . . fourth fingers . . . little fingers . . . hands and fingers are filled with space . . .

— that the region between the tips of your fingers and your wrists . . . between your wrists and your elbows . . . between your elbows and shoulders . . . between your shoulders is filled with space . . .

— that the space inside your throat is coextensive with the space between your shoulders and in your shoulders and arms, hands, and fingers . . .

— that the regions inside your shoulders, and the regions between your shoulders and fingertips are simultaneously filled with space . . .

— the space between your toes . . .

— that your toes are filled with space . . .

— that your feet and toes . . . the region between your arches and your ankles . . . between your ankles and your knees . . . between your knees and your hips . . . between your hips is filled with space . . .

— that your buttocks are filled with space . . .

— that your buttocks and the region between your hips and your legs and feet and toes are simultaneously filled with space . . .

— the space inside your anus . . .

— that your genitals are filled with space . . .

— that the region between your genitals and your anus is filled with space . . .

— that your lower abdomen . . . lower back is filled with space . . .

— that your body from the diaphragm down is filled with space, including your diaphragm, your genitals, your anus, and your feet and toes . . .

— the space inside your bladder . . .

— that the region between your kidneys . . . inside your kidneys . . . between your navel and your backbone . . . inside your stomach . . . inside your rib cage . . . between your ribs . . . between your shoulder blades . . . inside your breasts . . . between your breast bone and your backbone . . . between your shoulders and your ribs . . . inside your neck . . . between your shoulder blades and your chin is filled with space . . .

— the space inside your lungs . . . inside your bronchial tubes as you inhale and exhale . . .

— that your whole body, from the chin down, is filled with space, including your hands and fingers, your heart, your genitals, your anus, and your feet and toes . . .

— the space inside your throat . . . your nose as you inhale and exhale . . .

— the space between the tip of your chin and the inside of your throat . . . between the space inside your throat and the space inside your ears . . . between the space inside your throat and to the top of your head . . . between the space inside your throat and the space behind your eyes . . .

— that your jaw . . . cheeks and mouth . . . tongue . . . teeth and gums . . . lips are filled with space . . .

— the space between your upper lip and the base of your nose . . .

— that the region around your eyes and behind your eyes is filled with space . . .

— that your eyes . . . eyelids . . . nose and sinuses . . . bridge of your nose is filled with space . . .

— that the region between your eyes and the back of your neck . . . between the bridge of your nose and back of your head . . . between your temples is filled with space . . .

— that your forehead . . . brain . . . spine is filled with space . . .

— that your whole head is simultaneously filled with space . . .

— that your whole head and your face are simultaneously filled with space . . .

— that your whole head, face, neck, and your whole body, including your hands, genitals, and feet are simultaneously filled with space . . .

— that your whole being fills with air when you inhale and your whole being is left filled with space when you exhale . . .

At the same time that you are imagining the space inside your whole body, is it possible for you to imagine

— the space around your body, the space between your fingers and toes, the space behind your neck and back, the space above your head and beneath your chair, and the space in front of you and to your sides . . .

— that the boundaries between the space inside and the space outside are dissolving and that the space inside and the space outside become one continuous and unified space . . .

— that this unified space, which is coextensive inside and outside, proceeds in three dimensions, front to back, right to left,
and up and down . . .

— that, at the same time you imagine this unified space, you can
simultaneously let yourself attend equally to all the sounds
that are available to you, the sound of my voice, the sounds
issuing from you (and other members of the audience), and
any other sounds that you may be able to hear . . .

— that these sounds are issuing from and pervaded by unified
space . . .

— that at the same time you are attending to the space and the
sounds you can also attend simultaneously to any emotions,
tensions, feelings, or pains that might also be present . . .

— that these sensations and perceptions are permeated by space . . .

— that at the same time that you are aware of the space, the
sounds, emotions, and other body feelings, you can also be
simultaneously aware of any tastes, smells, thoughts, and imagery that might be present . . .

— that you can now admit also to awareness any sensation or
experience which may have been inadvertently omitted thus
far, so that you are now simultaneously aware of your entire
being, of all that is you . . .

— that all your experience is permeated and pervaded by space . . .

— that, as you continue to practice this Open Focus exercise, you
will increase your ability to enter into Open Focus more quickly,
more completely, and more effortlessly. . .

— that, as you continue to practice this Open Focus exercise, your
imagery of space will become more vivid and more pervasive . . .

— that, as you continue to practice this Open Focus exercise,
your ability to imagine space permeating all of your experience
will continue to become more vivid and ever present . . .

(Open Focus cassette tape)

While the client is practicing Open Focus exercises, changes in physiological processes mentioned in our laboratory indicate that positive changes
often occur even during the first session. During the course of the Open
Focus exercise, a gradual increase is often observed in the amplitude and
abundance of alpha activity from individual lobes and in the synchrony of
EEG activity between lobes. Large increases in synchrony and abundance of
alpha sometimes occur suddenly when certain regions of the body are imag-

ined filled with space. Hand temperature often rises dramtically even though imagery relating to warmth is not included in the exercise. Similarly, general muscle relaxation occurs even though no reference is made to relaxation. Other signs of well-being also become manifest, perhaps most notable of which is a reduction in blood pressure if previously high.

The Open Focus exercise may be rehearsed at home with the aid of cassette tapes. Significant deepening of the level of Open Focus can be achieved in one week of practice. After only one or a few practice sessions, clients often report feeling a greater degree of sustained relaxation than they had felt previously. As the effects of Open Focus become manifest, the experience of space pervading and permeating all sensory, perceptual, emotional, and mental experience can be maintained and enhanced. After repeated practice, clients can often enter a state of Open Focus without going through the exercise, by simply reminding themselves of that state through the use of a cue word or phrase, such as *open focus*. This phenomenon is analogous to the situation in which the thought of a stimulus or event evokes the associated affect and state of mind.

Practicing Open Focus exercises gives trainees the occasion to manipulate the direction and scope of their attention, processes which previously were manipulated without awareness. With awareness and practice comes the ability to transcend habitual modes and directions of attention. As a result, the client develops an ability to use his attentional abilities effortlessly and thus more appropriately.

Broadening one's attentional focus facilitates the diffusion and subsequent integration of stimuli and experiences upon which one was previously highly focused. This results in a reduction of the tension and associated states of self-consciousness which are concomitant with a narrowly focused attention. Clients report a reduction of extreme affective reactions to mind or body phenomena, with concomitant symptom mitigation. As a result, many intrusive sensations or experiences which have doggedly persisted in consciousness begin to diffuse. For example, various types of pain have quickly diffused and disappeared, to the considerable surprise of long-suffering bearers of pain.

As with other techniques which create the permissive conditions for general self-integration, including biofeedback training, practitioners often report what are called "release phenomena." Release phenomena may take the form of perceptual anomalies, shooting pains, jerks, tremors, numb or tingling feelings, perspiration, thoughts, memories, feelings, or emotional experiences which spontaneously come into consciousness. When release phenomena occur during Open Focus training, we explain to the client that, as a person relaxes, many experiences of which he was not previously aware come to consciousness. The client may experience these phenomena as pleasant or disturbing. The occurrence of release phenomena is similar to the appearance of experiences of pain or pleasure which occur in daily life after a stressful physical or emotional ordeal when one begins to let go and relax. For instance, in the excitement of an accident, one may be bruised or injured but discover this and the associated pain only later as the excitement abates.

The occurrence of release phenomena indicates that the clients' practice is effective in dissolving tension in its various forms, such as denial, negation, resistance, rejection, and inhibition. When such experiences occur, clients are encouraged to witness them without judgment, if possible, and include them in the Open Focus. Open Focus exercise encourages awareness of all sensations simultaneously, including the experience of space, rather than focusing upon one of them. Thus, it is possible for clients comfortably to maintain an accepting mode of relating to the occurrence of unusual or unpleasant experiences such as boredom, tension, anxiety, pain, or resistance by diffusing their energy into the larger arena of awareness.

Clients frequently express concern because their minds tend to wander occasionally during the exercise. They are assured that lapses of attention are natural and that no attempt should be made to rivet one's attention to the questions. However, when one realizes that one's mind has wandered and that one is involved in thoughts or processes other than those relating to the questions, one should gently include, along with these thoughts, the imagery associated with the questions. Clients are urged to bring themselves to regular practice with gentle persistence, or self-discipline if necessary, but to avoid self-reprimand or extreme self-discipline during the course of practice, because these observations are counterproductive.

In addition, clients are often concerned when they doze off for short periods during the exercise. Again, clients are assured that sleep is a natural occurrence during the exercise. Since the initial objective of Open Focus training is to move one's mind in the direction of sleep and away from hyperarousal, it is not unusual for people to overshoot this in-between state of mind, this state of Open Focus, and actually to fall asleep. Once one awakens, one should not abruptly bring oneself to extreme arousal. On the contrary, clients are encouraged to include the experience of drowsiness within the scope of their attention, which includes the Open Focus questions.

The clients need make no effort to resist sleep. The inclusion of a gentle awareness of sleepiness and associated processes into their Open Focus is quite effective in maintaining the desired state of arousal. When observing the clients' EEG waves and watching the video monitor in the laboratory, the trainer can quite easily recognize when a client has begun to doze. To assist reawakening, the trainer will include the client's name in the next question. For example, "George, can you imagine the space between your hips?" Stating the client's name is usually sufficient for arousal, while not eliciting hyperarousal. If light sleep or occasional dozing occurs during home practice, clients are assured that they need not be concerned, that there must be some need for them to sleep, and that they should continue their home practice.

The client usually finds that falling asleep gradually becomes less of a problem. However, if the tendency to fall into deep sleep persists, such that the value of the exercise is diminished significantly, a postural adjustment is recommended. For example, he or she is encouraged to sit in a relaxed but upright position in a straight chair, balancing the torso directly over and centered on the hips. Thus various body feedback mechanisms come into play so as to maintain a moderate level of arousal. At this point, it is emphasized that neither extreme tonus nor flaccidity is desirable. Rather, a middle level of body tonus evenly distributed throughout the body is desirable. An abundance of high amplitude brain wave activity depends upon the free and abundant flow of energy which is associated with an effortlessly erect posture.

Although a very similar procedure is followed for all clients during the early stages of training, exercises subsequent to the six-cassette series may be modified to suit individual personalities and symptoms. When the Open Focus state becomes natural and comfortable for the client, when the production of alpha has improved, and when the client has a sense of the state of mind associated with the production of the tone, then the exercise is modified to enhance the likelihood of symptom reduction if this has not already occurred. For example, a number of additional elements may be inserted for clients suffering from tension headache symptoms into the long and short form Open Focus exercise; these have to do with the head, face, or neck region. The content of the additional questions depends upon the offending symptom, the areas of the body involved, and the verbal preferences of the client. The "Dissolving Pain" (or dissolving experience) exercise of cassette tape 5 is also expanded upon, as is appropriate for symptom remission.

An important aspect of the form of this exercise is that the word *imagine* is most often used, rather than the word *experience* or *feel*. Even though the totality of direct experience, and not just visual imagery, is the goal of practice, *imagine* is used because it has a much softer, less effortful connotation than *feel* or *experience*. "Can you *imagine*" implies neither that a specific experience should be sought or expected nor that the experience should be rigidly defined. Thus, gentleness, permissiveness, and openness to one's experience and imagery are stressed through the form of this exercise.

Questions instead of imperative statements are used in the Open Focus exercises because it was observed that telling the client what to do or what to imagine has a demand quality to it which often arouses resistance. Use of the interrogative form generally circumvents this resistance and the associated ego defenses. In addition, the question form emphasizes the client's control of the procedure and suggests that success depends upon his own motivation and practice. Moreover, it is frequently emphasized to clients that symptom alleviation is the result of developing their own ability to diffuse focal attention and bring it into Open Focus, and that their own ability to continue to integrate experience in this way will help avoid the recurrence of stress symptomology.

Similar to various traditional meditative techniques, Open Focus exercises facilitate the dissolution of subject-object consciousness. Trainees have describes the occurrence of various transpersonal experiences, including feelings of union with the environment, "out-of-body" experiences, and other experiences of heightened and expanded realizations. Open Focus practice and other forms of attention training facilitate the permissive conditions for symptom remission, release of tension, and a broad spectrum of transpersonal phenomena, in spite of no specific direction or suggestion to these ends having been incorporated as part of the exercise.

Open Focus training has been used successfully with individuals and groups where the use of biofeedback equipment was not practical or possible. However, in our clinic, it is used conjointly with biofeedback training for most clients. During the beginning training sessions, Open Focus training is emphasized. During individual sessions, while the client is practicing Open Focus exercises, a feedback tone is presented which mirrors average alpha amplitude and synchrony from five cortical locations: mid-occipital, mid-parietal, mid-frontal, and left and right temporal lobes. The Open Focus exercise, by guiding the development of the permissive conditions for beneficial changes in relevant physiological processes, elicits effortless responses from the client which are signaled by the feedback tone. The feedback tone is both informative and positively reinforcing of the client's relaxed physiological state.

On occasion, galvanic skin response (GSR) activity, peripheral skin temperature, and electromyographic (EMG) activity are also monitored during Open Focus practice. The changes in these physiological measures provide additional evidence to both the client and the trainer that the quality of the practice is satisfactory and that Open Focus practice is achieving a positive effect. Moreover, there is evidence that the feedback tone itself may be arranged so that it augments alpha amplitude and synchrony (Selzer & Fehmi, 1975). Thus, through the combined use of Open Focus training and biofeedback, there occurs a kind of errorless learning of the ability to enter states of mind and body associated with high amplitude synchronous alpha wave activity, reduced GSR activity, higher peripheral skin temperature, and lower EMG activity.

Biofeedback Training

Open Focus and EEG biofeedback training have a reciprocally enhancing effect upon each other. Attention training, as manifested by the combined use of Open Focus and phase synchronous EEG feedback, is well suited to a patient population requiring symptom remission; to a population primarily interested in personal growth, enhancing functional capacity, and quality of life; and to a population seeking spiritual or transpersonal development.

Biofeedback training is a recently developed technique by which people may learn to control physiological processes not normally under voluntary control. In biofeedback training, participants are informed, by a sensory signal such as a tone or a light, of the fluctuating state of a particular aspect of their body's functioning—the level of muscle tension, blood pressure, skin temperature, or the frequency and amplitude of brain waves. By using the information contained in the feedback signal, the trainee can gradually learn to control the monitored function.

Commonly used physiological modalities of biofeedback training in the therapeutic setting include EEG and EMG activity, peripheral skin temperature, and GSR (Kamiya, et al., 1977). An increase in peripheral skin temperature and a decrease in GSR activity, which are reflective of decreased functioning of the sympathetic nervous system, are often easily initiated early in training. Therefore, GSR or temperature biofeedback is often utilized during the initial sessions of biofeedback training to demonstrate the possibility of control of the autonomic nervous system. EMG training is the primary biofeedback training modality indicated for symptoms associated with tension in the striate muscle system. GSR, peripheral temperature, EMG, and EEG activity reflect diverse aspects of system stress and, therefore, are often used in conjunction with desensitization procedures.

One of the more global physiological functions which has been investigated using biofeedback training techniques is EEG activity. The EEG records small changes in voltage on the cortex of the brain, via recording electrodes placed on the scalp. EEG recordings show four distinctive brain wave patterns in human subjects. These waves are distinguished and categorized according to the amplitude (size) and frequency (rate) of fluctuation of the voltage. Different types of EEG brain wave patterns have been found to be associated with different attentional states (see figure 22.1; cf. Lindsley, 1952). High frequency (above 13 Hz), low amplitude brain wave activity, called beta activity, is usually associated with a state of narrowly focused attention, high arousal, tension, and anxiety. Lower frequency (8–13 Hz), high amplitude activity, called alpha activity, is typically associated with a state of relaxed wakefulness, in which attention is diffused to include a broader field of one or more sense modalities, simultaneously. These two types of activity are present in the EEG records of most waking humans, in varying amounts. Lower frequency (4–8 Hz), high amplitude waves, called theta waves, are often associated with creative imagery, drowsiness, and daydreaming, and occur in most humans before falling asleep and before awakening. Delta

Brain Wave Activity	Frequency	Associated Mental States	Idealized EEG Record
BETA	above 13 Hz	effort concentration arousal anxiety focused attention critical attention	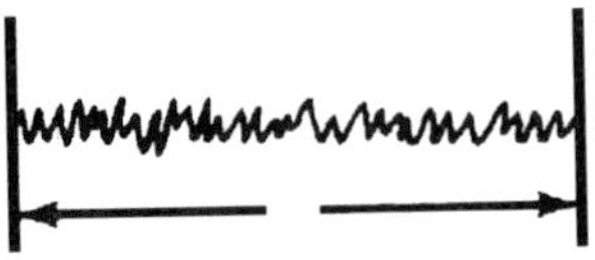
ALPHA	8–13 Hz	relaxed wakefulness diffuse attention meditative states into-it-ness Open Focus	
THETA	4–8 Hz	drowsiness daydreaming imagery deep meditation Open Focus	
DELTA	1–4 Hz	sleep	

Figure 22.1   Description of four brain wave activities and the associated mental states

waves (1–4 Hz) are high amplitude waves normally occurring only during deep sleep.

The verbal reports of subjects who receive biofeedback training and who achieve brain wave control often associate various EEG parameters with states of self-consciousness, attention, and concentration. These reports indicate that intentionally increasing and decreasing amplitude and frequency of brain wave activity are linked with an increase in attentional flexibility.

Most research in EEG biofeedback has involved training subjects to control their alpha wave activity. Consistent with the finding that alpha is associated with a state of relaxed wakefulness, trainees who have learned to increase the production of alpha wave activity have reported feeling more integrated and less tense after EEG biofeedback training. As the amplitude of alpha activity grows simultaneously larger in the major lobes of the brain, trainees report experiences of timelessness, energy, unity, and unself-consciousness. Large amplitude and synchronous alpha waves are concomitant with a state of mind which is not preoccupied with or attached to any single event that is occurring either internally or externally and is described as an unobstructed flowing of energy and experience throughout the mind-body system. Thus, EEG biofeedback training may serve as an effective tool in the service of transpersonal growth, and, more specifically, in the development of attentional flexibility. EEG biofeedback training has also been observed to facilitate the mitigation of various specific psychophysiological symptoms and neurotic conditions, such as anxiety, depression, mood swings, obsessive-compulsive behavior, stress reactivity, nausea, dizziness, tension, and physical or emotional pain and discomfort.

During EEG biofeedback sessions, one is comfortably seated in a softly illuminated, sound-attenuated room. When one closes one's eyes, one begins to hear a tone which occurs when one is producing alpha waves above a threshold level of amplitude. Trainees gradually begin to sense the association between their various mental processes and the volume of the tone. With practice, trainees gradually develop their ability to control the loudness of the tone. They learn to change relevant mental processes at will, as well as to sustain certain processes for longer periods. The development of this control allows trainees to become more subtly aware of the mental processes reflected by the feedback. Thus, by learning to sustain the feedback tone for a length of time and to modulate its loudness, trainees facilitate an experience of those mental processes associated with the parameters of the brain waves which generate the tone.

Persons who have practiced some discipline over a number of years, such as meditation, an art form or some athletic or martial art practice, do exceptionally well in producing large amplitude waves, controlling frequency and amplitude, and controlling the phase relatedness of their EEG activity recorded from the five major lobes of the brain. These highly practiced persons are more likely than others to report dramatic insights following a single session of EEG biofeedback training. For example, after only one session of EEG biofeedback training, a gifted composer realized that the exceptional state of concentration and flexibility of attention and awareness he had developed over many years of practice of his music could also be used in contexts outside the field of music. He stated that this illumination occurred as a result of realizing that his ability to attend was correlated with certain types of brain wave activity and that this activity was under his own control, irrespective of his field of attention.

According to reports from EEG biofeedback trainees, the most dramatic subjective effects associated with the production of alpha activity occur during the initial period following a sudden and sustained increase in alpha duration or amplitude which takes place simultaneously and bilaterally in all five lobes of the brain. The pleasant aspects of this experience appear to be associated with the feeling of release which accompanies an increase in amplitude and abundance of alpha activity. However, after becoming accustomed to periods of high alpha production, the pleasant aspects of the experience become less pronounced, culminating in the absence of affect associated with the tone. It seems that one habituates to the feeling of release and relaxation concomitant with the occurrence of newly achieved high amplitude and abundance of alpha waves.

When an increase in alpha amplitude or abundance is reached predominantly on one lobe of the brain while the other lobes remain for the most part at their previous low levels, the associated subjective experience is more subtle and more difficult to discern. Verbal reports suggest, however, that the alpha activity of each lobe, as signaled by feedback to the subject, has associated with it a unique experiential content. However, alpha increased in one lobe of the brain without corresponding small increases in the others are rare.

A recent double-blind experiment[2] involving middle management executives generally confirms earlier individual findings (Fehmi, 1974). Each trainee received twenty sessions of biofeedback training. Yoked control trainees received tape-recorded "feedback," which was not contingent upon their brain wave activity. During the course of training, the experimental subjects learned to increase and decrease their alpha wave activity as compared to their resting level of alpha activity (p<.05). In addition, their resting level of alpha activity increased across sessions (p<.05). These changes did not occur in the control subjects.

Before each session, each subject was asked to rate his state of mind on forty-five semantic differential scales. The responses on each semantic differential scale, averaged across the first two sessions, were statistically compared to the response averaged across the last two sessions.[3] The changes in the self-perceptions of the experimental subjects indicated that, after training, they had changed on ten scales. They experienced themselves as being more calm, less depressed, more able to concentrate, more self-initiating, more detached from their experience, more observant, more personal (as opposed to formal), more integrated (as opposed to alienated), more insightful, and more satisfied with life. The control subjects rates themselves as being less accepting of praise, less satisfied with life, more distracted (as opposed to absorbed), less self-conscious, and more even-tempered than they were at the beginning of training.

A Gottschaldt embedded figures test for field dependency, which measures distractability, was administered to the trainees before and after the twenty training sessions. The experimental group showed less field dependence after training than they did at the outset of the experiment, while the field dependency scores of the control group remained unchanged. Of two middle management executives beginning the experiment with somatic complaints, one reported mitigation of frequency and severity of headaches and subsequent alleviation of headaches. The other subject reported remission of "heart palpitations."

Training Protocol

In the typical training program, a series of Open Focus exercises is presented to the client during the first five sessions (cassette tapes 2 to 6). During the first session, the client is introduced to Open Focus exercises which emphasize the head and hands. A more complete form of the exercise, which promotes an Open Focus of the whole body and all sense modalities, is presented to the client during the second session. During the third session, a shortened version of a complete Open Focus exercise is presented. A special form of Open Focus, called "Dissolving Pain" is presented during the fourth session. With this tape, the client is guided to use Open Focus techniques in order to dissolve any lingering physical pain or experiential discomfort. A final Open Focus exercise series is designed to develop and facilitate the independent practice of Open Focus without tapes.

Beginning with the first session, clients are asked to practice the Open Focus exercises at home at least twice daily. Most clients are given cassette tapes of the five exercises used in the beginning sessions. Prior to each session, clients are questioned about their home practice: its duration, the nature of their subjective experience of the state of Open Focus, and any psychological or behavioral effects. This inquiry emphasizes to the clients the importance of home practice and also provides the opportunity for feedback in relation to questions they might have about their progress.

During the first five sessions, while clients are practicing the Open Focus exercises, their EEG's and/or other modalities of physiological activity are monitored. Auditory biofeedback signals are presented to them as they practice. During these sessions, the biofeedback signals are not emphasized. Rather, clients are encouraged to attend to the Open Focus exercises and the feedback signal simultaneously. By monitoring their physiological processes, both trainer and clients receive feedback regarding the clients' response to Open Focus training in general and to specific items in the series in particular. Thus, clients become broadly aware of their physiological environment, passively accumulating knowledge of the experiential concomitants of the feedback. As a result of effortlessly increasing the production of alpha feedback without trying, clients are more likely to be comfortable with the biofeedback setting and the training process when, in later sessions, they are asked to practice controlling the biofeedback signal.

Whether biofeedback training is sought for reasons of personal growth, general stress, or a specific psychophysiological disorder, the training program includes, with varying degree and timing of emphasis, Open Focus training, GSR, thermal, EMG, and EEG biofeedback training. Because of its relevance to attentional behavior, the development of control over EEG processes is generally emphasized; ability to attend flexibly develops naturally as clients learn both to increase and decrease its amplitude and frequency.

The particular needs of the client determine the specific emphasis for training in the program. In the case of a client suffering from migraine headaches, who has chronically cold hands and feet, peripheral skin temperature training may initially be emphasized. Chronic psychophysiological inflexibility, such as the chronic peripheral vasoconstriction associated with Raynaud's disease, is often difficult for the client to deal with directly, since the range and variability of physiological change is relatively small. In such a case, it is useful for the client to learn to increase the general level of relaxation while developing attentional control and flexibility in other physiological systems before attempting to develop control of the symptom-relevant vascular system.

For most clients, an intimate teacher-student relationship is an important aspect of training. Close personal contact is initiated at the outset of training and maintained throughout. Problems with home practice and the occurrence of motivational or affective responses are fully discussed in detail.

The relaxation of focused attention during training often results in clients becoming aware of past experiences and present emotions or problems. Many of these release phenomena take a form such as guilt or family memories which clearly reflect increases in psychodynamic awareness and integration. These releases may need to be integrated within a more comprehensive framework before the client will continue to allow attentional scope to broaden. Well-trained clients recognize these experiences as release phenomena and are able to include them into their Open Focus, in which the reintegration process occurs naturally. However, less experienced or more dependent clients may become focused on the affect associated with these experiences, which inhibits integration of the affect and inhibits their ability to attend openly to the biofeedback signals or the Open Focus exercises. In this case, the trainer facilitates the integration of these experiences by assuring the client that this new awareness is simply a reflection of increased openness to experience.

Highly charged release phenomena usually occur more frequently early in training, although they do occur from time to time throughout the training process. When release phenomena develop during later stages of training, they generally occur after a sudden increase in the breadth of the attentional field or after a sudden increase in brain wave amplitude or synchrony. When indicated, the client and the trainer explore in detail a particular emotion or other experience which is inhibiting the client's progress in training.

Open Focus and biofeedback training have been used to treat a variety of functional, psychosomatic, and stress-related disorders; the dynamics of the primary treatment, Open Focus and biofeedback training, are similar. As clients practice, the permissive conditions are created under which they are able to let go of physical bracing and mental or attentional stances which were previously habitual and which were resulting in an accumulation of tension. The physiological changes resulting from training are accomplished with varying degrees and foci of self-consciousness.

The relaxation and integration which occur as a result of Open Focus and biofeedback training are represented simultaneously in physiological and mental systems. Therefore, the trainee may experience the course of therapy in a variety of ways, depending upon the attentional orientation. One client with headaches may describe symptom remission occurring in association with his increasing awareness of physiological phenomena, such as hand temperature or muscle tension; another client may report remission of headache symptoms occurring as a result of a change in obsessive patterns of thought or attentional disposition. However, with increasing practice, awareness of the simultaneity and integration of mind and body phenomena continues to develop. This awareness is important for clients with psychosomatic disorders.

EEG biofeedback and attention training may be effectively used in the alleviation of chronic and severe symptomology, as well as in the facilitation of transpersonal growth. Brief clinical vignettes are presented below in order to describe the effectiveness and demonstrate the scope of utility of biofeedback and Open Focus training techniques.

Case Studies

CASE 1

D. is a forty-year-old married female, with two children. She has a responsible position with an accounting firm. D. came to my office with complaints of fear of an impending nervous breakdown and an inability to function at work. She complained that she was overworked at the office. Her husband was unresponsive, critical, and unsupportive of her in a crisis. In addition, her lover had recently found another girlfriend.

D. felt overwhelmed with physical and emotional pain. Various over-the-counter remedies were ineffective in relieving her symptoms.

Valium, prescribed by her doctor, had side effects which made it difficult for her to function at the level of accuracy required by her job. During her first session, it was noted that her hands were quite damp and very cold (72–75°F). She complained that her feet and hands were always cold. She felt that her emotional pain and physical distress were rapidly becoming worse and feared that she would not be able to hold her job much longer.

During the first ten sessions of Open Focus and biofeedback training, D. learned to enter an Open Focus state and to control GSR activity and hand temperature. On occasion, she was able to raise her hand temperature to as high as 96.5°F. She learned to control frontalis (forehead) muscle tension and was able to increase the production of alpha wave activity. Her emotional pain gradually diminished in frequency and intensity during that period (approximately six weeks). She was quite surprised both at her ability to transcend the pain and at the sense of well-being that emerged during practice sessions. This case is remarkable in that, after two training sessions with skin temperature biofeedback, she stated that her hands were never cold again, even though her hands and feet had been cold for as long as she could remember. Subsequent measurements of her temperature during office visits were always above 90°F.

After D. discontinued office visits (after twenty-seven sessions), she continued practicing twice a day, with occasional lapses. She had become very aware of subtle signs of stress, particularly as reflected by her hands. Therefore, following lapses in home practice, she became increasingly aware of her responsivity to stress, which then increased her motivation for home practice. D. also remarked, more generally, that her ability to function in stressful situations was greatly improved. She felt that, as a result of her practice, she did not work as hard but actually produced more. She remains less involved with her boyfriend. She has separated from her husband and is now in the process of divorce. D. has come for five additional sessions since termination of regular training one year ago. During her practice sessions, D. continues to produce relatively high amplitude alpha brain wave synchrony and to experience the associated states of unselfconsciousness and unitive Open Focus.

CASE 2

L., a forty-five-year-old, recently separated, female university professor, was diagnosed as having heart valve atrophy and scar tissue, which were thought to be responsible for her presenting symptom, tachycardia. At the outset of training, her resting heart rate was over 120 beats per minute. Moreover, her heart rate would exceed 160 beats per minute when she was even mildly excited. A cardiac specialist informed her that biofeedback would not help her tachycardia, since he felt that the cause was organic. He also informed her that eventually heart valve repair surgery would be necessary. On her own volition, but without discontinuing traditional medical treatment, she requested biofeedback training.

L.'s treatment program for the first ten sessions was similar to the others I have described in this chapter. During the second ten sessions, she occasionally received verbal heart rate feedback for a few minutes at a time. Direct heart rate feedback training was minimized because of her sensitivity to heart rate measurement of any kind, and because a generalized reduction in stress and tension was found to have a moderating effect on her heart rate.

After the first ten sessions, L. had reduced her resting heart rate to between 90 and 100 beats per minute. Following another ten sessions, her resting heart rate was occasionally in the low 70s. She currently reports that her resting heart rate continues to wax and wane concomitant with the stresses in her life. However, she is gradually learning to relate to stressful situations in a less extreme fashion. Tenure consideration in the coming year, a full teaching and supervisory load, and several experimental papers, grant proposals, and a book in preparation keep her quite busy. In spite of these stresses, her average resting heart rate continues in the range of 70 to 85 beats per minute. Various transpersonal experiences also are occurring with increasing frequency during her home practice.

CASE 3

T., a twenty-six-year-old woman in graduate school, had a history of depressions and one suicide attempt.[4] Her episodes of depression were precipitated by (1) feelings of discouragement and worthlessness, particularly when she felt unable to handle her work, since she was very conscientious and achievement oriented, and (2) feelings of rejection, particularly in heterosexual relationships. During periods when her work was going well, she described herself as being in a sustained hypomanic state. Because of indications of a manic-depressive pattern, she would not have been considered for biofeedback training except that her depression was triggered by severe anxiety. It was hypothesized that if the anxiety reactions could be avoided, the depressions might not occur. She initiated therapy following a suicide attempt. Lithium was also prescribed but was later discontinued.

After twenty-five sessions, T. was doing well. She described herself as being more at ease with herself and better able to function well even under a great deal of occupational pressure. She had no hesitation in characterizing herself as much improved. The following is a quotation from her self-evaluation:

> In the past my depressions were unpredictable, uncontrollable, and completely debilitating. The fear of depression was nearly as destructive as the depression itself. Gradually both the fear and depressions have dissipated. The second effect that became readily noticeable was a reduction in work anxiety and virtual elimination of extended periods of nonproductivity. . . . The problem of beginning tasks at work used to be horrendous. . . . Through training I have learned to relax with my work rather than push it. . . . My productivity has gone up markedly. Even though I may have several tasks in the mill, and a deadline to think about, I am quite able to work entirely on the project at hand, without being bothered by intermittent thoughts about other items.

By her own description, T. felt better able to handle mistakes, rejection, and failure. She reported her mood swings to have gradually diminished to the extent that she had greater self-control than she had had in a number of years. Although she reported that various feelings emerged over the duration of training, including intense feelings of unattractiveness, loneliness, and occasional bouts with anxiety, she was able to experience and assimilate these feelings without overreacting to them. Gradually, these feelings diminished in frequency and severity, and she reported that her emotional outlook took on a very comfortable tone. She enjoyed her favorite hobbies, cooking and woodworking, but remained more or less reclusive with regard to male companionship. This reclusiveness gradually decreased also, and her desire to continue her graduate studies was resumed.

Since her termination, she was admitted to medical school and has married. A number of postcards have been received from her describing her life. She reports that she is happily married and dealing with the pressures of medical school. At last report, she was still practicing her Open Focus and biofeedback exercises regularly. (Weber & Fehmi, 1974)

CASE 4

M., a male client in his late teens, was diagnosed as an essential hypertensive three years before beginning training. For the previous twenty-four months he had practiced Transcendental Meditation, with no measurable change in his condition. His intake blood pressure was 185/120. Diuretic medication had been prescribed, but various side effects led to its discontinuance. M. was highly motivated for biofeedback training, since he was very cncerned about the severity of his symptoms.

After three weeks of twice-weekly training sessions and daily home practice, his blood pressure had been reduced to 125/75. Subsequently, his blood pressure has remained in this region, with small variation during periods of stress. Aside from this remarkable and rapid change in blood pressure, M. has reported many other benefits from treatment. He is now able to take college exams without severe anxiety, and his concentration while studying has greatly improved. He reports a significant improvement in interpersonal relationships, and a bilateral hand and finger tremor has significantly improved.

One year of twice-monthly training sessions, at his own request, has enabled M. to control his brain wave activity and to become aware of subtle changes and shifts in frequency, amplitude, and synchrony of brain wave activity. For a person of his age, his level of self-awareness has become exceptional, even among well-trained individuals.

Headache Clinic

Open Focus and biofeedback techniques have also been used in group format. The treatment program begins with Open Focus attention training exercises, using the series of five cassette tapes described on page 395. The group is introduced to these cassettes during five sessions and asked to practice at home at least twice daily. Clients then receive biofeedback training during the group sessions. Smaller groups are formed in which participants use biofeedback instruments. Each client practices on two different biofeedback instruments during each session. As a result, all clinic participants receive experience using GSR, thermal, EMG, and EEG biofeedback. Several group programs of this type have been conducted, including four ten-session groups at the YMCA in Princeton, New Jersey, and one twenty-session group in the form of a Headache Clinic, as part of the Behavioral Medicine Learning Program at the Medical Center at Princeton.

In general, the results from group format training programs have been positive. At the most recent sessions of the Headache Clinic at the Medical Center at Princeton, it was observed that all clients who had migraine headaches showed significant symptom remission. Many of these clients had achieved and maintained complete alleviation of their headache symptoms. However, only one-half of the participants with muscle contraction (tension) headaches also achieved complete alleviation of their symptoms.

There were three participants with tension headaches who are noteworthy, due to their lack of success in affecting their symptoms. Each had suffered from tension headaches intermittently for a number of years. They felt that the headaches were work-related and occurred when they had a heavy work load and were required to focus very intensely on their work. Not surprisingly, these three clients tended to be "workaholics" and were inveterate problem-solvers. Moreover, they often felt bored by both the relaxation and the biofeedback procedures. Unfortunately, these clients reported no real change in their headache symptoms, although the trainers observed that they often became noticeably relaxed when practicing Open Focus and biofeedback techniques. The personality dynamics of this type of headache sufferer seem to be unique in his or her inability to derive lasting benefit from a combination of Open Focus and biofeedback training over ten weeks in a group setting. More prolonged and personal contact via individual sessions may be necessary in order to affect positively this category of headache sufferers.

CASE 5

R., a male dentist, began biofeedback and attention training after having suffered a continuous headache for three months. He was quite skeptical about the treatment since he felt that his headache had been caused by bending over patients while operating equipment with his hands and feet. It was explained to him that, although his headache might be due partly to the maintenance of tension-producing postures, if he attended and worked with less effort, he could maintain these postures longer with less tension and associated pain. Despite his avowed skepticism, he came for biofeedback treatment because he had been unable to obtain relief from the many other professionals he had consulted, including orthopedists and neurologists. Various organic maladies were suggested by these professionals as possible causes for his headaches, and surgery was suggested as a possible course in the event that his pain continued. Therefore, despite the client's skepticism, he was motivated to practice.

R. was to start treatment as a group participant in the Headache Clinic at Princeton Medical Center, but a scheduled vacation kept him from beginning along with the group. He therefore received individual training in order to catch up. After three individual sessions and two group sessions, his headache was completely alleviated, at which time he terminated treatment.

Since R.'s motivation for treatment was focused on headache symptoms and since he responded very rapidly to treatment, his motivation for regular home practice is minimal. Headache pain has returned on a few occasions, at which time R. was able to dissolve his pain during one Open Focus practice. He also practices Open Focus occasionally during his daily jogging, whenever he becomes aware of pain, stress, or tension. He reports that the use of Open Focus has enabled him to jog longer, with less pain and with a greater sense of well-being.

Open Focus training alone has been used successfully with individuals and groups where the use of biofeedback equipment was not practical or possible. The practice of Open Focus exercises is often used in conjunction with lectures or workshops. In this setting, participants with somatic symptoms often report mitigation or alleviation of symptoms. In addition, certain participants continue to practice Open Focus at home after only a single experience with cassette-guided practice. Many therapists and other individuals not involved in biofeedback training have effectively used Open Focus training in a variety of settings—as part of a Sunday sermon, before and during the birth process.

While Open Focus and biofeedback training have been used successfully in the treatment of many disorders, certain symptoms are particularly suited for this approach (Weber & Fehmi, 1974). In the clinical setting, we have found this type of training to be effective in the treatment of acute and chronic anxiety, tension states, rigid and distorted behavior patterns (compulsions, phobias, obsessions), tense and anxious depressions, psychosomatic reactions, and physical symptoms such as aches, pains, spasms, and most incapacities resulting from accidental injury or stroke. Since motivation and some capacity for veridical awareness by the trainee is necessary for a successful training experience, we have found that certain types of behavior problems are poorly suited for attention and biofeedback training—chronic depression with passive immobilization, passive-dependent and inadequate personalities, neurasthenic (low energy level) conditions, schizophrenia, psychotic reactions, acting-out problems of long duration, and neurotic and psychosomatic problems involving secondary gain. In these cases, biofeedback and attention training may be used adjunctive to other forms of treatment, in the hope of a beneficial synergistic result.

Although attention and biofeedback training are employed to effect the remission of a variety of symptoms and may effect a variety of functional and physiological benefits, the underlying process of change is common to each client. As clients learn to control their own attentional processes—to expand and narrow focus and to attend more flexibly—they are able to approach their life experiences with appropriate ease, clarity, and integration.

The practice of Open Focus training and the development of physiological self-control with the use of biofeedback training techniques are different approaches; their goals are identical. Using attention training and biofeedback techniques together increases the clients' opportunities for a new perspective on the disposition of attentional processes. The learning which occurs, as Open Focus training progresses, encourages clients to let go of their attachment to a specific scope of narrowed focus and to allow their attention to expand to integrate internal and external experience simultaneously. Biofeedback training, however, provides an opportunity for clients to practice and perceive the utility of expanded awareness and the attentional flexibility developed with Open Focus training and practice. This experience is developed in the context of biofeedback training because, in order to be successful at biofeedback-guided autonomic, muscular, and central nervous system equilibration, the client must be able to give up a narrow focus and effortful orientation to the training task. This practical experience in the biofeedback setting encourages the deepening realization of the effortless attentional disposition which is conducive to long-term optimum functioning.

Notes

1. This section was adapted from the paper "Open Focus Training," a workshop presented at the annual meeting of the Biofeedback Research Society, Monterey, California, February 1975.

2. This research was supported by a grant from Kane-Miller Corporation.

3. A Walsh test of difference scores was employed.

4. Portions of this vignette were included in Weber & Fehmi, 1974.

23

Relationship Psychotherapy
Lessons from the Spiritual Traditions

Seymour Boorstein

I believe that long-term, committed relationships can help and be helped by our spiritual life. Such relationships often bring to the surface remnants of our unresolved narcissism which get in the way of our spiritual development. These remnants are usually linked to early-in-life developmental problems with their ensuing fears—in a relationship, these fears will manifest most commonly as anger and frustration.

Anger and the Fear of Death, a chapter I wrote in the first edition of this book presaged what I now feel to be the core issue in Relationship Therapy: that behind our anger lie our fear systems which can be traced to a primitive fear of death or annihilation.

In this new chapter, I discuss theories and methods to understand and help get at the fear behind the anger and thereby minimize its expression. My experience leads me to believe that the overt or covert expression of anger is the most disruptive issue in relationships. Ideas stemming from recent research of how primitive brain functions feed into the rage potentials of a couple are presented, along with strategies to help patients cope with these.

My approach in couples' psychotherapy is focused on helping the two individuals rehabilitate the loving feelings they once had for each other, and "I ask for their support in the therapeutic enterprise by requiring them to relinquish the direct expression of anger, and try, as much as possible, to express their anger in terms of feeling frightened or saddened."

All of the great spiritual traditions speak of the importance of not expressing anger to others. Since, realistically, this is not a state that is easily achievable, strategies (again, from the great spiritual traditions) are presented, demonstrating ways for us to find our path to forgiveness and empathy.

Couples sometimes fail at first in our planned strategy to work with their anger, and I have found that introducing them to a forgiveness practice can be very helpful. The Christian, Buddhist and Jewish traditions all have techniques to work with anger and grudges. Remarkable changes can be effected through these practices—usually, at the least, increased understanding and compassion, which may give the couple a new sense of peace as they work toward finding a psychological path to, and through, their anger.

Traditional forgiveness practices are very helpful, too, in that they include self-forgiveness—a component that seems to be overlooked and undervalued in our society. A new awareness and acceptance of self-forgiveness can lead one directly to a more compassionate view of others.

The couples' case histories I present in this chapter illustrate approaches I have used from different spiritual practices. In each situation, I chose an approach that I felt would best help this couple go beyond rage and learn to communicate the fears and sadness that actually lie beneath their anger. The powerful combination of specific practices from spiritual traditions and psychotherapy can, I believe, be mutually reinforcing, and, in the end, they become inextricably linked.

"A committed, caring relationship offers one of the most powerful tools I know of for psychological, as well as spiritual, healing." It brings me tremendous pleasure, therefore, to be part of the process of a couple healing their relationship and rediscovering their love.

RELATIONSHIP PSYCHOTHERAPY can justifiably be acknowledged as transpersonal psychotherapy from three perspectives. The first is that developing a successful relationship, one in which both partners enjoy a sense of contented attunement with the other, is a mini-version of our spiritual aspirations, our desire for a sense of non-alienation, of resting contented in our lives. The second is that my work with couples is based on my belief that our fundamental essence is loving and compassionate, which is more a spiritual perspective than the traditional, instinct-driven psychology view. Based on this belief, my therapeutic work with patients focuses on those obstacles, primarily experienced as fears, that block the expression of their natural essence. The third perspective is that I encourage patients to use tools such as meditation or prayer—whatever they feel comfortable with—from religious or spiritual paths to help attenuate fear and anger when they arise. I am convinced that in doing so they can more effectively develop the communication that will heal their relationship.

I believe the essence of all spiritual paths is the experience of oneness with God or the All and the bringing of this experience back into the world. All spiritual practices strive to lessen the attachments to our individual egos which keep us from feeling at one with God or others. When we feel in love or loving of others, we begin to lessen these attachments and move in the direction of the experience of oneness.

My presentation of relationship work as spiritual practice sets a tone for the therapy that I do with couples. I do not think relationship is a requirement for spiritual development—the monastic or celibate life, by choice or circumstance, includes renunciation of sensual gratification, often a strong component for overcoming narcissism. But being in intimate relationship, if that is one's path, does provide a different, ongoing, direct challenge to one's narcissism, since relational life requires constant modification of one's own desire to accommodate the needs of the partner, as well as potentially providing the support of feeling loved. The spiritual paths that I know all urge the development of compassion and kindness toward others as a way to experience interconnectedness, and the path of generosity and virtue is presented as the path to the fullest happiness.

In relationship, we are constantly being called upon to express our own needs and desires in the context of what would be pleasing and helpful to our partners. Motivated by personal love and a desire to please, we can practice in relationship a one-on-one version of what we hope to be able to feel in a wider sense toward *all* beings. When I work with couples, especially those who have an interest in religious or spiritual expression, I emphasize this aspect of our work together. I explain that the benefits of working out the problems in their relationship are multiple and expansive. Not only will they experience personal pleasure if they are successful, but they will, at the same time, discover ways in which to relate in a more loving and compassionate way toward others.

My therapeutic work with couples focuses primarily on uncovering the fear and/or sadness that they both experience in relationship to each other. I believe that being loving is our basic nature, and the ruptures which develop between people who have formerly loved each other are a reflection of the ways in which the unconscious needs of both become expressed in demands that alarm or disappoint the other. People often choose relationship partners to help replay a childhood trauma, hoping to use this new experience to heal the earlier wounding. Since these choices are unconscious, the tensions that develop when the new relationship does not heal those wounds are not easily identified.

It is my experience that people often fight about irrelevant issues because they don't know what the underlying need truly is. Generalized unhappiness manifests as anger, and people unskilled in the expression of anger often compound their difficulties either by fighting, in a vindictive or destructive way, by withdrawing into a pouting, alienated distance, or by repressing (or *trying* to repress) the anger altogether. It is usually at this point—when any or all of these maladaptive attempts to deal with feelings of fear and sadness are activated—that couples come for therapy.

When I begin my work with a couple, I explain my conviction that the direct expression of anger is never helpful in resolving conflict. I make it clear that I do not advocate the suppression of, or non-truthfulness about, feelings. I tell them our work together will be their learning how to fully express their feelings in a way that can be metabolized constructively by their partner. The ideal, the goal, is for a patient to say things like: "When you said that, I felt very angry, so probably I am frightened or sad. And now I need to figure out why I felt frightened, so I can tell you about it." In reality, however, I consider it a major advance when someone can replace his or her explosive anger with the comment, "I'm scared."

I use every possibility in our sessions to help couples discern the unconscious derivatives of their reactions and to express those to each other. Often, it is these disclosures, these expressions of one's deepest vulnerabilities, that bring couples closer together. They will often be able to start with very mildly threatening expressions of the fears beneath: "When you left that soiled sponge in the sink, you felt that I should clean it. I took that to mean that I (and my time) were not important. When I was growing up, my mother [or father] never treated me as if I was important." This is obviously just an example of a typical irritating situation that couples frequently find themselves in. It usually takes much work before that kind of comment can be elicited.

Ideally, over a period of time, as they see more clearly and trust more deeply, one person is able to say, "I am frightened that you, like my father, will never have a kind word for me . . ." or "I am disappointed that you do not provide the unconditional love that my mother did not provide and that I thought you would. . . . " The partner hearing the fear and/or sadness (perhaps for the first time) is often moved to compassionate response. Again, if the initial disclosure is simply, "I'm scared," this person is on the way. It will take a while for a patient to reach the level of understanding reflected in the remarks above, but it does happen, over time.

One way in which I make it possible for people to admit their vulnerabilities is my explanation of the varying levels of response we have, based on different levels of brain physiology. Harville Hendrix in *Keeping the Love You Find* (p. 306) presents the idea that our most instinctive response to a threat is based in the amygdala, a part of the midbrain, and in the "old brain" or "reptilian brain." Perceptions on this level are processed in terms of threatening or non-threatening, with no modifying nuance. Our reptilian or most primitive brain sees things in terms of an automatic reflexive "eat or be eaten" view. The amygdala is part of the limbic system in the midbrain and is found in lower mammals as well as in man. It seems to be a very important part of our survival brain and is necessary to experience fear, which then sets up the fight or flight mechanism. Thus, anger and rage also seem to be involved with the midbrain or limbic system. The response to a threat perceived on this level can not be other than attack or flee.

Brain impulses are said to travel from this portion of the brain at least twice as fast as they do to and from the "newer" cerebral cortex, the more mature part of the brain which, literally, can think things over and make alternative choices. In addition, nerve impulses from our five senses travel directly to the amygdala without having to first travel to the neocortex, which is our highest brain and most developed in man. We can think of our reptilian and midbrain to be our reflexive and quick action regulators which help us survive danger. Evolution has wisely prepared us for survival by not requiring our neocortex to be operational in an emergency where our life is threatened. A bit later, our highest brain, our neocortex, can come into operation with planning, reflecting or even canceling plans of the reptilian and midbrains. In a situation which is perceived as a threat, the reptilian and midbrain may swiftly "kidnap" or take over the rest of the brain and counterattack.

In the lower animal world, this is an adaptive survival mechanism. In a love relationship, however, the survival brain (reptilian and midbrain) response is usually destructive. Here is a vignette that demonstrates this point.

> Joelle and Martha had been together as a lesbian couple for a very long time. Martha experienced physical rejection in her first year of life and used to scream loudly for food. As a young woman, she felt more comfortable when the refrigerator and freezer were well-stocked. Her more primitive anxieties most often showed up in her style of approach to life, rather than in any discernible psychopathology. Since Joelle was less worried and more relaxed in these areas, they didn't have too many conflicts.
>
> Together, they had done a good deal of psychological work on their relationship and knew where most of their "buttons" were. They decided to remodel a guest cottage on their property, and Martha wanted to make sure that they included a significantly large refrigerator and stove for the storage and preparation of food. Joelle, however, insisted that the aesthetics of the small room would be impaired by all of the kitchen equipment. Martha experienced instant rage at Joelle for her insensitivity to her viewpoint and wishes. Because of our work together, Martha contained the rage with some facial grimaces and a mild pout,

while she internally struggled to find out what so enraged/frightened her. As soon as she reminded herself of her lifelong anxiety about provisions, stocked larders, etc., the rage totally disappeared, and she was able to explain to Joelle what her feelings were and where they came from. Joelle had initially responded to Martha relatively slowly, a sign of new brain-cerebral cortex processing, and she herself never felt personally threatened. Martha had actually experienced Joelle's relatively mild negative comments about the proposed kitchen renovation as a death threat and was aware that she had become enraged in a split second. As frequently happens in these types of episodes, Joelle later felt compassion for Martha. She sincerely and lovingly told her to renovate the cottage in whatever way made her most comfortable. Likewise, Martha, having moved from reptilian and midbrain type of response to her more reasonable cerebral neocortex-cognitive thinking response, was able to see the unreasonableness of her position and was much more comfortable now with Joelle's aesthetic viewpoint.

It has been my experience that Martha and Joelle's communication dilemma is typically the root of relationship difficulties. Since we very often pick partners who will unknowingly help replay our childhood traumas, the reptilian-midbrain fears of our childhood will also be activated in our adult relationships. I also believe that the earlier in life one experiences psychological or physical trauma, the more strongly relationship conflict will be perceived as life-threatening, thereby activating our reptilian-midbrain system type of reflexive thinking and acting to "stay alive." Although the participants in a conflict believe they are disagreeing or arguing about a surface issue, the reptilian-midbrain reflex manifests as a way of "surviving." It is valuable for people to understand that the ways in which they respond and react are probably more related to experiences in the past than to the experience at hand.

Couples who have learned this are less likely to fight with each other and more likely to use their partner as a support for healing. This becomes all the more obvious when we realize that our partner also has a survival (reptilian-midbrain) brain. Depending on what traumas they may have had, our aggressive or angry communications will cause them to go into fight or flight mode. When couples fight, more often than not the survival brain of each person is directing the communication with varying amounts (from nothing to some) of the communication being directed by the highest or neocortical brain. In fact, couples usually report later, when things are calmer, that they don't know what was so upsetting. From the vantage point of our neocortex, this makes sense since so many of our survival techniques are not logical to be used in our relationship. Our fighting (verbally or physically) or fleeing (pouting, withdrawing or leaving) are remnants of these earlier mechanisms and are, I believe, not in the best interest of the relationship.

Even in a civilized world we would still need some of these survival mechanisms for emergency situations. But not, it seems to me, to the degree that so many of us seem to have them activated.

Our knowledge of post traumatic stress disorder (PTSD) gives us some valuable clues in understanding some issues in relational difficulties. For example, a Vietnam veteran with PTSD might be walking down the street in a city in the United States and hear a car backfiring. Before he could think in his neocortex, "There is no shelling going on here," he has hurled himself to the ground. That is the survival brain in action. When the earlier trauma is threatening or stressful enough, *we are incapable* of resisting the impulse to fight or flee. Fortunately for us, most relational problems are not of this severity.

I do not believe the expression of anger and rage by the reptilian-limbic system part of our brain helps the individual to grow, mature, and become more loving. Relationships heal *despite* the expression of anger and not because of it. The older survival brain tends not to *listen* to cognitive reasonableness, but rather reacts on the basis of direct *experience*. The reptilian-midbrain can begin to relax and become less reactive when it has the *experience* of safety and comfort over a relatively long period—a strength which becomes available in long-term, committed relationships.

I involve couples in a therapeutic alliance with me as we begin therapy, by being supportive of their attempt to reconcile and optimistic about their ability to do so when that seems reasonable. I tell people that if they ever felt loving toward each other and excited about being with each other, the chances are those feelings can be rehabilitated. I ask for their support in the therapeutic enterprise by requiring them to relinquish the direct expression of anger and try to express their anger in terms of feeling frightened or sad. I advise them that if they cannot manage a non-aggressive presentation of their feelings outside of therapy, they should wait until our therapy session to discuss it. I explain that I understand this will be difficult, as it means they are also relinquishing the tension relief that comes from an angry outburst. But I encourage them to work at it. I tell them I believe that at some level the anger they feel is a remnant of an old response to something life-threatening, and our work together will try to explore this derivative fully to heal it. I describe the reptilian-mid brain response and use this image to encourage them to soothe each other's more primitive feelings. I assure them that, as loving support replaces aggressive fighting, the old survival brains will become less reactive, and the new brain will be able to assume more power. This will enable them to listen and evaluate current experience with cognitive, discriminating abilities which will then allow for making sounder choices.

Part of my therapeutic technique is to help people see directly that their anger is a reflection of a fear that is fundamentally experienced as life-threatening. Since I sometimes need to push people to examine their responses much more closely than they would otherwise, I must solicit their help in doing this. I will say, before following a line of reasoning, "Please go along with me as we follow this feeling, even if the line of questioning doesn't seem clear or reasonable to you." Usually people agree and most often are surprised to find that a fear of death underlies their anger.

When the level of depression and/or rage in a patient is great, I have found that the judicious use of certain medications may be able to transform a totally unworkable relationship into one that has a chance for resolution. Some of the new anti-depressants (SSRIs) which act to increase our serotonin levels can, with *skilled* application, greatly facilitate the psychological healing of a relationship. I have seen a variety of positive results in patients including noticeable calming of the hyperrage, a significant lowering of the level of anxiety, a decrease in the depth of depression, and a lessening of perfectionism (which can often be a problem in a relationship).

Anger, even at the level of rage, is frequently experienced with righteous indignation, as if it made sense to be angry or as if the anger would help amend the situation. Patients of mine in couples therapy reported that they had just had a terrible week.

> Tim had been complaining and finding fault with everything that Sally said or did. He felt justified because, he said, "My boss is talking about downsizing the company, and I may lose my job. So, I'm edgy, and Sally isn't supportive."
>
> "Why would it bother you to lose your job?" I asked.
>
> He seemed startled by the question, but responded, "I'm not sure where I can get another one."
>
> "Why would that bother you?" Again, he seemed startled as my questioning seemed naive.
>
> "I'd have no money," he said. "My family would starve . . . My wife would leave me . . . No one would respect me . . . I would be embarrassed to tell my parents . . . If my parents and my wife don't love me, I'd be alone . . ."
>
> "Why would it bother you to be alone?"
>
> "I would die if I were alone."

Here we see uncovered the ancient fear of the small child who lives within the patient. Our adult, neocortical brain knows that we can drive to the supermarket to buy bread and milk and can survive quite well. Our child within us is closer to our survival brains' mode of thinking and tends to react from that place, leading to fight or flight mechanisms which for the moment can "kidnap" our adult, neo-cortical brain whose logic might otherwise mitigate our response to a more appropriate one that would benefit the relationship. On occasion, this fear provides a springboard to move into the spiritual dimension, to offer to the patient spiritual ways to cope with the fear and deal with questions about meaning and survival of consciousness.

What is important, I believe, is not the particular fears that people express. What seems transformative in the relationship is the discovery that what was previously experienced as anger is actually an expression of fear. When people see this directly, they are motivated to reframe their angry communications in terms of the fears they represent. This level of communication most often elicits sympathy and compassion instead of rebuttal and retaliation.

Ben and Wendy were Zen Buddhist meditators who had met in Japan while on a spiritual pilgrimage. They shared many values, supported each other's spiritual aspirations, and both were devoted to their young sons. Their marriage, however, seemed to be deteriorating under the strain of Wendy's style of nagging and Ben's sullen withdrawal response. They sought therapy because they hoped they could regain the affection and warmth they had originally shared.

One day the therapy session began with Ben reporting he had become enraged at Wendy for leaving a pile of papers on the floor in a "messy" way. Following the style of questioning of "Why would it bother you that there was a mess on the floor," Ben recalled that when he was a child his mother had beaten him for leaving messes. He remembered the anxiety he had felt when she came into his room, lest the room not be tidy enough. Since he identified himself with his household, he needed it to be tidy at all times to keep from feeling anxious. Although his mother had died five years previously, any mess made him feel in danger of incurring her wrath. His thinking-level brain knew that it was just a pile of papers on the floor, but his instinctive response, originating from the older reptilian-midbrain, was alarm about being beaten and unloved. As Wendy watched Ben's breakdown, she was moved by how she had, inadvertently, caused him to be frightened, and she reached out to comfort him. These poignant moments occur frequently in this type of therapy and seem to be significantly healing.

Working with this couple and with some others, too, it is clear that it is not always necessary to access the fear of death by one partner in order to elicit empathy in the other partner. Often, just seeing the childhood fear of a significant parent is enough to evoke this sympathy.

I am convinced that, if pushed further beyond the "fear of mother" situation that was tapped by Ben, the fear of death by the very-young-child Ben would have been accessed.

The question can be legitimately asked: What would the reaction be from a person who had a very positive early ego development where there was not any major breach of the empathic and trusting bond? In almost every situation I have worked with, the fear of death was accessed behind the anger. Where I have not been able to elicit this, I am not sure whether or not it was due to a resistance to my approach—which to some is annoying or bothersome because the line of questioning seems so stupid (and, I believe, threatening).

I have observed through my therapy work with couples and with individuals that there is often a surprising difference in the pace of the work I've not seen discussed. When working with a couple, I find that as a rule they can access their problems more rapidly than I see people do in individual therapy. A couple, practicing their transference distortions with each other day and night, come into a session together with their transferences already at a heightened pitch. In individual therapy, on the other hand, it tends to take a significantly longer time for events to occur to set off the transference responses that then lead to the healing work.

Furthermore, in couples' therapy, it seems to me that there are three patients: Patient A, Patient B, and Patient C (the relationship). This creates a distinctly different dynamic than that of individual therapy and also, I believe, contributes to the reasons that couples' therapy may often move appreciably faster, especially at the start, than one-on-one treatment.

I often reassure a couple by explaining to them that traumas stemming from early childhood may take a very long time (ten, twenty, or thirty years) to heal in a generally safe and caring relationship. Usually, as we become less frightened, we have more energy for, and are more open to, a spiritual pursuit, if we are so inclined. Unresolved psychological problems will often negatively distort the spiritual journey. A committed, caring relationship offers one of the most powerful tools I know of for psychological, as well as spiritual, healing.

Sometimes patients are not able to grasp at first the process of delving beneath their anger to find the fear. Their reluctance can stem from a variety of causes, and I have found that introducing them to forgiveness practice is often very valuable. In the major spiritual traditions, various techniques have been taught to work with anger. Forgiveness practice can pave the way for a couple to see each other not only more clearly, but with compassion. And, finding compassion for one's partner will certainly ease tensions and help free one to deal with the issues from a more peaceful place.

Furthermore, an important facet of the forgiveness practice is the discovery of *self-forgiveness*—an opening of one's heart to oneself. This discovery can be very important, and it can bring a new dimension of acceptance and love to a couple's process as they explore their anger together. It can even hasten their understanding that there are fears beneath the anger. Allowing themselves to have compassion for themselves (and each other) permits them to move *beyond* the anger.

How can a long-term, committed relationship help us advance along our spiritual path? All of the great spiritual traditions speak of how our attachments can stand in the way of spiritual advancement—attachments to our (small) ego, (small) self (as opposed to our higher Self), material needs and wants, bodily gratifications, etc. We are all imperfect individuals with varying degrees of selfishness or unhealthy narcissism.

There is no way one can be in a long-term, committed relationship without having to face and struggle with these issues. In short-term relationships, it is possible to hide these areas from view, but not in long-term relationships. I frequently tell couples that in their essence they are like two pure diamonds with varying amounts of psychological rough edges obscuring their brilliance. In a successful committed relationship, the couple needs to "skillfully" polish the roughness covering the brilliance of their respective diamonds. To rub too abrasively on each other can damage the diamonds and, conversely, to not rub at all leaves us with our inner brilliance and potential not realized.

If there are children in the committed relationship, the "rubbing" process, with the additional need to gratify the healthy requirements of child-rearing, can be even faster, though often more dangerous and threatening. The reptilian-midbrain of the adult will, unfortunately all too often, stand in conflict with the child, leading the adult to damage the child as we frequently see in child abuse. To optimally parent a child requires that there be a minimal amount of pathologic narcissism present in the parent.

Thich Nhat Hanh, a Buddhist monk, confirms this viewpoint when he says: "Interpersonal relationships are the key for success in . . . [spiritual] practice. Without an intimate deep relationship with at least one person, transformation is unlikely." (p. 107) Here again, we see how what appears to be a more traditionally-oriented psychotherapy of relationships is actually creating an important prerequisite for a successful spiritual practice. In fact, the danger of not being able to experience real intimacy with at least one person is that whatever spiritual gains are made will be expressed through pathologic narcissistic channels. This can be seen in spiritual communities where the leader(s) use their followers in destructive ways.

Michael Washburn, in *Transpersonal Psychology in Psychoanalytic Perspective*, also affirms the importance of developing intimate relationships with another, or others, as a prerequisite for the development of spiritual wholeness. This development of intimacy is not usually achieved until midlife when traditionally the final ascent along the path of spiritual transcendence begins. Washburn points out that the development of intimacy requires effective dualistic ego functions, i.e., seeing oneself as separate from others (usually during the first half of life), while the lessening of the dualism of the ego is then required in order to attain greater psychospiritual wholeness. To put in another way, as Jack Engler said, "You have be somebody before you can be nobody." (Wilber, Engler, & Brown, p. 24)

Sometimes, I work with couples who have no particular interest in spiritual development. In those instances, the therapy can proceed on the basis of uncovering fears and sharing vulnerabilities and still be very helpful. My experience has been that the therapy is potentiated when couples do have a spiritual interest, and I support these interests whenever there is an opportunity. For example, the great spiritual traditions that I know all teach about the harmfulness of the direct expression of anger. As I begin to work with patients, in addition to sharing my own conviction that spontaneous outbursts of anger are not helpful, I might underline my conviction with a reference to a tradition that I think is meaningful to them.

For example, traditional Christian teachings present Jesus as the model of forgiveness in all situations. Also, the Christian-based *A Course in Miracles* teaches that we should never express anger toward others because we are, in that moment, unable to see clearly our interconnectedness with others. If we saw clearly, if we knew all of the dimensions of our feelings, we would see that our anger is fear-based, that the situation would be best handled by clear explanation of need rather than by outrage.

Buddhist teachings clearly present anger as one of the "defilements" that cloud the mind. Verse Two of *The Dhammapada* reads, "All things have the nature of mind. Mind is the chief and takes the lead. If the mind is polluted, whatever you do or say leads to suffering which will follow you as a cart trails a horse." Verse Five says, "Your enemies will never make peace in the face of hatred. It is the absence of hatred that leads to peace. This is an eternal truth." Verse Six says, "We are but guests visiting this world, though most of us do not know this. Those who see the real situation are not inclined to quarrel."

Of more significance, I believe, is the role that specific practices from spiritual traditions play in people's attempts to communicate skillfully with each other. Those people who have a meditation or prayer practice often find periods of quiet reflection help them put whatever they want to say into a perspective that can be more positively communicated to their partner. Meditators in all traditions, who practice attentiveness to the sequence of thoughts and states that arise in the mind, are often more easily able to recognize the perception-thought-fear-anger sequence as it happens. Consequently, they are often more capable of expressing the underlying core of fear that led to angry feelings than are people without this training.

A specific practice from the Buddhist tradition is the cultivation of Right Speech, speech that is truthful *and* helpful. In the *Vinaya*, the catalog of monk's rules as taught by the Buddha, admonishing a person is permissible only after reflecting on whether the admonition is timely, truthful, gentle, useful, and kind. (Woodward, p. 24) People quickly realize that what this means is that negative speech can be destructive and, therefore, requires careful reflection.

Sometimes patients will object to my emphasis on meticulously careful speech, suggesting that this leaves no room for spontaneity. I believe emotionally mature couples (people who normally do not come for therapy) are able to metabolize momentary irritability between them without significant loss of closeness. These couples can be comfortable being spontaneous and relaxed. However, where there is significant early psychological trauma and/or a predisposition to hypersensitivity to criticism, even small outbursts of anger can lead to fear and loss of trust on a primitive level. I assure people I see in therapy that emphasizing Right Speech is a useful tool with which to build a relationship based on trust. It will allow the couple, some day, to feel more relaxed with each other.

Miriam and Irving illustrate that the "speech" in Right Speech includes the many subtleties of body language, tone, and other physical nuances.

Miriam, age thirty-five, and Irving, age thirty-nine, had been married eight years and worked together as psychotherapists. They had both had many years of individual psychotherapy before coming to see me, during which time they seemed to have resolved most of their significant neurotic conflicts.

Miriam came from an intact Jewish family. Her mother was the authority in the family—pushy and demanding. Her father was loving, but weak and passive. Miriam's subborness and pushiness seemed to stem from her conflicts and identification with her mother. Irving, like her mother, frequently scowled and made a "bad face" at Miriam when he was upset.

Irving also came from a non-observant Jewish family which exhibited the reverse dynamics of Miriam's. His father, a Wall Street stockbroker, was harsh and hypercritical, while his mother allowed herself to be bullied by her husband. When his father got angry, he mostly held it in and fumed silently, with little doubt in anyone's mind about what he was feeling.

Miriam had unconsciously picked her "mother" to marry, as Irving had selected his "father." Each seemingly did this to heal those childhood wounds still remaining, i.e., they recreated the original trauma, but now hoped to have it come out differently and be healed. Since they were both psychotherapists, they tried to use very calm, sophisticated language to communicate. Miriam was working to be different than her mother had been in her marriage, and Irving, who so frequently had been the butt of his father's anger, endeavored consciously to relate to Miriam in ways that differed from those his father used. However, when Miriam and Irving did upset each other, they reverted to earlier identification patterns. They had enough neocortical brain function to avoid open hostility: their telltale signals of anger would come with an eye movement, clenching jaw muscles, tightening neck muscles, a wave of the hand, or a glazed look on the face. As we probed under each of these "mole hills," we found the "mountain" that, when pursued, most often led to an underlying fear that was being hidden in the moment.

Buddhist Vipassana (mindfulness) meditation can be used as a technique to train the mind to witness the arising of anger and not react impulsively and destructively to it. Such techniques can be seen as methods to train the mind to *not* let itself be kidnapped by the reptilian and midbrain when the individual is frightened.

As what lies beneath the anger is uncovered, one's reaction to it can more easily be changed. Forgiveness practices from spiritual traditions can hasten and enhance the awareness or even provide an alternate route to the awareness when traditional talk therapy does not seem to be providing the necessary clarity of mind.

Ken and Fran consulted me because their fifteen-year marriage was in danger of falling apart due to the rage attacks Ken had during arguments with Fran in which he would lose his temper and throw things at her. The immediate precipitating event would often be Fran's emotional withdrawal or threats to leave the marriage.

Ken was a forty-year-old art teacher at the local junior college, and Fran was a successful stockbroker in a brokerage firm. They had two daughters, ages ten and thirteen. Both Ken and Fran came from homes where they experienced benign neglect and a sense of not being cared for.

In a classical fashion, they seemed to have "picked" each other to replicate the feelings of aloneness that they had experienced in their early childhoods. I questioned Ken about the rages he experienced when Fran threatened to leave him. As we tried to access the fear behind the rage, Ken suddenly had trouble breathing, began gasping and suddenly remembered that he almost died of asphyxiation as a seven-year-old child when he had pneumonia. His condition had necessitated being rushed to the hospital emergency room. He had stopped breathing, and it required emergency intubation and artificial respirators to revive him. Ken told me how he had an out-of-body experience during which time he watched the physicians working on him. He remembered that while in the out-of-body state his favorite grandmother, who had died a year before, came to him, saying that it was not his time to die yet and that he had much to learn in this life.

By now, in my office, Ken was breathing much more easily and could readily see how Fran's threatening to leave him activated his terror of being left alone—it had been during one of the periods of being left alone by his mother (who had gone away for the evening) that the asphyxiation event had occurred in his childhood.

Further work with Ken along these lines was very helpful in alleviating the rage reactions to Fran. He would say somewhat light-heartedly, "I guess my problem is that I am afraid to let go [of life]."

I believe that our DNA is programmed for survival. Even an amoeba will try to survive by swimming away from a noxious substance. As long as we identify ourselves with our physical body, our DNA coding will fear extinction and try to survive. Many advanced spiritual beings have little attachment to their bodies—seeing themselves as more attached to their spiritual essence—and therefore have no fear of dying. As a result of this, I believe they seem more loving.

During our initial interviews, I ascertained that Ken and Fran had a newly emerging interest in spiritual issues, though their main interest seemed to be in developing psychic powers.

Although *A Course in Miracles* was not a path devoted to the development of psychic powers, I suggested to them that it might be a route that could offer them some help. I chose the *Course* because Ken and Fran both had Christian backgrounds which were meaningful to them. Also, *A Course in Miracles* suggests we are here to learn different lessons from each other on the path to becoming more loving, and I believed this concept would be helpful to them. I felt that since there was a great deal of loving and feelings of friendship still in the marriage, this approach would begin to give them an arena in which they could begin to look at the negative aspects of their relationship.

Because of their early traumas in their families of origin, both had fears of intimacy, lest they be retraumatized. They, therefore, used a narcissistic character style which most often reflected in emotional withdrawal and "selfish" demandings from each other which were not fulfillable and served to keep intimacy at bay. Their study of *A Course in Miracles* began to give them the courage and positive attitude to help each other with the fears which lay behind their "selfish-looking" approaches to life. This new spark revitalized their enthusiasm to make the marriage work, even if it took a very long time to do so.

I gained a new understanding from my work with this couple. Because of Ken's near-death experience at the age of seven, he had no conscious fear of death and was even looking forward to it as he saw it as an opportunity to be united with his beloved grandmother and many other friends who had since died. From this, I conclude that our highest brain (neocortex) can transcend the fear of death with, for example, various spiritual practices. Rather, it is the survival brains (reptilian and midbrain limbic system) that have the fear of death or drive for the survival of our physical bodies encoded. This may have important theoretical implications for working with rage and fear.

Karl came to me alone for individual therapy and then together with his wife, Kathy, for couples' therapy. Their case illustrates a number of significant issues: 1) that psychological healing can be helped and potentiated with meditation and with judicious use of medication, 2) that many individuals are resistant to the use of medications: some people for the reasons in this case study (and others for reasons as outlined by Peter Kramer in *Listening to Prozac*), and 3) that certain medications can potentiate the meditative experience.

Karl initially came to see me for help with his failing marriage, although he did so with reluctance. He was in his mid-fifties, had a Masters degree in social work and had been working for twenty years at a clinic run by Catholic Social Services where he worked primarily with new immigrants from Central and South America. His reluctance about therapy had several components. One was chagrin over what he characterized as his "inability to choose wisely." He felt that he should have had enough psychological sophistication to see that his third (and current) wife replayed the same dynamics that had led to the failures of his first two marriages. In addition, he had a serious interest in Buddhism and meditation (and chose to contact me after meeting me at a Vipassana retreat), as well as a continuing, dedicated practice as a Catholic. He felt that he "should" be able to use his spiritual practices to develop sufficient calm and resignation to accept his current situation without resentment. He hoped to convince himself of the spiritual merit of renouncing his own needs and desires, but it wasn't working. His final resistance was his general distrust of Western therapies and Western medicine, and probably my presence at the meditation retreat allowed him to contact me.

Karl had grown up in a large Catholic family in a midwestern city. He was the second child, first son, with seven younger siblings. Karl's father was a surgeon. The family was financially secure, but Karl recalled that his father was away from home working long hours and characterized him as an absent father. He told me that, apart from appearing as a family together at Sunday Mass, his father was rarely at home.

He described his mother as seeming "perennially flustered" by her large family with its many demands, even though the family's finances allowed her to have extra household help. His mother had migraine headaches and periodically would need to retire to her bed for several days. Even as a fairly young boy, Karl would try to care for his mother during her headache times, tiptoeing into her room, bringing her cool compresses for her head. He told me that he knew, as a child, that he was her favorite child and that he both secretly enjoyed that status and also felt a little guilty about it. He remembered feeling especially good when she would need something—her reading glasses, an extra sweater—and look immediately to him to fetch it for her. He enjoyed the "special smile" she would give him as a reward.

As Karl became adolescent, his father became a significant factor in his life. According to Karl, his father became stricter, more heavy handed in his discipline. As a teenager in the early sixties, Karl participated in the prevailing mood of revolution against "everyone over thirty." It was a strong factor in Karl's choice to drop out of the local university after one year. Since it was near his house, he had lived at home as a freshman and felt he needed to get away.

Karl spent several years traveling, settled in San Francisco where he worked at a Catholic home for delinquent and/or orphan boys and became active in working as a counselor for men who, like himself, wanted conscientious objector status from the draft. As a devout Catholic, a vegetarian, and a pacifist, he achieved that status for himself.

Karl met his first wife while traveling, and she had been his first serious relationship outside the scrutiny of his family home. She had been drawn to his solicitous, caretaking nature, and he had particularly used his capacity to anticipate the whims of needy women—which he had learned in relationship to his mother—to charm her. They married after a brief courtship, since his religious upbringing made him uncomfortable about sexual freedom. He was soon feeling neglected and disappointed. Whereas his caregiving of his mother has resulted in her treating him as "most favored," his wife treated him with disinterest. The more depressed he became, the more demanding she became. Their arguments became heated, and she left him, quite suddenly, for another man. Because she disappeared, he was able to have the marriage annulled.

Depressed and angry, Karl returned to college, finished his undergraduate degree, and entered social work school. His caregiving capacity led him to choose community organization as his major, and he started his work with immigrants immediately after graduation. He married a woman he met in social work school, five years older than he was, once previously married with a five-year-old son. They had twins one year later, and their marriage lasted eleven years. As Karl looked back on it, he characterized the years as periods of shared delight in their children, heated fights about his feelings of being unappreciated, of feeling his wife was only interested in him as the source of support for herself and the children, and periods of depressed resignation. Karl's job was his only source of gratification, and as social legislation began to erode funding for his agency, his depression deepened. His community organizational activities also escalated, and he used planning meetings as a place to vent his generalized anger, spending less and less time with his family. Finally, his wife filed for divorce, a step his own lingering religious constraints had prevented him from taking, and he did not contest.

Karl had been convinced his third marriage would be a happy one. He had met his wife at a Vipassana meditation retreat. He had begun meditation practice after his divorce because he hoped it would calm his agitation and his increasingly volatile temper. He liked the silence of meditation retreats and scheduled his vacations around them. His wife shared his enthusiasm for meditation, and they meditated daily together. She had seemed, when they met, more devoted and less needy than Karl's previous wives, but after two years of marriage, the old pattern of "non-reciprocated relationship" had emerged, discussions quickly became battles, and Karl was distraught.

I saw Karl individually for several sessions and felt that he seemed to be using his intellectual awareness of the source of his quick temper—"I keep falling for needy women, but they don't reciprocate my caretaking"—as a justification for fighting. He felt depressed to be in an ungratifying relationship and too immobilized to leave it. I then suggested seeing Karl and his wife together, in an attempt to see if they could both modify their behavior so that the relationship could continue.

I was impressed with Karl and Kathy as a couple. They seemed genuinely affectionate with each other, less adversarial than I had imagined from Karl's description. They eagerly accepted my suggestions for working with "Right Speech," a concept they knew from their Buddhist practice. They incorporated into their speech pattern my idea that anger arises when we are frightened, so that they would say, "When you seem uninterested in my needs, I am frightened that you don't love me."

Therapy sessions were spent reviewing fights that had occurred during the week, and by reconstructing their feelings at the time, they were able to recognize the fear that had been the source of the anger. During the sessions, it was not unusual for Karl or Kathy to burst into tears as they recalled a frightening time of their childhood. At such times, the other partner would respond compassionately, and all three of us would feel moved and hopeful that this level of mutual support would continue. Even if they left my office with strong intention to never fight, they would often report that the "truce" had held only briefly and that some seemingly minor event had precipitated a new crisis. Three months passed, and I felt we had not made much progress.

The adventitious event of Karl suffering a coronary spasm, brought on by an episode of rage, was the turning point in the therapy. Although he did not need further coronary care, his internist insisted that he try Prozac for his depression and especially for his rage. I had suggested antidepressants at several points in the therapy, but Karl was adamantly opposed on several counts. His general mistrust of Western medicine was a strongly held value. He also felt that taking a medicine would make him the identified patient, and it would mean that he had failed in triumphing over his own mind, something he saw as a defeat. However, at his internist's insistence, he began Prozac (20 mg./day) and began to feel less depressed after one week. His most immediate result of taking the drug was the virtual disappearance of his quick temper. He continued to notice that he was upset, but his reaction was calm.

At this time, his therapy experience changed. His relationship with Kathy became smoother, more loving, and she decided to leave couples' therapy and continue her individual therapy with another therapist. I continued seeing Karl for one year, weekly, during which time he became aware of how profoundly lonesome he had felt during his childhood, how much he had missed, and resented, his absent father, and also how much he had resented his "special relationship" with his mother which had left him feeling guilty and estranged from his siblings.

I feel that the Prozac potentiated the psychotherapy in two ways. As he became less wrathful, his relationship with Kathy became loving and supportive. Also, the Prozac reduced his level of anxiety so that unconscious material emerged. Previously too frightening to experience, this then became available for therapy.

Another surprising result of the Prozac was that Karl's meditation practice thrived. He found that he was more able to maintain a focused attention and was less distracted by ruminative depressive thoughts. His overall mood improved enormously, he felt more vigorous, and therapy was terminated by mutual agreement.

Karl's taking Prozac clearly aided the therapeutic process. I think the judicious use of antidepressant drugs is an important adjunct to therapy when indicated. With many patients, however, there are "spiritual" antidepressants which I have discovered can be helpful. Practicing forgiveness, for example, can be utilized as an effective tool.

It is easy to bring people to see the amount of personal pain they experience by holding on to a grudge. But it is not so easy to let go of grudges, even when one would like to. Again, all the major traditions seem to provide forgiveness practices. In the Buddhist tradition, practitioners cultivate metta (lovingkindness) through the recitation of wishes for the well-being of oneself and others. A simple version of metta meditation is:

> "May I be happy, may I be peaceful;
> May you be happy, may you be peaceful."

These resolves start with wishes for oneself, for peace of mind and ease—the very repetition of the resolves acts as a calming agent in the mind. As the mind calms and the body relaxes, antipathy usually decreases, and natural forgiveness, or understanding, emerges. Even if one is too angry to say the metta resolve, "May you be happy, may you be peaceful," one can keep the focus on just oneself, i.e., "May I be happy, may I be peaceful." Repetition of just that half of the resolve will eventually lead to a softening of one's anger toward the other person.

A central focus of Christian prayer is examination of one's own conscience and the wish to be absolved of one's mistakes, e.g.: "Forgive us our trespasses, as we forgive those who trespass against us" (Lord's Prayer, Matthew, Chapt. 6, Verse 12). I have worked with patients using *A Course in Miracles* who found that they could let go of feelings of ill will by repeating to themselves the lesson, "I and my brothers are one with God."

Years ago, while on a retreat, I learned from Joseph Goldstein, noted American Buddhist teacher, a forgiveness meditation which can be effectively practiced when anger arises in a relationship:

> If I have offended or harmed anyone, knowingly or unknowingly, I ask their forgiveness—and—if anyone else [e.g., spouse] has offended or harmed me knowingly or unknowingly, I FORGIVE THEM.

Initially, the words may almost be unutterable, but with repetition and practice, it does get easier. Any mind moment we spend being angry precludes our having a happy mind moment. As with the metta meditation above, if it is impossible to verbalize forgiveness of the other person, one may keep the focus on oneself, and eventually the anger toward the other person will soften.

Recently I came across a Hebrew forgiveness prayer that closely parallels that given to me by Joseph Goldstein. Recognizing that anger and resentment are antithetical to a peaceful mind, the last prayers of the Jewish mystic's liturgical day include a prayer that begins:

> Master of the Universe, I hereby forgive anyone who angered or antagonized me or who sinned against me—whether against my body, my property, my honor or against anything of mine—whether accidentally, willfully, or purposely; whether through speech, deed, thought or notion; whether in this transmigration [incarnation] or another transmigration—I forgive everyone.
>
> May no man [or woman] be punished because of me. (Scherman, p. 319.)

If recited every night before bedtime, the tendency to carry grudges or harbor resentments will be undercut.

When I mention these practices to patients, I do so primarily in the spirit of inspiration. Some people actually begin to incorporate these practices into their lives. This usually happens when people are already pursuing a spiritual path and are pleased to feel that they are doing spiritual work as they heal their relationship. Even when people do not actively begin a formal forgiveness practice, just hearing about the value of forgiveness is often inspiring enough to begin to make the direct expression of anger ego alien.

I believe that doors can be opened with more than one key: if a psychological key does not yet seem to fit, a spiritual key may be the one to help turn the lock successfully.

As a final note, I want to mention the particular pleasure I have as a therapist when I help couples heal a relationship. Of course, there is great satisfaction in helping individuals heal from psychological pain, but there is, for me, an *extra* satisfaction in helping couples reclaim a love they once had for each other that had become hidden behind fear and resentment. Part of the pain of a failing relationship is the partners' disappointment that the loving feelings they once had seem to have disappeared. My hope in working with couples is that restraint in the expression of anger will help their minds to clear so their fears can be safely shared and love for each other rediscovered.

24

Past-life Regression Therapy

Roger J. Woolger

I met Roger Woolger at a conference on psychotherapy and spirituality and was immediately intrigued by his comments that Jung used the term "collective unconscious" for professional reasons, i.e., to cover his deep belief and understanding of reincarnation. I was even more curious when Woolger said that Jung had taught courses on the Vedanta.

From reading the author's personal background information, it is clear that the seeds for his later work were present before he started college at Oxford. His study of Freud, Eastern religions, the Gospels, mysticism, and, later on, his exploration of bodywork, Jungian and Gestalt therapy, hypnotherapy and birth release work (intensive breathing and hyperventilation) all presaged the evolution of Woolger's technique in using past-life regression to help his patients.

In the theoretical section of this chapter, a fascinating new way of thinking evolves to begin to explain to us the phenomenon of how emotions, thoughts, bodily feelings and disease processes can be transmitted from one body to another, that is, from one *incarnation* to another. Woolger's discussion of the mental, emotional, and etheric bodies or energy fields points the way for further therapeutic efforts in these areas.

Woolger makes the clear assumption that ancient ancestral dramas are already imprinted on the psyche at birth, "revealing unfinished business or karma derived from multiple lives of the soul." Patients who are stuck therapeutically and/or therapists who want to deepen their own processes are considered by Woolger as ideal subjects for his short-term, intensive, past-life remembering therapy.

Reprinted from *Regression Therapy: A Handbook for Professionals,* Vol. 1, *Past-life Therapy.* Edited by Winafred Blake Lucas. Crest Park, Calif.: Deep Forest Press, 1993.

The conditions that he feels can be helped by this therapy are *some* of the anxieties, fears, phobias, depressions, behavior problems, relationship difficulties, and chronic physical ailments. The freedom achieved by patients from exploring and, indeed, *reliving* their ancestral dramas is remarkable. He does *not* recommend this form of therapy for severely ego-impaired individuals.

Woolger vividly explains his induction techniques and provides valuable insights on how to manage problems that can arise. He describes linguistic subtleties the therapist can employ to help the client thoroughly experience the past-life remembering process. For him, awareness is the key word in processing what is happening, whether from Gestalt approaches or Buddhist Vipassana meditation.

In his five case presentations, Woolger describes and illustrates how he tries to clear negative samskaras or past-life patterning at the mental, emotional, and physical levels.

I believe it is important for all clinicians to examine the incredible implications for psychotherapy and medicine that this approach offers.

MY FIRST ENCOUNTER with past life-therapy and regression was a purely skeptical one. As a member of the British Society for Psychical Research I was asked in 1970 to review the book *The Cathars and Reincarnation* by Arthur Guirdham. I was not a believer in reincarnation at that time and, striking as Guirdham's case was, I nevertheless reviewed the book skeptically, citing Guirdham's obvious countertransference to his patient and his patient's unexplored relationship with her father, a medievalist. My impression was that Guirdham had fallen in love with his patient and enabled her to tune into her father's deep love of the Middle Ages. Today I am not so sure. All three may have interacted in a medieval lifetime.

My first personal experience of past lives was purely spontaneous and occurred during a two-week intensive Buddhist meditation retreat in 1976. During this time I underwent a mild cardiac crisis accompanied by horrible visions of what seemed to be witch burnings. My meditation teacher from Thailand informed me that they were simply past-life fragments and I should let them go. I followed his instructions and wasn't bothered further.

A year later in Burlington, Vermont, I agreed to experiment in a simple form of past-life regression with another therapist I knew personally. From my Jungian training I had done a great deal of "active imagination," which allows images from dreams and visions to be reactivated while one is in a receptive state not unlike meditation. From this experience I found it very easy, with the guidance of my friend, to go into a state where I would seemingly experience past lives. The very first memory to surface was the medieval story with the burning. It turned out to be the Albigensian Crusade and therefore was concerned with the burning of heretics and not of witches. I was a soldier taking part in the massacres and later converted to the Cathar faith. I was captured and burnt. My story was not remotely like Guirdham's though his book may have influenced it. The process of bringing this memory to consciousness was painful emotionally, and following it I began a personal exploration that continued for nearly two years. In the process I learned to regress not only fellow therapists but a number of other friends who were also intent on learning its therapeutic benefits. For another two years I continued my own past-life remembering and did private experimentation with other colleagues.

Theory

Philosophical Hypotheses

1. The personality consists of conscious and unconscious areas. The ego is presumed to be the center of consciousness, while the self is the center that integrates both the conscious and the unconscious (Jung, 1953b).

2. The unconscious psyche is multiple: it is made up of many energy nodes or archetypes that may be conscious or unconscious. Aspects of the archetypes that are activated during our lives are called "feeling-toned complexes," following Jung (Jung, 1960b).

3. Complexes are experienced in three major ways:

   a. As *projections,* involving others in neurotic dramas and acting out ("games" in the language of Transactional Analysis) (Berne, 1964).

   b. As *somatizations,* such as aches, pains, musculature rigidity, organic dysfunction (Jung, 1960b).

   c. As *personifications,* such as dream and fantasy figures and subpersonalities (Hillman, 1975).

4. Every complex has six aspects to it. Therapy may begin with any one of these aspects, which are all available to consciousness when appropriate techniques are applied (Woolger, 1987):

   a. The *existential* aspect of the complex: problems bothering a person in his or her life *now.*

   b. The *biographical* aspect of a complex: infant, childhood, adolescent or more recent unfinished business.

    c. The *somatic* aspect of a complex: physical manifestations such as illnesses, chronic pains, rigid muscular patterns, breathing and sexual dysfunctions, etc.

    d. The *perinatal* aspect of a complex: all intrauterine experiences and birth trauma residues, following Grof (Grof, 1975).

    e. The *past-life* aspect of a complex: what in Hindu terminology are called the *samskaras* or psychic residues from previous lifetimes (Hariharananda, 1984).

    f. The *archetypal* aspect of a complex: these are the universal structural patterns which include mythic and religious motifs such as the sacred marriage, the hero quest, the scapegoat, the wise old person, the mystical union, etc. (These last three aspects, the perinatal, the past-life and the archetypal, are also *transpersonal* phenomena.)

5. No one aspect of a complex is either temporally prior to another aspect or psychologically more fundamental. From the viewpoint of the psyche each aspect mirrors all the other aspects according to holonomic principles (Grof, 1985).

6. The *past-life aspect* of a complex arises where there was an event producing pain, hurt, loss, grief, bitterness, etc., in that lifetime; this would be the psychological equivalent of karma. A complex may also arise from fresh events in the current lifetime, the *biographical aspect* of the complex, hence creating new karma.

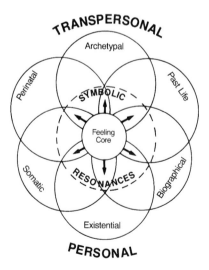

Figure 24.1   Every complex has six aspects to it, which are all available to consciousness.

7. There are three distinct levels of subtle energy: thought, feeling, and life energy which can be conceptualized or clairvoyantly perceived as subtle bodies or energy fields:

a. The *Mental Body*: This very broad energy field is the most subtle of the three and is the locus of all powerful mental contents or fixed thoughts. These thoughts may be conscious or unconscious and can radically influence an individual's overall life patterns or self-image. Such thoughts can be the residues of negative past-life experiences. They do not necessarily affect the lower bodies, but if they do, their influence is extremely strong.

b. The *Emotional Body* (sometimes called the astral body): This energy field is the locus of the *feeling* residues from past events, including, as with the mental body, past lives. These feeling residues may be sadness, rage, disappointment, apathy, etc. This energy level may be strongly affected by the negative thoughts from the mental body. The emotional body is more dense than the mental body. When its feeling contents become highly charged and are not released, the lack of release will affect the lower etheric energy body adversely.

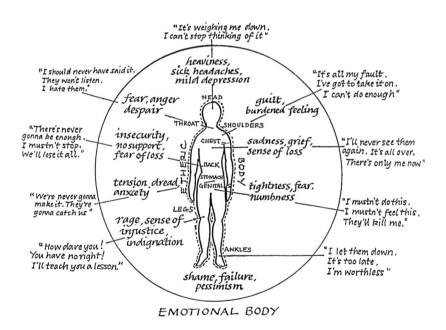

Figure 24.2   The Emotional Body is the locus of *feeling* residues from past events.

c. The *Etheric Body* (or energy field): This is the most dense of the three subtle bodies and is physically perceptible to many people as heat emanating from parts of the body. It is the field worked with in such healing practices as therapeutic touch and hands-on healing. Residues from physical traumas such as accidents and surgery, as well as past-life traumas, restrict release in this body. Repressed feeling from the emotional body will lodge at the etheric level to produce organic problems.

8. The imprinting of past-life traumas onto the body (violent death, mutilation, disease, rape, starvation, etc.) is transmitted at a subtle level to become part of the *somatic level* of a complex in the current life. Emotions associated with the physical trauma in the past life will also be imprinted along with the somatic residues.

9. Opposite types of past-life memories frequently occur sequentially. One memory simply constellates or brings forth its opposite, as a pair of psychic opposites (master-slave, parent-child, persecutor-victim, profligate-ascetic); they reverse into each other according to the principle of *enantiodromia* described by Heraclitus and by Jung in *Psychological Types* (Jung, 1971).

10. Integration of the opposites or wholeness is preferred to a goal of perfection or of "overcoming" negativity. Following Jung, the dark or shadow sides of the personality are to be integrated into consciousness and not banished or exorcised as if they are possessing entities (Jung, 1970).

11. Until a person can acquire a witness point outside patterns of opposites on all levels of the complex, he or she may experience a continuing spiral of lives of action, reaction, and counter-reaction that elude any resolution. The aim, therefore, is non-attachment to the complex.

12. Ultimately all opposites are to be united with the psyche, leading to a state of non-duality or oneness of being. This principle is directly derived from Advaita Vedanta, Mahayana Buddhism, and Tantrism:

> The Great Way is not difficult
> for those who have no preferences.
> When love and hate are both absent
> everything becomes clear and undisguised.
> Make the smallest distinction, however,
> and heaven and earth are set infinitely apart.
>
> (Sengstan, *hsin hsin ming*)

13. It is not considered important whether there is an individual soul that reincarnates or whether it is merely personality fragments or samskaras that are passed on to form new personalities; the work of psychotherapy is to deal with inherited residues, regardless of their origins. Since the archetype of reincarnation is traditionally a wheel, the search for a "first cause" of karma is seen as fruitless. Recourse could more profitably be made to archetypal doctrines of a fall from a higher state of being to a lower.

Psychotherapeutic Assumptions

1. Past-life therapy is like Gestalt and psychodrama in emphasizing the healing power of catharsis and re-enactment, but it goes deeper, following Jung and Grof, into ancestral dramas that seem to be imprinted on the psyche at birth, revealing unfinished business or karma derived from the multiple lives of the soul. Past-life therapy offers a highly concentrated depth process that can free up and transform the root metaphors or archetypal patterns that can govern our lives.

2. By using a straightforward induction process it is possible to arouse ancestral images from the collective unconscious and vividly recall detailed memories of other eras through an ego consciousness different from our present identity. This ego consciousness has all the characteristics of a full autonomous secondary personality or part-soul. This other self can be of either sex and complements the living ego psychologically in the same way as the familiar shadow, anima, and animus figures from dreams. The difference is that these secondary figures reveal, when asked, detailed and consistent historical biographies, the content of which is often mundane, rarely glamorous, but always full of situations where the subject's complexes are vividly enacted within the constraints of that historical period.

3. The regression technique expands the Jungian injunction to "stay with the image" by adding to it a metapsychological framework that allows more than one reality in which the individual's complexes can be played out imaginally. Moreover, it includes the crucial archetypal "rite of passage" experience of the death transition from one reality to another.

4. The past-life approach entails using a therapist to focus the story and ask questions "as if" it were a literal lifetime and not a fantasy, thus subjecting the story to the constraints of time, space, personal

identity, and history. It acknowledges, also, the limitations of the death experience and treats this, too, as a literal, bodily event when it occurs. The psyche responds with great facility to the "as if" of such suggestions and frequently gives quite spontaneous and surprising historical data.

5. Past-life remembering entails a deep projected identification with an inner or secondary personality. This involves imagination, as all remembering does, but in the fullest sense, so that the current personality must put itself in the place of the earlier one.

6. Past-life remembering brings our own inner cast of characters to the surface of consciousness with remarkable clarity, detail, and consistency, by allowing a drama to surface among the personified complexes.

7. To acknowledge and to experience the other in ourselves is the first step toward genuine psychological reflection and toward knowing for one's self that in deeper or fuller consciousness we are multiple beings, that we have many personalities within us.

8. It is essential for effective cathartic working through in past-life therapy that the subject fully re-experience the bodily sensations of the past-life trauma for emotional release to be complete. This means staying in the imaginal body of the other lifetime while being aware of this lifetime's body sensations as one remembers the other life.

   This overlay is the original cause of psychosomatic symptoms. Bringing the body image into a past-life scenario de-concretizes imprinting of the imaginal body and frees up energy for creative and spiritual purposes. Thus, in the sessions we move from the literal to the symbolic for release. Backache becomes a "broken back," becomes a discovery of new impetus for life. Migraine becomes a "head injury," becomes a freeing from burdensome and painful thoughts.

9. Remembering anger and other emotions and releasing them has a therapeutic effect but the more important release is at the level of understanding the symbolic nature of the complex.

10. There are three levels of experience in working with past lives:

    a. First is the reliving of past lives as though they were real. In this level there is real pain. Real executions are experienced, for example.

b. In the second level the symbolic or metaphorical content is explored. The pains in the neck, in the first level experienced as beheading, may indicate a feeling of being cut off from life. Feeling crippled and being starved for love may now be seen to be metaphors for our current life patterns.

c. There is also a third level which is symbolized by the well-known series of Zen ox-herding pictures where the person who has received enlightenment returns to the market place. Insight is here understood to be in the service of creative productivity and service. It does not exist as an end in itself.

11. When the patient has identified with the opposite personalities in past lives, either in the after-life review stage or at the end of a session when their symbolic meaning is explored, a major piece of the work is done. A shadow figure becomes integrated, a split is healed, a lost part of the soul is redeemed through love and acceptance.

Indications and Contraindications for Use

In considering the suitability of past-life therapy for different patients, I have come to regard it as a short-term intensive therapy that is best reserved for patients who have already made considerable headway in conventional psychotherapy. It is particularly helpful for someone who feels blocked in certain areas in ongoing therapy to have a new modality to help finish fragments of unfinished stories where the psyche seems, as it were, to be stuck in a groove. Many issues of abandonment and separation, for example, even though they have resisted conventional therapies at the infantile, primal, or birth trauma level, are seen to open up dramatically as soon as scenarios of infant death and abandonment from other lives are relived. Often a deep-seated phobia or a sexual blockage can be released cathartically and psychosomatically when scenarios of rape, torture, and violent death are relived by the secondary ego. Parental complexes reveal themselves in a different light within the power dynamics of entirely different family constellations in another age. Complexes surrounding issues of power or money take on another dimension when memories of famine, oppression, slavery, etc., come to consciousness.

Another group of subjects who respond well to past-life therapy are therapists of many orientations who wish to deepen their own process and to become more able to recognize fragments of past-life memories that may surface in their patients. Many therapists, bodyworkers, and healers frequently observe material from their patients that seems to be connected to past lives, perhaps a function of the strong stresses that are being borne by the collective unconscious at this very difficult period of humanity's growth. Past-life therapy can be considered a "therapist's therapy," since it requires openness and commitment of persons who are very advanced in their own psycho-spiritual development. Jung recognized that only the wounded heal, and the therapist needs constantly to work upon himself.

Whether the person is trying to move from a stuck position or trying to deepen generally, the work is best done within the context of some broader frame of ongoing therapy or spiritual discipline. Much of the material that emerges may take many months to integrate fully, and some of it may require a lifetime of meditation and reflection.

My regression work consists of a series of two-hour sessions. Most patients complete their work in from five to ten of these intensive experiences. The longer sessions give adequate time for various stages of the process, and so integration is actually a part of each session rather than being a separate process following regression experiences.

Problems responsive to past-life therapy include most of those commonly brought into psychotherapy:

1. *Anxieties, fears, phobias, and depression.* Insecurity and general fear of abandonment are often related to past-life memories of literal abandonment as a child, separation during a crisis or a war, being orphaned, sold into slavery, being left out to die in times of famine, etc. Phobias and irrational fears stem from every kind of trauma in a past life: death by fire, water, suffocation, animals, knives, insects, natural disasters. Depression and general low energy can result from past-life memories of loss of a loved one or parent, unfinished grieving, suicide memories, despair and rage as a result of war, massacre, deportation, etc.

2. *General behavior problems.* These include sado-masochism, a pattern of accidents, violence, and physical brutality, guilt and martyr complexes, eating disorders. Sado-masochistic problems are usually related to a past-life memory of torture, often with loss of consciousness, usually with sexual overtones. The pain and rage seem to perpetuate hatred and a desire to revenge oneself in the same way. Guilt and martyr complexes may stem from past-life memories of having directly killed loved ones or from feeling responsible for the deaths of others, as in a fire, human sacrifice of one's child, having ordered the deaths of others, etc. The entrenched thought is most often, "It's all my fault. I deserve this."

Accidents and violence are often a repetition of old battlefield memories from warriors' lives or from unfulfilled quests for power.

These can re-emerge as an *adolescent* neurosis in the current life-time because this age period is historically where many soldiers met deaths during other lifetimes. Eating disorders are often the rerunning of past-life memories of starvation, economic collapse, or inescapable poverty.

3. *Relationship difficulties.* Frequently problems of frigidity, impotence, and genital infections have past-life stories of rape, abuse, or torture behind them. Many incest and child abuse stories turn out to be reruns of old patterns where emotional release was blocked. Marital difficulties in general derive from past lives with the same mate in a different power class or sexual constellation: e.g., mistress, slave, prostitute, concubine relationship, often where the sex roles were reversed. Family struggles occur where there are old past-life scores to settle with parents, children, or siblings: betrayal, abuse of power, inheritance injustices, rivalry, etc. Most of the Freudian dynamics emerge here.

4. *Chronic physical ailments.* These often stem from the reliving of traumatic injuries or deaths incurred in past lives, especially trauma to the head, the limbs, and the back. Headaches may also relate to intolerable mental choices in other lives. Throat ailments, in addition to being caused by physical injury, may stem from verbal denunciations or unspoken thoughts. Neck aches commonly stem from hanging, strangling, or beheading. Reliving the past life often relieves the pain in these areas.

Past-life therapy does not work for everyone. To some the very idea of past lives is either intellectually bothersome or simply too alien, culturally speaking. But in addition to these cases in which the general attitude is the inhibiting factor, there are several categories of patients with whom I am wary about working at the past-life level.

1. I feel that regression therapy is contraindicated for patients with no therapeutic background because the material too easily feeds into a false literalism that upsets their ability to integrate the past lives as personified complexes. The ego becomes inflated or overcome with the glamor of the memories.

2. For some patients past-life work is too intensive, too overwhelming. They do not need to have the raw areas of their psyche exposed yet again. Instead, for them it is the personal factor in the therapeutic relationship that helps them rebuild their trust and confidence in life.

3. Others find imaging and working inwardly either too difficult or too dissociating. Even if they can remember past lives with ease, some patients do better to reinforce their connections with this life rather than to wander further off into another world.

4. Past-life therapy is not recommended for anyone seeking to confirm some prior metaphysical belief system. Usually it will provide experiences that are distressingly incompatible with fixed beliefs.

5. Past-life work is a moral problem that involves work with the entire ego-personality and requires a strong ego. Therefore, it is not indicated for anyone with psychiatric symptoms. In those with schizophrenic tendencies there is already a tendency for the psyche to become enamored, if not totally seduced, by the many sub-personalities within. It seems highly possible that many of the visions and voices that flood into the psyche of many a schizophrenic are indeed past-life fragments, but such a sufferer will be tempted to overidentify with such fragments and fall into a state of inflation. Such patients also attempt to turn readily available theories of reincarnation and metaphysics into grist for their own personal philosophical mills. Their wonderfully appealing theories often end up being nothing more than a huge and elaborate defense against the simple fact of being alive and present on this earth.

Induction

Preparation

Usually I start with an interview to explore any current or recurrent problems. In the first session I take a detailed personal history from birth through childhood up to the present, noting illnesses, accidents, or impairments such as deafness, the need for glasses, high blood pressure, etc. I ask if any emotional upheaval occurred shortly before or around the same period of life. This is my procedure for all patients, whether or not past-life work is to be undertaken. Usually I work with an individual patient for two hours.

Induction Techniques

After the initial interview to explore any current or recurrent problems, the patient is asked to stretch out and is gently guided through a relaxation exercise. In a relaxed state of light trance a number of simple guided imagery exercises or thematic phrases will lead easily and effortlessly into a past-life story where the patient is the protagonist. Sometimes I encourage the patient to focus on a recent memory or a person and start to say whatever comes to mind as if that situation were being confronted. I may feed them, Gestalt-wise, a phrase to sum up or intensify the affect, such as "I've had enough of this. Leave me alone!" Sometimes we may focus on a pain in the body, such as backache or stomach cramp, and allow images to emerge from that area.

As soon as images, words, and feelings start to intensify, I suggest they be followed into any story that emerges in this or another life. I tell my patient, "It doesn't matter whether you believe in reincarnation, or not. Simply follow the story as if it were real for the duration of the session." The unconscious mind automatically produces a story that reflects current life issues.

I do not use formal hypnosis in my practice, as I find it quite unnecessary for getting people into past-life memories. From years of dreamwork I can easily get patients to focus on their inner images, feelings, breath, or body sensations. No doubt this is trance inducing in the Ericksonian sense, but I do not offer it as such or claim it to be hypnosis. I would prefer to call it a kind of guided meditation.

Four Brief Inductions

1. Using Images

We may begin with a dream fragment, part of a waking dream, or guided fantasy, or even a subtle déjà vu feeling, such as, "It's as if I had lived in that castle."

> T: Find yourself back in the dream again with your eyes closed. Good. So you are standing on this bridge?
>
> P: Yes.
>
> T: What is the bridge made of?
>
> P: Seems to be stone.
>
> T: Are you crossing it, waiting, or what?
>
> P: I seem to be crossing into this town. There are people all around me.
>
> T: Describe them and their dress.
>
> P: They seem to be Oriental, maybe central Asia. Peasants.
>
> T: And you, how are you dressed?
>
> P: I'm wearing a long robe. Heavy material. A sort of cloth wrapped around my head, like a simple turban.
>
> T: How old are you, roughly? What kind of body do you have? Etc.

2. Using Words with Feeling States

If during the interview there is evidence that the presenting complaint is bringing up strong feelings, the patient can focus on those feelings and go immediately into the past life.

T: Give words to the feelings you have.

P: I'm so sad. I feel totally alone.

T: Say that again: "I feel totally alone."

P: I feel totally alone.

T: Keep repeating that until an image, or the sense of a story that belongs to these words, comes. Maybe you will find yourself in a story earlier in this life, or maybe you will find yourself in a past life. Etc.

(This approach derives from psychodrama and Gestalt and is influenced by the Netherton method. It also has elements of indirect suggestion derived from Ericksonian trance induction.)

The basic principle is to contact the image, whether it is easily available to consciousness, split off, or somaticized. Once the image is contacted, awareness should then be directed in such a way that affect is expressed *within the context of the image.* Once the image is enlivened by affect, a story is easy to elicit. This amounts to giving the unconscious full rein to express itself on all the levels necessary: symbolic, emotional, and somatic.

3. Using Feelings with Breathing and Posture

Sometimes the patient can only talk about feelings in a detached or split-off way. When this is the case, the direct use of words does not work. Breathing is used to activate the somatic level of the complex. Suggesting postures that mimic attitudes that normally belong to the feeling state also facilitates a connection.

T: I want you to breathe fairly fast, as though you are out of breath. Now clench your jaw and your fists. Good. Now start to let yourself feel really angry. Angry at anyone or anything. Good. Just keep going.

The patient may do this for five minutes or more. If it is uncomfortable, this is helpful, since the discomfort will usually trigger the split-off affect. Once the body seems fully involved in the exercise, the addition of words can be made by the patient.

P: I don't want to do it. Leave me alone. Don't you come near me.

T: Keep saying that until you seem to be saying it to someone.

P: It's a slavemaster. He's beating me. Etc.

4. Using Bodily Sensations and Pains

All somatic disturbances probably contain deeply repressed feelings that either symbolically express themselves or else mirror a past-life trauma. To access them requires taking sensate consciousness into the area of the disturbance. This may involve one of several approaches:

T: I want you to close your eyes and take your awareness right down into your hips, right into the painful areas. Good. What does it feel like down there?

P: It's as though I'm wedged, as though I can't move from side to side.

T: Does it feel like anything is constricting you from the outside, or is it held on the inside?

P: It feels like I'm stuck between something like rocks. I can't move.

T: Good. Repeat: "I can't move," and stay with the image of the rocks.

P: Oh, it hurts! I've been thrown down here. It's a crevasse! They wanted to kill me. Etc.

Or

P: My necks feels tight, I'm tensing my shoulders.

T: What are your shoulders trying to say, if they could speak?

P: No, don't do this, don't do this!

T: Exaggerate your shoulders—bring them up higher. Now say that again.

P: Don't do this. No, no, no! They're going to cut my head off. Etc.

Supportive and Deepening Techniques

With these relaxation and imaging techniques and the repetition of loaded phrases, the patient will soon find him/herself in a different body and personality, recounting the story quite dramatically *as that other self.* Then, following the principles of psychodrama, I encourage the reliving, in their fullness, of the major events and turning points of that other life, assuming that the catharsis and release will tend to come at these crucial points of conflict. Whatever arises, however confusing, incoherent, or bloody, I take the patient through to completion. If a particular story involves a violent death, I will ensure that it is fully relived at a physically conscious level on the same principle that has been used successfully with shell-shock victims, namely, that only a remembered trauma can be released.

If we read the stage directions to any play we find that everything is written in the present tense, linguistically speaking (e.g., "It is night. The old barn has a small lamp shining dimly above the door. The farmer and his son enter downstage. They are arguing fiercely.") In guiding a past-life session it is extremely helpful to follow this model of keeping the subject firmly in the present, having him recount the story as it happens, event by event, very much as if he or she were in the middle of a drama. Whenever the therapist poses a series of questions in any past tense, this acts as an unconscious trigger which can easily distance the subject from the events of the story so that imagery quickly loses it vividness.

Often during a past-life session, when a subject is being moved forward in time, he or she will overshoot large sections of the story and will spontaneously begin describing the events in the past as over and finished. More often than not, this indicates a strong resistance to reliving the painful core of the event. To counter this, the therapist simply needs to refocus in the present. A simple technique is to ask the patient to go forward to the next significant event. Then, when the habit of relating what is happening in the present is re-established, it is possible to go back to the traumatic event and remain in the present.

Sometimes the opposite resistance occurs. The subject does not want to go forward in time at all because the unconscious is already anticipating painful scenes. Here it is common for an earlier scene to be dragged out moment by moment almost in slow motion so that the subject appears frozen in time. To counter this kind of blocking, it is helpful to use connectors with the present tense, such as, "What do you find when you go up the stairs?" or "What happens when you go into battle?" An even more subtle linguistic way of dissolving this kind of block is to use the conditional tense, "And what would you find if you went upstairs?" or "What would happen if you rode into battle?" The reason these techniques work so effectively is that although the conscious mind interprets a hypothetical situation, the unconscious nevertheless produces an image. It is the image that encapsulates the feared event so that once in consciousness the scene can be worked with.

"How?" questions are among the most valuable for bringing the zoom lens right in close to the traumatic event. Therapists in training often avoid this type of question if a particularly gruesome scene of torture or mutilation is involved (usually the avoidance is because some past life of their own is unresolved on these issues). Nevertheless, in order for a trauma of this nature to be released fully at a psychosomatic level, the details of exactly how will have to be elicited by the therapist with all the precision of a surgeon removing shrapnel from the tissue of a bomb victim.

In addition to verbal cues, such as "how" questions and the use of the conditional tense or going backward or forward in time, I often find it effective to use rebirthing breathing and massage. Refocusing awareness on the bodily experience will frequently open up blocked or buried feeling states.

Processing

Psychotherapeutic and Transformational Techniques

I always insist that the past-life story be experienced fully in the body, not from the viewpoint of a detached observer. There will often be quite intense bodily convulsions and contortions that are part of the somatic process of spontaneous release—sweating, hot and cold flashes, cramping, temporary paralysis, sharp pains, and other sensations, such as numbness, trembling, shaking, or tingling. I tell patients that this is the release of blocked energy associated with an old trauma. The trauma at a physical level may be from birth, a past life, or a surgical operation in this life, and often all three. Whatever it is, the body is encouraged to express and let go of the shock and trauma. Although to an observer seeing a session for the first time this may seem frightening or even a little crazy, it has been my repeated and consistent finding that such release at a somatic as well as emotional level is absolutely crucial to the full healing process.

In general, if bodily sensations and their concomitant emotions are not fully experienced, the complex seeking to express itself will remain lodged in the body because of the imaginal imprinting. No amount of methodical understanding of the meaning or symbolic content or the "karmic" ramifications of the experience will help unless this bodily imagery is allowed to surface as well. On the other hand, if the physical and emotional levels of the trauma are released without a full understanding of their meaning, in whatever framework the subject is open to (psychological, karmic, spiritual), then the subject will tend to remain stuck in a meaningless repetition of the emotions of the past-life scenario and the recurrence of whatever psychosomatic symptoms exist.

In most sessions I attempt to complete the memory of a life story by taking the rememberer through the death of that particular personality. When a death agony is unfinished and is recorded in the imaginal body memory, it becomes re-imprinted in the current life body as if it were any other physical trauma. Also, going through the death brings a sense of completion and, more importantly, of detachment. The death transition is an opportunity to let go consciously of the obsessive and repetitive thoughts, feelings, or fears of that other self. In the after-death period there is usually valuable comparison of the themes of the other life with unresolved issues in this one. Every patient is encouraged to see the story as now finished, as a pattern that need not be repeated.

To start out, in guiding sessions it is necessary for the therapist to take all experiences as completely real—*as if they were literal experiences*. This is the first or *literal* level of past-life work. There can be no questioning of whether this is fantasy or imagination, only absolute respect for the psychic reality of the experience in order that this other life can be reconstituted and relived in all its fullness. The therapeutic "as if" provides an attitude of unconditional concern that is the basis for all successful therapy. Whatever embroidering, distortion, or reworking may occur, each patient's story needs to be heard totally without judgment or interpretation, fully encouraged to be told *as real*. Naturally, there will be painful, even shameful aspects of the self that may have to be faced. This is what is called shadow work—looking at unpleasant and often negative qualities in the self but accepting them as a moral challenge and not repressing them further.

To know the shadow when it has surfaced is a process of constant inner dialogue with this secondary consciousness. I am convinced that our past-life identifications with personalities whose lives have been far from illustrious or creative are a profoundly helpful extension of this process. Past-life remembering is possibly the most vivid and extensive way of facing the shadow—seeing and knowing the murderer, the prideful priest, the cruel soldier, the abandoning mother, the greedy merchant, the sadistic slave-owner—that we may carry in us. These are personifications of the darker but necessary parts of the psyche that all stand in need of acceptance, forgiveness, and redemption. Jung said that we do not become enlightened by imaging figures of light but by making the darkness conscious.

Not all shadows of the ego personality are dark, however. A person with a poor self-image—an abused wife, or a violent rapist—may find in their shadow personalities creative and fulfilled images of self. They may remember successful past lives as artists, leaders, innovators. The psyche compensates the ego personality as part of its tendency to seek balance and stability within the psyche as a whole. Persons who feel powerless or inadequate may be shown lives with extremely powerful political or religious status, power that may have been abused and for which the ego in this or another life feels a need for atonement.

At the first level of past-life work, in which we take all stories literally, it is as if there were a linear cause-and-effect sequence that operates within and across lives. Here the story behind the complex is seen as absolutely real, a product of hidden trauma that is in need of healing through being brought to consciousness. Such past-life complexes arise where there is an area of hurt or loss, of grief, anger, or bitterness. By bringing the traumatic incident to consciousness in all its horror and pain there is often a strong cathartic release and complete remission of symptoms.

However, for some patients this reliving is not enough. The causal, literal mode gets them unaccountably stuck. For such patients it is necessary to shift gears and go the second level of past-life work, which involves therapeutic and transformational approaches on a *symbolic* level. This second level is a total reversal from what is real to what is metaphorical. The aim here is to detach from the stuck place by deliteralizing the complex, by asking for meaning rather than catharsis. As the formulation goes in Sufi literature, "There is nothing in this world but is a symbol of something in the invisible world" (Al Ghazzali). By making use of the after-death state, it is possible to detach from the sub-personality or the complex and see what has been re-lived as more like a dream pregnant with meaning. By standing outside the whole story one can see exactly how one is caught up in the drama of one's complex, and that it *is* a drama. At a psychological level this use of a detached or "discarnate" perspective facilitates the development of what certain meditation disciplines call the witness point.

In effecting these integrating and transformational processes I have drawn from many modalities. Most important have been the contributions of Jung (1971), especially his view that all complexes manifest as sub-personalities that can be envisioned and dialogued with. Moreno's psychodrama has been extremely helpful because it aims for the catharsis of conflicting complexes (Fox, 1987). I have taken a great deal from the Gestalt theories of Fritz Perls because of their insistence on the contiguity of all complexes to awareness (Fagan and Shepherd, 1970), which was a reinforcement of similar ideas I had practiced in the Buddhist Vipassana meditation (Dhiryamsa, 1975). Finally, Reich's insight into bodily armoring and how the body holds attitudes at an organic level confirmed my impressions of how trauma is imprinted into the imaginal body and helped me work out techniques for releasing this (Boadella, 1973).

Integration into the Psychotherapeutic Process

Most of the work I do is short-term, intensive psychotherapy intended to relieve persistent symptoms that have resisted other therapies. Often it is enough to work only at the first or literal level of past-life remembering. Many patients, however, seek longer-term therapy in the broader perspective of Jungian analysis. For these patients a transition to the symbolic level is helped by dreamwork and by maintaining a certain attitude to the unconscious that Jung called "living the symbolic life." Such patients often return periodically for substantial periods of intensive work while they continue elsewhere in regular hourly therapy of a traditional Jungian sort.

For patients who have integrated a number of major complexes at the initial level and have begun to understand those "other selves" as part of the larger symbolic patterning of their inner and outer lives, a third level may emerge. This is what I call the *integrative level,* and it closely resembles what Jung called the individuation process—the process of becoming who one uniquely is. A subtle and almost indescribable movement of the recentering of the personality is experienced, which often brings spiritual openings and manifestations of the Greater Self in dreams and meditation. The human comedy of all lives past and present is then seen from a perspective of understanding, compassionate acceptance, and non-attachment. From this standpoint one begins to understand that there is in the end no real division between a literal and a symbolic world. There is simply the one world where "God is a sphere whose center is everywhere and whose circumference is nowhere." This is a point of view that would not have been possible without going through the first two stages.

When we can achieve such a consciousness, all is both one *and* many, and everything is in its place in the ever-transforming play of creation. We are called simply to know and embrace our part of this whole, to know that this part is perfect in and of itself. From such a perspective there is no reincarnation because the individual soul that is said to be reborn has no separate reality except as one of the billions of sparks of the greater mind. This is the realization that many of those who have had near-death experiences have reached. Regression therapy is challenging and many do not want to go all the way, even if it is possible, but however far any individual goes, the regression process can increase the level of freedom within which he functions.

Failures

Because past-life therapy does not work for everyone, it is important for the experienced clinician to be aware of categories of patients who have little chance of success in this modality (see contraindications). But even when patients for whom regression work is contraindicated are eliminated, there still can be failures. Three groups can be identified:

1. There are patients who are able to image other lives comfortably enough but do so rather flatly and with a certain rigidity in their bodies. They dutifully recover lifetimes and nothing changes. If the body is not alive and sensitive, the past lives that are reproduced will merely mirror back the emotional and somatic deadness of that patient with stories of characters like monks, hermits, outcasts, or others whose lives symbolized detachment, emptiness, and a reluctance to be embodied. In their case I usually prescribe a course of bodywork or some other kind of experiential work.

2. Stuckness and failure is sometimes a major metaphor in a patient's life, and therapy may be just another place to say, "There, I told you so." For instance, in some cases past-life therapy fails because a person is so deeply identified with a complex that neither in this life nor in any other does he seem willing to relinquish it. A man who had brutally killed in other lives and who had left his wife in this one when she was dying of cancer was so deeply entrenched in his guilt, being convinced that he deserved to suffer, that I could not bring him anywhere near the point of self-forgiveness. He had a negative inflation, seeing himself as "the greatest of all evil-doers," who felt he deserved to suffer to the end of time.

3. A third category of patient with whom I have limited success includes those who are psychologically healthy but who come to me

with all kinds of theories about their past lives, possibly derived from Cayce, Seth, Theosophy, or a psychic they have been to. It is not the origin of the patient's beliefs that I find myself suspicious of but a certain obsessiveness in their attachments to these beliefs. This kind of patient, a little like the schizophrenic, is already somewhat intoxicated, if not quite inflated, by some secret and glamorous fantasies about his or her past lives. *It is the ego that seeks to benefit, not the personality as a whole.* Past-life stories and personalities that emerge in the regression process are often far from flattering to the ego of the experiencer and produce characters that are rarely illustrious or famous. Because of this the regression experience is seen by the patient as a failure, even though the pattern which is exposed might be maximally helpful if it could be observed and transformed.

Cases

In all my past-life therapy work I aim to clear negative samskaras or past-life patterning at three levels: mental, emotional, and physical. There is not particular order to this process, but the key principle is that the client must fully experience the bodily sensations as well as the emotions until they are completely released. In addition to this, full mental understanding of the karmic or symbolic meaning of the patterns must occur or else the symptoms will simply recur in physical and/or emotional form. Directing the patient to relive a seeming past-life story *in the body of the past-life personality* amounts to enabling the patient to become aware of the subtle body of the sub-personality as if it were his or her present body.

Being aware of one's previous life through the subtle body is a two-pronged process. Staying in one's body has the dual meaning of (1) staying in the imaginal body of the other lifetime and (2) being aware of this lifetime's body sensations as you remember the other life. Therapy has to be sensitive to this overlay, since it is the cause of psychosomatic symptoms. Bringing the body image into a past-life scenario de-concretizes the unconscious imprinting of the subtle body and frees up libido (or orgone energy, or chi, or prana) for creative and spiritual purposes.

CASE 1. ARTHRITIS-LIKE SYMPTOMS FROM A BOMB EXPLOSION
The first case will illustrate the necessity of getting into the actual experience of trauma in the body and show techniques used to accomplish this. It will also illustrate the importance of working both on the level of bodily sensation and at the same time on the metaphorical level. This is a situation where a young woman recovered the memory of a bomb explosion. In her current life the physical feature that was

most salient was the arthritis-like pain in her arms and legs that was the expression of the particular stage of lupus erythematosus in which she was at that time. A colleague of mine who is both a Jungian analyst and a physician with considerable knowledge of alternative healing practices, was treating her and was somewhat pessimistic about her chance of recovery. When I met her, the slow spread of infirmity through her limbs had already become a serious threat to the pursuit of her career. I worked directly from her feeling of anxiety about this.

> T: Close your eyes and simply find yourself at any part that is vivid to you.
> P: [The whole of her body is trembling violently and tears well up in her eyes.]
> T: Where are you?
> P: I don't know. I think I've died. I know I've died. I don't know what happened.
> T: Repeat those last words.
> P: I don't know what happened.
> T: What went wrong?
> P: [Her body begins to twitch and convulse and she writhes from side to side.] I know what went wrong. The bomb went off too soon. I'm dying. Oh, the pain. Oh! Oh! My limbs . . . it's black. I'm not there.

I recognized that we were in a death experience of some violence in which, as the victim of a bomb, she kept losing consciousness. From the way her body reacted it appeared that, whoever the past-life personality was, he or she was horribly maimed. From many such experiences I knew that the body needs to reproduce the whole of the event for it to be released. Painful as it is, the victim must not become unconscious in her memory.

> T: Go back and relive the events leading up to the explosion.
> P: I'm with a group of young men. I'm about nineteen, a man. It's Russia. We're going to kill them. We hate them. They killed my father! *They killed my father!* Several of our group has been killed but we go on fighting. No more of this tyranny. It's time to fight back.
> T: What are you doing now?
> P: We're carrying bombs. They're for those bastards (soldiers) who killed my father.
> T: Go forward and tell me what happens.
> P: It's all black. I'm not there. I don't know where I am. But my body hurts. Oh! Oh!

Edith continued to groan as her body writhed from side to side in a state of utter terror, agony, and confusion. Was she dead? I kept urging her to get an impression of the situation, though she was in tears and resisting.

T: Go back and tell me how you died.

P: I'm looking down from outside my body. Oh, my God! It has no arms and legs. There's been an explosion. It's still moving.

T: Go back inside your body and tell me exactly how it feels.

P: I'm dying, lying here on the street. The pain is terrible. No arms, no legs . . . [Cries.] . . . Now I'm dead. No more movement. I'm leaving my body.

T: Be aware of your last words as you are dying and go to the point where your heart finally stops beating.

P: My arms and legs will never work again. Oh, no!

At this point Edith wept bitterly and I knew the possibility that her arms and legs would never work again lay behind her fear of progressive deterioration from the lupus. I guided her to becoming precisely aware of the last few seconds of being in that maimed body.

T: Were there any other thoughts you had been holding in your arms and legs before you left them?

P: Yes. I wanted to kill them. I wanted them to suffer like my father. [Crying.] But now I'm hurting.

T: Are you willing to let go of your anger at them?

P: Yes.

T: So let go of the anger and let go of all the pain and tell me when you are finally out of your body.

Edith took a deep breath and her body went limp. Then, to reinforce her awareness of what had happened, I proposed verbal affirmations to counter all the pain and negativity.

T: Make this affirmation: "These arms and legs are strong and healthy and can work for me perfectly."

Like most victims of explosions, the young anarchist had gone out of his body even though he was not yet dead. The death agony had been unfinished and was recorded in the imaginal body memory of the anarchist life that had, so it would seem, been imprinted on the young woman's body in this lifetime as part of the lupus symptoms of pain in her joints.

Letting go of the physical memories also entailed for her letting go of the vengeful feelings she (he) had carried as the young anarchist, which had symbolically turned against her as "explosive" rage. What is remarkable is that after this one session all the arthritis-like symptoms disappeared. Her doctor, who was present at the session, attests that the symptoms have not returned over two years later. In the case of this subject, it was just as essential for her to understand the symbolic meaning of the explosion as rage that had backfired against her in that lifetime, as to re-experience the death. But both were necessary for healing to occur.

CASE 2. DEATH IN A GAS CHAMBER

Not being in the body is another version of the defense we described earlier as the temporal distancing a subject will perform to avoid painful emotions. Such subjects have to be taken backward or forward to the crucial existential moment of the trauma and then drawn fully into the body, even to the extent of exaggerating the imaginal psychodrama. An illustration of this was a young woman who described a previous life when, as a twelve-year-old girl, she had been killed in a Nazi gas chamber.

This patient's initial account, in her first session, of her deportation to a concentration camp and subsequent death, though detailed, was extremely flat, detached, without catharsis. Painful as it was, we decided to re-run the memory, this time focusing both dramatically and physically.

> T: Where are you now?
> P: We're in a line outside this building. I'm no longer with my mother.
> T: What exactly are you doing?
> P: I'm holding the hand of this older woman.
> T: How do you feel?
> P: Terrible!
> T: Do you cry?
> P: No, I can't.
> T: All right. Then breathe very deeply and let any feelings you may be holding back come to the surface. [Coaches breathing.]
> P: [Breathes deeply.] I don't want to go in there [trembles, heaves].
> T: Say that louder.
> P: I don't want to go in there! [Sobs loudly.]

From then on a flood of emotion emerged and she described in detail the gassing: how it tasted, smelled, and which parts of the body it affected. For several minutes she went through the convulsions of choking, vomiting, and doubling up as she relived her death. By the end of the session, she had released so much fear, grief, and despair, as well as physical pain, that her chest had opened up to a much fuller pattern of breathing, similar to the release experienced in Reichian therapy and rebirthing. Later she reported that a deep-seated depression, which had affected most of her life, was gone and that her breathing was permanently changed. In her case, there had been no particular indication of the bodily blocks. Her breathing had been shallow, it was true, but not exceptionally so, so the clue to the block was the lack of affect.

CASE 3. SUICIDE

There are many cases where the body images advertise "trauma" very loudly, and when they do, direct intervention may be appropriate. An example of this is a woman of thirty-four, a professional artist, who sought out therapy to deal with a confused bag of complaints about her marriage, about the bad feelings she had about her mother, from whom she had moved, and her notion that it was all connected to a fragment she had glimpsed of a past life as a painter in Holland. As she told her story I was struck by how rigid and tense her shoulders were. It as as though they were held two or three inches higher than necessary.

During the relaxation part of my induction procedure she had great difficulty in letting go, so I offered to massage her neck and shoulders. She agreed, and I worked on the tight trapezius muscle and on her neck. Very soon she slipped into a male life as an impoverished Dutch painter during the seventeenth century. The painter had a wife and a very young baby whom he could barely support. In his obsession with finishing a certain painting he severely neglected both wife and baby, even when the baby became sick. To his horror, the baby grew worse and died and his embittered wife deserted him. The key scene in our work was as follows:

> T: Where are you now?
> P: I'm wandering along the canals. I can't find my wife. She's left me for good.
> T: Where do you go now?
> P: I think, back to the house. Oh, no! I don't want to go back there. [Her shoulders begin to tense up noticeably.]
> T: Breathe deeply and go back to the house and see what happens.

At this point the young woman, who had been lying on the couch, shot up to a sitting position, grabbed her neck, and began to scream.

T: What has happened?
P: Oh, God! I hanged myself. [Sobs deeply.]

For a short while we worked on letting go of the death experience and the emotions connected with the loss of wife and child. But this was not all. When asked to move forward she spontaneously found herself re-experiencing her birth in this life with the cord wrapped around her neck.

Full understanding came moments later when, as a baby, she looked up to her mother, having survived the second trauma.

P: I know why I'm here.
T: Why are you here?
P: To be close to my mother [sobs]. I know who she is now.
T: Tell me who she is.
P: She's the baby who died. I see that I've been trying to make it up to her all these years.

The guilt about the neglect and the death of the baby had been lodged, as an imaginal imprint, at the moment of the Dutch painter's remorseful suicide. It was reinforced in the birth trauma and carried in her body language to the present day. Also carried forward were her feelings about the baby, and these had colored her feelings about her mother. In subsequent sessions she was able to release her feelings of guilt and despair and felt enormous pressure taken off her marriage, to say nothing of how her shoulders noticeably dropped a couple of inches!

CASE 4. ORIGIN OF ULCERATIVE COLITIS

As more and more therapists are discovering, there are all kinds of neurotic complaints of both an emotional and a physical nature that simply refuse to be resolved through exploring infantile stories, no matter how far back we trace them. Many children are obviously born fearful, depressed, rage-filled, withdrawn, unable to eat (i.e., starving), desensitized, and so on. It is precisely in such cases that past-life exploration is proving particularly effective, now that we are free to ask the very questions that Freudianism and the *tabula rasa* doctrine of development have proscribed for so long.

Every part of the body, it would seem, has in one person or another revealed some old accident or wound. Past-life traumas always have a *specific* and *not a general* relationship to the current physical problem. Not all migraines derive from head wounds or all throat problems from strangling. A similar throat complaint in several people may carry quite different stories; in one it may be a death from a beheading, in another, a choking death, while someone else may remember having been hanged. In different people a painful chest or pains in the heart region will bring up memory traces of all kinds of stabbings, gun wounds, lances, arrows, shrapnel, etc. Sore legs and arms remember being broken in accidents or war, crushed by fallen trees, shattered by torture or crucifixion or the rack, or else ripped off by wild animals. A weak or sensitive belly area may recall cuts, slashings, and disembowelings, or else starvation or poisoning. Sensitive feet and hands have in past lives been subjected to every kind of accident and mutilation, to say nothing of performing horrible acts on others.

A young woman, whom I will call Heather, had suffered since early adolescence from ulcerative colitis. Naturally, every kind of dietary therapy had been tried and in more recent years, psychotherapy. Her psychotherapist, who referred her to me, admitted that she could find no cause of anxiety to account for the ulcers in Heather's present life, despite many months of probing, so we agreed to try a past-life session.

The story that immediately surfaced took us to Holland during World War II at the time of the Nazi invasion. Heather found herself an eight-year-old girl in a Jewish family living in the Jewish neighborhood of a small Dutch town. In the first scene to surface she was happily helping her mother bake bread when the sounds of explosions reached their ears. The Nazis were systematically blowing up and setting fire to the terraced houses to "flush out" the inhabitants onto the streets. The mother, panicking, pushed the children onto the street, telling them to run. The street was full of townspeople running in all directions. There were armored cars and jeeps following them, and everywhere the sound of gunfire.

The little girl ran down an alleyway, thinking it to be safe, and watched for a time from behind a wall, seeing some neighbors and friends shot, but mostly rounded up by the Nazis. Fleeing farther from the smoke and explosions, she turned a corner and almost ran into a van commandeered by the soldiers. They caught her and shoved her into the back with other captives.

Later, she and the others were herded out and lined up in front of trenches that had been dug as mass graves. Standing and watching lines of people being machine-gunned as she awaited her turn, she reported that her stomach was totally knotted in terror. Eventually her turn came and she fell back, shot, onto a pile of dead and dying victims. She didn't die immediately; other bodies fell on top of her, and she finally died of suffocation and loss of blood. Her stomach remained knotted in terror throughout this appalling ordeal. My approach during our session was to direct her to breathe deeply and to let go of all the fear and anguish as much as possible. Given this permission she broke into convulsive sobbing, screaming, and keening. As the young Jewish girl she had died, so it seemed, unable to express the terrible shock of losing her parents, seeing mass slaughter, and facing her own premature death. Phrases such as, "I'll never see them again," "Help me!" "I can't get away," "It's too late," surfaced spontaneously and her body went through violent convulsions and dry vomiting for a while.

When it was all over Heather was exhausted and depleted, yet she felt unburdened of a fear she had always dimly sensed and that she now understood. Her stomach condition improved radically after this and a couple of follow-up sessions.

The important principle that may be gleaned from this highly condensed description is that there is a descending order of influence from higher to lower among the three subtle bodies. In Heather's case the following pattern can be discerned:

1. The unconscious thought: "I am in danger" (mental level) makes Heather feel perpetually anxious (emotional level);
2. Heather's perpetual anxiety (emotional level) creates constant tension in her abdominal region (etheric level);
3. The constant tension in Heather's abdomen (etheric level) affects the gastro-intestinal (somatic) system to produce ulcers.

In many cases, once we shift our focus away from supposed early childhood traumas in this life and give the deeper unconscious permission to express itself, we find that, as in this case, the presenting symptom seems to be derived from a past-life memory. There had been no event in Heather's current life experience remotely severe enough to induce fear symptoms as heavily somaticized as ulcers; in fact her complaint was quite out of proportion to the relatively untroubled course of her current life. Yet immediately after the past-life story of the Dutch Jewish girl emerged, we found traumatic images that were entirely consistent with her symptoms.

CASE 5. STAGE FRIGHT

The subject, Mike, was a social worker who suffered terrible panic attacks every time he had to make any kind of presentation to his colleagues at meetings. About an hour before the appointed time of a meeting he would become uncontrollably nervous. His chest would tighten, his breathing would become constricted, and he would experience severe heart palpitations. In Mike's case I did not need to encourage him to be aware of his body as he described his problem: "My palms are starting to sweat as I talk about it," he said. He also described his tight chest and stomach.

Were these reactions new? By no means. Mike recognized them from childhood, where he remembered a painful experience at a talent show in which he had been forced to perform. The overriding feelings then as now were of fear and shame. And yet, neither as a child nor as an adult could he find any memory of anyone actually doing anything to humiliate or shame him.

Here is a condensed extract of how our exploration of these feelings and somatic reactions proceeded:

T: So what does it feel like every time you go into one of your staff meetings?

P: Terrible panic. I feel like I'm gonna die. [Touches his chest.] Everything feels like it's gonna shut down. I can feel my heart beating like crazy when I talk about it now.

T: So what thoughts go with this? You're clearly in a huge conflict.

P: I've got to do it, but I don't wanna do it. Oh, my God! No! How do I get out of it? [His stomach seems to be tensing up and his arms are becoming rigid.]

T: What does your stomach want to say?

P: I don't want to do it. How do I get out of this? Oh God! It's this terrible sinking feeling. My chest is all tight and my stomach feels like it's gonna drop out.

T: Stay with the feelings and what your stomach wants to say and just follow it.

P: I don't want to. I want to be left alone. Please don't make me! No, not in front of them all! I'm trapped. I can't get out of it. [He is noticeably writhing from side to side now.]

T: Let yourself go into any other life story these words apply to.

P: I get a church. And a crowd. Yes, lots of people. Oh no! I don't want to. Don't make me!

T: Say that to them, not to me. Stay with the images and your body.

P: It's terrible, I'm afraid. I'm not gonna show my fear. They're making me go there. Oh help! My hands and neck! They're really hurting.

T: What seems to be happening to you?

P: They've got my wrists bound behind me. Something touching my face. I can't see. Now it's my neck. Oh help! They're gonna hang me!

> T: I want you to go all the way through it until it's over. The pain will pass, but it needs to be released. Keep saying exactly what you feel as it happens.

Mike's breathing became intense as he lay writhing on my mattress. He reported tingling in his hands and feet and increasing panic in his stomach. His struggle increased until the end. He was obviously fighting the execution all the way. I encouraged him to do so, since this was where all his tension was locked up.

> P: I can't get out of it. I'm really stuck now. I don't wanna be part of this, but there's no way out. [There are clearly elements of birth trauma in this part of the story.]
>
> T: What is your stomach saying?
>
> P: I don't wanna do this. I don't wanna do this! I hate this. I can't get out of it. I wanna leave.

Mike continued his death struggle as the hanged man for some while. He experienced strong electrical tingling in his hands, face, neck, chest, and stomach. He kicked violently, reproducing the desperate attempts to touch the earth that his former self had been deprived of doing. A comprehensive etheric release took place as the parts of the body that had held the subtle body imprint of the trauma relived the event. Finally, his body went limp as he reached the moment of the past-life death. He wept, his chest heaving: "There was nothing I could do." There was more release and opening in his chest. His breathing expanded considerably when the trauma was past.

We took as long as he needed for the energy release to be complete and for all the feelings to be expressed and verbalized. Then we went back to the events that led up to the hanging. Mike remembered himself as an adolescent boy who had robbed a man and then in a tussle knifed him. He was caught by the villagers and brought to trial, where he was condemned to death by hanging.

Mike remembered the jail cell, his huge public humiliation, and above all the sense of doom and powerlessness that sat in his chest and stomach in the last hours before he was taken to the scaffold. Needless to say, as an adolescent in this story, his life force was very strong, which was mirrored in his physical resistance to dying. This was why I encouraged him physically to express all aspects of the struggle, to maximize the etheric release, aspects of which were clearly locked into his chest and stomach in the present lifetime.

The remainder of our work consisted of helping him dissociate the old trauma from its current-life parallels. I suggested affirmations such as: "I am on the earth. I am fully in charge [for his stomach]. I am proud of my work. There is nothing to be ashamed of any longer."

One interesting corollary to his experience was that Mike then remembered that he had several times stolen unimportant things as a child, always feeling deeply ashamed and unworthy when he was caught. He realized how he had been unconsciously replaying the old story, testing to see if stealing would be as fatal as it had been in the past life. He did not, until now, connect it to his public speaking anxiety.

In later sessions Mike reported almost total absence of panic feelings at meetings and a sense of greatly increased vitality and power in his life in general. The trapped and humiliated adolescent in him had been freed and was now contributing energy to his life instead of draining it.

CASE 6. SYMBOLIC BODY TRAUMA

There are many cases where the transformational and therapeutic aspect lies in the symbolic handling of the materials. In this sort of work, guides, who are representatives of a transcendent function, may intervene to assist in helping the person in regression to achieve the witness point. Such was the situation with a young man, a teacher, who had been experiencing an almost paralyzing stage fright whenever he lectured to audiences larger than a small class. A seemingly unrelated body problem was poor circulation in his hands and feet and constant stiff necks.

In a past-life session he relived a life as an influential wandering teacher in the Middle East, a man who had attracted such large crowds that he and his following threatened to disrupt the stability of a small caliphate. He was arrested and martyred, first by having his hands and feet cut off, then by being left crucified overnight on a gibbet, and finally by being beheaded in the morning.

For many months following this, he experienced an agonizing catharsis during massage sessions whenever his hands, feet, or neck were touched. But when he again went through the death in that lifetime, this remarkable experience occurred. He floated above the earth and was met by a loving group of guides, a phenomenon quite common in the after-death state. He asked these guides why he had died so horribly. The answer came back immediately:

You lost your hands because you were out of touch with the people.
You lost your feet because you were off the earth.
You lost your head because it was too puffed up with knowledge.

These words struck such deep chords within him that he spent nearly a year meditating on them. When he came to a resolution, synchronistically he was offered a job lecturing to a large audience and found that his stage fright had now disappeared. Gradually, also, as the circulation in his hands and feet returned, he began to show some talents as a healer.

In his case the breakthrough came in the after-death state when he was able to stand outside, detach from the sub-personality or the complex he had been dramatically reliving, and see the whole experience more as a story, a dream play pregnant with meaning. It is similar to a technique used in psychodrama where the protagonist appoints substitutes to play himself and all his alter-egos. By standing outside the whole story this teacher was able to see exactly how he was caught up in the drama of his complex and that it *was* a drama. In other words, he had reached the witness point. Guides, or a higher sub-personality, however one wishes to understand it, had given him wisdom and insight. In this past life was evidenced the polarization of the teacher's complex: it demonstrated how spiritual pride had constellated its opposite in an utterly humiliating death, in this instance within that same lifetime.

25

A Shamanic Christian Approach in Psychotherapy

Donald Evans

Donald Evans states that the energies and presences in shamanic spirituality are real—as real as people, trees and stars—and these include angels, discarnate spirits, and various cosmic energies. Although he feels that non-shamanic spirituality can be at least as helpful as the shamanic, it is clear that for those who can access and successfully work within this dimension an extra tool is available to help some of our patients. He feels that by "coming out of the closet" he may inspire some other transpersonal therapists to be more open about their work in this area and be less frightened about the potential of disapproval from colleagues. I noted that at a plenary session during a recent annual American Psychiatric Association meeting, Dr. M. Scott Peck spoke openly of evil entities and exorcism as being important issues in certain situations that therapists encounter.

Evans does not see spirituality as leading to the transcendence of bodily-emotional life, but rather "to let angels and God live in us and as us." I believe that this is quite similar to the Jewish mystical tradition and to the ten ox-herding stories of the Zen Buddhist tradition. The idea of being "born again" is used by Evans as a way of revisiting infancy (e.g., as shown by Grof, involving some experiential re-enactment of one's birth) in order to re-integrate it within the adult personality which can then more readily embody the divine.

In addition to many of the traditional psychotherapy approaches (Freudian, Jungian, Gestalt), Evans adds meditation which includes not only techniques of concentration and emptying of consciousness, but also awakening shamanistic awareness of spirit. Here, too, meditation is grounded in the emotional and bodily feelings so that ultimately meditation and psychotherapy can be helpful to each other.

Threshold Relaxation (TR) is a technique that Evans presents in great detail in a separate appendix at the end of the chapter and is one of his most valuable methods in working with the bodily-emotional and spiritual aspects of his clients. He emphasizes that "what the therapist personally brings or fails to bring to the application [of TR] matters greatly."

The second half of the chapter focuses on Evans' "Seven Principles for Shamanic Psychotherapy" and provides us with a variety of clinical vignettes. His principles cover: the awareness of our resistance to positive spiritual experiences; the integration of spirituality and sexuality; the awareness of our oneness with every creature in the universe; how bodily-energetic processes may need to occur, leading to a change of one's own identity; cutting ties with family members psychically; and, finally, one of the most esoteric ideas presented in this chapter—that demonic evil exists and requires an appropriate response.

Evans correctly cautions us that in order to safely work with Shamanic Psychotherapy, one should have "relevant experience."

IF YOU ARE NEITHER a shaman nor a Christian, this chapter may nevertheless be of considerable interest to you, provided that you are involved in a psychotherapeutic process that is open to a spiritual dimension. I do need to begin, however, with some indication of my own particular approach, explaining why in some respects it can be called "shamanic" and "Christian." And toward the end of the chapter I will return to distinctively shamanic and Christian themes.

A Shamanic Approach

First, "shamanic." In my own personal experience, a shamanic approach to psychotherapy involves drawing on spiritual energies and spiritual presences from many different traditions, especially Hindu, Buddhist, Christian, and Native American. These came to me spontaneously in relation to my ongoing bodily-emotional-spiritual process, though occasionally I would deliberately open up to an energy or presence which I sensed in another human being. Similarly for my clients, such awareness usually arises spontaneously, especially during relaxation or meditation, though occasionally, with their consent, I try to help them resonate with an energy or presence that is already accessible to me. Sometimes a client will, in effect, initiate me into a new awareness, but usually what comes spontaneously to them is not new to me, though the coming is frequently a surprise not only to the client but also to me. Some clients become shamans, able to follow their own intuitions in this spiritual dimension as they continue by themselves. Some, however, have minimal shamanic experience, and their meditative practice contributes to their process mainly in helping them feel safely centered and grounded, enjoying an inner equanimity to which they can return again and again as turbulent emotions and painful memories arise. This non-shamanic spirituality can be at least as helpful as the shamanic.

The spiritual energies and spiritual presences in shamanic spirituality are real. It is true that our experience of them is shaped by symbolic frameworks of words and images which we bring to them. It is also true that our repressed emotional conflicts distort our awareness of them, just as they distort our awareness of our lover, our boss, or ourselves. We are in contact, nevertheless, with independent realities which exist outside our minds, like people and trees and stars. Angels and discarnate spirits and various cosmic energies would continue to exist if humankind disappeared. They are distinguishable, though sometimes not easily, from archetypes and other powerful symbols which human beings create and sustain within their minds. The metaphysical reality of spiritual energies and spiritual presences can be defended philosophically against the prevailing skepticism of our culture. In *Spirituality and Human Nature* (Evans, 1993, ch. 2, 11), I showed that this skepticism arises from assumptions that can be questioned. I have an impression that many transpersonal therapists actually experience and work with such spiritual realities on occasion, but do not acknowledge this publicly lest they lose credibility with their colleagues. Perhaps my philosophical argument and my own "coming out of the closet" in this matter will encourage them in their work!

A Christian Approach

Indwelling Christ

I am a Christian shaman, and this in three respects. First, although I have been graciously helped in my own personal process by many presences from many traditions, the indwelling presence of Jesus Christ has been central. I fully accept, however, that for many clients other spiritual presences are either already paramount or will become so as they become more open spiritually. For example, a Hindu may already have a keen awareness of Shiva or Krishna. On the other hand, a nominal Buddhist or Christian may spontaneously be drawn into awareness of a discarnate Native American elder, or a secular Jew may have an encounter with Jesus (all actual examples).

This-worldly, Incarnational Spirituality

A second way in which my approach is Christian is in its emphasis on a this-worldly, incarnational spirituality. This emphasis can influence what kind of process I am willing to facilitate. Sometimes a person comes to me, moved either by personal predilections or by an inherited spiritualistic tradition, wanting to learn how to transcend bodily-emotional life, identify him/herself as pure spirit, and merge with the Ultimate, thereby anticipating in this life a future life after death. If it turns out that the person is deeply committed to this, I explain why I cannot in good conscience work with him/her, for it would be difficult not to be trying to dissuade him/her. What I want to try to facilitate is a conscious embodiment of spirit and of the Ultimate. This process can involve intensely spiritual states and even a time of mystical pure consciousness, but the essential task is to allow such awareness to penetrate to every living cell in the body. We are not here on earth so as to become angels and to disappear into God. *We are here to let angels and God live in us and as us.*

I am not claiming that embodiment of spiritual and mystical awareness is an exclusively Christian emphasis. I have observed something similar for example, in Aurobindo's Westernized Hinduism, in some Native American spirituality, and in some Tibetan or Zen Buddhism. Nor can I even claim that a thorough incarnational emphasis has been central in Christian contemplative tradition, for it has included much of the other-worldly, body-transcending aspiration which I have rejected. For example, we can learn much from St. Francis and St. Clare, but not how the indwelling Christ can become present in bodily-passionate sexual love—surely a test case for embodiment of spirituality.[1] Nevertheless, no other great religion emphasizes the centrality of the process of divine embodiment: God became human in Jesus, and this can happen to us. (Eastern Orthodoxy is very explicit about this "divinization" of the human, though, again, the physical body and sexuality do not seem to be fully included.[2])

Born Again

A third way in which my approach is Christian, though not exclusively Christian, is in its understanding of the requirements that we must be "born again." For me this conveys two crucial insights. First, as a *metaphor* it implies that ever since we came into the world our orientation has been distorted. We have from the very beginning been caught up in, and consenting to, an inbuilt proneness towards a path away from God. We need somehow to start out again, this time filled and motivated by the Spirit, replacing the foundations laid in the first birth. Then our inherently good tendencies, ourselves as the "image of God," can come into their own, moving us on the true path.

The second insight is that the call to be born again is not only metaphorical but also, in a sense, *literal*. As Grof (1975, 1985) has shown, the second, spiritual birth can involve some experiential re-enactment of the first birth, remembering one's movement down the birth canal, correcting what went wrong not only physically but also emotionally and spiritually. Also, the first year of life has to be re-experienced and revised, for it involved coming into the world as a consciously separate mental ego. In a process which Washburn calls, "regression in the service of transcendence" (1995, p. 21),[3] we regain an intimacy with God and with ourselves, and we integrate this with the individual mental ego which had blocked such intimacy. As Wordsworth said, "Heaven lies about us in our infancy" and "Trailing clouds of glory do we come."[4] We can reclaim this awareness while shedding our resistance to it and yet paradoxically retaining in a new way our sense of ourselves as distinct individuals. Individually, though not historically, we have "fallen" from an innocent, paradisal state, shutting ourselves out from it. But we can and must return, not to stay there, but to bring awareness of it into our adult lives.

Although my own version of the "born again" insights is no doubt influenced by my own Christian heritage, similar versions are held by non-Christians, and the theme is appropriately contrasted with some "Eastern" outlooks where the dominant metaphor is not being born again but rather awakening from a dream, an awakening that replaces illusion with reality and ignorance with enlightenment. According to such "Eastern" accounts, infancy is a primitive, material foundation on which human development builds, to which there is no point in returning. And eventually, like all non-ultimate states and stages, it can and should be set aside as useless scaffolding when one moves into the fully transcendent spiritual state (perhaps voluntarily re-incarnating so as to help others move into this state). In contrast with this, a born-again approach insists that infancy must be revisited, revised, and then re-integrated in an essentially new way within one's adult personality—which can then gradually embody the divine. (This brings us again to the theme of full incarnation, which is the goal.)

Psychotherapy and Meditation

My openness to the eclectic shamanistic experiences and my convictions concerning embodiment and being born again no doubt influence what I encourage and receive in clients, so I reveal where I am coming from to them when this seems appropriate, sometimes even in a first session. Typically, however, my concern in a first session is that in a very general way the client be open to *both emotional and spiritual* elements in his/her process. In my own personal experience, bodily-emotional and spiritual processes have been intimately interrelated. Psychotherapy has been my main access to the bodily-emotional and meditation to the spiritual. I am convinced that at the deepest level of each process the other process is involved. When I speak of *"meditation"* I am referring to a wide variety of practices, including the following:

1. *concentration* on the breath, with or without mantra, with eyes open or eyes shut;

2. *emptying of consciousness,* letting go of all its contents as one sinks into the Mystery;

3. *awakening awareness of spirit,* by means of body postures/movement, chanting through the chakras, or visualizing light with eyes shut;

4. *becoming receptive to spontaneous changes in consciousness,* including shamanic awareness, by using 1, 2, or 3 above as a preparation and then switching into an open stance.

Occasionally I meditate with a client during a session, but in general I recommend that the client learn meditation in a group workshop led by me or in an ongoing group with someone else to whom they are drawn. The background in *"psychotherapy"* on which I draw includes psychoanalysis, bioenergetics, primal therapy, therapeutic massage, reality-therapy, psychodrama, and dream analysis (Freudian, Jungian, Gestalt, shamanic). Each client, and each particular session with a client, draws forth different approaches from this varied background as I respond to what s/he brings and to what I intuit.

How Meditation Can Help Psychotherapy

Where a person's main focus is psychotherapeutic, it is specially appropriate to be aware of the many varied ways in which meditation can help the psychotherapeutic process. First, meditation provides *a safe context for emotional work.* The awareness of an unconditionally loving spiritual presence and/or one's own strong, still center can reinforce and eventually replace the reassuring presence of the therapist as turbulent emotions come up. Second, meditation provides *an additional access to the emotional unconscious.* For some people meditation is even more important than dreaming in providing clues from the unconscious. Third, meditation provides *a training in focusing the energy of one's attention.* One difficulty which often arises in psychotherapy is that the client becomes overly fascinated, engrossed, and preoccupied with the emotional states that arise. This blocks the emergence of more deeply repressed material, and it impedes the working through in his/her everyday life. Meditation helps one to focus the energy of his/her attention: at times fully on the emotional state, at other times elsewhere, yet without repression.

Fourth, meditation provides an *access to creativity*. Sometimes psychotherapy feels like having an extremely painful bowel movement and then examining the rectal fissures and the various kinds of feces which have come forth. Effective psychotherapy includes not only uncovering painful memories and destructive emotional conflicts but also uncovering and releasing the client's creativity. Meditation is often a major resource for this. Fifth, meditation provides an *access to intuitive abilities*. Psychotherapy is the art of teaching an art, the art of learning how to work with the unconscious. Although this process, like any art, involves rational reflection, there is much reliance on intuition, which meditation facilitates.

Although meditation can thus facilitate psychotherapy in various ways, it can sometimes hinder it. The most common problem is that concentrative, mind-emptying or spirit-focused meditations can reinforce someone's tendency to split off from emotions, especially embodied emotions. Two main remedies are available. One is to use such meditations, if at all, only as brief preparations to meditations which involve the meditator in the body: not merely observing what is happening there, but "going with the flow" through chanting, sounding, movement to music, yoga, or a martial art. The other remedy (as in meditation practice 4, above) is to follow up each brief concentrative, mind-emptying or spirit-focused meditation with a deliberate opening up to whatever is "ripe" in the emotional unconscious. This means that, for example, one's concentrative meditation has two stages. First, one is focusing attention on the breath and/or mantra, letting everything else, including emotions, drift off to the edge of consciousness. Then, in a deliberate switch, one allows any emotions that spontaneously arise to move into the forefront of consciousness.

How Psychotherapy Can Help Meditation

If a person's interest is mainly spiritual rather than psychotherapeutic, it is especially appropriate to be aware of the various ways in which psychotherapy can help meditation. Some people can only meditate in a very disembodied way which is either terrifying (so that they try it only once) or all-too-consoling (so that they become addicted to it). As I pointed out, some body-meditations can help remedy this tendency, but the most effective approach for many is some form of bodily-emotional psychotherapy such as bioenergetics or Reichian massage. Such psychotherapy can also help people become aware of the strength and protective boundaries of their own energies, and this may be necessary before they can open up to indwelling spiritual energies and spiritual presences.

Psychotherapy is often indispensable in spiritual processes because without it we tend to project onto spiritual presences or God the same repressed emotional conflicts that already distort our awareness of ourselves, our lover, or our boss. This is true whether we fear abuse from others or long for an absent parent or despair about ever being loved or rage because we feel helpless. Such unconscious patterns are brought by us not only to significant events and people in everyday life, but also to whatever occurs, or might occur, in meditative experience. Although some unconscious neuroses are dealt with unconsciously in profound meditation, typically they need to be brought to consciousness and deliberately relinquished in everyday life. The emergence into consciousness sometimes happens during meditation (which, after all, served humankind well in the centuries before Freud!), but psychotherapy is to some extent a new and necessary resource in any spiritual process that emphasizes embodiment.

This is not so, however, on some world-transcending spiritual paths in which the bodily-emotional dimensions of human existence are left behind as one identifies oneself solely with oneself as spirit ("a tiny point of pure white light," according to one devotee) and then as the Self (or not-self, or Godhead, depending on the tradition). On such paths psychotherapy is typically scorned, except perhaps at the very beginning for someone who is obviously very disturbed emotionally. The ultimate goal is to disappear into God, or to become like a perfectly clear, unnoticeable window pane, transparent to the divine light. If, however, the ultimate goal is to surrender the whole human self into God so as to be lived by God not transparently but translucently,[5] like a stained-glass window which is a particular expression of the divine light, then all dimensions of the self, including the bodily-emotional, must be acknowledged and included. If the goal is not to shed the human and uncover the divine, but rather to uncover both the divine and the human so that the human can be divinized in a process of transfiguring incarnation, then psychotherapy is relevant not only in preparation for spiritual process but also in embodying spiritual reality. In my own experience, preparation and embodiment initially coincide or alternate. Eventually, however, embodiment gradually becomes more prominent as successive exposures to spiritual influxes and descents into the Mystery are assimilated emotionally and bodily and in everyday life. Yet even during advanced stages in spiritual process, perhaps especially then, psychotherapeutic preparatory work may be essential. For example, a penultimate stage on many mystical paths is an inner "sacred marriage" of feminine and masculine, an inner balancing or harmony or dance. In order to move into this, one must have done some intensive work concerning what James Finley calls "the wounded father and mother living within"(1978, p. 29)[6] and concerning the recognition and renunciation of attachments to "god" and "goddess" projected onto other people. And at the ultimate stage, when one lets go of all clinging, craving, and the need to control so as to be lived by the Mystery, the most difficult and crucial letting go is usually a letting go of one's positive and negative attachment to mother. Psychotherapy can be very helpful in the process of separation that leads to this climax.

Of course, some forms of psychotherapy can detract from genuine spiritual change, especially if they encourage repression of spiritual awareness, or insist that the goals of psychotherapy must always predominate, or encourage a narcissistic preoccupation with one's emotions, or tolerate an addiction to this or that psychotherapeutic process, or continually reinforce the wounded child. In general, it is important that more psychotherapists become aware of these dangers and become as open as they can to the spiritual unconscious. It is also important, of course, that spiritual counsellors become more open to the bodily-emotional.

Threshold Relaxation

Openness to both the spiritual and the bodily-emotional is presupposed in what I call "Threshold Relaxation" (TR), which is outlined in Appendix A.[7] Often I introduce TR quite early in the work with a client, turning to it later on from time to time as occasion seems to demand. Since this is one thing that I do which I can commend virtually without reservation to other psychotherapists, I will discuss it at some length. I introduce it to the client in roughly the following way:

> By means of relaxation you can become aware of whatever, if anything, is at the "threshold" of your consciousness, something which you *need* to become aware of, and which you are *safely able* to become aware of, at this time. If there is nothing there at this time (which is sometimes the case) you will simply enjoy a pleasant period of renewal; so don't *try* to bring something up, just let it happen if it is there. If there is something there, it might have some direct relation to what you have been talking about, but it might not. It could be any one of the following: an image or series of images, a dream-like sequence, an emotion, a memory, a bodily-sensation, a spiritual awareness of some kind, or something else that I have not mentioned. The relaxed state is not an occasion for you to put some suggestion into your mind. Such auto-suggestion or "input" (e.g., saying "I am worthy of love") is recommended by some therapists, but the point to threshold relaxation is exactly the opposite. You are to trust your own inner wisdom to reveal to you what is going on, just below the surface of consciousness, in you: spiritually, emotionally, and bodily. If you have had experiences or spiritual resources around you or

within you, you are invited to trust them as well. It may help to think of your consciousness as a room. Many deeply repressed contents of your unconscious are outside the room, inaccessible directly to you at this time, but probably there is something at the threshold of the room.

Although eventually a client can learn how to use relaxation effectively in the absence of the therapist, the presence of the therapist is initially very important. A major factor is the therapist's conscious and unconscious openness to receive whatever might come up into the client's awareness, to receive it in an unruffled yet sensitive and empathetic way. Even when a client has not previously met the therapist, s/he unconsciously intuits whether the therapist is able or unable (willing or unwilling) to receive this or that repressed content. Thus, even if some emotional or spiritual material is actually at the threshold for the client, it is unlikely to emerge if the client senses that it would jar the therapist. It could emerge, however, with a different therapist. Thus, a client is severely restricted in de-repressing whatever is at the threshold if the therapist is wary of spiritual states or embodied emotions or sexual abuse traumas or archetypal images. Such constriction is also a factor within all parts of the overall psychotherapeutic process, including dreams. (During ten years of essentially Freudian therapy I had only one Jungian dream!) Ideally, a therapist will have personally worked through a very wide range of repressed memories, passions, bodily sensations, individual and archetypal images, and encounters with spiritual energies and spiritual presences. This enables the client to bring forth *whatever* is at the threshold.

Of course, the therapist's attitudes can subtly influence *which* accessible contents actually come forth. If one kind of content seems to please or fascinate or in any way gratify the therapist, the client may unconsciously favor these over others. Thus it is important for the therapist not only to have a wide "repertoire" of experienced access to the unconscious but also to be very alert not to be *attached* to any of these, whether in his/her own process or in work with clients. For example, when spectacular shamanic experiences first occurred for me, and a few years later for some of my clients, I had to recognize and let go of an attachment to them. It became clear that at a particular time—whether for me or for a client—it may be less important to receive an angel or a power-animal than to receive an insight concerning some emotional issue in everyday life.

Personal variables in the therapist thus include an openness to a narrow or wide *range* of unconscious material and an attachment, unrecognized or recognized, to some *kinds* of material. Another variable is the depth of relaxation into which the therapist can help the client to sink. Relaxation can become not merely a movement into a more centered state, but a revised version of the "emptying consciousness" kind of meditation, which is essentially a letting go of attachment to whatever is in consciousness, a sinking down towards the still inner point that opens into the Mystery out of which we all arise. The revision made by TR is that the client does not continue indefinitely, for its own sake, this mystical descent into Mystery. Instead, the client deliberately stops and opens up to whatever is at the threshold of consciousness, focusing on it the full energy of his/her attention.

Thus the application of TR is not merely a matter of learning some basic techniques which I outline in Appendix A. What the therapist personally brings or fails to bring to the application matters greatly. Nevertheless, it is an unusually safe approach. What comes up the client not only needs to deal with, but can deal with; and the therapist can receive it and deal with it. This is only true, of course, if both therapist and client restrain any impatient impulse to break down the client's defenses and if both are genuinely open to unexpected experiences. Above all, they must trust the wisdom of the client's unconscious, a trust which can grow with experience. I have noted again and again that such wisdom includes a shrewd sense of timing and appropriate sequence. On one occasion, for example, a secular-minded client who was struggling with emotions evoked by abandonment (by his spouse and, much earlier, by his mother) was heartened by a totally unexpected visit from a loving feminine spiritual presence. On another occasion, a spiritually minded client who was troubled by a pervasive sense of shame and contamination which prevented her from letting Christ in had a threshold experience in which she remembered childhood sexual abuse which had initiated the shame. She was able to ask Christ to help her clear out the contaminating energies which had been in her body since the time of the abuse.

Only rarely do I use TR in every session for several weeks. If plenty of material is emerging in dreams or at home or at work or in meditation, many sessions involve only chair/talking therapy. But TR is indicated if the client seems to be on the verge of something, or is apparently "stuck." What then emerges may take several weeks of sessions and everyday living to work through.

In my work with clients I have found that in TR both therapist and client must learn to expect to be surprised and not to assume that some already-known pattern can be appropriately imposed. Nevertheless, many insights concerning patterns in bodily-emotional processes have been provided by psychotherapeutic writers of various schools. And many insights concerning patterns in spiritual processes have been provided by spiritual writers of various traditions. Much less illumination, however, is available concerning the *dynamic interrelation* between bodily-emotional and spiritual processes.

My own earlier contribution concerning this interrelation was in *Spirituality and Human Nature* (Evans, 1993, ch. 1), where I linked together psychotherapeutic and mystical concepts of "narcissism" (closedness, self-separation, self-preoccupation with comparative status and power). What emerges is a fundamental and repressed motivation in human beings generally (though more clearly in men), a motivation best uncovered in an approach which involves both bodily-emotional and spiritual processes. More recently I discovered Michael Washburn's very insightful *The Ego and the Dynamic Ground* (Washburn, 1995), which accurately maps much of my own bodily-emotional-spiritual process of the past fifteen years and also confirms my incarnational and born-again emphases. Washburn, however, does not touch much on the shamanic.

Seven Principles for Shamanic Psychotherapy

In this chapter it seems appropriate to present some of my findings concerning shamanic ways of linking bodily-emotional and spiritual processes (even though some of my work with clients is minimally shamanic, and even though non-shamanic spirituality can be very helpful). I can offer seven guiding principles to psychotherapists and clients who are involved in bodily-emotional-spiritual processes that have some opening to spiritual energies and spiritual presences. I will present these principles, not necessarily in order of importance, but beginning with those which most readers are likely to find the least esoteric and ending with those which may seem "weird." There will also be both straightforward and esoteric versions of some of the earlier principles. Throughout, I must emphasize caution. *None of the principles can be safely and appropriately applied unless one has some familiarity with the relevant experiences.* Some advance "mapping" may, however, be helpful as you explore new territory, especially in opening up new possibilities and in warning concerning possible dangers. (All the principles are at least compatible with what I have referred to as the "Christian" elements in my approach.)

First Principle

Realize that we commonly resist positive spiritual experiences, either repressing our memory of them or keeping them at the threshold (or ceiling) of our room of consciousness. Such resistance may seem strange, but there are at least three different reasons for it:

1. As Washburn (1995, ch. 2–4) points out, even an ideal infancy involves an individualizing separation not only from the human mother but also from the energies of the Dynamic Ground; the construction of a mental ego then shuts out most of the energies.

2. As Reich points out (1970, ch. 3), most parents reinforce this process. The infant's radiant life-energies are a tantalizing reminder of a streaming, bodily-emotional delight that has for them become inaccessible. They cannot bear living with this (just as Judas could not bear to live with Jesus' radiance), so they force the infant to suppress and repress these life-energies.

3. Many people were "disappointed in love" during infancy, so they resist genuine love from others, whether it comes from a therapist, a friend, or a spirit. Their disappointment arose because they received some love from a parent who withdrew it, or turned it into an instrument of control ("If you're 'good' I'll love you") or ownership ("Whatever is creative in you belongs to me") or neediness ("I'll 'love' you if you give me the empathy and devotion that I didn't receive from my mother") or incestuous treatment ("Be my lover psychically and/or emotionally and/or physically").

I have noted these varieties of disappointment[8] because any of them may emerge into consciousness as a client opens up to a loving spiritual presence—who is thus both a resource in facing painful memories and a generator of these memories. It is understandable that someone may unconsciously cling to familiar patterns or "complexes" of experience, however miserable and self-destructive, and fear spiritual experiences which may upset these patterns.

Although spiritual presences often come, especially initially, to comfort and support, this gradually changes so that their indwelling is an alarming challenge to our narcissism, our self-preoccupied clinging and craving and need to control. They have come to help us undergo a psychic death, a radical surrender, so that we can be lived by the Ultimate (God, the Compassionate Void). As spiritual process becomes more and more genuine, resistance mounts, competing strongly with aspiration.

Second Principle

Realize that if you are reading this chapter you are probably a "puer" or a "puella" and that your main work is therefore very down-to-earth. If you are sufficiently interested in transpersonal therapy to be reading this chapter, you are probably to some extent what Marie-Louise von Franz (1981) calls a *puer* or a *puella*: a Little Prince or Princess who is a visitor on Earth from a spiritual planet. As von Franz points out so clearly, the main work for such people is not acquiring more spiritual experience but rather embodying what they already have in ongoing, everyday commitments to a job, a mate, a long-term creative project or vocation, and a meaningful life on Earth. It is true, however, that some people interested in transpersonal therapy are earthy types who would like to learn how to soar. For them what I say here will be relevant, if at all, only when having soared they realize their need to return.

A few years ago I co-led a day-long workshop: "For Puers Only." At the beginning of the day we invited our fellow puers to focus on an ancient puer, Jacob, son of Isaac, who had a famous dream in which he saw a ladder or stairway leading to the gates of heaven, with angels ascending and descending (Genesis 28:10–17). The men were instructed to go up to the gates of heaven and either give thanks for their gifts or explore beyond the gates for a short while. Then they were to *descend,* if possible finding an angel who could help them to descend. One man's spirit-guide refused to descend with him, but finally he found an angel who would! As the men descended, the room was filled with sounds of anguish, resentment, and misery. The rest of the day was spent working through each man's resistance to being in this world. Each man had a different personal history, trapped and enraged by a different aspect of life *in a body,* whether at work or in a relationship. The common task, however, is somehow to live *as a body* though not only a body, integrating the vision, creativity, and freedom of spiritual existence (and artistic and intellectual existence) with the limitations and opportunities of embodied existence. As von Franz points out, such an integration is not only desirable but in some mid-life crises necessary if one is to go on living. If all vision seems to have gone, earthly life comes to seem intolerably heavy and constricted. Freudian counsel to "Give up your grandiosity and be like other people" can be disastrous in such a situation. What is required is some minimal recovery of creativity and then—only then—a return to work on integration through commitments in the everyday.

I have focused on puers because I have been one. Puellas seem to have a roughly similar life-task, but the dynamics are different in two respects. First, a puella is typically a "Daddy's girl" whereas a puer is typically a "Mommy's boy." Second, a puella can sometimes become more earthy through womb-awareness, linking this with "Earth Mother" spiritual awareness. (The latter, however, is also accessible to puers. Indeed, they typically drop into it as they let go of their resentment at being here.)

Third Principle

Integration of spirituality and sexuality is rare and difficult, but possible. Three different approaches are appropriate for different people, or for the same person at different stages in his/her process:

1. *TR spirit-work:* For some extreme and gifted puers and puellas, Jesus or Mary or another spirit comes in vivid visions. Their presence, however, is not felt in the body except perhaps in the head.

Then a surprising change may happen spontaneously. The spiritual presence is felt moving into and through the body, especially the lower abdomen, helping the person feel that pleasurable sensual awareness is blessed and helping the person reclaim sexuality as part of him/herself. These astonishing experiences are so immensely reassuring that they may seem miraculous (which, in a sense, they are) but much more work of various kinds needs to be done on a bodily-emotional level before sexual intercourse itself is integrated spiritually. The blessing, though related to the body, takes place mainly on a heavenly-spiritual plane. It is a necessary beginning for some puers and puellas, though much embodied "shadow-material" remains to be dealt with, including the "nasty old (wo)man."

2. *Chanting through the chakras:* This meditative practice, which I have outlined in my book (Evans, 1993, pp. 82–88), is a relatively gentle way to become aware of the spiritual energies in various centers of the body and to facilitate their flow between the centers. In world-transcending uses of this meditation the goal is to draw on the energies of the lower chakras to provide a "rocket fuel" to thrust one's consciousness up and through the crown chakra and on towards heaven. In an incarnational approach, however, one brings together at the heart chakra the heavenly energies from the crown, the third-eye, and throat chakras and the early energies from the base, sexual, and navel chakras. Usually there are some bodily-emotional constrictions at some of the chakras and these are both reduced and brought into some awareness by the vibrations of the sound. The meditation is thus instrumental psychotherapeutically. But it also provides new possibilities for consciously moving energies in the body, for example, between the sexual and heart chakras.

3. *Shamanic sounding and drumming.* The vibrations from spontaneous sounding and drumming have immediate access to the constricting tensions within the body and the emotions buried therein. In this respect the effect is similar to group bioenergetics, which also increases the energy level in each participant and in the room as a whole. Shamanic meditation is also open, however, to whatever spiritual energies and spiritual presences can facilitate the process, and this intensifies the process considerably. In one workshop which I have co-led several times (entitled "Love in the Penis, Sex in the Heart"!), the men find themselves drawing on powerful masculine-divine energies, and sexuality is integrated on a bodily-emotional as well as spiritual level. Such workshops are unsuitable for anyone

whose boundaries feel porous and who therefore is likely to feel overwhelmed and invaded rather than invigorated. (Also, shamanic workshops, even if not focused on sexuality, are sometimes difficult for a mixed group of men and women. Women who have suffered from male violence in one form or another find it difficult to distinguish sounds of healthy male aggression from what they fear. And some men are very frightened by sounds of healthy female aggression.)

Fourth Principle

Realize that you are a microcosm, able to resonate from within yourself with every creature in the universe. Meister Eckhart experienced this in relation to angels: "Sink deeply into yourself until you understand the angel and give yourself up to that with all your being. . . . Then you will realize that you are one with the angels" (1980, p. 94). Shamanic spirituality opens us up also to other creatures. For some people the best way to start is by entering into a meditative state as one tries to resonate with the energies of a tree or an animal or the waves at a beach. Meditative practice can gradually make the energies of other visible creatures accessible, including human beings and maybe even the moon, sun, and stars. Then one can move on in meditation or relaxation to be open to invisible creatures. It might be a spirit-guide or a "power-animal" or a discarnate saint or angel. Although there is a kind of order here, moving from the visible to the invisible, it is better once one has moved toward the invisible to let awareness simply arise spontaneously as needed, for example in TR. If shamanic exploration becomes a wilful project, there is danger that the dominant motivation will be idle curiosity or thrill-seeking or a desire to impress and/or control others. Then one may attract mischievous or even evil spirits. But if one has a sincere desire to change whatever impedes one from becoming a more expansively caring human being, one will attract positive, powerful presences who will not only provide protection if any negative presences should try to interfere, but also provide strength in relation to the overall positive process, including bodily-emotional dimensions. They act with superb timing. For example, a client involved in some "inner child" work had a dream in which he tried to get to a baby bear alone in an attic, but a huge, menacing bear stood in the stairway leading up there. I encouraged him to go into TR so as to continue the dream, beginning with facing the big bear again. He realized that although he felt terrified by venturing near, he had to do more than that: he had to become the bear. So he moved into the bear and the bear moved into him, and then he climbed up to the attic, where he was able to draw on the powerful protective and caring energies of the big bear as he parented the baby bear. From then on, in everyday life, he could from time to time draw on these energies which had been evoked from within himself.

In my own shamanic experience during the past eleven years a wide variety of spiritual presences and spiritual energies have come spontaneously, especially during a weekly men's meditation group. There has been a resonating not only with angels and power-animals and discarnate saints but also with a variety of masculine-divine and feminine-divine energies, both earthly and heavenly, and with the energies of various stages of evolution which are still *within* us, going back through early human life, pre-human animal life, and primitive life to the almost-formless energies out of which the universe began.[9] All this has arisen unbidden as part of a process of transformation for me and my peers in the group. I have come to realize that it is an awesome privilege to be a human being, an amazing microcosm connecting with, and resonating with, the whole range of creation, envied by the angels because of the opportunities provided by our embodiment. For Eckhart, letting go into angelic being prepares us for letting go into what he calls "the primordial source of being" (1980, p. 94). So, too, can letting go into other creatures. Eventually it will be the whole, microcosmic self that is surrendered into God to be lived by God.

Fifth Principle

Bodily-energetic processes may be involved in changing one's sense of one's own identity. Sometimes in conventional psychotherapy it becomes clear that a client has not only become locked in to ways of responding to a parent which began in infancy, but also—sometimes predominantly—has interiorized the parent's feelings towards self and others. The client even feels (or represses) these feelings in the same way as the parent. This is not simply a matter of having learned to imitate the parent, for it involves having taken the parent's distorted energies into one's own body, so that one's very identity seems to include these energies. If and when this interiorized parent comes to feel alien to the client, so that the client exclaims, "I *must* get him/her out of my system!" shamanic work may be appropriate, but only if the client has both a fairly strong sense of identity distinct from this interiorized parent and if the client has access to spiritual resources to help both in expelling it and in replacing it. I will illustrate this with two examples, disguising the identity of the persons.

> Jane, a very competent and well-educated professional, was overwhelmed nearly every day by feelings of being a failure. She was overwhelmed by anxieties that someone might catch her making a mistake and then shame her. She gradually became aware of how similar this was to her

father, and then she realized that it felt as if he were inside her—not intruding psychically from outside, which would be a very different matter, but already inside her for as long as she could remember. She went into TR, asking Jesus to help her with whatever would happen. Neither of us had expected anything like what did happen. In brief, she gave birth to a very repulsive still-born infant, a mess on the floor—in imagination, of course, but the energies involved were intensely palpable to both of us.

From a very early age her father had asked her unconsciously to carry his infantile self in her womb, being mother to him. Jesus, who had previously laid his hand on Jane's to help her ease a discomfort in her lower abdomen, in this session helped her begin to feel her own inner child there, which could begin to receive from her some of the caring that had been drawn off to the father.

From an early age Jim had interiorized both his mother's anxious lust and his father's resentful shame, as well as the intense conflicts between his parents. Eventually in a session he was able to expel his mother. This was partly made possible by powerful, nurturing feminine energies which came through a woman who was assisting me. As he received these energies into various parts of his body they moved and replaced his mother's energies. When in a later session he expelled his father's energies, this process involved the help of some masculine-divine energies.

Although in each instance there was one dramatic, pivotal session, considerable additional purging took place later, as well as much emotional work to deal with the feelings of emptiness and lack of clear identity which emerged. His own shamanic sounding helped greatly in claiming and expressing his emerging sense of identity. Shamanic methods work best when the client can learn how to use them for him/herself to claim and express a true identity. Work with some clients must be very gradual and cautious if they can do little of the shamanic work themselves. (An experienced therapist working with multiple personalities and victims of ritual abuse helped me realize the dangers and limitations of shamanic interventions where what is expelled, though destructive, is important to the client's sense of identity.)

A third client, Alex, expelled a destructive sense of identity which he had picked up, not from a parent, but from a past life. In this life there had been much from his parents that had influenced him to feel a shame and guilt so relentless that he had once tried to take his own life and had often found life utterly intolerable. Much of this had been worked through in psychotherapy, and he was making progress in sustaining a love-relation for the first time, as well as coping better with everyday life and in deepening shamanic spirituality. But the bouts of paralyzing self-hatred still overcame him periodically until one day he came to a session in a state of desperate determination to face whatever it took to rid himself of this horror. He went into TR and immediately (to my surprise and his) was immersed in very vivid past-life experience. He was a white man, witnessing a massacre by white men of an Indian village full of women and children, doing nothing to stop it, and being spared. The shame and guilt and self-hatred which he felt at that time was still in his system. I invited him to continue in TR to see if some healing might occur. He found himself in a circle of native elders around a fire. A "Jesus-like" native shaman leader entered on a white buffalo, picked him up, and put him on the fire, where he was burned up. Immediately, however, he emerged from the fire as a radiant young man. He walked outside the circle, where his shamanic power-animal (a black buffalo) and shamanic human companion (a wise old native) awaited him. Together they went off in his search for a new direction in life.

Sometime later—in everyday life rather than in an altered state—he received counsel from a native wisewoman to do work helping women and children. (Such working out in daily life is often what matters most in replacing the old shameful identity with a new one.)

Sixth Principle

Cutting psychic ties with family members is sometimes one of the first things to do in psychotherapy. About twenty years ago a friend, who was in the same therapy group as I, suddenly had a phone call from his mother in England. He had not heard from her in five years, but he had just started some deep work concerning repressed feelings toward her. Sometimes instead of a phone call the contact is made psychically, usually unconsciously. The client feels a pressure not to go on with the process. Often this pressure is signalled by a headache, which I also become aware of. I then "tune in," sensing the intruder's anger or fear or pain. After a while some clients can become aware of the intrusion and its contents without any help from me. If the psychic link or open channel to the family member has not been closely linked with the client's sense of identity, the severing of this tie in a symbolic ritual is a relatively easy step for the client to take, and the disruptive intrusions into the therapeutic process can be stopped. Henceforth the client is dealing "only" with the interiorized mother, father, or sibling. Face-to-face contacts or phone conversations may continue as before, but on such occasions the client has some degree of conscious control concerning what s/he "lets in."

If, however, there has been a very close and symbiotic psychic intimacy since infancy or childhood so that the continued connection feels vital to the client's sense of personal identity, the ceremony of severing the tie may have to be long delayed even though the tie is a major obstacle in the whole process. Such a client should not be encouraged to sever the psychic tie unless s/he feels ready and determined, has a secure support network of friends, and has access to emotional and spiritual resources to replace the tie. I always emphasized to any client that cutting the tie involves letting go of his/her longing to receive a sense of intimacy from the other person through the tie. It also often involves letting go of one's longing for a kind of love which one never received from this person, but one has gone on hoping for. Such a renunciation may be quite impossible at a given stage in a client's bodily-emotional-spiritual process. And such a renunciation, if and when it occurs, may make it unnecessary for there to be any symbolic ritual, for the client thereby often cuts the tie unconsciously in any case.

The ritual is essentially quite simple. The client goes into TR resolved to cut the tie. In TR the client draws on the strength of his/her own center and on any spiritual resources available, and then tries to become aware of threads or cords originating in various parts of the body and going out like antennae from there to link with the other person. Then s/he uses the edge of the hands as if they were sharp, cutting the threads or cords. The client is invited to follow his/her own intuitions throughout. Sometimes the cutting is easy and quiet, sometimes much effort and sound seems to be required. Sometimes the client is calm, sometimes angry, but the anger is used to mobilize energy for cutting the tie, not to send anger to the other person along the tie! Once in a group a woman invited all the women present to surround her for support as she cut off the psychic tie with her father. To her surprise she found that it was a very thick rope and that it came like an umbilical cord from her father's navel. She needed a saw or an axe to cut it, which she did in imagination. The imagery in the ritual is, of course, subjective, but the energy component can be felt inter-subjectively as something tangible and real.

Sometimes when two people have been very co-dependent and one of them dies the psychic tie between them continues and greatly restricts both of them. The discarnate person remains earth-bound and cannot proceed with whatever spiritual process is appropriate, and the incarnate person lives only a half a life, unable to open up to new relationships. I am very rarely directive with clients, but I once counselled a man not to proceed with an impending marriage unless he first cut the tie with his dead mother, for otherwise it would be grossly unfair to his fiancée. Usually, however, it is a matter of waiting until the person feels ready, and then I will assist. This typically involves helping not only the person but also the deceased co-dependent to let go of the other. Counselling of discarnate human beings seemed very strange when I began it about fifteen years ago, but now it is routine, though not frequent. Some therapists who lack this psychic capacity find that they can rely on the *client's* capacity under relaxation, so that the response of, say, the client's deceased mother is "heard" and expressed by the client.

One client, Jason, had been shipped away from home with his sister Joan when they were still pre-schoolers. They developed a very intense co-dependency in which Joan became for Jason his main access to feminine life-energy. When she committed suicide in mid-life, Jason clung to her psychically, drawing on her energy to stay alive himself, but also longing to join her. His half-life was so miserable that he needed to cut the tie as soon as possible, but he could not do this until he had gone through an arduous process that included building a replacement structure. She, too, had her own reasons for hanging on, but in the end their genuine caring for each other prevailed. With her consent he cut the connecting threads. (Sometimes, however, consent is not granted, and the incarnate person has to go ahead without it.)

Sometimes a person comes to see me for specific help with psychic intrusion and it turns out that s/he is mistaken. John felt that even though he had moved his work to another location, a man who had been verbally threatening was still attacking him psychically. When I tuned in, I could intuit no such invasion, so I invited John to go into TR to see whether he might uncover something else going on. What emerged was some long-repressed rage, disowned by John, and projected out as if it came from the man, who seemed a probable source but who probably had forgotten John by this time. As John felt, claimed, and sounded forth his rage, the rage gradually changed into a very positive, confident, self-assertive roar. He later explained to me that he felt himself becoming a lion. This was his first shamanistic experience. When filled with lion-energy he was thereby neither a victim nor—as he had feared concerning release of his released rage—a victimizer.

Sometimes, however, psychic intrusion is not only real but very destructive. This leads to a seventh principle.

Seventh Principle

Demonic evil exists, and requires a distinctive response. I quote St. Paul: "We wrestle not against flesh and blood, but against principalities, against powers, against rulers of the darkness of this world, against spiritual wickedness in high places" (Ephesians 6:12). Although I am appalled by some evangelical Christians who see every spiritual energy or presence other than Jesus as demonic, I agree with them that demonic evil exists and that it is very appropriate to call upon Jesus to combat it. When I have encountered what I would call "demonic evil," I have discerned a motivation to destroy the divine light and love in human beings, or to turn human beings away from that light and love so as to join the forces of darkness against God. Demonic evil differs radically from "ordinary" evil which is at worst motivated by sadism or by revenge or by destructive hatred toward a particular person. Demonic evil is motivated by hatred toward God's light and love, and it involves *a deliberate choice to ally oneself with whatever presences and energies are available that are opposed to God.* Some people hover at the boundary of the demonic. They are very dangerous and destructive, but they have not taken the final step and may be open to pleas that they turn back.

I have encountered demonic evil mostly in contexts of sexual abuse: my own in early infancy, and that of other people with whom I have worked. Fortunately most sexual abuse does *not* arise from demonic evil, but from many diverse motives and emotional conflicts which are adequately understood in terms of various psychotherapeutic accounts. These accounts may involve references to "evil" insofar as human *responsibility* is emphasized, but need not refer at all to esoteric notions such as an alliance with "powers of evil." Occasionally, however, it is clear that an attempt has been made to destroy someone spiritually and/or to recruit that person into service against God by means of evil energies. This attempt may have occurred by means of sexual abuse, perhaps involving rituals, and the attempt may even be going on in the present, through psychic intrusion. In such cases shamanic methods are mandatory, drawing on positive spiritual presences and energies to protect the person in the present and to expel the evil energies which have contaminated the person.

In my own experience the astounding cosmic power of Jesus is usually very effective in responding to the demonic. I differ from evangelical Christians, however, in that sometimes I find it more appropriate to call on the Hindu goddess Kali, who is even more terrifying than Jesus for some men if their destructive hatred is focused primarily on the divine (and human) as *feminine.* Kali's divine-feminine energies are fiercely affirming of the feminine as they protect the feminine and drive out the contaminating energies. Caution is necessary in the process of expulsion, however, whether one calls on Jesus or Kali or some other powerful presence, for (as I have noted before) much of a person's sense of personal identity was linked with whoever invaded him/her when young. Indeed, in demonic abuse such an identification is deliberately sought by the perpetrators.

I have referred to already-existing demonically evil energies and presences. These are of two kinds. Some are human creations, built up collectively over many centuries as a source on which to draw by many people who hated God. The others are divine creatures, discarnate humans and angels, who have turned against God and who work either on their own or together. The human creations[10] can be, and ought to be, *destroyed* (in my experience, by the power of Jesus). The divine creatures cannot be destroyed, but they can be either *contained* or *banished* so as to be no longer a menace to their victim.

Occasionally psychotherapists may suspect that they may be up against demonic evil as they work with a particular client who seems to be invaded. Such a hunch should be taken seriously, for at the very least the therapist could become very drained, and serious illness could ensue. One minimal step in psychic self-protection is to surround and pervade one's whole body in imagination with white light. If the therapist's world view permits, prayers for help can help even if one has not previously had any experience of the spiritual reality to whom one prays. If possible, assistance from someone who is familiar with such esoteric processes should be sought.

Fortunately demonic evil is rare. Most psychic intrusion comes from people, whether alive or dead, who are not wicked. Their motivations, like those of most people in everyday life, are a mixture of good and bad, clear and confused. Sometimes some measures of self-protection are needed, but what is needed is quite remote from radical "exorcism." Rather, it is mainly a matter of common-sense counselling. Although the medium, telepathy, is for some people paranormal, the message is quite normal, as in everyday life!

Appendix A: Techniques for Threshold Relaxation

1. Explain TR to the client.

   On the first occasion something similar to my explanation (in quotes) in the chapter is appropriate. Afterwards, a briefer reminder.

2. State the intention for this particular TR.

   Sometimes the client states it, aloud, sometimes the therapist, asking the client for any revisions.

   TR is always open-ended, but there may be a particular intended focus which can be stated. For example, a client may want to renew contact with a particular spiritual presence. Having stated this, however, s/he must be open to something else being at the threshold, e.g., some emotional obstacle to such a renewal, or perhaps something quite unrelated, a pain in a part of the body that needs to be "pursued."

3. Relax the body and thereby the mind.

This is optional. Use it if the client is unusually stressed or is out of experienced relation with his/her body:

On a deep inhalation, tense your feet; hold the tension as you hold your breath; then release tension as you release breath. Repeat throughout the body, wherever you can tense a part (exaggerating whatever tension you find there already). e.g., calves, knees, thighs, buttocks, lower abdomen, chest, jaw and mouth, arms and hands, neck and shoulders, brow. Then once with the whole body. Pause between parts rather than rushing through it. Enjoy the sensations as you relax each time.

4. Relaxing using a verbal patter.

Examples of verbal patter are:

a. "Relax and rest, relax and rest. Every muscle and every nerve relaxes. Waves of heaviness sweep over you. Your muscles ease out their tension. Your nerves grow calmer, calmer. There is nothing you have to do now. No need to remember or to plan. Simply be. If you are aware of any distracting tension, emotion, or thought, let it go with an exhalation."

b. "Sinking down, down, down; down and in, in and down. Letting go, sinking down; toward your own center, where there is silence and security; toward your own center, where there is serenity and strength. Letting go, letting be. No need to cling to anything. Trusting in your own inner wisdom." (For some, add, "trusting in the spiritual resources around you and within you" or "trusting in so-and-so." For some, add, ". . . to your own center, where there is openness to the Mystery out of which we all arise.")

5. Counting down.

After (a), above, or during (b), say, "I am going to count from one to fifteen, and with each number you will sink into a deeper state of relaxation."

Count quite slowly, interspersing some of the patter from (b) between each number, or every other number, following your intuition. The client may, for example, need to be reminded to let go of distractions with each exhalation.

6. Relaxation at the threshold.

At the end of the count, remind the client that there may not be anything at the threshold this time. If so, they will simply enjoy a period of refreshing renewal.

Also remind the client that what arises from the threshold may differ from what s/he expects and may initially seem trivial.

The silence, which may go on for several minutes. Following your intuition, decide when to ask, "What has been happening?" adding, "Don't speak unless it feels right to you." Or the client may already have begun speaking. Encourage the client to focus full attention and to "go with" it. Do not offer any interpretations until after the client is out of the relaxation.

7. Counting up (CRUCIAL: never forget to do this).

When it seems clear to the client that the process has come to a sort of completion, say, "I am going to count backwards from fifteen to one, and with each number you will move up and out toward your everyday consciousness, able to remember clearly everything you have been aware of during the relaxed state." The count up can usually be relatively quick, except when the client finds it difficult to come up (a rarity). Intersperse, "Up and out, out and up" between some of the numbers.

Notes

1. Concerning this issue see Evans (1993), chapter 3, "Sexuality, Spirituality and the Art of Therapy."

2. See Nellas (1987). A fully incarnational theology is impossible for Nellas, it seems to me, because for him there actually was a pre-fall human state which did not include our animal and sexual characteristics. For example, we "multiplied in the same way as the angels" (p. 75). Hence any restoration to, and improvement on, that pre-fall state does not include these dimensions.

3. See also Washburn (1995), pp. 41–42, 126, and 171–202.

4. William Wordsworth, "Ode: Intimations of Immortality from Recollections of Early Childhood."

5. I explore the "translucency"/"transparency" contrast in Evans, 1993, pp. 242–245.

6. Finley is here expounding Thomas Merton.

7. In Evans, 1993, pp. 71–75 I explored the theoretical implications of the "threshold" analogy in its application within psychotherapy.

8. There are also varieties of response to the disappointment. I note five in *Struggle and Fulfillment*, part one, pp. 19–108; see summary on p. 86.

9. Warning: If you open yourself up to primitive, undifferentiated, and amoral energies, be sure that your purpose is to provide a positive, containing form for these energies in your heart and mind. According to Jacob Boehme this shaping of what he calls the *"Undgrund"* is an essential part of our human task. If you open up casually, or with impure motives, however, the outcome can be very destructive to you and to others. (The clearest access to Boehme concerning this that I know is in Michael Stoeber, *Evil and the Mystics' God* [London: Macmillan, 1992], chapter 9.)

10. See Anonymous, 1985. Drawing on Cabbalistic writings, he refers to such invisible, artificial, collectively "engendered beings" as "egregores" (p. 138; see also pp. 61–64, 138–144).

26

Healing Potential of Non-ordinary States of Consciousness

Observations from Psychedelic Therapy and Holotropic Breathwork

Stanislav Grof

In the first edition of *Transpersonal Psychotherapy* Stanislav Grof, one of the leading pioneers of transpersonal psychology, presented findings derived from his research with LSD and other psychedelic substances. Almost twenty-five years ago, he proposed the concepts of Basic Perinatal Matrices (BPM) wherein the stages of birth and the psychiatric clinical correlates were clarified. In this chapter "clinical" examples are given to further clarify these stages.

Unfortunately, research with LSD and other psychedelic tools has basically been stopped in this country. Now Grof has developed and is actively involved in Holotropic Breathwork, an approach which may rival and, in some ways, be superior to LSD approaches. This method "can facilitate profound holotropic [oriented toward wholeness] states by conscious breathing, evocative music, and focused bodywork."

Besides surveying many differing ways of achieving non-ordinary states of consciousness (NOSC), Grof points out that the therapeutic use of NOSC is both a recent development of Western psychotherapy and can also "be traced back to the dawn of human history."

Grof explains how condensed experience (COEX) systems work—layer built upon layer, a storage system of one's major experiences of high intensity "in the form of complex dynamic constellations."

He suggests a model or map of the psyche which contains the usual biographical level and two transbiographical realms: the *perinatal* domain, related to the traumas of biological birth; and the *transpersonal* domain. He points out that the holotropic approach tends to bring "into consciousness automatically the contents from the unconscious that have the strongest emotional charge and are the most psychodynamically relevant at the time."

This cartography Grof feels has "revolutionary implications for the understanding of emotional and psychosomatic disorders, including psychoses, and offers new and revolutionary therapeutic possibilities." He sees the manifestation of symptoms as the beginning of the healing process. Though often emotional and psychosomatic problems have their origin in the postnatal period, especially infant and childhood, many originate in the perinatal or prenatal (e.g., past-life) areas. In fact, many of the postnatal problems have a multidimensional structure with *additional* roots in the perinatal or prenatal (transpersonal) levels. Ideally, the resolution of a problem would mean allowing "oneself to experience all the layers of problems associated with it."

In summary, Grof feels that the therapeutic work with NOSC (e.g., psychedelic therapy, Holotropic Breathwork) tends "to activate the spontaneous healing potential of the psyche and of the body and initiate a transformative process guided by deep inner intelligence."

THE OBJECTIVE OF THIS CHAPTER is to summarize my experiences and observations concerning the nature of the human psyche and its healing potential which I have collected during more than thirty-five years of research of non-ordinary states of consciousness (NOSC). These states are characterized by dramatic perceptual changes, intense and often unusual emotions, profound alterations in the thought processes and behavior, and by a variety of psychosomatic manifestations. Consciousness can be profoundly altered in a wide variety of situations and in different ways; however, not all NOSC have heuristic significance and therapeutic potential. This presentation focuses upon a large and important subgroup of such states that are of great theoretical and practical significance. I have coined for them the name *holotropic* (literally "oriented toward wholeness" from the Greek *holos*, meaning "whole" and *trepein*, meaning "moving toward" or "in the direction of something") (Grof, 1992).

Holotropic States of Consciousness

In holotropic states, consciousness is changed qualitatively in a very fundamental way, but is not grossly impaired. This distinguishes them from trivial deliria accompanying traumas, intoxications by various poisonous substances, infections, or degenerative and circulatory processes in the brain. People suffering from delirant conditions are typically disoriented (not knowing who and where they are and what date it is), show a disturbance of intellectual functions, and subsequent amnesia. All such functions are intact in the holotropic states of consciousness. In addition, the content of holotropic experiences is often spiritual or mystical. It involves sequences of psychological death and rebirth and a broad spectrum of transpersonal phenomena, including feelings of oneness with other people, nature, and the universe, past-life experiences, and visions of archetypal beings and mythological landscapes as described by C. G. Jung (1960b).

Holotropic States of Consciousness and Human History

Ancient and aboriginal cultures have spent much time and energy developing powerful mind-altering techniques that can induce holotropic states. They combine in different ways chanting, breathing, drumming, rhythmic dancing, fasting, social and sensory isolation, extreme physical pain, and other elements. These cultures used them in shamanic procedures, healing ceremonies, and rites of passage—powerful rituals enacted at the time of important biological and social transitions, such as circumcision, puberty, marriage, or birth of a child. Many cultures have used psychedelic plants for these purposes. The most famous examples of these are different varieties of hemp, the Mexican cactus peyote and Psilocybe mushrooms, the African shrub eboga, and the Amazonian jungle liana Banisteriopsis caapi, the source of yagé or ayahuasca.

Additional important triggers of holotropic experiences are various forms of systematic spiritual practice involving meditation, concentration, breathing, and movement exercises that are used in different systems of yoga, Vipassana or Zen Buddhism, Tibetan Vajrayana, Taoism, Christian mysticism, Sufism, or Cabalah. Other techniques were used in the ancient mysteries of death and rebirth, such as the Egyptian temple initiations of Isis and Osiris and the Greek Bacchanalia, rites of Attis and Adonis, and the Eleusinian mysteries. The specifics of the procedures involved in these secret rites have remained for the most part unknown, although it is likely that psychedelic preparations played an important part (Wasson, Hofmann, & Ruck, 1978).

Among the modern means of inducing holotropic states of consciousness are psychedelic substances isolated from plants or synthetized in the laboratory and powerful experiential forms of psychotherapy, such as hypnosis, neo-Reichian approaches, primal therapy, and rebirthing. My wife Christina and I have developed Holotropic Breathwork, a method that can facilitate profound holotropic states by very simple means—conscious breathing, evocative music, and focused bodywork. There also exist very effective laboratory techniques for altering consciousness. One of these is sensory isolation, which involves significant reduction of meaningful sensory stimuli. In its extreme form the individual is deprived of sensory input by submersion in a dark and soundproof tank filled with water of body temperature. Another well-known laboratory method of changing consciousness is biofeedback, where the individual is guided by electronic feedback signals into non-ordinary states of consciousness characterized by preponderance of certain specific frequencies of brainwaves. We could also mention here the techniques of sleep and dream deprivation and lucid dreaming.

It is important to emphasize that episodes of NOSC of varying duration can also occur spontaneously, without any specific identifiable cause, and often against the will of the people involved. Since modern psychiatry does not differentiate between mystical or spiritual states and mental diseases, people experiencing these states are often labeled psychotic, hospitalized, and receive routine suppressive psychopharmacological treatment. Christina and I refer to these states as spiritual emergencies or psycho-spiritual crises. We believe that, properly supported and treated, they can result in emotional and psychosomatic healing, positive personality transformation, and consciousness evolution (S. Grof & C. Grof, 1989; C. Grof & S. Grof, 1990).

Although I have been deeply interested in all the categories of NOSC mentioned above, I have done most of my work in the area of psychedelic therapy, Holotropic Breathwork, and spiritual emergency. This chapter is based predominantly on my observations from these three areas in which I have most personal experience. However, the general conclusions I will be drawing apply to all the situations involving holotropic states.

Holotropic States in the History of Psychiatry

It is worth mentioning that the history of depth psychology and psychotherapy is deeply connected with the study of NOSC—consider Franz Mesmer's experiments with "animal magnetism," the hypnotic sessions with hysterical patients conducted in Paris by Jean Martin Charcot, and the research in hypnosis carried out in Nancy by Hippolyte Bernheim and Ambroise Auguste Liébault. Sigmund Freud's early work was inspired by his work with a client (Miss Anna O.), who experienced spontaneous episodes of non-ordinary states of consciousness. Freud also initially used hypnosis to access his patients' unconscious before he radically changed his strategies. In retrospect, shifting emphasis from direct experience to free association, from actual trauma to Oedipal fantasies, and from conscious reliving and emotional abreaction of unconscious material to transference dynamics was unfortunate and limited and misdirected Western psychotherapy for the next fifty years (Ross, 1989).

While verbal therapy can be very useful in providing interpersonal learning and rectifying interaction and communication in human relationships (e.g., couple and family therapy), it is ineffective in dealing with emotional and bioenergetic blockages and macrotraumas, such as the trauma of birth.

As a consequence of this development, psychotherapy in the first half of this century was practically synonymous with talking—face-to-face interviews, free associations on the couch, and the behaviorist deconditioning. At the same time NOSC, initially seen as an effective therapeutic tool, became associated with pathology rather than healing. This situation started to change in the 1950s with the advent of psychedelic therapy and new developments in psychology. A group of American psychologists headed by Abraham Maslow, dissatisfied with behaviorism and Freudian psychoanalysis, launched a revolutionary movement—humanistic psychology. Within a very short time, this movement became very popular and provided the context for a broad spectrum of new therapies.

While traditional psychotherapies used primarily verbal means and intellectual analysis, these new, so-called experiential, therapies emphasized direct experience and expression of emotions and used various forms of bodywork as an integral part of the process. Probably the most famous representative of these new approaches is Fritz Perls's Gestalt therapy (Perls, 1976). However, most experiential therapies still rely to a great degree on verbal communication and require that the client stay in the ordinary state of consciousness. The most radical innovations in the therapeutic field were approaches that are so powerful that they profoundly change the state of consciousness, such as psychedelic therapy, Holotropic Breathwork, primal therapy, rebirthing, and others.

The therapeutic use of non-ordinary states of consciousness is the most recent development in Western psychotherapy. Paradoxically, it is also the oldest form of healing and can be traced back to the dawn of human history. Therapies using holotropic states actually represent a rediscovery and modern reinterpretation of the elements and principles that have been documented by historians and anthropologists studying the sacred mysteries of death and rebirth, rites of passage, and ancient and aboriginal forms of spiritual healing, particularly various shamanic procedures. Shamanism is the most ancient religion and healing art of humanity, the roots of which reach far back into the Paleolithic era. Among the beautiful images of primeval animals painted and carved on the walls of the great caves in southern France and northern Spain, such as Lascaux, Font de Gaume, Les Trois Frères, Niaux, Altamira, and others, are figures that undoubtedly represent ancient shamans. In some of the caves, the discoverers also found footprints in circular arrangements suggesting that their inhabitants conducted dances similar to those still performed by some aboriginal cultures for the induction of NOSC. Shamanism is not only ancient, it is also universal; it can be found in North and South America, in Europe, Africa, Asia, Australia, and Polynesia.

The fact that so many different cultures throughout human history have found shamanic techniques useful and relevant suggests that they address the "primal mind"—a basic and primordial aspect of the human psyche that transcends race, culture, and time. All the cultures with the exception of the Western industrial civilization have held NOSC in great esteem and spent much time and effort to develop various ways of inducing them. They used them to connect with their deities, other dimensions of reality, and with the forces of nature, for healing, for cultivation of extrasensory perception, and for artistic inspiration. For pre-industrial cultures, healing always involves non-ordinary states of consciousness—either for the client, for the healer, or for both of them at the same time. In many instances, a large group or even an entire tribe enters a non-ordinary state of consciousness together, as it is, for example, among the Kung Bushmen in the African Kalahari Desert.

Western psychiatry and psychology does not see NOSC (with the exception of dreams that are not recurrent or frightening) as potential sources of healing or of valuable information about the human psyche, but basically as pathological phenomena. Traditional psychiatry tends to use indiscriminately pathological labels and suppressive medication whenever these states occur spontaneously. Michael Harner (1980), an anthropologist of good academic standing who underwent a shamanic initiation during his field work in the Amazonian jungle and practices shamanism, suggests that Western psychiatry is seriously biased in at least two significant ways. It is *ethnocentric,* which means that it considers its own view of the human psyche and of reality to be the only correct one and superior to all others. It is also *"cognicentric"* (a more accurate word might be "pragmacentric"), meaning that it takes into consideration only experiences and observations in the ordinary state of consciousness. Psychiatry's disinterest in holotropic states and disregard for them has resulted in a culturally insensitive approach and a tendency to pathologize all activities that cannot be understood in its own narrow context. This includes the ritual and spiritual life of ancient and pre-industrial cultures and the entire spiritual history of humanity.

Implications of Modern Consciousness Research for Psychiatry

If we study systematically the experiences and observations associated with NOSC or, more specifically, holotropic states, this leads inevitably to a radical revision of our basic ideas about consciousness and the human psyche and to entirely new psychiatry, psychology, and psychotherapy. The changes we would have to make in our thinking fall into several large categories:

1. *The nature of the human psyche and the dimensions of consciousness:* Traditional academic psychiatry and psychology uses a model which is limited to biology, postnatal biography, and the Freudian individual unconscious. This model has to be vastly expanded and a new cartography of the psyche has to be created to describe all the phenomena occurring in NOSC.

2. *The nature and architecture of emotional and psychosomatic disorders (or what is traditionally called "psychogenic psychopathology"):* Traditional psychiatry uses an explanatory model limited to biology and biographical traumas in infancy, childhood, and later life. The new understanding has to include additional realms of the psyche as potential sources of emotional problems. These are transbiographical and transpersonal in nature.

3. *Therapeutic mechanisms and the process of healing:* Traditional psychotherapy knows only therapeutic mechanisms operating on the level of biographical material—remembering of forgotten events, lifting of repression, reconstruction of the past from dreams, reliving of traumatic memories, analysis of transference, etc. The work with NOSC reveals many important additional mechanisms of healing and personality transformation operating in realms that lie beyond biography.

4. *Strategy of psychotherapy and self-exploration:* The goal in traditional psychotherapies is to reach an intellectual understanding as to how the psyche functions and why symptoms develop and then derive from this understanding a strategy for "fixing" the patients. A serious problem with this strategy is the amazing lack of agreement among psychologists and psychiatrists about these fundamental issues, resulting in an astonishing number of competing schools of psychotherapy. The work with holotropic states shows us a surprising alternative and a way out of this confusion, which I will discuss later.

5. *The role of spirituality in human life:* Western materialistic science has no place for any form of spirituality and considers it incompatible with the scientific world view. Modern consciousness research shows that spirituality is a natural and legitimate dimension of the human psyche and of the universal scheme of things. In this context, it is important to distinguish spirituality from religion.

6. *The nature of reality:* The necessary revisions which I have discussed up to this point were related to the theory and practice of psychiatry, psychology, and psychotherapy. However, the work with NOSC brings challenges of a much more fundamental nature. Many of the experiences and observations that occur during this work are so extraordinary that they can not be understood in the context of the Newtonian-Cartesian materialistic paradigm and undermine the most basic metaphysical assumptions of the entire edifice of Western science.

The Nature of the Human Psyche and the Dimensions of Consciousness

The phenomena observed in modern consciousness research cannot be explained by a model limited to postnatal biography and to the Freudian individual unconscious. The dimensions of the human psyche are infinitely larger than academic psychology would like us to believe. In an effort to account for the experiences and observations from NOSC, I have myself suggested a cartography or model of the psyche that contains, in addition to the usual *biographical level,* two transbiographical realms: the *perinatal domain,* related to the trauma of biological birth; and the *transpersonal domain,* which accounts for such phenomena as experiential identification with other people or with animals, visions of archetypal and mythological beings and realms, ancestral, racial, and karmic experiences, and identification with the Universal Mind or the Void. These are experiences that have been described throughout the ages in the religious, mystical, and occult literature.

Postnatal Biography and the Individual Unconscious

The biographical level of the psyche does not require much discussion, since it is well known from traditional psychology and psychotherapy; as a matter of fact, it is what traditional dynamic psychotherapy is all about. However, there are a few important differences between exploring this domain through verbal psychotherapy and through approaches using NOSC. First, one does not just remember emotionally significant events or reconstruct them indirectly from dreams, slips of the tongue, or from transference distortions; rather, one experiences the original emotions, physical sensations, and even sensory perceptions in full age regression. That means that during the reliving of an important trauma from infancy or childhood, one actually has the body image, the naive perception of the world, sensations, and the emotions corresponding to the age he or she was at that time. The authenticity of this regression is supported by the fact that the wrinkles in the faces of these people temporarily disappear giving them an infantile expression, the postures and gestures become childlike, and their neurological reflexes are characteristic for children (e.g., the sucking reflex and the reflex of Babinski).

The second difference between the work on the biographical material in NOSC, as compared with verbal psychotherapists, is that besides confronting the usual psychotraumas known from handbooks of psychology, people often have to relive and integrate traumas that were primarily of a physical nature. Many people have to process experiences of near drowning, operations, accidents, and children's diseases, particularly those that were associated with suffocation, such as diphtheria, whooping cough, or aspiration of a foreign object. This material emerges quite spontaneously and without any programming. As it surfaces, people realize that these physical traumas have actually played a significant role in the psychogenesis of their emotional and psychosomatic problems, such as asthma, migraine headaches, a variety of psychosomatic pains, phobias, sado-masochistic tendencies, or depression and suicidal tendencies. Reliving of such traumatic memories and their integration can then have very far-reaching therapeutic consequences. This contrasts sharply with the attitudes of academic psychiatry and psychology which do not recognize the direct psychotraumatic impact of physical traumas.

Other new information about the biographical-recollective level of the psyche that has emerged from my research has been the discovery that emotionally relevant memories are stored in the unconscious in the form of complex dynamic constellations, not as a mosaic of isolated imprints. I have coined for them the name *COEX systems,* which is short for systems of "condensed experience." A COEX system consists of emotionally charged memories from different periods of our life that resemble each other in the quality of emotion or physical sensation that they share. Each COEX has a basic theme that permeates all its layers and represents a common denominator. The individual layers then contain variations on this basic theme that occurred at different periods of the person's life.

The nature of the central theme varies considerably from one COEX to another. The layers of a particular system can, for example, contain all the major memories of humiliating, degrading, and shaming experiences that have damaged our self-esteem. In another COEX, the common denominator can be anxiety experienced in various shocking and terrifying situations or claustrophobic and suffocating feelings evoked by oppressive and confining circumstances. Rejection and emotional deprivation damaging our ability to trust men, women, or people in general, is another common motif. Situations that have generated in us profound feelings of guilt and a sense of failure, events that have left us with a conviction that sex is dangerous or disgusting, and encounters with indiscriminate aggression and violence can be added to the above list as characteristic examples. Particularly important are COEX systems that contain memories of encounters with situations endangering life, health, and integrity of the body.

The above discussion could easily leave the impression that COEX systems always contain painful and traumatic memories. However, it is the intensity of the experience and its emotional relevance that determines whether a memory will be included into a COEX, not its unpleasant nature. In addition to negative constellations there are also those that comprise memories of very pleasant or even ecstatic moments. The concept of COEX dynamics emerged from clinical work with clients suffering from serious forms of psychopathology where the work on traumatic aspects of life plays a very important role. The spectrum of negative COEX systems is also much richer and more variegated than that of the positive ones; it seems that the misery in our life can have many different forms, while happiness depends on the fulfillment of a few basic conditions. However, a general discussion requires that we emphasize that the COEX dynamics are not limited to constellations of traumatic memories.

When I first described the COEX systems in the early stages of my LSD research, I thought they governed the dynamics of the biographical level of the unconscious. At that time, my understanding of psychology was based on a superficial model of the psyche limited to biography that I had inherited from my teachers. In addition, in the initial psychedelic sessions, particularly when lower dosages are used, the biographical material often predominates. As my experience with non-ordinary states became richer and more extensive, I realized that the roots of the COEX systems reach much deeper. Each of the COEX constellations seems to be superimposed over and anchored in a particular aspect of the trauma of birth. As we will see later in the discussion of the perinatal level of the unconscious, the experience of birth is so complex and rich in emotions and physical sensations that it contains in a prototypical form the elementary themes of all conceivable COEX systems. In addition, a typical COEX reaches even further and has its deepest roots in various forms of transpersonal phenomena, such as past-life experiences, Jungian archetypes, conscious identification with various animals, and others. At present, I see the COEX systems as general organizing principles of the human psyche. The similarities and differences between the concept of COEX systems and Jung's concept of complexes has been discussed elsewhere (Grof, 1975).

The COEX systems play an important role in our psychological life. They can influence the way we perceive ourselves, other people, and the world, and how we feel about them. They are the dynamic forces behind our emotional and psychosomatic symptoms, difficulties in relationships with other people, and irrational behavior. There exists a dynamic interplay between the COEX systems and the external world. External events in our life can specifically activate corresponding COEX systems and, conversely, active COEX systems can make us perceive and behave in such a way that we recreate their core themes in our present life. This mechanism can be observed very clearly in experiential work. In non-ordinary states, the content of the experience, the perception of the environment, and the behavior of the client are determined in general terms by the COEX system that dominates the session and more specifically by the layer of this system that is momentarily emerging into consciousness.

All the characteristics of COEX systems can best be demonstrated with a practical example. I have chosen for this purpose Peter, then a thirty-seven-year-old tutor who had been intermittently hospitalized and treated in our department in Prague without success prior to his psychedelic therapy.

At the time we began with the experiential sessions, Peter could hardly function in his everyday life. Almost all the time, he was obsessed by the idea of finding a man of a certain physical appearance and preferably clad in black. He wanted to befriend this man and tell him about his urgent desire to be locked in a dark cellar and exposed to various diabolic physical and mental tortures. He hoped to find a man who would be willing to participate in this scheme. Unable to concentrate on anything else, he wandered aimlessly through the city, visiting public parks, lavatories, bars, and railroad stations searching for the "right man."

He succeeded on several occasions to persuade or bribe various men who met his criteria to promise to do what he asked for. Having a special gift for finding persons with sadistic traits, he was twice almost killed, several times seriously hurt, and once robbed of all his money. On those occasions, where he was able to experience what he craved for, he was extremely frightened and actually strongly disliked the tortures. In addition to this main problem, Peter suffered from suicidal depressions, impotence, and infrequent epileptiform seizures.

Reconstructing his history, I found out that his major problems started at the time of his compulsory employment in Germany during World War II. The Nazis referred to this form of slave labor using people from occupied territories in hard dangerous work situations as *Totaleinsetzung*. At that time, two SS officers forced him at gun point to engage in their homosexual practices. When the war was over, Peter realized that these experiences created in him preference for homosexual intercourse experienced in the passive role. This gradually changed into fetishism for black male clothes and finally into the complex obsession described above.

Fifteen consecutive psychedelic sessions revealed a very interesting and important COEX system underlying this problem. In its most superficial layers were Peter's more recent traumatic experiences with his sadistic partners. On several occasions, the accomplices whom he recruited actually bound him with ropes, locked him into a cellar without food and water, and tortured him by flagellation and strangulation according to his wish. One of these men hit him on his head, bound him with a string, and left him lying in a forest after stealing his money.

Peter's most dramatic adventure happened with a man who promised to take him to his cabin in the woods that he claimed had just the cellar Peter wanted. When they were traveling by train to this man's weekend house, Peter was struck by his companion's strange-looking bulky backpack. When the latter left the compartment and went to the bathroom, Peter stepped up on the seat and checked the suspect baggage. He discovered a complete set of murder weapons, including a gun, a large butcher knife, a freshly sharpened hatchet, and a surgical saw used for amputations. Panic-stricken, he jumped out of the moving train and suffered serious injuries. Elements of the above episodes formed the most superficial layers of Peter's most important COEX system.

A deeper layer of the same system contained Peter's memories from the Third Reich. In the sessions where this part of the COEX constellation manifested, he relived in detail his experiences with the homosexual SS officers with all the complicated feelings involved. In addition, he relived several other traumatic memories from World War II and dealt with the entire oppressive atmosphere of this period. He had visions of pompous Nazi military parades and rallies, banners with swastikas, ominous giant eagle emblems, scenes from concentration camps, and many others.

Then came layers related to Peter's childhood, particularly those involving punishment by his parents. His alcoholic father was often violent when he was drunk and used to beat him in a sadistic way with a large leather strap. His mother's favorite method of punishing him was to lock him into a dark cellar without food for long periods of time. All through Peter's childhood, she always wore black dresses; he did not remember her ever wearing anything else. At this point, Peter realized that one of the roots of his obsession seemed to be craving for suffering that would combine elements of punishment by both parents.

However, that was not the whole story. As we continued with the sessions, the process deepened and Peter confronted the trauma of his birth with all its biological brutality. This situation had all the elements that he expected from the sadistic treatment he was so desperately trying to receive: dark enclosed space, confinement and restriction of the body movements, and exposure to extreme physical and emotional tortures. Reliving of the trauma of birth finally resolved his difficult symptoms to such an extent that he could again function in life. The above COEX system also had some connections to elements of a transpersonal nature.

While the above example is more dramatic than most, it illustrates well the basic features characteristic for other COEX constellations. In experiential work, the COEX systems operate as functional wholes. While the person involved experiences the emotions and physical feelings characteristic of a particular constellation, the content of its individual layers emerges successively into consciousness and determines the nature of the experience.

Before we continue our discussion of the new extended cartography of the human psyche it seems appropriate to emphasize in this context a very important and amazing characteristic of NOSC that played an important role in charting the experiential territories and that also is invaluable for the process of psychotherapy. Holotropic states tend to engage something like an "inner radar," bringing into consciousness automatically the contents from the unconscious that have the strongest emotional charge and are most psychodynamically relevant at the time. This represents a great advantage in comparison with verbal psychotherapy, where the client presents a broad array of information of various kinds and the therapist has to decide what is important, what is irrelevant, where the client is blocking, etc.

Since there is no general agreement about basic theoretical issues among different schools, such assessments will always reflect the personal bias of the therapist, as well as the specific views of his or her school. The holotropic states save the therapist such difficult decisions and eliminate much of the subjectivity and professional idiosyncrasy of the verbal approaches. In the above example, this "inner radar" often surprises the therapist by detecting emotionally strongly charged memories of physical traumas and brings them to the surface for conscious integration. This automatic selection of relevant topics also spontaneously leads the process to the perinatal and transpersonal levels of the psyche, transbiographical domains not recognized and acknowledged in academic psychiatry and psychology. The phenomena originating in these deep recesses of the psyche have been recognized and honored by ancient and pre-industrial cultures of all ages. In the Western world they have been—I believe erroneously—attributed to pathology of unknown origin and considered to be meaningless and erratic products of cerebral dysfunction.

The Perinatal Level of the Unconscious

The domain of the psyche that lies immediately beyond the recollective-biographical realm seems to have close connections with the beginning of life and its end, with birth and death. Many people identify the experiences that originate on this level as the reliving of their biological birth trauma. This is reflected in the name *perinatal* that I have suggested for this level of the psyche. It is a Greek-Latin composite word where the prefix *peri-*, means "near" or "around," and the root *natalis* "pertaining to childbirth." This word is commonly used in medicine to describe various biological processes occurring shortly before, during, and immediately after birth. Thus the obstetricians talk, for example, about perinatal hemorrhage, infection, or brain damage. However, since traditional medicine denies that the child can consciously experience birth and claims that the event is not recorded in memory, one does not ever hear about perinatal experiences. The use of the term perinatal in connection with consciousness reflects my own findings and is entirely new (Grof, 1975).

Academic psychiatry generally denies the possibility of a psychotraumatic impact of biological birth unless the trauma is so serious that it causes irreversible damage to the brain cells. This is usually attributed to the fact that the cerebral cortex of the newborn is not myelinized—that means its neurons are not fully protected by myelin sheaths. The assumption that the child does not experience anything during all the hours of this extremely painful and stressful event and that the birth process does not leave any record in the brain is astonishing in itself, since it is known that the capacity for memory exists in many lower life forms that do not have a cerebral cortex at all. However, it is particularly striking in view of the fact that many current theories attribute great significance to nuances of nursing and the early relationship between the mother and the child. Such blatant logical contradiction appearing in rigorous scientific thinking is incomprehensible and has to be the result of a profound emotional repression to which the memory of birth is subjected.

People who reach this level in their inner explorations start experiencing emotions and physical sensations of extreme intensity, often surpassing anything they consider humanly possible. As I mentioned before, these experiences represent a very strange mixture and combination of two critical aspects of human life—birth and death. They involve a sense of a severe, life-threatening confinement and a desperate and determined struggle to free oneself and survive. The intimate connection between birth and death on the perinatal level reflects the fact that birth is a potentially life-threatening event. The child and the mother can actually lose their lives during this process and children might be born severely blue from asphyxiation or even dead and in need of resuscitation.

As their name indicates, an important core of perinatal experiences is the reliving of various aspects of the biological birth process. It often involves photographic details and occurs even in people who have no intellectual knowledge about their birth. The replay of the original birth situation can be very convincing. We can, for example, discover through direct experience that we had a breech birth, that a forceps was used during our delivery, or that we were born with the umbilical cord twisted around the neck. We can feel the anxiety, biological fury, physical pain, and suffocation associated with this terrifying event and even accurately recognize the type of anesthesia used when we were born. This is often accompanied by various physical manifestations that can be noticed by an external observer. The postures and movements of the body, arms, and legs, as well as the rotations, flections, deflections of the head can accurately recreate the mechanics of a particular type of delivery, even in people without elementary obstetric knowledge. Bruises, swellings, and other vascular changes can unexpectedly appear on the skin in the places where the forceps was applied, the wall of the birth canal was pressing on the head, or where the umbilical cord was constricting the throat. All these details can be confirmed if good birth records or reliable personal witnesses are available.

The spectrum of perinatal experiences is not limited to the elements that can be derived from the biological processes involved in childbirth. The perinatal domain of the psyche also represents an important gateway to the collective unconscious in the Jungian sense. Identification with the infant facing the ordeal of the passage through the birth canal seems to provide access to experiences involving people from other times and cultures, various animals, and even mythological figures. It is as if by connecting with the fetus struggling to be born, one reaches an intimate, almost mystical connection with other sentient beings who are in a similar difficult predicament. Experiential confrontation with birth and death seems to result automatically in a spiritual opening and discovery of the mystical dimensions of the psyche and of existence. It does not seem to make a difference whether it happens symbolically, as in psychedelic and holotropic sessions and in the course of spontaneous psycho-spiritual crises ("spiritual emergencies") or whether it occurs in actual life situations, for example, in delivering women or in the context of near-death experiences (Ring, 1984). The specific symbolism of these experiences comes from the Jungian collective unconscious, not from the individual memory banks. It can thus draw on any spiritual tradition of the world, quite independently from the subject's cultural or religious background.

Perinatal phenomena occur in four distinct experiential patterns characterized by specific emotions, physical feelings, and symbolic images. Each of them is closely related to one of the four consecutive periods of biological delivery. At each of these stages, the baby undergoes a specific and typical set of experiences. In turn, these experiences form distinct matrices or psycho-spiritual blueprints that later manifest in non-ordinary states of consciousness and that we find echoing in individual and social psychopathology, religion, art, philosophy, politics, and other areas of our life. We can talk about these four dynamic constellations of the deep unconscious that are associated with the trauma of birth as *Basic Perinatal Matrices* (BPMs).

	BPM I	BPM II	BPM III	BPM IV
RELATED PSYCHOPATHOLOGICAL SYNDROMES	schizophrenic psychoses (paranoid symptomatology, feelings of mystical union, encounter with metaphysical evil forces, karmic experiences); hypochondrias (based on strange and bizarre physical sensations); hysterical hallucinosis and confusing daydreams with reality	schizophrenic psychoses (elements of hellish tortures, experience of meaningless "cardboard" world); inhibited "endogenous" depressions; irrational inferiority and guilt feelings; hypochondriasis (based on painful physical sensations); alcoholism and drug addiction	schizophrenic psychoses (sado-masochistic and scatological elements, automutilation, abnormal sexual behavior); agitated depression; sexual deviations (sado-masochism, male homosexuality, drinking of urine and eating of feces); obsessive-compulsive neurosis; psychogenic asthma, tics and stammering; conversion and anxiety hysteria; frigidity and impotence; neurasthenia, traumatic neuroses; organ neuroses; migraine headache; enuresis and encopresis; psoriasis; peptic ulcer	schizophrenic psychoses (death-rebirth experiences, messianic delusions, elements of destruction and recreation of the world, salvation and redemption, identification with Christ); manic symptomatology; female homosexuality; exhibitionism.
CORRESPONDING ACTIVITIES IN FREUDIAN EROTOGENIC ZONES	libidinal satisfaction in all erotogenic zones; libidinal feeling during rocking and bathing; partial approximation to this condition after oral, anal, urethral or genital satisfaction and delivery of a child.	oral frustration (thirst, hunger, painful stimuli); retention of feces and/or urine; sexual frustration; experiences of cold, pain, and other unpleasant sensations	chewing and swallowing of food, oral aggression and destruction of an object; process of defecation and urination; anal and urethral aggression, sexual orgasm; phallic aggression; delivering of a child; statoacoustic eroticism (jolting, gymnastics, fancy diving, parachuting)	satiation of thirst and hunger; pleasure of sucking; libidinal feelings after defecation, urination, sexual orgasm, or delivery of a child
ASSOCIATED MEMORIES FROM POSTNATAL LIFE	situations from later life where important needs are satisfied, such as happy moments from infancy and childhood (good mothering, play with peers, harmonious periods in the family, etc.), fulfilling love romances; trips or vacations in beautiful natural settings; exposure to artistic creations of high aesthetic value; swimming in the ocean and clear lakes, etc.	situations endangering survival and body integrity (war experiences, accidents, injuries, operations, painful diseases, near drowning, episodes of suffocation, imprisonment, brainwashing and illegal interrogation, physical abuse, etc.); severe psychological traumatizations (emotional deprivation, rejection, threatening situations, oppressing family atmosphere, ridicule and humiliation, etc.)	struggles, fights, and adventurous activities (active attacks in battles and revolutions, experiences in military service, rough airplane flights, cruises on stormy ocean, hazardous car driving, boxing); highly sensual memories (carnivals, amusement parks and nightclubs, wild kicks and parties, sexual orgies, etc.); childhood observation of adult sexual activities; experiences of seduction and rape; in females delivery of their own children	lucky escape from dangerous situations (end of war or revolution, survival of an accident or operation); overcoming of severe obstacles by active effort; episodes of strain and hard struggle resulting in a marked success; natural scenes (beginning of spring, end of an ocean storm, sunrise, etc.)

Figure 26.1 Basic Perinatal Matrices

continued

Figure 26.1 (continued)

PHENOMENOLOGY IN LSD SESSIONS	*undisturbed intrauterine life*: realistic recollections of "good womb" experiences; "oceanic" type of ecstasy; experience of cosmic unity; visions of Paradise; *disturbances of intrauterine life*: realistic recollections of "bad womb" experiences (fetal crises, diseases and emotional upheavals of the mother, twin situation, attempted abortions), cosmic engulfment; paranoid ideation; unpleasant physical sensations ("hangover," chills and fine spasms, unpleasant tastes, disgust, feelings of being poisoned); association with various transpersonal experiences (archetypal elements, racial and evolutionary memories, encounter with metaphysical forces, past incarnation experiences, etc.)	immense physical and psychological suffering; unbearable and inescapable situation that will never end; various images of hell; feelings of entrapment and engagement (no exit); agonizing guilt and inferiority feelings; apocalyptic view of the world (horrors of wars and concentration camps, terror of the Inquisition, dangerous epidemics, diseases, decrepitude and death, etc.); meaninglessness and absurdity of human existence; "cardboard world" or the "cardboard world" or the gadgets; atmosphere of artificiality and gadgets; ominous dark colors and unpleasant physical symptoms (feelings of oppression and compression, cardiac distress, flushes and chills, sweating, difficult breathing)	intensification of suffering to cosmic dimensions; borderline between pain and pleasure; "volcanic" type of ecstasy; brilliant colors; explosions and fireworks; sado-masochistic orgies; murders and bloody sacrifice; active engagement in fierce battles; atmosphere of wild adventure and dangerous explorations; intense sexual orgiastic feelings and scenes of harems and carnivals; experiences of dying and being reborn; religions involving bloody sacrifice (Aztecs, Christ's suffering and death on the cross, Dionysius, etc.); intense physical manifestations (pressures and pains, suffocation, muscular tension and discharge in tremors and twitches, nausea and vomiting, hot flashes and chills, sweating, cardiac distress, problems of sphincter control, ringing in the ears)	enormous decompression, expansion of space, visions of gigantic halls; radiant light and beautiful colors (heavenly blue, golden, rainbow, peacock feathers); feelings of rebirth and redemption; appreciation of simple way of life; sensory enhancement; brotherly feelings; humanitarian and charitative tendencies; occasionally manic activity and grandiose feelings; transition to elements of BPM I; pleasant feelings can be interrupted by *umbilical crisis*: sharp pain in the navel, loss of breath, fear of death and castration, shifts in the body, but no external pressures
STAGES OF DELIVERY			

Each perinatal matrix has its specific biological, psychological, archetypal, and spiritual aspects. In addition to having specific content of their own, BPMs also function as organizing principles for experiential elements from other levels of the unconscious, namely for biographical material and for some transpersonal phenomena. Individual matrices thus have fixed connections with certain categories of postnatal experiences arranged in COEX systems. They have also associations with the archetypes of the Terrible Mother Goddess, the Great Mother Goddess, Hell, or Heaven, as well as racial, collective, and karmic memories, and phylogenetic experiences. I should also mention theoretically and practically important links between BPMs and specific aspects of physiological activities in the Freudian erogenous zones and to specific categories of emotional and psychosomatic disorders. All these interrelations are shown on the synoptic paradigm on pages 500–501.

BPM I. (Primal Union with Mother). This matrix is related to the intrauterine existence before the onset of delivery. Prenatal life can be referred to as "the amniotic universe." The fetus does not have an awareness of boundaries or the ability to differentiate between the inner and outer. This is reflected in the nature of the experiences associated with the reliving of the memory of the prenatal state. During episodes of undisturbed embryonal existence, people can have feelings of vast regions with no boundaries or limits. They can identify with galaxies, interstellar space, or the entire cosmos. A related experience is that of floating in the sea, identifying with various aquatic animals, such as fish, dolphins, or whales, or even becoming the ocean. This seems to reflect the fact that the fetus is essentially a water creature. One might also have archetypal visions of Mother Nature—safe, beautiful, and unconditionally nourishing like a good womb—such as luscious orchards, fields of ripe corn, agricultural terraces in the Andes, or unspoiled Polynesian islands. Mythological images from the collective unconscious that often appear in this context portray various celestial realms and paradises.

The persons reliving episodes of intrauterine disturbances, or "bad womb" experiences, have a sense of dark and ominous threat and often feel that they are being poisoned. They might see images that portray polluted waters and toxic dumps, probably reflecting the fact that many prenatal disturbances are caused by toxic changes in the body of the pregnant mother. Sequences of this kind can be associated with visions of frightening demonic entities. Those who relive more violent interferences with prenatal existence, such as an imminent miscarriage or attempted abortion, usually experience some form of universal threat or bloody apocalyptic visions of the end of the world. This again reflects the intimate interconnections between events in one's biological history and Jungian archetypes.

The following account of a high-dose psychedelic session can be used as a typical example of a BPM I experience, opening at times into the transpersonal realm.

All that I was experiencing was an intense sense of malaise resembling a flu. I could not believe that a high dose of LSD that in my previous sessions had produced dramatic changes—to the point that on occasions I was afraid that my sanity or even my life was at stake—could evoke such a minimal response. I decided to close my eyes and observe carefully what was happening. At this point the experience seemed to deepen, and I realized that what with my eyes open appeared to be an adult experience of a viral disease now changed into a realistic situation of a fetus suffering some strange toxic insults during its intrauterine existence.

I was greatly reduced in size, and my head was considerably bigger than the rest of the body and extremities. I was suspended in a liquid milieu and some harmful chemicals were being channeled into my body through the umbilical area. Using some unknown receptors, I was detecting these influences as noxious and hostile to my organism. While this was happening, I was aware that these toxic "attacks" had something to do with the condition and activity of the maternal organism. Occasionally, I could distinguish influences that appeared to be due to ingestion of alcohol, inappropriate food, or smoking—and others that I perceived as chemical mediators of my mother's emotions—anxieties, nervousness, anger, conflicting feelings about pregnancy, and even sexual arousal.

Then the feelings of sickness and indigestion disappeared, and I was experiencing an ever-increasing state of ecstasy. This was accompanied by a clearing and brightening of my visual field. It was as if multiple layers of thick, dirty cobwebs were being magically torn and dissolved, or a poor-quality movie projection or television broadcast was being focused and rectified by an invisible cosmic technician. The scenery opened up, and an incredible amount of light and energy was enveloping me and streaming in subtle vibrations through my whole being. On one level, I was still a fetus experiencing the ultimate perfection and bliss of a good womb or a newborn fusing with a nourishing and life-giving breast. On another level, I became the entire universe; I was witnessing the spectacle of the macrocosm with countless pulsating and vibrating galaxies and was it at the same time. These radiant and breathtaking cosmic vistas were intermingled with experiences of the equally miraculous microcosm—from the dance of atoms and molecules to the origins of life and the biochemical world of individual cells. For the first time, I was experiencing the universe for what it really is—an unfathomable mystery, a divine play of energy. Everything in this universe appeared to be conscious.

For some time, I was oscillating between the state of a distressed, sickened fetus and a blissful and serene intrauterine existence. At times, the noxious influences took the form of insidious demons or malevolent creatures from the world of fairy tales. During the undisturbed episodes of fetal existence, I experienced feelings of basic identity and oneness with the universe; it was the *Tao*, the Beyond that is Within, the *Tat tvam asi* (Thou art That) of the Upanishads. I lost my sense of individuality; my ego dissolved, and I became all of existence.

Sometimes this experience was intangible and contentless, sometimes it was accompanied by many beautiful visions—archetypal images of Paradise, the ultimate cornucopia, golden age, or virginal nature. I became a dolphin playing in the ocean, a fish swinning in crystal-clear waters, a butterfly floating in mountain meadows, and a seagull gliding by the sea. I was the ocean, animals, plants, the clouds—sometimes all these at the same time.

Nothing concrete happened later in the afternoon and in the evening hours. I spent most of this time feeling one with nature and the universe, bathed in golden light that was slowly decreasing in intensity.

BPM II (Cosmic Engulfment and No Exit or Hell). Individuals reliving the very onset of biological birth typically feel that they are being sucked into a gigantic whirlpool or swallowed by some mythic beast. They might also experience that the entire world or cosmos is being engulfed. This can be associated with images of devouring archetypal monsters, such as leviathans, dragons, giant snakes, tarantulas, and octopuses. The sense of overwhelming vital threat can lead to intense anxiety and general mistrust bordering on paranoia. Another experiential variety involves the theme of descending into the depths of the underworld, the realm of death, or hell. As Joseph Campbell so eloquently described, this is a universal motif in the mythologies of the hero's journey.

A fully developed first stage of biological birth is characterized by a situation where the uterine contractions periodically constrict the fetus and the cervix is not yet open. Each contraction causes compression of the uterine arteries, and the fetus is threatened by lack of oxygen. Reliving this stage is one of the worst experiences a human being can have. One feels caught in a monstrous claustrophobic nightmare, exposed to agonizing emotional and physical pain, and has a sense of utter helplessness and hopelessness. Feelings of loneliness, guilt, the absurdity of life, and existential despair reach metaphysical proportions. A person in this predicament often becomes convinced that this situation will never end and that there is absolutely no way out.

Reliving this stage of birth is typically accompanied by sequences that involve people, animals, and even mythological beings in a similar painful and hopeless predicament. One experiences identification with prisoners in dungeons and inmates of concentration camps or insane asylums, and senses the pain of animals caught in traps. He or she may even feel the intolerable tortures of sinners in hell and the agony of Christ on the cross or of Sisyphus rolling his boulder up the mountain in the deepest pit of Hades. It is only natural that someone facing this aspect of the psyche would feel a great reluctance to confront it. Going deeper into this experience seems like accepting eternal damnation. However, this state of darkness and abysmal despair is known from the spiritual literature as the Dark Night of the Soul, a stage of spiritual opening that can have an immensely purging and liberating effect.

The most characteristic features of BPM II can be illustrated by the following account.

> The atmosphere seemed increasingly ominous and fraught with hidden danger. It seemed that the entire room started to turn and I felt drawn into the very center of a threatening whirlpool. I had to think about Edgar Alan Poe's chilling description of a similar situation in "A Descent into the Maelstrom." As the objects in the room seemed to be flying around me in a rotating motion, another image from literature emerged in my mind—the cyclone that in Frank Baum's *Wonderful Wizard of Oz* sweeps Dorothy away from the monotony of her life in Kansas and sends her on a strange journey of adventure. There was no doubt in my mind that my experience also had something to do with entering the rabbit hole in *Alice in Wonderland,* and I awaited with great trepidation what world I would find on the other side of the looking glass. The entire universe seemed to be closing in on me and there was nothing I could do to stop this apocalyptic engulfment.

> As I was sinking deeper and deeper into the labyrinth of my own unconscious, I felt an onslaught of anxiety, turning to panic. Everything became dark, oppressive, and terrifying. It was as if the weight of the whole world was encroaching on me exerting incredible hydraulic pressure that threatened to crack my skull and reduce my body to a tiny compact ball. A rapid fugue of memories from my past cascaded through my brain showing me the utter futility and meaninglessness of my life and existence in general. We are born naked, frightened, and in agony and we will leave the world the same way. The existentialists were right! Everything is impermanent, life is nothing else but waiting for Godot! Vanity of vanities, all is vanity!

The discomfort I felt turned to pain, and the pain increased to agony. The torture intensified to the point where every cell in my body felt like it was being bored open with a diabolic dentist's drill. Visions of infernal landscapes and devils torturing their victims suddenly brought to me the awareness that I was in Hell. I thought of Dante's *Divine Comedy:* "Abandon all hope ye who enter!" There seemed to be no way out of this diabolical situation; I was forever doomed without the slightest hope for redemption.

BPM III (The Death-Rebirth Struggle). Many aspects of this rich and colorful experience can be understood from its association with the second clinical stage of the delivery, the propulsion through the birth canal after the cervix opens and the head descends. Beside the elements that are easily comprehensible as natural derivatives of the birth situation, such as sequences of titanic struggle involving strong pressures and energies or scenes of bloody violence and torture, there are others that require special explanation. This involves particularly a strong sexual arousal of a particular kind typically associated with this matrix.

There seems to be a mechanism in the human organism that transforms extreme suffering, particularly when it is associated with suffocation, into a strange form of sexual excitement. This explains why a large variety of sexual experiences and visions often occur in connection with the reliving of birth. One can feel a combination of sexual arousal and pain, aggression, or fear, experience various sado-masochistic sequences, rapes, and situations of sexual abuse, or see pornographic images. The fact that, in the final stages of birth, the fetus can encounter various forms of biological material—blood, mucus, urine, and even feces—seems to account for the fact that these elements also play a role in death-rebirth sequences.

These experiences are often accompanied by specific archetypal elements from the collective unconscious, particularly those related to heroic figures and deities representing death and rebirth. At this stage, many people have visions of Jesus, his suffering and humiliation, the Way of the Cross, and the Crucifixion, or even actually experience full identification with his suffering. Others connect with such mythological themes and figures as the Egyptian divine couple Isis and Osiris, the Greek deities Dionysus, Attis, and Adonis, the Sumerian goddess Inanna and her descent into the underworld, or the Mayan Hero Twins of the Popol Vuh.

The frequent appearance of motifs related to various satanic rituals and the Witches' Sabbath seems to be related to the fact that reliving this stage of birth involves the same strange combination of emotions, sensations, and elements that characterizes the archetypal scenes of the Black Mass and of Walpurgis Night: sexual arousal, aggression, pain, sacrifice, and encounters with ordinarily repulsive biological material—all associated with a peculiar sense of sacredness or numinosity.

Just before the experience of (re)birth, people often encounter the motif of fire. This is a somewhat puzzling symbol. Its connection with biological birth is not as direct and obvious as are many of the other symbolic elements. One can experience fire either in its ordinary form or in the archetypal variety of purifying flames. At this stage of the process, the person can have the feeling that his or her body is on fire, have visions of burning cities and forests, or identify with immolation victims. In the archetypal version, the burning seems to have a purgatorial quality. It seems to radically destroy whatever is corrupted and prepare the individual for spiritual rebirth.

Many of the symbolic themes associated with BPM III are described in the following account.

> Although I never really clearly saw the birth canal, I felt its crushing pressure on my head and all over, and I knew with every cell of my body that I was involved in a birth process. The tension was reaching dimensions that I had not imagined were humanly possible. I felt unrelenting pressure on my forehead, temples, and occiput, as if I were caught in the steel jaws of a vise. The tensions in my body also had a brutally mechanical quality. I imagined myself passing through a mon-strous meat grinder or a giant press full of cogs and cylinders. The image of Charlie Chaplin victimized by the world of technology in *Modern Times* briefly flashed through my mind.
>
> Incredible amounts of energy seemed to be flowing through my entire body, condensing and releasing in explosive discharges. I felt an amazing mixture of feelings; I was suffocated, frightened, and helpless, but also furious and strangely sexually aroused. Another important aspect of my experience was a sense of utter confusion. While I felt like an infant involved in a vicious struggle for survival and realized that what was about to happen was my birth, I was also experiencing myself as my delivering mother. I knew intellectually that being a man I could never give birth, yet I felt that I was somehow crossing that barrier and that the impossible was becoming a reality.
>
> There was no question that I was connecting with something pri-mordial—an ancient feminine archetype, that of the delivering mother. My body image included a large pregnant belly and female genitals with all the nuances of biological sensations. I felt frustrated by not being able to surrender to this elemental process—to give birth and be born, to let go and to let the baby out. An enormous reservoir of murderous aggres-sion emerged from the underworld of my psyche. It was as if an abscess of evil had suddenly been punctured by the cut of a cosmic surgeon. A

werewolf or a berserk was taking me over; Dr. Jekyll was turning into Mr. Hyde. There were many images of the murderer and the victim as being one and the same person, just as earlier I could not distinguish between the child who was being born and the delivering mother.

I was a merciless tyrant, the dictator exposing the subordinates to unimaginable cruelties, and also a revolutionary, leading the furious mob to overthrow the tyrant. I became the mobster who murders in cold blood and the policeman who kills the criminal in the name of law. At one point, I experienced the horrors of the Nazi concentration camps. When I opened my eyes, I saw myself as an SS officer. I had a profound sense that he, the Nazi, and I, the Jew, were the same person. I could feel the Hitler and the Stalin in me and felt fully responsible for the atrocities in human history. I saw clearly that humanity's problem is not the existence of vicious dictators, but this Hidden Killer that we all harbor within our own psyches, if we look deep enough.

Then the nature of the experience changed and reached mythological proportions. Instead of the evil of human history, I now sensed the atmosphere of witchcraft and the presence of demonic elements. My teeth were transformed into long fangs filled with some mysterious poison, and I found myself flying on large bat wings through the night like an ominous vampire. This changed soon into wild, intoxicating scenes of a witches' Sabbath. In this strange, sensuous ritual, all the usually forbidden and repressed impulses seemed to surface and were experienced and acted out. I was aware of participating in some mysterious sacrificial ceremony celebrating the Dark God.

As the demonic quality gradually disappeared from my experience, I still felt tremendously erotic and was engaged in endless sequences of the most fantastic orgies and sexual fantasies, in which I played all the roles. All through these experiences, I simultaneously continued being also the child struggling through the birth canal and the mother delivering it. It became very clear to me that sex and birth were deeply connected and that satanic forces had important links with the propulsion through the birth canal. I struggled and fought in many different roles and against many different enemies. Sometimes I wondered if there would ever be an end to my misery.

Then a new element entered my experience. My entire body was covered by some biological filth, which was slimy and slippery. I could not tell if it was the amniotic fluid, urine, mucus, blood, or vaginal secretions. The same stuff seemed to be in my mouth and even in my lungs. I was choking, gagging, making faces, and spitting, trying to get it out of my system and off my skin. At the same time, I was getting a message that I did not have to fight. The process had its own rhythm, and all I had to do was surrender to it. I remembered many situations from my life, where I felt the need to fight and struggle. In retrospect, that need to fight and struggle felt unnecessary. It was as if I had been somehow programmed by my birth to see life as much more complicated and dangerous than it actually is. It seemed to me that this experience could open my eyes in this regard and make my life much easier and more playful than before.

BPM IV (The Death-Rebirth Experience). This matrix is related to the third stage of delivery, to the final expulsion from the birth canal and the severing of the umbilical cord. Here one completes the preceding difficult process of propulsion through the birth canal and achieves explosive liberation as he or she emerges into light. Such a person often relives various specific aspects of this stage of birth as concrete and realistic memories. These can include the experience of anesthesia, the pressures of the forceps, and the sensations associated with various obstetric maneuvers or postnatal interventions.

To understand why the reliving of biological birth is experienced as death and rebirth, one has to realize that what happens is more than just a replay of the original event. Because the fetus is completely confined during the birth process and has no way of expressing the extreme emotions and sensations involved, the memory of this event remains psychologically undigested and unassimilated. Much of our later self-definition and our attitudes toward the world are heavily contaminated by this constant reminder of the vulnerability, inadequacy, and weakness that we experienced at birth. In a sense, we were born anatomically but have not caught up with this fact emotionally. The "dying" and the agony during the struggle for rebirth reflect the actual pain and vital threat of the biological birth process. However, the ego death that precedes rebirth is the death of our old concepts of who we are and what the world is like, which were forged by the traumatic imprint of birth.

As we are purging these old programs by letting them emerge into consciousness, they are becoming irrelevant and are, in a sense, dying. As frightening as this process is, it is actually very healing and transforming. Approaching the moment of the ego death might feel like the end of the world. Paradoxically, while only a small step separates us from an experience of radical liberation, we have a sense of all-pervading anxiety and impending catastrophy of enormous proportions. It feels as if we are losing all that we are; at the same time, we have no idea of what is on the other side, or even if there is anything there at all. This fear drives many people to resist the process at this stage; as a result, they can remain psychologically stuck in this problematic territory.

When the individual overcomes the metaphysical fear encountered at this important juncture and decides to let things happen, he or she experiences total annihilation on all levels—physical destruction, emotional disaster, intellectual and philosophical defeat, ultimate moral failure, and even spiritual damnation. During this experience, all reference points—everything that is important and meaningful in the individual's life—seem to be mercilessly destroyed. Immediately following the experience of total annihilation—hitting "cosmic bottom"—one is often overwhelmed by visions of light that has a supernatural radiance and beauty and is usually perceived as divine. The survivor of what seemed like the ultimate apocalypse experiences only seconds later fantastic displays of rainbows, peacock designs, and celestial scenes. He or she feels redeemed and blessed by salvation, reclaiming his or her divine nature and cosmic status. At this time, one is frequently overcome by a surge of positive emotions toward oneself, other people, nature, and existence in general. This kind of healing and life-changing experience occurs when birth was not too debilitating or confounded by heavy anesthesia. If the latter was the case, the individual has to do psychological work on the traumatic issues involved.

The following account of a death-rebirth experience describes a typical sequence characteristic of BPM IV.

> However, the worst was yet to come. All of a sudden, I seemed to be losing all my connections to reality, as if some imaginary rug was pulled from under my feet. Everything was collapsing, and I felt that my entire world was shattered to pieces. It was like puncturing a monstrous metaphysical balloon of my existence; a gigantic bubble of ludicrous self-deception had burst open and exposed the lie of my life. Everything that I ever believed in, everything that I did or pursued, everything that seemed to give my life meaning suddenly appeared utterly false. These were all pitiful crutches without any substance with which I tried to patch up the intolerable reality of existence. They were now blasted and blown away like the frail feathered seeds of a dandelion, exposing a frightening abyss of ultimate truth—the meaningless chaos of the existential Void.
>
> Filled with indescribable horror, I saw a gigantic figure of a deity towering over me in a threatening pose. I somehow instinctively recognized that this was the Hindu god Shiva in his destructive aspect. I felt the thunderous impact of his enormous foot that crushed me, shattered me to smithereens, and smeared me like an insignificant piece of excrement all over what I felt was the bottom of the cosmos. In the next moment, I was facing a terrifying giant figure of a dark goddess whom

I identified as the Indian Kali. My face was being pushed by an irresistible force toward her gaping vagina that was full of what seemed to be menstrual blood or repulsive afterbirth.

I sensed that what was demanded of me was absolute surrender to the forces of existence and to the feminine principle represented by the goddess. I had no choice but to kiss and lick her vulva in utmost submission and humility. At this moment, which was the ultimate and final end of any feeling of male supremacy I had ever harbored, I connected with the memory of the moment of my biological birth. My head was emerging from the birth canal with my mouth in close contact with the bleeding vagina of my mother.

I was flooded with the divine light of supernatural radiance and beauty whose rays were exploded into thousands of exquisite peacock designs. From this brilliant golden light emerged a figure of a Great Mother Goddess who seemed to embody love and protection of all ages. She spread her arms and reached toward me, enveloping me into her essence. I merged with this incredible energy field, feeling purged, healed, and nourished. What seemed to be some divine nectar and ambrosia, some archetypal essence of milk and honey, was poured through me in absolute abundance.

Then the figure of the goddess gradually disappeared, absorbed by an even more brilliant light. It was abstract, yet endowed with definite personal characteristics and radiating infinite intelligence. It became clear to me that what I was experiencing was the merging with and absorption into the Universal Self, or Brahma, as I have read about it in books of Indian philosophy. This experience subsided after about ten minutes of clocktime; however, it transcended any concept of time and felt like eternity. The flow of the healing and nourishing energy and the visions of golden glow with peacock designs lasted through the night. The resulting sense of well-being stayed with me for many days. The memory of the experience has remained vivid for years and has profoundly changed my entire life philosophy.

The Transpersonal Domain of the Psyche

The second major domain that has to be added to mainstream psychiatry's cartography of the human psyche when we work with NOSC is now known under the name *transpersonal,* meaning literally "beyond the personal" or "transcending the personal." The experiences that originate on this level involve transcendence of the usual boundaries of the individual (his or her body and ego) and of the limitations of three-dimensional space and linear time that restrict perception of the world in the ordinary state of consciousness. I have defined and discussed the phenomena originating on this level of the psyche in some detail in chapter 4 in this volume. In this context, I will only briefly mention their most important representatives.

According to their content, transpersonal experiences can be divided into three large categories. The first of these involves primarily transcendence of the usual spatial barriers, or of the spatial limitations of the body ego. In experiences of this category, individual consciousness can identify with any person, animal, or inorganic object and process (or group of them) that lies on the continuum between the body ego and the Mind at Large. The second category of transpersonal experiences is characterized primarily by overcoming of temporal rather than spatial boundaries, that is by transcendence of linear time. Here any event in human history, evolution of the species, or cosmogenesis can become available as a subjective experience; in some instances, this can even involve various aspects of the future. The third category of transpersonal experiences includes beings and realities that, according to the Western world view, do not have independent objective existence—archetypal beings, mythological landscapes, discarnate entities, spirit-guides, and inhabitants of parallel universes. In NOSC, all these types of experiences seem equally real and authentic and can reveal new information about the persons, animals, mythological figures and realms, and various events involved. Phenomena of this kind have been repeatedly described in spiritual literature of the world.

I firmly believe that the expanded cartography which I have outlined above is of critical importance for any serious approach to such phenomena as shamanism, rites of passage, mysticism, religion, mythology, parapsychology, near-death experiences, and psychedelic states. This new model of the psyche is not just a matter of academic interest. As I will try to show in the remaining pages of this chapter, it has deep and revolutionary implications for the understanding of emotional and psychosomatic disorders, including psychoses, and offers new and revolutionary therapeutic possibilities.

The Nature and Architecture of Emotional and Psychosomatic Disorders

Traditional psychiatry uses the medical model and the disease concept not only for disorders of a clearly organic nature, but also for emotional and psychosomatic disorders for which no biological cause has been found. Psychiatrists use quite loosely the term "mental" or "emotional disease" and try to assign various disorders to specific diagnostic categories comparable to those of general medicine. Generally, the time of the onset of symptoms is seen as the beginning of the "disease" and the intensity of the symptoms is used as the measure of the seriousness of the pathological process. Alleviation of the symptoms is considered "clinical improvement" and their intensification is seen as "worsening of the clinical condition."

The observations from the study of NOSC suggest that thinking in terms of disease, diagnosis, and allopathic therapy is not appropriate for most psychiatric problems that are not clearly organic in nature, including some of the conditions currently labeled as psychoses. To exist in a material form, to have experienced the embryological development, birth, infancy, and childhood has left traumatic imprints in all of us, although we certainly differ as to their intensity, extensity, and also availability of this traumatic material for conscious experience. Every person is carrying a variety of more or less latent emotional and bioenergetic blockages which interfere with full physiological and psychological functioning.

The manifestation of emotional and psychosomatic symptoms is the beginning of a healing process through which the organism is trying to free itself from traumatic imprints and simplify its functioning. The only way this can happen is by emergence of the traumatic material into consciousness and its full experience and emotional and motor expression. If the trauma that is being processed is of major proportions, such as a difficult birth that lasted many hours and seriously threatened biological survival, the emotions and behavioral expressions can be extremely dramatic. Under these circumstances, it might seem more plausible that it is a result of some exotic pathology than to recognize that it is a potentially beneficial development. However, when properly understood and supported, this process can be conducive to healing, spiritual opening, personality transformation, and consciousness evolution. The emergence of symptoms thus represents not only a problem, but also a therapeutic opportunity; this insight is the basis of most experiential psychotherapies. Symptoms manifest in the area where the defense system is at its weakest, making it possible for the healing process to begin. According to my experience, this is true not only in relation to neuroses and psychosomatic disorders, but also to certain conditions traditionally considered psychotic (psycho-spiritual crises or "spiritual emergencies"). It is interesting to mention in this context that the Chinese pictogram for "crisis" is composed of two others, one meaning "danger" and the other "opportunity." The idea that the symptoms are not manifestations of the disease, but are expressions of a healing process and should be supported is also found in a therapeutic system called homeopathy.

In traditional psychotherapy, emotional and psychosomatic symptoms that are not organic in nature, but psychogenic in origin, are seen as resulting from postnatal biographical traumas, especially those that occurred in infancy and childhood. Therapeutic work using NOSC reveals that they actually have a multidimensional structure with additional roots on the perinatal and transpersonal levels. Thus, for example, somebody suffering from psychogenic asthma can discover that the underlying biographical material consists of memories of suffocation during a near-drowning accident in childhood and an episode of diphtheria in infancy. On a deeper level, the same problem is also connected with choking in the birth canal and its deepest root can be a past-life experience of being strangled or hanged. To resolve this symptom, it is necessary to allow oneself to experience all the layers of problems associated with it. New insights concerning this multilevel dynamic structure of the major forms of emotional and psychosomatic disorders have been described in detail elsewhere (Grof, 1985).

Therapeutic Mechanisms and the Process of Healing

The work with NOSC has thus discovered that emotional and psychosomatic problems are much more complex than is usually assumed and that their roots reach incomparably deeper into the psyche. However, it also revealed the existence of deeper and more effective therapeutic mechanisms. Traditional psychotherapy treatments of psychogenic disorders recognize only therapeutic mechanisms related to various manipulations of biographical material, for example: lifting of psychological repression and remembering or reconstructing events from infancy and childhood; emotional and intellectual insights into one's life history; or transference neurosis and analysis of transference. The new observations show that these approaches fail to recognize and appreciate the amazing healing potential of the deeper dynamics of the psyche. Thus, for example, the reliving of birth and the experience of ego death and spiritual rebirth can have far-reaching therapeutic impact on a broad spectrum of psychological disorders. Similar beneficial results are often associated with various forms of transpersonal phenomena, such as past-life experiences and identification with various animals or archetypal figures and energies. Of particular importance in this sense are ecstatic feelings of cosmic unity which—if properly integrated—provide a healing mechanism of extraordinary power.

These observations show that the conceptual framework of psychotherapy has to be extended as vastly as the cartography of the unconscious. Freud once likened the human psyche to an iceberg, of which only the one-tenth visible above the water surface represented the conscious mind, while the submerged nine-tenths were the unconscious realms studied by psychoanalysis. In light of modern consciousness research (and ancient wisdom of perennial philosophy), we can correct this simile and say that all that Freudian psychoanalysis has discovered about the human psyche represents at best the exposed part of the iceberg, while vast additional domains remained hidden under water. In the words of Joseph Campbell, Freud was fishing, while sitting on a whale.

Strategy of Psychotherapy and Self-exploration

Modern psychotherapy is plagued by an amazing lack of agreement among its different schools about the most fundamental questions concerning the functioning of the human psyche, nature and dynamics of symptoms, and the strategy and technique of psychotherapy. This does not apply only to the schools based on entirely different philosophical assumptions, such as behaviorism, psychoanalysis, and existential therapy, but also the various branches of depth psychology that evolved historically from the same source, the original work of Sigmund Freud (the Adlerian, Rankian, Jungian, Kleinian, Reichian, and Lacanian schools, ego psychology, and many others). The world of modern psychotherapy resembles a large busy marketplace, in which it is difficult to orient oneself. Each of the many schools offers different explanations for the same emotional and psychosomatic problems and a different therapeutic technique. In each case this will be accompanied with the assurance that this is the scientific way to treat this condition, or the "method of choice." It is difficult to envision a similar degree of disagreement in one of the hard sciences. Yet in psychology, we have somehow learned to live with this situation and do not usually even question it or consider it strange.

There are no convincing statistical studies showing that one form of psychotherapy is superior to others. Psychotherapy is generally as good as the therapist; good therapists of all schools tend to get good results and bad therapists of all orientations have bad results. Clearly, the results of psychotherapy have very little to do with the theoretical concepts of a particular school and with what the therapists think they are doing—strategic use of silence, the content and the timing of interpretations, analysis of transference, etc. According to some researchers, the important factors might be of a completely different nature, such as the quality of human encounter between the therapist and the client, the client's feeling of being understood or unconditionally accepted, or even such an immeasurable dimension as love. Under these circumstances, if we opt as professionals for a certain school of psychotherapy, for example Freudian, Reichian, or Sullivanian, it is because we are attracted to it for very personal reasons. It is a purely subjective choice reflecting our own personality structure and it has very little to do with the objective value and scientific accuracy of that particular approach.

The work with NOSC suggests a very radical alternative: if the experts cannot reach agreement, why not trust one's own healing intelligence, one's own inner healer? This approach was first suggested by C. G. Jung. He was aware of the fact that it is impossible to reach an intellectual understanding of how the psyche functions and why the symptoms developed and derive from it a technique by which we can control and correct the mental functioning of a client. According to him, the intellect is just a small fraction of the psyche, while the psyche itself has cosmic dimensions *(anima mundi)*. Jung saw the task of the therapist in helping to establish a dynamic interaction between the client's conscious ego and what he called the Self; this takes the form of a dialectic exchange using the language of symbols. The healing then comes from the collective unconscious, and it is guided by an inner intelligence that surpasses that of any individual therapist or therapeutic school.

Therapeutic work with NOSC, as exemplified by psychedelic therapy or Holotropic Breathwork, supports in general Jung's understanding of the therapeutic process. However, it involves mechanisms which are much more powerful than those available by the methods Jung was using, such as the analysis of dreams and active imagination. NOSC tend to activate the spontaneous healing potential of the psyche and of the body and initiate a transformative process guided by deep inner intelligence. In this process, unconscious material with strong emotional charge and relevance will automatically emerge into consciousness and become available for full experience and integration.

The task of the therapist is simply to offer a method that induces an NOSC (e.g., a psychedelic substance or faster breathing and evocative music), create a safe environment, and support unconditionally and with full trust the spontaneous unfolding of the process. This trust has to extend even to situations where the therapist does not understand intellectually what is happening. Healing and resolution can often occur in ways that transcend rational understanding. In this form of therapy, the therapist thus is not the doer, the agent who is instrumental in the healing process, but a sympathetic supporter and co-adventurer. This attitude corresponds with the original meaning of the Greek word *therapeutes*, which means attendant or assistant in the healing process.

The Role of Spirituality in Human Life

Traditional psychology and psychiatry are dominated by materialistic philosophy and have no recognition of spirituality in any form. From the point of view of Western science, the material world represents the only reality and any form of spiritual belief is seen as reflecting lack of education, primitive superstition, magical thinking, or regression to infantile patterns of functioning. Direct experiences of spiritual realities are then relegated to the world of gross psychopathology. Western psychiatry makes no distinction between a mystical experience and a psychotic experience and sees both as manifestations of mental disease. In its rejection of religion, it does not differentiate primitive folk beliefs or fundamentalists' literal interpretations of scriptures from sophisticated mystical traditions and Eastern spiritual philosophies based on centuries of systematic introspective exploration of the psyche. It pathologizes spiritually of any kind and together with it the entire spiritual history of humanity.

The observations from the study of NOSC confirm an important insight of C. G. Jung. According to him, the experiences originating in deeper levels of the psyche (in my own terminology perinatal and transpersonal experiences) have a certain quality that he called (after Rudolph Otto) *numinosity*. They are associated with the feeling that one is encountering a dimension which is sacred, holy, and radically different from everyday life, and which belongs to a superior order of reality. The term *numinous* is relatively neutral and thus preferable to others, such as religious, mystical, magical, holy, or sacred, which have often been used incorrectly and are easily misleading.

To prevent confusion and misunderstandings that in the past have compromised many similar discussions, it is critical to make a clear distinction between spirituality and religion. Spirituality is based on direct experiences of other realities. It does not necessarily require a special place, nor a special person mediating contact with the divine, although mystics can certainly benefit from spiritual guidance and a community of fellow seekers. Spirituality thus involves a special relationship between the individual and the cosmos and is in its essence a personal and private affair. At the cradle of all great religions are visionary (perinatal and/or transpersonal) experiences of their founders, prophets, saints, and even ordinary followers. All major spiritual scriptures—the Vedas, the Buddhist Pali Canon, the Bible, the Koran, the Book of Mormon, and many others are based on revelations in holotropic states of consciousness.

By comparison, the basis of organized religion is institutionalized group activity that takes place in a designated location (temple, church), and involves a system of appointed mediators. Ideally, religions should provide for its members access to and support for direct spiritual experiences. However, it often happens that a religion completely loses the connection with its spiritual source and becomes a secular institution exploiting the human spiritual needs without satisfying them. Instead, it creates a hierarchical system focusing on the pursuit of power, control, politics, money, and other possessions. Under these circumstances, religious hierarchy tends to actively discourage and suppress direct spiritual experiences in its members, because they foster independence and cannot be effectively controlled. When this happens, genuine spiritual life continues only in the mystical branches and monastic orders.

From the scientific point of view, the main question here is the ontological status of transpersonal experiences. While mainstream psychiatry and psychology see them as indications of pathology, transpersonal psychology considers them important phenomena *sui generis* that have great heuristic and therapeutic value and deserve to be seriously studied. While much of what is found in mainstream religions and their theologies is certainly in serious conflict with science, this is not true in regard to spirituality based on direct transpersonal experiences. The findings of modern consciousness research show actually remarkable convergence with many revolutionary developments in Western science referred to as the emerging paradigm. As Ken Wilber (1982) has noted, there cannot possibly be a conflict between genuine science and authentic religion. If there seems to be a conflict, we are very likely dealing with "bogus science" and "bogus religion," where either side has a serious misunderstanding of the other's position and very likely represents a false or fake version of its own discipline.

The Nature of Reality

As we have seen, the observations from the research of NOSC represent a serious challenge to contemporary psychiatry and psychology and require a drastic revision of our thinking in these fields. However, many of them are of such a fundamental nature that they transcend the narrow frame of these disciplines and challenge the most basic philosophical assumptions of Western science and its Newtonian-Cartesian paradigm. They seriously undermine the belief that our consciousness is an accidental product of the neurophysiological processes in our brains and strongly suggest that it is a primary attribute of all existence. In this context, I cannot offer a comprehensive discussion of this important subject. Fortunately, I have already done it in my book *Beyond the Brain: Birth, Death, and Transcendence in Psychotherapy* (Grof, 1985), and I thus can refer all the interested readers to this publication.

When confronted with the challenging observations from modern consciousness research, we have only two choices. The first one is to reject the new observations simply because they are incompatible with the traditional scientific belief system. This involves an arrogant assumption that we already know what the universe is like and can tell with certainty what is possible and what is not possible. With this kind of approach, there cannot be any surprises, but there is also very little real progress. In this context, everybody who brings critically challenging data is accused of being a bad scientist, a fraud, or a mentally deranged person. This is an approach that characterizes pseudoscience or scientistic fundamentalism and has very little to do with genuine science. There exist many historical examples of such an approach: people who refused to look into Galileo Galilei's telescope, because they "knew" there could not be craters on the moon; those who fought against the atomic theory of chemistry and defended the concept of a non-existing substance flogiston; those who called Einstein a psychotic when he proposed his special theory of relativity, and many others.

The second reaction to such observations is characteristic of true science. It is excitement about and intense interest in such anomalies combined with healthy critical skepticism. Major scientific progress has always occurred when the leading paradigm was seriously challenged and failed to account for some significant findings. In the history of science, paradigms come, dominate the field for some time, and then are replaced by new ones. If, instead of rejecting and ridiculing the new observations, we would consider them an exciting opportunity and conduct our own study to test them, we might very likely find that the reports were accurate. At that point we would realize that we are something very different from what we were taught and from what the Western industrial civilization believes. It would also become clear to us that materialistic science has an incomplete and inadequate image of reality and that its ideas about the nature of consciousness and the relationship between consciousness and matter (particularly the brain) have to be radically reversed. We would literally find ourselves in a different universe.

Conclusions

I hope that I have succeeded in this chapter in presenting sufficient evidence that it is useful and important to study non-ordinary states of consciousness because of their great therapeutic potential and because they are a rich source of revolutionary new information about the psyche, human nature, and the nature of reality. In spite of some recent encouraging developments in Switzerland and in the United States, the future of clinical work with psychedelics, the most powerful means of inducing NOSC, remains uncertain. However, whether or not these remarkable tools will return into the psychiatric armamentarium, the discoveries made in the past are of lasting value. There exist powerful non-drug approaches that can induce similar states of consciousness and hold remarkable therapeutic promise. It is hard to imagine that Western academic science will continue indefinitely to ignore all the challenging evidence that has already been accumulated in the study of various forms of holotropic states, as well as the influx of new data. Sooner or later it will be necessary to face this new evidence and accept its far-reaching theoretical and practical consequences. It is my firm belief that we are rapidly approaching a point when transpersonal psychology and the work with nonordinary states of consciousness will become integral parts of a new scientific paradigm of the future.

V.

Transpersonal Implications of the Birth and Death Experiences

While chapters throughout this collection have dealt with birth-death-rebirth experiences in their many forms, this section devotes singular attention to these transformational events. Consideration of them involves consideration of ultimate beginnings, the ultimate end point, the ultimate silence, and the perfect circle of wholeness—all at once.

Charles Tart's chapter explores the process of dying, drawing on his personal experience with a friend's death as well as scientific research, leading to the conclusion that the consciousness' survival of death is possible.

Around this issue of death the transpersonal emerges, of course, in its most potent and awesome forms. They can often be found lurking behind manifestations of anger, the root of which, I contend, is fear of the unknown or the terrible. As an alternative simply to "working through" the fear or the anger, we can profit from looking at the unknown itself, at death and the possibilities of its transpersonal nature. Here we are confronted with our aloneness. No one else can face for us our fear of loss, our fear of ceasing to be, our essential aloneness. Here, perhaps more than in any other area, the transpersonal must be considered undeniably as part of traditional therapy.

27

Anger and the Fear of Death

Seymour Boorstein

I include "Anger and the Fear of Death" here for several reasons. This collection covers the whole spectrum of current transpersonal psychotherapeutic techniques, from the most radical to the most conservative, in order to provide a wide variation of styles and approaches. This particular chapter represents a conservative position, the Freudian or classical approach, and therefore will have most relevance for more conservative therapists who are evaluating elements of the transpersonal approach that they might find useful in their own practices. However, it received favorable response when presented to the Association for Transpersonal Psychology and appears to have relevance for more radical transpersonal psychotherapists as well.

The chapter demonstrates, first, how classical psychoanalytic thinking can be blended with a transpersonal approach, and second, how work in a specific area, such as fear, can provide the opportunity for exploring the important issue of facing death with all its transpersonal elements, thus stirring the potential seeker to action.

It is my thesis that, with few exceptions, the root of all anger is fear and that psychotherapy is most effective when it focuses on the fears behind the anger rather than on the anger itself. Insight into the nature of such fears is an alternative to both internalization and externalization of anger. These fears are often elemental and, as such, permeate the transpersonal issues of death, survival, and meaning. If the therapist can aid the patient's readiness to explore some of these issues, then the patient has a unique opportunity to wake the searcher within.

In this chapter, these basic fears and their treatment touch the transpersonal area in many ways. As Anthony Sutich has said in the chapter which opens this book, transpersonal therapy is "directly or indirectly concerned with the recognition, acceptance, and realization of ultimate states" together with "the psychological conditions or psychodynamic processes that are directly or indirectly a barrier [to realization of the transpersonal realm]."

In esoteric traditions, fear of death is considered part of the illusion of this plane of existence, an illusion which tends to prevent our experiencing the transcendent states described by Sutich. Psychotherapeutic work on this area of consciousness permits wider perceptions and breakdown of some of the barriers to these realizations. The deep psychological awareness that there is something beyond death can represent a giant leap in human beings' struggle to find ultimate meanings. The therapy described in this chapter can help nudge open that door of awareness.

THERE IS A STORY of a Zen master whose monastery and surrounding countryside were threatened by the savage destructiveness of a barbaric general. Everyone, except for the old Zen master, fled. When the general heard that the old monk had not fled, he was infuriated and came to confront the old master himself. With drawn sword he said to the old man, "Why haven't you fled? Don't you know that I can run you through with my sword without batting an eye?" The Zen master calmly replied, "And I can be run through with your sword without batting an eye." It is reported that the general turned and left. To face death serenely is to be able to live fearlessly without anger.

In classical psychotherapy, individuals coming for help generally are most occupied with working out the vicissitudes of anger in their lives. It is my thesis that, except for certain physiological or drug-induced states, the root of all anger is fear; and psychotherapy is most effective when it focuses on the basic fears rather than on the anger itself.

Many present psychotherapeutic methods involve teaching individuals to express their anger either directly to the other person(s) concerned or, through certain psychodramatic techniques (including therapies working with transference), to the representations of the persons towards whom the anger was originally felt. These methods teach and encourage the external expression of anger.

Such systems are predicated on the idea that the only alternative to direct expression is repression or suppression of the anger, which may lead to maladaptive solutions such as psychosomatic disorders and/or neurosis. Also, the impression is often given that direct expression of anger is always healthy. While verbal expression of anger may in some instances be helpful in clarifying communications, and while shouting at one's spouse or therapist or beating a pillow may be healthier than expressing anger covertly, physical expression of anger and often verbal anger as well can be painful, cruel, and destructive. Contrary to the notion that one feels better having "gotten it off one's chest," the expression of anger often leaves one feeling drained and demoralized.

I believe that the alternative to both internalization and external expression of anger is insight into the fears behind the anger and a transfer of energy and focus onto the struggle of dealing with these fears directly (Krantzler, 1977). They invariably include the transpersonal issues of death, survival, and meaning. In *Denial of Death*, Ernest Becker makes the point that all of neurotic anxiety is actually a cover for more fundamental existential anxiety (1975).

Psychotherapeutic technique to facilitate this conceptualization requires that the therapist constantly refocus the patient's attention, moving from dealing with the anger to recognition of the fear behind it. For example, when a patient becomes angry at me, I might ask, "How did I frighten you?" As we explore these fears—beginning with the currently perceived threat, moving on to their infantile roots, and ultimately perhaps, to the basic existential fears—the energy and effort of the psychotherapeutic endeavor are retained and redirected to issues central to personal evolution; otherwise it is drained off in the expression of anger. Naturally, considerable psychotherapeutic effort may be needed to deal with the fears related to the expression of anger. In psychodynamic literature, these are spoken of as resistances to the expression of affects.

These techniques for exploring deep-seated fears can be combined with standard techniques for helping people clearly communicate their thoughts and feelings. In marital counseling, for example the angry partner can be directed to explore how he or she experienced the other partner as frightening. This exploration of fear can help circumvent the power struggles in which couples often become involved. A person experiencing anger towards an employer, for example, may begin to be aware that this anger is linked to such fears as being discharged and left without means of survival. Another person, struggling to deal with anger over the death or departure of a loved one, may come to be aware that this anger is linked to fears of being left alone, fear for one's own survival, fear of death.

The classical psychotherapeutic model attempts to resolve neuroses and conflicts by bringing infantile fears and anxieties to the surface. This work rests on the premise that the now more mature person can cope with fears which in childhood were overwhelming. What generally emerges in such work are early fears of conflict with a parent, fears of killing or being killed, and fears of being separated from a caring or loved one.

These fears can—and usually are—explored in respect to their current interpersonal significance and their infantile roots. It is at this point that classical psychotherapy usually terminates. The patient may feel better and experience life as moving more successfully.

CASE 1

A forty-five-year-old social worker had come for treatment because of fears relating to some recent successes. Classical Oedipal issues concerning competition and surpassing his father predominated. These areas were quickly brought into focus for working through. I was impressed with his "style," which involved much shouting and expression of anger. Both in therapy and in personal life he screamed angrily when he was frightened of what always traced out to be fear of death (failure, starvation, or Oedipal victory resulting in punishment and death). As he was able to see the fears more directly, he ceased using anger as a way of coping and became far more effective professionally and interpersonally. Aside from being aware that our welfare system would prevent him from starving, he handled the idea that, if survival after death existed, it would be a pleasant surprise and that, if it didn't, he wouldn't know about it.

This is probably the way most individuals would cope with the anger-fear-survival sequence. Many patients find sufficient relief in their day-to-day lives by realizing that their distress is not anger directed at people or events but rather a reflection of the dis-ease they feel at the prospect of having to face questions of ultimate significance at some time in their life. For many of these patients, the concept of survival of consciousness is frightening and unacceptable.

CASE 2

O. L., a forty-year-old successful physician, sought treatment for certain obsessional traits. During the course of treatment he developed a tumor in the head which required surgical intervention and which could have been life threatening had it been cancerous. With this possibility in mind, and with a very short time available to us, I suggested that he browse through Moody's book *Life After Life* (1976), hoping that it might help him cope with the terror he had of dying. Contrary to the hoped-for relief, it caused even more anxiety because he could not be comfortable with the idea that there might be realities beyond those he had managed to control with his obsessional approach to life. He rejected the book as hogwash even though it did relieve his terror of death. Biopsy of the tumor proved it to be benign, and the issue was put aside for the time being.

With this type of individual there is some risk that premature exposure to concepts of survival of consciousness may strain the patient-therapist relationship. Such exposure should be done only when there is an overriding reason.

Patients with strong but oppressive religious backgrounds may have a tendency to equate exploration of these areas with the religion of their childhood. This can result in strongly negative and sometimes disruptive reactions. For some people, bringing questions of life after death into the open may initiate an active search for expanded self-awareness and for study into matters of transpersonal significance. Others, as in the first example, may handle anger more constructively as a result and allay their fears until later in life when old age, sickness, or the death of loved ones brings those fears into the open again.

The following examples help to clarify further how these issues are dealt with clinically.

CASE 3

F. M., a fifty-year-old psychologist, had lifelong anxieties relating to performance and shame. Many of his anxieties were expressed in his (*a*) drive to accumulate sufficient money to feel secure and in his (*b*) generally picky, sarcastic, and angry style. Although he was professionally and financially successful, his anxieties persisted and were often manifested by timidity. Despite a long and successful analysis, which brought to the fore the Oedipal rivalry with a weak and passive father, many of the anxieties persisted. Some of these could be traced to pre-Oedipal fears of dying and seemed to relate to a mother-child separation early in his first year. However, it was only with the exploration of death and possible survival that these earlier anxieties subsided.

Perhaps as a result of our later work, F. M. began studying and practicing Zen Buddhism, which further focused on impermanence and the fear of death. Whereas formerly he would get angry when he felt his security was threatened (the family spending money, household things breaking), he was now able to go automatically and immediately to the fear which was at the source of his anger and be calm internally and externally while doing what the situation required. It was interesting to note that his favorite boyhood and adult movie was *Lost Horizon*, which had, as one of its main themes, the avoidance of death by living in Shangri-La.

CASE 4

B. C., a thirty-year-old engineer, came for treatment of a severe depression, which recently manifested itself by a serious suicide attempt. His background included lifelong rejection by his mother, who used large amounts of drugs and alcohol to alleviate her own depression. Initially our work focused on his need not to be aware of strong affects. During regressions in the treatment, he came in contact with his rage at not being cared for, and his desire now for that to be made up to him. The exploration of maternal transference continually exposed his rage at not being loved and at his mother's even wishing (he thought) he had not been born. During treatment, B. C. began practicing Transcendental Meditation. The exploration of his rage exposed his fears of being deserted by his mother and therefore dying. Those realizations permitted him to face the infantile fear of death more comfortably and led him in the direction of active philosophical searching. A great deal of time was spent on the constant and repetitious working-through of the "rage-fear of desertion leading to death" equation. This permitted him to master the anxiety and rage sufficiently to resume his life with greater openness to the possibilities of loving and with a great decrease in angry, depressive episodes.

CASE 5

Mrs. A. is a thirty-seven-year-old housewife who came for help because of depression alternating with rages relating to a recent divorce. Much of the overt crisis stemmed from the financial pressures her ex-husband placed on her. In the transference many of the patterns of identification with father emerged. Despite being a successful businessman, her father viewed money as that which separated one from death. The level at which she functioned related to her childhood fears that she would starve to death unless she had an abundance of money. She was able to assure herself that she had the competence to care for herself and her two children. Her anxiety had the beneficial effect of getting her to return to business school, a long cherished wish. Mrs. A. obtained great relief from her rages and depressions. With the resolution of these earlier paternal identifications, the struggle with the deeper, existential anxieties regarding death will probably be postponed until some time when her stable adjustments are again threatened.

CASE 6

Mrs. R. is a thirty-one-year-old housewife and mother of three who came for treatment because of a resurgence of lifelong depression and low self-esteem alternating with attacks of rage. Each of her parents had had multiple divorces. Her attractive mother was extremely narcissistic, and her father and stepfathers were overtly seductive to her as she reached puberty.

Part of the depression was resolved as her guilt around her Oedipal wishes surfaced. In relation to this, her self-esteem improved when she could see herself as more than a sexual object (which she had secretly wanted to be in order to fulfill her Oedipal wishes and identification patterns with her mother).

As these more traditional neurotic patterns were resolved, she began to experience anxieties from an earlier period in which she had to care for her mother rather than her mother's caring for her. Because of these earlier fears, she had married a successful stockbroker. Their marriage, basically satisfying, provided her protection from these earlier fears. During times of even minimal marital friction she began to face her enormous childhood fears of dying. Many of the marital strains were related to this fear insofar as they made her feel uncared for and thus liable to die. Like other patients described here, she experienced some relief with the awareness by her infantile self that there was an adult to care for her. She also began reading some of the literature regarding survival of consciousness after death. Despite her traditional Catholic upbringing, the exploration of these areas permitted her to face the inevitability of her own death and even the possibility of her children dying before her. As a result, the rages greatly diminished along with the anxieties, and this permitted her to experience a greater sense of freedom from inner tensions and caused others to notice how loving she had become.

CASE 7

Mrs. M., a fifty-year-old teacher, had recently married a fellow schoolteacher following a divorce from a cold and unloving man. The marriage was successful except for her feeling that the welfare of her now-grown children was threatened by her new husband's seemingly uncaring attitudes. At times this feeling would make her fly into fits of anger, when she would berate him on other issues. In short-term psychotherapy it evolved that under the anger she was frightened that her son, who had been an unwanted child, would die. She was able to see that she feared her original wish for him to die and as a result tended to overindulge him. Verbalizing the reality that both she and her son would become corpses some day and be separated permitted her to stop clutching at a lifelong preoccupation with protecting him. The angry episodes with her husband quickly subsided as she saw that under most of the rages lay her fear of her child's death and/or her own through the unrealistic anticipation of desertion by her husband.

CASE 8

Mr. and Mrs. H., ages thirty-seven and thirty-five, had been seen in "marriage therapy" for the past two years. This was his first and her second marriage. The presenting complaints included much bickering, excessive drinking by Mrs. H., and a rigidity of affect in Mr. H., occasionally broken by rage attacks and even physical blows to his wife. Mr. H. was a biology professor and, prior to the marriage, Mrs. H. had been a secretary. Aside from working through the traditional transferences and their roots in childhood, the therapist was able to help them and the marriage itself by teaching the couple to shift from anger as soon as it was experienced to the fear behind it.

As the adult intellect faces the ideas of "permanent" death and/or survival after death, the infantile anxieties surrounding these issues usually diminish in varying degrees. I suggest that, where it seems feasible, all psychotherapeutic relationships include the exploration of these ultimate fears. Awareness of this need is already reflected in the recent upsurge in literature of death and dying issues. Traditional psychotherapists have usually held that the transpersonal areas are not within the province of therapy.

Apart from instances in which the patient's fear of and resistance to exposing this area may be so great that to do so might be unwise, I suggest that exploring these fears is entirely appropriate to the therapeutic process. This requires sensitivity in evaluating the readiness of the patient for this kind of work. It goes without saying that the therapist needs to feel comfortable with this type of exploration.

I specifically suggest that, wherever possible, the therapist help the patient to see that behind all anger is fear, and that the fear is usually a body-ego fear of death, cessation, or dissolution of the self or other cared-for persons. Far from suggesting that the therapist be responsible for providing answers, I believe that the patient's readiness to explore these matters is strength-giving in itself. Indeed, if further exploration in these areas is to be undertaken, the individual needs to do it alone in addition to or in place of therapy. The therapist can be seen as someone who helps clarify the matters that need ultimately to be dealt with and perhaps who serves as a resource for further study or exploration. The burgeoning amount of literature concerning the inner life and questions of meaning, life, death, and survival; the good media coverage of meditative techniques; interest in altered states of consciousness and other realities—all these provide ample resource material for people who wish to address themselves to some of these questions.

In summary, I believe that those of us who work with patients have a unique opportunity to awaken the searcher who exists within each of us. The exploration of the fear behind all anger can lead to this awakening.

28

Helping the Dying
Science, Compassion, and the Possible Survival of Death

Charles T. Tart

What do we think happens to us after death? This question confronts all of us and is perhaps one of the most profound issues we have to struggle with. How a patient copes with this issue can often have significant implications on how his or her personality manifests now. Through Tart's description of the death of a friend, many important considerations surface. It is clear that we need to be more honest than we have been around the dying process. Tibetan Buddhism has some of the clearest maps of and helpful approaches (chants, prayers, meditations) to the dying process.

Tart suggests that we can study the dying process much as we would study an altered state such as those produced by a psychedelic substance or a fevered delirium. Tart, Kubler-Ross, and Monroe have prepared a series of tapes to help prepare for death by giving the dying person "a sense of what it would be like to be a consciousness that is not confined to the body." Since we are all in the process of dying (some of us faster than others), Monroe, a major pioneer in out-of-body experiences, has developed week-long experiential seminars for those wishing to explore this area.

Tart gives an excellent overview of scientific research that indicates that consciousness is much more than the electrochemical operation of

This chapter is a revision of an article entitled "Compassion, Science and Consciousness Survival" originally published in the *Noetic Sciences Review*, Spring 1994. It is included here with the permission of the Institute of Noetic Sciences.

the brain, and it follows, therefore, that consciousness' survival of death is possible. In short, this "demonstrates the non-physical nature of consciousness," that "mind does *not* equal brain," and that "*the mind can do things that the brain can't do.*" The literature on research with mediums is reviewed and Tart concludes that in "*some cases there was extremely good evidence for the survival of a particular personality.*"

Tart concludes by summarizing his struggle (which, I think, reflects the struggle most of us have) to find a life that is meaningful, seeing how working with helping people face death can greatly help us in the ways we face life.

A FRIEND OF MINE DIED recently, and being with him during his last few months taught me a lot about both care for the dying and how I might integrate my scientific work on consciousness and the possible survival of death of consciousness with a compassionately human perspective. It is all too easy to use the abstractions and intellectual creations of science as a means of distracting ourselves from the *fact* of death. It confronts us all, and we all have a natural fear of annihilation and of the unknown. Yet by avoiding the actuality of death, taking ourselves away from the presence of mortality, we also shut out an opportunity for a profound and valuable experience— an experience that may transform the quality of our living.

Before turning to a scientific perspective, therefore, I want to begin with the story of my recent experience with my friend Ken. I first met him a couple of years ago through our common interest in Buddhism. We were both members of Sogyal Rinpoche's Rigpa Fellowship, although he was not someone I knew intimately. In 1993 he fell ill with AIDS-related symptoms. When he could not take care of himself anymore, I, along with a number of others, volunteered to come to his home occasionally and do what we could to offer practical help and spiritual support.

The Honesty of Death

I've had very little experience in caring for the dying—even though intellectually I know quite a lot about the process. My first reaction was "What am I going to say to someone who is dying?" All my conceptual knowledge about the biology and psychology of death and dying seemed so inappropriate when confronted with the real thing.

The first evening I went over to see Ken, however, the confusion I had about what to do vanished because of something very simple. He immediately asked me to help him with his will—he was having trouble seeing clearly, and he couldn't read the document. He wanted me to read it to him, take notes, and make corrections as he dictated. Somehow, his matter-of-fact acceptance of his fate, the imminence of his death, dissolved my awkwardness. I found I could unself-consciously talk to him about the fact that he was dying. It wasn't a big deal anymore. That initial moment of honesty simply cleared the air. The experience, however, also sensitized me to how *dishonest* we are about death in our culture, about how much we tend to avoid and suppress it.

I would visit Ken about one evening a week, first at his home and then in hospice. My interactions with him there led me to an even deeper appreciation of and insight into the power and possibilities available *if* we open up to the process of dying.

Ken had not been a student of Buddhism very long, perhaps three or four years, but he had become very serious about it. He intended to die in a Tibetan Buddhist way: taking death as an opportunity for spiritual growth; as a way to dedicate his suffering to relieve the suffering of others; to develop compassion and to use the process of dying to gain greater liberation.

His hospice room was arranged to evoke this atmosphere. He had pictures on the wall of Buddhist teachers he had known and a little shrine at the foot of his bed where he could see it easily. People would come in from the Rigpa Fellowship, and they would help him chant mantras or go through some prayers, meditate with him, or talk about spiritual matters. When he began slipping into what the medical staff called AIDS "dementia," where his mind would wander, the focused chanting, praying, and meditation were very helpful in keeping him communicative and coherent. Of course, people could not be with him all the time, so I helped out by recording on tape some of the chants and practices he was familiar with from Tibetan Buddhism, including simultaneous English translations, which he could play over and over. He found that very helpful, and I realized then how important audio tapes could be in assisting people through the dying process.

Dying as an Altered State

I learned a great deal from being with Ken. For one thing, I learned that what the doctors were calling "dementia," implying some form of stupidity or loss of coherent consciousness, could, at least sometimes, be something altogether different. From my perspective of years of studying spiritual practices and transpersonal psychologies, it was clear that he was going in and out of altered states of consciousness. By "altered" state I mean different, not necessarily better or worse (see Tart, 1975 for detailed discussions of my systems approach to understanding altered states). Sometimes he was right here in his ordinary state; he was sharp and had a great sense of humor. And sometimes he was way "out there"; to us, he seemed to be sleeping or unconscious, but when talking to him afterwards he would sometimes report that he had been aware and experiencing some very extraordinary conscious states. Sometimes he was kind of here and kind of there, in an altered state, and it was difficult to communicate with him unless we were careful about how we phrased things. I realized that this was like talking to someone during a psychedelic experience or who is delirious from a fever: we can communicate a lot, both ways, if we allow for the characteristics of the altered state, and we know something about doing that.

As I said, Ken was highly motivated to take his dying as an opportunity for practicing his spiritual path more and more deeply. For instance, he repeatedly asked the hospice staff to turn off the television set in his room, although their habit was to automatically turn it on if it was off. In fact, he wanted them to take the television out of the room altogether, but the staff could not understand his desire to be without it. At one point, they were so bemused by his requests they sent up an engineer to *fix* the set, when all he wanted was to be rid of the thing! They couldn't understand that he wanted it gone, that he wasn't interested in losing himself in television.

I noticed that every room of the hospice had a television, and it seemed the set was always on. The basic policy seemed to be to drug people up and distract them with an unending round of sit-coms and reruns. The hospice was giving good medical care and perhaps "good" psychological care but, with the exception of our activities in Ken's room, there seemed to be no recognition of the spiritual possibilities connected with death.

Soon enough, however, the hospice staff began to notice what was going on, and they began dropping into Ken's room whenever they had a break, because of the calm and the spiritual, loving atmosphere there. They noticed there was a meaningful process going on in his room, a different response to dying than the usual attitude "all we can do is make the patients comfortable."

I wasn't there at the very end. Ken wanted to share his last moments just with his family and Sydney, a remarkable lady from the Rigpa Fellowship who had been Ken's most devoted helper. But I was told the inspiring story of how he left. He knew his time was close, and he chose to listen to a tape of a Tibetan Buddhist practice called *powa*, a meditation designed to eject consciousness from the body in a way that is favorable to liberation or at least to the probability of a good incarnation (see Sogyal, 1992). Powa usually involves internally reciting mantras and visualizing energy flows, in a meditative frame of mind. Whether or not you happen to believe this particular spiritual doctrine, it strikes me as certainly more interesting to devote your mental energies to this kind of practice than wallowing in self-pity, distracting yourself with old reruns on television, or being with people who deny that you are dying!

Ken died while listening to the powa practice, breathing shallower and shallower, until, at the last round of the visualization, he breathed out and didn't breathe in again. He died with a smile on his face, and people said that his body was radiant for hours afterwards. Being in the room with his body was like a mystical experience. Yet this wasn't somebody who had been an advanced spiritual master; it wasn't as though Ken had been raised somewhere like Tibet and had lived his life immersed in exotic spiritual practices. He was an ordinary modern American, sharp and computer-literate, an analytical kind of guy. He had just opened himself up to Buddhist practices for a few years, and at the end had committed himself wholly to the spiritual possibilities of dying.

Improving How We Can Die

The experience of being with Ken inspired me to want to be more helpful to the dying. At first I thought—and often still do—"Who am I to think I can help the dying? What nerve!" I'm not somebody with extensive hospice training, and I don't have much practical experience. On the other hand, I started thinking, it doesn't take much at all to make a big improvement on the mainstream practice of "Drug 'em and distract 'em with old reruns"! I feel ignorant about so much; but I do know something about altered states, which people are going to experience as they die; and I do know something about spiritual practices concerned with dying and death.

Sogyal Rinpoche's best selling book, *The Tibetan Book of Living and Dying* (Sogyal, 1992), has alerted many people to the need for a more spiritual death, and, as one way of trying to help, I hope to be of some help in his plans to eventually create a hospice designed to offer more comprehensive *spiritual* care for the dying. Although it will be organized within a Buddhist context, he will attempt to generalize it so that people unfamiliar with Buddhism will still feel welcomed, without having to adopt a different spiritual philosophy. However, there are other ways I can be of help. As it happened, while taking care of Ken I heard from an old friend, Robert Monroe—founder of the Monroe Institute and author of three books on his and others' out-of-the-body experiences (OBEs) (Monroe, 1971, 1985, 1994)—and he, "coincidentally," had been thinking of developing techniques to help the dying, with no specific, formal religious framework involved, so they would be accessible to all people.

I've been working for some time now with Monroe and Elizabeth Kubler-Ross, and we have developed a series of training tapes for people who are dying. This series of cassette uses Monroe's "HemiSync"™ process of driving brainwaves via special sounds to help induce states of consciousness that will assist in making the suggestions and ideas on the tapes more effective. The training sequence starts with instructions designed to help people relax, to sleep better, and to have clearer inner experiences which remind them that we are more than our physical bodies—that there is a life of the mind, an inner life, that's very important and that doesn't seem particularly connected to the body. Some of the later exercises are designed to produce what we call OBEs or "inner journeys." The altered states induced by listening to these tapes are intended as a preparation for death by giving the person a sense of what it would be like to be a consciousness that is not confined to the body. Finally, when the person feels that he or she is ready to go, there is one tape which takes the listener through the now-familiar methods of "leaving," but this time with no instructions to return to their body on the tape. (They can always change their mind, of course, and come back on their own.)

In focusing here on the purpose of this *Going Home* series,[1] I am deliberately emphasizing the human side of dying, rather than the scientific side. Quite aside from the intellectual work I've done on altered states and research into the possibilities of survival of consciousness beyond biological death, my experience with Ken has awakened me to a deep desire to want to help people through the process of dying. The tapes will be an experiment in improving the quality of the way a person can die. At the very least, they will give people something far more interesting to occupy the final stages of a terminal illness than watching television. And at their best, they will ???????
This is one of the most interesting experiments I have ever been involved in, and I am looking forward to getting feedback from people who have helped loved ones die using these training tapes.

Scientific Research on Survival

Switching now from my heart to my head, I'd like to summarize my scientific perspective on the question of the survival of consciousness. For most of my thirty-plus-years career as a scientist, it has been obvious to me that the dominant materialistic view of consciousness as being nothing but the electrochemical operation of the brain, with possible survival of death ruled out as inherently nonsensical, is grossly inadequate—not just on theoretical or philosophical grounds, but in light of solid, factual evidence. There are two bodies of data that support this position: (1) the data on psi phenomena—extrasensory perception (ESP) and psychokinesis (PK); and (2) careful research with mediums.

The evidence from laboratory parapsychology shows that you can put human beings in isolation situations where, according to the conventional materialist view of the world, no communication with the outside can possibly happen and they cannot affect external physical processes. Nevertheless, it has been repeatedly shown that people sometimes *do* communicate with each other when all known sensory channels have been excluded (ESP), and sometimes *can* influence the behavior of physical systems without any physical contact (PK). For example, researchers have put people in isolated rooms, sometimes separated by thousands of miles, have tested to see if they could send telepathic messages, and have found that sometimes a message gets through. Readable accessible summaries of this kind of experimentation can be found in books by, e.g., Broughton, 1991; Edge, Morris, Palmer, and Rush, 1986; Jahn and Dunne, 1987; Targ and Harary, 1984; Targ and Puthoff, 1977; Tart, 1977. Note that it is important to distinguish this kind of rigorous, scientific parapsychological data from the popular use of "parapsychology" to mean any kind of unusual phenomena or ideas which may not have any scientific backing.

In other experiments, researchers tested to see if people could affect electronic devices incorporating randomizing elements simply by using their minds, and discovered that the behavior of the machine correlated with the intention of the subject significantly above the statistical laws of chance. In one type of experiment, for example, the subjects were asked to influence a sequence of randomly flashing red and green lights; they demonstrated an ability to produce a statistical bias in favor of one of the colors. In other words, we have here an instance of mind directly affecting matter.[2] Although such phenomena are typically dismissed as "trivial" or "inconsequential anomalies" by the scientist orthodoxy, the evidence for both telepathy and psychokinesis explodes the myth of reductionistic-physicalistic science that mind or consciousness is "nothing but" an epiphenomenon of the brain.

These results present a far greater challenge to current scientific paradigms than anything that has come out of relativity theory or quantum physics. In short, they effectively demonstrate the non-physical nature of consciousness. Mind does *not* equal brain. Even if we don't have a coherent theoretical framework for explaining this, the empirical evidence removes previous objections based solely on theoretical physicalist grounds. Given this, the exploration of survival of consciousness after biological death becomes a viable scientific venture.

More specifically, none of the evidence for the phenomena reported in the more than thirteen hundred articles on psi effects can be explained in terms of what a human brain and nervous system can do. You don't have to be a physicist to see that the minuscule electrical and magnetic energies generated by brain operation are totally insufficient to communicate ESP information or PK effects over distances.

Thus if you believe you fully understand what a human being is, and it's nothing but a function of material factors we know about, you are ignoring the very reliable data that tells us *the mind can do things that the brain can't do.* The empirical facts are that the mind can reach out and gather information and affect things when there is no way to explain this according to our current understanding of physics or any reasonably straightforward extension of it. Diehard materialists object that someday scientists may be able to explain mind in physical terms, but that is simply a case of what philosophers call "promissory materialism." Such a position is completely unscientific; there is no way ever to falsify a statement of promissory materialism. It is a statement of faith, on a par with saying that someday we'll be able to explain everything in terms of what God or the aliens from Arcturus Five do.

Based on the evidence from parapsychology, we can make a strong case, then, for believing that *the human mind is something more than the material body.* In principle, therefore, the idea that consciousness could survive death is not so outrageous and should not be beyond scientific exploration. Nevertheless, we may ask, what, specifically, can science do in this area?

Research with Mediums

To begin with, scientists could take note of reports of anomalous phenomena involving purported extra-corporeal consciousness. For instance, many apparently normal people—over 25 percent of the American population in one survey (Gallup & Proctor, 1982; Greeley, 1975; Haraldsson, 1985) believe they have had psychic contact with deceased relatives. Such spontaneous experiences, however, provide only weak data on which to build a science, due to possible distortions of memory and other factors. They may suggest directions to explore, but science ideally deals with an experimental method, which provides much stronger evidence than anecdotes.

Historically, attempts to establish experimental evidence for disembodied consciousness began in the last century with the rise of modern spiritualism. In the late 1800s, in Hydesville, New York, the Fox sisters generated a lot of attention internationally with claims and alleged demonstrations of communications with spirits of the dead. After a time, numerous other people were claiming they could go into some kind of altered state, usually called "mediumistic trance," could contact spirits of the deceased and get messages from them. (See Inglis, 1977, for a history of spiritualism.) The early Spiritualists emphasized that it wasn't necessary to *believe* in survival in order to investigate the apparitions. In fact, they discouraged unquestioning belief, inviting serious-minded people to "Test it for yourself." In principle, that sentiment reflects the essence of the scientific attitude. Of course, in attempting to actually apply this approach, investigators encountered many difficult procedural complications—such as how to rule out subjectivity, trickery, and self-delusion. Nevertheless, many experiments were done in a true spirit of scientific research.

Spiritualism was popular with a great number of Americans and Britons during the late nineteenth and early twentieth centuries, and attracted leading figures in the scientific community, such as psychologist William James in the

United States and physicist William Crookes in England. As in any field of life, the problem of fraudulent reports can never be overlooked, and, indeed, cases of charlatanism were uncovered in spiritualistic seances. But by no means should we decide, therefore, that all claims for spirit communications are false. However, even in cases where fraud was not an issue, the quality of the evidence was often weak scientifically.

To explain why, let me give a hypothetical example: You go to a medium in the hope of contacting your beloved but dead Uncle Ferdinand. Bear in mind that, like most people who go to mediums, you are there because you have recently lost a loved one. You are looking for comfort, even though you may insist you are skeptical and looking for proof. There is a very strong emotional desire to believe, and that is not the best way to collect evidence. Furthermore, if an outsider listens to the mediumistic communications that impressed you, in many cases it would not be very impressive. You may protest, "But I *know* it was Uncle Ferdinand because he said he loved me, and it sounded like him." You may be totally convinced, but evidentially that is extremely vague and weak data on which to base a scientific case.

Although your visit to a medium may serve an important psychological function, helping you cope with bereavement, if you are interested in strong scientific evidence a different approach is needed. Scientific investigation of good mediums has involved, ideally, sending a *proxy sitter,* not someone emotionally attached to the departed soul or, indeed, who even knows the deceased. The proxy could thus not ask leading questions that imply the correct answer and could not inadvertently give away part of the information being sought. This is important: even if the medium were honest but in an altered state, she (most mediums have been women) may not even know she got the information through your inadvertent cues and replayed it as part of an unconscious impersonation of Uncle Ferdinand. To be good science, of course, the entire interaction should be recorded—nowadays, on video tape if possible. Other clues, such as body language, for instance, may give the game away. A well-recorded session can help eliminate this artifact.

A fair amount of good quality research was done in this manner in the past, albeit before video tapes. Some years ago I looked at the data in great detail, and my main impression was that in *some cases there was extremely good evidence for the survival of a particular personality.* The alleged deceased communicator sometimes gave correct names, dates, memories, and specific personality characteristics which created a distinct impression of the deceased's identity. To give a sense of the standards of investigation used in much of this research, I sometimes use an analogy of a favorite cousin who disappeared a few years ago. Suddenly you get a long-distance phone call for help. The connection is very bad, it's hard to make out voice tone or complete sentences, and the caller, claiming to be your cousin, says he was hit on the head so he has a hard time remembering, but he needs urgent financial help. Wire money now! Naturally, you would want to be sure who the person is before you sent any money. The kinds of rational criteria which would need to be applied in this scenario have been applied in the cases of good mediumship that have been investigated in the past.

Spiritual Implications of Conscious Dying

At this point, I'd like to bring this chapter to a focus by trying to integrate the opening section illustrating a human perspective on death with the scientific discussion above. Together, they may help shed some light on the spiritual implications inherent in the altered states experienced during the process of dying.

A central question of many spiritual traditions, insofar as it can be expressed in the limited medium of words, is Who am I? What is my identity? All my studies, and my knowledge of other people's studies, have made me think that a *major* component of one's ordinary identity is the physical body. Our awareness is heavily influenced for the most part by the physical representations of who we are physically. There is a constant pattern of sensations from our body that we are not even conscious of for the most part, but which nevertheless molds our consciousness, which in turn reinforces habits of thinking, feeling, perceiving, and acting. Unfortunately, from a spiritual, or a psychology of liberation perspective, this is a problem.

More and more it becomes apparent to me as a psychologist and student of the spiritual that each of us has vast potentials. Quite apart from questions of survival of death, we have enormous potential to re-create, to expand, to transform our identity, our experience of self. But because we are socialized, enculturated into a particular set of beliefs and behaviors, each one of us has been squeezed down to a tiny fraction of that potential. The great tragedy is that we have been conditioned to believe that this tiny fraction is *all* we are. We live, therefore, in a cramped psychological space, in what Gurdjieff called "false personality." We think that is who we are; we think that is our personality and nature, but it is false in the sense that it ignores so much of the reality of what could be.

A major spiritual task in life is to begin to deeply realize how artificially cramped we are, to stop identifying so closely with that limited self, and begin to discover some of our other potentials. The task is to live what I like to call a more "spacious" life. Let me personalize this to illustrate what I mean. I'm manifesting right now as "Professor Charles T. Tart, Ph.D., authority on altered states and psychic research." But that's only one of many possible manifestations; if I'm totally immersed in this persona, I'm trapped. If, however, I can maintain a certain kind of spaciousness, I can realize that actually another part of who I am is somebody who would like to be helpful to people, who would like to be compassionate. If I'm following a spiritual practice, I can watch the part of me that is so involved in the technical persona. I can ask myself, for example: Am I presenting the ideas in this article in a way that is actually going to be helpful to people? Or have I become intoxicated with technical ideas and intellectual exposition, with doing things that mainly reinforce the Professor identification? When I open to the spaciousness, however, I can be aware of more points or aspects of who I am.[3]

When it comes to death, Tibetan Buddhism is the most interesting spiritual tradition to me because the lamas have thought a lot about it, have developed sophisticated techniques for dealing with it, and have fascinating psychological teachings about it. I don't know how much of it is literally true or false. But, whether I know that or not, what appeals strongly to me is that, according to the Tibetans, *the best way to prepare for death is to become more spacious in life, now;* to begin to relax, to become more natural, to get out of this artificial identification with our limited self. Becoming more spacious gives us opportunities to contact the more open, deeper, broader parts of our self.[4]

This letting go of self is, I think, a wonderful way to prepare for death. To the extent that I can stop identifying with the limited self of Professor Tart, even in social situations where it's appropriate to manifest it, and come more to realize the spaciousness behind ordinary mind and identification; to the extent that I learn to contact the basic ability to spaciously know before experiences get articulated into specific false personality patterns, then the less of a shock, I believe, death is going to be. What excites me about Tibetan Buddhism and working with the dying is the chance to contact these basic spiritual realities that make death an opportunity to grow, to expand, to be of help to other people.

Personally Dealing with the Fear of Death

Let me restate the results of our discussion so far in a more personal form. Here I am, a human being: I've got a physical body that I know is going to die. Most of the time I suppress that information, I don't want to think about it; I prefer to put it off until the indefinite future. But I'm getting older, and it's gradually coming home to me that death is not just a theoretical matter of intellectual interest. I am going to die. My friends are going to die. What do I do?

On one level I'm afraid of death and the process of dying. I know it's natural to fear death and dying. It will be a loss of what I know of my competence; I have a strong investment in being able to handle my world. I don't like the idea of being helpless and dependent, and of being in pain.

So how do I deal with that? One way, which is very common in our culture, is to believe in some version of the materialistic world view that says, basically, "life is just a biochemical accident, consciousness is nothing but chemistry, there's no meaning to it, and some day it's all over, so don't worry about it." Unfortunately, this credo doesn't take care of the fear very well. Instead, all our efforts go into preserving life at all costs. I don't buy that outlook. As I said earlier, to me the materialistic world view is simply not scientifically adequate, quite apart from its emotional distastefulness.

On the other hand, another way of dealing with the fear of mortality, a way which some people find comforting, is to follow the teachings of a conventional religion which promises some form of an afterlife. I'm happy for people who can do that, and sometimes I envy them. I don't have that strong a belief in any particular religion. But I do have an interest in what the general spiritual traditions have to say about dying, death, and afterlife. Not only does this help to alleviate some of the fear, but to me it's incredibly interesting. It offers more possibilities for growth. I like to learn things, and seventy-five to one hundred years of life is not much time to learn about myself or the universe. So, I like the idea of some kind of continued existence (discarnated or reincarnated) which leaves the way open to learn new things.

Also the older I get, the more important it becomes for me to ask, Am I being helpful to people? Living just for my own satisfaction becomes more and more hollow. There's nothing wrong in feeling personally happy, but being of service to others is somehow much more satisfying and meaningful. Spiritual teachings that seem to help people face death, therefore, are increasingly important to me.

At the same time, as a person who has always been interested in how my own mind works, as a person who doesn't like to be fooled, I'm aware of how my fear of death, my desire for continuity, may be leading me into investing in illusions about survival that may not be true. Consequently, the part of me that does not like to be fooled has spent a long time looking at what little scientific evidence we have. And, to the satisfaction of my emotional side, I have found that as a scientist—a scientist who knows how to do science well—there's enough evidence around to at least provisionally say it is likely that I and other people probably survive death in some form, even if it's an altered form. And that makes life and death and the whole universe very, very interesting.

Who Survives?

Taken together, although they are not *overwhelmingly* convincing, the evidence from psi research and the quality of communications from some mediums persuades me of the possibility that consciousness can exist independently of a physical body. I can sum up my position on this as follows: I will not be too surprised if, after some initial shock, suffering and maybe unconsciousness during my own death, I regain consciousness. But I will be surprised if "I" regain consciousness (Tart, 1987).

The "I" that I am mostly familiar with, the one identified with the personality that most of my friends and acquaintances know me by, is shaped to a great extent by information from my physical senses. My awareness is informed by external signals coming through my exteroceptors (sight, hearing, touch, smelling, tasting), and by signals from within my body (my interocepters). If most of this sensory information is shut out or greatly reduced—for example, as would happen in a sensory deprivation tank or during sleep—I would eventually experience a different state of awareness. Take away my access to sensory information completely, as will presumably happen when I die, then it is inevitable that whatever consciousness remains will be shifted into an altered state significantly different from my normal waking consciousness. That is what I mean when I say that I would be surprised if, after death, "I" regain consciousness.

As I watched my friend Ken slip in and out of altered states in his final days and witnessed how different he was at times from the man I had known, I could only wonder about his state of consciousness after he serenely left his body behind, graced with that radiant smile. Would it even matter to him, now, in a radically altered state, whether his friends and family could communicate with him, via a medium? Would he see any relevance, significance, or value in our philosophical, scientific, or even spiritual attempts to decide, once and for all, the issue of an afterlife? And if "he" could communicate, would his experiences have any recognizable meaning for us? Such, after all, may be concerns only of the living.

And yet . . . in some way beyond our ordinary understanding, we, our ordinary selves, seem to survive. As account after account from those who have died and been revived testifies, the near-death experiencer so often meets the spirits of deceased loved ones, meets them in a profound and loving way. Recognition is sure and deep and joyous. So we change, I think we *must* change after death, but yet something essential, something vital persists. I believe that having good evidence about whether we might survive death is important in deciding how you live. I advocate that we investigate death and survival as much as possible—it deserves a lot more effort than curing the common cold! And perhaps there are limits to what we can understand with our ordinary mind but, as I have proposed elsewhere (Tart, 1972b), we can develop state-specific sciences that allow good investigation beyond the ordinary mind . . .

Notes

1. The *Going Home* tape series is now available from the Monroe Institute, Box 175, Faber, Virginia 22938.

2. Now, of course, this happens every time you or I exercise our volition—for example, deciding to turn a page or switch off a light. But that is mind affecting the matter of its own brain, nervous system, and muscles which are in physical contact with the page or switch. In the situation just referred to, however, we have an instance of someone's *mind directly affecting matter beyond that person's brain and body.* Both of these situations—mind affecting its own brain, and mind affecting matter at a distance—remain completely inexplicable within the parameters of modern science.

3. More discussion of and practical techniques for creating this kind of spaciousness are discussed in my *Waking Up: Overcoming the Obstacles to Human Potential,* 1986, and my *Living the Mindful Life,* 1994.

4. A classical Buddhist, of course, would say letting go allows you to enter a state of or contact the "no-self." The concept of "self" tends to concretize and promote too much identification with the pathological habits of what has no permanent existence anyway.

Bibliography

Abramson, H. A. (ed.). *The use of LSD in psychotherapy and alcoholism.* Indianapolis: Bobbs-Merrill, 1967.

Aiken, J. Exploding the facade. *Weekend Magazine,* 1976, 26 (19), 12–14.

Alexander, F. Buddhist training as artificial catatonia. *Psychoanalytic Review,* 1931, *18,* 129.

Allport, G. *Personality and social encounter.* Boston: Beacon Press, 1960.

Angyal, A. *Foundations for a science of personality.* New York: Commonwealth Fund, 1941.

Angyal, A. A holistic theory. *Neurosis and treatment.* New York: Viking Press, 1965.

Anonymous. *Meditations on the Tarot: A journey into Christian hermeticism.* Amity, N.Y.: Amity House, 1985.

Arieti, S. *Interpretation of schizophrenia.* New York: Robert Brunner, 1955.

Assagioli, R. *Psychosynthesis.* New York: Viking Press, 1965.

Assagioli, R. *R. M. Bucke Memorial Newsletter,* 1966, 2 (2), 11–12.

Assagioli, R. *Psychosynthesis: A manual of principles and techniques.* New York: Viking Press, 1971.

Assagioli, R. *The act of will.* New York: Viking Press, 1973.

Assagioli, R. Self-realization and psychological disturbances. *ReVision,* 1986, Winter/Spring.

Avalon, A. *Principles of Tantra I.* Madras: Ganesh, 1914.

Avalon, A. *The serpent power.* New York: Dover, 1974.

Bakan, D. *Sigmund Freud and the Jewish mystical tradition.* New York: Schocken, 1958.

Baker, E. *Man in the trap.* New York: Avon, 1974.

Bandura, A. Self-efficacy: Toward a unifying theory of behavioral change. *Psychological Review,* 1977, *84,* 191–215. (a)

Bandura, A. *Social learning theory.* Englewood Cliffs N.J.: Prentice-Hall, 1977. (b)

Bandura, A. *Principles of behavior modification.* New York: Holt, Rinehart & Winston, 1969.

Banquet, J. P. Spectral analysis of the EEG in meditation electroencephalogram. *Clinical Neurophysiology,* 1973, *35,* 143–151.

Bates, C. *Ransoming the mind: An integration of yoga and modern therapy.* St. Paul, Minn.: YES International, 1986.

Bateson, G. Communication theories in relation to the etiology of the neuroses. In J. H. Merin (ed.), *The etiology of the neuroses.* Palo Alto, Calif.: Science and Behavior Books, 1966.

Becker, E. *The denial of death.* New York: Free Press, 1975.

Benoit, H. *The supreme doctrine.* New York: Viking Press, 1959.

Benson, H. *Relaxation response.* New York: William Morrow, 1975.

Benson, H., Beary, J. F., & Carol, M. P. The relaxation response. *Psychiatry,* 1974, *37,* 37.

Benson, H., & Wallace, R. K. Decreased drug abuse with transcendental meditation: A study of 1,862 subjects. *Congressional Record,* 92nd Congress, First Session, June 1971 (Serial #92-1). Washington, D.C.: U.S. Government Printing Office, 1971.

Bentov, I. *Stalking the wild pendulum.* New York: E. P. Dutton, 1977.

Bergson, H. 1914 presidential address (untitled), *Proceedings of the Society for Psychical Research,* 1914, 27.

Berne, E. *Games people play.* New York: Grove Press, 1964.

Bloomfield, H., Cain, M., Jaffe, D., & Kory, R. *TM: Discovering inner energy and overcoming stress.* New York: Delacorte Press, 1975.

Bloomfield, H., & Kory, R. *Happiness: The TM program, psychiatry and enlightenment.* New York: Simon & Schuster, 1976.

Bloomfield, H., & Kory, R. *The healing silence.* New York: Simon & Schuster, 1978.

Bloomfield, M. (Trans.) *Atharvaveda.* Delhi, India: M. Banarsidess, 1964 (UNESCO collection of representative works, Indian series).

Boadella, D. *Wilhelm Reich: The man and his work.* London: Routledge, 1973.

Bohm, D. Reality and knowledge considered as process. *Academy,* 1975, *19,* 13–18.

Boorstein, Seymour. The use of bibliotherapy and mindfulness meditation in a psychiatric setting. *Journal of Transpersonal Psychology,* 1983, *13* (2), 173–179.

Boorstein, Sylvia. *It's easier than you think: The Buddhist way to happiness.* San Francisco: HarperSanFrancisco, 1995.

Boorstein, Sylvia. *Don't just do something, sit there.* San Francisco: HarperSanFrancisco, 1996.

Boswell, J. *Life of Samuel Johnson.* In W. H. Auden and L. Kronenberger (eds.), *Viking book of aphorisms.* New York: Viking Press, 1966.

Braceland, F. Psychiatry and the science of man. In S. R. Dean (ed.), *Psychiatry and mysticism*. Chicago: Nelson-Hall, 1975.

Brenner, C. *An elementary textbook of psychoanalysis*. New York: Anchor, 1974.

Brookes, C. E. Group therapy: Jungian technique. In B. Wolman (ed.), *International encyclopedia of psychiatry, psychology, psychoanalysis and neurology*. New York: Van Nostrand Reinhold, 1977, 276–279. (a)

Brookes, C. E. Jung's contribution to psychiatry: Psychotherapy. In B. Wolman (ed.), *International encyclopedia of psychiatry, psychology, psychoanalysis and neurology*. New York: Van Nostrand Reinhold, 1977, 252–253. (b)

Broughton, R. *Parapsychology: The controversial science*. New York: Ballantine, 1991.

Brown, G. The farther reaches of Gestalt therapy. *Synthesis: The realization of the self #1* (rev. ed.). Redwood City, Calif.: Synthesis Press, 1977.

Brown, M. *An introduction to direct body-contact psychotherapy*. Privately published, 1971.

Brown, N. *Life against death*. Middletown, Conn.: Wesleyan University Press, 1959.

Buber, M. (M. Friedman, trans.). *Hasidism and modern man*. New York: Horizon, 1958. (a)

Buber, M. *I and thou*. Part 1 (R. G. Smith, trans.) New York: Charles Scribner & Sons, 1958. (b)

Bucke, R. *Cosmic consciousness*. New York: E. P. Dutton, 1901.

Buddhagosa. *The path of purity* (P. M. Tin, trans.). London: Pali Text Society, 1923.

Bugental, J. F. T. *The search for authenticity: An existential analytic approach to psychotherapy*. New York: Holt, Rinehart and Winston, 1965.

Bugental, J. F. T. *The search for existential identity: Patient-therapist dialogue in humanistic psychotherapy*. San Francisco: Jossey-Bass, 1976.

Bugental, J. F. T. *Intimate journeys: Stories from life-changing therapies*. San Francisco: Jossey-Bass, 1990.

Burr, H. S. Electrometrics of atypical growth. *Yale Journal of Biology and Medicine*, 1952–53, 25.

Burr, H. S. *Blueprint for immortality*. Sudbury, Mass.: Neville Spearman, 1972.

Burrow, T. *The social basis of consciousness*. New York: Harcourt Brace, 1927.

Byrom, T. *The Dhammapada: The sayings of the Buddha*. New York: Vintage, 1976.

Campbell, J. *Myths to live by*. New York: Viking Press, 1972.

Campbell, J. *The mythic image*. Princeton, N.J.: Princeton University Press, Bollingen Series, 1974.

Campbell, K. *Body and mind.* Garden City, N.Y.: Doubleday, 1970.

Capra, Fritjof. *The tao of physics.* London and Berkeley: Shambhala, 1975.

Carrington, P. *Freedom in meditation.* New York: Anchor Press/Doubleday, 1977.

Carrington, P. *Clinically standardized meditation: Instructor's kit.* Kendall Park, N.J.: Pace Books, 1978.

Carrington, P., & Ephron, H. F. Meditation as an adjunct to psychotherapy. In S. Arieti (ed.), *New dimensions in psychiatry: A world view.* New York: John Wiley & Sons, 1975.

Carter-Haar, B. Identity and personal freedom. *SYNTHESIS: The realization of the self* #2 (rev. ed.) Redwood City, Calif.: Synthesis Press, 1978.

Castaneda, C. *The teachings of Don Juan.* Berkeley: University of California Press, 1969.

Castaneda, C. *A separate reality.* New York: Simon & Schuster, 1971.

Castaneda, C. *Journey to Ixtlan.* New York: Simon & Schuster, 1972.

Castaneda, C. *Tales of power.* New York: Simon & Schuster, 1974.

Chang, S. K. Morita therapy. *American Journal of Psychotherapy,* 1974, *28,* 208.

Chessick, R. *Intensive psychotherapy of the borderline patient.* New York: Jason Aronson, 1977.

Chiang, H., & Maslow, A. H. (eds.). *The healthy personality.* New York: Van Nostrand Reinhold, 1969.

Chinen, A. B. *Once upon a mid-life: Classic stories and mythic tales to illuminate the middle years.* Los Angeles: J. P. Tarcher, 1992.

Chinen, A. B. *Beyond the hero: Classic stories of men in search of soul.* Los Angeles: J. P. Tarcher, 1993

Chu, D. C., & Chu, D. W. *The principles of Chinese acupuncture medicine.* Los Angeles: Life Science Medical Laboratories, Inc., 1975.

Cole, C. W. *This Week* magazine, March 1960.

Course in miracles. Tiburon, Calif.: Foundation for Inner Peace, 1975.

Crumbaugh, J. C. Cross validation of purpose-in-life test based on Frankl's concepts. *Journal of Individual Psychology,* 1968, *24,* 74–81.

Csikzentmihalyi, M. Play and intrinsic rewards. *Journal of Humanistic Psychology,* 1975.

Cushman, A. The shrinking of the guru: An ashram comes of age. *Yoga Journal,* 1994, *19,* November/December.

Deatherage, O. G. The clinical use of "mindfulness" meditation techniques in short-term psychotherapy. *Journal of Transpersonal Psychology,* 1975, 7 (2), 133–143.

Deikman, A. J. De-automatization and the mystic experience. In C. T. Tart (ed.), *Altered states of consciousness*. New York: John Wiley and Sons, 1969.

Deikman, A. J. Comments on the GAP report on mysticism. *Journal of Nervous and Mental Disease*, 1977, 3, 155, 165, 217–218.

De Ropp, R. S. *The master game*. New York: Delta, 1968.

Desai, A. *Kripalu yoga: Meditation in motion, Book II*. Lenox, Mass.: Kripalu Publications, 1985.

Desai, A. The Kripalu approach to psychological healing and personal transformation. *Spirit Journal*. Lenox, Mass.: Kripalu Publications, 1993.

Devereux, G. (ed.). *Psychoanalysis and the occult*. New York: International University Press, 1953.

Dhammapada. (E. Easwaran, trans). Petaluma, Calif.: Nilgiri Press, 1986.

Dhiryamsa. *The way of non-attachment*. New York: Schocken Books, 1975.

Dobkin De Rois, M. Ayahuasca: The healing vine. *International Journal of Social Psychiatry*, 1971, 17 (4).

Don, N. S. The transformation of conscious experience and its EEG correlates. *Journal of Altered States of Consciousness*, 1977/78, 3 (2), 147–168.

Dossey, L. *Healing words: The power of prayer and the practice of medicine*. San Francisco: HarperSanFrancisco, 1993.

Duke, M. *Acupuncture*. New York: Pyramid House, 1972.

Eccles, J. C. *The brain and the unity of conscious experience*. Cambridge: Cambridge University Press, 1965.

Eckhart, M. (M. Fox, trans). *Breakthrough: Meister Eckhart's creation spirituality in new translation*. Garden City, N.J.: Image Books, 1980.

Edge, H., Morris, R., Palmer, J., & Rush, J. *Foundations of parapsychology: Exploring the boundaries of human capability*. Boston: Routledge & Kegan Paul, 1986.

Edinger, E. *Ego and archetype*. New York: Putnam, 1972.

Eeman, L. E. *Cooperative healing*. London: Frederick Muller, 1947.

Ehrenwald, J. *Psychotherapy: Myth and method*. New York: Grune & Stratton, 1966.

Ehrenwald, J. *New dimensions of deep analysis*. New York: Arno Press (1st ed.) Grune & Stratton, 1954/1975.

Ehrenwald, J. *The history of psychotherapy: From healing magic to encounter*. New York: Jason Aronson, 1976.

Ehrenwald, J. *The ESP experience: A psychiatric validation*. New York: Basic Books, 1978.

Eigen, M. On breathing and identity. *Journal of Humanistic Psychology,* 1977, *17* (3), 38.

Eisenbud, J. *Psi and psychoanalysis.* New York: Grune & Stratton, 1970.

Eliade, M. *Rites and symbols of initiation: The mysteries of death and rebirth.* New York: Harper & Row, 1958.

Eliade, M. *Yoga: Immortality and freedom.* Princeton, N.J.: Princeton University Press, 1969.

Eliot, T. S. Burnt Norton. In *Four quartets.* New York: Harcourt, Brace, & World, 1943.

Ellis, A. *Reason and emotion in psychotherapy.* New York: Lyle Stuart, 1962.

Emerson, R. W., The over-soul. *Emerson's essays.* New York: Thomas W. Crowell, 1951.

Endicott, J., Spitzer, R. L., Fleiss, J. L., & Cohen, J. The global assessment scale. *Archives of General Psychiatry,* 1976, *33,* 766–771.

Epstein, M. *Thoughts without a thinker: Psychotherapy from a Buddhist perspective.* New York: Basic Books, 1995.

Erickson, M. H., Rossi, E. L., & Rossi, S. I. *Hypnotic realities: the induction of clinical hypnosis and forms of indirect suggestion.* New York: Irvington, 1976.

Erikson, E. *Childhood and society.* New York: W. W. Norton, 1950.

Erikson, E. *Insight and responsibility.* New York: W. W. Norton, 1964.

Evans, D. *Spirituality and human nature.* Albany, N.Y.: SUNY Press, 1993.

Evans-Pritchard, E. E. *Witchcraft, oracles and magic among the Azande.* Oxford: Clarendon Press, 1937.

Evans-Wentz, W. Y. (ed.). *The Tibetan book of the dead.* Oxford: Oxford University Press, 1960.

Fabry, J. B. *The pursuit of meaning: Logotherapy applied to life.* Rev. ed. New York: Harper and Row, 1980.

Fabry, J. B. The noetic unconscious. *The International Forum for Logotherapy* (1 Lawson Road, Berkeley, Calif. 94707), 1979, 2 (2), 8–11.

Fabry, J. B., Bulka, R. P., & Sahakian, W. S. (eds.). *Logotherapy.* New York: Jason Aronson, 1979.

Fadiman, J., & Speeth, K. Transpersonal psychotherapy. In R. Henrik (ed.), *Handbook of psychotherapy.* New York: New American Library, in press.

Fagan, J., & Shepherd, I. A. *Gestalt therapy now.* New York: Harper, 1970.

Fehmi, L. G. *EEG biofeedback training of middle management executives.* A paper presented at the annual meeting of the Biofeedback Research Society, Colorado Springs, 1974.

Fehmi, L. G. EEG biofeedback, multi-channel synchrony training, and attention. In A. A. Sugarman & R. E. Tartar (eds.), *Expanding dimensions of consciousness*. New York: Springer Press, 1976.

Feuerstein, G. The Yoga-Sutra of Pantanjali. *Inner Traditions*. Rochester, Vt., 1979.

Finley, J. *Merton's palace of nowhere*. Notre Dame, In.: Ave Maria Press, 1978.

Fisher, G., & Martin, J. The psychotherapeutic use of psychodysleptic drugs. *Voices: The Art & Science of Psychotherapy*, 1970, 5, 67–72.

Fortune, D. *The mystical Qabalah*. New York: Alta Gaia, 1979.

Fox, J. *The essential Moreno: Writings on psychodrama, group method and spontaneity*. New York: Springer, 1987.

Frank, J. D. Nature and function of belief systems: Humanism and transcendental religion. *American Psychologist*, 1977, 555–559.

Frankl, V. E. *Psychotherapy and existentialism*. New York: Touchstone, 1968.

Frankl, V. E. *The will to meaning*. New York: New American Library, 1970.

Frankl, V. E. *The doctor and the soul*. New York: Vintage Books, 1973. (a)

Frankl, V. E. *Man's search for meaning*. New York: Touchstone, 1973. (b)

Frankl, V. E. *The unconscious God*. New York: Pocket Books, 1976. (a)

Frankl, V. E. *The unheard cry for meaning*. New York: Pocket Books, 1976. (b)

Freud, S. [Project for a scientific psychology.] In J. Strachey (ed.), *The standard edition of the complete psychological works of Sigmund Freud*, Vol. 1. London: Hogarth Press, 1966. (Originally published, 1895.)

Freud, S. [Recommendations to physicians practicing psychoanalysis.] In J. Strachey (ed.), *The standard edition of the complete psychological works of Sigmund Freud*, Vol. 12. London: Hogarth Press, 1958. (Originally published, 1912.)

Freud, S. [Thoughts for the times on war and death.] In *Collected Papers*, Vol. 4. New York: Basic Books, 1959. (Originally published, 1915.)

Freud, S. [*Beyond the pleasure principle*] (J. Strachey, ed. & trans.). London: International Psychoanalytic Press, 1922.

Freud, S. [*The future of an illusion*] (J. Strachey, ed.; W. D. Robson-Scott, trans.). London: Hogarth Press, 1928.

Freud, S. [An outline of psychoanalysis.] In J. Strachey (ed.), *The standard edition of the complete psychological works of Sigmund Freud*, Vol. 23. London: Hogarth Press, 1964. (Originally published, 1940.)

Freud, S. [*Totem and taboo*] (J. Strachey, trans.). New York: W. W. Norton, 1952.

Freud, S. *The ego and the id.* London: Hogarth Press, 1961.

Freud, S. *New introductory lectures on psychoanalysis.* J. Strachey (trans.), New York: W. W. Norton, 1965.

Furth, H. G. *Piaget and knowledge: Theoretical foundations.* Englewood Cliffs, N.J.: Prentice-Hall, 1969.

Gallup, G. *Year 1976 could mark beginning of new religious revival in America.* Princeton, N.J.: American Institute of Public Opinion, 1976.

Gallup, G., & Proctor, W. *Adventures in immortality.* New York: McGraw-Hill, 1982.

GAP (Group for the Advancement of Psychiatry). *Mysticism: Spiritual quest or psychic disorder?* New York: Group for the Advancement of Psychiatry Publications, 1976.

GAP. *Mysticism and Psychiatry.* Washington, D.C.: American Psychiatric Association, 1977.

Garfield, C. *Psychothanatological correlates of altered states of consciousness.* Unpublished doctoral dissertation, University of California, Berkeley, 1974.

Garfield, C. Consciousness alteration and fear of death. *Journal of Transpersonal Psychology,* 1975, 7 (2), 147–175.

Garfield, C. *Rediscovery of the body: A psychosomatic view of life and death.* New York: Dell, 1977. (a)

Garfield, C. The impact of death on the healthcare professional. In H. Feifel (ed.), *New meanings of death.* New York: McGraw-Hill, 1977. (b)

Garfield, C. *Psychosocial care of the dying patient.* New York: McGraw-Hill, 1978.

Garfield, C. *Stress and survival: The emotional realities of life-threatening illness.* St. Louis: Mosby, 1979.

Gellhorn, E. The neurophysiological basis of anxiety: A hypothesis. *Perspectives in Biology & Medicine,* 1965, 8, 488.

Gellhorn, E., & Kiely, W. F. Mystical states of consciousness: Neurophysiological and clinical aspects. *Journal of Nervous and Mental Diseases,* 1972, 154, 399.

Gendlin, E. T. Focusing. *Psychotherapy: Theory, Research and Practice,* 1969, 6, 4–15.

Gibran, K. *The prophet.* New York: Alfred A. Knopf, 1966.

Glueck, B. C. *Current research on transcendental meditation.* Paper delivered at Rensselaer Polytechnic Institute, March 1973. (a)

Glueck, B. C. Quoted in the *Hartford Courant,* May 27, 1973. (b)

Glueck, B. C. Biofeedback and meditation in the treatment of psychiatric illnesses. In J. H. Masserman (ed.), *Current psychiatric therapies.* New York: Grune & Stratton, 1975.

Glueck, B. C., & Stroebel, C. F. Biofeedback and meditation in the treatment of psychiatric illness. *Comprehensive Psychiatry,* 1975, *16,* 303–321.

Goldstein, J. *The experience of insight.* Santa Cruz, Calif.: Unity Press, 1976.

Goldstein, K. *The organism.* New York: American Book Co., 1939.

Goleman, D. The Buddha on meditation and states of consciousness. Part II: A typology of meditation techniques. *Journal of Transpersonal Psychology,* 1972, *4,* 151.

Goleman, D. Meditation and consciousness: An Asian approach to mental health. *American Journal of Psychotherapy,* 1976, *30* (1), 41–54.

Goleman, D. Meditation and stress reactivity. *Journal of Consulting Clinical Psychology.* 1976.

Goleman, D. Back from the brink. *Psychology Today,* 1977, *4,* 56–59.

Goleman, D. *The Meditative Mind.* Los Angeles: J. P. Tarcher, 1988.

Goleman, D. *Emotional Intelligence.* New York: Bantam Books, 1995.

Goleman, D. & Gurin, J. *Mind, body, medicine: How to use your mind for better health.* Yonkers, N.Y.: Consumer Reports Book, 1993.

Goleman, D., Kaufman, P., & Ray, M. *The creative spirit.* New York: Dutton, 1992.

Grad, B., Cadoret, R., & Paul, G. I. The influence of an unorthodox method of treatment on wound healing in mice. *International Journal of Parapsychology,* 1961, *3* (2), 5–24.

Greeley, A. *The sociology of the paranormal: A reconnaissance.* Beverly Hills, Calif., and London: Sage Publications, 1975.

Greeley, A. M., & McCready, W. C. Are we a nation of mystics? *New York Times Magazine.* 1975.

Green, C. *Out-of-the-body experiences.* Oxford: Institute of Psychophysical Research, 1968.

Green, E., & Green, A. On the meaning of transpersonal: Some metaphysical perspectives. *Journal of Transpersonal Psychology,* 1971, *3,* (1).

Green, E., & Green, A. *Beyond biofeedback.* New York: Delacorte, 1977.

Greene, M. (ed.). Toward a unity of knowledge. *Psychological Issues,* 1969, 6 (2).

Greyson, B., & Flynn, C. P. (eds.). *The near-death experience: Problems, prospects, perspectives.* Springfield, Ill.: Charles C. Thomas, 1984.

Grof, C., & Grof, S. *The stormy search for the self.* Los Angeles: J. P. Tarcher, 1990.

Grof, S. *Psycholytic and psychedelic therapy with LSD: Toward an integration of approaches.* Paper presented at the Conference of the European Medical Association for Psycholytic Therapy. Frankfurt A. M., West Germany, Oct. 1969.

Grof, S. Beyond psychoanalysis: I. Implications of LSD research for understanding dimensions of human personality. Presented at the First World Conference on Scientific Yoga, New Delhi, India, Dec. 1970. Published in *Darshana International* (India), 1970, *10,* 55. (a)

Grof, S. Beyond psychoanalysis: II. A conceptual model of human personality encompassing the psychedelic phenomena. Presented as preprint at the Second Interdisciplinary Conference on Voluntary Control of Internal States, Council Grove, Kans., 1970. (b)

Grof, S. Beyond psychoanalysis: III. Birth trauma and its relation to mental illness, suicide and ecstasy. Presented as preprint at the Second Interdisciplinary Conference on Voluntary Control of Internal States, Council Grove, Kans., Apr. 1970. (c)

Grof, S. *The grotesque in human personality: Experiences from LSD psythotherapy.* Presented at the Symposium on the Grotesque, Perfidious, and Profound, organized by the Society for the Arts, Religion and Contemporary Culture (ARC), Riverdale, N.Y., Apr. 1970. (d)

Grof, S. LSD psychotherapy and human culture (Part I). *Journal for the Study of Consciousness,* 1970, *3,* 100. (e)

Grof, S. The use of LSD in psychotherapy. *Journal of Psychedelic Drugs,* 1970, *3,* 52. (f)

Grof, S. LSD psychotherapy and human culture (Part I). *Journal for the Study of Consciousness,* 1971, *4,* 167.

Grof, S. Varieties of transpersonal experiences: Observations from LSD psychotherapy. *Journal of Transpersonal Psychology,* 1972, *4,* 45–80.

Grof, S. Theoretical and empirical basis of transpersonal psychology and psychotherapy: Observations from LSD research. *Journal of Transpersonal Psychology,* 1973, *5* (1).

Grof, S. *Realms of the human unconscious: Observations from LSD research.* New York: Viking Press, 1975.

Grof, S. *The human encounter with death.* New York: E. P. Dutton, 1977. (a)

Grof, S. Perinatal roots of wars, totalitarianism, and revolutions: Observations from LSD research. *Journal of Psychohistory,* 1977, *4* (3), 270–308. (b)

Grof, S. Modern consciousness research and the quest for a new paradigm. *ReVision,* 1979, *2,* (1).

Grof, S. *LSD psychotherapy.* Pomona, Calif.: Hunter House, 1980/1994.

Grof, S. *Beyond the brain: Birth, death, and transcendence in psychotherapy.* Albany, N.Y.: SUNY Press, 1985.

Grof, S. *The adventure of self-discovery.* Albany, N.Y.: SUNY Press, 1988.

Grof, S. *The holotropic mind.* San Francisco: Harper, 1992.

Grof, S., & Grof, C. *Beyond death.* London: Thames & Hudson, 1982.

Grof, S., & Grof, C. (eds.). *Spiritual emergencies.* Los Angeles: J. P. Tarcher, 1989.

Guenther, H. V. *Philosophy and psychology in the Abhidharma.* Berkeley, Calif.: Shambhala, 1976.

Guirdham, A. *The Cathars and reincarnation.* Wheaton, Ill.: Quest Publications, 1970.

Halifax, J. *Adaptive and assimilative aspects of Santeria in southern Florida.* Paper presented at the Annual Meeting of the American Anthropological Association, New York, Nov. 1972.

Haraldsson, E. Representative national surveys of psychic phenomena: Iceland, Great Britain, Sweden, USA and Gallup's multinational survey. *Journal of the Society for Psychical Research,* 1985, *53,* 145–148.

Harding, D. *On having no head.* London: Penguin, 1986.

Harding, D. *Head off stress.* London: Penguin, 1990.

Hariharananda, Swami Aranya. *Yoga philosophy of Patanjali: Containing his yoga aphorisms with commentary by Vyasa and annotations and copious hints on the practice of yoga.* Albany, N.Y.: SUNY Press, 1984.

Harner, M. *The way of the shaman.* New York: Harper & Row, 1980.

Hartmann, C. *The function of sleep.* New Haven: Yale University Press, 1973.

Heath, D. H. *Maturity and competence: A transcultural view.* New York: Gardner, 1977.

Heath, D. H. The maturing person. In R. N. Walsh & D. Shapiro (eds.), *Beyond health and normality: An exploration of exceptional psychological well-being.* New York: Van Nostrand Reinhold, 1978.

Heider, J. Catharsis in encounter. *Journal of Humanistic Psychology,* 1974, *14* (4), 27–47.

Hendrix, H. *Getting the love you want: A guide for couples.* New York: Perennial Library, 1990.

Hendrix, H. *Keeping the love you find.* New York: Pocket Books, 1992.

Heywood, R. Attitudes to death in the light of dreams and other out-of-the-body experience. In A. Toynbee (ed.), *Man's concern with death.* New York: McGraw-Hill, 1968.

Hillman, J. Archetypal theory. *Loose ends.* Zurich: Spring Publications, 1975.

Hixon, L. *Coming home: The experience of enlightenment in sacred traditions.* Los Angeles: J. P. Tarcher, 1989.

Hjelle, L. A. Transcendental meditation and psychological health. *Perceptual and Motor Skills,* 1974, *39,* 623.

Hoffer, A. Group interchange on LSD. In H. A. Abramson (ed.), *The use of LSD in psychotherapy*. New York: Josiah Macey, Jr., Foundation Publications, 1960.

Hoffman, E. *The right to be human: A biography of Abraham Maslow*. Los Angeles: J. P. Tarcher, 1988.

Hoffman, E. *The heavenly ladder: Kabbalistic techniques for inner growth*. Commack, N.Y.: Four Worlds Press, 1991.

Hoffman, E. *The way of splendor: Jewish mysticism and modern psychology*. Northvale, N.J.: Jason Aronson, 1992.

Hoffman, E. *Alfred Adler and the founding of individual psychology*. Reading, Mass.: Addison-Wesley, 1994.

Hoffman, E. (ed.). *Opening the inner gates: New paths in Kabbalah and psychology*. Boston: Shambhala, 1995.

Holmes, O. W. Cited in G. Murphy, *Human potentialities*. New York: Basic Books, 1958.

Horney, K. *Our inner conflicts*. New York: W. W. Norton, 1945.

Horney, K. *Neurosis and human growth*. New York: W. W. Norton, 1950.

Hunt, W., & Issacharoff, A. History and analysis of a leaderless group of professional therapists. *American Journal of Psychiatry*, 1975, *132*, 1166.

Inglis, B. *Natural and supernatural: A history of the paranormal from earliest times to 1914*. London: Hodder & Stoughton, 1977.

Isherwood, C. *Vedanta for the Western world*. New York: Viking Press, 1969.

Jacobs, L. *Jewish mystical testimonies*. New York: Schocken, 1978.

Jacobson, N. *Life without death*. New York: Dell, 1973.

Jaffé, A. *The myth of meaning*. New York: Putnam, 1971.

Jahn, R. G., & Dunne, B. J. *Margins of reality: The role of consciousness in the physical world*. New York: Harcourt Brace Jovanovich, 1987.

James, W. *The varieties of religious experience*. New York: Collier Books, 1961. (Originally published, 1902).

James, W. *Psychology: Briefer course*. New York: Harper, 1962.

James, W. In G. Murphy & R. V. Ballon (eds.), *William James in psychical research*. New York: Viking Press, 1963.

Jaynes, J. *The origin of consciousness in the breakdown of the bicameral mind*. Boston: Houghton Mifflin, 1977.

Johari, H. *Breath, mind, and consciousness*. Rochester, Vt.: Destiny Books, 1989.

Jones, E. *The life and work of Sigmund Freud*, Vol. 3. New York: Basic Books, 1957.

Jones, E. *Free associations.* New York: Hogarth Press, 1959.

Jung, C. G. *Psychological types.* Collected Works, Vol. 6. Princeton, N.J.: Princeton University Press, 1971. (Originally published, 1921.)

Jung, C. G. *Modern man in search of a soul.* New York: Harcourt Brace, 1933.

Jung, C. G. *The practice of psychotherapy.* Collected Works, Vol. 16. New York: Pantheon, 1954, 15. (Originally published, 1935.)

Jung, C. G. *Psychology and alchemy.* New York: Pantheon, 1953. (a)

Jung, C. G. *Two essays in analytical psychology.* Collected Works, Vol. 7. New York: Bollingen-Pantheon Press, 1953. (b)

Jung, C. G. *The archetypes and the collective unconscious.* Collected works, Vol. 9.1. Princeton, N.J.: Princeton University Press, 1960. (a)

Jung, C. G. *The structure and dynamics of the psyche.* Collected Works, Vol. 8. New York: Pantheon, 1960. (Originally published, 1954.) (b)

Jung, C. G. *Memories, dreams, and reflections.* New York: Random House, 1961.

Jung, C. G. *The symbolic life.* Collected Works, Vol. 18. Princeton, N.J.: Princeton University Press, 1976. (Originally published, 1961.)

Jung, C. G. *The secret of the golden flower* (rev. ed.). New York: Harcourt, Brace and World, 1962.

Jung, C. G. *The archetypes and the collective unconscious.* Princeton, N.J.: Princeton University Press, 1968.

Jung, C. G. *Analytical psychology.* New York: Random House, 1970.

Jung, C. G. *Letters.* (G. Adler, ed.). Princeton, N.J.: Princeton University Press, 1973.

Kabat-Zinn, J. *Wherever you go there you are: Mindfulness in everyday life.* New York: Hyperion, 1994.

Kamiya, J., Barber, T. X., Miller, N. E., Shapiro, D., & Stoyva, J. (eds.). *Biofeedback and self-control, 1976/1977.* Chicago: Aldine Publishing Co., 1977.

Kao, F. China, Chinese medicine, and the Chinese medical system. *American Journal of Chinese Medicine,* 1973, *1* (1), 14–18.

Kapleau, P. *The three pillars of Zen.* Boston: Beacon Press, 1967.

Kapleau, P. (ed.). *The wheel of death.* New York: Harper & Row, 1971.

Karasu, T. B. Psychotherapies: An overview. *American Journal of Psychiatry,* 1977, *134,* 851–863.

Kasamatsu, A., & Hirai, T. An EEG study on the Zen meditation (zazen). *Folio Psychiat. Neurol. Jap.,* 1966, *20, 315.*

Kastenbaum, R. Temptations from the ever after. *Human Behavior,* 1977, *6* (1), 28–33.

Kastenbaum, R., & Aisenberg, R. *The psychology of death.* New York: Springer, 1972.

Keen, S. *The faces of the enemy.* New York: Harper & Row, 1986.

Keleman, S. *The human ground: Sexuality, self, and survival.* Palo Alto, Calif.: Science and Behavior Books, 1975.

Kelley, C. R. *Primal scream and genital character.* Santa Monica, Calif.: Interscience Work Shop, 1971.

Kelman, H. Kairos and the therapeutic process. *Journal of Existential Psychiatry,* 1960, *1* (2).

Kelsey, D., & Grant, J. *Many lifetimes.* New York: Pocket Books, 1968.

Kernberg, O. Notes on countertransference. *Journal of the American Psychoanalytic Association,* 1965, *13.*

Kernberg, O. Structural derivatives of object relationships. *International Journal of Psychoanalysis,* 1966, *47.*

Kernberg, O. Borderline personality organization. *Journal of the American Psychoanalytic Association,* 1967, *15.*

Khyentse, D. *The heart of the enlightened ones.* Boston: Shambhala Press, 1992.

Koestler, A. *The roots of coincidence.* New York: Vintage Books, 1972.

Koestler, A. Cosmic consciousness. *Psychology Today,* April 1977.

Kohut, H. *The search for the self: Selected writings of Heinz Kohut 1950–1978,* vols I and II. New York: International Universities Press, 1978.

Kohut, H. *How does analysis cure? Contributions to the psychology of the self.* Chicago: University of Chicago Press, 1984.

Kramer, P. D. *Listening to prozac: A psychiatrist explores mood-altering drugs and the new meaning of self.* New York: Viking, 1993.

Krantzler, M. *Learning to love again.* New York: Crowell, 1977.

Krishna, G. *Kundalini: The evolutionary energy in man.* Berkeley: Shambhala, 1973.

Krishnamurti, J. *Freedom from the known.* San Francisco: HarperSanFrancisco, 1969.

Kubler-Ross, E. (ed.). *Death: The final stage of growth.* Englewood Cliffs, N.J.: Prentice-Hall, 1975.

Kuhn, T. *The structure of scientific revolutions.* Chicago: University of Chicago Press, 1962.

Kurland, A. A., Savage, C., Pahnke, W. N., Grof, S., & Olson, J. LSD in the treatment of alcoholics. *Pharmakopsychiatrie Neuro-Psychopharmakologie,* 1971, *4,* 83.

Laing, R. D. *The politics of the family.* New York: Pantheon, 1971.

Laing, R. D. In J. White (ed.), *Highest state of consciousness.* New York: Anchor, 1972.

Langley, N. *Edgar Cayce on reincarnation.* New York: Paperback Library, 1967.

Lao-tzu. *The way of life.* (W. Bynner, trans.). New York: Capricorn Books, 1962.

Lao-tzu. *Tao te ching* (Gia-Fu-Feng & Jane English, trans.). New York: Random House, 1972.

Lee, M., & Reynalds, N. *Phoenix rising yoga therapy training manual.* Housatonic, Mass.: Phoenix Rising, 1992.

Lesh, T. V. Zen meditation and the development of empathy in counselors. *Journal of Humanistic Psychology,* 1970, *10,* 39.

Leuner, H. *Die Experimentelle Psychose.* Berlin: Springer Verlag, 1962.

Leung, P. Comparative effects of training in external and internal concentration on two counseling behaviors. *Journal of Counseling Psychology,* 1973, *20,* 227.

Levitan, H. The relationship between mania and the memory of pain: A hypothesis. *Bulletin of the Menninger Clinic,* Mar. 1977, *41* (2), 145–161.

Lewis, C. S. *A grief observed.* New York: Seabury, 1961.

Lidz, T. On the life cycle. In S. Arieti (ed.), *The American handbook of psychiatry.* New York: Basic Books, 1974.

Lilly, J. *The center of the cyclone.* New York: Julian Press, 1972.

Lindsley, D. B. Psychological phenomena and the electroencephalogram. *Electroencephalography and Clinical Neurophysiology,* 1952, *4,* 443–456.

Loevinger, J. *Ego development: conceptions and theories.* San Francisco: Jossey Bass, 1976.

Lowen, A. *The betrayal of the body.* London: Collier Books, 1967.

Lowen, A. *The language of the body.* New York: Collier, 1971.

Lowen, A. *Bioenergetics.* New York: Penguin Books, 1976.

Luborsky, L., & Bachrach, H. Factors influencing clinicians' judgments of mental health: Eighteen experiences with the health-sickness rating scale. *Archives of General Psychiatry,* 1974, *31,* 292–299.

Luborsky, L., Singer, B., & Luborsky, L. Comparative studies of psythotherapies. *Archives of General Psychiatry,* 1975, *32,* 995–1008.

Lucas, W. B. *Regression therapy: A handbook for professionals,* vol I *Past-life therapy.* Crest Park, Calif.: Deep Forest Press, 1993.

Lucas, W. B. *Regression therapy: A handbook for professionals.* vol II *Special instances of altered state work.* Crest Park, Calif.: Deep Forest Press, 1993.

Ludwig, A. M. Altered states of consciousness. In C. T. Tart (ed.), *Altered states of consciousness.* New York: John Wiley, 1969.

Lukas, E. Zur Validierung der Logotherapie. In V. Frankl (ed.), *Der Wille zum Sinn.* Bern-Stuttgart-Wien: Verlag Hans Huber, 1972.

Lukas, E. The four steps of logotherapy. In V. Frankl (ed.), *Festival of meaning.* Berkeley: Uniquest, 1977.

Luthe, W. *Autogenic therapy,* Vols. 1–5. New York: Grune & Stratton, 1969/1970.

Maby, J. C. *Physical principles of radiesthesia.* Gloucestershire, England: Stonehouse, 1966.

Mack, J. E. *Abduction: Human encounters with aliens.* New York: Charles Scribner's Sons, 1994.

Macy, J. *Mutual causality in Buddhism and general systems theory.* Albany, N.Y.: SUNY Press, 1991.

Maharishi Mahesh Yogi. *The science of being and art of living.* London: SRM Publications, 1966.

Maharishi Mahesh Yogi. *On the Bhagavad-Gita: A new translation and commentary.* Baltimore: Penguin Books, 1969.

Maharishi Mahesh Yogi. *Alliance for knowledge.* Seelisberg, Switzerland: MIU Press, 1973.

Mahoney, M. *Cognition and behavior modification.* Cambridge, Mass.: Ballinger, 1974.

Malan, D. H., Heath, E. S., Bacal, H. A., & Balfour, F. H. G. Psychodynamic changes in untreated neurotic patients. *Archives of General Psychiatry,* 1975, *32,* 110–126.

Mann, F. *Acupuncture: The ancient Chinese art of healing and how it works scientifically.* New York: Random House, 1973.

Maslow, A. H. *Religions, values, and peak experiences.* Cleveland: Ohio State University Press, 1964.

Maslow, A. H. *Eupsychian management.* Homewood, Ill.: Richard D. Irwin, 1965.

Maslow, A. H. *The psychology of science.* Chicago: Gateway, 1966.

Maslow, A. H. *Toward a psychology of being.* New York: Van Nostrand, 1968.

Maslow, A. H. *The farther researchers of human nature.* New York: Viking Press, 1971.

Masterson, J. F. *Psychotherapy of the borderline adult.* New York: Brunner-Mazel, 1976.

Mause, L. de. *Foundations of psychohistory.* New York: The Psychohistory Press, 1975.

McCain, G., & Segal, E. *The games of science.* Belmont, Calif.: Brooks Cole, 1969.

McKeen, J., & Wong, B. Individual responsibility in illness and health. *Cold Mountain Journal,* Spring 1977, 18.

Meher Baba. Discourses. *Sufism Reoriented* (1290 Sutter St., San Francisco), 1967, 2, 176–193.

Meher Baba. *Not we but one.* Meher Baba Foundation (21a Elliott St., Beacon Hill, N. S. W., Australia), 1977.

Mehta, et al. *Yoga the Iynegar way.* New York: Knopf, 1990.

Merton, T. *The way of Chuang Tzu.* New York: New Directions, 1969.

Miller, S. Dialogue with the higher self. *SYNTHESIS: The Realization of the Self* #2 (rev.). Redwood City, Calif.: Synthesis Press, 1978.

Mishra, R. *The textbook of yoga psychology.* New York: Julian Press, 1987.

Mitchell, E. *Philosophical significance of ESP.* Concluding address at the annual conference of the American Academy of Psythotherapists, entitled "Beyond the Senses," New York, Sept. 1972.

Miyazaki, Y., & Youngdahl, A. Community studies thesis, University of California, Santa Cruz, 1979.

Mohan, A. G. *Yoga for body, breath, and mind.* Cambridge, Mass.: Rudra Press, 1993.

Monroe, R. *Journeys out of the body.* Garden City, N.Y.: Doubleday, 1971.

Monroe, R. *Far journeys.* Garden City, N.Y.: Dolphin Books, 1985.

Monroe, R. *Ultimate journey.* New York: Doubleday, 1994.

Moody, R. *Life after life.* New York: Bantam Books, 1976, c1975.

Moore, B., & Fine, B. *A glossary of psychoanalytic terms and concepts.* New York: American Psychoanalytic Association, 1968.

Motoyama, H. *How to measure and diagnose the functions of meridians and the corresponding internal organs.* Tokyo, Japan: Institute for Religion and Parapsychology, 1974.

Muses, C. The limits of consciousness. *Journal for the Study of Consciousness,* 1968, *1,* 77.

Narada, T. *A manual of Abhidhamma.* Kandy, Ceylon: Buddhist Publication Society, 1968.

Naranjo, C. Present-centeredness in Gestalt therapy. In J. Fagan & I. L. Shepherd (eds.), *Gestalt therapy now.* Palo Alto, Calif.: Science & Behavior Books, 1970.

Natterson, J. *Beyond countertransference: The therapist's subjectivity in the therapeutic process.* Northvale, N.J.: Aronson, 1991.

Nellas, P. (N. Russell, trans.). *Deification in Christ.* Crestwood, N.Y.: St. Vladimir's Seminary Press, 1987.

Nelson, J. *Healing the split, madness or transcendence?: A new understanding of the crisis and treatment of the mentally ill.* Los Angeles: J. P. Tarcher, 1991.

Nelson, J. *Healing the split: Integrating spirit into our understanding of the mentally ill* (rev. ed.). Albany, N.Y.: SUNY Press, 1994.

Neumann, E. *The origins and history of consciousness* (Bollingen Series, Vol. 42). Princeton, N.J.: Princeton University Press, 1954.

Nhat Hanh, T. *Touching peace: Practicing the art of mindful living*. Berkeley: Parallax, 1992.

Nouwen, H. *Out of solitude*. Notre Dame, Ind.: Ave Maria Press, 1974.

Odajynk, V. W. *Gathering the light: Psychology of meditation*. Boston: Shambhala, 1993.

Olcott, H. S. *A Buddhist catechism*. Wheaton, Ill.: Quest Books, 1971.

Orme-Johnson, D. W. Autonomic stability and transcendental meditation. *Psychosomatic Medicine*, 1974, *35*, 341–349.

Orme-Johnson, D. W., & Farrow, J. T. (eds.). *Scientific research on the transcendental meditation program: Collected papers*, Vol. 1. New York: MIU Press, 1976.

Ornstein, R. E. *The psychology of consciousness*. San Francisco: W. H. Freeman, 1972.

Osborne, A. *For those with little dust: Selected writings of Arthur Osborne*. Encinitas, Calif.: Ramana Publications, 1990.

Osis, K. *Deathbed observations of physicians and nurses*. New York: Parapsychology Foundation, 1961.

Osis, K., & Haraldsson, B. *The hour of our death*. New York: Avon, 1977.

Ouspensky, P. D. *In search of the miraculous*. New York: Harcourt, Brace and World, 1949.

Pahnke, W. N., Kurland, A. A., Unger, S., Savage, C., & Grof, S. The experimental use of psychedelic (LSD) psychotherapy. *Journals of the American Medical Association*, 1970, *212*, 1856.

Pahnke, W. N., & Richards, W. A. Implications of LSD and experimental mysticism. *Journal of Transpersonal Psychology*, 1969, *2*. Reprinted from *Journal of Religion and Health*, 1966, *5*, 175.

Peck, M. S. *The road less traveled: A new psychology of love, traditional values and spiritual growth*. New York: Walker, 1985.

Peers, E. A. (ed.). *Dark night of the soul* by St. John of the Cross. Garden City, N.Y.: Image Books, 1959.

Pelletier, K. Influence of transcendental meditation upon autokinetic perception. *Perceptual and Motor Skills*, 1974, *39*, 1031.

Pelletier, K., & Garfield, C. *Consciousness: East and West*. New York: Harper and Row, 1974.

Penfield, W. *The mystery of the mind*. Princeton, N.J.: Princeton University Press, 1975.

Perls, F. S. *Ego, hunger and aggression*. San Francisco: Orbit Graphic Arts, 1966.

Perls, F. S. *Gestalt therapy verbatim.* Moab, Utah: Real People Press, 1969. (a)

Perls, F. S. *In and out of the garbage pail.* Moab, Utah: Real People Press, 1969. (b)

Perls, F. S. *The Gestalt approach.* Palo Alto, Calif.: Science & Behavior Books, 1973.

Perls, F. S. *Legacy from Fritz.* Palo Alto, Calif.: Science & Behavior Books, 1975.

Perls, F. S. *The Gestalt approach and eye-witness to therapy.* New York: Bantam Books, 1976.

Perry, J. *The far side of madness.* Englewood Cliffs, N.J.: Prentice-Hall, 1974.

Pierrakos, J. *Life functions of the energy centers of man.* New York: Institute for the New Age of Man, 1975.

Polanyi, M. *Personal knowledge.* Chicago: University of Chicago Press, 1958.

Polanyi, M. *Tacit knowing.* London: Routledge & Kegan Paul, 1967.

Popper, K. *Objective knowledge.* Oxford: Oxford University Press, 1972.

Prabhavananda, S., & Isherwood, C. (eds.). *Shankara's crest-jewel of discrimination.* Hollywood, Calif.: Vedanta Press, 1947.

Progoff, I. *The death and rebirth of psychology.* New York: Julian Press, 1956.

Proust, M. *The captive.* New York: Random House, 1932.

Proust, M. Remembrance of things past. In W. H. Auden & L. Kronenberger (eds.), *Viking book of aphorisms.* New York: Viking Press, 1966.

Radha, S. *Hatha yoga: The hidden language—symbols, secrets and metaphor.* Porthill, Id.: Timeless Books, 1987.

Rajneesh, B. S. *The way of the white cloud.* Poona, India: Rajneesh Center, 1975.

Rajneesh, B. S. Then you are it. In R. N. Walsh & D. Shapiro (eds.). *Beyond health and normality: An exploration of extreme psychological well-being.* New York: Van Nostrand Reinhold, 1978.

Ram Dass, B. *Love, serve, remember.* Santa Cruz, Calif.: Hanuman Tape Library, 1973.

Ram Dass, B. A talk at the San Francisco Gestalt Institute. In J. Downing (ed.), *Gestalt awareness.* New York: Harper & Row, 1976.

Ram Dass, B. *Grist for the mill.* Berkeley, Calif.: Celestial Arts, 1987.

Ram Dass, B. Preface. In D. Goleman, *The varieties of the meditative experience.* New York: E. P. Dutton, 1977.

Rama, S., Ballentine, R., & Ajaya, S. *Yoga and psychotherapy: The evolution of consciousness.* Honesdale, Penn.: Himalayan International, 1976.

Rank, O. *The trauma of birth.* New York: Harcourt, Brace, 1929.

Rappaport, B. Carnal knowledge. *Journal of Humanistic Psychology,* 1975, *15* (1), 49–69.

Ravitz, L. J. Changes in the electromagnetic field in health and disease. *Annals of the New York Academy of Sciences,* 1963, 1144–1201.

Redfield-Jamison, K. *Touched with fire.* New York: Free Press, 1993.

Reich, W. *The murder of Christ.* New York: Noonday Press, 1970.

Reich, W. *Character analysis.* New York: Simon & Schuster, 1972.

Reich, W. *Selected writings.* New York: Noonday Press, 1973.

Reich, W. *The function of the orgasm.* New York: Simon & Schuster, 1974.

Richards, W. A., Rhead, J. E., Di Leo, F. B., Yensen, R., & Kurland, A. A. The peak experience variable in DPT-assisted psychotherapy with cancer patients. *Journal of Psychedelic Drugs,* 1977, *9* (1).

Rieker, H. U. (ed.). *The yoga of light: Hatha Yoga Pradpika.* Los Angeles: Dawn Horse Press, 1975.

Rimm, D. C., & Masters, J. C. *Behavior therapy.* New York: Academic Press, 1975.

Ring, K. *Life at death: A scientific investigation of the near-death experience.* New York: Quill, 1982.

Ring, K. *Heading toward omega: In search of the meaning of the near-death experience.* New York: William Morrow & Co., 1984.

Ring, K. *Omega project: Near death experiences, UFO encounters, and mind at large.* New York: Quill, 1993.

Roe, C., & MacIsaac, D. *Empathic attunement: Techniques of psychoanalytical self-psychology.* Northvale, N.J.: Jason Aronson, 1989.

Roethke, T. *The far field.* Garden City, N.Y.: Doubleday, 1971.

Rogers, C. *On becoming a person.* Boston: Houghton Mifflin, 1961.

Rosen, D. Suicide survivors: A follow-up study of persons who survived jumping from the Golden Gate and San Francisco–Oakland Bay bridges. *Western Journal of Medicine,* 1975, *122,* 289–294.

Rosenberg, J., Rand, M., & Asay, D. *Body, self and soul: Sustaining integration.* Atlanta: Humanics, New Age, 1985.

Rosenthal, R. The Pygmalian effect lives. *Psychology Today,* Sept. 1973, 51–59.

Rudhyar, D. *Occult preparations for a new age.* Wheaton, Ill.: Quest Books, 1975.

Rychlak, J. F. The personality. In S. Arieti (ed.), *The American handbook of psychiatry.* New York: Basic Books, 1974.

Sabom, M. *Recollections of death: A medical investigation.* New York: Harper & Row, 1982.

Sannella, L. *Kundalini: Psychosis or transcendence?* San Francisco: H. S. Dakin, 1977.

Sannella, L. *The Kundalini experience: Psychosis or transcendence.* Lower Lake, Calif.: Integral Publishing, 1987.

Sarfatti, J. The physical roots of consciousness. In J. Mislove, *Roots of consciousness.* New York: Random House, 1975.

Satprem. *Sri Aurobindo or the adventure of consciousness.* New York: Harper & Row, 1968.

Savage, C., & McCabe, O. L. Residential psychedelic (LSD) therapy for the narcotic addict. *Archives of General Psychiatry,* 1973, *28,* 808–813.

Savage, C., McCabe, O. L., & Kurland, A. A. Psychedelic therapy of the narcotic addict. In C. Brown & C. Savage (eds.). *The drug abuse controversy.* Baltimore: National Education Consultants, 1972.

Sayadaw, M. *The satipatthana vipassana meditation.* San Francisco: Unity Press, 1972.

Schafer, R. *A new language for psychoanalysis.* New Haven: Yale University Press, 1976.

Schafer, R. The interpretation of transference and the conditions for loving. *Journal of the American Psychoanalytic Association,* 1977, *25,* 335–362.

Scherman, Rabbi Nosson, (trans.). The complete artscroll siddur. Sefard edition, Brooklyn: Mesorah Publications, 1985.

Schrodinger, E. *What is life? Mind and matter.* London: Cambridge University Press, 1969.

Schwartz, G. E. Biofeedback, self-regulation, and the patterning of physiological processes. *American Scientist,* 1975, *63,* 314.

Seeman, W., Nidich, S., & Banta, T. H. Influence of transcendental meditation on a measure of self-actualization. *Journal of Counseling Psychology,* 1972, *19,* 184–187.

Selye, H. *The stress of life.* New York: McGraw-Hill, 1956.

Selzer, F., & Fehmi, L. G. *Effects of amplitude modulated auditory stimulation on EEG activity.* A paper presented at the annual meeting of the Biofeedback Research Society, Monterey, Calif., 1975.

Shafii, M. Adaptive and therapeutic aspects of meditation. *International Journal of Psychoanalytic Psychotherapy* 1973, *2,* 364–382. (a)

Shafii, M. Smoking following meditation. Unpublished manuscript. University of Michigan Medical Center, Ann Arbor, 1973. (b)

Shafii, M., Lavely, R., & Jaffe, R. Meditation and marijuana. *American Journal of Psychiatry,* 1974, *131,* 60–63.

Shah, I. *Caravan of dreams*. London: Octagon Press, 1968.

Shah, I. *Tales of the dervishes*. New York: E. P. Dutton, 1970. (a)

Shah, I. *The way of the Sufi*. New York: E. P. Dutton, 1970. (b)

Shah, I. *The pleasantries of the incredible Mulla Nasrudin*. New York: E. P. Dutton, 1971. (a)

Shah, I. *The Sufis*. Garden City, N.Y.: Doubleday, Anchor Books, 1971. (b)

Shah, I. *The exploits of the incomparable Mulla Nasrudin*. New York: E. P. Dutton, 1972. (a)

Shah, I. *The magic monastery*. New York: E. P. Dutton, 1972. (b)

Shah, I. *Thinkers of the East*. Baltimore: Penguin Books, 1972. (c)

Shands, H. C. *The war with words*. The Hague: Mouton, 1971.

Shapiro, D. N., & Walsh, R. N. (eds.). *Meditation: Classic and contemporary perspectives*. Chicago: Aldine Press, 1984.

Sheehy, G. *Passages: Predictable crises of adult life*. New York: E. P. Dutton, 1976.

Sherrington, C. S. *Man on his nature*. Cambridge: Cambridge University Press, 1951.

Smuts, J. C. *Holism and evolution*. New York: Viking Press, 1926.

Sogal, Rimpoche. *The Tibetan book of living and dying*. San Francisco: HarperSanFrancisco, 1992.

Soma, B. *The way of mindfulness*. Colombo, Ceylon: Lake House Bookshop, 1949.

Speeth, K. Gurdjieff. In C. Tart (ed.), *Transpersonal psychologies*. New York: Harper and Row, 1975.

Spiegelman, J. M., & Vasavada, A. W. *Hinduism and Jungian psychology*. Phoenix: Falcon Press, 1987.

Stapp, H. *Are superluminal connections necessary?* Lawrence Berkeley Lab. Report No. 5559, Nov. 8, 1976.

Stcherbatsky, T. *The central conception in Buddhism* (2nd ed.). Calcutta: Susil Gupta, 1956.

Stein, J. *Meditation, habituation, and distractability*. Undergraduate honors thesis, Harvard University, 1973.

Stevens, J. R. An anatomy of schizophrenia? *Archives of General Psychiatry*, 1973, *29*, 117.

Stevenson, I. *Twenty cases suggestive of reincarnation*. Charlottesville, Va.: University Press of Virginia, 1974.

Stevenson, I. Research into the evidence of man's survival after death. *Journal of Nervous and Mental Disease*, 1977, *165* (3), 152–170.

Stolerow, R. D. & Atwood, G. A. (eds.). *Contexts of being: The intersubjective foundations of psychological life*. Hillsdale, N.J.: The Analytic Press, 1992.

Stolerow, R. D., Atwood, G., & Brandchaft, B. (eds.). *The intersubjective perspective.* New York: Aronson, 1994.

Stolerow, R. D., Brandchaft, B., & Atwood, G. (eds). *Psychoanalytic treatment: An intersubjective approach.* Hillsdale, N.J.: The Analytic Press, 1987.

Strachey, J. (ed.). *The standard edition of the complete psychological works of Sigmund Freud,* Vol. 21. London: Hogarth Press, 1961.

Strachey, J. (ed.). *The standard edition of the complete psychological works of Sigmund Freud,* Vol. 1. London: Hogarth Press, 1966.

Strachey, J. (ed.). *The standard edition of the complete psychological works of Sigmund Freud,* Vol 23. London: Hogarth Press, 1964.

Strachey, J. (ed.). *The standard edition of the complete psychological works of Sigmund Freud,* Vol. 24. London: Hogarth Press, 1974.

Sutich, A. J. Introduction. *Journal of Humanistic Psychology,* 1961, *1* (1), viii.

Sutich, A. J. The growth experience and the growth centered attitude. *Journal of Humanistic Psychology,* 1967, 7 (2), 156–157. Reprinted from *Journal of Psychology,* 1949, *28,* 293–301.

Sutich, A. J. Transpersonal psychology: An emerging force. *Journal of Humanistic Psychology,* 1968, 8 (1), 77–79.

Sutich, A. J. Some basic considerations regarding transpersonal psychology. *Journal of Transpersonal Psychology,* 1969, *1* (1), 11–20.

Sutich, A. J. Association for Transpersonal Psychology. *Journal of Transpersonal Psychology,* 1972, 4 (1), 93–97.

Sutich, A. J. Transpersonal psychology. *Journal of Humanistic Psychology,* 1975, *14,* 39–40.

Sutich, A. J. Emergence of the transpersonal orientation: A personal account. *Journal of Transpersonal Psychology,* 1976, 8, 5–19.

SYNTHESIS: The realization of the self #1 (rev. ed.). Redwood City, Calif.: Synthesis Press, 1977.

SYNTHESIS: The realization of the self #2 (rev. ed.). Redwood City, Calif.: Synthesis Press, 1978.

SYNTHESIS: The realization of the self #3–4, Redwood City, Calif.: Synthesis Press, 1977.

Taimni, I. K. The science of yoga. Wheaton, Ill.: Theosophical Publications, 1961.

Talbot, M. *The holographic universe.* San Francisco: Harper Collins, 1991.

Targ, R., & Harary, K. *The mind race: Understanding and using psychic abilities.* New York: Villard, 1984.

Targ, R., & Puthoff, H. *Mind reach: Scientists look at psychic ability.* New York: Delacorte Press, 1977.

Tart, C. A psychophysiological study of subject. *Journal of the American Society for Psychical Research,* 1968, 28–45. (a)

Tart, C. A psychophysiological study of out-of-body phenomena. *Journal of the Society for Psychical Research,* 1968, 62, 3–27. (b)

Tart, C. Scientific foundations for the study of altered states of consciousness. *Journal of Transpersonal Psychology,* 1972, 3, 93–124. (a)

Tart, C. States of consciousness and state-specific sciences. *Science,* 1972, 176, 1203–1210. (b)

Tart, C. Out-of-the-body experiences. In E. D. Mitchell & J. White (eds.), *Psychic exploration.* New York: Putman, 1974.

Tart, C. *States of consciousness.* New York: E. P. Dutton, 1975.

Tart, C. *Psi: Scientific studies of the psychic realm.* New York: Dutton, 1977.

Tart, C. *Waking up: overcoming the obstacles to human potential.* Boston: New Science Library, 1986.

Tart, C. Altered states of consciousness and the possibility of survival of death. In J. Spong (ed.), *Consciousness and survival: An interdisciplinary inquiry into the possibility of life beyond biological death.* Sausalito, Calif.: Institute of Noetic Sciences, 1987.

Tart, C. *Living the mindful life.* Boston: Shambala, 1994.

Tart, C. (ed.). *Transpersonal psychologies.* New York: Harper Collins, 1992.

Thera, N. *The power of mindfulness.* San Francisco: Unity Press, 1972.

Thera, N. *The heart of Buddhist meditation.* New York: Samuel Weiser, 1973.

Thomson, R. L. Psychology and science from the ancient East. *The Brook Postgraduate Gazette,* 1973, 2, 1–9.

Thoresen, C. E., & Mahoney, M. *Behavioral self-control.* New York: Holt, Rinehart and Winston, 1974.

Tiller, W. Devices for monitoring nonphysical energies. In E. D. Mitchell & J. White (eds.), *Psychic exploration.* New York: Putnam, 1974.

Tillich, P. *The courage to be.* New Haven: Yale University Press, 1952.

Tobias, M., & Sullivan, J. *Complete stretching.* New York: Knopf, 1992.

Tolstoy, L. *A confession, the gospel in brief, what I believe.* London: Oxford University Press, 1951.

Trungpa, C. *Cutting through spiritual materialism.* Berkeley: Shambhala, 1973.

Ullman, M., Krippner, S., with Vaughan, A. *Dream telepathy.* New York: Macmillan, 1973.

Ullman, M., & Zimmerman, N. *Working with dreams*. New York: Delacorte Press/ Eleanor Friede, 1979.

Unger, S. M. Mescaline, LSD, psylocybin, and personality change: A review. *Psychiatry: Journal for the Study of Interpersonal Process*, 1963, 26 (2), 111–125.

Vallée, J. *UFOs in space: Anatomy of a phenomenon*. New York: Ballantine, 1965.

Van Nghi, N., Fisch, G., & Kao, J. An introduction to classical acupuncture. *American Journal of Chinese Medicine*, 1973, 1, (1), 75–83.

Vargiu, J. Subpersonalities. *SYNTHESIS: The Realization of the Self* #1 (rev. ed.). Redwood City, Calif.: Synthesis Press, 1977.

Vaughan, F. Transpersonal perspectives in psychotherapy. *Journal of Humanistic Psychology*, 1977, 17 (2), 69–81.

Vaughan, F. *Awakening intuition*. New York: Doubleday, 1979.

Vaughan, F. *The inward arc: Healing in psychotherapy and spirituality*. Nevada City, Calif.: Blue Dolphin Press, 1995.

Vaughan, F. *Shadows of the sacred: Seeing through spiritual illusions*. Wheaton, Ill.: Quest Books, 1995.

Veith, I. *Huang Ti Nei Ching Su Wen (The Yellow Emperor's classic of internal medicine)*. Berkeley: University of California Press, 1972.

von Franz, M-L. *Puer aeturnus*. Santa Monica, Calif.: Sigo Press, 1981.

Walker, E. H. The nature of consciousness. *Mathematical Biosciences*, 1970, 7, 131.

Wallace, R. K. Physiological effects of transcendental meditation. *Science*, 1970, 167, 1751–1754.

Wallace, R. K. *Neurophysiology of enlightenment* (26th International Congress of Physiological Science, New Delhi). New York: MIU Press, 1975.

Wallace, R. K., & Benson, H. The physiology of meditation. *Scientific American*, 1972, 226, 84–90.

Walsh, R. N. Reflections on psychotherapy. *Journal of Transpersonal Psychology*, 1976, 8, 100–111.

Walsh, R. N. Initial meditative experiences: Part I. *Journal of Transpersonal Psychology*, 1977, 9 (2), 151–192.

Walsh, R. N. Initial meditative experiences: Part II. *Journal of Transpersonal Psychology*, 1978, 10, 1–28.

Walsh, R. N., and Shapiro, D. (eds.). *Beyond health and normality: An exploration of exceptional psychological well-being*. New York: Van Nostrand Reinhold, 1978.

Walsh, R. N., & Vaughan, F. Towards a transpersonal model of the person. In R. N. Walsh & D. H. Shapiro (eds.), *Beyond health and normality: An exploration of exceptional psychological well-being*. New York: Van Nostrand Reinhold, 1978.

Walsh, R. N., & Vaughan, F. (eds.). *Paths beyond ego: The transpersonal vision*. Los Angeles: J. P. Tarcher, 1993.

Washburn, M. *Transpersonal psychology in psychoanalytic perspective*. Albany, N.Y.: SUNY Press, 1994.

Washburn, M. *The ego and the dynamic ground: A transpersonal theory of human development* (2d ed.). Albany, N.Y.: SUNY Press, 1995.

Wasson, R. G. *Soma: Divine mushrooms of immortality*. New York: Harcourt Brace, 1972.

Wasson, G., Hofmann, A., & Ruck, C. A. P. *The road to Eleusis: Unveiling the secret of the mysteries*. New York: Harcourt Brace Jovanovich, 1978.

Watts, A. *The two hands of God*. New York: Collier Books, 1969.

Weber, E. S. P., & Fehmi, L. G. *The therapeutic uses of EEG biofeedback*. A paper presented at the annual meeting of the Biofeedback Research Society, Colorado Springs, 1974.

Wei, L. Y. Theoretical foundation of Chinese medicine: A modern interpretation. *American Journal of Chinese Medicine,* 1976, 4 (4), 369–371.

Wei Wu Wei. *All else is bondage*. Hong Kong: Hong Kong University Press, 1970.

Weisman, A. *The existential core of psychoanalysis*. Boston: Little, Brown, 1965.

West, L. J. Transcendental meditation and other nonprofessional psychotherapies. In A. M. Freedman & H. I. Kaplan (eds.), *Comprehensive textbook of psychiatry*. Baltimore: Wilkins and Wilkins Company, 1974.

White, J. (ed.). *The highest state of consciousness*. New York: Doubleday, 1973.

Whitehead, A. N. *Science and the modern world*. New York: Free Press, 1967.

Wilber, K. *The spectrum of consciousness*. Wheaton, Ill.: Quest, 1977.

Wilber, K. Where it was, there I shall be. In R. N. Walsh & D. Shapiro (eds.), *Beyond health and normality: An exploration of exceptional psychological well-being*. New York: Van Nostrand Reinhold, 1978.

Wilber, K. *The Atman project*. Wheaton, Ill.: Quest, 1980.

Wilber, K. *No boundary: Eastern and Western approaches to personal growth*. Boulder, Co.: Shambhala Press, 1981.

Wilber, K. *A sociable God*. New York: McGraw-Hill, 1982.

Wilber, K. *Eye to eye*. New York: Anchor Press, 1983.

Wilber, K. *Grace and grit: Spirituality and healing in the life and death of Treya Killam Wilber*. Boston: Shambala Press, 1991.

Wilber, K. *Sex, ecology, spirituality: The spirit of evolution.* Boston: Shambhala Press, 1995.

Wilber, K., Engler, J., & Brown, D. *Transformations of consciousness: Conventional and contemplative perspectives on development.* Boston: New Science Library/Shambhala, 1986.

Wilhelm, R. I. Ching (Book of Changes) (C. Baynes, trans.). Princeton, N.J.: Princeton University Press, 1967.

Williams, L. F. (ed.). *Sufi studies: East and West.* New York: E. P. Dutton, 1974.

Williams, W. C. *Pictures from Brueghel.* New York: Grove Press, 1972.

Winquist, W. T. *The effect of the regular practice of transcendental meditation on students involved in the regular use of hallucinogenic and "hard" drugs.* Unpublished manuscript. Department of Sociology, University of California, Los Angeles, 1969.

Wolpe, J. *Psychotherapy by reciprocal inhibition.* Stanford, Calif.: Stanford University Press, 1958.

Woodward, F. S. *Some sayings of the Buddha.* New York: Gordon Press. 1973.

Woolger, R. *Other lives, other selves.* New York: Doubleday, 1987.

Wordsworth, W. *Complete poetical works.* London: MacMillan Co., 1924.

Yensen, R. *Group psychotherapy with a variety of hallucinogens.* Paper presented at the Eleventh Annual Meeting of the Association for Humanistic Psychology, Montreal, Canada, 1973.

Yensen, R. *The use of 3, 4 methylenedioxyamphetamine (MDA) as an adjunct to brief intensive psychotherapy with neurotic outpatients.* Unpublished doctoral dissertation, University of California, Irvine, 1975.

Yensen, R., Di Leo, F. B., Rhead, J. C., Richards, W. A., Soskin, R. A., Turek, I., & Kurland, A. A. MDA-assisted psychotherapy with neurotic outpatients: A pilot study. *Journal of Nervous and Mental Disease,* 1976, *163* (4), 233–245.

Yogananda, P. *Autobiography of a yogi.* Los Angeles, Calif.: Self-Realization Fellowship, 1975.

Zohar (Sperling, H. & Simon, M., trans.) vols. 1–5. London: Soncino Press, 1931–1934.

Contributors

*Harold H. Bloomfield, M.D.,** is Director of Psychiatry and Preventive Medicine at the North County Holistic Health Center in San Diego, California. He is the author of six books: *TM: Discovering Inner Energy and Overcoming Stress; How to Survive the Loss of a Love; Happiness: The TM Program, Psychiatry and Enlightenment; The Holistic Way to Health and Happiness; How to Enjoy the Love of Your Life;* and *Inner Joy.* He is a founding member of the American Holistic Medical Association and the Association for Holistic Health.

Seymour Boorstein, M.D., is an Associate Clinical Professor of Psychiatry, School of Medicine, University of California, San Francisco. A Life Fellow of the American Psychiatric Association, he has been a member of the San Francisco Psychoanalytic Society for the past twenty-six years. He has conducted a private practice of psychoanalysis and psychotherapy for the past thirty-six years. Aside from writing many articles in the field of the transpersonal and psychotherapy, he currently has a book in press with SUNY entitled *Clinical Studies in Transpersonal Psychotherapy.*

Sylvia Boorstein, Ph.D., is a co-founding teacher at Spirit Rock Meditation Center in Woodacre, California, and has had a private psychotherapy practice since 1967. She has published articles in the *Journal of Transpersonal Psychology,* and her book *It's Easier than You Think: The Buddhist Way to Happiness* has just been published.

*Crittenden E. Brookes, M.D., Ph.D.,** is Associate Clinical Professor, Department of Psychiatry, School of Medicine, University of California, and assistant chief, Department of Psychiatry, Mount Zion Hospital and Medical Center (both located in San Francisco). He has a private practice as a psychiatrist and Jungian psychoanalyst and is a lecturer in the University of California Extension Division as well as a consultant to various mental health facilities in northern California. He is director of curriculum at the C. G. Jung Institute in San Francisco and a Fellow of the American Psychiatric Association and the American Academy of Psychoanalysis.

Stephen Cope, LiCSW, a clinical social worker, is a Program Director at Kripalu Center for Yoga and Health. He has designed and led many special programs including The Yoga of Recovery and Psychotherapy and Spirituality.

*Contributors' biographies unedited from first edition.

He integrates the teachings of the Buddhist Vipassana tradition with yogic philosophy. He is a writer creating a synthesis between the meditative traditions and psychotherapy.

*Olaf G. Deatherage, Ph.D., formerly Assistant Professor of Psychology, University of Lethbridge, Lethbridge, Alberta (Canada), is presently Director of Valley Mental Health Services in Creston, British Columbia. His research interests include the effects of long-term alcohol consumption, the functioning and interaction of the limbic and frontal cortex systems, and the clinical use of mindfulness meditation techniques in short-term psychotherapy. He has practiced Buddhist meditation for the past eight years and studied with Chögyam Trungpa and other lamas and teachers at Naropa Institute.

Arthur J. Deikman, M.D., is a psychiatrist in private practice in Mill Valley, California, and San Francisco, where he is Clinical Professor of Psychiatry at the University of California. Dr. Deikman is a pioneer in the scientific investigation of the psychological effects of meditation. In addition to his articles on meditation, mystical experience, and consciousness, he is the author of *Personal Freedom: On Finding Your Way to the Real World* and *Science of the Self: The Mystical Tradition and Western Psychotherapy*.

*Norman S. Don, Ph.D., is a psychotherapist in private practice and Director of the Laboratory for Psychophysiology, in Chicago. As a researcher he specializes in the psychophysiology of altered states of consciousness and in the study of persons with unusual yogic and parapsychological abilities.

*John B. Enright, Ph.D., after completing traditional training in clinical psychology at the University of California, Berkeley, branched out in three major directions—Gestalt therapy, Synanon, and *est*—with "side trips" into bioenergetics, psychosynthesis, and sufism. In addition to teaching and conducting a private practice in psychotherapy, he has developed a personal growth seminar for the public (ARC) and, through Manifest Learning Systems, serves government and industry as a consultant on responsibility, intention, and work satisfaction.

Donald Evans, Ph.D., Professor Emeritus of Philosophy at the University of Toronto, earned his Ph.D. from Oxford. His publications include *Struggle and Fulfilment: The Inner Dynamics of Religion and Morality* and *Spirituality and Human Nature*. He is a spiritual counselor and psychotherapist in private practice and has also led many workshops linking the approaches explored in his two books.

*Joseph Fabry, J.D., received his degree from the University of Vienna and later studied with Dr. Viktor Frankl. He is Director of the Institute of Logotherapy, Berkeley, editor of the *International Forum for Logotherapy*, and author of *The Pursuit of Meaning* and *Logotherapy in Action*. He is currently teaching logotherapy in the University Extension Division, University of California, Berkeley, as well as at the Psychosynthesis Institute (San Francisco) and John F. Kennedy University (Orinda, California).

*Lester G. Fehmi, Ph.D., was a postdoctoral fellow at the Brain Research Institute at UCLA and later served as Assistant Professor of Psychology at the State University of New York at Stony Brook, where he began research in biofeedback in 1967. He is presently Director of the Behavioral Medicine Learning Clinic at the Medical Center at Princeton and Director of the Princeton Biofeedback Clinic. He is an affiliate staff member of the Department of Rehabilitation Medicine at the Medical Center at Princeton. Dr. Fehmi is a licensed psychologist in private practice. He is a founding member of the Biofeedback Society of America and has directed workshops in biofeedback and attention training.

*John Firman, M.A., is a licensed marriage, family and child counselor and a Director of the Psychosynthesis Institute. He has taught at various colleges and universities, has worked at the Napa State Hospital and the Sonoma County Rehabilitation Program for Alcoholism, and conducts a private practice with individuals, couples, and groups. He had didactic training in psychosynthesis with Roberto Assagioli and completed advanced training with James and Susan Vargiu.

Daniel Goleman, Ph.D., reports on the brain and behavior science for the *New York Times*. He is the author of *Emotional Intelligence* and *The Meditative Mind* and co-author of *Mind, Body, Medicine* and *The Creative Spirit*.

Stanislav Grof, M.D., Ph.D., is a psychiatrist with experience of over thirty-seven years of research in non-ordinary states of consciousness. His early research was in the clinical uses of psychoactive drugs conducted at the Psychiatric Research Institute in Prague. There he was Principal Investigator of a program systematically exploring the heuristic and therapeutic potential of LSD and other psychedelic substances. He developed with his wife Christina Holotropic Breathwork™, an innovative form of experiential psychotherapy. Stanislav Grof is one of the founders and chief theoreticians of transpersonal psychology and founding president of the International Transpersonal Association (ITA). Among his publications are over one hundred articles in professional journals and the books *Realms of the Human Unconscious; The Human Encounter with Death* (with Joan Halifax); *LSD Psychotherapy; Beyond the Brain; The Adventure of Self-Discovery; Beyond Death; The Stormy Search for the Self* (the last two with Christina Grof); *The Holotropic Mind;* and *Books of the Dead: The Manuals for Dying and Living.* He also edited the books *Ancient Wisdom and Modern Science; Human Survival and Consciousness Evolution;* and *Spiritual Emergency* (the last with Christina Grof).

Edward Hoffman, Ph.D., is a licensed clinical psychologist in the New York City area. A long-time member of the Association for Humanistic Psychology, he has authored more than sixty articles and eight books in the fields of psychology and Jewish studies. These include major biographical works about Wilhelm Reich, Abraham Maslow, and, most recently, Alfred Adler. He has also authored several books on the psychological relevance of Kabbalah and Hasidism including *The Way of Splendor, The Heavenly Ladder,* and *Despite All Odds.* His latest book on this evocative subject is entitled *Opening the Inner Gates.*

W. Michael Keane, Ph.D., clinical psychologist, is co-founder and co-director of New Directions for yoga, health, and psychotherapy in Brookline, Massachusetts. He seeks an integration of Western psychology with Eastern philosophy and techniques, interweaving these two powerful traditions to create the space for more complete healing. As a certified Kripalu yoga teacher and yoga therapist, he has led many programs combining yoga and psychotherapy. He frequently directs programs at the Kripalu center in Lenox, Massachusetts.

*Gerald G. May, M.D., a psychiatrist in private practice, serves as consultant for Shalem, an Institute for Spiritual Formation in the District of Columbia, and is a staff member of Spring Grove Hospital Center in Maryland. Among his books are *The Open Way: A Meditation Handbook; Simply Sane;* and *Pilgrimage Home.*

John E. Nelson, M.D., is a practicing psychiatrist certified by The American Board of Psychiatry and Neurology. He has worked with the severely mentally ill since 1969 and has long been a student of Eastern philosophy and transpersonal psychology. He is the author of *Healing the Split: Integrating Spirit into Our Understanding of the Mentally Ill,* which applies the central ideas in his chapter to psychotic experience. He is currently co-editing an anthology on transpersonal aspects of depression.

*Stephen Schoen, M.D., is a teaching member of the Gestalt Institute of San Francisco and a psychiatrist in private practice. He trained with Harry Stack Sullivan, Gregory Bateson, and Fritz Perls. He has led Gestalt workshops for many years on the West Coast, and recently has conducted courses in psychotherapy at the Naropa Institute, Boulder, Colorado, and the Fritz Perls Institute, Düsseldorf, Germany. His psychological papers include chapters in *Ways of Growth* and *Gestalt Awareness,* and articles on LSD in psychotherapy, creative attention, and the approach to self in Gestalt therapy.

*Fern Selzer, Ph.D., has conducted research in biofeedback and attention training for eight years. She received her Ph.D. in physiological psychology from the State University of New York at Stony Brook in 1973 and presently is Assistant Director of the Princeton Biofeedback Clinic in Princeton, New Jersey.

*Anthony J. Sutich, Ph.D.**, was co-founder (with Abraham H. Maslow) of the *Journal of Humanistic Psychology* (1961) and the Association for Humanistic Psychology (1963). The re-emergence of his interest in mysticism and Eastern philosophies led to his later founding of the *Journal of Transpersonal Psychology* (1968), the Transpersonal Institute (1969), and the Association for Transpersonal Psychology (1971). He died on April 10, 1976.

Charles T. Tart, Ph.D., Professor Emeritus of Psychology at UC Davis, and currently Visiting Professor in East-West Psychology at the California Institute of Integral Studies and Core Faculty Member at the Institute of Transpersonal Psychology, is internationally famous for research with altered states, transpersonal psychology, and parapsychology. His ten books include two classics: *Altered States of Consciousness* and *Transpersonal Psychologies. Waking Up: Overcoming the Obstacles to Human Potential* synthesized Buddhist, Sufi, and Gurdjieffian mindfulness training ideas with modern psychology, and his latest book, *Living the Mindful Life,* extends these explorations.

*James G. Vargiu, M.A.**, is President of the Synthesis Graduate School, Founding Director of the Psychosynthesis Institute, and executive editor of the journal *SYNTHESIS: The Realization of the Self* (all in San Francisco). He was educated in physics, mathematics, and psychology, then underwent didactic training with Roberto Assagioli, working with him over a period of ten years and assisting him in the writing of his last book, *The Act of Will.* He has done research in applied physics, systems development, and creativity; has developed applications of psychosynthesis to psychology, education, medicine, and other fields; and has assumed primary responsibility for the Research and Curriculum Development Program of the Synthesis Graduate School.

Frances E. Vaughan, Ph.D., is a clinical psychologist in private practice in Mill Valley, California, author of *Awakening Intuition* and *The Inward Arc,* and co-author of *Paths Beyond Ego.* She was formerly on the clinical faculty of the University of California Medical School at Irvine and served as president of the Association for Transpersonal Psychology. She is on the board of editors of the *Journal of Transpersonal Psychology* and has published numerous articles on transpersonal psychotherapy.

Roger Walsh, M.D., Ph.D., is a physician who is Professor of Psychiatry, Philosophy, and Anthropology at the University of California at Irvine and has been a student of contemplative practice for two decades. His publications include *Meditation: Classic and Contemporary Perspectives; The Spirit of Shamanism;* and *Paths Beyond Ego: The Transpersonal Vision.*

Roger J. Woolger, Ph.D., is a British-born Jungian analyst trained at C. G. Jung Institute, Zurich, with degrees in psychology, religion, and philosophy from Oxford and London Universities. He leads workshops at the New York

Open Center and Esalen Institute and has taught at Vassar College, the University of Vermont, and Concordia University, Montreal. His book *Other Lives, Other Selves,* a definitive work on past-life therapy, has been translated into five languages. He runs professional trainings in Europe and America.

*Richard Yensen, Ph.D., conducts a private practice in Baltimore of psychotherapy and teaches Applied Behavioral Sciences at the Evening College of the Johns Hopkins University. He has served as consultant to the Clinical Sciences Division, Maryland Psychiatric Research Center, and to Friends of Medical Science Research (both in Baltimore), where he designed and conducted clinical studies using psychedelic drugs as an adjunct to psychotherapy.

INDEX